Cognitive Psychology

Third Edition

James F. Juola
Hideya Koshino

Publisher and Director of Development: Richard Schofield
Textbook Specialist: Chad Peterson
Production and Fulfillment Manager: Janai Escobedo
Textbook Development Coordinator: Tiffany Koopal
Copy Editor: Kimberly Wein
Permissions Liaison: Logan McDonald
Typesetter/Cover Designer: Tim Gerlach

For information address BVT Publishing, P.O. Box 492831, Redding, CA 96049-2831

Textbook^Plus (Loose-Leaf Bundle) ISBN: 978-1-5178-0058-1
eBook^Plus ISBN: 978-1-5178-0057-4
Loose-Leaf ISBN: 978-1-5178-0055-0
Soft Cover ISBN: 978-1-5178-0056-7

BR082017TG

Brief Contents

Table *of* Contents

Chapter Three

Perception   59

Chapter Four

Visual Imagery and Spatial Cognition   93

Chapter Five
Attention 117

Chapter Six
Short- versus Long-Term Memories 151

Chapter Seven

Long-Term Memory for Meaning and Knowledge   185

Chapter Eight
Long-Term Memory for Events 211

Chapter Nine
Cognitive Development and Language Acquisition 235

Chapter Ten

Language Development and Reading   263

Chapter Eleven
Higher Conceptual Processes   291

Chapter Twelve

Consciousness   319

Chapter Thirteen

Life-Span Development, Normal Aging, and Pathology   341

Chapter Fourteen

Current and Future Applications of Cognitive Science   363

Preface

Cognitive psychology is the study of the typical, adult human brain and how it interprets sensations, sorts out important inputs from background noise, brings its vast store of knowledge into play to interpret its surroundings, and decides what to do next. Many types of human activity have been studied by cognitive psychologists around the world for over 100 years; yet we are confronted by the fact that the human brain is the single most complicated organ in the known universe, and we cannot hope to understand all of what it can do, even in simple situations. Cognitive psychology has evolved to give us the theoretical and empirical tools necessary to construct models of what the brain does to handle the incredible complexity of tasks—such as recognizing objects; navigating in a dynamic, three-dimensional world; communicating across space and time; and applying the power of human reason to solving problems that threaten our lives and our planet. The world is growing increasingly complex, and it is a valid question to ask whether technological developments are increasing our ability to deal with this complexity or adding levels to make things worse. In fact, we are at the dawn of an era in which machine intelligence might approach or even surpass our own, perhaps to our ultimate peril.

Kurt Lewin is credited with the simple but profound statement that, "there is nothing so practical as a good theory." A good theory serves the purposes of summarizing a set of observations, explaining what they mean, and predicting future observations. One of the consequences of Einstein's Theory of Relativity was that gravity could bend a beam of light. This prediction could not be tested until sometime after the theory had been published, when the opportunity arose to measure the apparent position of a star as the sun moved to obscure it. Normally the star would be invisible against the sun's brilliance, but photographs taken during a solar eclipse confirmed the predictions of the theory. There was a slight deflection of the star's light when it neared the edge of the sun. The Theory of Relativity is both practical, in that it can summarize and explain many complex physical phenomena, and specific enough so that it could have been proven wrong by the measurement of a path of light as it neared the sun. Theories that are vague can never be refuted by data, and they can never be replaced with better ones, creating a situation in which science does not advance.

In cognitive psychology theories are constantly being evaluated against data collected in laboratory experiments and in the natural environment. Theories guide our selection of tasks, materials, instructions, response requirements, and the interpretation of results. It is imperative that research be designed to give theories a rigorous test so that weak theories can be rejected and replaced with stronger ones. In that way, theories should become continuously better approximations to reality. From its inception in the late 1950s, cognitive psychology has always benefited from theoretical inputs from other disciplines, including linguistics and computer science. New fields of cognitive ergonomics, psycholinguistics, and artificial intelligence have grown out of these early collaborations. Today we are reaping additional benefits from new methods of measuring brain activity in alert, conscious individuals while they are engaged in various tasks. Computer simulations and artificial intelligence systems that challenge our ideas about what it means to be a conscious, feeling human are also being developed. These efforts produce converging operations that give us different perspectives and approaches to solving common problems about how the mind works. The student of cognitive psychology must be conversant with research and theory in many disciplines, including philosophy, linguistics, computer science, neurophysiology, evolutionary biology, anthropology, and experimental psychology. We must also understand the meaning and limitations of research methods in these different areas. The mind that tries to understand itself proposes a daunting challenge to our theoretical and experimental efforts. The joint steps of research and theory presented in this book should guide the reader through the beginnings of this process. Certain problems in cognition—such as how we quickly perceive and understand words and objects, how we learn and comprehend language, and how we develop conscious experiences—may not be solved within our lifetimes, but we can never succeed if we do not begin.

About *the* Authors

James F. Juola is Emeritus Professor of Psychology at the University of Kansas (KU) and Emeritus Professor of Human-Technology Interaction at Eindhoven University of Technology (TUE) in The Netherlands. He received his PhD in psychology from Stanford University in 1972 and began a 42-year teaching and research career mainly at the University of Kansas. In 1985,

he received a Fulbright Fellowship to join the research faculty at the Institute for Perception Research at TUE and began a 29-year partnership with TUE and Philips Research Laboratories, also headquartered in Eindhoven, as a researcher and half-time professor. Dr. Juola also served as a Visiting Professor of Psychology at the Autonomous University of Madrid, Spain, and Gettysburg College in Pennsylvania. He has published over 90 papers and given lectures in 12 countries in the areas of attention, perception, memory, life-span development, human-technology interaction, and robotics.

Hideya Koshino is Professor of Psychology and co-director of the Learning Research Institute at California State University, San Bernardino (CSUSB). He received his PhD in cognitive psychology from the University of Kansas in 1994 and started a teaching and research career at CSUSB. He also received a postdoctoral

fellowship for training in brain imaging (fMRI) at the Department of Psychology at Carnegie Mellon University, Pittsburgh, Pennsylvania. In 2007, he served as a visiting associate professor at Waseda University in Tokyo, Japan, and also as a visiting professor at Osaka University in Osaka, Japan, from 2013 to 2016. He has published over 25 papers and book chapters and given lectures in the areas of attention, working memory, life-span development, and autism, as well as brain–imaging applications to the study of cognitive psychology.

This work is dedicated to the thousands of students whom we have been privileged to have in our classrooms for over 70 years between us.

RICHARD ATKINSON

Wikimedia Commons
By University of California
(Atkinson family)

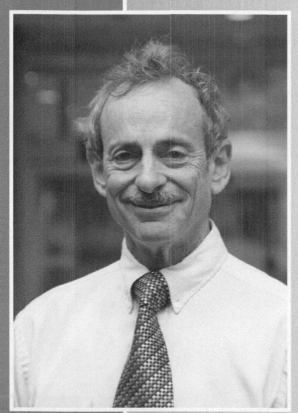

RICHARD SHIFFRIN

Photo courtesy of Richard Shiffrin

Chapter 1
Introduction and History

"As used here, the term, cognition, refers to all the processes by which the sensory input is transformed, reduced, elaborated, stored, recovered, and used. It is concerned with these processes even when they operate in the absence of relevant stimulation, as in images and hallucinations. Such terms as *sensation, perception, imagery, retention, recall, problem-solving,* and *thinking,* among many others, refer to hypothetical stages or aspects of cognition."

Ulric Neisser, *Cognitive Psychology,* 1967, p. 4

PREVIEW QUESTIONS

❖ *Where does knowledge come from?*

❖ *Is it possible to study mental processes if we cannot observe or measure them directly?*

❖ *Is cognitive psychology the study of human behavior or the study of the human mind?*

❖ *What roles, if any, do disciplines such as linguistics, computer science, anthropology, and neuroscience have in modern cognitive psychology?*

1.1 Introduction

Try to imagine, if you can, all that is going on around you and within you as you read these first few sentences. You might be seated in some quiet room, but undoubtedly there are other things going on that could distract you. Other people might be talking or you might hear music or traffic noises from outside. Nevertheless you continue on, but you are likely to turn away if someone calls your name, your telephone beeps, or you need to get a drink. As you read you might think of how your eyes move as you take in each new character and word in the line of print. Somehow these ink marks excite memories of words, language, and ideas, and you might generate original thoughts in your mind as you consider the meaning of the text. Finally you might reflect on what you have read, or discuss it with a friend, later to forget about it or recall some idea that might be interesting or important in addressing some problem. All of the acts involved in reading a few simple sentences and thinking about them include the topics that are actively researched and discussed by cognitive psychologists.

Cognitive psychology The study of how the human brain produces mental activity and observable behavior

Cognitive psychology, simply put, is the study of the human mind and how it works. It remains one of the most impenetrably difficult areas of research and theory in all of science. So difficult, in fact, that some psychologists in the early part of the twentieth century decided to study behavior, while at the same time, denying the very existence of the mind itself! This emphasis on behavior alone is an extreme view, but one that is nevertheless held by some scientists even today. The idea that the mind can study itself is fraught with methodological and theoretical problems that are a constant challenge for cognitive researchers. A strict behaviorist argues that observable facts are the only basis of knowledge. By this view, theory, at best, only suggests what observations are likely to be most important. Behaviorism, as set forth by John Watson (1913), maintained that human behavior should be explained only in terms of observable stimuli and responses. He claimed that any explanations based on appeals to hypothetical mental states or processes are simply speculative delusions, not based on observable, scientific facts. If such thoughts dominated psychology today, Neisser's (1967) insightful book, including the quote that begins this first chapter, would have been tossed into an academic trash heap rather than becoming one of the most important intellectual efforts defining the field of cognitive psychology.

It is our purpose in this book to impress upon students of cognitive psychology how modern methods of research and theory are capable of answering questions about what the human mind is like and how it works. We have a common advantage in exploring this discipline in that each of us has a mind to work with. Thus, we can appeal to you to think about what is involved in remembering, say, what you had for breakfast or where you last parked your car or bicycle. Similarly I might ask you to recall what you did on your 16th birthday, who your 3rd grade teacher was, what "vicissitude" means, or how to find the square root of 256. You can do these kinds of things, with more or less success, but it is interesting to introspect (i.e., look into one's self) about how they are done. Your introspections might be right or wrong, and they might agree with us or not, but they can result in interesting speculations that lead to testable theories of how the human mind works.

Introspection was a major scientific method used at the beginning of experimental psychology over 100 years ago. It was thought that the mind could study itself through careful thought and recording of one's experiences. Thus, when leaving a building, you might remember where you parked your car by remembering the route you took to approach the building after you parked it. Similarly, you might remember your 3rd grade school building, your classmates, and your teacher's face before recalling his or her name if in fact you can recall any of these very well. Memory sometimes seems to involve a kind of active recollection of one's thoughts or actions produced at an earlier time. Other memories are not so actively recalled, and we are sometimes perplexed about why we cannot remember certain things. Still other thoughts and memories seem to spring to consciousness without effort or will, or even to our own annoyance. It should be obvious that there are many aspects of memory that are hidden from one's own thoughts about the matter, and it is unlikely that we can agree about whether or not each of our memories work in exactly the same way. Introspection fails as a research tool because of this kind of variability across individuals, and behaviorism arose partly as a reaction against introspective research techniques. Cognitive researchers spawned a scientific approach to the study of memory and cognition that, rather than being based on subjective introspection, uses objective laboratory research to find out what we do when we try to perceive, learn, remember, and use information.

1.2 Historical Roots of Psychology

1.2.1 The Dawn of Epistemology

The study of the human mind has its origins in philosophy, particularly in the work of Greek philosophers, beginning about 2,500 years ago. They addressed a fundamental question that confronts us today: How does the mind acquire knowledge? Plato, a student of Socrates, argued that true knowledge could not possibly be based on experience because real-world objects are merely imperfect replicas of more general *ideas* or *forms*. Perfect forms, such a perfect sphere, exist only in our minds, and these are supposedly present from birth. Such internal forms help us to recognize what objects are and to understand how they can be used, but such knowledge generally precedes and is actually more important than any knowledge that can be gained from experience with objects. In fact forms are eternal and unchanging, unlike physical objects themselves, or even worse, our perceptions of them. Some philosophers have credited Plato with an important insight—true understanding of natural phenomena must go beyond mere observations alone. Indeed, our internal representations of object categories might be based on certain ideal members, or prototypes, which are parts of an important, modern theory of how we group things into categories. That is, our idea of whether a given object is a bird or a "good" red color might be based on how close the observed example is to an ideal or prototypical member of the respective category. Plato also anticipated a major contribution of the modern scientific method, namely scientific induction. The idea is that observations of real-world objects and events can lead to idealizations and generalizations that are the basis of theories that can eventually explain our perceptions (Cottingham, 1987).

Nativism The idea that much of our knowledge and behavior is inborn or biologically programmed to develop in a certain way

Plato advocated what came to be known as the **nativist doctrine** of knowledge. Nativists believe that much of what we know is innate. Such innate knowledge is necessary, according to the nativist view, since some aspects of our behavior are too complicated to be the result of learning. For example, it has been argued that our knowledge of language is too complete and acquired too early in life to be based on experience alone (e.g., Chomsky, 1959). Humans are also born with a variety of reflexes and behaviors that appear to be innate, such as startle, rooting (i.e., searching for a nipple when the face is stimulated), and grasping reflexes. These behaviors are common to other primates and have evolved presumably as a means to insure survival of relatively helpless newborns.

Empiricism The idea that much of our knowledge and behavior is learned through experience

Plato's student Aristotle argued, alternatively, that most knowledge could not possibly be inborn and shared by all of us. Rather, he believed that knowledge must be based on experience, a doctrine called **empiricism**. Aristotle originated the empiricist viewpoint that observation is the basis of all knowledge, and that learning is a product of experience. To Aristotle, even one's thoughts are the results of past experiences. He reduced all conscious processes to the internal manipulation of representations of the material world. The nativist-empiricist debate has persisted to the present day. This is at least partly due to the fact that there are hereditary, biological components to all human behaviors, even if they require appropriate experience for their full expression (e.g., Bridgeman, 2003). Although infants will show a stepping reflex if they are held over a hard surface, learning to walk occurs only much later and with appropriate practice after greater voluntary control of leg motions and balance is achieved.

1.2.2   Descartes and Rationalism

Rationalism The idea that much of our knowledge and behavior is created by mental activities alone and is the sole product of neither inheritance nor environment

Rene Descartes (1596–1650) and others developed the rationalist philosophy in the seventeenth century. **Rationalism** is the belief that true knowledge comes only from human reason, and that logical reasoning will reveal life's mysteries. Thus, rationalism denies both nativism and empiricism to some extent by making the human mind the creator of its own knowledge. Descartes was also the founder of the doctrine of dualism; namely that the body can be explained in terms of the physical laws of nature, but the mind exists as a transcendental spirit. Even though the mind and body interact in most behaviors, dualists believe that the human mind can never be reduced to mere biology. In that sense, knowledge does not come from experience alone, but from mental reflection upon experience that transcends physical limitations. It should be noted that not all rationalists were dualists. For example, Spinoza (1632–1677) rejected dualism, and proclaimed that the mind is a product of the body, yet he endorsed rationalism as a means for humans to ascend and prevail over animalistic behaviors. Further, rationalism asserts that we are not limited only to what we have been born with or to what has occurred to us in the past, but that we are capable of creating new ideas and bodies of information based on emergent properties of our inheritance and experiences.

1.2.3 British Empiricism

The ideas of Aristotle were rekindled in Britain in the seventeenth and eighteenth centuries in a reaction not only against rationalism, but also in opposition to centuries of spiritualism and mysticism. Francis Bacon (1561–1626) argued that knowledge grows only through induction of general principles from repeated observations provided through the senses. Since the physical world is supposedly a regular, law-abiding system, our careful observations should lead us to recognize these regularities. When we create formal statements that summarize these regularities, we have defined some of the laws of nature. Bacon was instrumental in separating science from philosophy by arguing that science must be based on rigorous testing of principles induced from observations. He anticipated the modern scientific method by rejecting the notion that we should seek only information that supports our ideas. By seeking confirmations of our beliefs, it would be possible to retain incomplete or erroneous theories indefinitely. Rather, he insisted that we must look for exceptions to proposed general principles in order to limit their generality or disprove them altogether.

John Locke (1632–1704) expanded on Bacon's views by tracing all simple ideas to their origins in specific sensory experiences. Simple ideas based on memories for specific objects and events could be combined through **association**, he argued, into complex concepts and abstract ideas. He also agreed with Isaac Newton that all objects and events in the universe obey lawful relationships of cause and effect. The associations among ideas in the mind were thought to reflect relations among objects in the real world. Further, mental associations could creatively represent imagined or even impossible physical events. The British empiricists' belief that simple associations form the basis of all knowledge has been used by cognitive psychologists today to explain many types of learning (e.g., Anderson, 1983). The empiricist tradition also has contributed to the general faith in the scientific method of inquiry to develop and test explanatory laws of nature, including theories of human behavior.

Associationism The idea that much of our knowledge and behavior can be reduced to simple associations among stimuli, their representations in memory, and responses

Intellectual giants like Galileo (1564–1642) and Newton (1642–1727) contributed to our understanding of natural laws based on observations under carefully controlled conditions. Their successes in physics encouraged the belief that the scientific method could be applied to the study of human behavior and mental processes. These views were supported by Charles Darwin (1871; 1872) despite criticisms from contemporaries that it "… would insult religion by putting the human soul in a pair of scales" (Gregory, 1987, p. 416). Yet, Darwin found himself forced to conclude that the mind has a physical basis in biology. He formed this conclusion from many observations of animal communication through facial expressions and bodily movements and posturing. He believed that not only our physical form, but also some of our abilities to communicate meanings and emotions were inherited from our nonhuman ancestors (Gregory, 1987, pp. 179–180).

1.3 **The Birth of Experimental Psychology**

1.3.1 Donders and the Subtractive Method

In the nineteenth century there was a flurry of developments to advance psychology as a separate domain of scientific inquiry apart from its roots in philosophy and physiology (Boring, 1950). The goal was to develop scientific psychology, modeled on physics, by using similar research methods, only applied to human behavior and mental processes. For example, F. C. Donders (1869/1969) in Holland sought a method to measure some properties of internal mental events. Although such mental processes remain hidden from direct observation, he thought that he could find a way to time their durations and then have at least something to say about how the mind works.

Donders began his research by using a simple stimulus, such as a light, and a simple response, such as hitting a button, and he timed how rapidly an observer could press the button when the light was turned on. Today we call this experimental procedure a measure of simple reaction time (RT), and for a normal young adult, simple RT can be as short as two-tenths of a second (200 milliseconds). Donders reasoned that if he could complicate this simple situation a bit and measure the RT for the more complicated task, he should be able to measure the time it takes for someone to deal with the complication. For example, he next used two different lights; say a green one and a red one. The observer was instructed to hit the button as rapidly as possible only if the green light appeared, and to do nothing if the adjacent red light turned on. Today we call this a go/no-go task, and it is not surprising that RTs on "go" trials in this task tend to be longer than those in simple RT tasks. The only difference between the two tasks is that in simple RT, there is only one light to attend to, but in the go/no-go task, there are two lights. Any difference in average RT between the two tasks should be equal to the time necessary for someone to make the discrimination between the green light and the red one.

Following this logic, Donders invented the **subtractive method**, whereby a specific mental event, like color discrimination, could be timed by performing the operation (see Figure 1.1).

The subtractive method can be used in any number of applications that are based on observable behaviors. In a simple example, if we notice that someone washes three plates in 45 seconds and four plates in 60 seconds, the difference between these two times should be the time necessary to wash a single plate. Of course, one could easily observe a human plate washer directly and measure the time to wash one plate with a stopwatch. The unique aspect of Donders's method is that it enables us to time mental events that are not directly observable. The subtractive method has been used in numerous laboratory studies to estimate the durations for a variety of different mental events. Although these times do not tell us exactly what is going on inside the head, they do allow us to compare times for different tasks and test theories about why some things should take longer than others.

Subtractive method A method of using differences in response times to measure the duration of mental processes (If two tasks differ in only one step, then their RT difference is equal to the time it takes to carry out that step.)

FIGURE 1.1

Example Application of Donders's Subtractive Method for Timing the Durations of Mental Events

---

(1) Simple reaction time (SRT) task: One stimulus and one response:

The subject is to push a response button as soon as a light (e.g., a green one) is turned on. Therefore, SRT consists of two processing stages: a stimulus encoding stage, in which the stimulus (e.g., the green light) is perceived, and a response stage, in which the response (push of the button) is executed.

SRT = elapsed time between onset of the green light and onset of the button press.

(2) Go/no-go response time (Go/no-go RT) task: Two stimuli and one response

The subject is to push a response button as soon as one of the lights is turned on (e.g., a green one), but is to withhold a response to the other one (e.g., red). Therefore the Go/no-go RT consists of three stages. The first stage is the stimulus encoding stage that is the same as the SRT. The second stage is a discrimination stage, in which the go stimulus and a no-go stimulus are discriminated. The third is the response stage that is the same as the SRT.

Go/no-go RT = elapsed time between onset of the green light and onset of the button press.

(3) Choice response time (CRT) task: Two stimuli and two responses

The subject is to push one response button for a green light, and a different response button for a red light. Therefore, CRT consists of four stages. The first and the fourth are the Encoding stage and the Response stage which are common across all three tasks. The second stage is the discrimination stage, which is the same as in the go/no-go task. The third stage is the Choice stage, in which the response button is selected.

CRT = elapsed time between the onset of the green light and the onset of the button press.

Therefore, the information processing stages in the three tasks are summarized as follows.

SRT = Encoding + Response

Go/no-go RT = Encoding + Discrimination + Response

CRT = Encoding + Discrimination + Choice + Response

Illustration of the subtractive method to time specific internal mental events:

Go/no-go RT − SRT = time to discriminate between two possible stimuli.

CRT − Go/no-go RT = time to choose between two possible responses

---

However, there are problems with using the subtractive method that were discovered shortly after its invention. The main problem is that the method assumes that the addition of some task component changes only how the observer deals with that component, and everything else remains the same. In some cases, however, additional components cannot be "purely inserted," but broadly affect other aspects of task performance. That is, the addition of another stimulus can produce qualitative changes in how the task is performed rather than merely quantitative changes. For example, taking a call on a mobile phone while driving might appear to take only a few seconds to pick up the phone and punch a button, but the diversion of attention away from driving for the entire length of the conversation can have serious consequences. A similar situation can occur when two different prescription drugs are taken that have predictable beneficial effects on their own, but their interaction is unpredictable and sometimes dangerous. It was not until 1966 that Saul Sternberg demonstrated how careful restrictions on Donders's method could lead to an improved method to study how the mind works (see Box 1.1).

BOX 1.1

Measuring the Speed of Mental Processes

In 1966, Saul Sternberg published a paper in the prestigious journal *Science* that had an enormous influence on cognitive psychology. In the first place, he refined a method for timing mental events that was based on the subtractive method of Donders. In the second place, he demonstrated how to develop theoretical ways to measure otherwise unobservable processes occurring in immediate or short-term memory.

The task he used was a simple one that can be approximated as follows: Think of your current telephone number. When you have it in mind, answer the following question as rapidly as possible—is there a five in it? Most people can make this decision rapidly and with few errors even if the numbers held in memory (the memory set, in Sternberg's terms) change from trial to trial and so does the single test digit (called the probe). In fact, Sternberg varied the size of the memory set from one to six items so that there would be few problems with forgetting or errors in the task, and the probe was a member of the memory set on half of the trials. People were told to hit a "yes" or "no" button as rapidly as possible to indicate whether or not the probe was a member of the memory set. Each subject was run for many trials with the memory set, and items varied randomly from trial to trial. The average response times (RTs) were then found, and the

RT data were plotted along the ordinate (Y axis) and the number of memory set items along the abscissa (X axis), as is normally done when observed data are plotted against experimental conditions.

The data showed one of the most striking results in all of modern psychology: The response times (RTs) were almost a perfect, increasing linear function of the number of memory items. Further, the slopes of the lines (average increase in RT for each additional memory item) were nearly identical for yes and no responses. This result was surprising for two reasons. First, most psychologists thought that immediate, short-term memory should be literally immediately accessible, so that there should be no increase in RT with increasing memory set size. Sternberg incorporated this idea in a parallel search model to reflect the fact that if all items in memory are accessed at once, the RT by set size functions should be flat. Since the functions had a positive slope, the simple parallel model was rejected.

An alternative model is based on the assumption that there is some kind of serial search process operating in short-term memory. If this search consists of an item-by-item scan looking for a match between the probe and each of the memory items, then the linear increase in RT across set size would be expected.

(Graph adapted from Sternberg, 1966)

Again, however, many psychologists objected. Why, they argued, should the linear increase be the same on yes and no trials, since the probe should match one of the memory items sometime during the scanning process on positive trials? On negative trials, the scan would have to go all the way through the memory set before a response could be made, but on positive trials, on average, the scan should have to go only halfway through the set. Therefore, there should be about twice as many comparisons on "no" trials as on "yes" trials. Since the increase in RT with increasing set size (slope of the line of best fit to the data) presumably reflects the number of comparisons that have to be made, the slope of the RT by set size function should be twice as large on negative trials as on positive trials. However, the data showed that the slopes were the same on "yes" and "no" trials. If the slope of the RT by set size function represents scanning time, then the results imply that all comparisons are made on both positive and negative trials even though a match is found sometime during the scan on positive trials.

Sternberg reasoned that on every trial some time is taken up by non-scanning processes that do not depend on the number of items in the memory set. That is, when the probe is presented, it must be visually processed and recognized before it can be compared with the items in memory. Further, when the comparison is complete, a decision must be translated into a motor response to hit the "yes" or "no" response button. Thus, probe recognition, decision, and response execution occur on every trial. The sum of their execution times yields a constant factor to overall RT. Only the number of comparisons changes from trial-to-trial. Thus, the slope of the RT by memory set size function represents the comparison time per item. Sternberg argued that since this comparison process is so fast (the slope was about 38 ms per item), it would make sense to execute all comparisons between the probe and the memory items before deciding whether a match had been found. Switching between a fast comparison process and a slow decision process after every comparison would only slow the whole process down. Sternberg argued that his data supported a serial, exhaustive scanning process operating in short-term memory for determining whether a probe matched one of the items held in memory. The exhaustive scan would be faster, on average, than a scan that checked for a match after every comparison and terminated with the discovery of a match on positive trials. Further, he demonstrated that the time to make a comparison between two codes in memory could be as little as about 38 ms, if his theory is correct.

There have been many replications of Sternberg's results over the past decades, and his theory has been challenged in various ways. Yet, he made several important, lasting contributions to cognitive science. He demonstrated that, with proper care, Donders's subtractive method could be used to measure the times needed for executing otherwise hidden mental processes. That is, by introducing only a simple change into an otherwise complex task, the change could be "purely inserted" to have an effect on only one process in the overall task. Varying the number of items in the memory set should affect only the memory comparison stage of processing, leaving probe encoding, decision, and response processes intact. Sternberg also developed a new methodology for the analysis of RT data to test theories of how mental operations are executed. Many advances and new applications have been made in the use of RT data to induce and test theories of cognitive processes based on Sternberg's original contribution.

1.3.2 Weber, Fechner, and Psychophysics

Ernst Weber and Gustav Fechner in Germany took a unique approach to using the scientific method to measure mental processes. They were interested in how our sensory responses are related to the strength or intensity of physical stimuli. In the mid-nineteenth century, Weber studied the just noticeable difference (jnd) between two similar stimuli, such as two lights that differed in brightness or two tones that differed in loudness. The jnd is the smallest change in stimulus intensity (up or down from some standard stimulus) that an observer can reliably report as a noticeable change. Weber made the important discovery that for almost all stimuli, the jnd was a linear, increasing function of the standard's stimulus intensity. He formulated the observed linear relation into what became known as **Weber's law**—the ratio of the jnd to stimulus intensity is a constant across stimulus intensity:

$$\text{jnd} = \frac{\text{Just noticeable change in stimulus intensity}}{\text{A standard stimulus intensity}} = \text{A constant value}$$

As an illustration, if 20 grams added to 100 grams is a just noticeable increase in weight, then 200 grams added to 1000 grams, which maintains the same ratio, should also be a just noticeable difference. This fact was confirmed in Weber's laboratory.

Fechner (1860) took these results one step further. He reasoned that an internal psychological scale must exist for every external physical scale that we are capable of perceiving. Our perceived brightness of a light, loudness of a tone, or heaviness of a weight must all be based on psychological values, not on physical values directly. That is, our sense organs determine the apparent intensity of a stimulus, and the apparent intensity need not change in a direct, linear relation with physical intensity. In fact, he proposed that the function relating psychological intensity to physical intensity should be logarithmic, rather than linear, in order to sustain Weber's law. The logarithmic relation describes diminishing increases in psychological intensity as physical intensity increases by constant increments [i.e., psychological intensity falls off as a negatively accelerating function of physical intensity (see Figure 1.2)]. This was a fundamental discovery—what we perceive is not a literal copy, nor even a simple linear transformation of object and event properties in the physical world. Rather, our senses transform aspects of physical objects and events into psychological variables that have different qualitative as well as quantitative properties than the underlying physical variables.

FIGURE 1.2

A Logarithmic Relationship between Psychological Intensity (ordinate) and Physical Intensity (abscissa) can Produce Equal jnds for Small Stimulus Changes at Low Intensities and Large Changes at High Intensities.

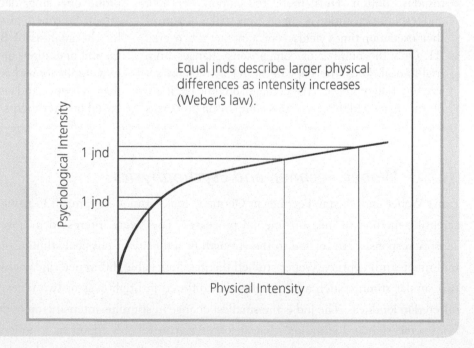

Equal jnds describe larger physical differences as intensity increases (Weber's law).

Psychological Intensity

1 jnd

1 jnd

Physical Intensity

The study of the relation between some physical variable and its psychological representation is called **psychophysics**. Plato was right in the sense that physical objects are imperfect representations of our mental ideas, but he was wrong in asserting that we could not learn about one from the other. Rather, research supported Aristotle's position that observations can determine what the world is like. There are lawful relationships between physical events and psychological interpretations, a fact anticipated by Fechner's psychophysics.

Psychophysics The study of the lawful relation between some physical property of a stimulus and the psychologically perceived property

1.3.3 *Ebbinghaus's Studies of Memory*

Other psychologists in Germany applied the scientific method to the study of learning and memory. One of these, Hermann Ebbinghaus, read Fechner's (1860) book and was duly impressed with the new application of the scientific method to mental processes. He decided to undertake a similar study of memory. His classic book (Ebbinghaus, 1885) describes a heroic study using himself as his only subject for many years of research. He daily studied lists of nonsense syllables (like DAF and KUD—chosen because they had no meaning and therefore were being learned for the first time in his experiment). His usual method was to study and test himself on each list repeatedly until he achieved perfect recall of the entire list. Then he put the list away and returned to it only after hours, days, or weeks had passed. Of course, he could recall very few items from the nonsense lists after long intervals between their original study and the subsequent tests, but he did show some memory for the lists, as they were usually learned more quickly the second time, even if he could not remember much about them when they were first recovered from his files. Thus, he discovered a type of implicit memory savings which became very important for later theories of human memory.

Ebbinghaus discovered many other facts about human learning and memory from his simple yet elegant studies using nonsense lists. He found that learning (and forgetting) is rapid at first, then slowly approaches some limit (see Figure 1.3). He also found that additional study even after perfect recall had been achieved (sometimes called *overlearning*) produced higher levels of memory later—a fact well worth considering in preparing for a test some days in the future.

Ebbinghaus also discovered what today is called the memory span—short lists of up to seven items or so can be remembered perfectly after a single study trial, but longer lists inevitably produce errors until they are studied several more times. Finally, he invented the method of **savings**, which is the most sensitive way to measure memory that has ever been devised. People can fail to recall or even recognize something like a game or a poem presented to them, but if they had ever played the game before or studied the poem for any length of time, it can usually be relearned with greater ease than if it never had been experienced before. This is but one example in which one's introspections about memory can be wrong; memory can be shown to exist for some things even when people deny ever having seen them before.

Savings The most sensitive measure of memory, developed by Ebbinghaus; the reduction in time to learn something a second time given that it was once learned earlier

FIGURE 1.3

Examples of Simple Learning and Forgetting Curves

From Hilgard, E. R., Atkinson, R. C., & Atkinson, R. L. (1975). *Introduction to Psychology,* 6th Ed. New York: Harcourt, Brace, Jovanovich, p. 214 (Figure 1.3.1) and p. 225 (Figure 1.3.2).

Figure 1.3.1 shows the proportion of correct responses after each study trial for a list of items. Learning is more rapid for the shorter list (50 items) than for the longer list (100 items), but the learning curve has the same shape. The data are from Atkinson (1972).

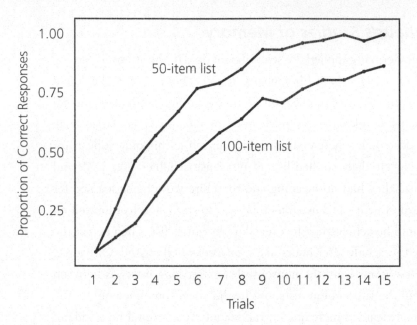

Figure 1.3.2 shows the amount of retention (measured as savings) for lists of nonsense syllables as a function of delay since the initial study to a level of perfect recall. The data are from Ebbinghaus (1885).

1.3.4   The First Laboratory in Experimental Psychology

Psychology as a formal discipline has often been traced to the founding of the first psychology laboratory by Wilhelm Wundt at the University of Leipzig in 1879. Many eminent psychologists began their careers in Wundt's lab, including James McKeen Cattell, the founder of the American Psychological Association and the American Association for the Advancement of Science. Wundt was a pioneer of many laboratory procedures that have remained in use to the present day. However, he is perhaps most famous for his unfortunate choice of **introspection** as a major method of studying mental events. He and his students were interested in reducing complex experiences to the simplest elements of conscious awareness. This choice was based on an analogy with physics—just as matter could be decomposed to its molecular and atomic components, Wundt hoped that introspection could reduce sensations to the "atoms of consciousness." Observers in his lab were presented with simple lights or tones and taught to think deeply about what they experienced. The method followed the rationalist tradition in that the power of human reason was supposed to reveal the true nature of mental processes. Further, it was believed that deep insight into one's mental processes could lead to the discovery of the elementary components of consciousness, just as physicists were discovering the fundamental structures of matter.

Introspection The subjective study of one's own mental processes by looking inward into oneself

Unfortunately, the method of introspection suffers from at least two fatal flaws. First, the method is unreliable. What you claim to experience and what I think I experience even in very similar situations is often different, sometimes startlingly so. Training in introspection was geared toward uniformity across individual experiences, so that one's success in graduate school could depend on having the same "mind's eye" as one's major professor. Yet, people can and do perceive things differently, even when trying to arrive at a consensus description of an observed event. Consider the common observation that different eyewitnesses of an accident or a crime often provide conflicting testimony.

A second fatal flaw for introspection is the fact that the method is insufficient to reveal many mental processes. Many things that we do in response to a stimulus, even a very simple one, occur too rapidly and at too low a level to be available to conscious introspection. For example, let's think about what happens when a light is suddenly turned on. Light striking the retina of the eye initiates a cascade of chemical and electrical processes that decades of study have failed to reveal completely. The first tenth of a second (100 milliseconds) after a flash of light results in propagation of millions of neural signals from the retina to several parts of the brain, most of which never result in conscious experiences. Introspection is obviously incapable of "shedding light" on early visual processes. Many other psychological processes, from simple reflexes to complex associations that come readily to mind, are also immune to conscious introspection about their origins and their effects on our behavior.

From this discussion you should not conclude that there is no use for introspection in psychology. All of us think about why we favor one friend over another or why we forget important appointments. However, our thoughts about these matters cannot be regarded as data in the sense that data are independently replicable observations. Nonetheless, introspections can lead to theories that are testable against data, as in the classic research of Sperling (1960), who asked how much information is visible in a single, brief exposure to a simple visual stimulus (see Box 1.2).

1.4 The Rise of Behaviorism

1.4.1 The Empirical Approach of Watson and Skinner

European psychologists' emphasis on introspection and conscious experience was one of the main causes of the rise of behaviorism in America early in the twentieth century. Scientists like John Watson and B. F. Skinner objected to the direction that psychology was taking, wandering far from its scientific beginnings in psychophysics (Fechner) and memory research (Ebbinghaus). In order to restore its place among the physical and biological sciences, they believed that psychologists should insist on replicability of research results. In other words, observations should be carefully made of the exact physical conditions of the stimulus environment, the exact properties of the subject's responses, and the relationships that exist between them. Only measurable stimuli and responses were to be included in behaviorism, along with manipulations of rewards and punishments that could influence the associations between stimuli and responses.

Behaviorists adopted the British empiricists' views that the acquisition of simple associations is the basis of all learning. For example, the repeated pairing of two stimuli, such as a bell and the presentation of food to hungry dogs in Pavlov's (1927) **classical conditioning** research, results in a learned association between the two stimuli. After repeated pairings, the bell alone could come to control the response—salivation in anticipation of feeding—almost as well as the original presentation of food alone. Pavlovian, or classical, conditioning shows that some types of learning can be based on the acquisition of associations between different, previously unrelated stimuli. Such associations are common in all of our experiences, such as when we associate an object or person with a name or associate fear with novel stimuli (e.g., a phobic fear of spiders or a prejudicial avoidance of members from another ethnic or religious group).

Operant, or Skinnerian, conditioning is also based on learning simple associations, but in this case, between a stimulus and a response that initially have weak or no associations. Skinner showed that a hungry rat would explore a cage thoroughly in search of food, and when it pressed a lever in the cage and a food pellet appeared, the rat would be likely to push the lever again. Very soon the hungry rat will push the lever rapidly and repeatedly when placed in the cage, demonstrating a learned association between the appearance of the lever and the response of pushing it in order to obtain

Classical (Pavlovian) conditioning The learned association between two stimuli due to repeated reinforced pairings (A bell followed by food leads to salivation to the bell alone.)

Operant (Skinnerian) conditioning A learned association between a stimulus and a response due to reinforced practice (A bar press followed by a food pellet increases the probability of a bar press in the future.)

BOX 1.2

Measuring the Duration of a Visual Image

Many experiments have been devised to answer the question: How much can we see in a single eye fixation? This question was addressed in Wundt's lab by James McKeen Cattell and also by Raymond Dodge and Benno Erdmann in Germany more than 100 years ago (see Huey, 1908/1968, for a thoughtful review of early research on word perception and reading). They used various types of apparatus to present words or letters very briefly that then were to be reported. The general conclusion was that the amount reported depended on the meaning and familiarity of the material. For unrelated consonants, however, only four or five items could reliably be reported even if there were many more letters in the display.

(a) Whole report

(b) Partial report
Tone immediate

(c) Partial report
Tone delayed

Procedure used in Sperling's (1960) experiment. (a) In the whole report task, subjects report as many letters as possible from a brief (50 ms) display—about 4.5 is the average number. (b) If a cue is given to report the top row (high tone), middle row (medium tone) or bottom row (low tone), performance is almost perfect (4 out of 4) if the tone occurs as soon as the display is offset. (c) If the tone is delayed for as little as half a second, however, performance drops precipitously. [From Goldstein, E. B. (2005). *Cognitive Psychology.* Belmont, CA: Thomson/ Wadsworth, p. 144.]

Continues

From the behaviorist tradition, the number of letters reported should be taken as the number seen, since correct report is a reliable behavioral response. Yet almost everyone who has ever participated in these types of experiments has complained that many letters can actually be seen, but they gradually fade away before they can be reported. What can an experimental psychologist do if observers' introspective reports disagree with the data that are collected? What was done for almost a century was to ignore the subjective reports and record the actual data. The number of letters correctly reported after a single brief exposure of a multi-letter display was taken as a measure of what was actually seen.

In 1960, George Sperling published the results from his doctoral dissertation in a paper that became one of the hallmarks of the cognitive revolution. He took his observers' introspections to heart and tried to invent a way to measure how much information was actually available immediately after a brief visual display. He hit on the clever idea that rather than asking his participants to report all the letters in the display (whole report task), he would only ask for part of the display to be reported (partial report task). The trick was that the observers never knew which part was to be reported until after the display was turned off!

Sperling used displays of unrelated consonants in rows and columns centered on the display. For example, the display could include four consonants in each of three rows. Sperling used a tone, sounded shortly after the display ended, to cue the observers which row to report. A high tone indicated the top row, a medium pitch indicated the middle row, and a low tone indicated the bottom row. He found that people could accurately report letters from the cued row if the tone was presented within a fraction of a second after the display was shut off. However, if the tone was delayed further, observers could only guess from the four or five letters that they could remember in short-term memory (whole report level). That is, the partial report technique showed an advantage over whole report that was statistically significant for cue delays up to almost a half second after the display was physically gone.

The important deduction that Sperling made was that since his subjects could report three to four letters from the single cued row, without knowing which row was to be cued, then they must have had three to four letters available for a brief time from each of the rows. This very-short-term visual memory came to be called *iconic memory* to indicate its

sensory nature. The icon is a brief image of a display that persists for some time in sensory memory after the display is gone. The iconic image can be scanned with attention much like an actual display can be scanned with eye movements, but its duration is very brief. Once the icon is gone, and Sperling found that little useful information persisted beyond about 300 ms in most conditions, only those letters remain which have been coded into a more durable form, such as letter names in verbal short-term memory.

The importance of Sperling's research rests on its demonstration that although introspections might be unreliable, they nonetheless can be sources of theories to be tested in the laboratory. In this case, people's introspections are correct. A brief visual display is stretched out in time by persisting sensory activity, and as long as it lasts, the sensory image can be looked at by the "mind's eye" in much the same way that we examine a concrete image with eye movements. Since the time of Sperling's research, it has been shown that other sensory modalities, such as hearing and touch, also have brief memories. Sensory memories serve the likely function of lengthening the time that sensory information is available so that we can attend to selected parts and code them into a more permanent form for later use. The image of a tiger illuminated by a flash of lightning or the flickering light of a campfire would be useless if it could not be retained long enough for us to figure out what it is. Similarly, speech sounds cannot be recognized as words or sentences unless we have some type of memory available to integrate them over time. The first operation performed on selected sensory information is to try to match or categorize it with respect to known information in memory. We call this categorization process perception, and it is the topic of Chapter 3.

a reward. In general, operant conditioning relies on behavior coming under control of its consequences. Many human behaviors are similarly shaped by the consequences that follow them. Talking at the dinner table is much more likely to be reinforced by one's companions than talking in a movie theater, resulting in different behaviors in the two situations.

Behaviorists developed the scientific method of inquiry to a high level in psychology. They are largely responsible for the scientific rigor we demand in research today, based on careful recordings of the stimulus environment and exact specifications of how a response is defined and measured. They also insisted on strict controls in laboratory science, so that ideally all variables (both environmental and subject variables) could be controlled but one, and that one was deliberately manipulated to observe its effects on behavior. Such precision and control enables research results to infer causal relations among variables, and it allows data to be collected in similar ways in different laboratories to test the generality of causal laws. Then results can be replicated (or not) and theories can be tested in a way that enables knowledge in the field to accumulate.

1.4.2 Limits of Behaviorism

Behaviorism's insistence on observables excluded most of the topics of interest to modern cognitive psychologists, as listed in the quote from Neisser (1967) at the beginning of this chapter. Mentalism was excluded from the scientific endeavor since behaviorists believed that there was no way to measure mental events, only their consequences in observable behaviors. Thus, the study of processes, like thought and imagery along with much of perception and problem solving, were dismissed as unscientific because the underlying variables could not be controlled or directly observed.

To modern cognitive psychologists, behaviorism appears to have "thrown the baby out with the bath water," as mental structures and processes are at the heart of all interesting human behaviors. Further, new methods have been developed to observe and measure mental events, however indirectly (e.g., Sperling, 1960; Sternberg, 1966—see Boxes 1.1 and 1.2). Nevertheless, behaviorists had many positive contributions to make. Mainly, these include insistence on rigorous methodology, precise definition of stimulus and response conditions, replication of results over many trials and with new participants, and the search for lawful relations expressed as associations among stimuli and responses that depend on past learning situations.

1.5 The Cognitive Revolution

1.5.1 The Relevance of Animal Models

Between about 1940 and 1960 psychologists and other scientists in related fields began to have some misgivings about the generality of behaviorism to human psychological issues. The behaviorists were interested in describing basic laws of behavior derived from experiments on learning and forgetting of simple associations. For their research, they commonly used animals, such as rats and pigeons, since the discovery of behavioral laws required tight control of the experimental environment as well the animals' past history of rewards and punishments. Such controls could be unethical for research with humans. Thus, the research was necessarily restricted to simple association learning, and uniquely human abilities—such as language, reasoning, decision making, and complex problem solving—were largely unstudied. Another problem with behaviorism as a model science was its limitation to descriptive laws of behavior rather than more general theories that could explain and predict behavior in a wider variety of situations (see Box 1.3).

Researchers concerned with understanding human abilities were particularly dissatisfied with behaviorism's accounts of how we learn things like our native spoken language. Behaviorists believed that the acquisition of individual words and short phrases developed through imitation of adult speech. Linguists, however, produced convincing evidence that children's speech was very much unlike any adult's. Young children tend to say things like "She goed out the door," "I losted it," and "I no find it" that indicate that rules (however different from the grammatical rules of an adult) rather than specific word combinations are being learned. Linguists, such as Chomsky (1959), marveled at the speed of first language learning and the number of universals across all human languages—both indictors that there is a large innate, biological capacity behind human language acquisition and use. The acknowledgement of inherited abilities and the demonstration that people can learn general rules in addition to specific habits demanded change from the tenets of radical behaviorism.

1.5.2 *The Advent of the Computer Age*

Another important development occurred in the mid-twentieth century: the construction of the first large computers that were designed to be general-purpose machines. That is, rather than being useful merely for crunching numbers, the machines were designed to read inputs, store them temporarily while various operations were performed, retrieve additional information from memory, and use the results to produce new information for storage or to execute some task, such as producing a useful output. The goal was to manufacture a symbol-processing device with various memory systems and computational abilities that could be programmed to do things that, if a human did them, we would label them as "intelligent." It should be no surprise that intelligent beings generally created intelligent machines in their own image, at least in terms of overall architecture (see Box 1.4).

Of course, in order to program a computer to do something intelligent, we usually want to know what intelligent behavior is. This often requires that we understand what the most intelligent response would be in some situation, at least in terms of

BOX 1.3
The Place of Theory in the Scientific Method

A theory is a general principle induced from a variety of observations that summarizes and explains a body of knowledge. That is, unlike its everyday use, it is more than a mere guess or a hypothesis about some specific observation. Rather, a theory has some scope that depends on its consistency with a large body of observations, such as the theories of motion and inertia, the relativity of space and time, the conservation of matter and energy, and biological evolution. A theory also can be used to predict observations in new situations. That is, theories go beyond mere description of data to include explanations that are the basis of predictions in new circumstances. If the predictions are correct, then the theory is maintained, and new generalizations are incorporated into the theory. If the predictions are incorrect, however, the theory must be reconsidered and perhaps changed or rejected entirely and replaced with a better description and explanation of natural phenomena.

The strength of the scientific method of inquiry is to develop, by deductive logic, hypotheses from a theory that are specific enough that they can be compared with data collected in an experiment. That is, theories are useful not only if they provide an explanation of behavior, but if they are capable of being disproved in the face of observational data (i.e., they are falsifiable, see Popper, 1959). The concept of falsifiability is crucial, as a theory is of no use if it can explain everything and never be proven wrong. For example, a conspiracy theory is difficult to eliminate, because the theorist could always say that the right evidence has not yet been collected (and often cannot be) to disprove it. The idea in science is akin to natural selection in determining the survival of the fittest. Hypotheses die out through competition in the field or in the laboratory. The goal of science is to develop cumulative knowledge about some area of importance, such that explanatory theories continually are refined or rejected as more observations are made. Science progresses much like Sherlock Holmes in solving a mystery—when the impossible is eliminated, we are left with the possible.

Sweeping theories of behavior were never goals of behaviorism (with some exceptions; e.g., see the review of Hull's learning theory in Hilgard & Bower,

1975), but such theories were needed when psychologists faced demands for applications of their science to important human problems. Important issues arising in the twentieth century include: (1) What is the best way to teach our children to read? (2) What is the best way to teach inexperienced people to use new technology, such as radar equipment, flight traffic controls, and instruments in cockpits or nuclear power plants? (3) How should such new technology be designed to make it easy to use while minimizing costly human errors? (4) How can we build computers and write programs to do intelligent things like solve problems, translate messages from one language to another, and provide advice in uncertain situations? Behaviorism offered some suggestions in these areas, but many scientists found it to be inadequate on both practical and theoretical grounds. For example, during World War II, the question was raised about how to design sights and guidance systems to improve accuracy of bombs and missiles. B. F. Skinner suggested using a trained pigeon in the nosecone of a missile that could control its direction by pecking at part of touch-sensitive display if the missile lurched off-target. Although his system might well have worked, it was rejected by the military as fantasy and science fiction conjured up by a crackpot professor. Animal conditioning also said little about the larger issues of how to train novices to use high-tech equipment creatively in uncertain situations.

Having general theories of human behavior serves several purposes. First, if the theories are valid, we have a way of summarizing and understanding some body of observations about human cognition and behavior. Second, theories allow us to generalize and predict behavior in new situations, in which no observations have previously been made. Third, theories provide a means of communicating ideas among researchers within and across disciplines, so that their short-hand descriptions reduce ambiguities in discussing research. Finally, theories allow us to carry out simulations of human behavior by intelligent machines that can do useful things for us in distant or difficult situations, such as underwater, in the centers of power plants, in outer space, inside the human body, and so on.

how we would react ourselves. Only then can the behavior be duplicated in computer codes that might well execute the process much more rapidly and accurately than humans can. What resulted from this enterprise was a kind of symbiosis based on computer simulations of human behavior. That is, in order to program a computer to

---

BOX 1.4
A General Theory of Human Memory

One of the goals of cognitive psychology is to develop theories of mental structures and processes that summarize and explain existing data as well as make predictions about what should be observed in new situations. In the late 1960s, several researchers had decided that enough had been discovered to begin the task of developing a general theory of human memory. These theories borrowed concepts of information processing theory as realized in early computer systems. Perhaps the most influential of these theories was that of Atkinson and Shiffrin (1968; 1971).

Atkinson and Shiffrin expanded on William James's (1890) distinction between what he called primary memory and secondary memory. According to James, there is a difference between those thoughts that are immediately available to us and those that can be brought to mind only with some effort and uncertainty. Atkinson and Shiffrin called these two types of memories, short-term and long-term memory. To these they added sensory memories, of the type that Sperling (1960; see Box 1.2) had discovered for vision. Thus, there were three memory structures in their model: sensory memory, short-term memory, and long-term memory.

Sensory memories exist for all modalities, but they provide more information than we can possibly attend to at one time. Only some of the information available is selected for inclusion in short-term memory. Short-term memory has a limited capacity; it can handle only those few ideas or images that are actively maintained in conscious awareness. Long-term memory, on the other hand, is the enormous repository of everything we have ever learned, including specific details about our past as well as all general knowledge about things like language and mathematics.

To these three structures, Atkinson and Shiffrin added a number of processes for transforming information and shunting it among the memory systems. In this way, their model was analogous to a computer that has several types of memory structures to hold information temporarily or permanently and a set of software programs for controlling the contents of the memories and the operations performed on these contents. Thus, the memory structures in the Atkinson-Shiffrin model are analogous to the hardware components of a computer, and the proposed memory processes are analogous to its software. The structural and processing components of a revised version of their model are shown

A Proposed Model of Human Memory (after Atkinson & Shiffrin, 1968)

The structural components include sensory memories, short-term memory, and long-term memory. They differ in their properties as indicated in the following table.

	Capacity	Type of Code	Duration	Forgetting
Sensory	Large	Precategorized Sensations	1/2 to 2 secs	Decay or Overwriting
Short-term	Small	Subvocalizations Imagery	15 secs without Rehearsal	Replacement
Long-term	Unlimited	Semantics, Episodes, Procedures	Lifetime	Possibly none, retrieval failures due to Interference

The processing components include the following, as numbered in the above figure:

1. Sensation: the process by which physical stimuli are encoded into sensory messages that are sent to the brain

2. Attention: the process by which one or a few sensory inputs are selected for further processing by entering them into short-term memory

3. Automatic activation: the process by which some sensory signals activate corresponding codes in long-term memory without attention or awareness

4. Rehearsal: the process by which some codes are maintained in short-term memory by continuous processing, such as subvocalization or refreshing images

5. Forgetting from short-term memory: the loss of information through lack of rehearsal and spontaneous decay or overwriting by new inputs

6. Storage: the copying of new codes into long-term memory (learning)

7. Retrieval: the copying of old codes into short-term memory (remembering)

8. Controlled responses: the execution of some responses under control of conscious processes

9. Automatic responses: the execution of some responses without intention or awareness (e.g., a reflex)

All aspects of this version of the Atkinson-Shiffrin theory are based on research carried out over the last four decades of the twentieth century. The theory forms the basis for the consensus view of cognitive psychologists as we research new areas of human behavior and mental life. Although all cognitive psychologists have some disputes with the exact structure and terminology put forth here (for example, short-term memory has evolved into "working memory" to emphasize its complex processing capabilities beyond mere storage), the model is a good theoretical summary of human cognition. It summarizes much common jargon and beliefs that cognitive psychologists share in discussing their subject, and it forms a consolidating basis for what will follow in the rest of this textbook.

solve a problem, we must understand and recreate problem-solving strategies used by people (i.e., a theory of human problem solving ability needs to be developed). At the same time, to complete the symbiotic relationship, effective programs and subroutines created by computer scientists can be used as models of human behavior. Of course, their usefulness in psychology depends on how well these computer models can explain and predict people's behaviors.

1.5.3 Cognitive Neuroscience

Another research area that has made important contributions to cognitive psychology is neuroscience. Biologists have long been studying how the nervous system works in animals and humans, and important advances in understanding neural processes have recently been made. Since cognition and behavior are controlled by the actions of nerve cells (neurons), it is of fundamental importance for psychologists to understand the basic structures and processes of the central nervous system. These include the study of normal as well as brain-damaged individuals. Head injuries, tumors, strokes, and other types of damage to the brain offer insights into normal brain function when we observe the loss of functions associated with damage to specific areas. There have also been tremendous advances in our ability to record neural activity in both the peripheral and central nervous systems of normal people. Existing methods can now yield fairly precise information about electrical and metabolic activities in the brains of alert, conscious individuals while performing various tasks. These measures can be used to indicate which cerebral areas are active in performing the tasks, as well as the sequence in which different brain areas coordinate their activities. The combination of results from brain-damaged individuals and observations of activity in normal brains gives a two-pronged approach to the problem of relating brain activity to observable behavior.

1.5.4 Cognitive Science

According to Howard Gardner (1982), 1956 is viewed as the first year of cognitive psychology because of three epoch-making events that took place in this year. The first event was the publication of the seminal paper by George Miller titled "The Magical Number Seven Plus or Minus Two", in which he proposed a common capacity limit for many memory and judgment behaviors. We will discuss his paper in more detail in Chapter 6. The second was the publication of the book titled "Syntactic Structures" by Noam Chomsky. His book revolutionized linguistics and created the new field called *psycholinguistics*. The third was the conference of computer scientists held at Dartmouth College, in which the term "artificial intelligence" was coined.

Today, we are witnessing the growth of a new scientific discipline called cognitive science, which pools data and theory from several sources. At the heart of this endeavor is laboratory science, in which theories are tested against the behavior of people in controlled situations. Psychologists' efforts have profited from converging operations in related fields, such as linguistics, computer science, anthropology, philosophy, and neuroscience, to develop increasingly complete theories of human mental processes. The challenge is to understand the very complex behaviors that are uniquely human, or sometimes present in an abbreviated form in other animals or artificially-intelligent devices, such as problem solving, the use of tools, the design of new technologies, and the development and use of language. The goal of research and theory in cognitive science is to understand all aspects of human behavior based on models of human mind-body systems. Success in this task will enable us to design new technologies in the fields of science, education, and entertainment that are able to extend human capabilities while compensating for human limitations.

Chapter **Summary**

Cognitive psychology is as old as people's abilities to think about where knowledge comes from and as new as the most modern methods of neuroscience and artificial intelligence. In the past people argued about whether knowledge is inborn, comes from experience, or is created anew in each person's thinking brain. In truth, we realize today that knowledge comes from many places, and almost all human behavior is a joint product of nature, nurture, and the power of human reason.

Any system as complicated as the human brain can best be studied using several different methods. Cognitive psychologists are proficient in testing information-processing models against human performance in strictly controlled laboratory experiments. In this way, proscribed parts of the entire cognitive system can be tested in relative isolation without the complications of trying to explain behavior in the immense and variable natural world. The problem of studying human behavior is greatly simplified by the strategy of divide and conquer. Such efforts can also lead to problems, however, in that any complex human behavior is the result of concerted contributions from a variety of neural substrates. In addition, textbooks, such as the one in your hands, can suffer from presenting "… a series of disconnected phenomena, a rag-tag collection of curiosities—what you might find at a psychologist's garage sale" (Rosenbaum, 2014, p. ix). Larger systems, such as the Atkinson-Shiffrin theory, result from attempts to put the pieces back together again, however premature such general theorizing might be given our current state of knowledge.

At the same time, psychologists appreciate the power of converging operations in applying different scholarly and laboratory disciplines to understanding the human mind and how it works. Tremendous insights into the design of intelligent systems have been gained from attempts to program computers to mimic and exceed human capacities for processing information. Similarly, the challenge of understanding how people come to learn and use language has produced contributions from laboratory experiments, computer speech production and comprehension systems, linguistic theory, and studies of the physiological processes occurring in normal and injured human brains. A new cognitive science is developing that combines these and other disciplines into a joint effort to gain an understanding of the structures and processes of the human brain, and how they come together to produce behavior, thoughts, feelings, and conscious awareness of the physical and social world.

Review Questions

- **Where does knowledge come from?**

  Knowledge traditionally has been ascribed to three different sources. Nativists argue that much of what we know is inborn or develops naturally as biological systems mature. Empiricists assert that knowledge results from experience with the outside world, including our social environment, and rationalists say that much of what we know we derive ourselves through mental effort and the power of human reason. There is at least some truth in all of these claims, as most human behavior results from multiple causes. There is room for explanation from many sources for the vast amount of knowledge and computational power that all of us carry around inside our heads.

- **Is it possible to study mental processes if we cannot observe or measure them directly?**

  The history of experimental psychology provides both classic and recent examples of how theory and experimentation go hand-in-hand to derive explanations of how the mind works. Over 100 years ago, Donders and Fechner demonstrated that we could measure mental processes, however indirectly, in a way that eliminated some theoretical explanations in favor of others. Similarly, Ebbinghaus used the scientific method to discover some of the basic properties of human learning and memory. Recent demonstrations of the power of theory to develop models of how the mind works include Sperling's demonstration of the existence of sensory memory and Sternberg's studies of the speed of comparisons in working memory. Theories and their rigorous tests in the laboratory have allowed us to build complicated information-processing systems, such as the Atkinson-Shiffrin theory, that go a long way toward explaining experimental data and providing direction for further research to correct and expand our theoretical understanding of mental life.

- **Is cognitive psychology the study of human behavior or the study of the human mind?**

  In truth, human behavior is the observation window into the mind that perceives and remembers information, and plans, controls, and executes behaviors. Therefore, behaviors are the data against which theories of the underlying mental operations that produce them can be tested. Cognitive psychology is thus a study of both behavior and the mental processes that give rise to it.

- **What roles, if any, do disciplines such as linguistics, computer science, and neuroscience have in modern cognitive psychology?**

  Linguistics is the study of language structure, and psycholinguistics is the study of linguistic behavior. Learning to speak and to read a natural language are two of the most important things that we learn in all our lives. Therefore, linguistics will always play a central role in developing theories of the kind of knowledge that children must acquire to master their native language and adults must have to communicate effectively.

Computer science is intimately related to cognitive psychology in that both research areas are centered on the design of intelligent systems, albeit natural versus artificial. Although some useful analogies can be made between software and mental processes and between hardware and mental structures, most advances in both fields are obtained at more abstract levels. Common problems are confronted in attempts to understand both human and artificial intelligence, such as in trying to define what we mean by intelligence, how language is used productively to communicate ideas, and how we can learn to navigate in a three-dimensional world filled with different static and moving objects. Solutions in one area frequently give rise to applications in the other, thus fostering a synergy across disciplines.

Finally, any theory of human behavior must be consistent with known facts of human physiology. The brain is an immensely complicated organ that is slowly yielding its secrets through applications of new techniques that measure activity in living, intact human brains and those that evaluate the performance of people with brain damage. Theories of human behavior increasingly incorporate neural-systems components in order to forge a closer approximation to the actual structures and processes of the human brain.

Key Terms

Associationism   5

Classical (Pavlovian) conditioning   14

Cognitive psychology   2

Empiricism   4

Introspection   13

Nativism   4

Operant (Skinnerian) conditioning   14

Psychophysics   11

Rationalism   4

Savings   11

Subtractive method   6

Weber's Law   10

Associated Press

Chapter 2

The Peripheral and Central Nervous Systems: Elementary Cognitive Neuroscience

"I wish you to consider ... that all the functions which I attribute to this machine, such as digestion ... respiration, waking, and sleeping; the reception of light, sounds, odors ... the impression of ideas in the organ of the common sense and imagination, the retention of these ideas in the memory; the inferior ... appetites and passions; and finally the movements of all external members ... I say, that you consider that these functions occur naturally in this machine solely by the dispositions of its organs, not less than the movements of a clock."

Rene Descartes (1596–1650), quoted in Blakemore (1977) pp. 22–23.

PREVIEW QUESTIONS

❖ *How do sensory systems inform the brain about the outside world?*

❖ *How do we know what information from the physical world is selected for further use?*

❖ *How can we measure activity inside the brain of an active, alert human?*

❖ *What are the behavioral consequences of damage to different areas of the brain?*

2.1 Introductory Neuroscience

Human behavior often begins as a response to external stimulation. The brain exists in a dark and quiet world, yet it has the power to recreate vivid images of objects and events around us. Specialized sensory organs have evolved to inform the brain about environmental lights, sounds, and other physical disturbances. Different parts of the brain are specialized for receiving and interpreting sensory signals about sights, sounds, touches, smells, and tastes. Other parts of the brain coordinate information

Neuron A specialized cell in the nervous system that has three main parts, namely a cell body that includes the nucleus, branching fibers called dendrites that receive inputs from other neurons, and an axon fiber that ends in branches that release transmitter substances to communicate with other neurons

Synapses The tiny spaces between the axon terminals of one neuron and the dendrites of another; when a spike is propagated along an axon, it releases neural transmitters when it reaches the terminals; these can either excite or inhibit subsequent neurons when the transmitters are absorbed into the dendrites

from various senses and decide how to respond to them. Still other parts direct motor responses, controlling bodily functions such as eye movements, walking, reaching, and grasping. In short, all of our behaviors, from simple reflexes to complex thoughts and their intricate expressions, are the result of activity in the nervous system. For this reason, a basic understanding of the brain and how it learns about the world through the senses is an indispensable part of cognitive psychology.

The sensory systems possess specialized cells that transform physical events into neural codes. In most of the nervous system, these codes are simple spikes, or rapid changes in the electrical charge difference between the inside and outside of a nerve cell (**neuron**). When a spike travels along a neural fiber (axon), it eventually reaches its end, resulting in the release of chemical transmitter substances into the tiny spaces called **synapses** between nerve cells (see Figure 2.1). These transmitter substances have the potential to increase (excite) or decrease (inhibit) the activity of neurons that take them in. It is the change in rate of firing, measured in number of spikes per second, that is the only information provided by sensory neurons to the brain. These spikes are sent rapidly along sensory peripheral nerves to various parts of the central nervous system. Eventually they result in brain activity correlated with our conscious perceptions of the outside world and our reactions to them.

There are essentially five ways that cognitive scientists study processes occurring in the human brain:

(1) Behavioral studies of how average people (i.e., non-neurological patients) perform various tasks

(2) Recordings of electrical activity in individual neurons or groups of neurons during task performance

(3) Sophisticated imaging techniques to record brain metabolism while alert subjects perform those tasks

FIGURE 2.1

The Transmission of Sensory Information

Schematic diagram showing the transmission of sensory information from a receptor cell along a nerve fiber to a synapse with a typical neuron. Chemical information taken up by the dendrites can lead to excitation or inhibition of the neuron, leading to a change in the number of impulses (spikes) it sends along its axon to the dendrites of other neurons.

Adapted from Goldstein, E. B. (2005). *Cognitive Psychology.* Belmont, CA: Thomson Wadsworth, p. 29.

(4) Observing any performance decrements in brain-injured people in performing the same tasks

(5) Testing theories of task performance against any of these data as well as using the theories to predict behavior in real or artificial systems

The use of data and research methods from a number of related disciplines gives scientists the power of converging operations to attack a problem from several different approaches. Combining behavioral, neurophysiological, and theoretical studies of brain function in normal versus brain-damaged individuals should lead to better and more complete explanations of the relation of brain activity to conscious experience and resulting behavior.

Although there are a large number of innate reflexes that result in orienting (e.g., turning the eyes and body toward a loud sound or a sudden flash of light), many behaviors have to be learned. The brain learns to associate sensory inputs with specific environmental objects and events. We need to learn to recognize our caregivers when we are young and the differences between desirable and dangerous objects as we mature. We also must learn which stimuli are most important and which are unimportant or safe to ignore. Unimportant sensory events need to be filtered out, and important ones need to be attended in order to maintain effective interaction with the environment. If we could not separate important sensory inputs from unimportant ones, we would experience information overload and interference with accomplishing even simple goals. We might not even live to pass on our genes if we were not able to tell the difference between a stick and a snake. We will begin the study of neuroscience by first exploring sensory processes and then the resulting activity in the central nervous systems of normal and brain-damaged individuals.

2.2 Sensory Processes

Sensation begins with some physical signal making contact with specialized receptor cells in various parts of the body. Receptor cells are directly affected by physical events or objects, such as electromagnetic energy (vision), mechanical pressure waves (hearing), pressure and temperature (skin senses), and various chemicals (taste and smell). Receptor cells are also called transducer cells, since they change (**transduce**) physical matter or energy into biochemical energy and eventually into electrical spikes transmitted along sensory nerve cell fibers.

In vision, some of the individual photons of light energy that enter the eye through the pupil eventually pass into the rod and cone receptor cells in the inner lining of the eye, called the retina. Some of these are then absorbed by the photopigments that are located in the 120 million or so receptors in each eye. When a pigment molecule inside a rod or cone absorbs a photon, a cascade of chemical reactions begins that changes the way the receptor cell relates to other nerve cells in the retina. These

Sensation Activity in the peripheral and central nervous systems that results directly from physical stimulation

Transduction The conversion of external, physical sources of energy into internal biochemical and electrical activity by sensory receptor cells changes are eventually communicated via a number of intermediary cells to special neurons called ganglion cells, of which there are about 1 million in each eye. The axons of the ganglion cells join together to form the optic nerve that leaves the eye at a point called the blind spot (see Figure 2.2). Although the blind spot contains no receptors, we are usually not aware of it for two reasons. First, the spots correspond to two different locations in space for the two eyes. Second, the visual system tends to fill in the blind spots with best-guesses of their contents based on their immediate surroundings (Ramachandran & Rogers-Ramachandran, 2005).

In hearing, sound waves in the air are converted to mechanical pressure waves in the fluid inside the cochlea of the inner ear. These pressure waves produce vibrations along a cochlear membrane in which tens of thousands of transducing hair cells are embedded. The bending and shearing forces applied to the hairs result in internal changes in the cells, beginning the train of neural impulses that eventually reaches the brain (see Figure 2.3).

In order to sense heat, cold, pressure, and pain, our skin is embedded with a variety of receptor cells that detect physical changes in skin conditions. Again, the skin's transducer cells convert these mechanical forces into neural signals that wind their way to the spinal cord and brain. The chemical senses (taste and smell) also depend on specialized receptors that make use of molecular structures on their cell membranes to bind and interact with chemicals in food or in the air. Other tastes and odors are detected by changes in the porosity of receptor cells' membranes. The transduction process is not as well understood here as in the other senses, but the general principles are the same (Goldstein, 2001).

It is a fact that the only information the brain receives about the outside world is a train of neural impulses arriving from different sensory pathways through various relay stations along the way. A faculty member once asked one of my (JJ's) students in a master's oral examination: "How can you tell if you are seeing something or hearing something?" The mystified student had obviously never given much thought to such a question, and he did a lot of embarrassed hemming and hawing for several minutes. Finally, the committee rescued him—we admitted that it was a difficult question! The simple answer is that the only cognitive difference between sights and sounds depends on what part of the cerebral cortex receives the input relayed from the stimulus. The actual answer, of course, is a lot more complex than that, so let's start with the sensory pathways and see how external information is conducted to the brain.

2.3 **Pathways to the Brain**

2.3.1   Subcortical Sensory Pathways

For the remainder of this chapter, and the next one on perception, we will concentrate on vision and hearing only, as these senses are the best understood and the source

FIGURE 2.2

The Eye and the Retina

Figure 2.2.1 shows a cross section of a human eyeball into which light enters the eye through the pupil on left and is focused by the lens onto the inner lining of the eye—the retina. Visual information is carried to the brain via the optic nerve.

Figure 2.2.2 shows a schematic representation of a cross section through the retina, showing the receptor cells (rods and cones) at the top of the drawing, which represents the outermost neural cells in the retina. Intermediate cells, including horizontal, bipolar, and amacrine cells, relay information to the ganglion cells whose axons leave the eye in a bundle called the optic nerve.

Figure 2.2.1 from Goldstein, E. B. (2005). *Cognitive Psychology*. Belmont, CA: Thomson Wadsworth, p. 30; Figure 2.2.2 from Kalat, J. W. (2007). *Biological Psychology*, 9th Ed., Belmont, CA: Thomson Wadsworth, p. 167.

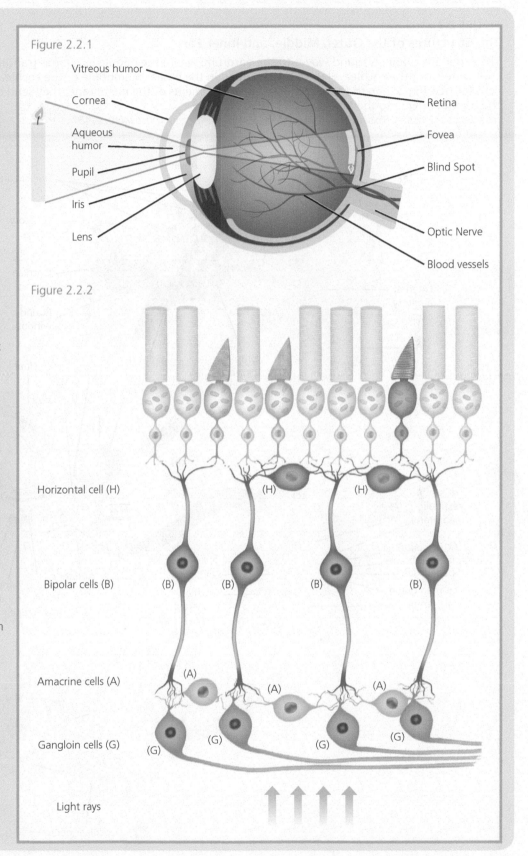

Figure 2.2.1

Vitreous humor
Cornea
Aqueous humor
Pupil
Iris
Lens
Retina
Fovea
Blind Spot
Optic Nerve
Blood vessels

Figure 2.2.2

Horizontal cell (H)   (H)   (H)

Bipolar cells (B)   (B)   (B)   (B)   (B)

Amacrine cells (A)   (A)   (A)   (A)

Gangloin cells (G)   (G)   (G)   (G)   (G)

Light rays

FIGURE 2.3

The Structures of the Outer, Middle, and Inner Ear

The outer ear channels sound waves to the eardrum, where the middle ear bones transmit the waves to the oval window of the cochlea. Hair cells embedded in the basilar membrane of the cochlea are the transducer cells for hearing. When they are stimulated by movements of the membrane, they send neural impulses along the auditory nerve to the brain.

From Kalat, J. W. (2007). *Biological Psychology,* 9th Ed., Belmont, CA: Thomson Wadsworth, p. 197.

of by far the majority of information of interest to us in cognitive psychology. Several brain structures lying below the cerebral cortex are important for initial processing of sensory inputs and their conveyance to cortical areas. Some very primitive structures in the brain stem (the enlarged top of the spinal cord lying just below the brain) are involved with orientation and attention. That is, the medulla and reticular formation have the special function of alerting us to new or important stimuli without telling us anything about what they are. Identification of a stimulus depends completely on finding relevant information stored about it in the cerebral cortex (see Figure 2.4).

FIGURE 2.4

Diagram of the Surface and Cross Section of the Human Brain

Adapted from J. Ward (2015). *The Student's Guide to Cognitive Neuroscience* (3rd Ed.). Psychology Press.

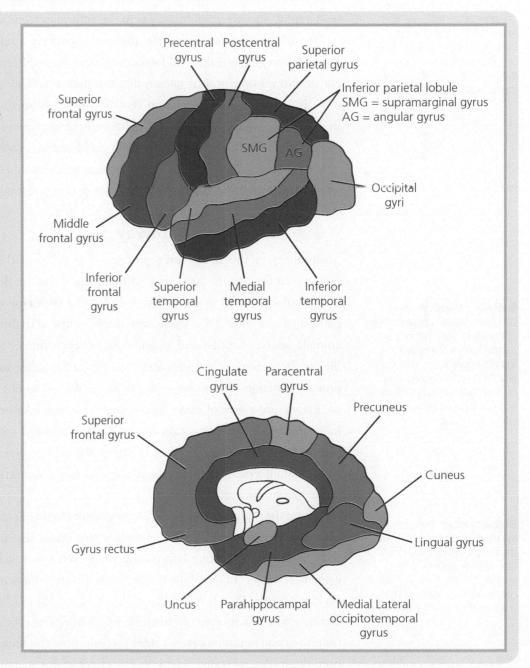

Thalamus A bilateral structure in the center of the brain, between the brainstem and the cortex that serves as a relay station for all senses except olfaction, and has a large amount of two-way communication with the cerebral cortex

Lateral geniculate nuclei Layered bundles of neurons on the sides of the thalamus that receive inputs from the optic nerve and send outputs to the occipital cortex in the back of the brain. The LGN also receives inputs from several cortical areas

Although most sensory inputs have primary projection areas in the brain (i.e., where the axons of sensory nerves terminate in different parts of the cortex), all senses but one (olfaction) first send their trains of neural impulses to the **thalamus**. The thalamus consists of two structures located in what is called the diencephalon, below the cortex on either side of a point in the center of the head (see Figure 2.4). Parts of the thalamus, the **lateral geniculate nuclei** (LGN), have maps of the visual environment laid over them, so that neighboring cells in the thalamus receive information about neighboring objects in the visual scene. This kind of mapping is called *retinotopic*, since the areas of the retina that are stimulated by light are traced over topographically corresponding areas in the central nervous system.

It used to be thought that the thalamus is merely a relay station taking sensory inputs from each modality and forwarding them on to different regions of the cerebral cortex. Now, however, it is known that the thalamus does some computations of its own. It also receives information sent downward from the cortex that might help in selecting certain sensations for enhancement or suppression. That is, all sensory inputs from new objects or from some object of interest, such as the face of a friend in a crowded room, might be passed through or even enhanced on their way to the cortex, whereas sensory messages about old objects or uninteresting ones are damped out.

2.3.2   *The Visual Pathway*

Superior colliculi A pair of structures situated near the top of the brain stem that receives a small part of the output from the optic nerve, they play no role in conscious vision in humans, but can direct attention and eye movements to new or interesting objects

Most fibers in the optic nerve proceed directly from the eyes to the thalamus. However, a few (about 10%) split off beforehand and are directed to a pair of primitive visual structures in the midbrain called the **superior colliculi** (techtopulvinar pathway, see Figure 2.5). These structures are the actual primary organs of sight in animals, such as reptiles and amphibians, but their role in conscious vision is strictly limited in mammals and primates. As with some other midbrain structures, their primary function in humans seems to be to alert us to changes in the environment so that we are aware of new visual objects or events. Automatic orienting is usually indicated by a shift in attention along with eye and head movements toward the new object. In order to identify what the new stimulus is, however, we have to process additional information about it by passing sensory information through the thalamus to the cerebral cortex.

Occipital lobes The lobes of the cerebral cortex that are in the far, back part of the head; they receive input from the eyes via the thalamus and are concerned exclusively with vision and visual imagery

From the thalamus, visual pathways connect to the far back parts of the **occipital lobes** of the cortex, which are the primary projection areas for vision (see Figure 2.5). It is of some interest that information from each eye is kept separate in the lateral geniculate nuclei (LGN) of the thalamus; the first true binocular cells are located in the occipital cortex. That is because each LGN is divided into separate layers, somewhat like an onion, that receive, alternatively, information from the nasal halves of the retinas from the contralateral (opposite side) eye, and from the temporal halves of the retinas from the ipsilateral (same side) eye. The effect of this mapping is to channel all information from the right half of the visual field to the left side of the thalamus and all information from the left visual field to the right side of the thalamus (i.e., it is not

FIGURE 2.5

The Visual Pathway from the Eyes to the Brain.

The optic nerves from the two eyes converge at the optic chiasm, where there is a partial cross-over of the fibers. The fibers from the temporal halves of the two retinas remain on the same side of the brain (ipsilateral connections), whereas the fibers from the nasal halves cross to the other (contralateral) side of the brain. Some of the fibers split off toward the superior colliculi of the midbrain (techtopulvinar pathway), but most go to the lateral geniculate nucleus of the thalamus (geniculostriatal pathway). From the thalamus, new nerve fibers make up the optic tract to the primary projection area for vision—the back part of the occipital lobes

From *Sensation & Perception,* 3rd Ed. by J. Wolfe et al. (2012), Sinauer Associates, Sunderland, MA.

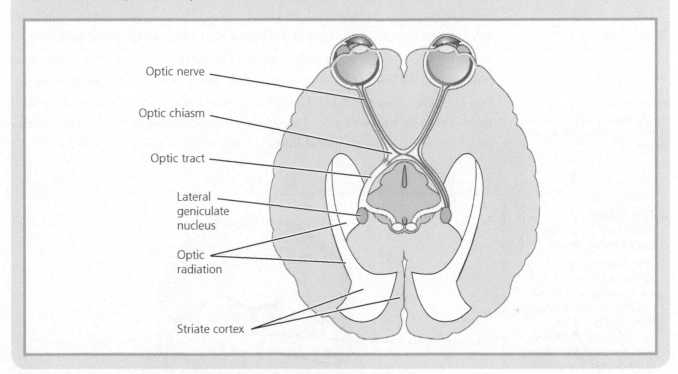

Optic nerve

Optic chiasm

Optic tract

Lateral geniculate nucleus

Optic radiation

Striate cortex

the case that the *right eye* communicates only to the *left brain* and vice-versa, as is commonly misconstrued). This separation continues on to the brain, such that both cerebral hemispheres receive information from the contralateral visual field. Here, however, many cortical cells receive information from both eyes (i.e., the cells receive binocular inputs). The overlapping of information from both eyes is important for depth perception in primates, as the slightly different views of the world provided by the two eyes provide one of the most important cues for relative depth of nearby objects.

As in the LGN of the thalamus, a map of the visible world is laid out across the primary visual projection area in the occipital cortex. The mapping scheme also projects the left half of the visual field onto the right occipital lobe and vice-versa. The one exception is for information that we are looking at directly. The area devoted to central (foveal) vision, is represented in both hemispheres and is much larger, proportionally, than that afforded to peripheral vision. This cortical magnification, as it is called, indicates the importance that the brain gives to the object of central focus in the field of view.

2.3.3   *The Auditory Pathway*

The auditory pathway to the brain is a bit more complex than that for vision. The auditory nerve leads from the cochlea of the inner ear to the brain stem and from there to the inferior colliculi on either side of the midbrain (see Figure 2.6). As their name implies, the inferior colliculi are located just below the superior colliculi, and this proximity enables multi-modal cells in the midbrain to coordinate orientation responses to the locations of sights and sounds that come from the same place. Subsequent auditory pathways include both ipsilateral (same-side) and contralateral (opposite-side) connections from the ears to the medial geniculate nuclei of the thalamus. As in the colliculus, the auditory and visual areas of the thalamus are close together; an indication of the importance of integrating the separate senses in the common perception of a single object or event. Once the pathway leads to the thalamus, all connections remain on the same side of the brain while proceeding to the primary auditory projection areas in the **temporal lobes** of the cerebral cortex (see Figure 2.6).

Temporal lobes The lobes of the cerebral cortex that are located in the sides of the head, inward from the ears, that receive auditory inputs and are important for understanding the meaning of sights and sounds, including spoken and written words

FIGURE 2.6

The Auditory Pathway from the Ears to the Brain

The auditory nerves from each ear project to the cochlear nucleus in the brain stem, from which both ipsilateral and contralateral pathways flow through the olivary nucleus and the inferior colliculi of the brain stem before passing through the thalamus on their way to the primary auditory projection areas in the temporal lobes of the brain.

From Kalat, J. W. (2007). *Biological Psychology*, 9th Ed., Belmont, CA: Thomson Wadsworth, p. 200.

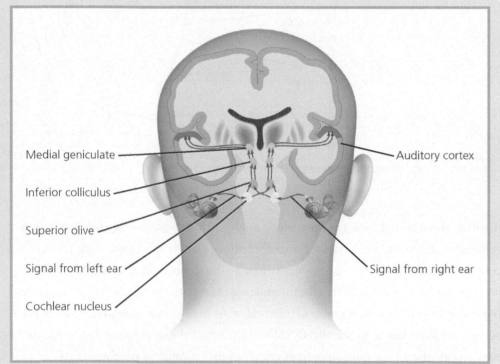

Medial geniculate

Inferior colliculus

Superior olive

Signal from left ear

Cochlear nucleus

Auditory cortex

Signal from right ear

2.4 **Methods in Cognitive Neuroscience**

2.4.1   *Single-Cell Recordings in Peripheral Visual Nerves*

There are a number of ways to study the physiological processes involved in sensation. Among the most elegant is to record the activity of individual cells in the sensory pathways in order to find out what aspects of visual and auditory stimuli control their responses. Such techniques were developed over 50 years ago by using a fine wire placed next to, or actually inserted into, a living animal's nerve cell and recording its activity when the near-by receptor cells were stimulated. Hartline, Wagner, and Ratliff (1956) discovered fundamental principles of brightness perception and **lateral inhibition** in this way. Lateral inhibition has been shown to be an important biological process that has apparently evolved to help the visual system recover edges from a blurred and noisy retinal image (see Box 2.1).

2.4.2 Single-Cell Recordings in the Visual Cortex

Perhaps the most famous research based on the single-cell recording technique was that of the Nobel Prize-winning team of David Hubel and Torsten Wiesel. They recorded from single cells in the occipital cortex of anaesthetized animals that were presented with a variety of visual stimuli. Hubel and Wiesel (1959, 1977) found a great degree of specificity in the response functions of individual cells. Most cells were found to be sensitive to lines, edges, or bars at specific locations and orientations in the visual field. Changing the slant of the line by 20 degrees or its location by a few millimeters in the field of view would greatly diminish the response rate of the cell. Other cells were sensitive to motion, often in only one direction, and still others were found to be sensitive to colors and to differences in information available mainly from the left or right eye. Some cortical cells were sensitive only to combinations of features, such as a bar at a particular orientation that stopped at a precise location within the **receptive field** of the cell. This tremendous degree of specialization was found to be laid out in a very orderly way across the visual cortex and replicated hundreds of times to represent each small area of the visual field (see Box 2.2).

Further research has shown that more than half of the cerebral cortex is involved in some way with vision (e.g., Enns, 2004). There are two main pathways leading from the visual cortex in the occipital lobes to other brain areas. The pathway linking the occipital lobes to the **parietal lobes** in the top, back part of the brain is called the **dorsal pathway**. It seems to be specialized for the processing of spatial information, and is perhaps involved in guiding hand and body movements. The **ventral pathway** connects the occipital lobes to the temporal lobes of the cortex, and seems to be involved in identification rather than localization processes. This distinction between the dorsal-parietal visual path and the ventral-temporal path has become known as the "where versus what" dichotomy in vision (Ungerleider & Mishkin, 1982).

2.4.3 Single-Cell Recordings in the Auditory Pathway

Similar single-cell recording techniques in hearing have shown that cells in the auditory nerve have "tuning curves," indicating a limited range of tonal frequencies to which they are responsive. Cells receiving inputs from hair cells near the beginning of the **cochlea** show maximum responsiveness to high-frequency sounds, whereas those communicating with hair cells near the end of the cochlea are most sensitive to low frequency sounds. These separate frequency pathways are maintained all the way to the primary

---

Lateral inhibition The tendency of active neurons to inhibit their neighbors; in vision, this process has been shown to enhance the perception of edges

Receptive field (of a neuron) The specific location and type of stimulus that must be presented in order to observe a change in firing rate (excitation or inhibition) of a nerve cell in a sensory system

Parietal lobes The back, upper parts of the brain that are responsible for spatial and tactile perception and directing spatial orienting, attention, and reaching

Dorsal visual pathway The pathway linking the occipital lobes to the parietal lobes of the cortex (It has been called the "where" pathway because of its role in spatial processing in vision.)

Ventral visual pathway The pathway linking the occipital lobes to the temporal lobes of the cortex (It has been called the "what" pathway because of its role in object identification and naming.)

Cochlea The fluid-filled, structure shaped like a snail's shell in the inner ear that contains hair cells embedded in a membrane that spans its length (The hair cells are the receptor (transducer) cells for hearing in that they convert sound vibrations into neural impulses.)

BOX 2.1
The Discovery of Lateral Inhibition

Among the first researchers to record activity from individual neurons in a living eye was H. K. Hartline (e.g., Hartline & Ratliff, 1957; Hartline, Wagner, & Ratliff, 1956). Hartline and his colleagues chose to work with *Limulus*, the so-called horseshoe crab, although it is actually an ancient form of arthropod and not a crab at all. Limulus was chosen as a test animal because of its large and accessible compound eye containing many individual facets. Each facet is covered with a lens and contains a number of receptors communicating with a single nerve fiber that connects the facet to the brain. The research involved shining a single, small spot of light onto individual facets or neighboring facets and recording the number of spikes propagated along the nerve fiber in response to the light. The recordings were made from a thin wire lying adjacent to or inside the neuron's axon (see the figure below).

The initial research showed that a small spot of light, when shone onto a facet, produced an initial burst of activity, eventually slowing down to a steady-state firing rate. The firing frequency of both the initial burst and the final equilibrium state were proportional to the intensity of the light; that is, the brighter the light, the higher the observed firing rate

both immediately and over the long term. Hartline and his colleagues were interested in determining what kind of spatial relations, if any, existed among neighboring cells in the Limulus eye. They found that each faceted eye is connected to one and only one nerve fiber. Moving the light onto a neighboring cell increased the firing rate of the neighbor, while the firing rate of the original cell fell to baseline (almost all living nerve cells have a baseline firing rate in the absence of outside stimulation; inactive nerve cells are usually damaged or dead). Therefore, they found no evidence for lateral summation in the Limulus eye. Lateral summation would occur if any cell fiber showed an increase in firing rate when its neighbor was stimulated.

When Hartline's research group tried shining a pair of lights onto two neighboring eye facets, they found a very interesting and important result. Rather than demonstrating lateral summation between two neighboring illuminated cells, they found that lateral inhibition was the rule. That is, whenever a nerve cell increased its firing rate in response to a light, and then its neighbor was stimulated, the original cell's firing rate decreased rather than increased. This general finding has held true in almost all experiments

Action potentials are recorded from neurons by microelectrodes placed in or near an axon. (b) Each potential changes the cell's resting charge from −70 millivolts to slightly positive and back again as it moves along the axon. These potentials appear as spikes when viewed over a longer time span. [From Goldstein, E. B. (2005). *Cognitive Psychology*. Belmont, CA: Thomson Wadsworth, p. 31.]

involving higher animals, including monkeys and humans—lateral inhibition is a basic fact that is found throughout the evolution of animal vision.

But why, you might ask, do adjacent cells in the eye tend to inhibit one another rather than pool their energies by increasing their firing rates when neighbors are stimulated? The answer appears to be due to a remarkable result of lateral inhibition; it is a process that modifies images projected onto the eye by increasing apparent contrast at edges. Lateral inhibition is one of the most important biological phenomena that begins the process of sharpening and improving the eye's imperfect optics and blurred visual details captured from ambient light.

Let's consider how lateral inhibition might work to sharpen images. If we can represent an edge by a field of bright light next to dark field, then there are a number of cells that fall entirely in the light and entirely in the dark, and so do their immediate neighbors. Near the edge, however, we find two kinds of cells: one type will be in the light but some of its neighbors will be in the dark, and another will be in the dark and some of its neighbors will be in the light. A cell in the light away from an edge will be stimulated, but its neighbors that are also in the light will inhibit it. Near an edge, only some of the neighbors will be in the light, so it will receive less inhibition than cells whose neighbors are all in the light. Similarly, a cell in the dark away from an edge will not be excited and neither will its neighbors if they are also in the dark. They should all be firing at or near their baseline rates. Near an edge, however, a cell in the dark will have some neighbors in the light, and these will produce inhibition. Thus, a cell in the dark near an edge will fire below its baseline rate. The result is that there is nothing so apparently bright as a white surface near a dark one, and there is nothing so dark as a black surface near a white one. These increases in contrast produce a well-known illusion called Mach bands, named after their discoverer, Ernst Mach (See figure, and also Cornsweet, 1971, pp. 276–277).

In the figure, four retinal cells are positioned such that two are on the dark side of the edge and two are in the light. The dark side units output 10 arbitrary excitation units, and the bright side units report 20 units (arrows). These are decreased by lateral inhibitory connections (circles) that are weaker from adjacent units in the dark (−1) than from those in the light (−4). The sum of direct excitatory and lateral

inhibitory connections produces net activations that enhance contrast of the edge.

An example of lateral inhibition in which illusory dark spots appear at the intersections of light lines between dark squares [from Kalat, J. W. (2007). *Biological Psychology*, 9th Ed., Belmont, CA: Thomson Wadsworth, p. 169].

It is interesting to point out that similar properties of lateral inhibition were incorporated into early image-processing programs designed to improve the quality of photocopies and telescopic images. Although these image-processing routines were not based on their inventors' knowledge of biology, they did recapitulate millions of years of evolutionary history driven to improve the quality of biological optics.

BOX 2.2

Mapping the Occipital Cortex

In 1981, David Hubel and Torsten Wiesel were awarded the Nobel Prize in Physiology and Medicine for their pioneering work in vision. They perfected the technique of recording the activity of single neurons in the visual cortex of the brain in living mammals. At the time of their initial work (Hubel & Wiesel, 1959), no one had any idea what kinds of stimuli would excite individual neurons in the brains of animals. Earlier work recording from cells in the optic nerve had shown that retinal cells respond optimally to small black spots on a white background or to white spots against a black background (e.g., Kuffler, 1953). That is, the receptive fields of retinal cells had circular center-surround areas, with an excitatory center surrounded by an inhibitory ring, or vice-versa. When Hubel and Wiesel recorded from cells in the visual cortex of anaesthetized, but alert, animals, they found hardly any responses at all when the stimuli were spots of light.

Hubel (1982) reports an anecdote from his laboratory in which dozens of slides were shone onto a screen in front of a cat while they were searching for a pattern that would excite a nerve cell in the occipital lobe of the cat's brain. Finally, one slide produced a torrent of spikes from the cell, and the researchers seized it to see what had elicited the response. It turns out to have been an improperly mounted cardboard slide that projected the edge of the cardboard onto the field of view rather than the spot of light that was supposed to have been shone. Hubel and Wiesel had serendipitously discovered a fundamental difference between retinal cells and cortical cells. Retinal cells detect "pixels" (tiny light or dark points or circles that contrast with their backgrounds) that vary in intensity, whereas cortical cells prefer elongated edges or bars in one of a full circle of possible orientations.

With this example in mind, Hubel and Wiesel produced a variety of elongated stimuli and found that most cells in the cat's brain were sensitive not to spots, but to edges and bars of particular orientations and locations in the field of view. That is, each cell showed extreme selectivity in its responsiveness. First, the stimulus had to fall within its receptive field, the area on the retina where a stimulus image must be projected in order to change the firing rate of the cell. Most cortical cells have receptive field areas

that correspond to only a few minutes or degrees of visual angle relative to the 360-degree inner surface of the eyeball. Within these receptive field areas, cells are responsive only to certain types of stimuli. Hubel and Wiesel identified "simple" cortical cells as those responsive to lines, bars, or edges of specific orientations. Changing the orientation of the stimulus by 20 degrees or more would greatly diminish the response rate of the cell. Other, complex cells were sensitive to edges or bars in motion, often in only one direction across the receptive field. Still other hypercomplex, or end-stopped cells were maximally responsive only to combinations of features, such as a bar at a particular orientation that stopped at a precise location within the receptive field of the cell, or a corner moving in a particular direction through the receptive field.

This extreme degree of specialization was puzzling at first, since it seemed to indicate that the visual scene is parsed into hundreds of elementary components made up of simple lines, edges, bars, and corners and their static or moving properties. How could this immense array of piecemeal bits possibly relate to our experience of a 3-D world of holistic objects against a smooth background? At first, theorists argued that Hubel and Wiesel's data supported a particular theory of object recognition based on feature analysis. Essentially the theory states that there is a finite set of elementary features that make up our internal representations of all possible visual objects. Hubel and Wiesel's findings were taken as support for such a feature-based theory of recognition, since they had found "feature detectors" in the visual cortex of higher mammals. Later theorists pointed out problems with both feature theory and the assumption that cortical cells detect features, rather than merely providing evidence for the relative likelihood of different components in the visual scene. The conclusion from this debate, covered in more detail in Chapter 3, is that it is difficult to decide the merits of any major cognitive theory on the basis of one set of data alone. Rather, issues as complex as deciding how we recognize objects from retinal images will be resolved only when we consider converging evidence from a number of areas, including behavioral research and neurophysiology.

auditory projection area in the temporal cortex. Here, individual cells also have been shown to have a large amount of specificity in terms of the types of stimuli that produce a maximum response in each cell. Some cells respond only to certain frequencies, whereas others respond most to tones that increase or decrease in frequency within their preferred ranges. Others in adjacent regions of the auditory cortex seem most responsive to idiosyncratic sounds like chirps or clicks (Whitfield & Evans, 1965).

2.4.4 *The Importance of Single-Cell Recordings*

It is an important question to determine how higher cognitive processes begin with the outputs of single cells in the visual and auditory cortex, and from them derive recognition of complex stimuli, such as spoken words and faces. Since people can perform such feats so quickly and accurately, it is of more than purely theoretical interest that motivates us to find out how it is done. Such knowledge would enable us to do things like design better software for machines so that they could recognize faces and understand human speech. It should also be possible to design better training programs to help stroke and accident victims recover recognition and comprehension processes as they are rehabilitated from their injuries. These applications depend on our understanding of how we interpret initial sensory signals that record basic physical features, which by themselves have no meaning. It is only when elementary features are integrated into internal representations of objects and events that they come to be recognized and understood. The process of recognizing and understanding the meaning of sensory events is the topic of perception, which is covered in the next chapter.

2.5 Imaging Electrical Activity in the Brain

Individual neurons in the brain communicate by sending spike potentials along their axons just as sensory and motor nerves do. Sensitive detectors placed on the scalp can pick up the results of these electrical discharges, and they can be amplified and stored for later analysis. What is recorded is the simultaneous activity of many thousands of neurons lying under the skull in the vicinity of each detector (the technique is called electroencephalography, or **EEG** recording). EEG recordings appear to be more-or-less random accumulations of activity resulting from neural impulses that cause ions to flow across neural membranes (Woodman, 2010). Indeed, when successive intervals of such activity are summed, the result is a fairly flat line, indicating that the negative and positive voltage fluctuations tend to cancel each other out. However, when this brain activity is time-locked to some event, such as a flash of light, the resulting electrical field can show regularities over time. The electrical activity measured in the brain relative to the onset of some event is called an event-related potential (**ERP**). An ERP is a series of waves that vary in strength and polarity (positive or negative charges) in a fraction of a second after the event occurs (Hillyard, 1993; Luck, 2005).

EEG Electroencephalography, or the recording of electrical activity of large groups of neurons in the brain ("brain waves") through electrodes placed at various locations on the scalp

ERP Event-related potential or changes in EEG patterns as a direct result of the presentation of some stimulus; these usually occur within 50 to 1000 ms after stimulus onset

Because activity is recorded from a variety of neural responses, the usual technique is to record activity after a large number of similar events and then average the resultant ERPs. This averaging procedure eliminates the random noise in the EEG and reveals the common peaks and valleys in the ERP that are present in the majority of the signals. The result is a regular series of positive and negative waves that are characteristic of how the brain responds to certain stimuli, thoughts, and actions.

Some particular peaks and valleys in ERPs show up consistently across many experiments and have been labelled with letters and numbers to reflect their usual time course and appearance. By convention, N refers to negative deflections and P refers to positive deflections around a baseline or average voltage, usually measured before the stimulus is presented. P1 usually occurs about 100 milliseconds (ms) after an auditory or visual stimulus and reflects sensory registration and initial perceptual processing. N1 occurs almost 100 ms later, and represents early perceptual discriminations. Later positive and negative peaks have been identified as representing attentional processes and categorizations leading to response decisions (see Figure 2.7).

Although somewhat different patterns of ERPs can be obtained by recording from different areas across the scalp, the technique does not reveal the precise brain

FIGURE 2.7

Electroencephalography (EEG Recording)

(Left panel) A picture of a person wearing an electrode cap with 129 separate recording electrodes distributed over the scalp and several reference locations away from the brain. Each electrode records activity from many thousands of neurons in its vicinity.

(Right panel) When recordings are made after the presentation of some stimulus, they are called event-related potentials (ERPs) and are timed from the onset of the event (0 ms on the abscissa of the graph). Averages of many trials reveal smooth up (negative) and down (positive) recordings. The N400 peak shown in the figure differs for hearing two words that fit (lower function) or do not fit (upper function) the context of the sentence in which they were embedded. This result indicates that 400 ms after hearing a word in a sentence, its grammatical role is either understood, or an anomaly is detected.

Adapted from Goldstein, E. B. (2005). *Cognitive Psychology.* Belmont, CA: Thomson Wadsworth, p. 47.

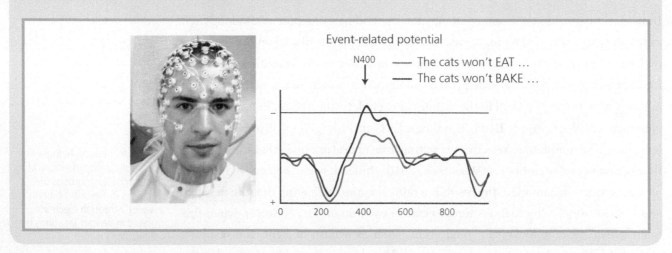

area active at the time of recording. However, this lack of spatial precision is more than made up for by the fine degree of temporal resolution of the ERP. Events can be measured precisely in ms, and they show great consistency across individuals for simple visual and auditory stimuli. Further, the sequence of peaks and valleys recorded at different scalp locations can be used to determine the flow of relevant information processing activities following the sensory registration of any stimulus in the relevant cortical areas for each modality.

2.6 Imaging Metabolic Rates in the Brain

Other brain–imaging techniques have made use of the fact that whenever certain brain structures are active in performing some task, they demand an increase in metabolic resources. Thus, active brain areas consume more oxygen and receive increased blood flow relative to inactive areas. Several techniques have recently been developed to measure these relative increases and decreases in brain activity while observers perform some task. These measures have yielded precise information about which brain areas are most heavily involved in different types of cognitive activities.

One of the brain imaging techniques is called positron-emission tomography (**PET**). The technique involves injecting minute amounts of radioactive nutrients into the bloodstream that can later be detected by instruments that measure the relative amounts of radioactivity in different neural tissues. Test participants are asked to engage in some task while the substance diffuses through the bloodstream and is taken in by cells as they need nutrients from the blood. Brain areas that are most radioactive shortly after completion of the task indicate those areas that had been most active and during task performance (see Figure 2.8).

A similar method of brain imaging that developed at about the same time as PET-scan technology is called **fMRI** for functional magnetic resonance imaging. Magnetic resonance imaging (MRI) is based on the fact that various tissues of the body have different chemical makeups that react differently to the presence of strong magnetic fields. These differences can be used to create images to reveal different soft tissues, unlike X-rays that typically reveal mainly dense tissues, like bone. The fMRI technique measures changes that occur in brain activity in response to some stimulus or task that the subjects are asked to perform. The idea is called the neurovascular coupling, which refers to the fact that changes in neural activity affect changes of the blood flow in the particular brain regions. For example, when we look at visual stimuli such as pictures, activity of the neurons in the occipital lobe increases, and this change results in an increase of the blood flow into the occipital lobe.

A measurement that is commonly used in fMRI is called Blood Oxygen Level Dependent (BOLD) signals. This is based on the different speed of changes between blood flow and actual oxygen consumption. When a brain region is not working, the amounts of oxyhemoglobin (hemoglobin carrying oxygen) and deoxyhemoglobin (hemoglobin without

PET Positron-emission tomography; a method of determining which brain areas are most active in performing some task. Radioactive tracers attached to nutrient molecules are injected into the bloodstream and are taken up by active neurons in the brain. Brain images from radioactive decay detectors then reveal differential patterns of activity involved in the task.

fMRI Functional magnetic resonance imaging; a technique for measuring brain activity indirectly by comparing BOLD (blood oxygen-level dependent) differences observed in two tasks that differ by a single component. Excitatory and inhibitory processes involved in the task difference are revealed in false-color images.

FIGURE 2.8

Sample PET Schematic

PET-scan records obtained from subtracting blood flow levels measured in observers performing a neutral task, such as viewing a blank screen, from those measured while performing some task. The tasks used for each panel were (A) viewing a word silently and (B) listening to a spoken word. In the next two panels, the patterns obtained for viewing a word silently were subtracted from those obtained when (C) speaking the viewed word and (D) generating a related word from memory (after Posner & Raichle, 1994) From Matlin, M. W. (2005). *Cognition,* 6th Ed. New York: Wiley

A. Second Level, Visual (Viewing Words)

B. Second Level, Auditory (Hearing Words)

C. Third Level (Speaking Words)

D. Fourth Level (Generating Verbs)

oxygen after oxygen release) are about the same. When the brain region becomes active (e.g., the occipital lobe when looking at a picture), the blood with oxyhemoglobin starts flowing into the region within a few seconds. However, the speed of oxygen consumption (oxygen intake into cells) is much slower. Therefore, there are more oxyhemoglobin than deoxyhemoglobin in the region when it becomes active compared to when it is resting. The oxyhemoglobin and deoxyhemoglobin have different magnetic traits; therefore, the magnetic property of the region is also different between the task period and the rest period, and this difference appears in a brain activation map (see Figure 2.9).

Both PET and fMRI imagery make use of the subtraction method, similar to Donders's method of analyzing reaction times in the nineteenth century. That is, images are taken of the brain during a control task (e.g., passively viewing words) and during an experimental task (e.g., deciding whether or not the words are animal names). The two images are then compared by taking the difference in relative activity levels between them. This difference should show which brain areas are more active, or less active, when performing the experimental task relative to their activity in some control task.

PET and fMRI scans and ERPs yield complementary information about brain function, in that the electrical changes picked up by the EEG measures used in ERP research show millisecond-by-millisecond resolution of changes in brain activity. Unfortunately, the spatial resolution of such techniques is not precise, so there is

FIGURE 2.9

fMRI Images of Brain Activity

Figure 2.9.1 from From Kalat, J. W. (2007). *Biological Psychology,* 9th Ed., Belmont, CA: Thomson Wadsworth, p. 109, and Figure 2.9.2 from Goldstein, E. B. (2005). *Cognitive Psychology.* Belmont, CA: Thomson Wadsworth, frontispiece.

Figure 2.9.1 For an MRI machine in operation, successive images can reveal changes in blood-oxygen levels that reflect different metabolic rates in corresponding areas of the brain.

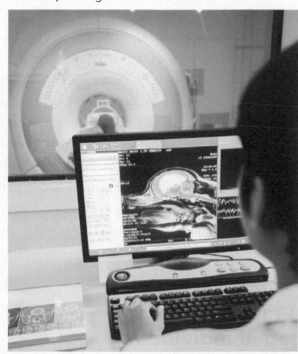

Figure 2.9.2 Blood-oxygen level dependent (BOLD) measures determined by differences between brain metabolism when observers were looking at a picture versus a blank screen. The small, bright areas located mainly in the ventral portions of the temporal lobes represent areas that were more active when pictures were present.

uncertainty about exactly which brain areas under the scalp are responsible for positive or negative changes in electrical potentials. On the other hand, PET and fMRI scans show a relatively high degree of precision in locating which brain areas are active or inactive, but the time scales of these changes reflect modulations in blood flow that can vary over large fractions of seconds. It is likely that combining these two types of techniques so that changes in brain activity over time can be mapped throughout the cortex and in subcortical brain areas as well will enhance our understanding of brain function in normal, alert observers (Raichle, 2001; Woodman, 2010).

Recently more refined imaging techniques have been developed based on magnetoencephalography (**MEG**), which gives improved spatial and temporal resolution over fMRI recordings. MEG recordings are made of the minute magnetic fields produced by electrical activity in the brain itself. Although the method is limited to only certain areas of the brain, its high spatial and temporal resolution combine some of the best features of ERP and fMRI techniques. An entirely different procedure for studying brain processes involves **trans-cranial magnetic stimulation** (**TMS**)

Magnetoencephalography (MEG) A brain imaging technique that records the activity of groups of neurons by measuring the magnetic fields that they produce when electrical impulses travel through them; it gives high resolution of both where and when this activity occurs in the brain during performance of some task

Transcranial magnetic stimulation A method of stimulating specific areas of the brain by placing a strong magnetic field over the surface of the skull; can temporarily disrupt neural activity in the stimulated area, producing stroke-like effects that can be used to study brain function

which uses a powerful magnetic field to temporarily disrupt brain processing in local areas under the scalp (Driver, Blankenburg, Bestmann, Vanduffel, & Ruff, 2009). Although the effects are only temporary, the technique allows the simulation of localized brain damage in otherwise healthy individuals. In effect, TMS can produce the temporary effects of a stroke by eliminating the contributions made by the affected brain area. These newer techniques promise to extend future capabilities of neuroscientists to study brain activity and relate it to observable behavior.

Although these mapping processes can tell us about what brain areas are active and when this activity occurs while some task is being performed, they cannot tell us how the brain is processing information or what intermediate processes are involved in transforming sensory inputs into internal decisions and external responses. That is, any brain area active in performing some task could well be the major site where the task is performed, or it could be a link between two or more sites where the task is actually performed, or it could be the initiator or receiver of information before or after the task is completed elsewhere (Uttal, 2001; Wade, 2006). Brain imaging research provides only one clue for the task of relating brain activity to behavior. Much work remains for cognitive psychologists to test neurophysiologically-driven theories against human behavior as well as for cognitive neuroscientists to observe the effects of various types of brain damage on this behavior. It is to this latter area of research that we now turn.

2.7 Behavioral Changes in Brain-Damaged Individuals

2.7.1 Individual Differences in Normal and Damaged Brains

Theories relating brain activity to conscious experience and observable behaviors depend on converging evidence from different sources. One of the most important sources of such information comes from individuals who have suffered brain damage due to accidents, disease, surgery, or strokes. Although data collected from such patients can be of great interest and importance, it must always be used with caution. There are several reasons for such caution. First, just like any other human attribute, all brains differ from one another, and generalizations from one specific patient to all other people are difficult to justify. Second, anyone with brain damage is likely to be special, with unique patterns of normal and abnormal brain functions. When an individual suffers a head injury in an automobile accident or experiences a rupture or blockage of a cerebral artery, the extent and location of the damage is unlikely to be the same as that for any other patient. Further, patients at different stages of recovery from damage are likely to show different patterns of behavior. Only when the results from several patients with similar brain lesions are compared can we begin to make general statements about the relation between brain structures and human behavior. With these warnings in mind, we should nevertheless review some of the classic case studies of brain-damaged individuals to trace the history of these observations in the developing field of cognitive neuroscience.

2.7.2 Frontal Lobe Damage

Phineas Gage was a foreman working on a construction gang building a roadbed for a new railway line in Vermont in 1848. One of their jobs was to blast away rock formations that lay in the path of the railroad line. On one occasion, Phineas Gage took over the task of tamping down a gunpowder charge into a hole in a rock so that it could be blasted away. Unfortunately for Mr. Gage, a spark from the tamping iron ignited the powder prematurely with the result that the tamping rod was fired out of the hole with the force of a cannon shot. The tamping rod was about a meter in length and almost 4 cm (1.5 in) in diameter. It weighed about 8 kilograms (13 lbs). The force of the explosion shot the rod into Phineas's face just below his left eye, and the rod continued through the front part of his head and landed some 40 meters away (see Figure 2.10).

Perhaps the most surprising thing about this incident is that not only was Phineas Gage not killed outright, but he barely lost consciousness. He was able to walk, and, after a few weeks in recovery, mainly spent dealing with a dangerous infection, he resumed a relatively normal pattern of activity. This was despite the fact that he had suffered a terrible, permanent injury to much of the frontal lobes of his brain (see Figure 2.10).

However, the Phineas Gage who survived was not the same honest, hard-working foreman who had experienced the accident. In the words of John Harlow, a physician who treated him:

Frontal lobes The front parts of the brain extending back from above the eyes to the parietal and temporal lobe boundaries; responsible to control motor activities, including speech and eye movements, and are responsible for executive functions, such as planning and execution of sequential activities; also strongly influence judgment, decision-making, and personality

FIGURE 2.10

Phineas Gage

Photograph of Phineas Gage with the tamping rod that penetrated his head and images showing the path that it took as it passed through his skull (see Damasio, Grabowski, Frank, Galaburda, & Damasio, 1994).

From http://onlinestorybank.com/2014/03/the-strange-case-of-mr-phineas-gage/

His physical health is good, and I am inclined to say that he has recovered … [but] the equilibrium or balance, so to speak, between his intellectual faculties and animal propensities, seems to have been destroyed. He is fitful, irreverent, indulging at times in the grossest profanity (which was not previously his custom), manifesting but little deference for his fellows, impatient of restraint or advice when it conflicts with his desires, at times pertinaciously obstinate, yet capricious and vacillating, devising many plans of future operation, which are no sooner arranged that they are abandoned … In this regard his mind was radically changed, so decidedly that his friends … said that he was "no longer Gage" (Blakemore, 1977, pp. 3–4).

Subsequent research on patients with frontal lobe damage has confirmed the general findings indicated by Phineas Gage's case study. Although the posterior parts of the frontal lobe are primarily involved with motor control functions, the anterior part (sometimes called the prefrontal region) of the frontal lobes seems to control executive functions—such as planning, sequencing, voluntary attention, and some aspects of language and memory. Damage to the anterior frontal lobes can also lead to personality changes. Dorsolateral lesions (damage to the top and sides of the frontal lobes) are more frequently associated with apathy, lethargy, and reduced emotionality. Damage to the orbitofrontal regions (near the eye sockets) is more commonly associated with inappropriate social behavior, increased motor activity, and sexual disinhibition (Benson & Miller, 2000). It is these latter personality changes that were noted in Phineas Gage.

2.7.3 *The Frontal Lobe and Broca's Speech Area*

Broca's area Typically in the left frontal lobe near the temporal lobe that controls speech and expressive language; damage to this region produces Broca's aphasia, which is characterized by the inability to speak

Other nineteenth-century scientists studied behavior deficiencies in individuals whose brains had been damaged by strokes or disease. In the 1860s in France, the surgeon Pierre-Paul Broca had occasion to test the then new hypothesis that language production is controlled by the frontal lobes. He examined eight different patients whom had been rendered mute or whose speech had been severely curtailed by stroke or other brain injury. The speech of Broca's patients, if present at all, was halting, difficult, and function words were often omitted. In severe cases, speech was almost impossible. These people did not necessarily lose all of their language abilities, however, as they often could comprehend speech more or less normally. Such loss of productive language with retained comprehension skills has been called Broca's aphasia. All of these individuals showed similar brain damage found in post-mortem examinations—lesions in the left frontal lobe near the frontal-temporal lobe boundary. The brain region associated with productive aphasia has become known as Broca's area in honor of his discoveries (see Figure 2.11).

The posterior part of the frontal lobe (precentral gyrus) is the primary motor cortex, which controls movements of our body parts. The superior part of the superior frontal gyrus is associated with motor programming, including eye movements (the frontal eye fields). The lower part of the superior frontal gyrus is associated with initiating and planning actions. The middle central gyrus is associated with working memory

FIGURE 2.11

Broca's and Wernicke's Areas

Locations of Broca's and Wernicke's areas schematically indicated on the surface of the cerebral cortex.
From Goldstein, E. B. (2005). *Cognitive Psychology*. Belmont, CA: Thomson Wadsworth, p. 41.

Wernicke's area

Broca's area

and thinking. The inferior central gyrus is associated with sequential motor control including language production (Broca's area). The lower and medial parts of the frontal lobe include the orbital frontal cortex, and these are associated with social values and judgments. Damage or dysfunction in these areas can cause impairments in social judgments, as will be seen in the famous case of Phineas Gage, and in cases of psychopathology or sociopathy. The lowest part of the medial frontal lobe is the anterior cingulate cortex (ACC), which plays an important role in various forms of cognitive and social-emotional monitoring. The area anterior the ACC is associated with the default mode network (DMN), which is associated with social and personal information processing.

2.7.4 *The Temporal Lobe and Wernicke's Aphasia Area*

Within ten years of Broca's findings, Karl Wernicke in Germany identified a second type of language disability, in which language production might be fluent, although meaningful content is severely disrupted (e.g., "word salad"). The main feature of Wernicke's aphasia is very poor language comprehension. The damaged brain area most closely identified with Wernicke's aphasia is in the temporal lobe (Figure 2.11), and depending on the extent of the damage, both speech comprehension and reading ability can be affected. Both Broca's and Wernicke's aphasias result much more commonly from damage to the left cerebral hemisphere than to the right, indicating that language is lateralized in the left hemisphere of the brain for the vast majority of individuals.

The posterior, inferior (back, lower) part of the temporal lobe is a part of the ventral pathway, which is associated with visual recognition of objects. Damage in this area can produce visual agnosia—the inability to recognize common objects by sight, although they might well be recognized by touching them or listening to the sounds they make. The middle temporal lobe is related to biological and social information processing. The superior (upper) temporal lobe includes the auditory cortex

Wernicke's area An area typically in the left temporal lobe near the temporal-parietal junction that controls language perception and comprehension; damage to this area produces loss of language understanding and Wernicke's area. The anterior and medial (front and middle) parts of the temporal lobe are associated with long-term memory.

2.7.5 *The Occipital Visual Area*

As one might expect, since the occipital lobe of the brain is the primary projection area for vision, damage in this area can produce permanent visual disabilities. This type of blindness is termed cortical blindness, compared to blindness caused by damage to eyes. Occipital lesions can produce **scotomas**, or regions of blindness in the visual field corresponding to the area of damage in the visual cortex. Small scotomas, such as that associated with the blind spot on the retina, might go unnoticed and be unimportant for most vision. Large scotomas, however, are noticeable by brain-injured patients, and they must learn to adjust their behavior to compensate for their disability. The loss of vision in specific areas following occipital damage should not be surprising, as the visual world is mapped onto the occipital cortex, with the main distortion being a disproportionate expansion of the area devoted to fovea vision.

There is an interesting phenomenon associated with cortical blindness. Imagine a patient with cortical blindness who has a large scotoma, and he cannot see anything in his right visual field. However, if he is presented with a dot in his scotoma, moving up, down, left, or right, and asked to guess the direction of movement of the dot, he

Scotomas Literally, "holes" in the visual field caused by damage to areas in the occipital lobe; since the visual field is mapped out over the occipital cortex localized brain damage produces loss of vision in the corresponding part of the visual field

FIGURE 2.12

An Example of the Visual Effects of a Scotoma

From shutterstock.com

can guess more than a chance level, even though he is not aware of it. This phenomenon is termed *blind sight*. Blind sight is related to the function of the superior colliculus. Remember our discussion on the two visual pathways (geniculostriatal and techtopulvinar pathways). In the patient with cortical blindness, the geniculostriatal pathway is damaged, but not the techtopulvinar pathway, and the superior colliculus is associated with orienting reflex and detection of motion. However, the pathway is not associated with our conscious awareness. Therefore, the patient can detect movement in his scotoma, but is not aware of it.

2.7.6   *The Parietal Spatial Area*

The main functions of the parietal lobe include spatial information processing (the superior parietal lobe), sensory integration (inferior parietal lobe), and somatosensation (sensation from body parts in the postcentral gyrus). Parietal lesions can result in curious problems in spatial vision such as visual neglect. Neglect patients commonly show attention failures in one half of the visual field, usually the left field following right parietal damage. These patients will sometimes eat food on the right half of their plates, leaving the other half full while complaining that they are still hungry. They might also miss visual objects in the left half of the visual field, especially if something is presented simultaneously to the right side. These results are consistent with the spatial role ascribed to parietal function in vision.

The main functions of the parietal lobe include spatial information processing (the superior parietal lobe), sensory integration (inferior parietal lobe), and somatosensation (sensation from body parts in the postcentral gyrus).

2.7.7   *Conclusions*

Studies of brain-damaged individuals have provided important evidence for our understanding of brain function in normal, healthy adults. By itself, this body of data would not be very useful, as every type of brain insult or injury is different, and people with brain damage often have other health and emotional problems that make assessment of their abilities difficult. Nonetheless, such information can be extremely useful if combined with brain imaging techniques for the study of normal cortical activity. Finally, the development and use of precise behavioral measures that involve specific cognitive functions serve as analytical tools for studying mental processes. The convergence of evidence from behavioral studies, from brain imaging techniques, and from observing the disabilities associated with various types of brain damage allows us to develop more general theories about the relation between brain activity and mental processes than any one of these areas of research could achieve by itself.

Chapter Summary

For over 100 years scientists have studied responses of individual cells as well as coordinated activities of large groups of cells in the central and peripheral nervous systems of animals and humans. These have included observations of normal individuals as well as those people and animals that have suffered some loss of function due to surgery, injury, tumors, drug abuse, or strokes. This wealth of knowledge has provided us with detailed information about what kind of information is detected in the environment, how this information is channeled to the brain, and what parts of the brain receive the incoming sensory information. Further studies have shown that the four main regions of the brain have specialized functions in interpreting and responding to this sensory information. The occipital lobes are primarily involved in vision and recording the spatial layout of features, such as line and edge orientations, colors, motion, and depth. This information is relayed to the parietal lobes and temporal lobes that have different roles to play in interpreting visual input. The parietal lobes function to process spatial relations among seen objects as well as to direct attention to potential objects of interest. It is also the center of somatic information relayed from the skin receptors and other sensors from all parts of the body. The temporal lobes function to interpret the functions and retrieve names and other meaningful information about objects of interest. Auditory information is channeled to the temporal lobes, which also include information about object meaning and function. Language comprehension is mainly localized in the left temporal lobe for most people, and language production depends on coordinated activity in the left frontal lobe. The frontal lobes function as directors for many processes essential for planning tasks and executing those plans as well as controlling behavioral responses relating to judgment and personality.

Our knowledge of brain structures and processes has come from a variety of studies of humans and various animal species, but, by itself, it cannot answer all questions about how brain processes are related to human behavior. Rather, the neurosciences contribute a piece to the total puzzle of how we describe the relation between some external event and someone's response to it. Behavioral research is necessary to confirm or refute theories of how brain processes are related to observable behavior. Only then can theoretical mechanisms be derived that are consistent with both overt behavior and the underlying neuroscience. By using such converging operations guided by theory, cognitive scientists hope to make continual progress in understanding the human mind and how it works.

Review Questions

- **How do sensory systems inform the brain about the outside world?**

Sensory systems begin with transducer cells that transform physical matter and energy into biochemical and electrical activity in neural pathways to the brain. In vision, the transducers are rods and cones in the retinas of the eyes, and in hearing, the transducers are hair cells in the cochleae of the inner ears. The transducers communicate through synaptic connections to other neurons in the auditory and visual pathways to the brain. Most sensory pathways are relayed to the thalamus, and the thalamus has a rich set of forward and backward connections to the cortex. Each sense modality has a primary projection area in the brain—the temporal lobes for hearing and the occipital lobes for vision. The initial representation of information in the sensory projection areas is in terms of fundamental features, such as frequency components and frequency changes in hearing, and edge orientation, motion, and color in vision. Neural activity derived from sensory processes forms the basis for all that the brain learns about sights and sounds available in the outside world.

- **How do we know what information from the physical world is selected for further use?**

Selection begins in the transducers by limiting the range of stimulation that can be detected in the physical stimulus. Stimuli of adequate intensity must fall within certain ranges (e.g., frequency for hearing, wavelength for light) or they will not stimulate the transducers. Recordings of single cells in the visual and auditory pathways reveal that individual neurons show great specificity for responding only to certain events within narrow ranges of variation. Thus, the brain sorts out the visual world into lines and edges, colors and motion, size and location, and the audible world is similarly reduced to frequency components, rising or falling pitches, and certain idiosyncratic sounds. Somehow these fundamental components are reassembled into experiences of real-world objects and events. Recordings of electrical or metabolic activity in the sensory areas of the brain reveal what is detected in the environment, and behavioral studies reveal what people report they see and hear and what they are capable of responding to.

- **How can we measure activity inside the brain of an active, alert human?**

Two major techniques have been developed for recording brain activity in active alert subjects, namely EEG or ERP recordings of electrical activity and PET and fMRI measurements of metabolic activity. Both methods depend on the assumption that brain structures involved in some task will respond differently when that task is performed than they will in some control task or during rest. ERP measurements offer precise temporal determinations of sequences of neural events in response to some stimulus, but they do not produce good spatial resolution. PET and fMRI techniques, on the other hand, are excellent at localizing the sites of increased or decreased brain activity, but their temporal resolution is poor. The combination of the two methods, or the application of newer methods based on magnetoencephalography (MEG) or transcranial magnetic stimulation (TMS), offer the promise to increase our understanding of brain processes in active, alert humans in a variety of task environments.

- **What are the behavioral consequences of damage to different areas of the brain?**

Damage to the frontal lobes can produce a variety of symptoms depending on the location and extent of the injury. These can include losses of judgment, decision-making ability, planning and execution of plans and other executive functions. Changes can also be observed in personality, motor behavior, and speech. Damage to the temporal lobes can result in loss of hearing, loss of recognition of words, pictures, and objects, and the loss of language comprehension. Parietal lobe damage can result in diminished abilities to attend to particular regions in space, and the loss of sensory-motor coordination and spatial abilities. Finally, damage to the occipital lobe can result in complete blindness or lack of vision in specific areas or for specific details, such as color or motion.

Key Terms

Broca's area   50

Cochlea   39

Dorsal visual pathway   39

EEG   43

ERP   43

fMRI   45

Frontal lobes   49

Lateral geniculate nuclei   36

Lateral inhibition   39

Magnetoencephalography (MEG)   47

Neuron   30

Occipital lobes   36

Parietal lobes   39

PET   45

Receptive field (of a neuron)   39

Scotomas   52

Sensation   31

Superior colliculi   36

Synapses   30

Temporal lobes   38

Thalamus   36

Transcranial magnetic stimulation   48

Transduction   31

Ventral visual pathway   39

Wernicke's area   51

IRVING BIEDERMAN

Photo courtesy of Irving Biederman

Chapter 3

Perception

"Seeing is one of the most rapid operations possible: it embraces an infinity of forms, yet it fixes on but one object at a time."

Leonardo da Vinci (1452–1519) as cited in *Bramly*, 1991, p. 255

"… the function of the brain and nervous system and sense organs is in the main eliminative and not productive. Each person is at each moment capable of remembering all that has ever happened to him and perceiving everything that is happening everywhere in the universe. The function of the brain and nervous system is to protect us from being overwhelmed and confused by this mass of largely useless and irrelevant knowledge, by shutting out most of what we should otherwise perceive or remember at any moment, and leaving only that very small and special selection which is likely to be useful."

C. D. Broad (1887–1971), as cited in *Huxley*, 1956, pp. 22–23.

PREVIEW QUESTIONS

❖ *What are the differences between sensation and perception?*

❖ *Is perception based on analysis of simple features of objects, or are objects recognized as wholes?*

❖ *What can the analysis of single-cell recordings tell us about perception?*

❖ *Are there any computer simulations or neural network models that actually perceive things as humans do?*

3.1 Introduction: Sensation versus Perception

The brain's dark and quiet world is disturbed only by patterns of neural discharges, many triggered by external events and the nervous system's responses to them. Most of these sensory events are of little or no interest to us, but others are important because of what they tell us about the environment or because they relate to our current needs and desires. For example, if we are looking for a certain pair of brown socks in a drawer, anything brown is likely to draw our attention for a closer look. Also, even if one is happily daydreaming, it is important to note a book falling toward one's head, or when driving, if your car is drifting off the road.

Different parts of the brain are involved in storing memories of sensory events for later use in recognizing new sights and sounds. Still other parts are involved in planning and directing responses to these stimuli. Many cells in sensory projection areas of the brain respond maximally to very specific features of environmental stimuli. Recent research in neuroscience has discovered *multimodal cells* in various brain centers that respond most strongly to, for example, sights and sounds that can be localized in about the same place and occur at about the same time. We take advantage of multisensory correspondences when, for example, we understand a speaker better when we can also see his or her face. Similarly, one modality can come to dominate another, as in the *ventriloquist effect* in which a sound source appears to move towards the location of a visual event that occurs at about the same time.

All of these phenomena show that the brain tries to make the best possible interpretation of sensory inputs by imposing regularities on them that reflect the structure of the natural world. The world is a regular place, governed by natural laws of physics and structured such that similar things tend to occur together. Even simple events tend to produce related experiences in the separate sensory modalities. Striking a match in front of your face produces an integrated percept that includes a scratchy sound, a flash of light, the smell of burning sulphur, and heat on the fingers. The regularity of life's experiences allows us to make educated guesses and inferences that limit the possibilities and direct our interpretations of what could be causing our sensations. We come to know much more about our environment than we possibly could if we merely recorded incoming sensory signals passively and responded to them in a rigid, habitual way. **Perception** is the interpretation of physical objects and events as recorded by the senses. Human perception is vastly different from that of other animals and the best of our machines with artificially-endowed intelligence. This fact is due to the enormous amount of knowledge that each of us possesses about the physical world and our previous interactions with it. Further, we rapidly and automatically bring much appropriate knowledge to mind when interpreting each new experience.

Perception The interpretation of a sensory message, based on memory of past experiences, and its entry into conscious awareness

3.2 Deriving Perceptual Experience from Sensory Inputs

3.2.1 Perception Depends on Sensation and Memory

Unlike sensation, in which every unique physical event produces an equally unique sensory response, perception depends on treating different things as similar or belonging to the same category. That is, some stimulus properties are ignored and others are unimportant for perceptual processes. Not all visible aspects of a chair in front of us are important enough to analyze in detail before we decide to sit down. The important thing is to categorize the input to decide if it satisfies our current needs. We use internal concepts to identify things that belong to external categories at a global level of analysis—in fact, many objects can be categorized as soon as they are detected (Grill-Spector & Kanwisher, 2005). Recognition of objects occurs when a best-matching example or best-fitting concept is found in memory for the stimulus as encoded by the senses. Perception thus depends on memory, and our perceptions change as we learn about the world. What to us looks like a small bird is a zebra finch to an ornithologist, and a wine expert can distinguish different vintages from a taste that leaves most of us only with the impression of ordinary, good, or excellent.

3.2.2 Is Perception Analytic?

When Hubel and Wiesel (1959, 1962; Hubel, 1963; Box 2.2) found cells that looked like *feature detectors* at the cortical level in mammals, some psychologists hailed the discovery as support for an analytic theory of pattern recognition based on **feature analysis**. It was argued that, rather than storing copies of every possible stimulus in memory and scanning through this enormous list for a match with a new object, a much smaller number of feature tests could be made that would pinpoint the identity of any object. For example, we would have to store 50,000 or more idealized patterns ("templates") just to recognize words in our vocabulary, but tests for the presence or absence of merely 20 features could distinguish among over a million different items (i.e., sorting something based on 20 features that are present or absent in the stimulus allows for $2^{20} = 1,048,576$ different possibilities). Hubel and Wiesel's discovery was treated as a blow against the holistic or template theory of recognition. It was argued that, besides having to be very numerous, object templates in memory would have to be incredibly detailed to match any incoming sensory pattern. Also, we would have to be capable of transforming the sensory image (or its corresponding template) in terms of its size, location, and rotation in 3-D space in order to match sensations with the varieties of visual experiences stored in memory.

Feature analysis A step in a theory of pattern recognition in which an object is analyzed into its component features, which are then compared with stored lists of features representing object concepts in memory

3.2.3   *Selfridge and Neisser's "Pandemonium" Theory*

Among the best ways to test theories of how complex human processes work is to force them to be specific enough to make predictions about human behavior. Even better, if the theory can be formalized as a working model that actually simulates the behavior we are trying to model, then the simulation's predictions and the data from human participants in an experiment can be compared directly. Among the first to create a computerized pattern-recognition device were Selfridge and Neisser (1960) who wrote a program to recognize hand-written letters of the alphabet. They chose not to test **template matching** theory because they thought it would be unacceptably demanding of both memory storage and information processing capacity. If every possible recognizable pattern had to be stored in memory and compared exhaustively with each new input in a search for a match, the storage and processing demands could easily have exceeded limits established for computers of their time. However, both modern computer systems and some current theories of human behavior can handle such demands. Nonetheless, they rejected template theory and used a small number of feature detectors to sort out the identity of individual hand-printed letters.

Features were defined as horizontal, vertical, or oblique lines, along with curves and corners that help to distinguish among printed letters. When a letter was presented to the computer, it was first broken down into its linear and curvilinear components. The idea was to analyze the features in the stimulus to be compared with letters in memory that were each represented by unique lists of features. As each new feature was detected in the input, all letter categories in the computer's memory that contained that feature in their lists received one unit of activation. Since all these activations were effected in parallel (i.e., all letter categories in memory that had a detected feature would be activated at once), the system converged on a most-active letter category more quickly than if the target image had to be scanned serially against all letter categories (i.e., one at a time). (The analogy suggested for understanding the model was to imagine a set of "feature demons" all calling out to "cognitive demons" when their particular feature was detected in the input. Similarly, a "decision demon" listened for the shouting of the "cognitive demons," and tried to pick the loudest one out of the pandemonium—see Figure 3.1). By picking the most active category in memory, their pattern-recognition program was able to achieve a high level of success—comparable to that of a person trying to identify the same hand-printed characters (Neisser, 1967).

3.2.4   *Is Perception Holistic?*

Feature analysis theory contrasts, however, with our subjective impression that we see whole patterns and objects, and seldom their individual components unless we deliberately focus on them. We also know that we can recall vivid images of certain people's faces and common objects in our environment, and we can bring to mind songs or other types of music from beginning to conclusion, at times hardly missing

Template matching A step in a theory of pattern recognition in which an image of an object is compared holistically with stored patterns representing object concepts in memory

FIGURE 3.1

A Fanciful Representation of the Pandemonium Model of Selfridge and Neisser (1960)

A sequence of "demon" processors respond to inputs by shouting their findings to the next level, which includes demons that pick out the loudest shouting demon from among the pandemonium that ensues. In this way, the decision demon usually picks the correct category in memory for matching what was seen by the image demon and handed on to the successive feature demons and cognitive demons.

From Friedenberg, J. & Siverman, G. (2006). *Cognitive Science*. Thousand Oaks, CA: Sage, p. 104.

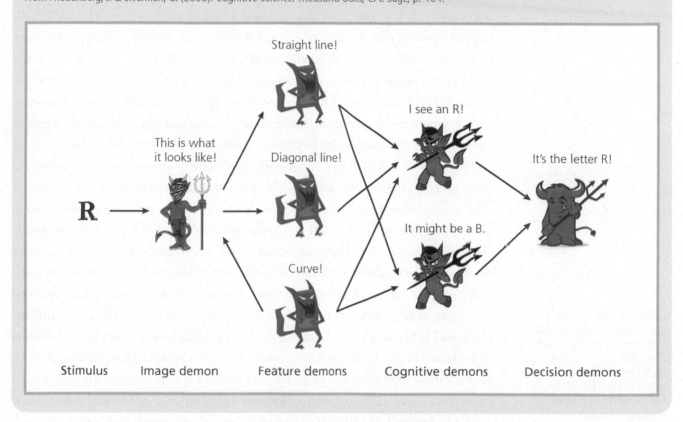

a beat. It is reported that the pianist Arthur Rubenstein was riding in a train one day and was going through a Mozart piano concerto in his mind. His thoughts were interrupted by another passenger who engaged him in conversation for a time, before going back to his newspaper. Rubenstein was amused to observe that the concerto had continued on its own, unchecked, and was nearing its conclusion just as if the intervening conversation had never occurred. Perhaps you have noticed something similar when a popular song is "going through your head."

One could imagine that such self-contained visual and auditory memories could facilitate pattern and object recognition by providing a holistic spatial or temporal template for comparison with global aspects of the environment. You might imagine what is involved when you describe a building that you are trying to find or turn a map around inside your head to direct a friend to take a right or left turn at the next intersection. These results are at least suggestive that holistic images are involved in perceiving real-world objects and scenes and manipulating these images internally. However, suggestive and introspective accounts of perception must be formalized into testable theories before we can determine how objects are recognized.

3.3 Features versus Templates

The discussion so far suggests that the issue of whether pattern or object recognition is based on prior analysis into elementary features, or on construction of an internal image to be compared with stored templates, merits further consideration. It is undoubtedly true that any complex visual scene or auditory experience is literally analyzed into its components by individual cells in the sensory pathways that show great specificity in terms of what stimuli affect their response rates. Cells in the visual cortex respond only to lines, edges, or bars of specific orientations in specific locations in the visual field. Others respond specifically to certain colors or to motion, often only in a certain direction. Similarly, cells in the auditory cortex respond only to sounds of specific frequencies or changes within a specific frequency range.

Faced with this evidence for analytic specificity in sensory coding, it is hard to argue with the theory that perception begins with feature analysis. However, it is not at all obvious that these feature detectors feed directly into pattern and object recognition processes (see Box 3.1). It is entirely possible that other brain regions assemble elementary features into higher-order units, such as candidate objects before they are recognized. For example, recordings of single cells in both auditory and visual association cortex (i.e., areas adjacent to the primary sensory projection areas) have revealed specificity of responding to complex and idiosyncratic stimuli. Cells in the **inferotemporal (IT) cortex** (the parts of the temporal lobes tucked away near the bottom of the brain) in monkeys have shown preferences for a variety of specific stimuli, such as black disks with thin bars projecting out of them at certain angles, or star-shaped patterns at particular orientations (Tanaka, Siato, Fukada, & Moriya, 1991; Young, 1995; see Figure 3.2). Other IT cells respond best to important, familiar objects, such as hands and faces. Similarly, recordings of single cells in auditory areas have found neurons that specifically respond to unusual sounds, such as keys jangling, paper tearing, or animal cries and screams (e.g., Rauschecker, Tian, & Hauser, 1995).

These results have led scientists to question seriously whether there could be grandmother detectors or yellow Volkswagen cells! In fact, a recent study of single cell responses in the medial temporal lobe of a human subject showed some cells with remarkable specificity—some fired only to pictures of the actress Jennifer Aniston, and others to pictures of Halle Berry or the Sydney Opera House (Quiroga, Reddy, Kreiman, Koch, & Fried, 2005). The question is whether the cells' responses indicate that they are the sole responders for particular stimuli, or that they are part of a complex network, parts of which might serve to recognize other people or places as well. In response to questions like that, we should consider the specific versus distributed notion of information representation in the brain. That is, it would seem to be more economical as well as far safer for the maintenance of memories and other abilities if information could be represented by the relative activity of a number of

Inferotemporal cortex Part of the temporal cortex located in the lower part of primate brains that plays a role in visual object recognition; it includes thousands of cells that are tuned to a variety of idiosyncratic shapes

BOX 3.1

Are Orientation-Specific Cells Feature Detectors?

Certain cells in visual, auditory, and other sensory systems are sometimes referred to as "feature detectors" because of the narrow range of stimulus variation within which their response is maximal. Thus, a cell in the visual cortex will respond maximally, say, to a black stripe between two white ones, all oriented at 30 degrees clockwise from vertical, and the response rate falls off as the orientation is changed 10 or 20 degrees from the preferred angle. One might easily assume that this cell therefore detects only dark stripes at a specific location and orientation in the visual field, and if the cell is active, its preferred stimulus must be present. This assumption is not correct. The problem with the feature detection assumption is that it is based on the view that cells in sensory or perceptual systems specifically code for certain features in the environment. Specificity coding means that cells only show all-or-nothing responses to their stimuli. No cell in any sensory system responds like that; all show a gradation of responses around some range with their preferred stimulus in the center of the range. Thus, a cell might respond moderately to a low-contrast stimulus of the preferred orientation, and just as moderately to a high-contrast stimulus rotated 10 degrees away from the preferred orientation (see figure). Exactly what stimulus is presented to the receptive field of the cell cannot be determined by its response alone.

The conclusion to be reached is that the response rate of any individual cell, or even a small group of cells, is insufficient to determine the unique properties of any stimulus. Only by determining the relative rates of firing activity across a large sample of neurons can a general picture be obtained of what stimulus properties exist in the environment. This is the principle of distributed coding, which is viewed as being more efficient, more resistant to brain injury and cell death, and a more likely candidate for how we represent and store information in the brain (see Box 3.2).

Are Simple Cells Feature Detectors?

(A) Imagine that the receptive field of a cortical cell looks like this (where "−" means an inhibitory area, and "+" means an excitatory area:

(B) Then the cell's response rate for different stimuli below might look like (the horizontal axis the line is time, and the vertical lines are neural spikes)

Time

Continues

(C) It is obvious that similar patterns of responses can be elicited by different stimuli (e.g., preferred orientation, low contrast versus 20 degrees off preferred orientation, high contrast). Therefore, a single cell cannot be a feature detector.

neurons, perhaps those that participate in a particular network. Then, no individual cell would ever have the sole responsibility for any cognitive ability, yet each cell could contribute to a number of different functions (See Box 3.2—connectionism).

There is an area termed the Fusiform Face Area (FFA) in the inferior temporal lobe, which shows activation during face recognition (e.g., Kanwisher, McDermott, & Chun, 1997). There is also an area termed the Parahippocampal Place Area (PPA), which responds to images of landscapes and buildings.

FIGURE 3.2

Inferotemporal Cortex

Location of the inferotemporal cortex in a macaque monkey brain (dark region in figure) and the responses rates of an individual cell in this region to the onsets of seven different stimuli presented in its visual receptive field (after Tanaka et al., 1991)

From Goldstein, E. B. (2002). *Sensation and Perception*, 6th Ed. Pacific Grove, CA: Wadsworth, p. 113 (monkey cortex) and p. 119 (single-cell response rates).

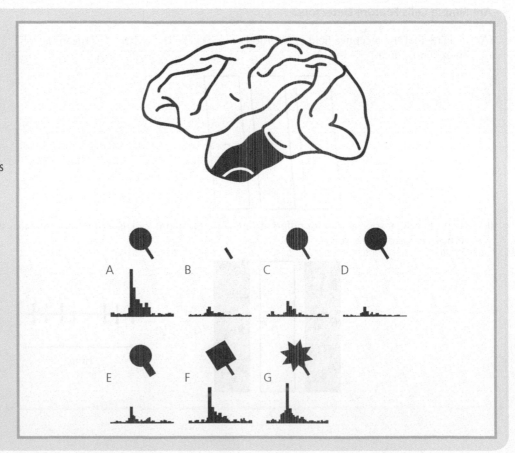

BOX 3.2

Parallel and Distributed Information Coding—Connectionism

For over 100 years attempts have been made to link behavior with underlying neurophysiology. Much success in understanding the basic architecture of sensory systems has been based on the single-cell recording technique. However, it is clear that higher mental processes, such as perception and language, require the concerted efforts of millions of cells working together. Obviously, initial attempts at building models of how neural circuits might code and process information began with simple systems. The seminal work in this area was done by Donald Hebb, described in his book, *The Organization of Behavior* (1949).

Hebb used the term *cell assemblies* to refer to networks of interconnected neurons that could change their structure and function as they learned to perceive and remember sensory events. Hebb followed a long tradition in psychology that based learning on the acquisition of simple associations: if two or more cells are repeatedly active at about the same time, later activation of one will tend to activate the others (hence the expression, "cells that fire together wire together"). This change in activation potential, Hebb argued, would be due to structural changes in synaptic connections among cells, with cell assemblies having lower synaptic

resistance than unrelated cells. In this way, common structures in the environment would be represented by analogous structures in the brain.

Later theorists (e.g., Rosenblatt, 1958) developed Hebb's ideas into artificial networks of units (or nodes) and connections among them that at least superficially resembled actual neural networks. These typically consist of a set of input units (cells that receive input directly from the stimulus), a set of intermediate (or hidden) units, and a set of output units that determine the response to the stimulus. As shown in the figure, all input units can be connected to all hidden units, and all hidden units can be connected to all output units. The system begins with a set of connection weights associated with each inter-unit connection. If a weight is zero, then no activation can flow along the connection. If the weight is one, the activation of the input unit is conveyed directly to the output unit, whereas if the weight is −1, the activation level of the input is reversed, and the connection becomes inhibitory rather than excitatory, and vice-versa. Each unit sums up the weighted activations it receives from all of its input sources, and this sum determines the strength of its output.

An Example of a Neural Network

The network is in the process of learning to replicate a specific input pattern of black and white squares arranged into a column. The input layer nodes receive 0s (black) as inputs, and the links to the hidden and output layers have weights that result in activations of the output nodes that can vary from -1.0 (inhibitory) to +1.0 (excitatory). With feedback, the weights should gradually change to produce an accurate copy of the input; that is, the network will have "learned" the pattern. (From http://ecee.colorado.edu/~ecen4831/lectures/NNdemo.html)

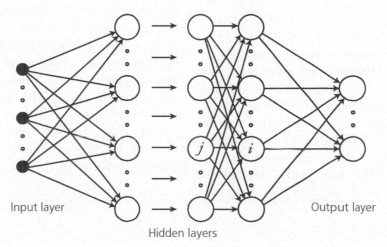

Input layer   Output layer

Hidden layers

Continues

The network learns by receiving feedback from the responses that it makes to a set of input patterns. In early network theory, weights that led to incorrect responses were decreased, and those that led to correct responses were increased. The output pattern for each stimulus is compared with the input pattern, and the discrepancy is called the *error signal*. The goal is to drive this error to zero by continuously adjusting the weights over learning trials (see figure).

Artificial networks bear only superficial similarity to human neuronal systems, in that nodes are like neurons and connections are like synapses, and model networks are necessarily much simpler than neural networks in the human brain. However, research with neural nets has led to some fascinating discoveries and unanticipated results that have encouraged an increasing amount of research in this area. Some of these results are discussed below.

Parallel-distributed representation Memory in a neural net consists of a pattern of weights among connections in the network. That is, there is no central memory node or specific location where the memory is stored. The stimulus consists merely of selective activation of some of the input nodes, and the weights determine which nodes in one or more hidden layers are activated and their levels of activation. These, in turn, propagate activation or inhibition along links to the response nodes, and the final activation levels of these nodes represent the response. Thus, all information in the network is contained in the weights of all connections between input and output layers. Information is not stored locally, but rather globally over the network; and activation proceeds not in a serial way from a single start node to an eventual response node, but rather from an input vector of values to an output vector, with all nodes in each level activated in parallel.

Back propagation Whenever an error occurs in the output pattern that distinguishes it from the desired response, there is no way of knowing which of the many weights in the network contributed to the error. This problem has been solved in principle by developing algorithms that begin with the set of weights that connect the units in the last hidden layer to the output units. These are then altered to minimize the discrepancy between the actual and desired output. This procedure is iteratively repeated to the next hidden layer, and so on back to the input layer. The algorithm is designed to achieve learning in the network by systematically modifying those weights most responsible for errors.

Resistance to noise and graceful degradation Block (1962) taught a simple network to discriminate between the letters E and X. He then introduced noise by (1) randomly switching on 30% of the input units in addition to those activated by the test pattern and (2) giving incorrect feedback on 30% of the trials. Although learning performance was impaired, both types of noise only slowed development, but eventual perfect pattern discrimination was not eliminated.

In another demonstration, Block systematically removed units from a network after the discrimination had been learned. He found that performance declined gradually rather than all at once, and the degree of degradation was directly proportional to the number of units removed. This is a big improvement over loss of information units in serial systems, as any missing link in a chain can cause the system to crash.

Simulation of figure segmentation in object recognition Grossberg and Mingolla (1985) developed a model of shape perception based on layers of units roughly corresponding to the different kinds of cortical cells identified by Hubel and Wiesel (1977). The first layer consists of filters, like simple cells that respond maximally to edges with a dark surface next to light surface presented at a certain location and orientation on the input grid of units. Units at the second layer are analogous to the hypercomplex cells identified by Hubel and Wiesel. Activations at one orientation and place at this layer produce inhibitions of orthogonal orientations. At a third level, like-oriented filters activate others of similar orientations at a distance across the input field. This long-range cooperation produces detection of linear components of larger figures, and is posited as a possible explanation of some interesting phenomena, such as illusory contours (see figure).

An Example of Illusory Contours

Do you see a white triangle? Is it in front of the black blobs and lines? Is it brighter than the rest of the page? (From www.newworldencyclopedia.org/entry/Kanizsa_triangle)

Connectionist modeling has a short but active history, and the field is full of promise for developments in many areas of cognitive science. Neural networks have been proven to be adept at learning some of the most impressive perceptual abilities of humans, such as voice recognition, speech understanding, and 3-D object recognition (see Quinlan, 1991 for an excellent review of the early work in this area). Research in neural networks has the two-fold promise of unveiling a deeper understanding of how biological systems come to learn and code information as well as providing practical means to develop a host of intelligent systems with wide applications in the future.

3.4 Beyond Feature and Templates— Structural Component Theories

3.4.1 Features Alone Are Not Enough for Perception

Groups of neurons firing together in patterns of activity tell us nothing about whether they are coding individual features or holistic patterns from the stimulus environment. Several researchers (e.g., Biederman, 1987; Juola, 1979; Reed, 1973) have pointed out a particular flaw in a radical feature theory that puts all its stock in recognition of patterns from individual features alone. It is likely that the way features are combined is just as important for object recognition as what those features are. Some combinations can be simple and symmetric; other combinations of the same features can be complex. Let us consider a simple example: the letters "T" and "L" contain the same features: a horizontal and a vertical line that connect to form a right angle. At the most elementary level of feature analysis, they are identical, yet these two forms (and many other examples) are easily differentiated and apparently effortlessly recognized by adult readers and named as "tee" and "ell."

Features can also be combined to yield emergent properties that sometimes cannot be predicted from analysis of individual features alone. This principle was what Wertheimer had in mind when he noted that, "I stand at the window and see house, trees, sky. Theoretically I might say that there were 327 brightnesses and nuances of color. Do I have 327? No. I have sky, house, and trees" (1923, p. 71).

The Gestalt psychologists in early twentieth-century Germany [i.e., Koffka (1886–1941), Kohler (1887–1967), and Wertheimer (1880–1943)] recognized the fact that we see objects, not features, and made it an axiom that "the whole is greater than the sum of its parts" (Koffka, 1935). Such properties as symmetry and global orientation depend on how features are arranged. How features are perceptually grouped depends on properties such as similarity of their shapes, sizes, or colors, as well as good continuation and common fate motion (as a flock of birds in flight is grouped). Figure 3.3 shows examples of some of the **Gestalt principles** of grouping and how they can reveal structures in what would remain separate, unrelated items if

Gestalt principles A descriptive set of rules that perception seems to follow in order to force the simplest, most symmetric, and most likely interpretation of sensory input, including grouping features by proximity, similarity, good continuation, common fate motion, and others

---

FIGURE 3.3

Do You See Columns or Do You See Rows?

Gestalt principles of organization describe our tendency to group things on the basis of similarity. (A) below should be viewed as ambiguous; that is, you should be able to imagine the grid as being organized into either columns or rows (but not both at the same time). But (B) appears as columns because of color (or brightness) similarity, and (C) appears to be organized into rows because of shape similarity. (D) is organized into columns because of good continuation (straight lines preferred over wavy lines). (E) is organized into columns because of size similarity, and grouping by proximity causes (F) to appear as rows.

similarities among separate features were not noticed and used by the visual system. It also appears that such grouping principles occur early in vision, as they form the basis for integration of features into more holistic representations that only later are recognized as familiar patterns or objects. Further, the Gestalt principles make sense from the ecological point of view in that things that are similar in size, shape, color, orientation, and common fate motion in nature are most likely to belong together as components of a single object.

Although the Gestalt psychologists were primarily interested in visual perception, one would think that what is useful in early perceptual organization in one modality might work just as well in another. In support of the generality of these principles, musical illusions have been found that demonstrate Gestalt principles of grouping by similarity (Wessel, 1979) and good continuation (Deutsch, 1975) (see Figure 3.4).

3.4.2 David Marr's Artificial Intelligence Approach to Vision

Perhaps one of the most important applications of Gestalt rules of organization in perception occurs in the work of David Marr. He was a vision scientist working in artificial intelligence approaches to recognizing objects, and wrote one of the most influential books in the area, namely *Vision* (1982). It is a heroic effort on many dimensions, just one of which was his construction of a computer simulation model of early processes in vision. Marr tried to make as much use as possible of **bottom-up processes** working on information available in the two-dimension retinal image. He assumed that elementary features, such as lines and edges, could be combined by higher-order cells in the visual cortex that use Gestalt grouping principles, such as similarity and good continuation. Indeed the presence of such cells was discovered after Marr had completed his work (e.g., "continuation cells" that connect cells sensitive to similar orientations across different regions of the cortex, Gilbert & Wiesel, 1989; and cells that fire in synchrony when they detect the presence of similar features in nearby regions of the visual field, Engel, Konig, Kretier, Schillen, & Singer, 1992).

Marr called the retinal image and the features and groupings in it the "raw primal sketch." In his theory, many Gestalt-like organizational principles work at this early stage of vision to recover global structures by accumulating information across individual units. These processes produce the next representational stage: the "2½-dimensional sketch." The 2½-D sketch benefits from organizational tools that help to separate objects in depth, including figure-ground separation. There are many cues in the environment that help us to decide whether one object is in front of another. The most important of these is occlusion (when one object hides part of another object that stands behind it). Occlusion is signaled by a sharp edge or boundary between two figures that clearly belongs to the figure in the foreground. Other cues include the usual fact that figures are brighter than backgrounds, they have more details visible on their surfaces, and they are more likely to be symmetrical than partially occluded

Bottom-up processes Processes usually determined only from sensory analysis of the stimulus (also called "data-driven" processes), although they can also be affected by the observer's adaptation level (e.g., number of minutes in the dark) and amount of attention directed to the stimulus

FIGURE 3.4
Gestalt Principles of Organization in Hearing

From Goldstein, E. B. (2002). *Sensation and Perception*, 6th Ed. Pacific Grove, CA: Wadsworth. p. 397 (Figure 3.4.1) and p. 399 (Figure 3.4.2).

Figure 3.4.1 Wessel's (1979) illusion The open notes (a) stand for tones with one timbre (e.g., a trumpet) whereas the black notes stand for tones of a different timbre (e.g., a flute). When the tones are played slowly (b) they are heard as separate ascending sequences with alternating timbres. When the tones are played quickly (c) they are heard as overlapping descending sequences of the same timbre. At a sufficient rate of presentation, grouping by similarity overrides grouping by temporal proximity.

Figure 3.4.2 Deutsch's (1975) scale illusion Although the high and low notes alternate between the two ears as presented by headphone (a and b), the listener hears a smoothly ascending or descending scale in each ear (c). In this case, grouping by pitch proximity wins out.

background objects. These cues for relative distance are likely to be consistent with each other, reinforcing the various visual processes involved in determining what is foreground and what is background. Depth cues are rarely inconsistent in the real world, although they can lead to amusing distortions of perception in the laboratory and in some clever examples from the illusion literature (see Figure 3.5).

FIGURE 3.5

Figures with Global or Local Ambiguity in Depth and Figure-Ground Relations

Shutterstock.com (Figure 3.5.1 and 3.5.2), adapted from W. H. Freeman, p. 81 (Figure 3.5.3).

Figure 3.5.1 A drawing in which the black parts can be seen as background behind the white faces, but it can also be seen interpreted as a foreground figure (i.e., as a black tree with a twisted trunk). The two interpretations should alternate; seeing both interpretations at once is difficult.

Figure 3.5.2 A triangle drawing with inconsistent relative depth information. It is impossible to resolve into a real object.

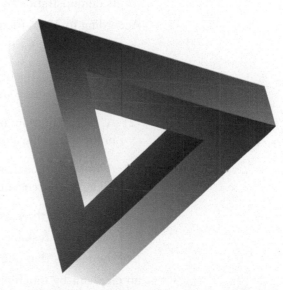

Figure 3.5.3 A Drawing of a Pseudo-Greek Temple with Depth and Good Continuation Ambiguity in the Surfaces of the Columns

Top-down processes Those aspects of perception that use information beyond what is in the stimulus alone, such as the context in which it occurs and any prior knowledge about it retrieved from memory

The 2½-D sketch ends with the segregation of the field of view into likely objects that are near and those that recede into the background. Only at the last stage of visual analysis does Marr allow for **top-down processes** to occur. At the level of a 3-D model of the world, candidate objects are identified by a holistic matching processes that choose the most closely-corresponding representation in long-term memory. Marr did not consider other top-down processes in his initial model, but he was well aware of the effects of prior knowledge and use of context that contribute greatly to human perceptual abilities (to be considered in section 3.7.4).

Marr's (1984) theory is important not only for its contribution to vision, but also for its demonstration of how theory can best be applied to solve scientific problems. According to Marr, there are three aspects of a theoretical attack on a problem that must be included for the theory to be successful. These are:

(1) A summary of the behavior that one is trying to understand, including a description of the procedures used, measurements taken, and their quantitative analysis

(2) A representation of the underlying processes that determine the behavior, preferably using algorithms based on known physiological mechanisms

(3) A working model, in his case, a computer simulation based on the processes understood to occur in (2) that predicts the data described in (1)

Without all three aspects in place, Marr argued that a theory is incomplete and not adequately testable in any science. To use a metaphor, incomplete theories are like the results that one might obtain if seven blind-folded persons were to examine an elephant by touching it and then reporting what it was like. One would feel the trunk and describe it as a snake, another would touch the ear and describe it as a fan. Still others would describe it as a tree (leg) or a rope (tail), and so on, each being confused by examining only part of the problem.

Much theorizing in psychology and other disciplines suffers because of an inadequate approach to the whole issue involved. Marr made an example of Gibson's theory of visual perception (1966) that places all the work at the bottom-up level. Gibson argued that perception is direct in the sense that all information necessary to resolve 3-D space and the objects in it is available in the ambient visual array, particularly as viewed by a moving observer. He stated that there was no need for theorizing about how higher-order rules and knowledge are brought to bear on the retinal image and how top-down processes examine its contents in search for a best match in memory. Gibson added some useful viewpoints to our understanding of perception, particularly in emphasizing the value of observer motion in disambiguating two-dimensional retinal images. This behavior is illustrated by the snake that appears to be charmed by imitating the motions of the flute player in front of it. In reality the cobra is moving back and forth in order to gain a better judgment of whether the snake charmer is within striking distance! Gibson's view that vision is direct, in the sense that everything necessary for vision is present in the stimulus, ignores the enormous amount of knowledge we have that can influence our perception in a top-down way. In fact, Marr dismisses some of his work with the remark that Gibson simply did not understand the complexity of human vision. The main problem is to specify the form in which perceptual memories exist and how they are used to enhance vision, for without such memories, human perception cannot take place.

3.5 Theories of Object Recognition

3.5.1   Features versus Templates Revisited

There are several reasons that issues, such as features versus templates, are so important to cognitive scientists. One reason is obvious: We want to understand how we can confront an absolutely unique stimulus object, yet almost always quickly and accurately decide what it is, name it, and come up with some useful functions for it. Every day, sometimes every minute, we see new people and things, but we seldom have any difficulty in knowing what they are. If we knew how people performed such feats, we might be able to duplicate them in automatic systems that also could recognize important stimuli, such as voices, faces, and other complex objects and events, rapidly and with few errors. Of course, technology is becoming increasingly successful in exactly such areas, and studies of human perception have contributed greatly to this effort. Nevertheless, there remain large aspects of human perceptual abilities that remain mysterious despite our best research efforts, and cannot be duplicated by artificial-intelligent systems (see http://captcha.net for examples in vision).

3.5.2   Processing Stages in Recognition

Pattern and object recognition can occur only when a correspondence can be found between the current sensory impressions of some physical object or event and stored traces of past experiences in memory. Psychologists have identified three processes that must occur between presentation of the stimulus and its recognition. These stages are encoding, comparison, and decision. The encoding stage is largely a bottom-up sensory process that informs the brain about featural components and global properties of the object under examination. The decision process picks the best-fitting object representation from candidates in memory. The main work occurs in the comparison processes, which by its very name means that there must be some way to compare sensory codes with memory codes in looking for the best match or category for the stimulus. Then it becomes obvious why the feature versus template and other issues of pattern recognition are so important. Simply stated, a theory of pattern or object recognition is more than just a theory of how physical objects are represented in the sensory code. It is also a theory of what memory structures are like for previously experienced objects and events. That is, sensory codes and memory codes must be literally comparable for perception to take place.

Extreme views of object recognition based on features alone have been criticized as being too simple—the ways features are combined can and do influence how we interpret what is presented. Similarly, extreme template theories have also been criticized as being too cumbersome, requiring literally millions of entries in memory that must be kept and updated for recognizing even everyday things. Yet, it is obvious that many things can be identified by a single feature, such as a skunk by its odor and a traffic signal by its color. Other things are subjectively, but just as convincingly, recognized as whole objects, such as the face of a friend, the value of a coin, or the opening chord of a symphony

3.5.3 Biederman's Recognition-by-Components (RBC) Theory

Recognition-by-components
Biederman's theory of object recognition based on use of a set of "geons," or geometric solid primitives, that are components of all natural and artificial objects

Both research efforts and introspective reports such as those listed above have led psychologists to favor theories of object recognition that fall between the extreme views of feature analysis and holistic template matching. One of the most influential of such theories has been the **recognition-by-components (RBC) theory** of Biederman (1987; Biederman & Cooper, 1991). Biederman's idea is that since features by themselves are often ambiguous in determining an object's identity, and since object templates would need be too numerous and cumbersome to match to all possible stimuli, some intermediate level of visual components could serve as the basis of object recognition. By analogy, thousands of different words can be learned and recognized based on their unique combinations of a few basic building blocks like letters in writing and phonemes in speech. Biederman argued that there are certain volumetric properties of objects (i.e., basic 3-D shapes) that remain invariant despite changes in an object's location, distance, and rotation in space—just as a pyramid or a cube retain their basic structures as they are moved about. That is, these basic shapes are viewpoint-invariant, since they have the same apparent structure from a variety of different perspective views. He further argued that only a small set of primitive shapes in isolation or combination is sufficient to recognize almost all natural and artificial objects. He termed these primitives *geons* for geometric icons, and he argued that only about 30 are sufficient to capture nearly all possible object shapes. Examples of some of these geons and their inclusion in some familiar objects are shown in Figure 3.6.

Proposing any theory of object recognition on logical grounds alone is insufficient for its acceptance as a useful theory of human perception. That is, even though Biederman's recognition-by-components theory is an elegant solution to the features versus templates dilemma, it remains only a conjecture until it can be tested against relevant data and shown to have predictive and explanatory power. In addition, any physiological mechanisms known to identify geon-like components in the visual array would provide further support for the theory. As it turns out, there are both empirical and physiological supports for the theory.

FIGURE 3.6

Recognition-by-Components Theory

Biederman's recognition-by-components theory supposes that all recognizable objects can be constructed from a small set of volumetric primitives that he called "geons" (from geometric icons). These geons can be combined in various ways to produce an effectively infinite variety of objects. Sample geons are shown on the left, and how they might combine to form objects is indicated on the right (adapted from Biederman, 1987).

Adapted from Goldstein, E.B. (2005). *Cognitive Psychology.* Belmont, CA: Thomson Wadsworth, p. 71.

Research by Biederman and Cooper (1991; Biederman, Cooper, Hummel, & Fiser, 1993) measured recognition speed and accuracy for outline drawings of common objects that had half of their line segments removed. In one case, the segments removed were selected from the middle parts of lines, such that corners and other vertices (where lines intersect) were left intact. For these items, the volumes and shapes of components could be determined by inspection. In the other case, the lines removed were selected from areas at corners and vertices, and longer line segments were left intact. For these items, volumes and shapes were more difficult to derive from the visible lines. As expected, performance was much worse in the latter condition since corners and vertices are the important parts of line drawings as well as real objects that define structural components of objects, as geon-theory predicts (see Figure 3.7).

In another experiment, Biederman and Cooper (1992) showed line drawings of two objects twice each in separate blocks of trials. In this case the data were the naming times for objects. It has been shown in many experiments that the time taken for someone to name an object, picture, drawing, or even a common word is shorter if the same stimulus has been presented earlier in an experiment (this is called "the repetition priming effect"). Biederman and Cooper demonstrated that repetition priming worked if a line drawing of an object was repeated, even with different line

FIGURE 3.7

The Importance of Vertices for Object Recognition
Two views of the same outline drawings of familiar objects, with the one on the right obscured by a mask such that the major vertices are covered, and only some line segments remain. In the middle column, the same proportions of the objects are obscured, but this time the major vertices are revealed, making it much easier to recognize the objects (adapted from Biederman, 1987).

segments deleted from the drawing on the two repetitions. That is, the repetition priming effect is just as strong if the same line segments are shown both times or if the complementary set of line segments is shown the second time. This result indicates that whatever we use to recognize objects from line drawings, it must be more than the simple features represented by line segments themselves. It simply did not matter whether the same features were shown the second time or not—repetition priming effects were just as strong in either case (see Figure 3.8).

A second experiment was designed to find out what was remembered from the first presentation to prime the second, if it was not the features represented by line segments. In the second experiment, half the line segments were also shown in each presentation, but this time the deleted segments were carefully chosen to preserve parts of the object that correspond to geon-like components. In this case, repetition priming was stronger for the drawings that had the same components in both repetitions. Objects with different components were recognized no faster than totally new objects of the same category. It appears that recognition of an object depends not so much on recognizing its features, but on recognizing its components. This conclusion is based on the observation that repeating features or showing new features has no effect on the repetition priming effect. However, repeating components produces strong repetition priming, but showing new components of the same objects does not. Biederman and Cooper's result is clear support for a component theory of object recognition.

FIGURE 3.8

Examples of the Stimuli and the Average Results from the Experiment of Biederman and Cooper (1992).

Biederman, I., & Cooper, E. E. (1991). Priming contour-deleted images: Evidence for intermediate representations in visual object recognition. Cognitive psychology, 23(3), 393-419.

Figure 3.8.1 Line-complement priming An example stimulus shown in the first series of trials included a drawing of a grand piano with half of its line segments missing. In the second series of trials, either the same drawing or the complementary one (same piano, different set of line segments) was shown, along with a drawing of a new, upright piano with half of its segments missing. All three stimuli showed a reduction in naming time (priming effect) on the second series of trials, but the effect was larger and equal (168 versus 170 ms) for the two grand pianos than for a different piano version (93 ms). The equivalent priming effect for the two grand pianos shows no memory for the specific line segments (features) shown in the first series of trials, but the priming effect shows that some categorical information was remembered.

Figure 3.8.2 Part-complement priming An example stimulus shown in the first series of trials was a drawing of a grand piano with half of its geon-like components missing. In the second series of trials, either the identical drawing or the complementary one (same piano, completely different set of components) was shown, along with a drawing of a new, upright piano with half of its components missing. All three stimuli showed a naming time advantage (priming effect) on the second series of trials, but the effect was larger for the grand piano version with the same components repeated (192 ms) than for the same piano version with different components shown (108 ms). The latter priming result was no different than that found for an entirely different piano with half of its components missing (110 ms). The results show that it is memory for the specific components that yields the largest priming effect, strongly supporting the component view of object recognition and memory.

3.5.4 Neurophysiological Support and a Critique of RBC

Physiological support for Biederman's RBC theory comes from studies of single-cell recordings in higher visual centers in monkeys. Recordings of neural activity indicates that cells in the inferotemporal cortex (IT) show remarkable specificity for specific shapes, from simple to complex, that could form the basis of object recognition (Tanaka, et al. 1991; Young, 1995). There are cells that respond maximally to extremely idiosyncratic patterns, such as a circular disk with a thin bar extending from it at a particular direction or a picture of a face at a particular orientation. Such specificity can presumably be afforded because of the massive numbers of cells in areas such as IT that can each signal the likelihood of certain components in a scene.

Biederman's theory is not without its critics. For example, Enns (2004) points out some difficulties that the theory has in explaining how people recognize objects that cannot easily be decomposed into simple convex solids, such as crumpled newspapers, articles of clothing, fruits, and trees. Tarr (2003) also challenges the assumption that geons are viewpoint-invariant structures, since his research indicates that viewpoints of past experiences can and do influence object recognition processes in subsequent experiences. Yet RBC remains a classic example of a theory that is worked out in sufficient detail that it (1) can predict and offer an explanation for data collected in object recognition experiments, (2) is consistent with known physiological mechanisms in primate vision, and (3) can provide a working formalization, in this case a computer neural-network model, that simulates human data (Hummel & Biederman, 1992). These three components are all necessary pieces of a complete theory, as originally argued by David Marr (1982).

3.6 The Where and What of Object Recognition

3.6.1 Organization of Occipital Cortex

Over half the human brain is completely or heavily involved in visual information processing (e.g., Enns, 2004). The occipital lobe includes the primary visual cortex that receives visual input from the eyes via the lateral geniculate nuclei of the thalamus. From there, neural pathways pass on various types of information to other centers located in various parts of the brain. An important concept here is modularity of function. That is, the visual system seems to be composed of several more-or-less independent modules that handle specific attributes of the visual world. This **modularity** exists in the primary visual cortex in the form of *hypercolumns* that replicate bundles of modules hundreds of times across the outer layers of the occipital lobe. These hypercolumns correspond to adjacent, small areas of the retina (and hence the visual field) and include cells specialized for the detection of orientation, color, motion, and depth. Fine details and color information are conducted mainly along the ventral pathway to the temporal lobe of the brain that specializes in object recognition. Gross details and motion information are conveyed mainly along the dorsal pathway to the parietal lobe that specializes in spatial representation and motion perception.

Also, the ventral pathway includes V4 (color perception) and V5/MT (motion perception). Other visual features, such as color and motion, are processed in the occipital lobe; and therefore, damage to those regions is associated with specific deficits in perception. For example, damage to area V4 can cause a symptom termed "achromatopsia", which is different from color blindness caused by a cone deficiency. Severity of achromatopsia may depend on severity of damage; for example, partial damage to V4 may make colors appear dirty or washed out (See Sacks, 1997).

Modularity a characteristic of sensory channels in which different individual or bundles of neurons respond to different specific aspects of a stimulus; e.g., in vision, there are separate modules for location, orientation, color, motion, and size (or spatial frequency).

TABLE 3.1   Summary of the Two Visual Pathways Beyond the Primary Visual Cortex

	Ventral pathway	Dorsal pathway
Functions	Object recognition	Spatial cognition
Brain regions	Primary visual cortex	Primary visual cortex
	Inferior extrastriate	Superior extrastriate
	Inferior temporal lobe	Superior parietal lobe
Neurological disorders	Apperceptive agnosia	Visual neglect
	Associative agnosia	Simultagnosia
	Prosopagnosia (face)	

3.6.2   Deciding "What?" versus "Where?" in Vision

Support for separate "what" versus "where" systems in perception originally came from ablation studies in monkeys. In ablation studies, part of the brain is destroyed to mimic types of stroke damage or other cerebral injuries that can occur in humans. Ungerleider and Mishkin (1982; Mishkin, Ungerleider, & Macko, 1983) reported studies in which monkeys had been trained to select one of two objects in order to receive a food reward. In one case, the two objects differed in appearance; and in the other case, the two objects differed in their distance from a third, landmark object. After training produced nearly perfect discrimination in the two tasks, the monkeys were operated on to produce a lesion in either the temporal or parietal regions of their brains (see Figure 3.5). Monkeys with temporal lesions failed more often at the object discrimination task, but performance was undiminished for the landmark task. Monkeys with parietal lesions showed the opposite effect; the landmark task was now performed poorly, whereas the object recognition task showed no impairment (see Figure 3.9).

Similar results have been observed in human patients with localized brain damage. Milner and Goodale (1995) describe the results from patient D.F., a 34-year-old woman who suffered damage to her ventral visual pathway as a result of carbon monoxide poisoning. She demonstrated a deficit known as visual form **agnosia** that showed itself in her poor ability to recognize simple geometric forms and pictures of objects. Her ability was not due to loss of memory for objects, as she could easily identify some objects when they were placed in her hand, even though she could not name them by sight alone. She also retained some ability to draw objects from memory, even though she later was unable to recognize what her own drawings represented.

Patient D.F.'s dorsal pathway remained intact, and she was able, therefore, to navigate in space and walk though an obstacle course with no apparent difficulties. In one impressive demonstration of the dissociation of dorsal and ventral abilities, she was handed a card and asked to orient it to the same oblique angle visible in a

Agnosia The loss of certain perceptual abilities, such as the ability to name objects or faces or the ability to see motion or color, due to localized brain damage

FIGURE 3.9

Research Demonstrating Independent Visual Pathways for Object Discrimination and Object Location Information (after Mishkin, Ungerleider, & Macko, 1983)

From Goldstein, E. B. (2007), *Sensation and Perception*, 7th Ed. Belmont, CA: Thomson Wadsworth, p.79.

Figure 3.9.1 In the object discrimination task (a), monkeys learn to reach for food under an object of a specific color and shape. In the location discrimination task (b), monkeys learn that food is under the object either nearer to or farther away from the cylinder landmark. After surgical removal of the indicated parts of the brain, monkeys with lesions in the inferior temporal lobe lost the ability to perform the object discrimination task, and monkeys with lesions in the posterior parietal lobe lost the ability to perform the landmark discrimination task. In both cases, performance on the other task was unaffected by the lesions.

Area removed
(temporal lobe)

(a) Object discrimination

Area removed
(parietal lobe)

(b) Landmark discrimination

Figure 3.9.2 Traces of two visual pathways in the monkey cortex. The dorsal pathway leads from the occipital lobe to the posterior parietal lobe and reflects neural activity involved in locating objects in space and perceiving spatial relations among objects. The ventral pathway leads from the occipital lobe to the temporal lobe and reflects activity involved in pattern recognition and object identification.

Where/How
Parietal lobe

Dorsal
pathway

Occipital lobe
(primary visual
receiving area)

Ventral
pathway

Temporal lobe
What

slot in a box. She was unable to do this, as she held the card in orientations that were essentially randomly distributed around that of the slot. However, when she was then asked to place the card in the slot, like mailing a post card, she was able to execute the appropriate rotating wrist motion to align the card and slip it into the slot without error. This result indicated that the dorsal visual pathway, which remained intact in D.F., allowed her to reach and grasp for objects and put things in their proper places without conscious control.

There are several types of agnosias. One is termed apperceptive agnosia and the other associative agnosia. Patients with apperceptive agnosia show inability to distinguish between two objects, to copy and to name objects. They tend to have lesions in the inferior extrastriate cortex of the occipital lobe. Patients with associative agnosia typically can copy objects, but they cannot name objects. They tend to have lesions in the inferior temporal lobe. However, other cognitive functions of these patients of agnosias are intact; for example, they can easily identify objects by touch.

There is another variation of agnosia termed prosopagnosia, which is an impairment in face recognition. Patients cannot recognize people by looking at their faces, including their family members, close friends, and even themselves in the mirror or in pictures. They tend to have lesions in the inferior temporal lobe, a location known as the Fusiform Face Area (FFA).

A different disorder, called motion agnosia, can result from damage to the dorsal visual pathway as reported by Zihl, von Cramon, Mai, and Schmid (1991). They describe a 43-year-old woman who suffered a stroke that damaged her brain near the temporal/parietal boundary. Her ability to see continuous motion was replaced by the disturbing experience of having objects appear suddenly at different distances, such that she could no longer pour coffee into a cup without resulting in either too little or an overflow. Crossing the street was frightening, as cars that appeared to be at a safe distance when she started across would suddenly seem to jump closer without warning.

These examples illustrate a dissociation between object recognition and motion perception abilities in human vision. That is, the ventral pathway leads to the temporal lobes of the brain that are important for naming and other language functions as Wernicke (1874) demonstrated. A separate processing module leads eventually to the parietal lobes that function in motion perception and 3-D spatial representations. The data from studies of human brain-injured patients thus support the distinctions of separate ventral/temporal "what" versus dorsal/parietal "where" pathways discovered in monkeys by Ungerleider and Mishkin (1982).

3.7 Multimodal and Contextual Influences on Object and Event Perception

3.7.1 Perceiving Objects and Events

Perception has not evolved merely to locate objects or to identify patterns from their features, components, or overall shapes. Neither is its main purpose to recognize sounds, tastes, smells, or information obtained by touch. Rather, perception has evolved to inform us about objects in the real world and how they interact in real-time events that have causes and consequences. We are aware of the world at the object and event level, and perception grants us this awareness so that we can identify objects and understand events. Further, the role of perception is to use this understanding in order to predict functions of objects and consequences of events so that we can respond appropriately to them. Perception, thus, has the dual role of interpreting environmental objects and events and directing appropriate responsive actions.

3.7.2 Locating Objects in a 3-D World

One of the most important aspects of event perception is localization of relevant objects in space. Localization is important not only for understanding object interactions in events, but also in avoiding dangerous objects and in reaching out for desirable ones. Meredith, Nemitz, and Stein (1993) found cells in the colliculus of monkeys that responded most strongly when an auditory and visual event occurred at about the same time. Neither the auditory nor visual modality alone produced much of a response in these cells, so they appeared to be sensitive mainly to events that were both visible and audible. Other researchers have found visual, auditory, and tactile maps of the environment laid out across parallel collicular layers (Enns, 2004). Since most nearby events tend to produce multimodal sensations, these cells seem to function as sensory integrators, to call our attention to events with greater certainty than if the same event were either silent or not visible.

3.7.3 Integrating Information Across Modalities

Besides the multimodal cells found in the colliculus of the brain stem, multimodal cells in the parietal cortex also signal the presence of auditory and visual events taking place at about the same time (Andersen, Snyder, Bradley, & Xing, 1997). Other parietal cells integrate over visual and tactile modalities, and still others integrate across modalities in order to plan movements. Graziano and Gross (1995) found cells in monkeys that responded either to a touch on the side of the face or a visual stimulus near the face on the same side. Other cells responded to a touch on the hand and to a visual stimulus near the hand. They report the even more interesting finding that the visual stimulus that excites the parietal cell moves with the hand, so that the particular area in the environment in which a visual stimulus must be located in order to excite the cell depends on where the monkey's hand is! If the hand is placed behind the monkey's head and out of sight, the cell becomes unresponsive to visual stimuli. These results indicate that just as most real-world events produce multi-modal sensations, many cells in midbrain and cortical structures are specifically sensitive to the spatial and temporal properties of these events.

3.7.4 Context Effects on Perception

Perhaps only in certain psychology experiments do objects and events occur in complete isolation from a structured, meaningful context. Stimuli are often presented in isolation in order to study responses that are influenced only by the stimulus itself. That is, contextual variables are known to have effects on perception, and the inclusion of uncontrolled variables in any experiment can lead to uninterpretable results— we cannot tell which of several variables or their combination produced the results at hand. However, once simple experiments have indicated how we recognize objects, then contextual factors can be added to determine their effects as well.

Several experiments have shown that an object embedded in a related context is recognized more quickly and accurately than one presented alone or in an irrelevant context. Palmer (1975) has shown that a loaf of bread, for example, was recognized more accurately after a brief presentation if it had been shown in a typical kitchen scene than if it had been presented in a farmyard scene (see Figure 3.10). Reicher (1969) has similarly shown that a letter is recognized more accurately in a brief display if it is contained within a familiar word than in a nonsense string of letters.

Contextual effects are presumably due to the redundant information present in context that helps to narrow down what the stimulus is likely to be. Redundancy is the presence of the same or similar information in more than one source. Thus, relevant context aids perception by reducing the candidate set for alternative categorizations of the stimulus. A common model of object recognition includes both comparison and decision processes, and both of these can be influenced by context. Context usually reflects the normal structure of things in the environment, and this structure makes certain objects more likely to occur than others. We are more likely then, to compare the coded stimulus with more probable items, reducing the comparison time when an object fits the context. We are also more likely to allow contextual bias to help us converge on a decision for what something is, at least by eliminating impossible objects. For example, an object passing overhead is likely to be a bird (or a plane or even Superman), but not likely to be a tortoise; and an object moving below the surface of a lake is more likely to be a fish than a banana. The experience we gain every day of our lives allows us to make rapid use of context to predict what a stimulus is and be correct even without seeing the stimulus itself, as if I were to ask you what is the next letter in the word "acq___," or what the next syllable is in the phrase "nuclear disarma___ ."

FIGURE 3.10

Examples of Visual Context on Perception

Adapted illustration by Palmer, T. E. (1975). The effects of contextual scenes on the identification of objects. Memory & Cognition, 3, 519-526.

Figure 3.10.1 If you read the following character strings quickly, you might not notice that both pairs include identical ambiguous characters. The context leads you to interpret them in a way that makes them belong to the same set as their neighbors, indicating that categorization can occur before identification.

Figure 3.10.2 An example of contextual priming The scene on the left was presented briefly followed by the brief presentation of an object that was appropriate or inappropriate to the contextual scene. Contextually appropriate items were identified more accurately (about 85% of the time) than were items without a context (about 65%) or following an inappropriate context (about 50%). (After Palmer, 1975.)

Context effects generally aid perception because we have learned associations between things that commonly occur together in the environment. If two objects have a common co-occurrence, then the presentation of one leads us to expect the other, just as in Pavlovian conditioning, in which the sound of a bell causes dogs to expect to be fed through repeated associations of the bell and food. These associations work between modalities as well as within modalities, with perhaps the most common example occurring in speech communication. It is well known that a speaker is understood better in most situations if we can also see the speaker's face than if we have the audio input alone. This is particularly true if the speech is degraded by a noisy environment, such as in a TV transmission from a busy city or in a conversation at a noisy party. In fact, McGurk and MacDonald (1976) demonstrated that we clearly use both visible facial gestures and the auditory speech code in understanding a speaker. When a video of a person saying the syllable "ga" was shown at the same time that an audio message of the syllable "ba" was played, most persons reported that the combined experience was of the intermediate sound "da." (Try saying "ba-da-ga" a few times to convince yourself that "da" is an intermediary between the other two sounds.) This shift in perception to produce an experience unlike either sensory input is a result of the perceptual system's attempt to integrate two information sources that normally yield the same information. When either input strays from the normal ideal, it is accommodated as best as possible in a holistic percept, even if what we experience is technically inaccurate. The so-called **McGurk effect** is an error only because it results from an unusual stimulus situation. In normal situations, redundant signals can safely be integrated to improve our perceptual accuracy.

A similar example comes from the **ventriloquist effect** in which an actor moves parts of the face of a mechanical dummy in synchrony with his or her spoken words, which are ideally uttered without lip movements. The overwhelming illusion is that the voice occasionally emanates from the dummy, and the actor and the dummy can carry on a realistic-appearing conversation. In fact, laboratory research has shown that a simple visual stimulus can capture the apparent location of a tone coming from a significant distance away, but only if they also occur at about the same time (Choe, Welch, Gilford, & Juola, 1974). Again, things that seem to occur at about the same place and at about the same time probably emanate from the same event, and it makes sense for our perceptual system to integrate such experiences across modalities. The supposition that two slightly different sensory events actually originated from the same physical event is likely to be correct more often than not, so this bias produces errors only in unusual situations.

McGurk effect The tendency to integrate visual and auditory information from a speaker, such that if the two are in conflict, the listener "hears" an intermediate speech sound.

Ventriloquist effect The tendency to perceive an auditory stimulus as coming from the same location as a visual stimulus, even if they occur in separate locations; the visual capture of perceived auditory location is stronger the closer they occur together in time

Chapter Summary

Perception has been defined as the interpretation of sensory signals, and this interpretation depends on many kinds of knowledge. Perception depends not only on what is detected in the environment, but also on what we know about the world based on our previous experiences. We know that if something is dropped, it will fall to the ground; and that if something is nearby and small enough, we can reach out and grasp it. Similarly, we know by an object's shape and size whether it can be picked up and thrown with accuracy, used to extend our reach to bring another object closer to us, or sat upon as a chair. Perception has, as its ultimate goal, the understanding of real world objects and events and knowing how we can use them to meet our needs and avoid discomfort. Integrating information across the senses and using context to reduce uncertainty about what is out there and what it means shows that perception is more than interpretation of sensory inputs. It is the use of knowledge of objects, the categories to which they belong, and how they enter into predictable events that gives the true value to perception. Perception enables us to create a fairly complete and veridical model of the world within our minds. This model allows us to understand the meaning of objects and events, predict the outcomes of future events, and anticipate how our actions will change objects and events to suit our needs. The real purpose of perception is to determine our actions. How effectively we deal with the world is determined by how we perceive it.

Review Questions

- **What are the differences between sensation and perception?**

Sensation is an innate, biologically-programmed response of specialized neurons that transduce physical stimuli into neural impulses that travel along different sensory channels to the brain. Each sensory modality has a different primary projection area in the brain, located in the occipital lobes for vision and the temporal lobes for hearing. Sensation is determined in a bottom-up way by the stimulus alone, but it can be modified by the adaptation level of the observer or the amount of attention paid to the stimulus.

Perception is a learned response to a stimulus that depends on memory for past experiences. It depends on the observer's interpretation of the stimulus. Unlike sensation, it is likely to be more variable across individuals, as one's conscious awareness of what something is depends on memory, context, and personal biases.

- **Is perception based on analysis of simple features of objects, or are objects recognized as wholes?**

This apparently simple question has a complex answer, as there are likely to be some very familiar objects (e.g., words and faces) that are recognized as wholes and others (e.g. unfamiliar stimuli) that can be recognized only by examining their details. In general, neither theory gives an adequate explanation of the scope of human pattern and object recognition abilities. Perhaps an intermediate approach, such as Biederman's recognition-by-components theory, best summarizes the widest range of data and physiological evidence for how we recognize common objects.

- **What can the analysis of single-cell recordings tell us about perception?**

Just as single-cell recordings in the sensory pathways can tell us about what kinds of features are encoded and signaled to the brain along various sensory pathways, single-cell recordings in the occipital, temporal, and parietal lobes of the brain can tell us about neural correlates of perception. Although sensory neurons seem to be analytic and narrowly selective in their responding, cells in the higher visual centers of the brain respond maximally to a variety of shapes and sounds, some with unexpected complexity. Other cells in the brain respond maximally only when different sensory channels report the presence of an object or event as sensed by two or more sensory modalities. Single-cell recordings in perceptual processing support the subjective impression that we perceive objects and events, and typically not isolated features, such as color and pitch.

- **Are there any computer simulations or neural network models that actually perceive things as humans do?**

  Since perception is ultimately a subjective experience, we can never know how machine vision or any other simulation relates to human perceptual experience. However, we can do behavioral tests of the discrimination performance of computer models and machine object recognition performance along the lines of Marr's (1982) artificial intelligence approach. Similarly, new methods of neural network modeling have produced systems that can learn from experience to do an increasingly better job of discriminating among a set of similar patterns (see Box 3.2). As in all theoretical approaches to problems, if we have a good theory of how people recognize patterns and objects, then the theory should be capable of being implemented into an artificial system that can duplicate human behavior.

  The real trick is to develop an adequate theory that can summarize, explain, and predict human behavior in a situation as difficult as object recognition. It is still largely a mystery how people can so quickly and effortlessly recognize any of a potentially infinite variety of objects while making so very few errors.

Key Terms

Agnosia 81	Modularity 80
Bottom-up processes 71	Perception 60
Feature analysis 61	Recognition-by-components 76
Gestalt principles 70	Template matching 62
Inferotemporal cortex 64	Top-down processes 74
McGurk effect 87	Ventriloquist effect 87

ROGER SHEPARD

Photo courtesy of Roger Shepard

Chapter 4
Visual Imagery and Spatial Cognition

"Visual mental imagery is 'seeing' in the absence of the appropriate immediate sensory input; imagery is a 'perception' of remembered information, not new input … images cannot be actual pictures in the brain; there is no light in there, and who or what would look at the pictures even if they were there? … these are knotty problems indeed."

(Kosslyn, 1990, p. 73)

PREVIEW QUESTIONS

❖ *What is an image, and how does it differ from other kinds of memories?*

❖ *How can we prove that images exist if we cannot measure them directly?*

❖ *What is the relation between visual perception and imagery?*

❖ *Are there different kinds of visual/spatial perceptions and memories?*

❖ *Does brain damage that affects vision also affect imagery, and vice-versa?*

4.1 Introduction: What Is an Image?

Few people doubt the psychological reality of memory images. Most of us can do things like imagine the front of our childhood home (say, where we were living at about 10 years of age) and report how many windows were visible from the street. We can also usually imagine our mother's face, or the *Mona Lisa*, for that matter, and describe whether the face is a full frontal view, slightly off to one side, or in profile. Most of us are able to manipulate images as well, such as by imagining what a trumpet would look like if you were playing it yourself or watching a friend play it while facing you. We can also imagine following a familiar route, such as walking from one's bedroom to the front door or driving or walking from home to school or to work.

Despite the ability that most of us have to imagine and manipulate visual images without needing an actual object or picture in front of us, they remain subjective impressions that are very difficult to study empirically. For example, I can ask you to describe your childhood home, and record your verbal description. This description could then be compared with that of a parent or sibling, and we could score points of similarity and differences. But how could we possibly compare your image with that of another person? Certainly we cannot ask you both to draw them so that someone else can compare them objectively, because individual differences in drawing ability are probably at least as great as differences in the abilities of individuals to form images. The point is that since imagery is such a difficult, subjective topic to investigate, many researchers, including the behaviorists in the first half of the twentieth century, rejected the topic as being impervious to scientific inquiry.

With these objections about the subjective nature of visual images in mind, many researchers have been challenged to attempt a proof, or at least to collect strong evidence, for their existence. To do this, clever tasks have been invented that presumably can be performed only by generating and manipulating images in the mind, as such mental operations seem to provide the simplest explanation for performance in such tasks. These tasks are like the ones described at the beginning of this chapter—it is most unlikely that you ever counted the windows visible on the front of your childhood home and stored this number away in memory so that you could answer the question about how many there were. Rather, it is much more plausible, and consistent with one's introspections, that an image is conjured up and the count of windows is made from this image rather than from looking up the number in some stored list of facts about one's former home. Artists, athletes, and scientists also commonly report the use of imagery in preparing for a performance or solving a problem (e.g., Shepard, 1990). Imagery in one form or another has probably been with us a long time. It is quite likely that early humans could pick up a rock or a stick and fashion it into a useful implement by imagining how its shape could be changed to make it more functional. Similar imagination is required for making and designing tools of all types, including modern technological innovations. Thus, the ability to generate and manipulate visual images might indeed have been important throughout human history for the adaptation and survival of our species.

4.2 Visual Images in Long-Term Memory

4.2.1   *Images as the Basis of Recognition*

For perception to occur, we must be able to compare new sensory experiences with traces of previous experiences. In other words, we must have memory to perceive what we see. Without memory, every new experience would be truly unique, and we could never learn how to interpret or respond properly to each new object or event. Thus, perception depends on the more-or-less permanent storage of perceptual information in a form that enables object and event recognition.

When we think of a common category of objects, like *bird* or *lamp,* we often generate an image of a typical bird sitting in a tree or an average lamp that one might see in a friend's home. That such images exist is strongly supported by research in which pictures of objects are given to adults who are to classify them as belonging to a certain category. It is true that pictures of robins and table lamps are classified as being members of their respective categories faster than are pictures of penguins or chandeliers. One might take this as evidence that categories are represented by prototypical images, and objects that are much like these prototypes are classified as belonging to the category faster than pictures of unusual category members (Rosch, 1975; Rosch & Mervis, 1975). There is a problem with this interpretation however, in that if the word *robin* is substituted for a picture, it is still categorized as a bird faster than the word *penguin* (Smith, et al., 1974). However, true to the interpretation that prototypical images of categories exist in long-term memory, it has also been shown that regular (**canonical**) views of common objects are recognized faster than unusual views (Palmer, Rosch, & Chase, 1981). Examples of canonical and unusual views of common objects are shown in Figure 4.1.

Canonical view of an object the most common view of an object, the one that we most typically envision when generating an image of that object, and the one that is most rapidly recognized when an object is presented.

FIGURE 4.1

Examples of Canonical Views (left) and Non-Canonical Views (right) of Two Common Objects

Most objects have a certain canonical view that corresponds more closely to the view spontaneously generated when subjects are asked to form an image of the object. These views also typically result in faster and more accurate identification times than other views.

From Goldstein, E. B. (2007). *Sensation and Perception,* 7th Ed. Belmont, CA: Thomson Wadsworth, p. 110 (teapot); http://pi4.informatik. uni-mannheim.de/pi4.data/ content/projects/moca/ Project-ObjectRecognition.html (tricycle).

4.2.2   *Viewing Images with the Mind's Eye*

What kind of experiment can be done to indicate the reality of internal mental images? Kosslyn, Ball, and Reiser (1978) provided some evidence that images must exist in long-term memory by using experiments in which participants first memorized a novel scene, such as a map of a desert island (see Figure 4.2). When the map was then removed and the participants were asked to imagine themselves at the location of some prominent feature of the map, such as near the well, they could do so with apparent ease. Then the critical manipulation was made. The participants were asked to imagine that they were to travel to another place on the map and push a button when they arrived at that location. The results clearly indicated that the time to travel from one place to another on the memorized map was a direct, linear function of the distance between the two locations on the physical map. This result is most easily explainable by assuming that the participants actually generated an image of the map from memory and traced a path from location A to location B. The critical assumption

FIGURE 4.2

Image Scanning Research

The island image used in Kosslyn et al. (1978) image scanning research (a). The results showed that times to scan an image from one point to another across an internal image were directly proportional to distances between the corresponding objects on the physical map (b). Adapted from Goldstein, E. B. (2005). *Cognitive Psychology.* Belmont, CA: Thomson Wadsworth, p. 317.

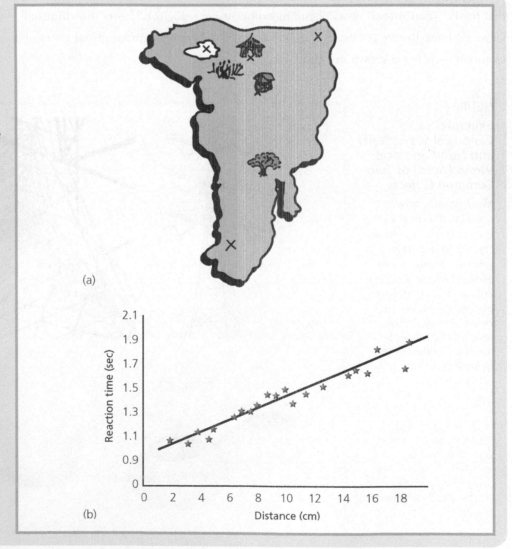

(a)

(b)

is that the time needed to trace this path across a mental image is proportional to the time taken to trace one's finger from point to point along the physical map, and by extension, the time needed to walk across the actual environment depicted by the map. You should be able to demonstrate a similar effect yourself if you imagined driving from Chicago to Minneapolis, say, versus from Chicago to Los Angeles.

Similar results have been reported in experiments using images of natural objects. For example, Kosslyn (1975) asked participants to imagine animals of different sizes, like a fly, a goose, or an elephant. He then asked people to form an image of two animals side-by-side, such as a goose and a fly or a goose and an elephant. When the participants were asked to verify if their image contained a specific feature, such as "Does the goose have a bill?" they were faster in their responses when the goose was imaged next to the small animal than when it was paired with the large animal (i.e., they were faster when the goose was relatively large in the "mind's eye") Just as with pictures, viewing fine details is harder with small images than with enlarged versions of them.

A thought experiment that we all can perform also seems to involve an image, in this case a mental map of a familiar location. Let's imagine that we are lying on the bed in the room of our house in which we lived while we were in high school. That is many years ago for us, but we can still clearly imagine the layout of our rooms and the locations of the bed, window, and door. We would not be surprised if you could generate a rich image full of such things as bookshelves and playthings, stuffed animals and favorite posters. Now, as an experiment, imagine yourself relaxed on this bed, lying on your back, and then, as quickly as you can, point to the nearest bathroom! Most of us can do so readily, and it is difficult to conceive of how this could be done if we did not have some kind of image or spatial layout of our home stored in memory. This image can be scanned even if it involves pathways that we have never traveled (through walls, for example). Similar internal maps presumably exist to help us navigate across campus, walk through familiar neighborhoods, or drive through familiar cities.

4.3 Manipulating Visual Images in Short-Term, Working Memory

Perhaps the most famous and influential of all studies of visual imagery are those of Roger Shepard and his students. Shepard argued for a **second-order isomorphism** between real-world objects and mental images. A **first-order isomorphism** would be some variant of the idea that images are literally like pictures in the head that can be retrieved and examined at will. Although many of us share some ability to generate and manipulate mental images, these images cannot be like pictures. Literal pictures in the head would demand that they be viewed by some mind's eye, and that eye would produce an image that would have to be viewed by someone or something, and

Second-order isomorphism for imagery The idea that whatever images are in the mind can be manipulated with mental processes in an analogous way to how objects are manipulated in our hands

First-order isomorphism for imagery The idea that images exist as "pictures" in the head to be examined with the mind's eye much as objects are examined with our actual eyes so on without ever arriving at a solution as to what an image is (Kosslyn, 1990). To put aside the difficult question of representation, Shepard argued that whatever an image is, the mental operations performed on an image should mimic the manual operations performed on an object. In that way imagery follows perception, and both are determined by physical properties of real objects and their manipulations over time. Properties of objects, such as changes in their apparent size as they are drawn towards us and changes in their apparent shapes as we turn them in our hands, should be reflected in the properties of images as we imagine an object looming toward us or turning in front of us. This is the second-order isomorphism that Shepard predicted and demonstrated so effectively in his research with Metzler and others (see Box 4.1).

Of course, the question still remains of what exactly an image is. The representation issue is a difficult one that we know is ultimately based on neural coding. Our ideas of symbolic codes, such as names and images for things and mental operations performed on them, are far removed from biology; thus, the link between theories

---

BOX 4.1
Shepard and Metzler (1971)

Roger Shepard, in his book *Mind Sights* (1990), draws and describes several splendid analogies between thinking and perception. He gives examples of how both perception and thought depend on the context in which an object is embedded and one's knowledge about it. He describes how images have presumably functioned in scientific discovery. For example, imagery might well have spawned understanding of ideas such as Archimedes's principle (buoyancy) and Pythagoras's theorem (right triangles) as well as the discovery of structures, such as the benzene ring, atoms themselves, the solar system, and the DNA molecule. The role of images in human thinking implies that they exist and that they can be manipulated, transformed, and compared in some way, much like the real objects they are meant to represent.

It is difficult to think of how one could design an experiment to demonstrate the existence of something we cannot observe directly. One idea is to measure

some process that might work in a similar way for viewing objects manipulated by hand and for imagining an object from different perspective views or transformed in some other way. The mental transformation that Shepard & Metzler (1971) chose to measure was the speed with which images of objects could be rotated around some axis. They used perspective drawings of blocks that implied a 3-D structure (see figure). These were shown in pairs that appeared to be either similar or very different perspective views of the same object, or different objects altogether. The main measure of interest was the RT for a "same" response as a function of degree of rotational angle separating the two views of the same implicit object. The classic result that has been replicated many times is that RT increases as a positive linear function of the degree of angular separation, for perspective views differing by 0 to 180 degrees.

Simular objects pairs to samples used in the Shepard & Metzler (1971) experiment

(a)   (b)

Results of the Shepard and Metzler (1971) study showing mean RT plotted against the degree of angular separation between two matching objects

Shepard and Metzler's experiment has been cited by some as a defining moment in cognitive psychology—the point at which an undeniably mental process, such as image rotation, could be timed and understood. Further, the results confirmed the introspective reports of many participants in mental rotation experiments. They commonly had the phenomenological impression that they were rotating one image until it could be placed into alignment with the other, and then performing a congruity check. One participant even reported that there was an upper limit on the speed of mental rotation—if they were turned too fast, blocks would fall off the image! If not proving the existence of images in the head, the results are certainly consistent with analogous relations between the visual consequences of manual manipulations of objects and the manipulations of mental images themselves.

and neurological underpinnings is severely stretched, perhaps most of all in difficult topics, such as perception, imagery, and language. Nonetheless, there have been numerous efforts to approach the problem of internal representations of external objects and events. Let's begin with a discussion of whether there is a single, fundamental representational system, or if different systems are needed for different kinds of information.

4.4 **Visual/Spatial versus Verbal Coding**

4.4.1 *Paivio's Dual-Coding Theory*

Paivio (1969, 1971) studied how people remembered lists of words versus lists of pictures of common objects. After having participants study a list of such items for a time, and then asking them to recall the list, Paivio found that people tended to recall items from the list of pictures better than from the list of words. Shepard (1967) showed the same thing for long lists of words or pictures that were shown only once. Later recognition was tested by showing a pair of items and asking participants to pick which of the two they had seen in the previous list. People were much more accurate in picking the correct picture from a pair of pictures than the correct item from a pair of words, and this advantage for pictures was found immediately after study and for days and weeks afterwards.

Paivio's dual-coding theory A theory of memory that proposes different stored representations for verbal materials (e.g., words) and imaginal information (e.g., pictures)

Paivio claimed that there are at least two different coding systems in long-term memory that emphasize different aspects of the outside world. His dual-coding theory accounts for the advantage of pictures over words for at least two reasons. First, imaginal codes of pictures are likely to be more distinct than verbal codes for words because each picture tends to be more or less unique, whereas words are used hundreds and thousands of times in our lives in many different contexts. Second, whereas words are usually stored as verbal codes, a picture can be stored both as an image and as a verbal code of its name or the names of salient objects in the picture. If retrieval can be thought of as a search through memory, then two codes are better than one since we are more likely to encounter either one of two codes for a picture than the single code for a word.

Support for dual-coding theory was obtained by Paivio who showed that simply instructing people to try to form images while studying a list of words tended to produce much higher levels of recall than if the participants were told to try to learn a list without any specific instructions. Even among participants who were given no instructions, those who tended to recall the most words often volunteered that they had used images while studying them. These results indicate that images can be formed in memory in the absence of pictorial input. Such images can improve recall of verbal materials as well as pictorial stimuli, presumably because they provide additional, durable codes of the studied items that can be used in addition to any verbal coding that had been made.

4.4.2   *Imaginal versus Propositional Storage*

All theories, including memory theories, should be parsimonious; that is, any phenomenon should be explained with as few assumptions as necessary. Assuming the existence of two different coding schemes in human memory is more complicated than relying on a single scheme. Thus, there has been some pressure for theorists to incorporate all memory phenomena into a single scheme if it is at all possible to do so. For example, Anderson & Bower (1973) assumed that all information in memory could be represented in a single, propositional format. A **proposition** is a simple, meaningful unit that can be expressed with concepts and relations among them.

Proposition The smallest unit of meaning that can be true or false (For example, a proposition can be most simply represented by two concepts and a relation between them, such as "A bird is an animal" or "A rhinoceros is a bird.")

To define propositional storage, let's begin with a simple example in which "robin" and "bird" are concepts, and "is" and "has" are relations. A simple proposition is often defined as the smallest meaningful unit that can have a truth value. Therefore, we can agree that simple expressions, like "A robin is a bird" and "A bird has feathers," are true propositions, whereas "A robin is a mammal" and "A bird has scales" are false. Of course, the actual words that are used to represent propositions are only useful for the communication of ideas; we are talking about a fundamental way of representing meaning in the mind, and this is a level deeper than words. That is, at the propositional level of meaning, the elements are concepts (represented in language mainly by nouns and adjectives) and relations (mainly represented by verbs and prepositions).

However, propositions are more basic than language and presumably underlie our thoughts, beliefs, and feelings that are not necessarily represented in language. The general idea is that if such propositional structures lie at the heart of understanding language, then perhaps, they also form the fundamental representations of objects, images, events, and other kinds of memories as well.

What followed was a well-known, and continuing, debate between adherents of Paivio, who insisted that dual coding was a descriptive fact of human cognition, and those following Anderson and Bower, who, at least initially, held the premise that a single coding scheme was sufficient to account for all memory phenomena. Pylyshyn (1973, 1981) has been perhaps the strongest advocate of the unified view, arguing that there is a single basic code that represents most information in memory, and that it is propositional in nature. This level is generally below the level of conscious awareness, but it forms the basis of conscious thoughts. Higher-level mechanisms can call up these propositions and convert them to inner thoughts, words, or conscious images. These higher-level representations can then be used to retrieve other related information. For example, we all know what a square is, from which we could form an image of a line drawing, or perhaps the central square of some well-known city, or a section of a chessboard. Similarly, we could retrieve a verbal description, tell a child how to make one, or even produce a definition from plane geometry. The point is that each of these apparently different processes could all draw on the same basic information in memory to generate different types of representations of the meaning of "square."

Other theorists reject the notion that there is a basic, unitary representational system that stands behind all memories. They point to the types of perceptual coding operations in the different sensory modalities that emphasize different aspects of a stimulus. For example, a sound pattern is generally stored and recognized as a change in acoustic intensity levels over time, whereas a visual pattern is a change in light intensity levels over space. These aspects of the stimuli are initially registered in the temporal and occipital cortices of the brain, respectively, and different modules are hard-wired into perceptual systems to analyze temporal frequency, intensity, and timbre in hearing, and spatial frequency (level of detail), orientation, motion, and color in vision. By this notion, imagery in the auditory modality, such as in the imaginative recollection of a song or a friend's voice, makes use of some of the same brain structures and processes as does auditory perception, and the same holds true for vision. Since these two perceptual processes are so very different, it makes sense to assume that auditory and visual imagery are also different and therefore not reducible to a common underlying representation.

At this point there can be no final resolution to the debate about whether there are separate storage systems for imaginal and verbal memories. However, the data are certainly suggestive that the modularity present in stimulus encoding is maintained in higher cortical centers. That is, damage to specific regions of the brain produces rather specific losses of productive speech, receptive language, visual object recognition, face recognition, vision, hearing, and associated imagery abilities. The idea that there is a single coding system for all memories is simply untenable given the variety of things that we have stored in memory and how both brain imaging studies and studies of individuals with brain damage indicate specific loci for specific memory processes (see, for example, Anderson, 2000).

4.5 **The Relation of Imagery to Perception**

Brain imaging studies have shown that many of the same cortical areas involved in perception are also active in tasks that require forming and manipulating images of perceived objects (Farah, Peronnet, Gonon, & Giard, 1988; Kosslyn, 1994; Kosslyn, Thompson, Kim, & Alpert, 1995). Further, when observers are directed to change the size, orientation, or location of their images, PET and fMRI studies have generally shown that metabolic activity in the occipital lobe of the brain is very similar to that observed when actual objects are presented in corresponding sizes, orientations, and locations (Ganis, Thompson, Mast, & Kosslyn, 2004). That is, the topographic mapping of the environment onto the primary projection area for vision in the occipital lobes of the brain reflects similar types of activity when viewing an actual object and merely imagining it. In addition, Martha Farah and colleagues (Farah, Soso, & Dasheiff, 1992) have shown that persons with brain lesions in primary visual cortex also show disruptions of visual imagery ability.

A related set of studies by Kosslyn and colleagues made use of transcranial magnetic stimulation (TMS) to temporarily disable brain functions in localized parts of the cortex for volunteer subjects. They report that when applied to the occipital cortex, TMS disrupts visual perception and visual imagery in similar ways and to similar extents (Kosslyn, Pascual-Leone, Felician, Camposano, Keenan, Thompson, Ganis, Sukel, & Alpert, 1999). These results support the general findings that patients with occipital lesions show similar losses in vision and imagery. Further, tasks that require subjects to imagine changes in spatial relations, such as mental rotation, show an increase in brain activity in the parietal lobes, whereas tasks that require visualizing object shapes show increased metabolic activity in the temporal lobes (Ganis, et al., 2004). There is general convergence in cortical processing for imagery and visual perception in both early visual processes and higher-order processes involved in object recognition and manipulation. Although there is not a perfect correspondence between brain processes in seeing and imagining, sufficient overlaps exist to conclude that visual perception and visual imagery share many processes in common.

4.6 Spatial Imagery and Memory

$4.6.1$ *Imagery for Identification versus Imagery for Location*

Visual imagery and memory seem to be involved in recollections of shapes and colors of things, so that we can recall and perhaps draw, more or less well, a robin or a skunk with appropriate proportions and colors from memory. This ability depends on memory for objects and patterns, which we know is stored in the temporal lobes of the brain. Damage to the pathway leading from vision to the temporal lobe (i.e., the occipitotemporal region) due to trauma or stroke can produce agnosias, or failure to recognize and name familiar objects, even if their spoken names are understood and other knowledge about them is retained (see Box 4.2). Damage to the parietal lobe, on the other hand, often results in failures to attend to certain locations in space or to be able to use landmarks to locate places and objects. This dissociation between object memory and spatial memory has indicated that these visual processes are distinct and respectively handled by the ventral ("what") and dorsal ("where") visual pathways in the brain (Mishkin, et al., 1983; see Figure 3.9).

However, it has been shown that the ventral and dorsal pathways are not entirely independent of each other. For example, object recognition associated with the ventral pathway and tasks, such as mental rotation, associated with the dorsal pathway seem to interact with each other. In an fMRI study (Koshino, Carpenter, Keller, & Just, 2005), figural complexity (simple versus complex figures) and the degree of mental rotation (0 degrees versus 90 degrees) were manipulated between pairs of objects that were to be judged same or different (see Figure 4.3). Figural complexity is associated with activity in the ventral pathway, and mental rotation is associated with that in the dorsal pathway. However, there were interactions between the two factors in these three brain regions. An increase of activity in the ventral pathway from single to complex figures was greater for 90 degree rotation than for 0 degree rotation. Also, an increase of activity in the dorsal pathway from 0 degree to 90 degree rotation was greater for the complex figures than for the simple figures. These interactions

---

FIGURE 4.3

Examples of stimuli used by Koshino et al. (2005) in which objects were to be judged as same (bottom) or different (top) despite differences in angular orientation

Simple figures
0 degree rotation

Complex figures
90 degree rotation

BOX 4.2

Agnosia and Prosopagnosia

It has been known for over a century that damage to certain areas of the brain can result in syndromes or mental difficulties involving perception, language, memory, and personality. Agnosia is the difficulty that some patients experience in naming common objects. The disruption can be slight, such that only unusual views of some objects go unrecognized, or it can be profound, in that neither drawings nor the objects themselves can be named with any regularity. Reading also becomes impossible for some patients, although understanding speech and the ability to participate in a conversation are sometimes spared. Most such patients have damage somewhere in the temporal lobe, although other areas of the brain can be involved. Further, different parts of the temporal lobe appear to be responsible for recognizing different kinds of objects, with one area apparently specialized for facial recognition.

There is no denying that facial recognition is a skill important for our survival, and it is present in human infants at a very early age. Individual cells that respond maximally to faces and facial features have been found in the temporal lobes of macaque monkeys. Hand-like stimuli also seem to elicit responses from other groups of cells.

In humans, specific agnosias have been reported in different stroke patients who can recognize animate things, but not manufactured artefacts, and vice-versa (e.g., Warrington & Shallice, 1984). A farmer has been reported to have lost his ability to recognize his cows, but regained the ability to recognize faces, whereas another farmer lost the ability to recognize faces, was able to recognize his cows (Humphreys & Bruce, 1989). Sergent and Signoret (1992) reported that a patient who was profoundly deficient in recognizing previously familiar faces, nonetheless retained a fine ability to discriminate and name different models of automobiles. These and other cases have suggested that face recognition is special, and that visual processing of faces has its own dedicated brain centers that are separate from those used in recognizing other objects. This view is supported by the results from a patient studied by Moscovitch, Winocur, and Behrmann (1997). Their patient suffered brain damage, resulting in severe disruption of object recognition along with an acquired reading disability; yet, face recognition ability was undisturbed. Prosopagnosia (Bodamer, 1947) is the name used for a specific disorder in face recognition, in which even close family members might go unrecognized after a localized brain injury.

Kanwisher and others (see Kanwisher, Downing, Epstein, & Koutzi, 2001) have tried to identify the specific locus of facial recognition abilities in the brain. Studies using brain imaging methods and those using patients and appropriate control participants have converged on a common locus for facial recognition processing. It is in the fusiform gyrus of the temporal lobe, or Fusiform Face Area (FFA), a structure located far underneath the back part of the brain (see figure). This region of the brain shows greater activity as measured by fMRI when viewing faces as opposed to other complex patterns, such as letter strings (Puce, Allison, Asgari, Gore, & McCarthy, 1996) or pictures of common objects (Grill-Spector, Knouf, & Kanwisher, 2004; Kanwisher, McDermott, & Chun, 1997; but see also counter-arguments by Tarr, 2003). Further, De Gelder and Kanwisher (1999) found no evidence for FFA activity in two patients who had minimal brain damage with small lesions, yet showed deficits consistent with prosopagnosia.

The location of the fusiform facial area in the inferior temporal lobe (view of the brain from below)

From Kalat, J. W. (2007). *Biological Psychology*, 9th Ed. Belmont, CA: Thomson Wadsworth, p.178.

It appears that faces are special in some sense both in terms of their importance for human social behavior and their unique processing by a dedicated, special-purpose brain structure. Other complex visual stimuli do not show these unique factors, which puts face recognition in a dominant position of importance for human evolution and survival.

indicated that there is a complex interplay between the dorsal and ventral pathways in manipulating object representations in memory.

Spatial memory in animals was studied by Tolman (1932, 1948), who rejected some aspects of Watsonian behaviorism in favor of more cognitive theories of learning. He collected data indicating that rats could learn to run mazes to seek places where food was to be found, rather than merely executing a series of left-right turn responses that had been previously reinforced. He did this simply by turning a tunnel maze that rats had learned to run upside down from the start box to a goal box, such that the goal box remained in the same place, but the tunnels were mirror-reversed from what the rats had learned. Most rats ran to the correct place rather than executing the learned sequence of left and right turns. These results were among the first to indicate that cognitive maps of the environment could be learned and used when necessary in rats as well as higher mammals.

4.6.2 *Cognitive Maps*

Thorndyke (1981; Thorndyke & Hayes-Roth, 1982) studied how humans learn to navigate a familiar environment and found that people tend to use at least three different sources of information, to different extents, when planning a route or actually moving from place to place. These include: (1) landmark knowledge, based on images of specific significant features and their relative positions; (2) route knowledge, based on familiar roads or pathways taken in the past in traveling between two places; and (3) map knowledge, which is an overall plan that includes both landmarks and routes in their relative positions, among other information. Others have distinguished between so-called *egocentric* and *allocentric* means of coding spatial relations. Egocentric coding relies on a representation from the navigator's point of view, and includes routes and landmarks visible from one's own perspective from a specific location in space. Allocentric coding, on the other hand, views spatial relations from some overall map or plan that is external to the observer. This functional distinction in spatial processing and way finding has been supported by brain imaging and lesion studies in humans that have identified separate egocentric and allocentric processing centers in the medial temporal and hippocampal regions of the brain (Panagioti & Berthoz, 2006).

Sometimes we make errors in judgments about relative spatial positions and distances based on internal images and other spatial knowledge. For example, places that include a large number of landmarks along a route tend to produce impressions of greater distances (Thorndyke, 1981; Wagner, 2006). Similarly, judged distances between two locations are heavily influenced by the normal route taken to travel between them, and these judgments can be very different from actual ("as the crow flies") distances. Such errors indicate the functional properties of spatial memories, rather than their veridical quality, even if people think they can produce a good map-like image from memory.

4.6.3 A Taxonomy of Spatial Cognition

Tversky (2005) has identified four different types or modes of spatial cognition. These are based on functional distinctions between knowledge that we have or are able to use about the environment. Three of these are commonly used by many animals, namely (1) bodily space (kinesthetics and proprioception that give feedback about bodily position and movements, as well as tactile and visual senses that give us information about bodily contact with nearby objects), (2) the perception of spatial relations around the body (to guide orientation, movement, and grasping), and (3) the space of navigation (to find one's way, especially back home). Another type of representation is uniquely human, and uses (4) symbolic representations—such as maps, charts, diagrams, and graphs—to represent both spatial structures and non-spatial ones (such as an organizational chart of a company). She further distinguishes these kinds of spatial representations from visual images, since spatial cognition emphasizes the function of each type of representation, whereas images are mainly used to represent structures.

Bodily space has been identified with specific neurological structures for processing information about one's own and others' bodies. Parts of the lateral occipital/temporal lobe seem to be especially active when viewing human bodies (Downing, Jiang, Shuman, & Kanwisher, 2001), and damage to the parietal lobe can lead to difficulties in locating the position of one's own body parts (e.g., Berlucchi & Aglioti, 1997). These distinctions follow the traditional roles of ventral and dorsal pathways in vision for processing "what" and "where" information separately.

The space around the body is represented internally by values on the cardinal directions of up/down, front/back, and left/right. Tversky (2005) reviews much research on how such directions are represented internally from knowledge of some space, such as a room full of objects. This knowledge can be given to a research participant through various means, including reading a narrative description, viewing a model of the room with a doll at its center, or viewing the room itself from a central position. Participants are then told to imagine the studied scene as retrieved from memory from different perspectives in the room. Finally, they are asked to describe the locations or actually point to specific objects as if they were standing in the room and viewing it from the instructed perspective. The results have consistently rejected two theories of space perception for information located around the body, namely the equavailability theory and the imagery theory. Equavailabilty theory asserts that all cardinal directions relative to the body are equally available. It was rejected because not all cardinal directions were responded to equally. For example, objects that are in front of the adopted perspective view were routinely responded to more quickly and accurately than objects behind the adopted viewpoint. Imagery theory was rejected because people did not tend to respond as an outsider imagining the room with themselves as one of the objects in it. Rather, the preferred way of answering questions about objects in the room was to assume the same perspective view of a person standing in the room, and view objects with the mind's eye from that perspective. This theory is called the spatial framework theory. Tversky admits that people can adopt an external viewpoint and imagine themselves as an object in the room if they are instructed to do so. But, in accordance with spatial framework theory, the preferred way for most people to recall a familiar scene is to adopt the position of an observer in the scene itself and describe the relative locations of objects with respect to the imagined self (see also Frith & Frith, 2007).

The space of navigation serves to guide us as we move about either under our own power or as a driver or passenger in some vehicle. This space can be too large to be perceived all at once, and it can be internalized either through direct experience or from indirect experience with a map or a set of directions. Levinson (1996) has described three ways in which a navigable space can be envisioned, namely from an egocentric route perspective, as in traveling through the campus by car or foot, or from an allocentric external viewpoints, as viewing a campus from the entrance gate or from a height, in which the campus plan is imaginable as if from a tall building or an airplane. People can and do freely change from one perspective to another in imaging a route and in describing it to others. However, the choice of perspective can lead to systematic errors of judgment. Most people are familiar with the egocentric view one has of geography, such that distances between familiar locations are judged to be greater than similar distances between far away ones. For example, people living in the Midwestern United States are likely to judge that the distance between, say, Kansas City, Missouri and Chicago, Illinois is greater than the distance between Boise, Idaho and Seattle, Washington, when in fact they are about the same. Further, two cities are likely to be judged to be further apart when they are in different countries than when they are in the same country, even if the actual distances are the same in both cases (Friedman & Montello, 2006).

People also make mistakes in judging distances and directions due to schematization of geographical information to conform to axes of orientation and symmetry and broad categories, such as continents (e.g., Friedman, Brown, & McGaffey, 2002). For example, people often judge South America to be directly south of North America, because there is a bias to place both continents along the same axis of elongation. In fact, New York City is actually west of Santiago, Chile, which is a surprise to most people. Similarly, American students tend to judge European cities to be farther south than their American counterparts (e.g., Madrid and Philadelphia both fall at about 40 degrees north latitude, but most people would guess that Madrid is further south). Further, natural features, such as rivers and mountain ranges, depicted on maps are often remembered as being aligned with respect to one of the cardinal directions and symmetrically organized more than they are in actuality.

The space of external representations is distinctly human, and the use of trail markers, calendars, tallies, and pictographs extends into the mists of prehistory (e.g., Marshack, 1972). These serve both as a more permanent record of objects and events and a means to offload significant amounts of knowledge into a representational form that can be used repeatedly to jog memory and as an aid to computation. Indeed, language itself, in both its spoken and written forms, is a type of external representation of internal thoughts and desires. Although maps are intended to portray landmarks and spatial relations in the real world, they are often drawn and used in a schematic way, with long distances of uneventful terrain abbreviated, and areas full of interesting and important details exaggerated in their spatial extents. Maps have evolved into graphs and charts that retain some of their characteristics in novel applications, metaphorically converting distances in space to differences along other dimensions, for example. Both adults and children prefer to align quantities with the north-south axis, so that larger values are on top, and time is most typically portrayed as a progression from left to right, although there is no inherent reason for this preference. The advent of computer graphics gives us new opportunities to include 3-D displays and animations in external representations of a variety of information domains. Yet, research has shown that unless such applications map naturally onto the information that they are trying to convey (such as a sequence of weather patterns organized temporally), the additional information is likely to add confusing complications rather than informative resolution to our ability to understand and use graphical information (Lowe, 1999; Palmiter & Elkerton, 1993).

4.7 Disorders of Spatial Perception and Memory

4.7.1   *Visual Neglect in Patients with Parietal Damage*

Since the dorsal pathway from the occipital to the parietal lobes of the brain seems to be specialized for handling spatial information, it should not be surprising that parietal lobe damage results in severe spatial processing deficits. Among the most severe is a syndrome called **neglect**, in which the patient seems to be totally unaware of any stimuli presented to the field of view opposite the lesion (i.e., the contralesional field). That is, if the right parietal lobe is damaged, a patient with neglect will appear to be blind to any visual stimulus presented to the left of the centerline. There appears to be an important hemispheric asymmetry to the expression of neglect. The deficit is more common and usually more severe following right parietal damage than after damage to the left parietal lobe (De Renzi, 1982).

A similar deficit can be produced if there is unilateral damage to the visual sensory pathway. For example, if a lesion exists in the left or right pathway from the lateral geniculate nucleus to the primary visual cortex, or if one half of the occipital cortex is damaged, the visual field on the side opposite the lesion (the contra-lateral side) will not be seen—a condition known as **hemianopia**. However, there are several critical distinctions between neglect and hemianopic patients. First, neglect is seldom complete or permanent, and the area of neglect usually does not perfectly follow the midline. Second, neglect patients are seldom aware of their deficit, whereas

Visual neglect A result most typically of damage to the right parietal lobe that causes an inability to attend to the contralateral (left) visual field as well as to the left sides of imagined objects or scenes

Hemianopia The loss of vision on one side of the visual field due to damage in the visual centers of the brain in one hemisphere hemianopic patients complain bitterly that they cannot see well on one side of space (Husain, 2001).

Since sensory processes up to and including primary visual cortex are intact in most neglect patients, the question has been raised as to whether the deficit is attentional rather than perceptual. Support for the attentional deficit notion has come from several sources. Driver (1999), in a review of data from neglect patients, has reported that some patients show deficits in reporting the left halves of objects even when the entire object is presented in the non-neglected field of view. Such results clearly show an attentional bias to the right rather than a localized spatial deficit.

Similar conclusions were drawn from a classic study by Bisiach and Luzatti (1978). They demonstrated neglect in patients who were asked to remember a stored image rather than an actual visual scene. They asked two patients with right-hemisphere damage to describe the buildings in the main square in Milan, Italy, a city very familiar to both of them. First, they were asked to imagine themselves standing in front of the cathedral. Consistent with their apparent attentional deficits, they described buildings that would have been visible on the right side of the square and omitted ones on the left. When they were asked to cross over mentally to the other side of the square, turn around, and imagine what they would see, they now described the buildings they had previously omitted, by again concentrating on ones that would have appeared on the right side only. The similar results obtained in neglect patients for real and imagined scenes eliminate a perceptual explanation for the phenomenon. Instead, parietal damage in the right hemisphere clearly reduces attention to the left side of real or imagined images.

4.7.2   Visual Extinction

Further evidence for an attentional deficit in right-parietal patients comes from individuals showing a similar but less severe deficit called extinction. Indeed, some patients who initially show symptoms of neglect soon after a brain injury, can recover to a condition in which only extinction is shown. Like neglect patients, people with visual extinction primarily have damage to the right parietal lobe of the brain, but unlike such patients, they can and do report seeing objects presented to the contralesional (left) visual field. The deficit shows up, however, when two different objects are presented at the same time, one to the left side and one to the right. The classic finding in the extinction literature is that the left-side object now becomes invisible, or at least unreported, whereas the ipsilesional (right) side object is reported (Posner, Walker, Friedrich, & Rafal, 1984; 1987). It is as though attention is drawn to the right side to such an extent that when there is a competing stimulus, only objects on the ipsilesional side are noticed and reported. When the right-side field is empty, however, attention is free to engage contralesional, left-side objects, and they are then reported accurately.

4.7.3 Bálint's Syndrome

A related attentional deficit resulting from brain damage also shows a tendency for patients to ignore parts of a display, but in this case, the neglected part or parts cannot be predicted in advance. Rather, all parts of a complex display might be ignored but one, yet this part is reported in great detail. The disorder has come to be called simultagnosia, or **Bálint's syndrome**, after the initial report of symptoms of individuals who had suffered bilateral parietal damage (Bálint, 1909). Farah (1990) later identified two types of simultagnosia associate with bilateral damage either to the dorsal (parietal) or ventral (temporal-occipital) visual pathways. Bilateral parietal damage can produce Bálint's syndrome, which, rather than being linked to a particular spatial region, as is neglect and extinction, is characterized by the inability to perceive more that one object at a time (Husain, 2001). Damage to the ventral pathway can result in agnosias that are often quite specific, such as prosopagnosia, which is the inability to recognize faces of familiar people (see Box 4.2).

Bálint's syndrome Also called simultagnosia; it is most commonly due to bilateral damage to the parietal lobes. Patients with this syndrome usually report seeing only one object at a time, even when many objects are presented simultaneously.

FIGURE 4.4

Examples of Drawings Made by a Patient with Right Parietal Damage When Asked to Copy the Figures Shown on the Left.

Representations of a copying task by a patient with visual neglect. In this illustration, information from the left side is ignored.

Source: BVT Publishing

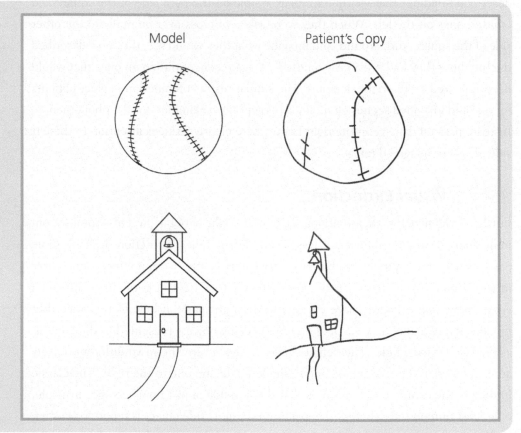

Model   Patient's Copy

Further support for the non-spatial nature of simultagnosia was reported by Humphreys, Romani, Olson, Riddoch, and Duncan (1994). They studied two patients with Bálint's syndrome, one having suffered from bilateral strokes in the parietal region and the other having suffered from anoxia. When single words or pictures of objects were presented to the central field of view, they could name them easily. However, when the words and pictures were superimposed, the patients either reported the picture alone or both the word and the picture. Words alone were almost never reported, indicating that the word information was sometimes extinguished by a picture, even though they occupied the same spatial location. Husain (2001) used these results to make an important generalization about neglect, extinction, and simultagnosia. He argued that the spatial bias in patients showing neglect or extinction is due to the asymmetric nature of their disability. The field of view contralateral to the lesion suffers from delayed processing, and thus, its representation is inhibited by attention and perceptual processes that reach completion for the ipsilateral side first. In contrast, with bilateral damage, there is no spatial bias, yet the first item processed again tends to inhibit perception and recognition of other objects in the field, regardless of their relative spatial positions. In an intact dorsal brain system there is less likelihood of an overpowering winner-take-all perceptual process, and we are able to attend to several things at once, or at least in a rapid sequence. Normal perceptual processes are freed from the trap of focusing on one position or one object to the exclusion of information readily available elsewhere in the field of view. Normal perception of a world populated by objects and events centered on the point of fixation depends on our ability to distribute attention over the visible scene.

Chapter **Summary**

Imagery is a purely subjective phenomenon that exists only in our conscious experiences. Therefore, it is very difficult to examine empirically, as there are no external measures of images. Yet, we can appeal to our shared introspective claim that we can "see" things with our mind's eye, as when we call up remembrances of favorite people and places from our past. The method of study used by imagery researchers has been to define tasks that presumably involve the maintenance and manipulation of images in the mind, and then measure observable results that can be explained most parsimoniously by assuming that analog images are indeed used and manipulated and are responsible for the observed results. Shepard and Metzler's (1971) study of mental rotation is the hallmark example of an experimental result that can be explained in no easy way except by assuming that people can manipulate mental images in their minds, much as they do objects in their hands.

Imagery is also used in other types of tasks, such as in recognizing objects and people, remembering certain concrete types of information, navigating through space while avoiding or reaching for objects, and drawing or interpreting charts and graphs. Neuroscience has shown that brain areas involved in perception are also involved in imagery, and damage to specific brain areas can result in loss of object identification by sight or the inability to attend to parts of the visual field. These brain areas are separate from those that enable verbal processing of information, indicating that there are indeed separate verbal and visuo-spatial neural substrates, as Paivio and others have suggested.

Review Questions

- **What is an image, and how does it differ from other kinds of memories?**

  An image is an internal representation of a visual stimulus or an imagined scene that differs qualitatively from a verbal description. Images presumably function in the recognition of familiar visual objects. They also can be used to imagine what things would look like if they were changed in form. Thus, they can be manipulated at will to some extent. They also include visual scenes and maps of familiar places that can be scanned and used to plan routes. Thus, images have some of the spatial (extensive and volumetric) properties of the objects they represent, and these affect the mental operations that can be performed on them

- **How can we prove that images exist if we cannot measure them directly?**

  Images are subjective experiences, and as such, they cannot be measured directly. Experiments have been designed, however, to show that if a task involves scanning or manipulating an image, then the time needed to perform the mental imagery task should be proportional to the time needed to perform an analogous manual or other physical task. The assumption is that if mental operations performed on images represent the kinds of physical operations that we can perform on real objects, then the analogies should be obvious in the data as well as in the introspective reports of subjects. Research by Shepard, Kosslyn, and others has shown that this assumption is correct.

- **What is the relation between visual perception and imagery?**

  Images are presumably based on visual experiences that have been stored in memory. Our richest visual images are often based on things that we have experienced frequently, such as the face of a friend or details of a house that we have lived in for a long time. Images also presumably function in visual perception, as we most quickly recognize objects that map directly onto the canonical or prototypical image that we think of when the object category is named. Finally, mental operations performed in imagery experiments seem to recapitulate the visual experiences one has when one manipulates an object manually while observing it.

- **Are there different kinds of visual/spatial perceptions and memories?**

  Tversky has argued that visual images mainly portray structural aspects of remembered objects, whereas spatial memories have evolved to handle functional aspects of dealing with our environment. She distinguishes between spatial images of our own bodies, of the space around our bodies, and navigational space. These serve different purposes necessary for controlling movements, avoiding dangerous situations and objects while reaching for desirable objects, and hunting and foraging before returning home, respectively. Unlike these basic spatial operations that we share with many other animals, humans have added another spatial processing domain, namely the representational space of maps, charts, diagrams, and eventually language. These representations allow us to maintain and manipulate symbolic representations that would be too large or complicated to work with in memory alone. As such, they are aids to planning and executing a variety of actions, many not related to space at all except in a metaphorical sense (top of the food chain, right hand of the president, etc.)

- **Does brain damage that affects vision also affect imagery, and vice-versa?**

Although vision and imagery are similar, and Farah, Kosslyn, and others have argued that there are many brain processes in common between imagery and vision, they are clearly different. Damage to the peripheral visual system, including the eyes, optic nerve, and occipital lobes, can produce full or partial blindness (e.g., scotomas), but leave imagery intact. Similarly, damage to the parietal lobes of the brain can affect visual imagery when vision remains fairly normal. In fact, the visual disturbances that result from right or bilateral parietal damage are more likely due to attentional processes than the ability to see by itself. Still, our ability to recognize and understand many different objects and patterns is probably due, in part, to our ability to form links between current sensory images from the retina and stored images in long-term memory.

Key Terms

Bálint's syndrome 110	Paivio's dual-coding theory 99
Canonical view of an object 95	Proposition 100
First-order isomorphism for imagery 97	Second-order isomorphism for imagery 97
Hemianopia 108	Visual neglect 108

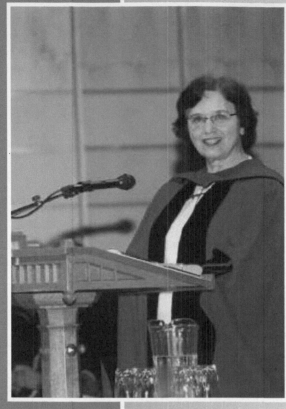

ANNE TREISMAN

Wikimedia Commons
UBC Library-University Archives

Chapter 5
Attention

"Everyone knows what attention is. It is the taking possession by the mind, in clear and vivid form, of one out of what seem several simultaneously possible objects or trains of thought. Focalization, concentration, of consciousness are of its essence. It implies withdrawal from some things in order to deal effectively with others, and is a condition which has a real opposite in the confused, dazed, scatter-brained state ...

William James, *Principles of Psychology*, 1890–1952, p. 261

PREVIEW QUESTIONS

❖ *Is there one kind of attention, or does attention do different things in different situations?*

❖ *What is the purpose of attention? How does it help us to deal with the outside world?*

❖ *Does attention change over space and time, or does it follow where we are looking and our current level of alertness?*

❖ *Can we learn something without paying attention to it?*

❖ *What changes in brain activity can be observed as attention changes from one focus to another?*

5.1 Introduction and Definition of Attention

Everyone *does* know what attention is. When someone asks you to "Pay attention!" you usually have no doubt about what is meant. James further described attention as a process that determines the contents of consciousness. In other words, the only things that we know, in some sense, are those of which we are consciously aware, and attention directs our awareness. Since attention follows or actually determines much of what we are doing, learning itself relies on attention, and poor attention can interfere with learning. Of course, there are many things that we can learn to do expertly that are not conscious or attended to in any specific way. One could think of how we learn to ride a bicycle or learn to walk, speak, swim, or hit a ball with a bat. Perception and language are only two of the immense human capabilities that are present in some form at birth, but develop prodigiously at the hand of experience, with or without our attention to many details of what is being learned and how. As these important skills become so well-learned that much of their execution becomes automatic (that is without our needing to attend to them), attention can be freed to deal with other tasks, such as understanding and responding to what we see and hear.

Attention A process that selects information from the environment and from memory for entry into limited-capacity conscious awareness

Attention has been defined in several related ways. The most common meanings of attention in psychology are in terms of selection and capacity. Selection is necessary because the environment is simply too full of information for us to attend to all of it simultaneously in any meaningful way. For example, as you are reading this sentence, you might be trying to attend to its meaning while trying not to attend to background noise from conversations or the TV. It is also possible to be distracted by a sudden itch or by noticing that the room is cold. Some of these interruptions of our attentional focus are important—in special circumstances our survival can depend on being able to avoid an obstacle in the road, or reaching out for a handrail when tripping on the stairs. At other times such interruptions are annoying, as when our train of thought is broken into by some recurring worry about relationships, school, or finances. In general, attention serves to select some important information for us to process deeply, while the vast majority of sensory inputs and recurrent thoughts are not so selected and have only fleeting effects on our conscious awareness if we are ever aware of them at all.

Capacity limitations are related to selection, as humans are notoriously incapable of doing two or more demanding things at once. Selection is used to channel the information that we need for accomplishing current tasks into conscious, working memory while preventing information overload from irrelevant information. Kahneman (1973) proposed that such capacity limits place strong constraints on how well we can do two or more things at a time. Wickens (1980) refined this idea by defining capacity limits at different levels in the human attentional system. He argued that attentional capacity could be viewed as having separate pools of processing resources for perceptual processing, cognitive/decision processing, and verbal versus spatial processing. The idea is that resources are consumed more rapidly if two tasks both demand the same type of perceptual resources or cognitive resources, than if one is primarily perceptual and the other is primarily cognitive. Further, with practice, an attention-demanding process can become automatized such that it requires fewer resources to operate than when it was first being learned (e.g., Schneider & Shiffrin, 1977; Shiffrin & Schneider, 1977).

Sometimes we are capable of doing two well-learned activities at once, such as driving an automobile along a familiar route while conversing with a passenger. If, however, a car swerves in front of us or a small child runs into the street ahead, the quality of our conversation is likely to take a sudden downturn. Likewise, when our attention is directed more toward an ongoing conversation than the simultaneous task of driving, then it is the quality of our driving that is likely to suffer. This is one reason that many governments around the world are assessing the wisdom of allowing car drivers to use mobile telephones. Some research has indicated that talking on a phone while driving increases the risk of accidents to about the same extent as alcoholic intoxication (i.e., a fourfold increase; Redelmeier & Tibshirani, 1997; see also Strayer, Drews, & Johnston, 2003), and there is no safety advantage in limiting use to hands-free telephones (e.g., Strayer & Johnston, 2001). Anything that requires our full attention literally leaves no capacity for doing much of anything else at the same time.

5.2 Attention and Consciousness

Attention acts as a gatekeeper to determine the contents of consciousness. Our conscious processes are limited (who can listen to a lecture and read an email from a friend at the same time?), so attention works to keep us focused on the task at hand while preventing unwanted thoughts and perceptions from interrupting us. Attention deficit disorders in children and adults as well as the **inhibition deficit hypothesis** of normal aging (e.g., Hasher & Zacks, 1988) indicate that we all have problems to varying degrees in attempting to maintain the focus of attention in the face of numerous distractions. Undergraduates in a class that I (JJ) have taught on reading sometimes report that they have read a page or more of a book before noticing that the mind had wandered onto other topics, yet their eyes had methodically continued to plow through the text. Unwanted thoughts as well as annoying environmental stimuli can be sources of distraction when we are trying to maintain the focus of attention on the task at hand.

James's definition of attention was based on an introspective appeal ("Everyone knows …") that rang as true to laypersons of his day as it does to most contemporary researchers in cognition. Attention determines our conscious experiences and recollections. Yet, we do not seem able to agree on a definition of **consciousness**. We can talk freely about consciousness that can be raised, lost, or come to again, but precise definitions escape us, as do related issues of whether animals are conscious or whether computers will ever develop consciousness. We will address such issues later (in Chapter 12) when we will consider how philosophers have viewed consciousness as aided by research in biology, psychology, and artificial intelligence.

Inhibition-deficit hypothesis A theory of cognitive aging proposed by Hasher & Zacks that attributes one of the difficulties that older persons have with the inability to ignore irrelevant information, such as in trying to follow a specific conversation at a noisy party

Consciousness The subjective feeling that we have an inner self that experiences the physical world, recalls past experiences, and acts as an agent in making decisions and carrying them out

Filter theory of attention Broadbent's theory that there is an early filter placed between most sensory channels and perceptual awareness, such that typically only one information source at a time is channelled into conscious awareness and working memory; contrasted with late filter theories that allow selection after information has been channelled to long-term memory for identification

For now, let's equate consciousness with most of what goes on in working, short-term memory (Box 1.4; see also Chapter 6), as we attempt to remain focused on current, important tasks. As the capacity of working memory is limited, attention serves many roles in maintaining focus and determining what is important enough to override the current contents of memory with new information. Broadbent (1958) described how attention controls working memory contents in his classic **filter theory of attention** (see Figure 5.1). He argued that since the environment is filled with many sources of information that cannot possibly be encoded fully, we need some kind of mechanism to sort things out. For Broadbent, attention to him acted like a filter or gate that could be set at will to allow some information source to feed directly into working memory, whereas non-selected sources would literally be filtered out and the information lost and gone forever. Much of Broadbent's theory was based on the results of selective listening experiments (see Box 5.1), but the theory can easily be generalized to other sensory modalities. To begin, let's focus on visual attention, and review how it was first studied empirically.

FIGURE 5.1

A Schematization of Broadbent's (1958) Early Filter Theory of Attention

Information in short-term sensory store (e.g., iconic memory for vision) feeds into an adjustable filter that selects a single message for entry into a limited-capacity perceptual system. The outputs from the perceptual system adjust the sensory stores (selective attention), consult memory for past conditional probabilities (e.g., environmental correlations), and determine the eventual responses made by the effectors. The filter theory is known as one of the first information-processing theories in psychology.

Adapted from Palmer, S. E. (1999). *Vision Science.* Cambridge, MA: MIT Press, p. 63.

5.3 Visual Attention

Most often we can freely attend to any part of the visual environment, and this freedom can lead to the illusion that everything is visible and perceptible at once (i.e., that we have a photographic record of the visual scene). This phenomenon

BOX 5.1

The Cocktail-Party Phenomenon

We are sure that you have all experienced the problem of trying to carry on a conversation in a noisy room. The noise can be due to traffic, a rock concert, a sporting event, or even several people who are talking at once. The latter situation was chosen as the paradigm case for a large body of research on a topic known as the cocktail-party phenomenon. The results led to the first theories of how we use attention to filter unwanted information from impinging on conscious awareness.

At a party, there are typically many people speaking simultaneously, and you, as any other guest, might attempt to follow or join in on one of these conversations to the attempted exclusion of others. With attention, this can be done, but it is sometimes difficult. Difficulties arise in situations in which you might be trapped with a bore while you notice that a much more attractive and interesting person has entered into the room. In other cases, a conversation away from the one to which you are supposed to be attending becomes suddenly salient, for example, if you hear your own name mentioned behind you.

The cocktail party was simulated in simplified laboratory situations in which stereo speakers or headphones were used to present two different spoken messages simultaneously. The participant was instructed to attend to one of the messages and warned that memory for the attended message would be tested later. To insure that participants were indeed attending to one of the messages throughout, one of the messages was to be "shadowed," that is, reported back aloud as it was heard. Results from experiments by Broadbent (1952, 1954) and Cherry (1953) showed that people were able to shadow one message and repeat it back fairly accurately while ignoring the other message. The more surprising result, however, was the almost complete lack of memory or even awareness of the non-shadowed

message. Almost nothing could be recalled from the unattended message, and people did not even notice if the non-shadowed message was changed to a different language or replaced by backward speech!

These results formed the basis of Broadbent's early filter model of attention (see Figure 5.1). The term *early* is the idea that unattended messages are filtered out before they can activate memory representations to produce recognized words in conscious awareness. The early filter theory was soon challenged by other theories that allowed many different familiar items in the external world to be encoded to the level of recognition. Then, a late filter selects those items relevant for the ongoing task, resulting in decay or active suppression of unwanted, irrelevant codes in memory. Late selection models (e.g., Deutsch & Deutsch, 1963; Norman 1968) are based on the assumption that familiar stimuli, like spoken or written words and common objects, are encoded automatically, so it does not matter if we are attending to them or not. The role of attention in late selection models is to channel the most important and relevant meanings of items into working memory so that we can maintain focus on a single task.

Some ingenious experiments by Anne Treisman (1960, 1964) offered proof that early selection is incomplete as a theory of human attention. Rather, she argued that if an early filter exists, it operates only to attenuate responses to some stimuli while emphasizing the encoding of others. Then, important or relevant information always has an opportunity to get through the filter, even if it comes from a non-attended channel. She demonstrated the effects of relevance by switching the two messages in mid-stream between the attended and unattended channels. Participants in her research commonly followed the message, rather than the channel, thus

Continues

indicating a level of control based on meaning (a late filter effect), rather than on the physical feature of location (early filter).

Treisman also showed that if the same message was presented in both channels, but was out of sync by several seconds, listeners did not notice that they were the same. However, if the relative speeds of the two tapes were changed so that the two messages gradually caught up with each other, listeners would eventually notice that the same message was being presented to the two ears. She also found an interesting asymmetry of some theoretical importance. If the unattended message was leading, the two messages had to be played within about 1.5 seconds of each other before the identity was noticed. However, if the attended message was leading, a lag as much as 4.5 seconds could pass, yet listeners still noticed the identity. This asymmetry points out one fact of early versus late (or deep) processing: Stimulus inputs that are ignored may be processed to the level of meaning, but they do not remain in memory for a very long time before they are lost and forgotten. With attention, however, inputs are processed to a deeper level and remain in active, working memory for at least 4.5 seconds, on average, in the shadowing task, and even longer in a more permanent memory system as demonstrated by later tests for recall of the contents of the shadowed message.

In summary, we have evolved with an attentional system that serves two purposes. First, there is a deliberate attempt to seek out what is important for the task at hand and to maintain focus on this information while attempting to attenuate irrelevant information. At the same time, there is a tendency for information to impinge on conscious awareness if it is related to the current task or if it is potentially important for our survival (e.g., a sudden sound or appearance of a new object).

has been called "the grand illusion of complete perception" (e.g., Enns, 2004). It is merely an illusion, and it is clearly false. People can and do miss things that are quite obviously present, most commonly because our eyes record more information than we can attend to or report. *Change blindness* (Rensink, 2001; Simons & Levin, 1997) and *inattentional blindness* (Mack & Rock, 1998) are two well-known phenomena showing how people can completely miss an otherwise easily detectable target if their attention is focused elsewhere.

The classic change blindness paradigm involves viewing a sequence of pictures in which one scene is alternated with another in rapid succession, and there is one obvious difference between them (e.g., the presence or absence of a tree in the background). Observers often take several seconds or even minutes to detect the difference, even though it is obvious once they notice it. It appears that contrary to the *grand illusion* most of the visual scene is represented in a sketchy gist form, and details are available only for a small area on which attention is focused (see Figure 5.2).

In the inattentional blindness demonstration, subjects are given a difficult perceptual task, such a brief presentation of two lines that cross in the center of the display and they have to judge which is longer—the horizontal line or the vertical one. On one of the trials, a geometric form is presented along with the lines, and the subjects are asked afterwards if they could identify it (see Figure 5.3). In fact, most subjects are surprised that there was anything other than the lines presented at all! The conclusion

FIGURE 5.2

An Example of Change Blindness

The two photographs represent successive shots in a film used in a change blindness experiment (typically the two scenes are alternated with a short blank or mask between them). Most such changes go unnoticed by observers unless they are specifically attending to them when the change occurs.

From shutterstock.com

FIGURE 5.3

An Example of the Inattentional Blindness Paradigm Used by Mack and Rock (1998)

Several trials of the main task (judging which of two crossing lines is longer) were followed with a single trial with an unexpected geometric form included in the periphery. Subjects performed poorly on a form memory test, indicating a lack of stimulus recognition without attention.

Trial sequence

is that we have the illusion of complete perception of a complex stimulus only because we can use our attention to select any component of the visual or auditory scene and experience it at an arbitrary level of detail. In this way, the stimulus functions as a back-up memory from which we can select and direct our conscious awareness to any of a number of specific components (see O'Regan & Noë, 2001).

To test the grand illusion of complete perception idea, an important question to ask is: how much information is recognizable in a single eye fixation (e.g., Cattell, 1900)? Eye fixations occur at a more-or-less regular pace of two to five per second, interspersed between eye movements called *saccades,* but shorter and longer ones can be present in any task. Information presented clearly for about 200 milliseconds (ms) is presumed to represent what is visible in a single eye fixation. Of course, in the real world, our fixations follow a path determined by internal goals or strategies as well as by salient external events. Our perceptions are built up cumulatively over a succession of fixations to generate an internal 3-D model of the environment. Nevertheless, as we look closely at each successive step in an old building as we walk up a dimly-lit staircase, our eyes can dart to the location of a sudden movement in a corner. We can also trace a regular pattern of fixations separated by rapid saccadic eye movements in certain tasks like scanning an instrument panel or reading a paragraph.

The classic experiment that showed beyond any doubt that people could see more than they can report, even if they cannot see everything clearly, was Sperling's (1960) study of partial report (see Box 1.2). In such controlled environments, the effects of attention on what we see and what we are able to report can be cleanly measured. Attention can be focused on some aspects of a visual display, and the region attended will result in better performance for recognizing objects in that region (see Box 5.2). Although we usually fixate (look directly at) the current object of our attention, much research has shown that attention serves a role in deciding where to fixate next. That is, attention operates covertly (without any outward signs) in determining what object or area in the visual field is worthy of more detailed inspection. The selected location then becomes a target for the next overt eye movement. An advantage for information processing in the attended region is often profited at a loss for non-attended regions of the field. Thus, in agreement with Broadbent's (1958) theory, Posner (1980) argued that attention's most important role seems to be the selection of what information should be directed to conscious, working memory where it can be encoded more deeply for recognition and response decisions. This selection results in improved detection and recognition even before the eyes start to move, and even if the item of interest disappears before the eyes can fixate it (see Box 5.2).

Besides selection, attention serves as a monitor of conscious processing, always at the alert to detect new or important information. There is nothing so powerful in attracting one's attention as a sudden, unexpected sound or the sudden appearance of a new object in the field of view (Jonides & Yantis, 1988). Other unattended stimuli that have high personal salience, such as one's name, frequently result in a change of attention, even in defiance of one's current focus (e.g., Moray, 1959). Such selection is limited, however, by the ongoing processing capacity of short-term working memory.

BOX 5.2

The Spotlight Model of Attention

Helmholtz (1850/1962) was among the first to speculate that attention and the direction of one's gaze are not necessarily correlated. He claimed that if he entered his office in the dark and looked straight ahead, he could prepare himself to attend either to the left or right of his point of fixation. To prove this fact to himself, he then briefly lit his office with an electrical spark and satisfied himself by being able to name more objects visible to the left or right of fixation, in the direction he had been attending. It was as if attention functions like a functional fovea to temporarily emulate the physiological fovea in the center, back part of the eye onto which things that we are looking at directly are imaged. Although the foveated object normally is represented in greater detail in the brain than any peripheral object, attention can function to override this predominance, such that items presented to the fovea are sometimes seen less well than objects presented to attended peripheral locations (e.g., Juola, Bouwhuis, Cooper, & Warner, 1989).

The first empirical work to study Helmholtz's claim in controlled situations was designed by Posner and his colleagues (Posner, 1980; Posner, Snyder, & Davidson, 1980). They defined several areas around the fixation point where a single target could appear. The defined areas were marked by boxes, and the target was a small, bright square that could appear in one of the boxes. The task was to hit a response button as quickly as possible when the small, bright square appeared (a simple RT task). On some trials, one of the boxes brightened briefly before the target was presented. This was a cue that the target was likely to occur within that box, although the cue was not 100% valid. Posner and colleagues found that if the target square subsequently appeared within the cued box, response times were shorter than if the square appeared in a non-cued box (invalid cue). The

response times on no-cue trials were in between the responses for valid and invalid cue trials.

An important point to keep in mind is that the entire time for cue presentation followed by target onset and then target offset was kept below 200 ms, so the observers did not have time to move their eyes before the cue and display were shown and disappeared. Nonetheless, people's behavior indicated that something moved in the direction of the cue. Posner asserted that this something was attention, and that it moves like a spotlight moves across a stage to illuminate part of the visual field, while leaving other parts in comparative darkness. If a target is presented within the spotlight of attention, it is detected and responded to quickly. If, however, the target is presented elsewhere, the spotlight usually has to be redirected to the target location, which takes time and slows responses. On no-cue trials, there is no spotlight, as observers attempt to spread their attention in a diffused way over the entire display in preparation for a target that could occur anywhere.

Later research has shown that the spotlight metaphor, while useful, does not capture the full flexibility of how we distribute attention over the visual field. Depending on display characteristics, and task demands, attention can be distributed more or less evenly over the field, concentrated around central vision (i.e., the fovea), concentrated at some location or over some object in space, or even distributed over rings around the fixation point or in different locations at the same time. Such a high degree of flexibility emphasizes two important characteristics of visual attention. First, attentional systems have evolved to enable us to attend to a variety of different objects and events that are important for our survival. Second, what we see and respond to is determined not only by what is present in the visual world but also by what we are looking for and are determined to find.

5.4 Theories of Visual Attention

5.4.1   *Exogenous versus Endogenous Attention*

Exogenous The bottom-up, automatic attraction of attention to a salient aspect of the environment, most certainly to a sudden sound or the sudden appearance of a new object

Endogenous attention The top-down, voluntary direction of attention toward information that is likely to be related to one's goals or needs

Posner (1980) differentiated between what he called **exogenous** (environmentally-generated, or bottom-up) and **endogenous** (self-generated, or top-down) controls of attention. Exogenous controls are mediated by lower brain systems, such as the colliculi in the midbrain, and they can result in rapid and automatic orienting of attention to an exogenous cue. Stimuli that most clearly attract attention automatically are sudden sounds or the appearances of new objects in the visual field. These primitive orienting responses have evolved early in animals, since being aware of new objects is an important determinant of survival. In fact, the superior colliculi of animals, such as fish and frogs, are the main processors of visual stimuli in their central nervous systems. It has been said that a frog will starve to death in a cage filled with dead flies, because they literally are not visible as food. Similarly, characters in the movie *Jurassic Park* were warned to remain still so that they would not be spotted by the Tyrannosaurus Rex. In mammals, and especially primates, these primitive brain-stem systems remain functional, but they are largely augmented, especially in conscious awareness, by visual centers in the cerebral cortex.

Endogenous controls of attention include deliberate searching for specific items, such as looking for a pair of red socks in a drawer full of multi-colored stockings and other articles. Stimuli with features that match what we are looking for attract attention, but in a slower and less certain way than do exogenous cues (e.g., Jonides, 1980). This difference is primarily due to the fact that exogenous cues trigger responses in a reflexive, bottom-up way under direction from automatic, hard-wired systems in the brain stem. Endogenous responses, on the other hand, are determined by search strategies under top-down control of executive systems and the frontal eye fields in the frontal lobes of the brain that direct the actions of lower visual systems.

5.4.2   *Treisman's Feature-Integration Theory (FIT)*

Preattentive stage Iin FIT, it is essentially the information available in sensory (e.g., iconic) memory. The features are briefly available in different modules or "feature maps" of the environment that are registered and maintained in parallel.

Many theorists have expanded on the argument that attention operates at different levels in the cognitive system. For example, Treisman and Gelade (1980) developed Neisser's (1967) argument that attention follows two successive stages in selecting items to be examined closely. The first stage is a **preattentive stage** in which a broad swath of the environment is processed in parallel. Most features in the field of view, including such things as color, orientation, size, depth, and motion, are coded by separate modules into feature maps that represent those specific aspects of the visible stimuli. In addition, there is a master map of locations to which all of the individual feature maps can be related. This relation, however, is achieved only in a second stage, called *focal attention* (see Figure 5.4)

FIGURE 5.4

Treisman's (e.g., Treisman & Gormican, 1988) Feature-Integration Theory (FIT) of Attention

All features in the visual field are registered in parallel in separate "maps" for color, orientation, motion, size, and other fundamental features. A master map of locations can be scanned with an attentional spotlight. Wherever attention is focused on the location map, features in the other modules at that location are bound together into an object file. In other words, attention acts like a glue that binds features into a recognizable object.

Palmer, Stephen E., Vision Science: Photons to Phenomenology, figure, page 557, © 1999 Massachusetts Institute of Technology, by permission of The MIT Press.

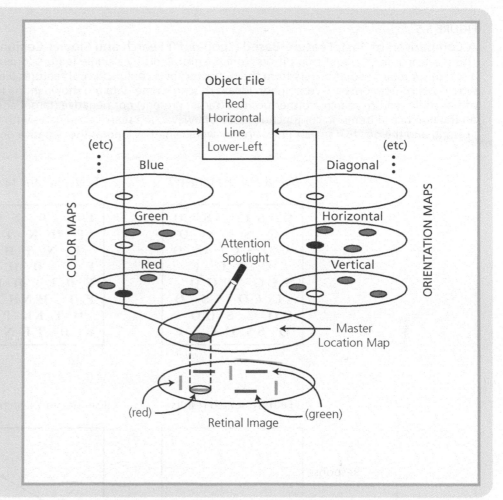

In Treisman's theory, focal attention is limited to a succession of small areas in the visual field, much as a spotlight is moved around a large stage to illuminate specific settings. When the spotlight of attention falls on a particular location, all features represented in the preattentive stage are integrated into a single, object-level representation. For this reason, Treisman's theory is called the *Feature-Integration Theory (FIT)* of attention. It is as though specific features are free-floating in a preattentive field, and attention acts as the glue that binds them into recognizable objects. Objects usually can be recognized only one at a time, however, making the second, focal stage of attention a serial process unlike the parallel feature processing that occurs in the earlier, preattentive stage (see Figure 5.5).

Treisman and Gelade (1980) based their theory on two related findings from studies of visual search. First, it is well known that search is fast and easy for a target that differs from all other items in the visual field by a single feature. Try the tasks shown in Figure 5.5 to see that finding a target **T** among letters with curved features and no horizontal elements is quite easy. However, finding an **L** among letters with horizontal and vertical features is not so easy. Treisman and her colleagues argued that if the target differs from background distractor items by a single salient feature,

FIGURE 5.5

A Comparison of Fast, Feature-Based ("pop-out") Search and Slower Conjunction Search
This is a search for a target that differs from the distractors by a single feature (orientation, left panel) versus
a search for a target that differs from the distractors by a conjunction of features (i.e., how vertical and
horizontal components are combined). Idealized search time data are shown in the lower panels for each type
of search. In feature search, neither positive (target present) nor negative (target absent) search times depend
on the number of items. In conjunction search, however, the search terminates with finding a target if it is
present, and the positive search times are on average half as long as the negative ones

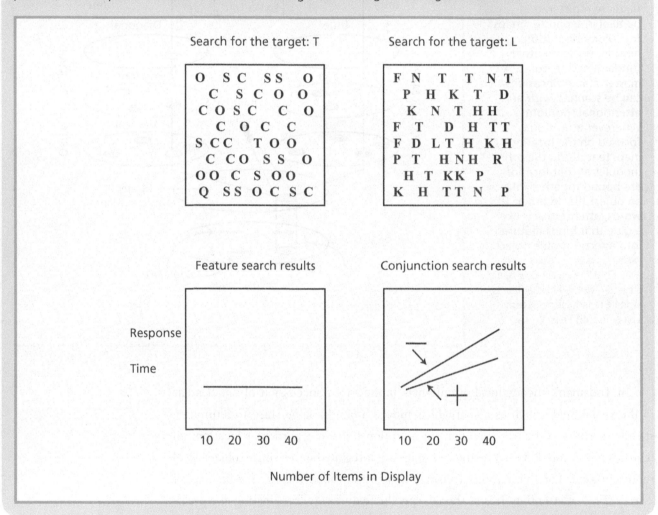

then search should be parallel (all items examined at once), based on information
obtainable preattentively. That is, a single red X will pop out from a field of blue Xs
when one is looking for a red item. And it will be just as easy to decide that there is no
target when there are only blue items in the display. However, if the target is defined
by a unique combination of features, such as a red X among blue Xs and red Ns, and
the target features exist by themselves in other display items, then the target can
be found only in the second, focal stage of attention. In other words, if the target is
defined by features that have to be combined by focal attention, in order to integrate
all its components, then search proceeds serially (one at a time) until the target is
found or until all items have been examined without finding a target.

Treisman and Gelade proposed a simple test to determine whether a target can be found at the preattentive level or only at the later, focal attentive stages of processing. The test is based on an examination of a plot of response times (RTs) in search tasks against the number of items in the display. In these search tasks, the target is present either once or not at all, so the person's task is to respond positively as soon as the target is found and to respond negatively when the search is completed without finding the target. The results are generally straightforward: If the target is defined by a single, unique feature (**feature search**), search times are independent of the number of items in the display [i.e., the response time by display size (RT by set size—see Figure 5.5) functions are flat.] If, however, finding the target is possible only after focal attention has integrated the display items' features (**conjunction search**), the slope of the RT by set size function is greater than zero. In some search tasks, especially those with more than about five items in the display, it seems as if we quit as soon as the target item is found, and the slope is about twice as large on negative (no target) trials as on trials containing the target. This result is expected, since if the display items are searched serially, the search should terminate as soon as the target is found, which would be, on average, about halfway through the search (see Box 1.1). On no-target trials, however, the search would have to cover all display items until a negative response could be made.

A second result Treisman used to support FIT was the occasional report of **illusory conjunctions** in a search display. That is, if a display is presented too briefly, or if an observer's attention is focused elsewhere, some display items will be processed only preattentively. If they do not undergo focal attentive processing, their features should be free floating, and they should be almost as likely to combine with features from neighboring items as with features from their own item. If a person is asked to name an object from an unattended region containing red Xs and blue Os, for example, the response "Blue X" is likely to be made, even though no such stimulus was shown.

5.4.3 Modifications of FIT

Like any good theory, FIT generated much research that eventually led to revisions of the theory. The main reasons for the revisions were the unreliability of some findings that were its main supports. That is, parallel search, as defined by a flat RT by set size function, is not limited to feature search. Some conjunctions apparently pop out as well (e.g., Nakayama & Silverman, 1986; Wolfe, Cave, & Franzel, 1989). Nakayama and Silverman showed that target items differing from distractors in depth or motion could be found quickly, without having to search through irrelevant items at a different depth or relative motion from the target. The crucial aspect in visual search appears to be whether or not the display can be segmented into potential targets and items that can be easily rejected. If some non-targets can be rejected as a set by having a salient feature or two that eliminates them from being possible targets, then the

Feature search The search for a target object that differs from the background distractors by a single, salient feature; the target appears to pop out, and search time is independent of the number of distractors in the display

Conjunction search The search for a target object that differs from the background distractors by a unique combination of features that are individually present among the distractors; search time increases linearly with the number of distractors in the display

Illusory conjunctions According to FIT, features that are not bound together by focal attention can be combined incorrectly, and subjects might report seeing objects that were not actually present remaining items can be searched more efficiently. Searching through the remaining items can now be parallel if the target is defined by a single feature among these items (e.g., Egeth, Virzi, & Garbart, 1984).

In a different rebuttal to FIT, Cohen and Ivry (1989) challenged the notion that illusory conjunctions occur frequently. They found that subjects reported such conjunctions only rarely, and when they occurred, they usually were miscombined features from neighboring items. They claimed that the effects of attention are small, at best, and the results are inconsistent with the idea that features are bound into an object only with focal attention and freely dissociated without it. Donk (1999) has also claimed that when features are processed, they include coarse, absolute location information as well as good relative location information. When feature conjunction errors are reported, they are most likely to be confusions between targets and distractors in the display, rather than miscombinations of free-floating features.

5.4.4 *Wolfe's Guided Search Theory*

Wolfe (1994, Wolfe et al., 1989) has proposed a revision of FIT that he calls the *guided search model*. In guided search, there are two sources of information that aid selection of potential targets. One source is bottom-up information from the stimulus. This information is represented as a two-dimensional salience map of the visual environment. Salience is determined primarily by contrast, such that features or objects are highly salient if they contrast strongly from their neighbors in brightness, color, orientation, motion, or other features. The second source of information is the top-down activation of objects or features that closely match a target template. Top-down activation is a deliberate, strategic process that can call attention to objects that belong to the target category. Bottom-up and top-down information are combined to produce an overall activation map (see Figure 5.6). The peaks on the map are objects that are most salient and match most closely with what we are looking for. Attention then selects items one at a time from those most active in the overall map in a serial search for the target. If salience and top-down information activate the target most highly, it pops out, and the search is fast and accurate. If, however, many distractors are also highly salient and they appear to be similar to the target, then the search can be a slow, tedious examination of many items before the target is found. Thus, different types of search results (including serial or parallel at the limits; see Figure 5.5) can be produced by special cases of a single model in which search difficulty is determined by item salience and item similarity to a desired target (see Duncan & Humphreys, 1989, for a similar model).

FIGURE 5.6

Wolfe's (1994) Guided Search Model of Visual Attention

Similar to Treisman's FIT, the visual stimulus is assumed to be analyzed by separate modules into feature maps for color, orientation, etc. Bottom-up activation of locations is determined by feature salience (i.e., the degree to which features contrast with their immediate neighbors.) In addition, top-down activation is added to the feature maps in proportion to their similarities to the target of the search. Bottom-up salience and top-down target-similarity activations combine to produce an overall activation map. Attention then scans this map by beginning at the highest peak, and continuing to lower activated regions until a desired target is found or the search is abandoned.

From Wolfe, J. M, (1994). Guided search 2.0: A revised model of visual search. *Psychonomic Bulletin and Review,* 1, p. 205.

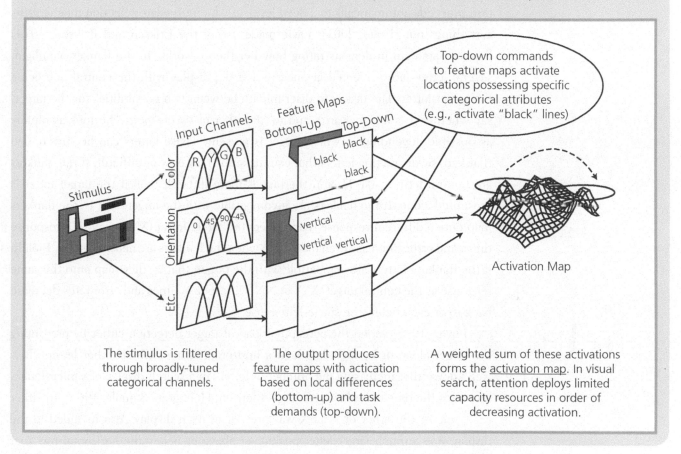

The stimulus is filtered through broadly-tuned categorical channels.

The output produces feature maps with actication based on local differences (bottom-up) and task demands (top-down).

A weighted sum of these activations forms the activation map. In visual search, attention deploys limited capacity resources in order of decreasing activation.

5.5 **The Effects of Perceptual Load on Attention**

5.5.1 *Lavie's Perceptual Load Theory*

Lavie (1995, 2001) has suggested that the scope of attention depends largely on the perceptual load of any given task. She was interested in addressing the question of whether Broadbent's (1952) early filter or Norman's (1968) late filter were more general descriptors of how selective attention works (see Box 5.1). That is, if one is engaged in a fairly simple perceptual task, like reading a single word in the middle of an otherwise empty page containing a few scattered random digits, attention might

Lavie's perceptual load theory The idea that easy perceptual tasks result in irrelevant information being processed deeply, requiring late selection; whereas difficult perceptual tasks result in early selection and filtering of irrelevant information.

act like a late filter, selecting the meaning of the word from among the competing characters. If, however, the task is difficult, like trying to read a small letter embedded in a cluster of distracting letters, and presented only briefly, then attention might behave like an early filter, separating out irrelevant information before it can compete with information derived from the target.

Lavie (1995) proposed a hybrid model of attention that combines early and late selection models into a flexible framework. The model acknowledges that human perception has some capacity limits (early selection), but within these limits, perception proceeds automatically to a deep level, at which time late selection mechanisms sort things out (Lavie, 2001). Lavie made use of the Eriksen and Eriksen (1974) flanker paradigm in demonstrating how her theory works. In the flanker paradigm, several letters are presented at once in a visual display with the central one being the target letter. The task is to discriminate between two possibilities for the target, say whether it is an N or an X and to hit either of two response buttons as rapidly as possible depending on which target is present. These letters can be surrounded (flanked) by distracting letters that can make the task easy or difficult. If the flankers are neutral letters, like H or Y, the task is more difficult than if the target letter is presented alone. If the flankers are incompatible with the target, that is, the flankers map onto a different response than the central target letter (XNX or NXN), response times and errors increase even more than when the flankers are neutral letters. Finally, if the flanking letters are compatible with the target, that is, they map onto the same response as the central target (XXX or NNN), response times and error rates decrease back to or even below the single-letter case.

Lavie (1995) varied the perceptual load of target detection either by presenting the target alone or by including it in a horizontal string with six other letters. It is well known that increasing the number of letters in a search display of similar letters increases the time to find a target (e.g., Atkinson, Holmgren, & Juola, 1969). In either case, one or the other of N or X was present in each display. Also included in the display was a much larger letter positioned above or below the horizontal row that contained the target. Participants were told to ignore the large letter, and it was either neutral (H), or it was an N or an X. On compatible trials the large letter matched the target (central letter) shown on that trial, and on incompatible trials it did not match the target. Lavie expected that when perceptual load was low (single target condition), attentional capacity would not be limited, and there would be a strong chance that the large, peripheral letter would be recognized and show compatibility effects on response times. When the perceptual load was high (target embedded among six distractor letters), the search for the target would take more capacity, and less would be left over for processing the peripheral letter (see Figure 5.7).

The results were exactly as Lavie (1995) predicted. When the peripheral letter was incompatible with the target presented on any trial, the incompatibility effect showed up on only on low load trials. When the perceptual load was high, no compatibility effect was found. Lavie argued that if any task does not use all of the attentional

FIGURE 5.7

Manipulation of Perceptual Load in the Flanker Task (after Lavie, 1995)

The task is to hit a left-hand button for one letter (e.g., "N") and to hit a right-hand button for the other letter ("X"). These target letters are always presented in the center of the display. In the high-load condition, six flanker letters are added to the central target. To test the distribution of attention, large peripheral letters (which should be ignored) that are shown in some trials are either neutral, compatible, or incompatible with the central target. Compatibility of the peripheral letters affected response times in the low-load conditions only. Examples of the conditions are shown below.

Low-load control	High-load control
X	DFKXMTP

Low-load neutral	High-load neutral
H X	H DFKXMTP

Low-load compatible	High-load compatible
X X	X DFKXMTP

Low-load incompatible	High-load incompatible
N X	N DFKXMTP

capacity available, other information in the environment might be encoded automatically and unavoidably such that it will compete for later selection. However, if any task is demanding enough to command all of one's attentional resources, irrelevant or extraneous stimuli will not be processed to a deep level—they will be weeded out by early selection. Thus, Lavie holds that both early and late selection theories of attention are true, but a better theory is a hybrid that predicts under what conditions selection will be early or late.

Lavie's theory is relevant for understanding human performance in dual-task situations (see also Johnston & Heinz, 1978). If two tasks are only minimally demanding of attentional capacity, then it is possible to do both at the same time without much loss of performance on either. One might be tempted to say that driving at a moderate speed on a good highway with light traffic would be manageable enough for a skilled driver to engage in a conversation with a passenger (or even with someone via a mobile phone) without much damage to either driving or conversational skills. However, if the conversation turns to a stressful topic with high emotional content, driving performance is likely to suffer, as is conversational quality if the traffic suddenly becomes congested or road conditions become dangerous. In these cases, high loads in one task can reduce performance in the other. Similarly, if you are trying to read in a room with a TV on, you might find that you can share your attention between the two if the reading and TV programs are both light in content. But if the text is highly relevant to an important midterm examination the next day or if the TV suddenly breaks to an important international development, attention is likely to be more clearly focused on one medium or the other, with the non-attended information blocked out by an early filter.

5.5.2   *Neurophysiological Support for the Perceptual Load Theory*

An interesting demonstration supporting Lavie's theory was reported by Rees, Frith, and Lavie (1997). They used displays of familiar words displayed on a background of small dots. On some trials, the dots appeared to move outward from the center of the screen, and on other trials the dots were stationary. While the participants viewed these displays, their brain activity in different regions was measured by fMRI techniques. As expected, different levels of brain activation for stationary versus moving displays were found in known motion processing centers, such as the medial temporal gyrus, **area MT** in the cerebral cortex.

Area MT The medial temporal gyrus of the cortex; an area that has many cells that are sensitive to the speed and direction of motion

The main manipulation in Rees et al.'s experiment was perceptual load demanded by the words presented in the middle of the screen. On some trials, the load was low, as participants were asked to determine simply if the words were printed in upper or lower case letters. On other trials, the load was high, as the participants had to hit one response button if the word contained two syllables and another button if it contained either one or three syllables. An important control was that the words shown were exactly the same in the two conditions; the only difference was the task that the subjects had to perform. Therefore, any difference observed between tasks must be due to the different cognitive processes involved and not to the stimulus or response aspects of the task. The results were clear: Motion-sensitive areas of the brain (i.e., area MT) were more responsive in the low-load conditions than in the high-load conditions. It is apparent that the low-load task freed attention to process other areas of the display, and motion detection centers of the brain were highly activated. When the task demanded a high level of attention however, less capacity was available for processing other information in the display, and motion-sensitive brain areas were less activated. It seems as though attention-demanding tasks can prevent us from noticing irrelevant information through active suppression of normal sensory coding. Although such a mechanism should generally be useful in focusing attention on the task at hand, it can sometimes lead to problems, with the common example being what can happen when one is engrossed in an important phone conversation while driving!

5.6 Location versus Object Theories of Attention

Another theoretical issue of some interest to those who wonder how visual attention works is whether attention is directed to locations in space or to objects that occupy various locations. In other words, does object segregation determine where attention is allocated, or is attention needed to find out where objects are? In Treisman's FIT, attention is allocated to a master map of locations, and object identity is revealed only after attention binds the features at that location into a recognizable whole. In other theories, objects are segregated, and even recognized, preattentively, and attention is directed to objects, not locations.

The debate can obviously become quite complicated because, of course, objects occupy specific locations, and attention to an object necessitates attention to its location. One approach to simplify things has been to ask participants to identify two target features that are equally close to each other, but sometimes fall on the same object and sometimes fall on different objects. For example, Duncan (1984) asked observers to report two features about a superimposed line and rectangle (see Figure 5.8). Two of these features belonged to the line (it was a dotted or a dashed

FIGURE 5.8

Stimuli Like Those Used in Duncan's (1984) Experiment

Subjects had to judge whether the rectangle was tall or short or had a gap on the left or right, or whether the line was dotted or dashed, or oblique to the left or right of vertical. Judgments were more accurate for two features if they were reported from the same figure (rectangle or line) than if or one feature was to be reported for each figure.

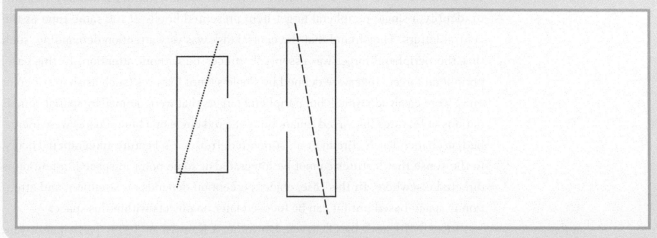

line that was tilted clockwise or counter clockwise from vertical) and two features belonged to the rectangle (it was either tall or short and had a gap on the left or right side). After a brief presentation of a stimulus pair, decisions were consistently more accurate if the two features to be reported were either both on the line or both on the rectangle. Discriminating between one feature on the line and one on the rectangle presumably required attending to two different objects and required more attentional capacity. Even though the lines and rectangles were overlapping such that all relevant features were equidistant, attention seemed to move along one object more easily than between two objects. This result supports the object-based theory of attentional allocation over a space-based theory, since attention directed solely on the basis of location should be indifferent to object relations within its focus.

Duncan's (1984) conclusion was qualified by Lavie and Driver (1996) who showed that spatial cues presented before the onset of a pair of objects could eliminate the object advantage. They used a pair of intersecting lines as objects, and the task was to determine whether two breaks in the lines (which could be either an empty gap or a gap with a dot in the middle) were the same or different. The breaks could occur either both in the same line or one in each line. The same-different judgment was easier when both gaps were in the same line, a result supporting Duncan's findings. However, when spatial cues were given in advance to direct participants' attention to the locations of the gaps, the same-object advantage disappeared. It is clear that attention can be directed to locations in space, and if enough time is given to segregate objects from the background, attention will spread from its initial location to encompass any object near its focus. Thus, space-based descriptions of attention are likely to be true of early stages of attentional allocation, before objects are segregated from their background. Object-based descriptions of attention are more descriptive of processes occurring later in vision, after objects have been segregated and integrated from their component features.

Braun, Koch, Lee, and Itti (2001) reached a similar conclusion. They used a task in which a central cluster of letters at various rotations had to be classified as being either all the same letter or a mixture of two different letters. A secondary task was to identify a single peripheral target item presented briefly at the same time as the central letters. They found that the central task was very attention demanding, such that the peripheral target was essentially processed without attention. In this case, peripheral targets that were defined by single salient features (such as shape or color only) were easily identified, but peripheral targets that were defined by spatial combinations of features (like a red square but not a red circle or a blue square) were identified at chance levels. Braun et al. supported Treisman's Feature Integration Theory, in the sense that features cannot be integrated at some point in space if attention is directed elsewhere. In this case, object perception depends on attention, and attention is space-based until it can be focused later on objects within this space.

In an fMRI study by, O'Craven, Downing, & Kanwisher (1999), participants were shown pictures on which a face and building were superimposed (like that shown in Figure 5.9). They were asked to pay attention to either the face or the building. Face recognition is associated with the Fusiform Face Area (FFA), whereas perception of building is associated with the Parahippocampal Place Area (PPA). The FFA showed activation when participants paid attention to the face, whereas the PPA showed activation when they paid attention to the building. So, their results showed the neurological foundations of different types of object attention.

FIGURE 5.9

An Example of an Overlapped Image of a Face and Buildings

From shutterstock.com

5.7 Distribution of Attention Over Time

5.7.1 Attending to Important Moments

Initial studies of attention were directed towards discovering how attention is distributed over space or directed to certain channels or objects. It is clear, however, that our attention is distributed over time as well as space. Most people have experienced a frightening event, such as a near or actual auto accident, in which there might have been a moment in which time appeared to stand still or at least slow down as one tried to take in the full importance of what is happening at a single moment (e.g., Tse, Intriligator, Rivest, & Cavanagh, 2004). Similarly, in certain sporting events, many minutes can pass with little action, but suddenly a crucial play occurs that can determine the outcome of the entire game (e.g., a penalty shot in ice hockey or soccer, or a close play at home plate in baseball). Most people share an introspective awareness that such an experience can create a vivid image of the scene, with events preceding and following the special event literally being crowded out of memory.

The introspective feeling that some particular experiences jump out, seem to occur more slowly, and are retained better than other events is supported by laboratory studies of how attention changes over time. It is well known from studies of worker and student performance that attention cannot remain focused at a high level on any task indefinitely. Lecturers are encouraged by their students to offer breaks in classes that run for an hour or more. Similarly, people have difficulty maintaining attention during demanding tasks, like managing an air-traffic control station or engaging in

Vigilance The attempt to maintain attention at a high level of focus on a single task for extended periods of time

RSVP (rapid, serial visual presentation) This is the presentation of a succession of different visual stimuli to a single, central point in the field of view. Rates of presentation can vary, but they usually are set at about 100 ms per item (10 items/sec) to prevent masking found at faster rates and naming and rehearsal likely at higher rates. Items typically are seen clearly enough to be identified, but are gone too quickly to be consolidated into memory.

simultaneous translations of one language into another as is done at large international meetings and at the United Nations. Periodic swings in attention over time have been studied in the experimental literature on human **vigilance**. In detecting the presence of rare events, such as radar or sonar signals against a background of noise, performance often shows a significant drop in a half hour or less after beginning the task (Broadbent & Gregory, 1985; Mackworth, 1948).

5.7.2   *Attending to a Rapid Sequence of Events*

Perhaps of even more interest than long periods of attentional variation are the moment-to-moment changes in memory for events that are attended to and remembered, whereas others apparently escape attention and are lost from memory. Lawrence (1971) studied how well people could identify words when they were presented one at a time at a high rate to a single place in the middle of a visual display. This research procedure has come to be called Rapid Serial Visual Presentation (**RSVP**). In RSVP presentations, the time between successive items is measured in milliseconds (ms). The stimulus onset asynchrony (SOA) is the time between the onsets of successive items, and the interstimulus interval (ISI) is the blank time (if any) between two successive items. Thus, SOA = (any item's exposure duration + ISI).

The SOA is the crucial variable in much RSVP research. At very short SOAs, on the order of 50 ms or less, successive items tend to run together and become difficult to differentiate, much less to identify and remember. This phenomenon is known as integration masking, and it is due to the fact that the visual system tends to integrate information over time in intervals approaching 100 ms. If the SOA is set to about 100 ms or so, each item appears distinctly visible and recognizable, but each of them occurs too rapidly to be remembered for very long. Still, Lawrence (1971), Potter (1976; Potter & Levy, 1969), and others have shown that even though very few of the items in an RSVP sequence could be reported from memory after the sequence was completed, perception and recognition of each of the items was fairly complete. This conclusion was reached from experiments in which a specific target (e.g., a picture of a boat) or a target category (e.g., an animal name) was given before an RSVP sequence of pictures or words. Even at rates of 10 items/sec (100 ms/item), target detection is often very good, with report accuracy of 90% or more for young adult participants. Lawrence even noted that search for targets in an RSVP stream could be 50% more efficient than a similar search through a list of words printed down the center of a piece of paper. This result prompted some people to wonder if tasks such as reading could also be made more efficient if the text were presented in the RSVP mode rather than being read with normal eye movements (see Box 5.3).

Potter later argued that successive items presented at a rate of 10 per second result in complete perception and recognition of each of them, as long as they are familiar items such as letters, digits, words, or pictures of common objects. However, they are quickly replaced in memory by successive items before they can be consolidated into a retrievable form. In other words, RSVP lists of items can be processed well enough to pick out one or two salient target items, but only because these targets receive additional processing do they survive the destructive interference from succeeding items in the stream.

BOX 5.3

Reading Text Presented in the RSVP Format

Text is normally read with a sequence of fixations, lasting about 150 to 350 ms, interspersed with saccadic eye movements, which are considerably shorter, about 20 to 50 ms. Most of these saccades are progressive, leading to fixations that land in the next word or two after the one previously fixated, but some are regressive (to earlier parts of the text), some are to other parts of the word currently fixated, and others are return sweeps to the next line of text. Thus, the visual input to a reader is a sequence of snapshots of text segments occurring at a rate of about four to five per second. Research by Rayner and others (e.g., McConkie & Rayner, 1975; Rayner, 1998) has shown that we are sensitive to only a small part of the text at any time. McConkie and Rayner used a computer display that changed with each eye fixation to reveal text in only a narrow window around the point of fixation. The rest of the text was represented by rows of Xs. This window can be arbitrarily small, with reading speeds and comprehension rates falling precipitously for very small windows of only a few characters. They found that reading is fairly normal in speed and comprehension if the window is expanded to about 15 to 20 character spaces around the fixation point, with most of the window extending to the right. Further, it appears that only the left-most word or two is processed to the level of meaning, whereas the rightmost part of the window is primarily used for determining the landing point of the next eye movement.

These facts about reading, as well as the high levels of performance that can be achieved in searching through RSVP lists of words, suggest that reading sentences and paragraphs in the RSVP mode might promote efficient reading for comprehension. That is, entire passages of text could be presented one or a very few words at a time to a central location on a computer screen, and the text could be read without the need for eye movements. Indeed, work by Forster (1970) and Gilbert (1959) showed that text could be read when presented this way by adults and children, respectively.

Most people, when first hearing about reading text presented in the RSVP mode, object that it would be both unnatural and difficult. On the other hand, it could be argued that reading with eye movements is hardly a natural act, since the ability to read has been limited to only relatively few members of our species in all our history. Besides, eye movements could be inefficient due to the lack of perfect oculo-motor control, the loss of information during saccades (e.g., saccadic suppression, see Volkmann, 1976), and the fact that some attention must be diverted from the main process of text comprehension in order to control eye movements themselves.

In our lab at the University of Kansas, a number of students and I (JJ) spent about 10 years trying to discover the optimal means of enhancing readability of text presented in the RSVP mode. We varied the presentation rate and window size of text selected from standardized tests of reading comprehension and found the optimal presentation format. The optimum method is to present one long word or two or more short words for about 250 ms each in single windows left-justified, so that people tend to fixate a point a few character positions from the left-hand border. Further, the text should be parsed as much as possible so that short syntactic phrases are preserved rather than being split between two successive windows (i.e., "The girl threw the red ball into the street" would be parsed: The girl / threw / the red ball / into the street.) Any phrases more than 15 characters in length were arbitrarily split near the middle in order to prevent showing windows too long to be read in a single eye fixation.

The combination of an average of two words every 250 ms equals eight words a second, or 480 words per minute (WPM). This is almost twice as fast as a normal reader usually processes text, so the presentation rate can be slowed as needed to

Continues

match readers' abilities. Several studies have shown that text presented in this optimal RSVP format can be read just as easily and with equivalent comprehension as text presented for the same total time in a normal page format to be read with typical eye movements (Juola, Ward, & McNamara, 1982). Moreover, we found the RSVP method to result in superior comprehension performance for readers of lower than average verbal ability among college students (Chen, 1986), and for middle-school students who were classified as disabled readers (Juola, 1988). The method has also been shown to be an optimal way of presenting text when the viewing area is extremely limited, as in some small electronic devices (Juola, Tiritoglu, & Pleunis, 1995). Reading RSVP text should remain a viable option for electronic displays in various contexts, for instructional purposes for beginning and remedial readers, and for the use as a tool in the study of cognitive processes involved in reading.

5.7.3   *Chun and Potter's Two-Stage Theory*

Chun and Potter (1995, 2001) expanded on these ideas to propose a two-stage model for how items are processed in RSVP streams. In a first stage of processing, each item is processed automatically, as deeply as possible, until it is replaced by the succeeding item. For familiar items, this first stage includes perception and recognition of the item so that its meaning in long-term memory is accessed and understood. However, before any more processing beyond simple recognition can be accomplished, the next item is presented and recognized, and so on to the end of the stream. If a certain item is salient in some way—such as by being presented in a different location, size, or color from the other items—it can be entered into a second stage of memory that is protected from being overwritten by new inputs. In this second stage, more attention is directed to elaborate coding of the item, such that it is maintained in memory longer and is more likely to be recalled at the end of the RSVP sequence than items that had received only stage 1 processing.

Chun and Potter's (1995) model was initially developed to explain a finding that demonstrates our ability to select items from a temporal sequence of events. The selected items are processed more deeply, but other items must necessarily receive less processing, resulting in their loss from memory. This loss due to the attentional selectivity of events distributed over time has come to be called the **attentional blink (AB)**, and it is the topic of the next section.

Attentional blink (AB) The finding that if two targets are present in an RSVP stream, the second target is frequently missed if it follows too closely on the heels of the first target

5.8 **The Attentional Blink**

It is known from the work of Posner (1980; Box 5.2) and others how attention can be distributed over space. Recently, some of the principles that guide our distribution of attention over time have been determined as well. Just as spatial attention selects some region or items in the visual scene for further processing to the detriment of others, certain events occurring in time can be selected with the consequence that other events might be lost from memory. Broadbent and Broadbent (1987) and Raymond,

Shapiro, and Arnell (1992) had observers monitor an RSVP stream of words or letters, looking for predefined targets. When two successive targets were separated in the stream by about 180 to 540 ms (i.e., at a lag of about 2 to 6 items at 90 ms per item), the second one was often missed, although the first was identified with more than 90% accuracy. Curiously, if the two targets occurred in immediate succession, the two were usually both reported, a phenomenon known as Lag 1 sparing (see Figure 5.10).

Visser, Bischof, and Di Lollo (1999) proposed a model for the attentional distribution over time in which specific episodes are defined by critical events that match what we are looking for or are otherwise important to us. Objects or events included in these episodes are selected for further processing, and while they are being handled, new objects or events can be missed, or only processed to a relatively shallow level. However, the selection mechanism can be relatively sluggish, so that if two targets occur in close succession, they are likely both to be included in the same attentional

FIGURE 5.10
The Attentional Blink

1.

2.

The task originated by Raymond et al. (1992) was detection of one or two targets in a rapid, serial visual presentation (RSVP) stream of characters. The first target (T1) was always present, and it was the only white letter among a stream of black letters. The second target (T2) was the black letter X, and it occurred on only 50% of the trials. When it was present it appeared 1–8 positions after the first target.
Adapted from Harris, I. M., & Little, M. J. J. (2010). Priming the semantic neighbourhood during the attentional blink. PLOS ONE, 9/14/2010. http://dx.doi.org/10.1371/journal.pone.0012645

In the graph, the probability of detecting the T2 when it was present is plotted against the position where it occurred relative to the first target (i.e., position 1 is 80 ms after the white letter, position 2 is 160 ms after the white letter, etc.). The results show that if the subjects have to detect only T1, performance is good across all relative positions of its location. However, if both T1 and T2 are to be reported, detecting T2 (T2|T1 means the proportion of times that T2 was correctly reported given that T1 was reported correctly on the same trial) is much harder, especially in the 160 to 600 ms or so attentional blink window.
Adapted from Nieuwenstein, M., Theeuwes J., Wyble, B., & Potter, M. (2009). Temporal constraints on conscious vision: On the ubiquitous nature of the attentional blink. *Journal of Vision*, 18, 1–14.

episode, and thus report probability is high for both targets. If there are one or more intervening items between the two targets, however, the episode is unlikely to include both targets, and the second will not be selected for deeper processing. It will then be less likely to be available for later report. After the first target has been recognized and consolidated into working memory, attention is freed to examine the incoming stream for new targets. Theories such as these (Chun and Potter, 1995, Visser et al., 1999) are consistent with the U-shaped decrement in reporting the second target after the first is detected (Figure 5.10).

5.9 Brain Mechanisms of Visual Attention

5.9.1   *The Visual Pathway Revisited*

Over 50% of the primate brain is involved in visual sensation, perception, recognition, and eye movement control (see Figure 5.11). Projections from the retinas of both eyes make up the optic nerve that travels mainly to the thalamus except for a small proportion of the fibers that break off and head to the superior colliculus in the brain stem. From the lateral geniculate nuclei of the thalamus, there are projections along the optic tract to the far, back regions of the occipital lobes; an area called V1, the

FIGURE 5.11

Brain Areas Associated with Visual Processing and Visual Attention (after Posner & Raichle, 1994)

The three main centers of visual attention include the posterior parietal cortex, the pulvinar nucleus of the thalamus and the superior colliculus in the brain stem. These have respectively been identified with the disengagement of attention from the current focus of attention, the movement of attention to a new focus of attention, and the selective enhancement of attended information.

From shutterstock.com

1. Posterior parietal lobe: **Disengage**

2. Superior colliculus: **Move**

3. Pulvinar: **Enhance**

primary projection area for vision. The thalamus also receives input fibers from many parts of the cortex as well as from the cerebellum. The superior colliculus connects directly with the eye movement control centers in the brain stem and seems to be involved with rapid and automatic movements of attention and the eyes. All these visual areas, and many others, show retinotopic mapping (i.e., there is a one-to-one correspondence between areas on the retina and areas on the thalamus, superior colliculus, and area V1 in the cerebral cortex). Although these areas show distortions, mainly to reflect greater analysis of central vision near the foveal areas of the retinas, they all have a more-or-less veridical map of the visual world laid over them.

From V1, visual pathways follow to association areas in the occipital lobe, including areas labeled V2 and V3. From there, visual information follows the dorsal pathway to the parietal lobe of the brain for functions mainly related to spatial analysis and motor programming. Other pathways follow a ventral pathway to the temporal lobe for processes related to object recognition and naming (see Chapter 2; Mishkin, Ungerleider, & Macko, 1983). Further connections travel in both directions to and from the frontal lobes, including areas called the frontal eye fields that are involved in voluntary attention and direction of eye movements to specific objects and locations in space. Research has shown that activities in all of these brain areas can be modulated by attention (Braun, Koch, & Davis, 2001).

5.9.2 Neurophysiological Evidence for Attentional Effects in Vision

Although there is some controversy about whether early visual processing centers in the brain, like the thalamus and area V1 in the occipital lobe, can be influenced by attention, recent research has supported the view that attentional influences exist. For example, changes in blood flow measured using the fMRI technique can be observed when subjects alternatively view a display passively or view it in order to make some visual discrimination. Heeger, Gandhi, Huk, and Boynton (2001) used this technique while presenting a series of ring-like stripes that cycled between inward and outward movement, continuously, around a fixation point. In the passive condition, participants simply observed the display, and in an experimental condition, observers had to discriminate between subtle changes in the rings' speed of motion. Measurements of blood flow using fMRI showed that during the discrimination phase, neural activity was higher in both areas V1 and MT (the medial temporal lobe that has many cells responsive to motion) than when the same displays were viewed passively. However, it is likely that, rather than being modulated directly by attention, activity in the primary visual cortex (V1) is prepotentiated by feedback from higher-level, extrastriate areas (Hopf, Heinze, Schoenfeld, & Hillyard, 2009).

Studies using single-cell response measurements in monkeys have also indicated that individual neurons respond differently to the same stimulus when it is attended and when it is ignored. McAdams and Maunsell (1999) recorded the activities of neurons in area V4 of the occipital lobe in macaque monkeys when they viewed a display containing color patches on one side and striped patterns on the other. The monkeys were trained to look straight ahead but attend to either the left side or the right side of the display on individual trials. They then alternated between performing either a color discrimination task or an orientation discrimination task. In the color task, the monkeys were to push a lever in one direction or the other to indicate whether or not two successive color patches were the same hue. In the orientation task, they indicated whether or not two successive bands of stripes were oriented in the same direction. The important point is that on all trials, color patches and stripes were shown in the two successive displays, so that comparisons could be made of responses to the same stimuli when the monkeys were attending to the color patches or to the stripes.

McAdams and Maunsell (1999) recorded from individual cells in area V4 that they found were tuned to various orientations. That is, a cell that shows a maximum response to a stripe aligned 70 degrees clockwise from vertical, shows a diminished response to stripes aligned at 50 or 90 degrees. The same cell might actually be inhibited below its baseline rate of firing when confronted with stripes of 30 or 110-degree orientations. The important result is that all such cells showed an average increase in firing rate of 22% when the stripe discrimination task was performed as when the same stripes were presented to the same cells, but the monkeys were attending to the simultaneous color discrimination task (see also Maunsell & McAdams, 2001).

Similar studies of individual neurons' response rates in the frontal eye fields (FEFs) of monkeys have shown that these cells are involved in attentional selection and motor control. Thompson, Bichot, and Schall (2001) trained monkeys to discriminate between a colored target and an array of distractors in another color. The task for the monkeys was to fixate the uniquely colored targets on some trials (go trials) and to withhold the fixations on other trials (no-go trials). When the target item appeared in a FEF cell's receptive field, it showed a more vigorous response than when a distractor was present. The level of responding was less vigorous for both kinds of items on no-go trials than on go trials. Thompson et al. concluded that cells in the frontal eye fields show greater responses for items that are to be the targets of subsequent fixations than for similar items for which a target response has not been trained. Further, an additional increase in responding was recorded when this selection was followed by an actual eye movement than when the movement was suppressed. These results support the notion that cells in the frontal eye fields of primates, including humans, are involved both in covert orienting (selecting possible targets for subsequent inspection) and overt orienting (directing a fixation toward the selected target).

In humans, brain-imaging studies have revealed that many parts of the brain, including subcortical structures, are involved in visual attention. Endogenous, or top-down attention, seems to be controlled by executive functions of the left frontal lobe, whereas exogenous, or bottom-up attentional capture, is a function of the superior colliculus in the midbrain and projections to the parietal lobe. These roles are reflected in the hypotheses that the prefrontal cortex executes control functions for focusing on task-relevant information, whereas the posterior parietal cortex has a visual salience map; a distinction reminiscent of the top-down and bottom-up components of Wolfe's (1994) guided search model. Both frontal and parietal lobe structures seem to be involved in alerting and orienting to new stimuli, in response to inputs from the superior colliculus and the pulvinar nucleus of the thalamus. These latter structures are also involved in automatic control of eye movements to novel stimuli, thus suggesting that human attentional systems evolved from more primitive mechanisms designed for eye movement control (Baars, 2007).

Braun et al. (2001) provide a cogent summary of many studies that support the notion that attention can modulate the activity of individual neurons and concentrated populations of neurons in all known visual centers of the brain. Traditionally, early brain imaging studies identified different aspects of attention with widely divergent cortical processes. That is, alerting is presumably signaled by activity in the frontal and parietal lobes, primarily in the right hemisphere, orienting is associated with activity in the superior parietal lobes, the temporal-parietal junction, and the frontal eye fields, and executive control is maintained by the anterior cingulate and lateral prefrontal cortex. Certain automatic responses that influence attention, like orienting to a highly salient stimulus, are mediated subcortically (e.g., by the superior colliculi) (Carrasco, 2011; Knudsen, 2007; Posner & Petersen, 1990). Some of these changes are due to hard-wired systems that have evolved to alert us to important changes in the environment, others are due to learned associations between simple stimulus patterns and arbitrary responses. It is clear that attention is a highly-evolved mechanism for enhancing neural responses to important stimuli while inhibiting responses to stimuli that are irrelevant in a given context (Tsotsos, Culhane, & Cutzu, 2001).

Attention also seems to affect different cortical areas when it is directed to spatial locations and when it is directed to specific features or objects in the field of view, regardless of their location. Spatial attention has its effects earlier both in time and in levels of the visual system than feature-based attention, particularly when signaled by an external, peripheral cue. Exogenous cues can result in enhanced signal processing in the cued area, and suppressed responses to noise in the areas surrounding the target that peak at about 100 to 120 ms after the cue. However, these responses are transient, and the attentional response can dissipate and even be suppressed in the cued area, a phenomenon known as inhibition of return (Posner & Cohen, 1984). Desimone and Duncan (1995) formulated the biased-competition hypothesis to describe attentional effects at many levels of the visual system. Within any level, neurons associated with the cued location are activated, whereas neurons with receptive fields in adjacent areas are inhibited. Therefore, one of the primary roles of spatial attention is to increase the signal-to-noise ratio by enhancing signal processing while also excluding external noise in the target region—in effect, setting up spatial filters. Attention has also been shown to increase the amplitude of neural impulses in attended regions, as well as to increase the synchronization of neural responses in successive layers of the visual system tuned to the target location (Fries, Reynolds, Rovie, & Desimone, 2001). The result is that attended regions appear as if they are brighter and more salient than unattended areas.

Feature-based attention, on the other hand, is more likely to be based on endogenous cues related to basic visual primitives, such as color, orientation, and direction of motion. Attending to different features can modulate activity in cortical areas specialized for processing those dimensions (Carrasco, 2011). That is, attending to motion results in enhanced activity in the medial-temporal region (MT), color results in modulation in extra-striate areas V4 and V8, and orientation affects responses in V1 and V2. Bichot, Rossi, and Desimone (2005) showed that individual neurons in monkey cortex responded more strongly to an attended feature presented to their receptive fields than when the same feature was shown but not attended. Similarly, aftereffects resulting from prolonged exposure to specific colors, orientations, and motion directions are stronger when the relevant features are attended than when they are viewed but not attended. Furthermore, feature-based attention "… has the remarkable property that its effects are not constrained to the locations of the stimuli that are voluntarily attended; they spread across space" (Carrasco. 2011, p. 1510). Neuronal modulations have even been observed in cells responding to spatial locations where no stimuli are present (McManis, Fehd, Emmanouil, & Kastner, 2007; Serences & Yantis, 2007). Even when observers are directed to attend to one or the other visual hemifield, brain activity to items presented to the unattended field show larger responses if they match the feature attended on the other side. Further, the motion aftereffect can be found in non-adapted areas of the visual field (Arman, Ciaramitaro, & Boynton, 2006), indicating wide-spread selection for relevant visual features.

These results affirm the main assertion held by modern theories of attention—it is not a unitary construct that can be identified with a simple underlying brain mechanism. Further, attentional effects can be found both far and wide in the visual field as well as in its various cortical representations.

Chapter Summary

Attention apparently serves a dual purpose in enabling us to perform many complex tasks in a noisy environment. First, it selects items of importance, either for the task at hand or because they are of potential significance for survival (e.g., sudden onsets of new objects or events). Second, it monitors the capacity and focus of working memory to prevent us from being overloaded with information and incapable of responding appropriately. Attention is guided by endogenous strategies and goals as well as exogenous alerts from the environment. Attention also seems to serve as a binding process that unites the various features of an object into a holistic representation when attention is focused on its location. Neurophysiological studies of attention have shown that it can affect most cerebral processes by priming relevant channels and inhibiting irrelevant ones for the task at hand. Attention has truly evolved as the gateway to consciousness, as envisioned by James.

Review Questions

- **Is there one kind of attention, or does attention do different things in different situations?**

  Although attention has been defined as the gateway to consciousness, it does not appear to be a unitary concept. Attention can select things from the environment based on different information, such as an item's location, size, color, loudness or pitch. We can look for red items in a drawer or listen for a flute in a symphony. Further, attention can be distributed over space and time, as certain objects or locations are processed to the exclusion of others, and certain events are selected and processed more deeply than preceding or following ones. Finally, attention can be goal-directed and under conscious control, or it can be captured automatically by salient objects or events in the environment, especially abrupt onsets of new stimuli.

- **What is the purpose of attention? How does it help us to deal with the outside world?**

  The main purpose of attention is to maintain conscious awareness of objects and events of current interest or importance, including those important for survival. It is an obvious fact that both the physical environment and the contents of memory contain far more information than we can process at any one time. Further, information in both of these sources varies greatly in their current importance values. Attention serves to select and maintain a small set of important information in conscious, working memory so that we can direct our limited central processing capacity to the task at hand. Still, attention can and must be diverted to important changes in the environment so tasks can be interrupted when necessary. It does us no good to carry on a clever conversation while driving if we do not notice the truck crossing into our lane.

- **Does attention change over space and time, or does it follow where we are looking and our current level of alertness?**

  Since attention controls the contents of working memory, it is likely to be the driving force behind selection of where to look next or when to listen for a critical sound. It is also more likely that attention directs eye movements as attention can shift to new objects or locations in the visual field within 50 to 150 ms, whereas the response latency of an eye movement to a visual target is around 250 ms. Attention presumably examines the periphery for items of interest and then guides eye movements to those locations one at a time.

- **Can we learn something without paying attention to it?**

  Although information can be selected by attention or even bypass attentional processing and automatically activate representations in long-term memory, it is believed that learning is something different. The learning of new information involves a structural change or addition to information in long-term memory, not merely the activation of existing memories. Of course there are different kinds of memories, and some of these can be acquired without attention, such as the implicit learning of certain motor skills, but the storage and retention of real life events and encyclopedic knowledge of the world seems to be laid down through conscious processing in working memory, and its contents are determined by attention.

- **What changes in brain activity can be observed as attention changes from one focus to another?**

  Just about all areas of the brain involved with perception can have their levels of activity modulated by attention. Attention to a stimulus can enhance the neural activity measured by ERPs or fMRI at the earliest stages of perceptual analysis (i.e., at the primary sensory projection areas of the cortex), and it can result in inhibition of the neural activity associated with brain areas responding to unattended information. It is likely that excitation and inhibition of sensory channels reflects the selective aspect of attention to direct important information to deeper processes of analysis while attempting to filter out unwanted or irrelevant information. Attention has also been shown to modulate brain activity in the dorsal pathway, leading to object selection by location, and in the ventral pathway, leading to object selection by features, such as color or orientation. Finally, selection of objects for inspection is indicated by activity in the frontal lobes of the brain known to control voluntary eye movements; thus, all major lobes of the cerebral cortex show modifications of their activities by changes in attention.

Key Terms

Area MT   134

Attentional blink (AB)   140

Attention   118

Conjunction search   129

Consciousness   119

Endogenous attention   126

Exogenous   126

Feature search   129

Filter theory of attention   120

Illusory conjunctions   129

Inhibition-deficit hypothesis   119

Lavie's perceptual load theory   131

Preattentive stage   126

RSVP (rapid, serial visual presentation)   138

Vigilance   138

ALAN BADDELEY

Wikimedia Commons
From Alan Baddeley

Chapter 6
Short- versus Long-Term Memories

"An object which is recollected … [from secondary memory] … is one which has been absent from consciousness altogether, and now arrives anew. It is brought back, recalled, fished up, so to speak, from a reservoir in which, with countless other objects, it lay buried and lost from view. But an object of primary memory is not thus brought back; it never was lost; its date was never cut off in consciousness from that of the immediately present moment."

(William James, 1890–1952, pp. 646–647)

PREVIEW QUESTIONS

❖ *What differences are there between memory over the short term and memory for the distant past?*

❖ *Is there any evidence that short- and long-term memories are stored and accessed differently?*

❖ *Why do we forget some things that happened just a short time ago?*

❖ *What is amnesia, and how is it different from ordinary forgetting?*

❖ *Are there any differences between memory for words and memory for pictures, objects, and scenes?*

6.1 Introduction to the Theory of Two Memory Systems

William James was among the first to argue for the existence of different kinds of memory systems. In his classic work, *Principles of Psychology*, he distinguished between **primary memory**, which for him held the current contents of consciousness, and **secondary memory**, which included all other memories. Further, as Ebbinghaus (1885) had shown, the contents of primary memory are severely limited. Maintaining

Primary memory A term used by James to describe the current contents of consciousness; the terms short-term memory (STM) or working memory are more commonly used today for similar concepts of a limited-capacity immediate memory

Secondary memory A term used by James to describe all other memories, from which retrieval is sometimes difficult and always uncertain; the term long-term memory (LTM) is more commonly used today for the more-or-less permanent and practically infinite storage system for all our knowledge

Encoding The process of representing external stimuli by internal codes for possible entry into STM

Retrieval The process of finding codes in LTM and entering them into STM

Retrograde amnesia The loss of memory for information learned prior to some traumatic event

Anterograde amnesia The loss of ability to form new memories after some traumatic event

about seven or so items in conscious awareness is about as difficult for the average person as keeping a large number of balls aloft is for a skilled juggler. As with the act of juggling, which uses the hands to increase the altitude of some balls while others fall, active rehearsal promotes the memory strength of some items, while others fade until they can be rehearsed again or are forgotten (as when we try to remember a telephone number between looking it up and tapping the key pad). Although the contents of secondary memory are, by definition, not currently conscious, they can potentially be recalled into consciousness. However, such recall requires effort, and retrieval can be fraught with uncertainty, just as the juggler wishing to change balls might encounter difficulty while reaching into a bag filled with objects searching for one in particular.

The distinction between the current contents of consciousness and other memories that can be recalled into conscious awareness was formalized in the Atkinson-Shiffrin theory (see Box 1.4, Chapter 1). Current terminology has replaced primary memory with short-term (or working) memory, to be distinguished from the much larger and more permanent secondary memory (or long-term memory) containing everything that we have ever learned. Rehearsal of material in short-term memory is the mechanism, in their theory, for maintaining information while copies are stored in long-term memory. Similarly, **encoding** and **retrieval** are processes that select information from the environment or activate information in long-term memory, respectively, for entry into short-term memory. The distinction between short- and long-term memories has been gleaned from various sources. Although James relied on introspection to convince himself that primary and secondary memories are different, the Atkinson-Shiffrin theory relied primarily on experiments involving people's abilities to remember lists of letters, digits, nonsense syllables, or words. Finally, there is a convincing set of evidence from neuroscience that supports the separation between short- and long-term memories.

6.2 Evidence from Cognitive Neuroscience for Short- and Long-Term Memories

6.2.1 Anterograde and Retrograde Amnesia

There have been many reports in the literature for a type of amnesia, or loss of memory for certain recent events, following brain injury, surgery, or trauma. In these cases, memories for the more distant past might remain fairly intact, whereas information for events that occurred just before or after the trauma might be forgotten. Memory losses include **retrograde amnesia** (loss of memory for events preceding the incident) and **anterograde amnesia** (loss of ability to learn some new things after the injury or trauma). This latter type of disability has been popularized in some recent movies (e.g., *Memento, Finding Nemo,* and *50 First Dates*). The most famous case of amnesia resulted from surgery and was reported by Milner and her colleagues

(Corkin, 1984; Milner, Corkin, & Teuber, 1968; Scoville & Milner, 1957). These published reports detailed the unfortunate results observed in patient H.M. following surgery for intractable epilepsy.

6.2.2 Amnesia in Patient H.M

Epilepsy is a seizure disorder that sometimes responds to drug therapy. Unfortunately, in some patients, the disorder is so severe and unresponsive to treatment that surgery to remove the focus of the seizures in the brain is sometimes considered. In these cases, the quality of life without surgery has to be compared with the consequences of the proposed treatment. In H.M.'s case, the consequences were unknown as the epilepsy had a bilateral locus in the medial temporal region (i.e., the **hippocampus** and adjoining temporal lobe structures were involved on both sides of the brain.) Removal of these structures in monkeys reportedly showed no severe memory or behavioral deficits (Parker, Easton, & Gaffan, 2002). Moreover, H.M.'s epilepsy was so severe and disabling that he consented to risk the uncertain consequences and underwent surgery.

The immediate results of the surgery seemed to indicate that it was a success— H.M. showed almost complete recovery from epilepsy. He also showed normal vision, object recognition, language skills, and above average intelligence (even somewhat higher than before surgery!). However, he suffered from retrograde amnesia, retaining little memory for anything that had happened for a period of about 2 years before the surgery. Even more devastating, however, was his almost complete inability to learn anything new (i.e., he showed anterograde amnesia as well). Although he could engage in a conversation and participate in various tasks given to him, each conversation, each memory of someone he met, or the activities he engaged in on any day were lost as soon as they were gone from immediate attention. It is as though long-term memory (at least for some period before surgery) and short-term memory for the immediate present are intact in H.M., but there is no remaining mechanism for the transfer of new memories from a short- to a long-term store. There is no new learning of people, events, and places experienced after the surgery despite H.M.'s apparently normal perception and responses. These results indicated that short- and long-term memory systems are separate and can be completely isolated in individuals with a missing or damaged hippocampus (see Figure 6.1).

Despite obvious memory difficulties, H.M. did manage to demonstrate some skills learning even without remembrance of the tasks or his participation in them. For example, he was asked each day to copy geometric forms while viewing an image of his hand in a mirror. His performance in this mirror-drawing task improved steadily, despite his lack of memory for ever having done the task before. From these results it was concluded that the hippocampal area of the medial temporal lobe is important for transferring only certain memories from short-term memory to permanent storage. These memories include memories for people, places, events, and vocabulary items (usually called **declarative memories**). However, certain other behaviors, such as

Hippocampus Small, curved structures on either side of the thalamus that are part of the medial temporal lobes of the cortex; they seem to be of fundamental importance to the learning and permanent consolidation of new long-term (declarative) memories

Declarative memory Memory for concepts and events that have been stored in long-term memory and can be consciously retrieved and described verbally; typically divided into semantic memory (for words and concepts) and episodic memory (for life-time events), as described in Chapter 7

FIGURE 6.1

Hippocampus and MRI Brain Scan of Patient H.M.

(a) A drawing of a section along the lateral midline of the brain with the left lobe of the hippocampus intact; the dotted line represents the location of the missing, overlying left temporal lobe (b) A photograph of a human brain with the left cerebral cortex removed revealing the hippocampus as it wraps around the top and rear of the thalamus before disappearing below it (c) An MRI scan of H.M.'s brain in three successive "slices" from more anterior to more posterior, showing the large lesions (dark areas) on either side of the central thalamus where tissue has been surgically removed

From Kalat, J. W. (2007). *Biological Psychology*, 9th Ed. Belmont, CA: Thomson Wadsworth, p. 391.

(a)

Corpus callosum
Thalamus
Offactory bulb
Offactory tract
Mamillary body
Left temporal lobe
Hippocampus

(b)

Cerebral cortex
Thalamus
Horizontal section through left posterior cerebrai cortex
Hippocampus

(c)

Location of the missing hippocampus

perceptual-motor skills, can be learned, but often without any awareness of exactly what is being learned (usually called **procedural memories**).

H.M.'s case is not unique, as other instances of temporal lobe damage have been reported with similar devastating memory effects. For example, Clive Wearing was a young musician who suffered a severe case of viral encephalitis in 1985 that destroyed brain areas similar to those removed surgically in patient H.M. He retains many memories of people and events from the time before his illness, and he can competently play the piano from sheet music and carry on an intelligent conversation. He is, however, completely incapable of learning anything new and seems to live eternally in the present. His notes and phone messages indicate that he continually feels as if he has just awakened from a sleep or mental fog and is perplexed about what is happening to him. Anything from which he is distracted appears to be completely lost from memory (Moscovitch, Chein, Talmi, & Cohn, 2007; Wearing, 2005). A similar case has recently been described by Foer (2007), in which a patient known as E.P. suffered brain damage due to a herpes simplex infection. Although the infection destroyed his medial temporal lobes and adjacent structures in 1992, his memories of the past include events only up to about 1960. He can recall his childhood, his service in the merchant marine, and events that occurred in World War II, but he cannot recall what happened a few minutes ago or the names or faces of researchers who visit him nearly every day to test his memory.

Procedural memory Memory for sensory-motor skills and other behaviors that have been learned and can be retrieved without conscious awareness

6.2.3 The Role of the Hippocampus in Memory Consolidation

Since damage to the hippocampus prevents certain kinds of learning, one should consider which aspect of learning is affected by this damage. The argument is that failure to remember something could be due to (1) inadequate storage, (2) failure to consolidate a memory after it is stored, or (3) failure to retrieve it at an appropriate time. Simply failing to remember something does not pinpoint the locus of the failure. Because people like H.M., Clive Wearing, and E.P. are able to perform short-term memory tasks as long as they maintain attention to them, the hippocampus does not seem to be necessary for most types of short-term memory processes per se. Therefore, initial encoding operations necessary for storage are presumably intact.

Research using single-cell recordings in the hippocampal region in animals has shown that individual cells respond to very specific spatial and temporal components of a task that is being learned. For example, as a rat learns to run through a maze, certain hippocampal cells fire when the rat is at specific positions or after specific relevant events have occurred (Eichenbaum, 2002). The hippocampus seems to be involved in storing components of complex episodes, but it is not the site where the episodes themselves are stored. Rather, the circuitry that connects the hippocampus to many parts of the cortex seems most likely to be involved in re-establishing memories as each component is activated whenever some event is experienced again. Therefore, its principal role in memory might be to consolidate memories by recirculating them among various cortical sites involved in their more permanent storage (Eichenbaum, Dudchenko, Wood, Shapiro, & Tanila, 1999). Without proper consolidation, which might take a considerable amount of time, certain memories are transient, and eventually will not be available for recall. Such a lack of consolidation could explain certain types of retrograde amnesia for events occurring before a traumatic brain injury.

6.3 The Limits of Short-Term, Working Memory

6.3.1 Miller's Magical Number Seven (Plus or Minus Two).

In 1956, George Miller wrote a famous paper in which he claimed that, "… I have been persecuted by an integer. For seven years it has followed me around, has intruded in my most private data, and has assaulted me from the pages of our most public journals" (p. 81). What he was asserting was that numerous tasks that people do every day show a certain limit, or channel capacity, of about seven items, letters, digits, categories, or, conventionally, chunks of information. We can more-or-less accurately sort things into seven categories, more-or-less reliably use a seven-point rating scale, and usually report back about seven simple characters (letters or digits) after a single presentation. All of the research methods and data that Miller reviewed indicated to him that there is some fundamental capacity limitation for people's abilities to handle information. Anything more than about seven chunks overtaxes our capacity and leads to errors in performance. Why else are local telephone numbers seven digits long and not eight, if not to prevent a continuing plague of wrong numbers?

According to Miller, the only way that this capacity can be exceeded in practice is to learn some way to increase the size of the chunks. If more information could be packed into a chunk, such as by combining letters into an acronym or word, then the higher-order words could be rehearsed in short-term memory, and unpacked later to recover their original letters. For example, a shopping list of milk, onions, lettuce, tomatoes, eggs, napkins, liquid soap, alfalfa sprouts, vegetable oil, and apples could be stored as the words "molten lava" and (hopefully) unpacked correctly at the grocery store.

Of course, one could always jot down a shopping list, but there are other situations in which referring to lists is inconvenient or unacceptable, such as in going through a set of arguments in a speech or recalling some information in an examination.

6.3.2 An Example of Chunking

I (JJ) attended a conference about 35 years ago in which Bill Chase presented some research results from a memory experiment (see Chase & Ericsson, 1982). The task he used was a simple one, called an immediate memory test. It consists of a sequence of digits read by the experimenter, and then the subject attempts to recall them in the order in which they were read. The results are sometimes used to measure the so-called memory span, which again, is about seven, plus or minus two, for most people. Chase played a tape recording during the meeting that proceeded somewhat as follows: "Repeat after me … 2, 5, 3, 7, 7, 9, 4, 3, 2, 8, 6, 6, 5, 1, 7, 0, 5, 4 …" and so on, continuing at the rate of about one digit per second for a long time. After hearing the first nine or so digits on the recording, there was an uncomfortable restlessness in the audience, followed by talking and laughter as the sequence continued until the experimenter finally stopped. This was followed by the sound of the subject's voice, who after a short hesitation, began to say, "2, 5, 3, 7, 7, … 9, 4, 3 …" and so on, emitting the digits in small groups followed by hesitations. Of course, no one in the audience could possibly have known whether the subject was recalling them correctly or not. Chase assured us that his subject generally recalled lists of random digits accurately for sequences of up to about 80 digits!

What could lead anyone to accomplish such an astounding feat of immediate memory? Chase and Ericsson's subject was no savant, but rather a well-trained student of a particular memory skill. That is, he had learned to chunk individual items into groups that were organized into a structure that could later be recalled and unpacked. The training had gone on for many hours a week for many weeks, during which time the person's apparent memory span gradually increased a few digits at a time. It turns out that their subject was an athlete whose speciality was running. He used the technique of chunking each set of three to five or so digits into a particular time or distance for track and field events, such as converting the first five numbers into 2 hours, 53 minutes and 77 seconds—a good time for a 50 km road race. The next step was to imagine the sequence of events as a large track meet, which served both to set down the order of the chunked times and distances and to recall them again by remembering the order of the events in the track meet. Although this sounds improbably complicated, the facts stand on their own as an example of how a particular mnemonic (memory-aid) device can lead to amazing feats of memory after many hours of practice.

A further demonstration that the technique of Chase and Ericsson's subject was based on the track meet model was its lack of generality to different materials.

Indeed, when confronted with a set of random letters from the alphabet, the skilled memorizer of lists of up to 80 digits could only recall seven, plus or minus two, letters, much like anyone else!

6.3.3   *The Generality of Capacity Limitations*

Miller (1956) intended his magical number to be a limit on more than just the span of immediate memory. Rather, he claimed that it represented an upper limit on just about anything that we try to maintain in active, working memory. For example, studies of absolute judgments of loudness of a tone or its pitch, the heaviness of a weight, or the concentrations of salt in water all show similar results. People are quite accurate if the number of discriminable categories is four or five. However, as the number of categories increases to seven or more, mistakes in absolute judgments are common, such that the same stimulus (e.g., a certain weight or a specific salt concentration) is not reliably judged in the same category on separate presentations. Similarly in studies of "subitizing," or reporting the number of spots in a brief display, people seldom make errors in judging the number if there are about six or fewer spots. If more are shown, however, they must be presented long enough for people to count them, or errors are routinely observed.

These and other observations led Miller to believe that there is a fundamental limit to working memory capacity, and tasks that exceed this limit inevitably lead to diminished performance. This limit has been with us throughout history as exemplified by "… the seven wonders of the world, the seven deadly sins … the seven ages of man, the seven levels of hell, the seven primary colors, the seven notes of the scale, and the seven days of the week" (Miller, 1956, p. 97).

6.4 **Retrieval and Forgetting in Short-Term Memory**

6.4.1   *Retrieval from Working Memory Takes Measurable Time*

One aspect of primary memory pointed out by James was its sense of immediacy—that its contents could be recovered without effort. In other words, it might be assumed that the contents of working memory are automatically available to consciousness. Sternberg (1966, see Box 1.1 in Chapter 1) showed that the contents of short-memory are by no means accessible all at once. Rather, the time to confirm that something is in working memory is a linear, increasing function of the number of similar items in memory (at least for fewer than seven items). Again, our introspections on this point are not quite accurate, and it goes without saying that consciousness and working memory should not be thought of as equivalent concepts (see Chapter 12).

6.4.2 Forgetting in the Brown-Peterson Task

Another limitation on short-term memory was revealed by a seminal codiscovery by Brown (1958) and by Peterson and Peterson (1959). They were interested in studying forgetting from short-term memory, which sounds like an oxymoron since the contents of working memory are, by definition, available and not forgotten. In order to cause forgetting, the **Brown-Peterson paradigm** makes use of a concurrent task to eliminate rehearsal processes in working memory. For example, a short list of items (say the letters BVK) is presented to start a trial. Then, a distracting task is used for a few seconds, before the observer is asked to repeat the three letters. Peterson and Peterson (1959) asked their subjects to count backwards (by threes) from a given three-digit number to begin the retention interval. The length of the counting task was varied from trial to trial so that sometimes the letters were to be recalled almost immediately, and on other trials, as much as 18 seconds of counting time could elapse before the subject was asked to recall the letters.

Not surprisingly, the counting task had a deleterious effect on memory. Although almost anyone can reliably repeat three letters immediately after hearing them, counting backwards for 5, 10, or 15 seconds resulted in a tremendous drop in performance in their experiment. Averaging over many trials and subjects, Peterson and Peterson found that recall accuracy dropped to about 10% after 18 seconds (see Figure 6.3). One aspect of these data seized the imagination of psychologists who believed that there were fundamental differences between short- and long-term memories. That is, it appeared that forgetting in short-term memory followed a spontaneous decay function, unlike forgetting in long-term memory, which was supposedly due almost exclusively to interference (see Box 6.1). The argument was that

Brown-Peterson paradigm An experimental procedure designed to study forgetting in short-term memory by preventing the subjects from rehearsing the material during the retention interval; usually done by having them do a rehearsal-prevention task, such as counting backwards aloud

FIGURE 6.2

Forgetting in the Brown-Peterson Task

The data (Peterson & Peterson, 1959) show the mean proportion of consonant trigrams that were recalled correctly as a function of the recall interval. The recall intervals were filled with a counting backward task that prevented rehearsal. With immediate recall (0 seconds of counting) recall was almost 90% correct, but it rapidly fell to about 10% correct after 15 seconds of counting.
From Lachman, R., Lachman, J. L. and Butterfield, E. C. (1979). *Cognitive Psychology and Information Processing: An Introduction.* Hillsdale, NJ: Earlbaum, p. 247.

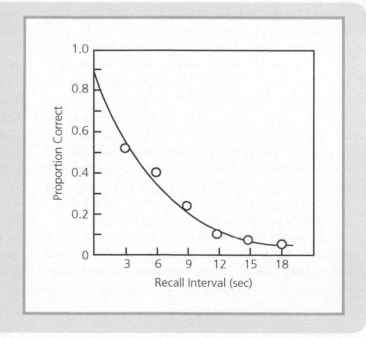

BOX 6.1

The Interference Theory of Forgetting

It is clear that we forget many things every day, from where our keys are to what appointments we have coming up. There is no need to go into things like what we had for breakfast 11 days ago or what score we had on our third spelling test in second grade. Yet, the dominant theory of forgetting for the past 75 years is based on what sounds like an absurd assumption: Nothing is every really forgotten, but rather, some memories might be inaccessible at a particular time (Bower, 1966; McGeoch, 1932).

In fact, it is very difficult to prove that some past event has been forgotten. Simply being unable to recall something could be due to a temporary problem with accessibility. That is, it is impossible to determine whether a retrieval failure is due to an actual loss of memory or merely to a momentary loss of access. Any given fact or event, if not recalled at once, might be recalled at a later time or if a better retrieval cue is given. The interference theory of forgetting was developed to explain why access to something stored in memory could be temporarily blocked.

McGeoch's (1932) theory was discussed in the terms of his day, in which all learning was thought to be reducible to simple associations. We can think of A as any stimulus and B as any response that might have become associated with A through repeated pairings. Thus, A-B is a simple stimulus-response association, such as day-night or red-flag, and other associations that we could bring to mind. Association learning can be studied in the laboratory by preparing lists of paired-associate words, such as dog-ball, house-tree, etc., that are presented for study. The task is then to later recall the B term when given the A term, such as "dog-__." This procedure is called cued recall because, unlike free recall tests in which no cues are given, the word originally studied as the first member of each pair is given as a cue to recall the second member. The A-B list can be studied for arbitrary lengths of time or until cued recall is perfect, and then memory can be tested at a later date.

If cued recall is not perfect, interference theory accounts for failures by asserting that the learned association (A-B) must not be as strong as some other association (A-C) learned at some other time. There are undoubtedly extra-experimental associations among words that might intrude on the ones specifically learned in the laboratory, as in the examples used above, a more likely response to dog would be "cat," and to house, "home" if the studied responses could not be recalled.

In the laboratory, interference theory has been tested using experimental designs specifically set up to produce forgetting. These are of two types:

(1) learn A-B, learn A-C, test A-B

(2) learn A-C, learn A-B, test A-B

These are to be compared with the control condition: learn A-B, test A-B. The interesting result is that both experimental conditions produce poorer performance than the control condition. In condition (1), associations acquired after original learning interfere with recovering the earlier associations, producing what is called retroactive interference (RI). In condition (2), associations learned prior to learning the A-B associations interfere with their recovery, producing proactive interference (PI).

Years of research have shown that almost all forgetting that occurs in long-term memory can be explained by the presence of competing associations between some stimulus situation and a set of possible responses (Bower, 1966). Any stimulus produces a host of associations learned separately or in combination over one's lifetime. Recall is often then a search for the correct association among many possible candidates. Imagine running into a familiar person at a party, but you are not sure if you have met before. Trying to recall a person's name after seeing him or her for the first time in years is likely to produce a wrong answer if an interfering incorrect association is available, or a lack of response if no associations are strong enough to retrieve into conscious awareness. Interestingly enough, if the person says, "Remember me? I'm Sarah Jones," one is likely to reply, "Of course I remember," and be telling the truth. Providing the correct association is enough to raise its strength above the level of competing associations and eliminate the effects of interference.

since counting backwards should not interfere with memory (letters and digits are so different, how could they interfere with each other in memory?), counting serves only to prevent rehearsal. Without rehearsal, the contents of short-term memory are not refreshed, so they **decay** with time until they are gone (in 18 sec or so). Long-term memories are thought not to decay with time, so the type of forgetting process is one of the differences between the two types of memory.

6.4.3 *Is Forgetting Due to Decay or Interference?*

It was not long before researchers began to challenge the idea that forgetting followed different rules in short- and long-term memories. Some people thought that attributing forgetting in short-term memory to spontaneous decay was unacceptable. It is an empty theory, because it provides no mechanism other than the passage of time. It is as though one were to explain that what happens to an iron nail left in the back garden for a year is due to the passage of time, or that if I drop my pencil, the passage of time causes it to eventually hit the floor. Saying "decay" instead of the passage of time is no help, since an iron nail rusts through a process of oxidation, and a dropped pencil hits the floor due to gravitational attraction towards the center of the earth. Even tooth decay and radioactive decay are based on physical processes with known causes and time courses. Decay, in most cases, is another word for an unknown or unspecified mechanism that acts over time (Bower, 1966).

A direct attack on the question of what happens to information in short-term memory over time was made by Waugh and Norman in 1965. They had subjects listen to a sequence of 15 random digits that was followed by a single probe digit. When the probe digit was heard, the subjects were to report which digit had been presented after the first occurrence of the probe. That is, in the sequence: "2, 4, 7, 6, 8, 4 ..." followed by the probe "7," the correct answer is "6" since it occurred after the first 7. Waugh and Norman varied the rate of presentation of the digit sequence, arguing that if short-term memory decays over time, then only the elapsed time, and not the number of digits presented, should affect performance. On the other hand, if each succeeding digit interferes with memory for previous ones, then the number of digits, and not the amount of time passed, should determine performance. The results of their experiment were clear: memory performance depended only on the number of intervening digits presented before the probe and its matching number, not the amount of elapsed time. This result clearly supports **interference** as an explanatory mechanism rather than the passage of time alone; the more events that occur in a given amount of time, the greater the amount of forgetting.

A similar experimental attack was waged on the results of the Brown-Peterson task itself. Keppel and Underwood (1962) refused to believe that the task was free from interference, and they designed a clever experiment to prove their case. They used a similar procedure in which three letters were presented to be remembered, and then the participants counted backwards by threes until told to stop counting

Decay theory of forgetting
A theory of forgetting in which information in memory is supposed to spontaneously decrease as time passes

Interference theory of forgetting A theory of forgetting in which information is made more difficult to retrieve due to the destructive effects of similar information that gets in the way during memory search and decision processes and recall the letters. However, their subjects participated in only three trials, rather than the long series of trials as in the Brown-Peterson studies. The data from these three trials, in which different groups of subjects counted for 3, 9, or 18 seconds before recalling the letters is shown in Figure 6.3. As you can see, the data show that everyone was very good at recalling the letters on the first trial, but performance fell on trials two and three. Further, in the second and third trials, performance also was worse the longer subjects counted, from 9 to 18 seconds. Clearly, something is happening across trials in the Brown-Peterson task, but what is it?

Keppel and Underwood argued that performance on the first trial was very good regardless of how long subjects were counting because the letters were unique—they were the only things presented to be remembered in the experiment thus far. On the second and third trials, however, the presentation of more letters destroyed this uniqueness, and the task changed to one in which the *most recently presented letters* had to be recalled when counting was halted. This confusion between the most recent items and others not quite so recent is a classic component of the interference theory of forgetting. The more things that are stored away in similar places in memory (because they are similar in content and they occurred in a similar context), the less likely it is that the correct ones will be recalled. The negative effect of prior items on recall of the most recent ones is called **proactive interference (PI)**, and the amount of this interference should increase as more trials are presented. This is exactly the result that Keppel and Underwood found.

Proactive interference (PI) The negative effects of information learned at some prior time on learning and retention of later information

---

FIGURE 6.3

Forgetting in the Keppel and Underwood (1962) Experiment

The data are the average number of consonant trigrams recalled correctly after 3, 9, or 18 seconds of counting backward. Unlike the Peterson and Peterson (1959) experiment, which continued for many trials, Keppel and Underwood examined the data from the first three trials only from different subjects in each retention interval group.

From Adams, J. A., (1967). *Human Memory.* New York: McGraw-Hill, p. 115.

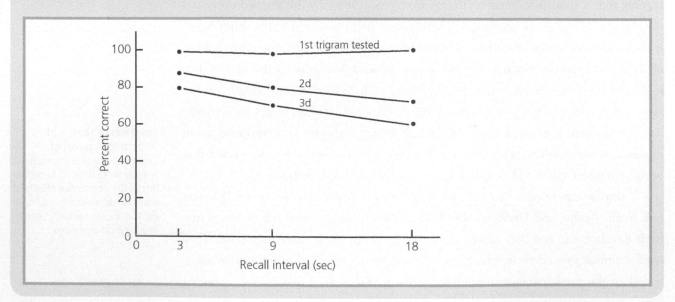

The counting backwards task was designed to prevent rehearsal, and it was thought that since digits and letters are not so readily confusable, any forgetting caused by counting would be due to decay, and not due to interference from counting. However, the fact that counting digits and rehearsing letters are both verbal tasks means that they cannot occur together without interference. This kind of interference of one task acting backward to reduce performance on prior information is called **retroactive interference (RI)**. Thus, Keppel and Underwood argued that the Brown-Peterson task resulted in forgetting from both RI and PI, just as these interference mechanisms produce forgetting in long-term memory.

Retroactive interference (RI) The negative effects of information recently learned on retrieval of information learned earlier

6.4.4   *Wickens's "Release from PI" Demonstration*

Another demonstration that forgetting in the Brown-Peterson task is due to proactive interference is the "release from PI" research by Wickens and his colleagues (e.g., Wickens, Born, & Allen, 1963). In their research, subjects were presented with groups of three words to remember on each trial before being given a number from which to count backwards. In order to study a build-up of PI, the words were specifically chosen from a common semantic category, such as fruit. Thus, the first trial might consist of the words "orange, peach, pineapple ... 547," to which the subject was to reply "547, 544, 541 ..." and so on until asked to recall the words. Naturally, recall was fairly high on the first trial. On the second trial, the subject was given the words "apple, grape, melon ... 632," and so on. As Keppel and Underwood had demonstrated, performance deteriorated over the first several trials due to an assumed build-up of PI. That is, the names of fruit were stored in long-term memory as the counting task eliminated any representation in short-term memory. Then, because fruit names are all related members of a single category, they would be stored in similar ways and places, and the task would be to pick out the most recent fruits from an expanding set of recently experienced fruit names.

The new manipulation introduced by Wickens was to change the category of the words on the fourth trial for half of the subjects while maintaining the same word category for the other half. If interference in memory is due to storing similar things in similar places so that it is hard to tell what occurred most recently, a change in categories would result in the most recent items being stored differently in memory. Therefore, there should be less PI for new-category items ("goat, bird, fish....727"). This is exactly the result Wickens found (see Figure 6.4). In fact, the greater the difference in word category for the items presented on the fourth trial from those presented on the previous three, the greater the improvement in performance (the amount of release from PI).

FIGURE 6.4

Release from Proactive Interference: The Wickens (Wickens, Dalezman, Eggemeier, & Thomas, 1976) Paradigm

Five groups of subjects participated in a Brown-Peterson short-term memory task. The items to be recalled were three words from the same category (e.g., fruits). Performance decreased across trials presumably due to a build-up of PI. On the fourth trial, the experimental groups received three words from a new category (i.e., professions, meats, flowers, and vegetables), whereas the control group received three more fruit names. The experimental groups demonstrated release from PI, at least for the categories that differed substantially from fruits.

From Willingham, D. T. (2004). *Cognition.* Upper Saddle River, NJ: Pearson, p. 158.

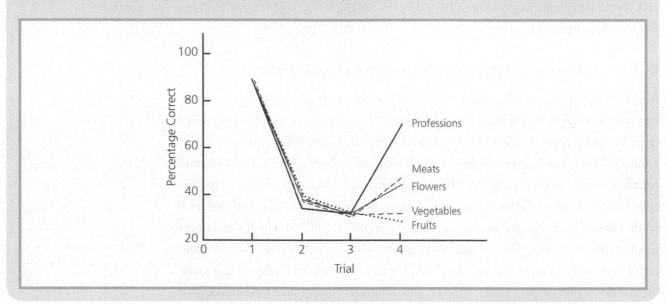

6.4.5 *PI and RI in Everyday Things*

Each of us has sometimes purchased or borrowed a new cell phone or computer and been stuck for a moment about exactly how to operate it. The natural assumption is that it should work just like the previous one, but often it does not. In this case, we are experiencing PI, or a type of negative transfer from our previous experience with a similar device to the new one we are working with. Any differences in keyboard layout, command sequences, menu options, and passwords are likely to lead to errors until the new system in mastered. In fact, if PI is great enough, we might even find ourselves making more mistakes than a novice user of the system. Later, after some time of using the new device, we might find ourselves using the old system again. We are then likely to have a new problem—the practice with the intervening system has resulted in new patterns of behavior that now might be incompatible with the old system. Then, we would be experiencing RI—the negative effect of our most recent experience on recovering something that we had learned before. I often experience such transfer problems when I switch between my PC at home and my iPad at work. Whenever we find interference between what we are trying to do and something else that we have learned, the interference is most likely either PI or RI.

6.5 Rehearsal and Retrieval in Long-Term Memory

6.5.1 Recalling Lists of Words

The formal distinction between short- and long-term memories in the Atkinson-Shiffrin theory was based mainly on research involving memory for lists of words. This research followed in the tradition of Ebbinghaus, who showed, among many other things, that recall was generally perfect after a single study trial for lists of seven or fewer items. For longer lists, the finding was that performance differed depending on where in the list the items to be recalled were presented (the serial position effect). In general, immediate free recall (i.e., the subject is allowed to recall the words in any order as soon as the list is completed) tended to be better for items at the beginning of the list (**primacy effect**) and for items at the end of a list (**recency effect**) than for those items in the middle (see Figure 6.5). If recall were delayed for as little as a few minutes while some distracting task was introduced before the list was to be recalled (delayed free recall), the recency effect usually disappeared, whereas the primacy effect remained. Clearly, there are different causes for the observed primacy and recency effects in the serial position curve.

Primacy effect The tendency for material presented early in a list to be recalled better than material presented in the middle of a list; usually found both in immediate and delayed free recall tasks

Recency effect The tendency for material presented near the end of the list to be recalled better than material in the middle of a list; usually found in immediate free recall only

---

FIGURE 6.5

The Serial Position Effect in Free Recall

If people study a list of about 20 words presented one at a time for a few seconds each, and then attempt to recall all of them in any order, they can usually recall about half of them. However, the order in which they are presented influences the likelihood that they will be recalled. The data below are from Murdoch (1962) and show a typical serial position effect. Recall tends to be better for the first items presented (primacy effect) and for the last items presented (recency effect) than for words in the middle of the list.
From Goldstein, E. B. (2005). *Cognitive Psychology*. Belmont, CA: Thompson Wadsworth, p. 147.

6.5.2   *Dissociating Short- and Long-Term Memories*

If free recall makes use of different types of memories in producing primacy and recency effects, then these should be dissociable (i.e., it should be possible to find experimental manipulations that affect only one or the other of these two effects.) One observation that points to this difference is how the words are recalled. In immediate free recall, the last few items are usually recalled rapidly and first, followed by a more reflective output of earlier items in the list. It is as though the contents of short-term memory are dumped first, and then an active search of long-term memory is made with uncertain results. If the recency effect is entirely due to recall from a separate, short-term memory, then eliminating the short-term contribution from recall should also eliminate the recency effect. This is exactly the result that has been found in delayed recall. Glanzer and Cunitz (1966) had their subjects perform a counting task for either 0 seconds (no-counting control) or 10 or 30 seconds after briefly studying a list of 15 words. As you can see in Figure 6.6, 30 seconds of counting was enough to eliminate all of the recency effect. Notice that recall levels for the early (primacy) and middle portions of the list were not affected at all by the short counting task. These results clearly support the idea that the recency effect is produced by recall from short-term memory, and anything that prevents rehearsal of items in the short-term store eliminates its contribution to recall.

If free recall has response components from short- as well as long-term memories, then it should also be possible to find a manipulation that affects the long-term memory component while leaving the short-term components intact. According to the Atkinson-Shiffrin theory, the amount of rehearsal an item receives in short-term memory determines its long-term memory strength and ultimate retrievability. One way to affect long-term memory strength would then be to limit the amount of rehearsal time, such as by limiting the amount of time available for study. Such a manipulation was tested by Murdock (1962) who presented words one at a time at rates of 0.5 second to 2.5 seconds per item. As expected, immediate free recall showed no effect of presentation rate on the recency part of the serial position curve, but the primacy and middle portions were reduced as presentation rate increased (see Figure 6.6).

Additional support for the role of long-term memory in determining the shape of the primacy and middle portions only of the serial position effect in free recall comes from the dissertation study of Rundus (1971). He asked his subjects to rehearse aloud as they studied a list of words presented one at a time. Their overt rehearsals were tape-recorded for later analysis and comparison with the free recall data. Rundus's results were clear: The more rehearsals a word received, the higher the later recall probability. Further, early items tend to be rehearsed more often than middle or late items because the first few items have no competition for entry into short-term memory. Only after the rehearsal buffer is full do the first items get dumped to be replaced by new ones. Therefore, the primacy effect is due entirely to the greater amount of attention and additional rehearsals that the first few items receive. Rundus observed an almost perfect correspondence between the number of rehearsals and recall probability along the serial position curve for delayed free recall (i.e., with no recency effect present).

FIGURE 6.6

Effects of Separate Manipulations on Different Parts of the Serial Position Effect in Free Recall

The top figure shows the effects of a 30-second delay on the start of recall, which affected the recency portion of the curve only. The bottom figure shows the effect of presentation rate, which affected the primacy and middle portions of the curve only (data from Glanzer & Cunitz, 1966).
From Goldstein, E. B. (2005). *Cognitive Psychology.* Belmont, CA: Thompson Wadsworth, p. 148

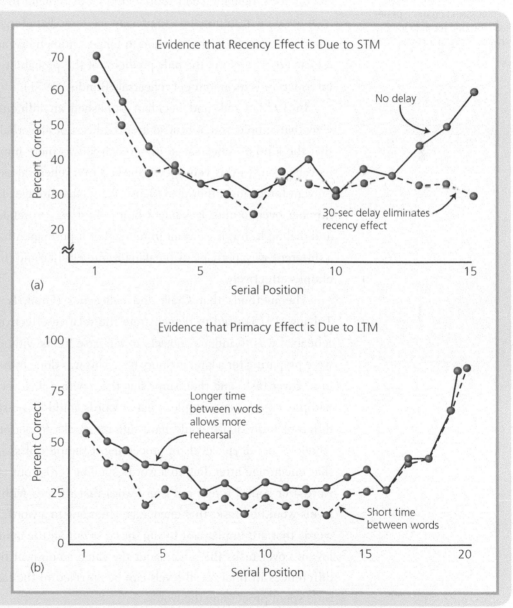

6.6 Contemporary Views of Working Memory

6.6.1   Levels-of-Processing Theory

Levels-of-processing theory
A theory developed by Craik and Lockhart in which the degree of long-term storage is determined more by the type of rehearsal than the amount of rehearsal; deep (e.g., semantic) levels of processing promote better learning and recall than do shallow (e.g., phonemic) levels

Although the Atkinson-Shiffrin theory was successful in accounting for many of the list-learning results from which it was derived, many researchers were dissatisfied with its generality and sought to expand or replace the theory with alternatives. One of the earliest attacks was directed to the role of short-term memory in the theory. Originally, short-term memory was thought to serve two related purposes: maintenance of information to prevent its immediate forgetting and the more-or-less automatic transfer of information to long-term memory, as long as anything is being rehearsed. Therefore, the only predictor of the probability of long-term recall of any information is its amount of rehearsal (Rundus, 1971).

In 1972, Craik and Lockhart published an influential paper challenging the view that simple, rote rehearsal is at the heart of all verbal learning. Their thesis was that the kind of rehearsal an item received was more important than the amount of its rehearsal. In this vein they criticized rote rehearsal as a tool designed mainly to prevent forgetting rather than to insure effective storage. Thus, repeating a telephone number over to ourselves might be the best way to retain it between looking it up and dialing it, but if we want to remember it permanently, we might want to study it a different way, perhaps by breaking it into chunks and thinking of ways to code the chunks effectively.

The methods that Craik and colleagues (Craik & Lockhart, 1972; Craik & Tulving, 1975) used to demonstrate the relative effectiveness of different kinds of rehearsal was to induce subjects to rehearse items without them knowing that they were preparing for a later memory test. This was done by having people process words in a "cover task" and then surprising them with a final recall task for the words they had processed. For example, a list of words could be presented to each subject, and different individuals would have different tasks to perform that encouraged either "shallow" or "deep" levels of processing. Examples of shallow levels would be tasks that encourage attending to a word's spelling (cross out every letter "t" in the list of words) or sound (cross out every word that rhymes with "hay"). Examples of deep levels would be tasks that encourage attending to a word's meaning (cross out all the words that are unpleasant to you, or cross out all the animal names). The trick is to invent cover tasks that take about the same amount of time to execute so that any differences in final recall levels can be ascribed to the task, and not the amount of time spent processing the words.

The results in the final, surprise recall test showed that deeper levels of processing (to the semantic or meaningful level) produced higher levels of recall than did shallow processing. Further research has even shown that if subjects can be induced to process words at a semantic level, final recall can be just as good as that for another group of subjects who are told to study the words for a final recall test. In this case, incidental learning (without intention to learn) can sometimes be as good as intentional learning (Hyde & Jenkins, 1969). Therefore, the conclusion is that learning and long-term retention depend more on the type of studying that is done, more than merely on the amount of time spent in studying.

6.6.2 Multiple Codes in Short-Term Memory

Theories of short-term memory have usually emphasized the role of verbal processes, such as sub-vocal speech in rehearsal. Part of this bias has been due to emphasis on the use of verbal materials in studies of human learning and memory. Another has been due to the demonstration that subvocalizations are apparently the preferred method of retaining information, even if it is presented visually. Conrad (1964) demonstrated this fact when he presented lists of letters to be recalled immediately after a brief presentation. His results showed that the vast majority of the errors were confusions based on auditory similarity rather than visual similarity (i.e., C and Z were more likely to be confused that M and W). More importantly, the patterns of errors in recall were the same for both auditory and visual presentations of the study lists. That is, it did not matter if the letters to be remembered were shown on a screen or spoken over headphones—auditory confusions were more frequent than visual confusions in both cases. Conrad's results have frequently been used as evidence for the phonological or subvocal bias for maintaining information in short-term memory.

Supporting evidence for phonological or inner-speech based coding in short-term memory comes from studies of immediate memory for word lists. Although immediate recall of seven or so words is relatively unaffected by whether or not the words are related semantically, phonological similarity has a large effect. Lists such as "cat, hit, hat, shut, met, mat, shop" produce more immediate recall errors than lists like "dog, boy, sun, pin, top, light, man" (Howes, 2007, p. 55). Also, words that have more syllables in them and take longer to pronounce result in smaller measured memory spans than one-syllable words (Baddeley, Thomson, & Buchanan, 1975).

It is clear from other research, however, that visual codes or images can be maintained and manipulated in short-term memory as well (as certainly is the case in long-term memory, see Box 6.2). Shepard & Metzler's (1971, Box 4.1) famous studies of mental rotation provide perhaps the strongest evidence for the maintenance and manipulation of visual codes in short-term memory. The equation of short-term memory with a repository of various types of codes that can be worked on in various ways has led to new models emphasizing the flexibility and multi-faceted nature of short-term memory. Chief among these has been the working memory model of Baddeley and colleagues (Baddeley, 1986; Baddeley & Hitch, 1976; see Figure 6.6).

BOX 6.2

Long-Term Memory for Pictures versus Words

It is perhaps interesting that the scientific study of memory began with Ebbinghaus's (1985) efforts to learn lists of nonsense syllables. He used meaningless stimuli in an attempt to eliminate any interfering effects from pre-existing knowledge and associations. However, researchers soon complained that nonsense syllables introduced a wide range of idiosyncratic associations that people naturally make to materials to be learned, thus leading to even more uncontrolled variation in the data than if familiar words had been used (e.g., Bartlett, 1932). Thus, a large body of data about human learning, memory, and forgetting has been accumulated from studies of how well people can recall lists of words and other verbal materials.

Most studies revealed that people tend to use rote rehearsal as a study strategy for learning verbal information. Further, typical results in free recall studies show that people can recall about 50% of the words from lists of 20 or so immediately after a single study trial, and that 20% correct is a typical score if recall is delayed for an hour or more (e.g., Craik, 1970). Free recall is a stringent test of memory, however, and better results can be obtained by using more sensitive tests. For example, recognition tests of memory usually result in higher performance scores than recall. In recognition tests, one or more items are presented at a time, and the subject is to indicate which of them occurred in the earlier study phase. Results in immediate recognition tests are frequently much higher than the 50% typically obtained in free recall tests.

The dominant theoretical explanation for a recognition advantage over recall is that the retrieval process is more difficult in recall tests of memory. In free recall, there is a search of a relatively indefinite subset of memory, whereas in recognition, the presentation of the stimulus to be remembered provides direct access to its representation in memory. Research and theory have supported the idea that memory search processes are different in recall and recognition (e.g., Atkinson & Juola, 1973, 1974)

Within verbal learning research, much has been made of the fact that rote rehearsal is a particularly ineffective way to study a list of words for later recall. For example, the simple additional instruction to "try to form visual images of the words as you study them" has been shown to produce dramatic increases in recall scores (Bower, 1972; Paivio, 1972). According to

Paivio's dual-coding theory, forming mental images of verbal items yields two different kinds of information that are potentially retrievable in a memory test: verbal codes for words, and visuo-spatial codes for images of the objects named by the words. If these two types of codes are stored even somewhat independently, then a search of memory is more likely to succeed than if only one memory code is to be found.

Paivio's explanation is open to another possibility, however. Perhaps images differ from words because they are more distinct and are therefore less likely to suffer from the destructive effects of interference from other items stored in memory. After all, we experience each common word (e.g., tree) hundreds or even thousands of times in our lives, but visual images can be as distinct as different pictures of trees are from one another.

If the distinctiveness explanation for the advantage of images over verbal codes in memory is correct, then we should see a large advantage in memory for pictures over words, just as we see an advantage for images. Perhaps the most famous demonstration of the correctness of this expectation comes from an experiment reported by Shepard (1967). Shepard compared memory for words, sentences, and pictures over both short and long-term retention intervals. He used hundreds of stimuli that subjects examined for study, one at a time, for as long as they wished. When finished, they were tested using a sensitive recognition memory procedure called an old-new test. The test sequence consisted of a number of pairs, each containing one old (previously studied) item and one new one. The task is to pick out the old one. Using this procedure, Shepard showed that soon after testing, recognition memory is extremely good for all types of materials; 95% or more of the test pairs resulted in the correct choice. Shepard also tested some of the items after much longer retention intervals. Subjects were returned to the lab for testing 2 hours, 3 days, 7 days, or 120 days after the initial study period. Over these longer retention intervals, a strong advantage for pictures was found over the verbal materials. Standing, Conezio, and Haber (1970) replicated Shepard's experiment with 2,560 color slides and found that recognition scores ranged from 97% to 63% (chance is 50%) over a retention interval of one year.

Clearly, there is an advantage in long-term memory for pictures over words, and this is one of the main reasons for an imagery advantage when memorizing verbal materials. Images can be as distinct from similar items as pictures are, and this distinctiveness prevents their memory representations from being eroded by interference to the extent that verbal memories are.

6.6.3 Baddeley's Theory of Working Memory

Baddeley's (1986, 1990, 1992, 2000) theory emphasizes the multi-tasking capabilities of conscious, attentional processing. Humans have the ability to encode stimuli from various modalities, retrieve relevant information from memory, combine these two sources of information, create new knowledge from this combination, and finally store some of it away for later use while acting on the current state of knowledge. These processes seem to be too complex to fit into the earlier version of short-term memory with the limited roles of maintenance and storage of information. Rather, a more flexible system seems to be called for. This more flexible system has come to be called working memory to distinguish it from early theories that emphasized only the storage capacities of short-term memory.

Baddeley's solution to the limits of earlier short-term memory models was to broaden the theoretical scope to include both storage and processing components within a single memory system. His most recent model of working memory (Baddeley, 2000) includes a **central executive** function to monitor the activities of three different storage systems, which he labeled a **phonological loop**, a **visuo-spatial scratch pad**, and an **episodic buffer** (See Figure 6.7). The executive decides how to allocate limited resources over the three memory components and makes decisions about what actions to take. Depending on the task at hand, the phonological rehearsal loop can be used to rehearse or temporarily store verbal information, and the visuo-spatial scratch pad can be used to retain and manipulate visual images or other spatial information. The episodic buffer works to integrate information from these two stores, along with relevant information from long-term memory, in order to maintain a coherent representation of the current task in terms of its current operation and future goals.

Central executive The process that directs and monitors activity in the three processing and storage components of Baddeley's working memory theory; namely the articulatory loop, the visuo-spatial scratchpad, and the episodic buffer

Phonological loop The theoretical processing component of working memory that rehearses and manipulates verbal information

Visuo-spatial scratchpad The theoretical processing component of working memory that rehearses and manipulates visual images and spatial information

Episodic buffer The theoretical storage component of working memory that integrates currently active information and related information retrieved from long-term memory into a coherent representation of current activity

---

FIGURE 6.7

Major Components of Baddeley's Working Memory Model (e.g., Baddeley & Hitch, 1974; Updated by Baddeley, 2000)

The central executive controls the storage and processing capacities of two independent processors, the visuospatial sketchpad and the phonological loop. A third system, the episodic buffer, combines information from the two processors and from long-term memory to maintain a coherent, integrated version of the task at hand.

Adapted from Matlin, M. W. (2005). *Cognition*, 6th Ed. New York: Wiley, p. 110.

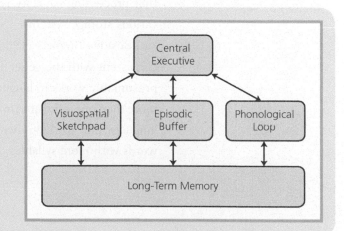

6.6.4 *Empirical Support for Baddeley's Working Memory Model*

Research supporting Baddeley's model had been reported by Brooks (1968). He asked subjects to perform two tasks at once, and the two tasks could be either both spatial, both verbal, or one spatial and one verbal. This demonstration works well enough so that you can try it yourself with a little bit of preparation. First you will need to write down on a sheet of paper 10 rows with two letters in each of them (a "Y" and an "N"). The two letters should be haphazardly placed in the rows so that they do not line up neatly from the top row to the bottom. Each row should contain the letter Y somewhere on the left and the letter N somewhere on the right.

The spatial tasks were (1) to imagine following a path around a visual image and (2) to point to a set of response alternatives in a pseudo random arrangement. For example, one could imagine the block letter "F" as a race track, and, starting from the lower left corner, one could race around the track until returning to the starting point, indicating "yes" for each right turn and "no" for each left turn (by pointing to the "Y" or the "N" in each row) while traveling around it. The verbal tasks were (1) reciting a sentence subvocally and (2) saying "yes" or "no" to oneself as each new component was tested against some criterion. For this example, imagine repeating the sentence "A bird in the hand is worth two in the bush" while saying "yes" for each noun and "no" for each word that is not a noun while working through the sentence. Then, each task can be repeated, only this time, verbal responses are to be made to turns in the race track task, and pointing responses are to be made to the words in the sentence task.

Brooks's (1968) results were clear in showing that doing two spatial tasks or two verbal tasks at the same time was more interfering than combining one verbal task with a spatial one. In terms of Baddeley's theory, there should be more competition for limited storage and processing resources between two tasks within a working memory module than if they are distributed between two modules (i.e., the visuo-spatial sketchpad and the phonological loop), all else being equal. In refining this idea, Bayliss, Jarrold, Gunn, and Baddeley (2003) have argued that storage capacity between verbal and visuo-spatial storage systems is not shared. However, they believe that processing capacity is not specific to either module, and it is shared over the various storage systems.

Besides Brooks's (1968), demonstration, there is a substantial body of research consistent with the general architecture of Baddeley's model. The phonological loop presumably works in language comprehension and reading, as we have to hang onto more than one word at a time if we are to understand a sentence. The relation between language and working memory has been shown in a number of studies. In general, words with more syllables, and hence longer pronunciation times, take more working memory capacity than words of fewer syllables. For example, Schweickert and Boruff (1986) tested the immediate memory span for a variety of different stimulus items that differed in numbers of syllables, such as digits, consonants, words, and nonsense words. They found the very impressive and important result that the number of items that could be repeated back immediately after their presentation was consistently equal to the number of them that could be spoken aloud in 1.5 seconds. A similar result was found in a cross-cultural study by Naveh-Benjamin and Ayres (1986). They found that some languages, such as English, have very short names for the digits (one syllable except for "seven"), but others (such as Spanish) have names of intermediate length, and still others, such as Hebrew and Arabic, average about two syllables per digit name. Consistent with Schweickert and Boruff (1986), they found that the pronunciation rate was slower (fewer than three digits per second) and the memory span smaller (about six items) for languages that have longer digit names. In English, observed pronunciation rates were almost four digits per second and the memory span about seven. These results support the view that verbal memories have a phonological- or articulatory-based (or inner-speech) memory representation, at least for short-term, working memory.

The visuospatial sketchpad component of working memory has been distinguished from the phonological loop by experiments demonstrating people's capacity for maintaining and manipulating visual images in working memory [e.g., Shepard & Metzler's (1971) mental rotation experiments]. Direct estimates of visual memory capacity have pegged its limit as somewhat less than that of the phonological loop. For example Luck and Vogel (1997) showed observers successive views of a number of simple objects, such as a green square, a black triangle, and a blue circle. The task was to indicate whether or not the two displays were the same, or if one of the objects had changed its shape or color. People were very accurate for an array sizes of up to four items, but after that, errors increased with the number of items, indicating that visual capacity for objects is limited to about four items.

In studies of the visuospatial sketchpad, the phonological loop component is sometimes deliberately disabled by making use of an articulatory suppression task. That is, subjects are given a phrase or a word or two to repeat continuously during a trial so that they would be unable to recode stimuli verbally and rehearse them in the phonological loop. For example, Brandimonte, Hitch, and Bishop (1992) showed subjects a set of six pictures of common objects (e.g., a pipe) that they were to study. A control group viewed the pictures silently whereas an experimental group was instructed to repeat aloud an irrelevant sound ("la-la-la …") the entire time they were studying the pictures. In this way, the phonological loop component of working memory would presumably be unavailable for stimulus coding in the experimental group. In the second part of the experiment, all subjects were told to remember each picture and then perform a mental manipulation of its image. Specifically, they were told to remove some specified part of the image and describe the object that remained. For the pipe example, they were told to remove the stem, which would result in a perfectly good bowl in the original picture. The interesting result was that the control group correctly named 2.7 of the objects formed by subtracting a part form the original image, whereas the experimental group was correct on 3.8 of the six objects, on average. That is, even though the experimental group had an extra task to perform, they performed at a higher level than the control group. The concurrent articulatory suppression task (saying "la-la-la …") somehow improved performance in the image manipulation task. This result is presumably due to the fact that the pictures were named and encoded verbally when the phonological loop was available, but the coding was exclusively visual when the phonological loop was busy doing something else. The reliance on visual coding alone then produced superior images for the later manipulation task, in agreement with Baddeley's theory.

Although the laboratory tasks describe in this section were aimed at separating the verbal and spatial components of working memory, Baddeley and others have argued that working memory more commonly operates as an integrated system. That is, the phonological loop and the visuospatial sketchpad are more likely to be engaged in similar activities than in different ones in typical situations. Think of how you might respond if someone is describing an amusing incident that occurred at a party last night. Your phonological loop would be engaged in understanding and maintaining the words that the speaker is saying, and your visuospatial sketchpad might be forming an image of the people and settings involved. If you know the people and place involved (especially if you were at the party yourself) you might be able to construct an accurate internal representation of the episode itself in the episodic buffer. All of these operations would be under control of a central executive, which would enable you to focus your attention on the people involved, the actions that occurred, or something entirely different, like—"I'm late for class, I have to go!" The point is that Baddeley's model is a more complete representation of all of the structures and processes that we have at our disposal in dealing with everyday experiences than earlier theories of short-term memory (e.g., Atkinson & Shiffrin, 1968; 1971).

6.7 Working Memory Capacity

6.7.1 How Large Is the Working Memory Capacity?

How should we measure the working memory capacity? George Miller claimed that short-term memory capacity is seven, plus or minus two, chunks. It means that healthy human adults could probably maintain seven, plus or minus two, chunks of information with rehearsals. If we use some mnemonic techniques, as we discussed before, we may be able to remember more information. In his paper titled "The Magical Number Four in Short-Term Memory" Cowan (2001) suggested that working memory capacity is about four items. There are several paradigms that support his estimate of working memory capacity. For example, Luck and Vogel (1997) used a change detection task, in which a group of objects is shown, and after a brief interval, another group is shown that is either the same group or one of the objects has been changed in some way. They found that memory accuracy remained high up until about four items, but sharply drops beyond that point. This memory capacity seems to be independent of materials (Alvarez & Cavanagh, 2004). Also, in the whole report paradigm (e.g., Sperling, 1960), memory span is about four items. *Subitizing* is the ability to identify the number of items without counting (Trick, & Pylyshyn, 1994). For example, if I drop a number of pennies on the floor, you can probably judge the number of items accurately at a single glance if they are four or less. However, if there are more items, then you would need counting. Multiple Object Tracking (MOT) is another area in which the capacity is about four (Pylyshyn, & Storm, 1988). In this paradigm, as shown in Figure 6.8, participants are shown a number of objects on a computer display, then some of them are highlighted, indicating that they are required to track them. Then the objects start moving at random for a while. When they stop, participants are asked which are the objects that they were supposed to track. People can track objects quite accurately up to four items, but beyond that point, accuracy rates drop.

FIGURE 6.8

Multiple Object Tracking (from Scholarpedia)

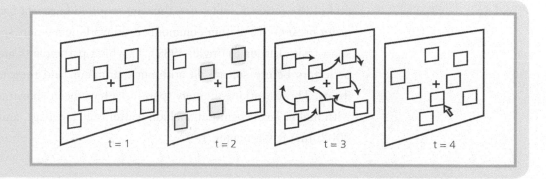

Why then is working memory capacity limited to about four items? This could be related to the capacity of the brain, especially the posterior parietal cortex. Todd and Marois (2004) used fMRI to investigate brain activation during the Luck and Vogel change detection task. Their results showed that there was a steady increase of brain activity in the posterior parietal cortex from one to four items; however, brain activity levelled off after four items. This pattern of brain activity nicely corresponded to the behavioral performance. Memory accuracy rate was almost perfect up to four items, and dropped afterward. They suggested that the underlying neural mechanism of working memory capacity is closely associated with the function of the posterior parietal cortex.

6.7.2   *Measures of Working Memory Capacity*

This type of short-term memory capacity (memory span) is typically measured with forward recall of digits, letters, or words, such as the one in the standard intelligence tests, including Wechsler Adult Intelligence Scale. In this case, a test administrator may read a number of digits one per second at a time, then a participant is asked to recall the digits in the same order as presented. Therefore, these short-term memory tasks are called "simple span tasks," because they involve only the maintenance aspect of memory. On the other hand, working memory involves two components: maintenance and processing. In other words, working memory allows for the manipulation of stored information, while traditional short-term memory span tasks are concerned only with the short-term storage of information and do not entail the manipulation of material held in memory.

Because working memory involves maintenance and manipulation of information, working memory span tasks contain these two components. In other words, working memory tasks are typically dual tasks and called complex span tasks. Daneman and Carpenter (1980) were the first to develop this type of task. Their task is called a reading span task, in which participants are asked to read a number of sentences (usually between two and six) and to remember the last word of each sentence. At the end of the series of sentences, they are required to repeat back the last words in the order presented. Another commonly used working memory span task is the operation span task (Turner & Engle, 1989), in which participants are asked to study words or letters before solving an arithmetic problem, and then to remember the initial items. These working memory span tasks have been shown to have high correlation with higher level cognition, including attention, language, and reasoning (e.g., Engle, 2002; Just & Carpenter, 1992).

6.8 Working Memory and Attention

Recently, some researchers have expanded upon the claim that attention and working memory are closely related. In this view, working memory is viewed as attention directed to internal representations (e.g., Awh & Jonides, 2001; Chun, Golomb, & Turk-Browne, 2011; Gazzaley & Nobre, 2012; Kiyonaga & Egner, 2013; Oberauer & Hein, 2012; Postle, 2006). In other words, attention can operate over representations of items that are no longer present in the environment, and therefore must be activated endogenously. This framework predicts that working memory and attention might interact with each other such that the contents of working memory should affect processing of visual information (e.g., Awh, Jonides, & Reuter-Lorenz, 1998; Awh & Jonides, 2001; Downing, 2000; Pashler & Shiu, 1999). For example, Awh et al. (1998) required participants to remember the position of a single letter on a screen, then a target stimulus was presented followed by a memory probe for the original location. The main task was discrimination between two letter-like target stimuli. They found that RTs were shorter and responses were more accurate for judging whether or not the test letter appeared in the same position before and after the discrimination test when the first two stimuli were presented in the same location than when the discrimination stimulus was presented at a position adjacent to the original letter (see Figure 6.9).

FIGURE 6.9

An Example of a Trial Sequence (adapted from Awh, Jonides, & Reuter-Lorenz, 1998)

In this case the two letters are presented in the same location, but they occur away from the position of the target stimulus. Responses were faster and more accurate to the memory probe when all three stimuli occurred in the same position.

Pashler and Shiu (1999) reported that an image stored in working memory can capture attention in an attentional blink task. In their study, an image cue was presented at the beginning of each trial, and participants were asked to form an image of a particular type of object (e.g., an elephant). Then, an RSVP stream of stimuli (eight line drawings and a digit) was presented, and participants were told to report the digit. The stream contained a picture of the same type of object that the participant had just imaged (e.g., an elephant), either before or after the target digit. When the picture appeared before the digit, an attentional blink occurred and digit detection was impaired. As expected, the image held in working memory focused attention on the relevant picture in the stream, which limited the amount of attention available to detect and identify the digit, but only if the relevant picture occurred before the digit.

Other researchers have demonstrated that irrelevant items held in working memory can affect the capture of attention in visual search tasks (e.g., Soto & Humphreys, 2007). In these tasks, observers are asked to hold onto one or more memory items during visual search. Then, a display is presented in which they are to search for the presence or absence of a target, after which they are to report the initial memory items. The main manipulation is whether or not one of the memory items appears in the search display. The general finding is, if one of the memory items appears as a distractor, responses in the search task are slowed, indicating that the contents of working memory can automatically lead to attentional capture of items in a search task, even when they are irrelevant to the target search. Subsequent research has shown that the effect is strongest if the memory items are visual images, rather than verbal descriptions (Calleja & Rich, 2013), and if only a single memory item is maintained or highlighted in working memory (Moorselaar, Theeuwes, & Olivers, 2014). Distributing working memory over several items or verbal labels seems to diminish the salience of the working memory content. If working memory contains a single image, however, a close match between this image and a search distractor can capture attention and interfere with visual search.

6.9 Neurophysiological Support for Working Memory Components

If there are identifiable subcomponents in human working memory, then brain-imaging techniques should be able to map out these components and show some of their differences, if any. Indeed, increased frontal lobe activity has been recorded in a number of working memory tasks. For example, Rypma, Berger, and D'Esposito (2002) have shown that prefrontal lobe activity increases with the number of items that must be held in memory for a short time. Such activity does not seem to be associated with storage per se, but rather in executive control of other cortical regions where the storage is taking place (Moscovitch, et al., 2007). In tasks involving the articulatory or phonological loop, the associated subvocal activity has been shown to result in bilateral activation of the frontal and parietal lobes (e.g., Cabeza & Nyberg, 1997) and activation in the left temporal lobe (Gazzaniga, Ivry, & Mangun, 2002; Schacter, 2001). The interpretation is that the frontal lobe activity reflects executive functions, directing the verbal processes involved in inner speech; that the temporal lobe processes semantic aspects of the speech code; and the auditory aspects of inner speech results are at least temporarily stored in the parietal lobe (Matlin, 2005; Moscovitch, et al., 2007).

In has been shown that visuo-spatial tasks result in activation of brain areas different from those involved in verbal tasks. Smith and Jonides (1997) compared brain activity measured during the performance of three different types of tasks. One task measured verbal memory for a set of letters, whereas the other two measured spatial memory or object memory. The verbal task showed increased activity in the left frontal and parietal areas, and the object memory task also produced more cortical activity in the left frontal and parietal regions, but in areas different from those involved in the verbal task. In addition, the object memory task produced increased activity in the left occipital-temporal boundary region. On the other hand, the spatial memory task consistently showed increased activity in the right hemisphere only, but again in frontal and parietal regions. Tasks requiring maintenance of visual information across time also show increased activity in the parietal and left frontal lobes (Haxby, Ungerleider, Horwitz, Rapoport, & Grady, 1995). In fact, the dorsolateral prefrontal cortex (i.e., its upper sides) has been implicated in most working memory tasks that involve monitoring and active manipulation of items in working memory (Ranganath & Knight, 2002).

In summary, executive functions seem to be under the control of structures in the frontal cortex, visuo-spatial tasks involve occipital and parietal structures, and phonological tasks involve parietal, temporal, and frontal regions. The activation of different brain areas for different components of working memory provides broad support for the overall architecture of Baddeley's theory (see Moscovitch, et al., 2007, for a review; and Vandierendonck, 2016, for alternative interpretations).

Chapter Summary

William James speculated that there must be two different kinds of memories, since he thought that some things that we are currently thinking of can be described with ease, whereas other things have to be dredged up with some effort and no guarantee of success. Today, the difference between short-term, or working, memory and long-term memory is a well established component of cognitive theory. Evidence has been gained from neurological studies of amnesic patients, who can show intact short- and long-term memories, but no way to transfer information from the immediate present into long-term memory. Other evidence has come from studies of verbal learning, which have consistently shown differences in recall from short-term and long-term components of memory in recalling lists of words.

Although the early theory of Atkinson and Shiffrin viewed short-term memory as a rehearsal buffer used to maintain items and transfer information to long-term memory, more recent theories have emphasized the central role that working memory plays in all cognitive abilities. Baddeley's model of working memory is fairly generally accepted as a good summary of behavioral and neuphysiological evidence to date. It incorporates a central executive function that determines the allocation of limited resources to three separate processors. One is a phonological loop than includes the functions of Atkinson and Shiffrin's rehearsal buffer as well as other, more active and elaborative verbal coding strategies. Another is a visuo-spatial scratch pad that enables the maintenance and manipulation of visual images and other spatial information. A third component is an episodic buffer that integrates information from the other stores with that from long-term memory. Different tasks require different levels of involvement of these systems, and their levels of involvement are managed by the executive function of the theory. Although limited in capacity, short-term, working memory is the focus of our conscious, cognitive involvement in the tasks of daily life.

Review Questions

- **What differences are there between memory over the short term and memory for the distant past?**

  James made the distinction between things that are currently in consciousness, and can be retrieved quickly and certainly, as opposed to things that have occurred beforehand, and can be retrieved only with effort and not with any certainty. Today we view the contents of short-term or working memory in much the same way that James did, and we understand some of the mechanisms, such as rehearsal, that are designed to maintain the contents of working memory while they are manipulated and/or stored in permanent long-term memory. The difficulty with retrieval from long-term memory has to do with the large amounts of information that are stored away, along with the great deal of similarity that exists among many items in storage. Retrieval then depends on difficult search processes among interfering information, such that it is not certain that the desired information will be found at any given time.

- **Is there any evidence that short- and long-term memories are stored and accessed differently?**

  The greatest differences between short- and long-term memories are their huge difference in capacities and the likelihood that their contents can be reported accurately. Short-term memory is limited to about seven or fewer chunks of information—such as digits, letters, or words—whereas the capacity of long-term memory is best thought of as infinite. On the other hand, the contents of short-term memory are immediately available by definition, whereas much of what is stored in long-term memory is relatively inaccessible without the right kind of retrieval cue. It was once thought that there were different preferred coding schemes and forgetting mechanisms for the two memory stores, but it is now believed that any kind of information that can be remembered (articulatory, semantic, visual, etc.) can be stored in and retrieved from either store. Similarly, both memory systems seem to be sensitive to the same kinds of interference explanations of forgetting, although the limited capacity of short-term memory means that sometimes information must literally be pushed out to make way for new inputs.

- **Why do we forget some things that happened just a short time ago?**

  By definition, short-term memory contains the information that we are currently retaining from the recent past, either abstracted from the environment, retrieved from long-term memory, or retained by active rehearsal. If something that has occurred in the recent past is not currently remembered, then one of two things must have happened: (1) The information was never attended to and entered into short-term memory in the first place or (2) the information was attended to, but was replaced by new information before it could be adequately coded into long-term memory.

- **What is amnesia, and how is it different from ordinary forgetting?**

  Amnesia is of two types, typically defined relative to some point in time when an incident, such as accident or stroke, damaged part of the brain, most likely the interior temporal lobes and hippocampus. Retrograde amnesia is forgetting of some information that occurred just prior to the injury, extending backward in time from that point, and anterograde amnesia is the inability to construct new (typically declarative) memories from the point of injury onward. Unlike ordinary forgetting, amnesia tends to be complete and relatively permanent for the information stored during the periods of amnesia, so that repeated attempts at recall over different periods give the same negative results. Further, there is no other forgetting like anterograde amnesia in which information just does not seem to be stored or consolidated into a normal format, so there is nothing learned to forget.

- **Are there any differences between memory for words and memory for pictures, objects, and scenes?**

  Much research has shown that memory for pictures and objects is better than memory for words, even when the words are the names of the objects studied. One argument, advanced by Paivio, is that words are encoded and remembered only verbally, whereas objects, pictures, and scenes could include both verbal labels and visual images in memory. Any memory search for stored information is more likely to encounter something if it is stored in two ways than if it is stored in only one format. These differences are also emphasized in Baddeley's model of working memory, which includes separate processing systems for verbal information (a phonological loop) and visual or pictorial information (a visuospatial sketchpad).

Key Terms

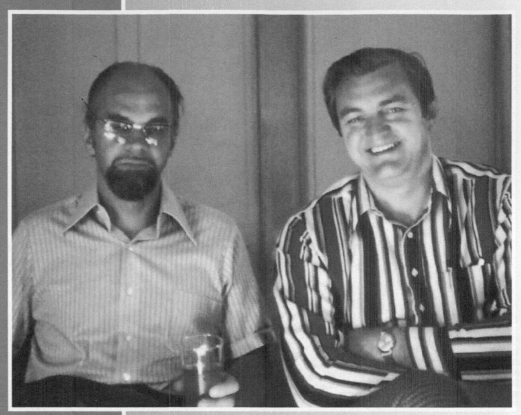

ENDEL TULVING & GORDON BOWER

Photo courtesy of Gordon Bower

Chapter 7

Long-Term Memory for Meaning and Knowledge

"The dissolving power of modern research seems to have split Memory into a number of variously related functions. Remembering is not ... entirely distinct from perceiving, imaging, or even from constructive thinking, but it has intimate relations with them all."

F. C. Bartlett, *Remembering*, 1932–1967, pp. 12–13.

PREVIEW QUESTIONS

❖ *Is human long-term memory a unitary structure, or are there multiple types of memories?*

❖ *How is meaning represented in memory?*

❖ *How are simple sentences represented and understood?*

❖ *Are there representations in memory for large structures like maps or stories?*

❖ *What brain processes are involved in storing and retrieving meaningful information?*

7.1 Introduction to Long-Term Memory

We have memories for words, faces, music, and mathematical operations. We know that robins are animals, dandelions are plants, and that Los Angeles is in California. We also know what we did yesterday, and most of us know how to hit a ball with a bat and ride a bicycle. We might even remember who won the 2003 World Series or where we were when we heard about the September 11, 2001, World Trade Center and Pentagon attacks. How are these different kinds of knowledge learned, stored, accessed, and used when we need them? Surely there must be multiple types of memories, only some of which we can recall to consciousness. Other memories might affect our behavior, but they are likely to remain unconscious if we cannot trace their origin or verbalize much about them, such as our memory for how to ride a bicycle.

Psychologists have argued that there are differences between general knowledge (semantic memory) and memory for events (episodic memory), between verbal and visuo-spatial memories, and between declarative (knowledge-of) and procedural (knowledge-how-to) memories. Some memories seem to be the result of explicit attempts to attend to and learn information, whereas others seem to be acquired implicitly, without awareness or intention to learn (see Figure 7.1). Studies of brain-damaged individuals support some of these distinctions. Some studies have even suggested that different kinds of information are stored in different parts of the brain, as specific types of memories can be affected in patients with damage to certain brain areas, but other memories can be spared. For example, damage to parts of the temporal lobes can result in a patient's inability to recognize the faces of familiar people, but objects might be readily named. Other patients with different injuries might be able to recognize family members, but common tools might be unrecognizable. Imaging studies of brain activity in healthy people have corroborated these findings, as different parts of the brain are active when we learn

FIGURE 7.1

Taxonomy of Long-Term Memory for Meaning and Knowledge

Taxonomy of memory by Larry Squire (From Gazzaniga, Ivry, & Mangun, 2002).

and remember different kinds of things. These results help us to develop and test theories of memory to explain why some things are easy to learn and other things are difficult, and why we remember some things well while others we seem to forget.

7.2 Semantic versus Episodic Memories

Over 40 years ago, Endel Tulving (1972) chaired a meeting of prominent memory researchers at the University of Pittsburgh and could not help noticing that they had aligned themselves into two groups. One group followed the tradition of Ebbinghaus (1885/1913) and studied how people learn and recall lists of verbal items, most commonly words that were specifically chosen to be unrelated to one another. The other group followed the tradition of Bartlett (1932/1967) and studied how people learn and remember meaningful sentences and stories. Tulving generalized beyond these differences to conclude that these two groups were in fact studying different kinds of memories, not just memory for meaningless versus meaningful collections of words. He was among the first to make the distinction between what he called "semantic memory" and "episodic memory."

According to Tulving's theory (1972), **semantic memory** is the general knowledge that we all have about the physical world and its symbolic representations, including language and mathematics. This common store of knowledge enables people to agree about how we perceive and identify objects and events and how we describe them to each other. We can witness a dog chasing a ball, and we will agree with one another about the basic perceptual facts of what a dog and a ball are. We are even likely to share inferences and attributions that are not directly perceptible, such that the ball belongs to the dog's owner and that the dog is enjoying the game of pursuit and retrieval. Both our memories of common events and our later discussions about them are likely to reveal the commonalties of our perceptions, interpretations, and recollections of everyday occurrences.

Episodic memory, on the other hand, is the personal, autobiographical record of our daily experiences that is stored away in a type of individual memory journal. Rather than being general knowledge about dogs, balls, and what fun is, episodic memories are specific to particular experiences as witnessed by us. For example, we might remember the most recent time that we played fetch with a dog, whose dog it was, and where the event took place. Episodic memories tend to be unique to each one of us. However, despite the uniqueness of our individual experiences, we all live in a world with similar physical properties, similar animals and objects, and similar interactions among people, artifacts, and other living things. Therefore, semantic memories that store the general properties of our experiences and knowledge are likely to be similar across members of a common cultural and linguistic community, if not across all people generally.

Semantic memory The permanent repository of all general knowledge in memory, according to Tulving's (1972) theory; the basis of understanding the meanings of objects, events, words, and sentences, as well as the basis of mathematical and encyclopedic knowledge

Episodic memory The personal memory of our experiences, according to Tulving's (1972) theory; it records events with date and setting information, and as such it is unique to each of us

If semantic memory is the part of long-term memory that contains all general knowledge, including mathematics, music, language, and familiarity with the three-dimensional physical world and the objects and living things that inhabit it, where does such knowledge come from? The obvious answer is that semantic memory is developed through some combination of biological predisposition and environmental experience, just as we learn to speak our native language and recognize members of our family. We cannot dismiss a large, inherited tendency to encode the world in a certain way, and this tendency also helps us to understand how we come to learn so much so fast. We will address some of these issues of nature versus nurture in Chapter 9 on language acquisition, and similar arguments can be raised to explain learning in other domains.

It is likely that semantic memory is built up through abstractions and generalizations from the set of experiences that make up episodic memory (Moscovitch et al., 2007). Indeed, nothing could be recognized at all if the currently encoded stimulus did not resemble a stored representation of a previous experience. Repeated experiences presumably result in stored traces, and a number of similar traces based on similar episodes are likely to be stored together in some sense. That is, the nervous system is hardwired to direct similar sensory experiences to similar parts of the brain. Repeated activations of brain structures due to repeated experiences are likely to produce changes in the brain itself (e.g., Hebb, 1949; Squire, 1987; captured in the phrase "neurons that fire together wire together"). These changes could include synthesis of new synapses and the development of large-scale interactions among different brain regions (e.g., Johnson, 2004). The repetition of familiar events promotes learning of general concepts that are central to the development of semantic memory. Any group of people living in a world with similar physical properties and filled with similar natural and artificial objects, who enjoy a common cultural and linguistic heritage, could well be expected to induce internal representations of their world that are more similar than different across individuals. That is, although the specific experiences that determine episodic memory will indeed differ across people, the abstracted generalities will be largely the same. This sameness is our shared semantic memory system.

7.3 **Models of Semantic Memory**

$7.3.1$ *The Collins and Quillian Model*

If semantic memory is an abstract representation of the commonalties of human experience, then it should include the processes and structures of human knowledge based on that experience. Any theoretical account of such memory structures and processes should detail the contents of the structures and how they are accessed, retrieved, and used in making judgments about real-world events. One of the first attempts to create such a theory, and also one of the first **network models** of human memory, was realized in Quillian's (1966) PhD dissertation, the "Teachable Language Comprehender." The model was later expanded (Collins & Quillian, 1969) and is today recognized as one of the first successful computer simulation models of human memory.

The structural components of the model included nodes, arranged into a hierarchy, that are accessed through a network of links connecting the nodes. Collins and Quillian chose to represent only a small part of semantic memory (i.e., some of the knowledge that we have about animals.) The nodes represent concepts, such as "animal" and "bird," and the links between them reflect relations among the concepts, such as subset/superset relations and property relations. Simple ideas can be represented by nodes and the associations between them. For example, propositions, such as "A bird is an animal," "A robin is a bird," and "A bird has feathers" are represented in a hierarchical network by two or more nodes and the relations that link them. There are two main types of relational links. Subset/superset relations define a concept's level in a hierarchy, to show, for example, that a robin is a type of bird and a bird is a type of animal. Other relations point to properties or features of the concept such as whether it can fly or has feathers. A schematic representation of such a model is shown in Figure 7.2.

The processing components of the model include search and decision processes. Search is simply an automatic spread of activation along the links from one node to others in the network that gradually diminishes as it extends out from its source like ripples in a pond around the splash of a stone. Activation can be regarded as a graded tendency for stored information to become available for further processing. Relatively inactive concepts remain below some threshold for influencing one's thoughts and behaviors, whereas highly activated concepts contribute to our current thoughts and perceptions. Activation is initiated either externally, as when we hear or see a word or encounter a familiar object, or internally, when we think of some concept. In either case, related concepts are activated to progressively lower levels as *distance* increases from the activated node. Distance is commonly equated with the number of links that have to be traversed between any two concepts in moving through the network. These mechanistic analogies should not be taken too literally, as the theory proposes only to represent a neural network in the brain, not to describe its actual structures and processes.

A decision is made whenever the search process is terminated or redirected. For example, Collins and Quillian (1969) originally tested their model by asking people to judge whether or not certain test sentences were true. They compared times taken by people to verify sentences of the form "A robin is a bird" versus "A robin is an animal." In either case, the search should terminate whenever the search process finds a link or links between the subject and predicate concept nodes. At that time, a decision could be made about whether or not the links existing in memory are consistent with the relation expressed in the test sentence. Since the sentence involving robins and birds is more direct than the one involving robins and animals, spreading

Network model A structural description of some domain (e.g., a part of semantic memory; Collins & Quillian, 1969) in which concepts are represented by nodes that are connected to other nodes via relational links; subsequent processing assumptions can include activation that spreads through the network from an input node along the links to other nodes in a diminishing wave of excitation

FIGURE 7.2

A Schematic Representation of Part of Semantic Memory as Modeled in the Theory of Collins and Quillian (1969)

Nodes representing concepts are arranged into a hierarchy with some links representing subset-superset relations (e.g., "a bird is an animal"). Other links identify concept properties (e.g., "a bird can fly" and "a fish has fins"). If the model is a good representation of human semantic memory, it should be able to predict how long people take to verify or refute simple sentences based on concepts and relations contained in the model.

From Goldstein, E. B. (2005). *Cognitive Psychology*. Belmont, CA: Thompson Wadsworth, p. 287.

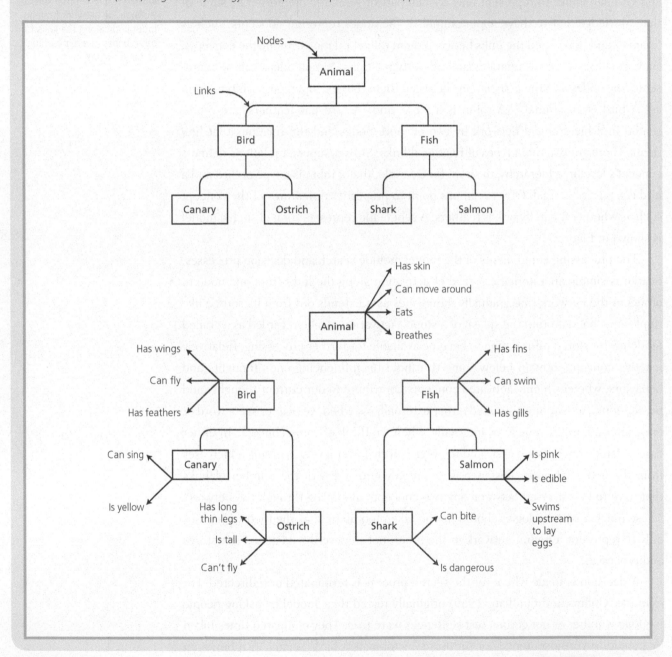

activation should make the search process shorter and the decision quicker for the first sentence. Similarly, a proposition such as, "A canary has skin" should be verified more slowly than "A canary has feathers" since all animals have skin, but only birds have feathers (see Figure 7.3).

FIGURE 7.3

Sample Results from Collins and Quillian's (1969) Experiment
People verified whether or not certain simple sentences were true. The data shown are mean response times for verifying sentences about properties (upper line) and sentences about category membership (lower line). In both cases, response times increased with the number of links that hypothetically should be traversed in a semantic memory network before the statement could be verified.
From Goldstein, E. B. (2005). *Cognitive Psychology.* Belmont, CA: Thompson Wadsworth, p. 289.

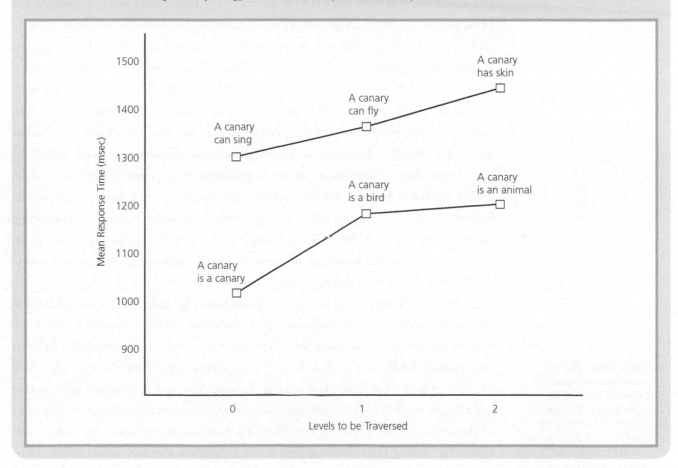

Collins and Quillian (1969) argued in favor of **cognitive economy** by asserting that it would make more sense to store general properties at their highest level of generality rather than at the level of every exemplar of a category that shares the property. That is, the property "skin" should be stored with animal, and the links between canary, bird, and animal would have to be traversed before the fact that canaries have skin could be evaluated as true. The proposition, "A canary has feathers" would involve only the links between canary, bird, and feathers before the proposition could be verified, thus the time should be shorter for determining that a canary has feathers than that it has skin.

These and other predictions were tested in experiments involving human subjects. The results showed consistencies between the structures and processes of the network model and the times that human subjects took to verify sentences. This demonstrated support for the Collins and Quillian theory. That is, by adding a certain amount of time for each stage of processing in the computer network, it

Cognitive economy A principle adopted by Collins and Quillian (1969) in their network model of semantic memory; asserts that any property that is true of more than one concept node in the hierarchy should be stored only at the highest-level (i.e., most general) node in the network over which the property is found was possible to simulate human behavior involved in understanding and verifying simple sentences.

7.3.2   *Feature-Based Models of Semantic Memory*

Of course, it was not long before problems were identified within the Collins and Quillian (1969) theory. For example Conrad (1972) disputed the generality of the principle of cognitive economy. It seems that unlike in an optimal computer network, properties in human memories are not stored only at the highest level of generality. Rather, they might be stored at multiple levels and with multiple specific concepts, especially if they are salient or prominent features of the concept (e.g., a peacock's feathers or a shark's teeth). One usually does not have to decide that a shark is an animal and that most animals have teeth before the fact that a shark has teeth comes to mind. Conrad's thesis presaged a more general attack on such network models by arguing in favor of distributed information storage as opposed to localized storage within semantic memory. That is, more recent neural network theories of semantic memory replace the notion that a concept node encapsulates all of our knowledge about some object. Rather, it is more likely that a variety of nodes and their inter-connections code the meanings of common objects and events in a more realistic portrayal of the neural basis of human memory.

Other problems for Collins and Quillian's theory include the fact that all links in human memories are apparently not equal. Sentences such as, "A robin is a bird" are verified much faster than ones like, "A penguin is a bird," a phenomenon known as the **typicality effect** (e.g., Rosch, 1975). In general, typical members are identified as belonging to a category more quickly than are less typical members. This is true even if care is taken to make sure that the words themselves are matched in frequency of usage in English. The typicality effect has been accounted for in revisions of the theory by making links between typical items and their category nodes shorter or by allowing activation to spread more freely along them than along links from less typical category exemplars (e.g., Collins & Loftus, 1975). Further, people sometimes make errors—for example, in saying "true" to sentences such as, "A bat is a bird" or "A whale is a fish," or saying "false" to sentences such as, "A sponge is an animal." Often people realize such errors and try to correct them, but other times errors like these seem to be based on faulty knowledge represented in memory. These results indicate that there needs to be something more than nodes and links to account for such semantic similarity and typicality effects on sentence comprehension.

An alternative to simple network models was proposed by Ed Smith and his students (e.g., Smith, Shoben, & Rips, 1974). Their model replaced nodes and links with a more homogeneous, multi-dimensional semantic space. Concepts are represented by specific locations in this hypothetical space, and their meanings by the values that each concept has on the various dimensions. One could imagine that related concepts would be located near one another, and that relative differences

Typicality effect The fact that some members of a category are judged to be better exemplars of a category than are other members; also reflected in speed of judgments (e.g., "A fox is a mammal" is judged to be true faster than "A whale is a mammal")

between concept meanings could be captured by their distances computed along the different relevant dimensions. To illustrate this notion, an example is shown in Figure 7.4 using familiar kinship terms. In this figure, the terms are differentiated along dimensions of gender, relative age, and relative closeness of relation. Arbitrarily putting the term *son* at the origin of this 3-D space, all eight kinship terms can be identified with different points in the space, with their meanings indicated by their respective locations. Further, distances are short between kinship concepts that are close, such as between son and sister and between father and mother, and greater distances reflect the lesser degree of kinship between, say, son and aunt. Of course, more general realizations of semantic memory would require many more dimensions of meaning and thousands of points within the space.

The feature model of Smith et al. (1974) can handle typicality effects, since robins should be located closer to the central concept of bird than penguins in the feature space. Also, the similarity effect, such as the fact that people are slower or more likely to make errors for sentences like "A bat is a bird" could be explained by the relative closeness of the bat and bird concepts in the feature space. However, it is unclear that distance between two concepts is sufficient to serve as the sole basis for the sentence verification process. To handle this problem, Smith and his colleagues differentiated between so-called characteristic features of concepts that influence their similarities, such as flying for both bats and birds, and defining features, such as laying eggs for birds versus giving birth for bats, which are important for the final decision about categorization processes.

Although the network representation in Figure 7.2 and the multidimensional feature space represented in Figure 7.4 are oversimplifications of parts of semantic

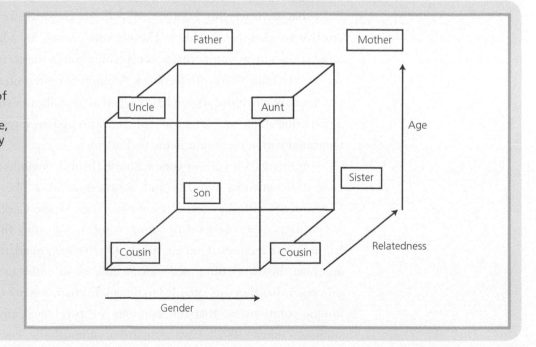

FIGURE 7.4

An Example of a Feature-Based Model of Part of Semantic Memory
A 3-D representation of English kinship terms, with dimensions of age, gender, and immediacy of family relations
The terms are defined relative to the "son."

memory, the theories can be extended to arbitrary complexity in principle. Networks can theoretically include nodes for thousands of different concepts with many different kinds of links among them. Similarly, a feature space could include dozens of dimensions of meaning with a range of values represented along each of them. Either model could represent millions of nuances of meaning. However, both models share a property that has come under increasing scrutiny as an unlikely candidate for a structural description of human memory, namely local storage of meaning. If the meaning of a concept were defined as a single node or the relations it has with other nodes, then a literal interpretation of the model would locate conceptual meaning within a few neurons and their links to others. Similarly, the **multidimensional feature model** would appear to locate meaning within a structure as a single point in space, again apparently equating it with a single neuron or small set of neurons in the brain. Although such interpretations may not have been intended by the theories' authors, they seem to follow naturally from the structural descriptions. Such localist ideas have been rejected on numerous grounds, including the facts that a concept's meaning can be accessed in many different ways (from any sense modality, for instance). Further, forgetting and cognitive aging effects show partial or intermittent recall of concepts and their meanings, along with graceful degradation of information storage in aging or injured brains.

Multidimensional feature model A model proposed by Smith et al. (1974) as an alternative to network; representing concepts, such as locations in a space, in which the dimensions are different aspects of meaning (semantic primitives), and features are the specific values that any concept has on the various dimensions

7.3.3   *Distributed Model of Semantic Memory*

The major alternative to such localist conceptions of semantic memory is a distributed model with connectionist architecture (see Box 3.2). Such neural network theories specify different layers of nodes—typically an input layer, an output layer, and one or more intermediate, or hidden, layers. Each node is connected to other nodes by links that have weights between −1 and +1. Negative weights are inhibitory, and positive weights are excitatory. The network "learns" by adjusting weights until the input results in an output that is acceptably close to the correct response after a large series of training trials with feedback. Memory is represented by the set of weights in the network when the system has reached an equilibrium state, thus the memory for a particular item, such as a concept, is distributed over a network rather than being identified with a small unit in the architecture.

Arguments supporting connectionist theories include their superficial appearance: the networks look like and behave somewhat like part of a human brain. Experiments with the computer networks (i.e., Monte Carlo simulations) are almost as useful as experiments with human subjects in testing theories about perception, learning, and memory (Quinlan, 1991). On the other hand, the networks are complex, and how they work often becomes as difficult to understand as the human mental processes that they are intended to model. Further, it is not certain that they produce unique solutions, or that the solutions are psychologically meaningful. Theorists, such as Pinker (2002), have argued that although "… connectionist networks can manage impressive displays of memory and generalization … they are simply too underpowered to duplicate more realistic feats of human intelligence like understanding a sentence or reasoning about living things" (p. 79). Also, researchers often find it easier to talk about important psychological phenomena, such as priming, discussed next, in the context of a simpler network of the Collins and Quillian (1969) type, than in the more abstract language of connectionism.

7.4 Priming in Semantic Memory

Natural events, including physical, social, and linguistic interactions, include structures and sequences of related items. That is, we tend to see tables and chairs together, people congregate in theatres and restaurants and behave in predictable ways, and adjectives tend to precede nouns in English. It is extremely likely from any reasonable theory of human memory that our internal representations of objects, people, events, and language should reflect these natural relations in the external world. Therefore, it should not be surprising that in semantic memory models, concepts in memory are linked to related concepts, and they can activate each other when any one of them is activated. The natural situation of perceiving related words or objects is mimicked in the laboratory by presenting pairs of stimuli that are either related in some way or unrelated. Then, the speed or accuracy of the response to the second member of the pair is measured. If responses are faster and more accurate for trials with related pairs than for unrelated pairs, the difference is a measure of the amount of **priming** produced by the related stimulus.

In a typical laboratory task involving words, the prime stimulus is a word presented before or at the same time as a target stimulus, and the target word requires a response of some kind. Tasks that have been used are categorization (is the second word an animal name?), naming (say aloud the second word), and making lexical decisions (is the second item a real word or not?), with response time (RT) being the primary measure. The usual result found is that related primes produce faster responses to the target (facilitation or benefits), whereas unrelated primes can result in a small amount of inhibition (costs) when compared with a no-prime control condition. In the context of network models, priming is explained by automatic spreading activation produced by the first item of the pair, and this activation makes related concepts more available in memory. If these activated concepts match the target, it is processed more rapidly, leading to higher levels of performance than in no-prime control trials. If the prime is unrelated to the target, costs can occur because of the diversion of memory activation to parts of semantic memory that are irrelevant to the target, resulting in dilution of resources needed to identify it.

Among the first studies of priming effects on access time for words in semantic memory was that of Meyer and Schvaneveldt (1971). They used a lexical decision task

Priming The effect that any stimulus (prime) has on the speed or accuracy of responding to another stimulus (target) that is presented at the same time as the prime or later; effects on the target can either be beneficial (positive priming) or detrimental (negative priming) (Priming can also be perceptual —prime and target related in form—or conceptual—prime and target related in meaning or associated to each other.)

in which participants had to decide whether or not two letter strings were both words. That is, they were to say "yes" when both strings were words, and to say "no" if either or both of them were nonwords. They found that the time to say "yes" on trials when both strings were words was almost 100 ms shorter when the two words were related (e.g., nurse, doctor) than when they were unrelated (e.g., bread, doctor; see Figure 7.5).

FIGURE 7.5

Sample Stimuli and Mean Response Times (RT, in milliseconds) for the Types of Stimulus Pairs Used by Meyer and Schvaneveldt (1972).

The task is to say "yes" only if both letter strings are words and to say "no" otherwise. Responses were fastest if the stimuli were two words related in meaning.

"YES"	RT	"NO"	RT
nurse	855	nurse	1087
doctor		doctum	
bread	940	doctum	904
doctor		bread	
		doctum	884
		corday	

A similar result was reported by Neely (1976), who also used the lexical decision task to measure the speed of word recognition. In Neely's experiment, the prime was presented before the target by a variable amount of time, the so-called stimulus onset asynchrony, or SOA. That is, the onset of the prime occurred between 200 and 2000 ms before the onset of the letter string that was to be judged a word or nonword. Similar to Meyer and Schvaneveldt's results, related priming words produced facilitation, and unrelated priming words produced inhibition relative to a neutral prime condition ("XXXX" presented before the target). Priming was maximal at a prime-target SOA of about 600 ms. This result indicates that it takes on average just over half a second for spreading activation to maximally excite the concept represented by a related target word, and that activation spontaneously dissipates afterwards.

In another experiment, Neely varied the relation between the prime word and the target word or nonword letter string that followed it. He told his participants that, in the normal condition, (1) a prime word would be likely to be followed by a word from the primed category (e.g., "BIRD" followed by a bird name, or a nonword). In a somewhat perverse condition (2) a prime word would be likely followed by a word from some other specific category (e.g., "BIRD" followed by a name of a body part or a nonword).

The interesting condition is the one in which a category prime was usually followed by a word from another category. That is, "BIRD" was usually followed by the name of a body part, like "ARM," but sometimes it was followed by a word from the same category as the prime, like "CANARY," and of course, many trials included nonwords, like "BORT." In this case, Neely's subjects knew what category to expect, presumably by thinking something like, "Bird—oh—that means body part" after the cue. Although when "BIRD" was followed by a real word, it nearly always was the name of some body part, but on a few rare trials, it was actually followed by the name of a bird. Neely found that naturally related words that occurred only occasionally ("BIRD" followed by "CANARY," for example) showed priming at short SOAs (200 to 400 ms), and "reversed" priming effects ("BIRD" followed by a more commonly-occurring and expected example, "ARM") showed up only at longer SOAs (700 ms or more).

The importance of these results is that intentional swapping of a priming cue's meaning for another (BIRD to BODY PART) takes time, but eventually, the reinterpreted cue produces priming much like a naturally-associated category label and an exemplar. However, the translation process cannot prevent automatic priming from initially facilitating the recognition of a related word, even if it is unexpected. In summary, related words produce fast automatic priming, and unrelated but rule-based primes result in slow, voluntary priming. In general, priming helps us to deal with sequences of events that occur in physical actions as well as in normal sentences. That is because sequences in both contexts usually contain related items. These relations can be used to prepare (prime) us for upcoming words or events, such that they are interpreted and understood more rapidly than if no priming had occurred.

7.5 The Neuroscience of Semantic Memory

Since semantic memory lies at the heart of the meaning of things and events, it is not surprising that it is intimately linked with the semantic aspects of language. In fact, one of the most common ways in which semantic memory is activated is through internal, lexical representations of written and spoken words. Warrington (1975) was among the first to provide clinical evidence supporting Tulving's distinction between semantic and episodic memory systems. She reported data from three patients with progressive dementia due to neurological disease who showed specific semantic memory impairments. Whereas these patients suffered little loss in intellectual ability, perception, and expressive language, they demonstrated severe losses in understanding the meaning of objects represented by words or pictures. Many of these results can be summarized by describing the losses in terms of accessing stored semantic memories, not in losses of the actual representations themselves. Further, certain types of semantic information were more vulnerable than others [i.e., property relations ("a canary has feathers") were more impaired than were subset/superset relations ("a canary is a bird")]. Subsequent research with patients suffering from strokes or diseases, such as herpes encephalitis, have also found semantic dementias characterized by difficulty in producing names of objects represented by pictures, by verbal descriptions, or by categories from which patients were to cite examples. All of the patients were subsequently shown to have damage in the left temporal lobe of the brain (Hodges, Patterson, Oxbury, & Furnell, 1992; Martin, 2001).

These conclusions have been supported by neuroimaging techniques using non-patient subjects. A critical manipulation has been to present pictures of familiar versus meaningless, nonsense objects while the amounts of metabolic activity in different brain areas are measured. The idea is that both types of stimuli should activate brain regions associated with processing visual input, but only those areas involved with processing conceptual and verbal information about objects should be active for the real items. The research showed two major brain areas that are more active for the familiar objects, namely the left inferior frontal cortex (Broca's area) and the posterior temporal lobe. Temporal lobe activity was bilateral in some studies (e.g., Martin, Wiggs, Lalonde, & Mack, 1996) and more heavily left-lateralized in others (e.g., Zelkowitz, Herbster, Nebes, Mintun, & Becker, 1998). Similar studies showed greater temporal lobe activity for silently reading real words as opposed to consonant letter strings (Price, Wise, & Frackowiak, 1996). In a review of these results, Martin (2001) concluded that primary storage of semantic information about words and objects is in the left temporal lobe for most people, whereas the left frontal cortex is responsible for directing retrieval of information from semantic memory (see also Moscovitch et al., 2007; Wagner, Bunge, & Badre, 2004).

Further studies of brain-damaged individuals have shown that semantic difficulties can sometimes be very specific. For example, some patients show selective deficits for naming animals, while retaining the ability to name tools, whereas others show a reverse effect: greater difficulty for manufactured artifacts and less for living things (Forde & Humphreys, 1999). Other areas of the ventral part of the temporal lobe seem to be particularly involved in face recognition (e.g., Kanwisher, McDermott, and Chun, 1997), and damage there can result in prosopagnosia—the inability to recognize faces, even those of one's own family. These differences might be due to the fact that different parts of the temporal lobes are associated with categorical information about visual features (relevant for animals) and with information about functional use (relevant for tools). This conclusion is supported by evidence that patients who show difficulty in identifying animals also have difficulty in identifying other objects that are defined by small visual differences, such as precious stones (Haxby, 2004; Martin, 2001).

In a recent review of the neuroscience of semantic memory, Yee, Chrysikou, and Thompson-Schill (2013) have argued that there is evidence for at least two theories of semantic memory formation and use. One is domain-specific, in the sense that semantic categories of the Collins and Quillian (1969) type exist in a generalized, modality-free structure that has abstracted the general properties of living things, artifacts, tools, etc. and their individual exemplars. The other type of theories emphasize the link between sensory-motor based interactions with environmental objects and their resulting general properties as food items, tools, clothing, predators, etc. For example, different parts of the temporal lobe are activated more for animal terms (an area associated with visual information processing) and for tools (am area related to action information). Studies of brain-damaged individuals have supported the claim that sensory-motor areas in the brain are associated with at least some components of semantic memory, whereas other areas, particularly the anterior temporal lobe, are associated with more abstract categorical relations. The picture that emerges is that semantic memory is distributed over a variety of different brain areas that are differentially activated depending on the task environment (e.g., naming, describing a function, use in a sentence, etc.) in which a common object or its name are processed.

In summary, deficits associated with specific types of brain damage, and neuro-imaging studies of non-patients have lead to similar conclusions. Many of the brain areas associated with production and comprehension of language are the same as, or closely linked with, areas involved in semantic memory. This relationship is consistent with the main function of language: the exchange of meaningful ideas among members of a linguistic community.

7.6 Interactions Between Semantic and Episodic Memory

Semantic and episodic memories interact in comprehending and remembering everyday events. Research has shown that semantic memory performance is better in tests of items that also have some associated episodic memories (e.g., Westmacott, Black, Freedman, & Moscovitch, 2004). Further interactions have been observed in abstract memories for structures larger than mere concepts and relations (i.e., from repeated experiences with complex events or event sequences). That is, it is believed that not only do the specific elements (e.g., concepts and relations) of semantic memory derive from experience with common objects and events, but larger memory structures are also derived from repeated experiences with common, everyday occurrences. In theory, common experiences can lead to higher-order structures called **schemata** or **scripts,** which serve both to predict and understand events in real time as well as to organize, store, and retrieve information in long-term memory. The term *schemata* (or schemas) usually refers to familiar structures, such as an internal map of your home town, whereas a script is used to refer to a familiar sequence of actions, such as what you might do to get ready for school or work in the morning. However, these structures can incur some costs, as when we "remember" things that simply did not happen, because they plausibly fit with familiar experience.

The idea of memory schemata derives from the work of Bartlett (1932/1967). He reported the first detailed studies of memory for folktales, stories, and pictures. The procedure that he used was to provide a single study episode followed by repeated memory tests hours, days, and years later. Perhaps the most famous of the materials

Schemata Theoretical structures in semantic memory that have developed to represent commonly-occurring objects and events, such as stories, maps or routes for familiar journeys, and layouts of familiar structures, such as faces, kitchens, buildings, and gardens

Scripts Theoretical structures in semantic memory that have developed to represent commonly-occurring sequences of events, such as dining out at a restaurant or attending a theater, lecture, or party he used was the Native American story, *The War of the Ghosts,* although he chose different kinds of materials that varied in their familiarity to the Cambridge students who participated in his research over 80 years ago (see Box 7.1).

BOX 7.1
Bartlett's *The War of the Ghosts*

F. C. Bartlett published an influential book called *Remembering: A Study in Experimental and Social Psychology* (1932/1967). In this book, he described a variety of ideas and experiments that he undertook to study some of the vagaries of memory evidenced by his colleagues and students at Cambridge University in England. One of the most famous examples concerns his use of a native North American folktale. In his studies he used the method of an initial reading (actually two readings at the subject's own pace) followed by repeated recollections at various intervals. The original version of the story, as translated by Franz Boas, reads as follows:

The War of the Ghosts

One night two young men from Egulac went down to the river to hunt seals, and while they were there it became foggy and calm. Then they heard war-cries, and they thought: "Maybe this is a war-party." They escaped to the shore, and hid behind a log. Now canoes came up, and they heard the noise of paddles, and saw one canoe coming up to them. There were five men in the canoe, and they said:

"What do you think? We wish to take you along. We are going up the river to make war on the people."

One of the young men said: "I have no arrows."

"Arrows are in the canoe," they said.

"I will not go along. I might be killed. My relatives do not know where I have gone. But you," he said, turning to the other, "may go with them."

So one of the young men went, but the other returned home.

And the warriors went on up the river to a town on the other side of Kalama. The people came down to the water, and they began to fight, and many were killed. But presently the young man heard one of the warriors say: "Quick, let us go home: that Indian has been hit." Now he thought: "Oh, they are ghosts." He did not feel sick, but they said he had been shot.

So the canoes went back to Egulac, and the young man went ashore to his house, and made a fire. And he told everybody and said: "Behold I accompanied the ghosts, and we went to fight. Many of our fellows were killed, and many of those who attacked us were killed. They said I was hit, and I did not feel sick."

He told it all, and then he became quiet. When the sun rose he fell down. Something black came out of his mouth. His face became contorted. The people jumped up and cried.

He was dead.

Bartlett used stories like *The War of the Ghosts* in his research because they provided a number of useful features of theoretical interest for his research. First, the stories represented a fairly alien culture and social environment with respect to his Cambridge students. He was interested in what might happen to a story as it is transmitted from one culture to another. Second, he was interested in how apparently unconnected events might be interpreted and recalled by his subjects. Third, he thought that the supernatural occurrences and vivid imagery that were evoked by some descriptions in the stories might influence memory for them.

Bartlett used the method of repeated reproduction, in which the first attempt at a complete recall of the story was made within about 15 minutes after the two initial readings. Further recalls were attempted at irregular intervals, but typically included two weeks, six weeks, and further months and years after the initial readings with no additional study of the original material. Bartlett noted several changes that occurred in the initial recalls of the story, and these generally became more pronounced as the recall interval increased.

(1) Although the initial recalls tended to be fairly accurate, the stories were often shortened, mainly by omissions, and the vocabulary and grammar tended to be recalled in more modern forms.

(2) The title and proper names all dropped out either with the initial recall or soon afterward.

(3) There was a strong tendency to rationalize unusual or supernatural events, so that they were either omitted or explained in a more natural, satisfying way. Such inferences and explanations are generally added to make the stories more coherent.

(4) More rarely, elaborations and other constructions were offered, usually to give a more dramatic sense to the story and add to its interest and coherence.

In general, the successive reproductions from different readers tended to converge on acceptable, understandable, comfortable, and straight-forward narratives with their puzzling elements removed. Literal accuracy of recall was clearly a rare exception, with both language and content shaped toward the more familiar and conventional. Elaborations and constructive inferences were more present in later recall, indicating that they were added as part of the recall process itself, and not as part of the original attempt to understand the story. Eventually, the story was actually replaced with a constructed revision of it, and this construction tells us about as much about the reader's mental schemata, beliefs and biases as it does about the story on which it is based.

Bartlett discovered many basic facts about memories for episodes that are active research topics today. One is that immediate or short-term recall tends to be largely reproductive, with most errors being omissions. Also, early memory tests can show **hypermnesia**, in which repeated tests without additional study can sometimes produce better recall in the short term. Delayed recall tends to be more reconstructive, with major errors introduced by combining story information with related information in long-term memory. Further, reconstructive errors tended to **normalize** story recall (with regard to cultural norms), making the stories more modern and conventional, by adding distortions and including information that was not in the original story. Normalization processes are evident in that different people's delayed recalls tend to become more alike within a given community or culture than they were in their initial recall. That is, they tend to rationalize or explain odd and supernatural occurrences in the story according to their common internal components of semantic memory.

Bartlett introduced the term memory schemata to describe sources of changes and additions observed in people's memories for stories. A schema is an active organization of related past experiences, and as such, it is a higher-order structure in semantic memory than simple concepts, associations, and propositions. Any new experience is compared with and sometimes integrated into an existing schema. Often, the new information is modified in some way to explain away discrepancies between the input episode and its interpretation. Similar processes are known to happen in pattern and object recognition, as when we recognize a car or person based on an incomplete or distorted image (e.g., if the object of interest is partially occluded by other objects or viewed briefly as it passes by a small window). Similarly, Gestalt principles of organization tend to improve an internal image of a perceived object to make it appear smoother, more continuous, and more symmetric than it actually might be. Both

Hypermnesia The tendency in repeated recollections of a certain event or story to introduce things present in the original that were not recalled in earlier retellings

Normalize The tendency to change characters, settings, and events in recall of a story to make them more consistent with one's own knowledge, beliefs, and cultural norms perception and memory tend to regularize our experiences to make them more like the average of our past encounters with similar objects and events.

Walter Kintsch (1977), discussed memory processes that can cause differences between the actual stories, movies, novels, and real-world events experienced by people and their later recall. He discriminated among (1) *reproductive memory*—which is more-or-less verbatim, accurate recall for some aspects of the original, (2) *constructive memory*—which includes additional *inferences made during the original event* that are incorporated into our memories, and (3) *reconstructive memory*—which includes additional knowledge incorporated into the original after the fact and added as *elaborations during recall* of the original.

Inferences and elaborations presumably arise from relevant knowledge structures in semantic memory that are activated both when the original material is experienced, and later, when it is recalled. Bartlett's schemata are theoretical structures that can affect memory for stories primarily through their influence on story recall. Other structures could influence both initial encoding as well as later recall, as Kintsch suggested. Schank and Abelson (1977) used the term scripts to describe certain sequences of events that occur in common situations (a birthday party, dining out, going to the movies, attending a lecture, and many other familiar events). In their theory, scripts have *headers* that alert us to particular major components of the script. These include the initial situation or plan of action that prepares us for what we should encounter as we enter a restaurant, attend a social event, or enter a sports arena. They can also be the initial acts of a speaker or a movie that leads us to generate certain expectations about a theme, genre, or story line. A script has *frames* or *slots* that are subcomponents executed in a stereotyped order. Thus, when we enter a restaurant, we expect to be greeted by someone, then shown to a table, handed a menu, etc., all in a fixed order that we have learned to anticipate. The various events are slotted into the frames of the overlying script structure as we proceed through the components of the event. If certain expectations are unconfirmed or omitted, *default values* are assigned to occupy the frames unless they are later replaced by actual objects or events in the episode (see Box 7.2).

The benefits or higher-order structures in semantic memory, like schemata or scripts, are that they facilitate prediction and comprehension of frequently occurring events (and almost all events that we experience share components with past experiences). Scripts also provide a retrieval plan so that we can recall events as they have occurred. The costs of such structures include the occasional activation of an incorrect script, perhaps by failing to recognize an important header, or the choice of a default value when a particular event is omitted or the event includes an unusual entry. Bower, Black, and Turner (1979) presented their participants with short stories that included familiar scenarios, such as a visit to a doctor's office. They were later tested with sentences that were or were not included in the original story. When the data for new sentences were examined, they found that people were much more

BOX 7.2

An Example of Following a Script

This is an example of the use of a script to encode a common experience that resulted in an embarrassing mistake. I (JJ) was driving my car in Lawrence, Kansas, and needed to stop for gasoline. I pulled into a gas station that I had used many times, and stopped next to the pump, opened the lid to the gas tank, and removed the pump handle in order to fill up the tank. Unfortunately, the pump had not been cleared from the previous purchase, and I could get no gas. After a few failed attempts to get the attendant's attention, I went inside the shop and asked the attendant to clear the pump, which he did. I then filled the tank of my car and drove off.

My next stop was across the street at a grocery store, and I picked up a few items and returned to my car. I was somewhat surprised to see a police car parked next to mine, with a female officer looking in the windows. "Did you forget something?" she asked me. I thought for a moment before the horrible realization struck that I just might have driven off from the gas station without paying. I admitted it,

and she said that she didn't think I was actually trying to get away with theft, since I had immediately parked just across the street. To be sure, however, she accompanied me back to the gas station.

That gave me the opportunity to offer a logical explanation for my absent-mindedness. "You see," I told her, "I am a psychology professor, and we believe that we have these structures called scripts in our heads that prepare us to do a certain number of things in a certain order when doing some routine task. One of the things you do at a gas station is to go inside to pay the attendant for the gas you pumped. Well, I had already gone inside once to ask the attendant to clear and turn on the pump, and when I had finished, I had already filled the slot in the script for going into the store to take care of the bill. Therefore, I drove off thinking that all the required acts had been taken care of." She was so impressed with my story that she stayed to make sure I paid the bill, in case I absent-mindedly followed some other script!

likely to say that such a sentence had actually been presented if it could logically be included in the script than if it were a new, non-script based sentence. That is, people were much more likely to say that they remembered a sentence like, "The patient removed his clothes," than one like, "There was a large plant in the waiting room," even though neither sentence or anything like it had actually been included in the story about a doctor's visit.

Results supporting the use of higher-order memory structures indicate that these structures have been incorporated into our memories because they generally serve useful purposes. That is, we live in an orderly world with numerous scenarios that follow a regular script. Just think about the routines you go through in getting up and getting ready for school or work in the morning, driving to work or school, parking and entering your building, encountering friends and co-workers, executing familiar tasks, carrying on a light-hearted, perhaps cliché-riddled, conversation, and all the other routine tasks that fill our days. The use of scripts and schemata can help us to deal with these situations by providing maps and action sequences that we can choose to follow. These guidelines enable us to interact with the environment in a more efficient way, as most details do not need to be processed to high levels if they can be correctly anticipated. More processing resources then should remain available for processing the unexpected anomaly or less typical events that occur and demand our attention, such as dangers on the road, or being asked a question. Unfortunately, as Kintsch (1977) and Bower et al. (1979) have shown, higher-order knowledge can also sometimes lead us astray. In some situations we can actually produce false memories that can be "remembered" with as great or even greater certainty than actual events if they are consistent with the relevant script. The idea of false memories, as well as forgetting of actual memories, is much more the province of episodic than of semantic memory, and they will be covered in the next chapter.

Another characteristic of semantic memory that distinguishes it from episodic memory is that it appears to be more permanent, and resistant to change. The most common changes in memory are learning and forgetting. These processes are slow developing in semantic memory, but the addition to, and apparent loss of information from, episodic memory is a very common aspect of our lives.

7.7 **Non-Declarative Memories**

Although much of what we mean when we talk about memory includes things like encyclopedic knowledge and recollection of events, it is clear that we learn and remember many other things that cannot be so easily be described. Squire (1992; see also Schacter & Tulving, 1994) and others have distinguished between **declarative** and **non-declarative** memories (see Figure 7.1). Declarative memories are things that we have learned and can retrieve with awareness. As such, we can describe them verbally, such as the meaning of a word or where we ate dinner last night. Both semantic and episodic memories are included within the set of declarative memories. Non-declarative memories, on the other hand, are often acquired implicitly, without necessarily an intention or even the awareness of learning. Such memories include sensory motor skills, such as riding a bicycle or catching a ball, and broad generalizations about specific experiences, such as biases, preferences, and judgments. Priming effects, such as repetition (or perceptual) priming (e.g., Biederman & Cooper, 1991) and semantic (or conceptual) priming (e.g., Meyer & Schvaneveldt, 1971), are also examples of changes that can occur in memory without our intention or awareness. Another difference between declarative and non-declarative memories is that the types of amnesia resulting from medial temporal lobe damage are largely restricted to declarative memories, whereas the retention and acquisition of procedural memories remain largely intact (Moscovitch, et al., (2007).

Declarative memories Things that are learned and retrieved with awareness and intention, and their retrieval promotes verbal descriptions of their contents; both semantic and episodic memories are declarative memories

Non-declarative memories Things that are learned and retrieved without awareness and intention, such as perceptual-motor skills, biases, habitual responses and value judgments

Chapter Summary

Human long-term memory is a rich repository of an amazing variety of information that seems to have no limits on storage capacity nor a proven means of information loss. In order to understand its complexity, psychologists have used the strategy of *divide and conquer* in order to limit investigations to manageable components. Tulving argued that a major subdivision of long-term memory should be semantic versus episodic memories. Semantic memory is the structure that enables us to summarize past experiences and interpret new ones based on abstracted commonalities of experience. It is the basis of understanding, symbolic thought, and communication, and of necessity, it is similar across individuals. On the other hand, episodic memory is the record of the individual experiences themselves, and is therefore unique to each of us.

Semantic memory has been modeled as a neural network of interconnected concepts and relations among them, as a multidimensional feature space with concepts defined as locations in the space, or as a parallel-distributed network of nodes and associated weights. Whatever the theoretical representation, it is clear that semantic memory is highly associated with language and is represented in the left temporal lobe of the brain for most of us. In any case, the theories need to account for basic facts, such as how we decide whether propositions expressed in simple sentences are true or false, how we understand and remember stories, and how we understand and interact with other people and objects in natural environments. Theorists have found the need to hypothesize the existence of high-order structures, such as schemata or scripts, to explain how easily we interact with common situations and remember them later. Such structures aid our understanding and memory because they are usually adequate architectures to fit with experience, but when the fit is not perfect, these structures can lead to misunderstanding of situations or errors in memory of them. Although most memory research has concentrated on declarative memories, such as episodic and semantic memory, researchers are becoming increasingly aware of the vast amount of information that can apparently be learned implicitly, without awareness and without verbalization during recall, such as the learning and retrieval of perceptual-motor skills.

Review Questions

- **Is human long-term memory a unitary structure, or are there multiple types of memories?**

Although parsimony dictates that we should not adopt a theory more complicated than necessary to explain the existing data, it is clear that the data from research on human memory points to the existence of different kinds of memory systems. In the Atkinson-Shiffrin theory, a distinction had been made between sensory, short- and long-term memories. Within long-term memory, Paivio's dual-coding theory presumed the existence of different kinds of memories for verbal and visuo-spatial information. Tulving further argued that semantic and episodic memories demonstrate different structural and processing components. Finally, there is evidence that declarative knowledge which we deliberately learn and can describe verbally, is different from procedural knowledge, which we often learn implicitly and usually cannot describe verbally.

- **How is meaning represented in memory?**

There is general consensus that meaning is represented in a type of semantic memory that is identified with left-temporal lobe processes in most people. Semantic memory theories include primary forms of representation, which entail the conceptual base of knowledge. This conceptual base has been represented alternatively as a simple network of concept nodes and relations among them, a multidimensional feature space in which concepts are locations in the space defined by the values that they have on the various dimensions, or a complex neural network in which concepts are represented by sets of weights distributed over a population of nodes existing at different levels. In any case, these primitive concepts must be combined in some way into propositions and higher-order structures called schemata or scripts. Propositions code simple ideas for expression or comprehension, whereas schemata and scripts code abstract generalizations of large structures or event sequences that have occurred with some regularity in our environments.

- **How are simple sentences represented and understood?**

Simple sentences are formed by one or more propositions linked into a meaningful set of phrases. Let us consider a simple sentence of the form "A weasel is an animal." In order to understand this sentence, it is necessary to have some internal representation of the meanings of "weasel," "animal," and the relation ("is") between them. We can, for the moment, ignore the articles "a" and "an" as pertaining to individual noun categories. If the meanings can be thought of as locations in a semantic memory space (or activations in a web of interconnected neurons), there must be some way for determining the relation between them and whether this relation is consistent with the verb in the sentence. In a simple network model, the relations among concepts in the memory model (a weasel is a mammal, and a mammal is an animal) can be compared with the relation expressed in the sentence. If they are analogous, the sentence is understood by being consistent with existing knowledge. If there is an inconsistency, the sentence, as it is understood, is deemed to be false.

- **Are there representations in memory for large structures like maps or stories?**

  Researchers have provided evidence for the existence of large-scale structures, such as schemas and scripts in human semantic memory. The evidence has come from studies of story comprehension and recall, which indicate that people make predictable errors in their recalls after various retention intervals. The errors tend to be consistent with interpretations made at the time of reading as well as reconstructions made at the time of recall. Both are influenced by normalizing memory structures that shape perception and memory toward an ideal form based on sets of related experiences. Thus, in reading a story, we expect to be introduced to a setting and characters, the development of themes and problems that need resolution, and an eventual resolution and conclusion. That is, we expect stories to fit into a general scheme, or predictable structure. The same is true for maps, blueprints, diagrams, automobile dashboard controls, and apartment and home layouts. In addition, there are certain sequences of events that we have experienced many times that result in scripts being entered into semantic memory. We have gone to a restaurant many times and expect the sequence to include being greeted by a host or hostess, being shown to a table, being offered a menu and a drink, placing an order, receiving some food, eating it, paying for the meal, and leaving. Repeated sequences like this presumably lead to script-like structures that serve the dual purpose of helping us to understand each episode as it unfolds in time while we are experiencing it as well as to recall the events at a later time should we choose to do so. Thus, as Bartlett argued almost 80 years ago, such higher-order memory structures have been acquired because they help us to understand and remember experiences in our daily lives.

- **What brain processes are involved in storing and retrieving meaningful information?**

  Much research has shown that many parts of the brain are involved in encoding, storing and retrieving memories. Results from brain-damaged individuals and imaging studies of normal, control subjects have converged on painting the same complicated picture. Memory begins with sensory coding areas in the temporal lobes for hearing and the occipital lobes for vision. These sensory events result in perceptual experiences that are stored in many parts of the brain. From these, semantic memory systems seem to be localized in the left temporal lobe for most people, and spatial relations seem to be bilaterally represented in the parietal lobes. Much of the actual work in storing and retrieving information is performed in the frontal lobes, with some evidence to support the notion that the left temporal lobe is more involved with verbal materials, and the right temporal lobe is more involved with spatial materials.

Key Terms

Cognitive economy   191

Declarative memories   204

Episodic memory   187

Hypermnesia   201

Multidimensional feature model   194

Network model   189

Non-declarative memories   204

Normalize   201

Priming   195

Schemata   199

Scripts   199

Semantic memory   187

Typicality effect   192

ELIZABTH LOFTUS

Chapter 8

Long-Term Memory for Events

"A well-known pedagogical principle is that vivid impressions are easily recalled. With frequency, recency, and emotional congruity, vividness plays an important role in association. In order to test the abiding character of a vivid experience, 179 middle-aged and aged people were asked in personal interviews the following question: "Do you recall where you were when you heard that Lincoln was shot?" ... 127 replied in the affirmative, and were able to give full particulars ... Inasmuch as 33 years have elapsed since Lincoln's death, the number who made an affirmative reply must be considered large, and bears testimony to the abiding character of vivid experiences."

F. W. Colgrove, Individual memories, *American Journal of Psychology*, 1899, 10, 228–255.

PREVIEW QUESTIONS

❖ *What is long-term memory for events like, and how does it differ from semantic memory?*

❖ *Are flashbulb memories different from memories for typical daily events?*

❖ *What are some of the major causes of forgetting?*

❖ *Do false memories really exist, or are they merely the results of suggestive questioning?*

❖ *Are there other kinds of long-term memories besides semantic and episodic memories?*

❖ *What brain processes are involved in storing and retrieving memories of events?*

8.1 Introduction to Memory for Personal Events

All of us have personal memories that include details of experiences that we have had and in which we have actively participated. Unlike semantic memory, which is a type of shared memory for general information, episodic memory is a private memory for specific events. It is, in effect, time and place stamped, as it is a record that retains the perceptual flavor of the actual experience that produced it. As such, episodic memories are unique to each of us, unlike the general similarity across individuals for semantic memory and its higher-order structures. Further, such episodes are stored and recalled with great variability. Some especially vivid, traumatic, or emotionally-wrenching events seem to be permanently impressed upon our memories, such as the *flashbulb* experience illustrated above (see Brown & Kulik, 1977). Others seem to occupy a fleeting moment on the stage of consciousness and then are apparently lost and gone forever. What causes this variety, and does the fact that we remember some events well and forget others have any resolution in theories of memory?

Although all life events produce some episodic traces, we often have difficulty recalling specific details of past experiences. While it might be possible for us to recall many events that occurred yesterday, the details of our daily activities seem to fade and become less memorable as each day passes. Most of us would be hard-pressed to recall what we did on Tuesday, August 17, 2004, for example, unless it was somehow special to us, like a birthday or a memorable party or vacation date. Other dates, however, seem to have etched indelible images into our memories, such as where we were when we first heard about some incredible event, such as the death of a close friend or relative or the 9/11 disasters. Still other events seem to be "remembered" when in fact they never occurred at all, yet we sometimes refuse to believe that they did not actually happen. Theories of episodic memory have to account for all of these phenomena: what we can recall accurately, what we recall falsely, and why we sometimes seem unable to remember anything at all about some event in which we had participated.

8.2 Experimental Studies of Episodic Memory

Laboratory studies of episodic memory have typically used materials that are unique in some way so that memory for them can be more easily measured. Ebbinghaus's (1885) solution was to use lists of nonsense syllables, like DAX and BIF, so that their learning would not be contaminated by previous learning and associations. Bartlett (1932/1967) rightly commented that rather than eliminating pre-existing associations,

Ebbinghaus merely increased their variability. That is, there is a natural tendency for people to try to interpret things that are presented to them, even if they are thought to be meaningless. When confronted with nonsense materials, we try to make sense out of them, such as by trying to associate a nonsense syllable with a familiar word: DAX = "Desk," for instance. Psychologists sided with Bartlett about 50 years ago when they came to realize that rather than eliminating people's associations with the stimuli, nonsense materials inevitably produced endless and uncontrollable variety in the associations that people produced to them. Most researchers studying verbal learning since have used words, sentences, or stories as their materials. At least we should find greater similarity across individuals about how the materials are encoded, learned, and remembered.

Research using lists of unrelated words replicated and extended many of Ebbinghaus's findings. These include the results that (1) about seven (plus or minus two) items can usually be recalled perfectly after a single, brief study trial, (2) the first and last several items in a list are recalled better than items in the middle (serial position effect), and (3) both learning and forgetting increase rapidly at first and then decelerate to an asymptotic level. Although Ebbinghaus's studies were based on lists of nonsense syllables, the general conclusions seem to be valid for other kinds of episodic memories. For example, Sehulster (1989) reported a serial position effect in his own memory for performances of the Metropolitan Opera attended over a period of 25 years. The earliest memories and those of the most recent performances were recalled in the most detail.

Memory research has pioneered several different methods to assess memory strength. The method favored by Ebbinghaus was **savings**, the time taken to learn something a second time relative to the time taken to first learn it. Formally, savings is defined as the difference in study time between first and second learnings, divided by the time for first learning. If someone first learned a poem to perfection in one hour, and five years later was able to learn the same poem in half an hour, the savings would be (60 min − 30 min)/60 min, or 0.50. Multiplying 0.50 by 100 would convert this amount of savings to 50%, a reduction in learning time by one half due to previous practice.

Savings The most sensitive measure of memory yet devised; the time it takes to learn something a first time, minus the time taken to learn something the second time, divided by the time to learn it the first time, multiplying the result by 100 yields the percentage of savings

Ebbinghaus's method of savings is the most powerful measure of memory known, as savings can be shown to exist in situations in which people have no apparent memory, either through recall attempts or even in recognition of what it is they are trying to learn. It is quite possible to be able to recall nothing of a previous story, movie, or game, but a second experience will often result in better performance and, therefore, a type of memory for a repeated episode than if there had been no prior exposure. In contrast, uncued recall of past events is often very poor, as can be demonstrated by asking for details of what you did on some day three weeks ago or being asked to write down the names of all the students who were in your high school class. On the other hand, recognition tests of memory usually produce better levels of memory performance than recall tests because the item presented for recognition serves as a cue to help the search for related information in memory. For example, at this minute you probably should not be able to recall who was present at your ninth birthday party, but if the family album were opened to the right place, you might immediately be able to recognize and name most if not all of the guests.

8.3 Memory for Real-Life Events

Bahrick, Bahrick, and Wittlinger (1975) tested memory for names and pictures of high school classmates for nearly 400 people, 17 to 74 years of age. They found that recognition memory for pictures and names was very high throughout one's lifetime. Recognition scores were about 70% to 90% accurate, with most of these losses not occurring until 25 to 35 years after graduation. Although most people could not recall individual names with this level of accuracy (average percentage of names recalled was about 15%), high levels of recognition were possible. Such high levels of recognition accuracy were due to the repeated and prolonged experiences that people had with their classmates throughout their school years. Other than the measure of savings, recognition tests of memory are among the most sensitive known—faces and names can be recognized after many years of no experience with them even if they had not been recalled in an initial memory test.

Shepard (1967) demonstrated phenomenal recognition ability for people who had experienced only a single study trial, particularly for visual information. He asked his subjects to look through a series of 612 different pictures at their own pace, and later tested their memories. The test consisted of a pair of pictures, including one old one from the set of 612, and one new one shown for the first time. Subjects were able to pick the old ones out with over 98% accuracy immediately after study, and accuracy remained over 90% even if the test was delayed for a week. Shepard's demonstration indicates that a sensitive memory test (recognition rather than recall) can produce surprisingly strong memories of specific objects and events, just as was shown by Bahrick, et al. (1975).

One difference between recall and recognition tests of memory that has been proposed by memory researchers is the type of retrieval process that locates the desired information. Whereas recall demands a search of a potentially large part of memory, recognition provides a cue—a token copy of what might be found in memory. Indeed some theorists have said that the main difference between recall and recognition is the difficulty of the search process in recall, and that it is all but eliminated in a recognition test—the test stimulus itself determines the memory location searched first (e.g., Atkinson & Juola, 1974). Recall of desired information can be made easier by the use of certain strategies that facilitate the three necessary stages of memory— encoding, storage, and retrieval (see Box 8.1).

BOX 8.1

Mnemonic Devices

Mnemonic devices are strategies for improving memory. It has often been stated by memory researchers that memory involves three stages, all of which must be executed successfully in order for information to be retrieved when needed. These stages are encoding, storage, and retrieval. Very little is remembered of any object or event if it is not attended to and coded properly. Common feelings of absent-mindedness, like where on earth we have put our keys or glasses, are often due to not attending to actions when they are performed. Encoding strategies that work are usually the product of directed attention and also involve some elaboration of the stimulus that adds to the information stored about it. That is, additional verbal associations or visual images can be deliberately generated and encoded with the experience to yield a richer code than what would be generated from passive, unattended processing.

Storage is most effective if new information can be integrated with existing knowledge rather than being stored as an isolated entry. Integrated memory codes provide both greater protection from destructive interference and multiple ways to access such information later on. Finally, the best encoding and storage strategies one can use will be ineffective if there is no retrieval plan for gaining access to the information when needed. Tulving and Thomson (1973) have argued that the best retrieval cues are those that were also present during initial encoding, a theory known as the encoding specificity principle. Retrieval is best when the conditions present during the memory test match those present at study as much as possible. These and other mnemonic principles were reviewed effectively by Gordon Bower (1970), and they will be summarized here. However, it should be kept in mind that, as Schacter (2001) points out, there are no memory tricks that will improve memory the way putting on a pair of glasses can improve eyesight. Like any other skill, memory aids work best when practiced and pursued with effort.

Perhaps almost all of us remember such phrases as "i before e except after c, except when sounded like 'a' as in neighbor and weigh, (except for the exceptions)" or "all cows eat grass," or even "on old Olympus' towering top a Finn and German viewed some hops." These are all examples of mnemonic devices that help us with such things as the vagaries of English spelling, the names of the lines and spaces of the bass and treble clefs, and the order of entry of cranial nerves into the central nervous system. The last example is a bit unusual, as it is most commonly used by medical students in learning neuroanatomy. Yet, the majority of mnemonic devices apparently were designed to assist children to learn basic facts of spelling, music, science, etc. The general belief seems to be that children need such artificial devices to aid their learning and memory, whereas adults have more advanced memory skills that are not helped as much by mnemonics. Nothing could be further from the truth. Mnemonic devices of various types have been shown to be very effective for adults as well as children, and could help college students to master material necessary for exams and for applying their knowledge to practical problems.

Bower's (1970) paper, "Analysis of a Mnemonic Device" summarizes his research and observations of how certain people have trained themselves to become extraordinary memorizers of information. There are certain commonalties to all successful memory tricks, including the following general principles:

1) Organize the material to learn and relate it to what you already know.

2) Practice relating the new to the old using a scheme or device, like a rhyme or an image.

3) Develop a retrieval plan based on this device and practice using it to retrieve the original information.

Some examples of mnemonic devices have been with us for centuries, such as the so-called method of loci. Supposedly a Greek poet named Simonides of Ceos was the featured speaker at a banquet and was called outside before a great earthquake struck and leveled the banquet hall. Distraught relatives of the victims were at a loss to identify their loved ones until Simonides was able to recall who they were from remembering the seating arrangement. The method of loci works by having a set of locations that are already memorized, such as a set of houses on your hometown street or the buildings along the main drive of your campus. During encoding, the items to be remembered are studied in conjunction with each item in the set of locations. Forming an interactive image between the items and the loci is among

Continues

the most powerful link, if the item to be recalled is concrete and imageable. When it is time to recall the list of items, a mental walk is taken along the route and each site is examined to retrieve the image.

Similar methods have used a rhyming scheme ("one is a bun, two is a shoe, …") or a story line to both provide an initial sequence of known items on which to append a new list, and to serve a retrieval cue when it is time to recall the items. In all cases, relational images between the known items and the new ones provide links that most are resistant to forgetting.

Other methods use acronyms, such as ROYGBIV for the seven spectral hues of the rainbow, and FACE for the names of spaces in the treble clef. The best mnemonic devices all use methods of elaborative coding, including imagery whenever possible, and an encoding scheme that also serves as a retrieval plan. The methods have definite benefits in aiding memory when external memory aids, such as lists, are unavailable or inconvenient. However, like most skills, they work best when practiced with proper application.

8.4 Flashbulb Memories

In 1899, Colgrove presented impressive data showing that most adults who were alive at the time of President Lincoln's assassination had detailed memories of where they where and what they were doing when they first learned about it. Similar results were reported by Brown and Kulik (1977) who asked 80 adult subjects to recall where they had been and what they had been doing when they first heard about some major historical events, like the assassinations of President John F. Kennedy on November 23, 1963, or Martin Luther King on April 1, 1968. They used the term **flashbulb memories** to describe the unique type of memory that has a "… 'live' quality that is almost perceptual. Indeed it is very like a photograph that indiscriminately preserves the scene in which each of us found himself when the flashbulb was fired" (Brown & Kulik, p. 74). Participants were scored as having flashbulb memories if they answered "yes" to the question "Do you recall the circumstances in which you first heard that …?" and if they could also recall at least one of the following details: (1) where they learned of it, (2) what they were doing at the time, (3) who told them the news, (4) the effects on themselves, (5) the effects observed in others, and (6) some details of the aftermath of receiving the news.

Brown and Kulik (1977) reported that using their scoring methods, 79 of 80 participants had flashbulb memories of hearing of President Kennedy's assassination. In addition, 47 reported a similar type of memory for another personal, unexpected, shocking event, and more than half of the subjects reported flashbulb memories for hearing about the assassinations of Robert Kennedy and Martin Luther King. As Neisser (1982, p. 48) described the phenomena, "… such memories are not so much momentary snapshots as enduring benchmarks. They are the places where we line up our own lives with the course of history itself and say 'I was there.'" Although the results are suggestive, especially in terms of the details that many people confidently reported about the circumstances of hearing the news, it remains to be established whether or not flashbulb memories are different from other memories, in some

Flashbulb memories Presumably special types of memories for events that are particularly vivid and memorable that include the details of when and where people were when they learned of the event, who was present, and other details of the situation and events; most commonly associated with momentous or shocking events, such as personal tragedies or disasters of international importance special way. That is, are they qualitatively different from other memories or are they merely exceptionally vivid examples that fall along a continuum of different types of memories of past events?

Some reasons that certain memories could qualify as being of the *flashbulb* type is that they are emotionally powerful, which results in immediate and sustained attention to the original event, to the exclusion of possible interfering events. Further, they are likely to be of some personal or even international significance; therefore, they are likely to be reinforced by continued retrieval, reflection, and restorage, including discussions of similar memories among friends and relatives (Schacter, 2001). Descriptions of the events in news and other media are likely to rekindle the original memory and further reinforce its imagability and vividness. Memory research has been consistent in showing that the spacing of an experience over repeated episodes, and in different contexts, as well as practice in retrieving something are both powerful ways to increase memory for an event. This combination of personal, or social, importance and the repeated experiences that we have of certain recollections are likely reasons that flashbulb memories are merely quantitative extensions of more typical memories, rather than being in a qualitatively different class by themselves (Hirst & Phelps, 2016). This conclusion is supported by the fact that people's subjective reports of the shocking nature of the original event or the vividness of such memories do not correlate well with the accuracy of their memories. Talarico and Rubin (2003) reported that people's flashbulb memories of the World Trade Center attacks showed the same kind of decline in accuracy as everyday memories over a period of several months after the attack, and Neisser and Harsch (1992) found similar levels of forgetting for details of the *Challenger* explosion when measured three years after the accident. Although flashbulb memories might appear to be special and subjectively different to those who experience them, they seem to follow the same patterns of forgetting as other memories.

8.5 Forgetting

Despite the impressive feats of memory that many of us occasionally demonstrate, there are at least as many situations in which we clearly make mistakes. Errors of omission (forgetting) are common of course, but perhaps even more serious and disturbing are errors of commission, in which things are apparently recalled or recognized with confidence, when they did not occur or even could not possibly have occurred. Let's consider omission first, and some of the reasons that we might forget things we wish we had remembered. In his book, *The Seven Sins of Memory,* Daniel Schacter (2001) attributed omission errors to three factors, transience, absent-mindedness, and blocking.

8.5.1   Transience

Transience The general tendency for memories of daily events to decline with time; although some events seem to be retained with great clarity, the majority seem to gradually fade away

We all know that memories for daily events seem to get worse as time passes. Ebbinghaus (1885) was the first to demonstrate the quantitative properties of the forgetting curve, tracing out the rapid loss of memory for lists of nonsense syllables that he had learned to perfection, as the days and weeks of the retention interval passed by. Many studies have replicated his demonstration that forgetting follows an exponential decay function—rapid losses at first, followed by a slower decline to a low asymptotic level. Even if materials are learned to a high level of proficiency, forgetting follows the same general function. For example, Bahrick (1984) found just this type of forgetting for vocabulary words learned in high school Spanish classes. Those people who very infrequently or never used Spanish again after high school showed a rapid drop in memory for vocabulary items in the first few years after high school. However, the losses after that were very small for many years, and the losses that did occur between 35 and 49 years after completing high school could be attributed more to declines in general levels of memory associated with aging rather than true forgetting (Anderson, 2000; see Figure 8.1 and Chapter 13).

Several psychologists have more recently attempted to replicate some of Ebbinghaus's (1885) findings, using themselves as subjects for periods ranging from 4 to 6 years (Linton, 1978; Wagenaar, 1986). They kept diaries of significant, unique events that occurred each day and then tested themselves later for memory. Although

FIGURE 8.1

Example of a Forgetting Curve for Information Learned to Three Levels of High Proficiency

The three curves represent performance on a Spanish vocabulary test for students who had taken one, three, or five courses of Spanish in high school. Scores are highest immediately at the end of school, show a rapid drop in the first three years, and then remain flat until over 30 years after finishing high school. Note that the forgetting functions are the same for the three different levels of original learning (Bahrick, 1984).

From Anderson, J. R. (2000). *Cognitive Psychology and its Implications, 5th Ed.,* New York: Worth, p. 205

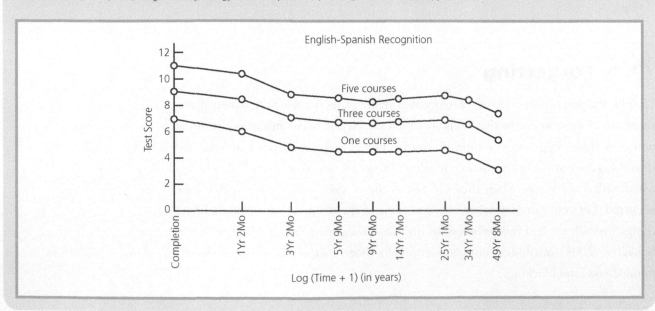

memory was found to fail increasingly with elapsed time, there is some question about whether such forgetting is due to interference or to true loss of information from memory. Wagenaar tested himself for memory at the end of a four-year period, using cues such as *who, what, where,* and *when*. He found that recall of the stored event increased with each additional cue, but there were some items that he could not recall, despite using all of the cues. In order to test himself further, he asked acquaintances who had participated in the original events to provide additional information about them. In all cases, such additional information was sufficient to enable him to recall the original event. As Schacter summarized these results, it seems as though "As time passes and interference mounts, information may be gradually lost to the point that only a powerful reminder can breach the seemingly inexorable effects of transience by dredging up the remaining fragment of an experience from ever-weakening neural connections" (2001, p. 33).

The transient aspect of memory can be combated by a variety of strategies and behaviors. First, attention and elaborate encoding at the time that the events occur can improve all event memories. Visual imagery and elaborations based on relevant knowledge can inure a memory from the destructive effect of interference from similar experiences over time. Second, repeated recollections and retellings can bring memories to life and renew their strength for subsequent retrieval (Karpicke & Roediger, 2008; Soderstrom, Kerr, & Bjork, 2016). Finally, the presence of a suggestive cue or reminder of the original event can lead to its recollection even if earlier attempts to recall it have failed.

8.5.2 *Absent-Mindedness*

Each of us has had moments of **absent-mindedness**, from forgetting where our glasses or keys are to forgetting appointments or things to pick up at a shop. Many of these memory lapses seem to be due to inadequate attention to details at critical moments. For example, if we should walk into our home or apartment and find the phone ringing, it is less likely that we would attend to where we drop our keys in the rush to answer the phone. Later, the misplaced keys might be difficult to find because no notice was taken of where they were put down. Research has shown that when attention is divided over two or more tasks, encoding new information is drastically reduced (Craik, Govoni, Naveh-Benjamin, & Anderson, 1996). It follows that when doing something that could produce a mini-disaster if forgotten, like putting one's glasses in an unusual place or parking one's car in a large parking lot, it pays dividends to attend to the details necessary to insure reliable retrieval.

There is a special name given to the attempt to do something in the present that should help to remember something in the future. **Prospective memories** are based on establishing some type of reminder that will be encountered in the future that should trigger the recovery of what one was supposed to do. These reminders can be event-based, such as trying to remember to stop at the grocery store as you pass

Absent-mindedness The tendency to forget daily activities, often soon after they have occurred; most likely due to inadequate storage of the information in the first place, probably due to distraction or lack of attention to the original event or behavior

Prospective memory The deliberate attempt to do something in the present that should help us to remember to carry out some action in the future; depends on the use of various reminder cues based on future times or events that should trigger the desired memory it on the way home from work, or time based, such as trying to remember to take a prescription medication at 9AM and 9PM (Einstein & McDaniel, 1990; McDaniel & Einstein, 2007).

Reminders usually take the form of setting up some cue in advance that should be informative and distinctive. When the cue is encountered in the future, it then should serve its proper role as a reminder to take the appropriate action. For example, if I were trying to remember to call a friend in the evening after work, I could take either an event-based approach, and say to myself that I must remember to call John after dinner, or a time-based approach, and say that I must remember to call at 8:00. In either case, when dinner is finished or 8:00 arrives, it must by itself trigger the memory to make the call. Obviously, there is nothing informative or distinctive about either cue, so I am very likely to forget. What I could do is form an image of the last time I had dinner with John, and think of him eating dessert—that might help me to recall the Chinese restaurant and dessert scene that I have stored prospectively when dessert is set out at home. Alternatively, I could imagine 8:00 as an eight-ball and imagine the last time I played a game of pool with John, so that I can try to retrieve that image when the clock strikes eight. Obviously, cues depending on time-based prospective memories are generally harder to make distinctive and informative, and they more often fail to produce the desired result than event-based cues. It is much more reliable, especially as we all get older and our lives seem to become more complicated, to rely on external memory aids. A calendar or messages taped to the door or programmed into some hand-held device can make us more certain that tasks we set out to do at certain future times are actually accomplished.

8.5.3   *Blocking*

Although absent-mindedness can prevent memories from being stored properly, and transience describes the inevitable loss of information that has been stored, blocking describes problems with the third stage of successful memory—retrieval.

Blocking can occur whenever a specific item must be recalled in a given situation, such as an answer on an exam when you are sure you know it, or the location of a favorite shop or restaurant when you cannot find it. However, the most common situation in which people find themselves blocking is in name retrieval. We are sure that most of us have had the embarrassing experience of meeting someone who addresses us by name and initiates a lively conversation, and we cannot remember exactly with whom we are talking. The person might even be very familiar to us, and the situation can become even worse when another friend comes up and we find ourselves needing to make an introduction. I (JJ) had a professor in graduate school who famously handled this situation by saying, "Why don't you two introduce yourselves?" whenever the occasion presented itself!

Perhaps the most well-known study of blocking was reported by Brown and McNeill (1966), who deliberately tried to produce retrieval failures by giving definitions

Blocking The inability to recall to mind some fact that is actually stored in memory (It most commonly occurs for names of people and things.)

of obscure words to their participants who were supposed to come up with the correct answer. For example, subjects were asked to recall the name of "a nautical device using the angle of the sun and horizon to find your position." Occasionally such definitions produced the **tip-of-the-tongue (TOT) state** in which the participants claimed to know the word, offered similar, but incorrect words (like "compass"), and could offer some details such as the beginning letter or number of syllables. If they eventually recalled the correct word, or if it finally was presented by the experimenter, the subject seemed to experience genuine relief that the frustrating period of fruitless effort had ended. (The correct answer is *sextant*, by the way.) Such TOT states are commonly reported by individuals, with diary studies showing that it occurs about twice as often for elderly persons (about 3 times a week) as for college students (about 1.5 times per week; Schacter, 2001). Again, the TOT state is more frequently reported for people's names, but it also occurs for names of books, movies, places, songs, and common words.

What is the explanation for blocking failures like the TOT state? Clearly, the result is not loss of memory, for people in that state frequently can offer partial knowledge about the target item, including aspects of its sound, spelling, and meaning. Rather, it seems to be a problem with retrieval of a specific memory code, in this case a name of someone or something. For example, people who are shown a photograph of a famous movie star will identify the person as an actor, and maybe even name a few movies the person has starred in, yet be unable to name the individual. It is almost never the case that the name is correctly retrieved without the participant being able to say what he or she does for a living. Names are also special in that they typically have only one exact representation in memory. When presented with a picture of an animal, we might say "dog," "coyote," "wolf," "German shepherd," "Alsatian," "police dog," or even "Rin-Tin-Tin," and not be committing an obvious error of memory. However, when shown a picture of Sean Connery, our response possibilities are much fewer, perhaps including "James Bond" or "Agent 007," besides his proper name. Brédart (1993) has reported that fewer retrieval blocks occurred for famous movie stars if people were allowed to identify the actors with either their real name or one of their character's names (like Sean Connery or James Bond) than if only their proper name would do.

Other explanations for retrieval blocking include the negative effects of retrieving similar, but incorrect information. Each act of retrieval produces activation of the retrieved concept or word, and this information can perseverate in memory. The unwanted, but highly active information can literally crowd out other information in working memory to the detriment of retrieving the desired information. Only with the passage of time, to let the interfering material dissipate in activation or with the deliberate attempt to approach the retrieval problem from a new angle, can blocking from competing information be released. Indeed, the presentation of a cue that introduces new, previously unretrieved information, such as the first letter of the person's name or his or her occupation, can sometimes unblock retrieval to everyone's relief.

Tip-of-the tongue (TOT) state The subjective experience that sometimes occurs while blocking; that the desired word to be recalled is literally "on the tip of the tongue" in that aspects of it such as its initial letter, number of syllables, vowels sounds, and aspects of meaning might be readily available, but its exact articulation cannot at that moment be produced

8.6 **False Memories**

$8.6.1$ *Demonstration of False Memories in Laboratory Settings*

The other kind of memory error, unlike omissions, is the apparent recall of information that never really happened. Schacter (2001) refers to these as the "sins" of misattribution (i.e., attributing information to the wrong source) and suggestibility (i.e., incorporating new information into an old memory). In the laboratory, there are several ways to demonstrate how such false memories can be constructed. For example, Deese (1959) had participants study lists of words like: "bed, desk, pillow, cushion, sheets, towel, dream, idea, tired, awake, night, blanket ..." Later tests showed that "sleep" was recalled with high probability and great confidence as having been on the list, even though it had not been presented. Apparently, many high associates in the list primed the word "sleep" and *activated* it during study. Roediger and McDermott (1995) confirmed this result and showed that people sometimes actually claimed to have remembered seeing or hearing words like "sleep" if many high associates of it had been presented in the list. Such high associates of list words, even though they were not included in the studied list, are often recognized falsely as having been on the list even more often than actual list words. This type of priming result is just one of many examples of how false memories can be induced in people. Even though their recollections are incorrect, such memories can be recalled and described convincingly and with high confidence by people who truly believe that their memories are valid.

Although laboratory studies of false memories can verify whether or not the recalled information actually occurred, it is generally impossible to determine whether memories produced in more natural situations are based on fact or not. This issue is particularly important in cases involving recovered memories of crimes or abuse. When an adult remembers incidents of childhood abuse after long periods of not recalling (or even deliberately repressing) them, it is a legitimate question to determine the veracity of the memories, particularly when they involve possibly disastrous consequences for the people involved. A study by Clancy, Schacter, McNally, and Pitman (2000) compared different groups of people on their susceptibility of making false recognition responses in the Deese/Roediger-McDermott (DRM) paradigm. The groups included people who had a continuous memory for childhood abuse (i.e., no period of forgetting or repression), people who had a recovered memory of previously forgotten childhood abuse in later adulthood, and a control group that claimed no abuse. Clancy et al. found that the recovered memory group had a higher tendency to falsely recognize associated words in the DRM task than did the other two groups. A follow-up study also found higher false recognitions of words for a group that had reported being abducted by space aliens than for a control group with no such reported experiences (Clancy, McNally, Schacter, Lenzenweger, & Pitman, 2002). McNally (2003) cautions us against over-interpreting such results, but they are indicative that some people, when questioned by therapists and investigators, might be more suggestible than others, and some recovered memories are therefore likely to be false.

8.6.2 The Incredible Eye Witness

Elizabeth Loftus has shown for over 30 years that eyewitness' memories and testimony are literally incredible. For example, Loftus and Palmer (1974) had people view videos of real and apparent (staged) automobile accidents. They then measured the effects of certain types of leading questions on responses that people made, supposedly based on their recollections alone. When asked questions like, "How fast was the red car going when it hit the green car?" the average answer was about 20 mph. However, when subjects who had viewed the same film were asked, "How fast was the red car going when it smashed into the green car?" the average speed estimate rose to 35 mph! Similarly, when subjects were asked later if they had seen any broken glass (there was none visible in the film), those who had been asked the "hit" question answered "yes" 14% of the time, whereas those who had been asked the "smashed into" question said "yes" 34% of the time.

Other types of leading questions can be more subtle. For example, a simple change in question format from, "Did you see any broken glass?" to "Did you see the broken glass?" can cause an increase in positive responses. The word *any* indicates no presumption of either possibility, whereas the definite article the indicates that broken glass was in fact present, and an astute observer certainly would have seen it (Loftus & Zanni, 1975). The inclusion of information that occurs before or after some event into the memory of the event itself is called the **misinformation effect**. For example, when a verbal description of an event is given after viewing the event, it is possible to introduce some details that were not present in the original experience. Yet, it is a common observation that subjects will sometimes report having *seen* the verbally-presented information in a photograph or video (Belli, 1989; Loftus, 1979; Loftus, Miller, & Burns, 1978). Such susceptibility can be especially high in young children. Ackil and Zaragoza (1998) showed elementary school children a video, and followed it with a set of questions, some of which were designed to be very suggestive so as to produce answers that were inconsistent with what had been seen. Later, many of the children confused their own answers with events in the video, showing powerful effects of suggestive questions on their memory for what happened (see Figure 8.2).

Such suggestibility in children and adults is worrisome given the great weight put on eyewitness testimony in social and legal circles. Part of the problem is that witnesses can be made to feel overly confident about their memories, and are capable of convincing themselves, not to mention judges and juries, that their memories are correct. Wells and Bradfield (1999) showed how, after identifying a culprit in a line-up, a simple comment, such as "Good job. You are a good witness," can have enormous consequences on the witness' confidence without improving his or her memory. And it is this confidence that is subsequently so convincing (and often convicting!) in a

Misinformation effect The inadvertent combination of information from two or more different sources into a false memory of a single event; for example, information learned after an event can change the memory of the original event

FIGURE 8.2

An Example of the Misinformation Effect

Loftus, Miller, and Burns, (1978) showed subjects pictures of accident scenes like the one below. Later, they were given verbal descriptions that either reinforced one of the components in the actual scene (i.e., the accident was described as occurring at an intersection marked with a stop sign) and other were given a verbal description that included an incorrect reference to a yield sign at the intersection. In a final test of the information presented in the original photo, subjects in the yield-sign condition were much more likely to report having actually seen a yield sign than those who had not had such misinformation presented in the verbal description.
From Goldstein, E. B. (2005). *Cognitive Psychology*. Belmont, CA: Thompson Wadsworth, p. 249.

trial situation. With encouragement, people's thoughts or imaginations can be crafted into memories, and the faith put in eyewitness testimony results in as many as 10,000 people per year falsely convicted on that basis (Cutler & Penrod, 1995; Loftus & Ketcham, 1991). As Schacter (2001) points out, "… leading questions can contribute to eyewitness misidentifications; suggestive psychotherapeutic procedures may foster the creation of false memories; and aggressive interviewing of preschool children can result in distorted memories of alleged abuses by teachers and others" (p. 114). Mistaken eyewitness testimony remains the single most common cause of erroneous convictions (Howes, 2007). With these problems in mind, we can be somewhat reassured that psychological research is beginning to have an impact on the legal system in the United States. The Department of Justice recently convened a panel that issued a set of national guidelines for recommended ways of collecting and using eyewitness testimony in order to minimize the effects of false memories and other biases incorporated into witness statements (Technical Working Group for Eyewitness Evidence, 1999).

8.7 **The Neuroscience of Episodic Memory**

Attempts to find brain sites that store memories for specific events have had an interesting history. Karl Lashley (1929; 1950) conducted a famous series of studies with rats that were taught to run quickly and without errors through a maze to earn a food reward. They then had parts of their brains surgically removed in a search for the *engram* where maze learning had been tucked away. The classic finding was that it did not matter so much which parts of the brain were removed, but rather the total amount of tissue that was taken away in determining the decline in maze performance. In Lashley's own words, "… the maze habit, when formed, is not localized in any single area of the cerebrum and … its performance is somehow conditioned by the quantity of tissue which is intact. It is less certain, though probable, that all parts of the cortex participate equally in the performance of the habit … " (Lashley, 1929, p. 107).

Although more recent studies have refined this rather grim conclusion, it is still likely that many areas of the brain are involved in learning even the simplest task. One theory holds that the posterior part of the brain (temporal, parietal, and occipital lobes) emphasize the storage of perceptual representations of past experiences, whereas the frontal regions emphasize storage of executive and action-related memory processes. Large-ranging synaptic connections could integrate these different brain processes into learning and storing away new memories (Fuster, 2004). Naghavi and Nyberg (2005) have argued that common frontal-parietal systems are involved in a number of related activities, such as attention, working memory, and episodic retrieval. In a review of neuroimaging studies of episodic memory processes, Gabrielli (2001) stated that, "… it is likely that all parts of the brain make some sort of contribution to episodic memories" (p. 255). These views underscore the fact that episodic memory includes perceptual representations as well as abstract interpretations of the events recorded in memory. For example, Sadeh, Ozubko, Winocur, and Moscovitch (2016) have argued that recollection of specific memory traces depends mainly on hippocampal processes, whereas nearby extrahippocampal structures are involved with judgments of familiarity and a feeling of knowing without necessarily recovering episodic details of the memory itself. However, the most devastating brain injury for episodic memory is clearly bilateral damage to, or surgical removal of, a small part of the medial (inner) portion of the temporal lobes. This region includes the hippocampus, which if bilaterally damaged, produces anterograde amnesia—the inability to acquire new episodic memories. It is this region, along with adjoining tissue in the medial temporal lobe area, that was removed bilaterally in patient H.M., resulting in severe and permanent anterograde amnesia (Scoville & Milner, 1957; see Figure 6.1).

Although retained many abilities and memories, he could not learn to recognize new people or objects or remember what had transpired more than a few minutes ago. Interestingly enough, he was able to learn procedural information, such as how to draw copies of figures while viewing his hand in a mirror. Improvement occurred in certain procedures and skills from day to day, even though H.M. denied ever having tried the tasks before each time they were presented. That is, he showed differences between memories for things that he could describe versus things that he could do (see Box 8.2). Thus, the medial temporal lobe area, while important for acquiring new episodic knowledge, is not required for all kinds of learning, such as procedural or implicit learning. Damage to additional tissues in the medial temporal lobe can produce anterograde amnesia as well, leading to memory loss for events preceding the damage by a decade or more (Corkin, Amaral, Gonzalez, Johnson, & Hyman, 1997).

BOX 8.2
Implicit versus Explicit Memory

Most of what has been discussed in the episodic memory sections of this chapter fall into what psychologists would call explicit memory. That is, it is memory for things that were deliberately studied, or at least attended to, prior to a subsequent recall or recognition test. Remembering seems to bring to mind the original learning experience, and we can verbally describe or imagine the things we are trying to remember. Implicit memory, on the other hand, is memory for things that were not learned intentionally and sometimes cannot even be described very well, despite obvious evidence for learning. Examples of implicit memories include procedural memories (how to do things), classical conditioning (the learned association between two stimuli due to their repeated pairing), conceptual and perceptual priming, and implicit learning (Howes, 2007).

Many skills, such as riding a bicycle, are learned implicitly and we would be at a loss to describe exactly what it is that we learn as we progress from a novice to a skilled cyclist. Ebbinghaus's method of savings is an example of implicit learning in an intentional task. For some of his lists of nonsense syllables, he was unable to recall any of the items after a delay of some weeks. They looked, for all practical purposes, like new lists of items. Yet, Ebbinghaus was able to show that some memory must have been retained, as learning a list that had been learned previously was mastered more quickly the second time—evidence for implicit memory measured by savings. Savings is as easily demonstrated in skill learning, as it has often been remarked that one never forgets how to ride a bike!

Another example of implicit learning has been demonstrated by Reber (1967; Reber & Allen, 1978). He used a set of mathematical rules to generate letter strings of various lengths and also generated a similar set of letters that were formed by random combinations of the same letters. Participants had to sort them into two piles, those strings that followed the unknown rules and those that did not. Of course, people had to guess at first which were which, but after many trials, they seemed to learn the rules and became very good at deciding which letter strings looked right and which seemed to be wrong in some way. That learning was implicit was determined by the fact that none of the subjects could specify what the rules were that they were using, yet they behaved as if the rules had become internalized in some way. By extension, one could argue that the grammatical rules of natural language are learned in the same way, as we usually can easily decide whether or not any English sentence is grammatical, but be hard pressed to explain exactly why in some cases (Howes, 2007).

Other forms of implicit memory are measurable in an incidental learning format. Incidental learning can be demonstrated in a surprise memory test that follows an initial task set up by the experimenter. For example, some words can be presented in various cover tasks that are described as if they are the main part of the experiment. These words are presented in different sets with instructions to process them to a deep (semantic), moderate (phonemic), or shallow (graphemic) level. For example, the respective tasks could be to report a synonym, a rhyming word, or the type font (upper or lower case) of the target word. In an explicit memory test, subjects would then be given a surprise recognition test. Usually words are tested in pairs in which one of the words had been included in one of the cover tasks, and the other word in the pair is a new word that had not previously been

Continues

used in the experiment. The explicit task would be to pick the member of each pair that had been seen previously in the experiment. An implicit memory task would be set up to be apparently unrelated to a memory test. For example, subjects could be asked to guess what a briefly presented word is or to complete a word given its first two or three letters. No mention is made about the relation of the guessing or completion tasks to the previous cover tasks. These kinds of experiments have consistently shown that depth of encoding affects explicit memory performance: Items coded to the semantic level are recalled and recognized better than those processed to a shallow level (e.g., Jacoby & Dallas, 1981). However, tests of implicit memory, such as recognizing briefly-presented words, show no depth of processing affects. That is, the depth manipulation that affects the relative levels of recall has no affect on the identification probability of briefly presented words. This is true even though the brief targets are typically recognized more often than words that had not been shown in the cover tasks. The conclusion is that the type of memory that supports implicit advantages for previously seen words is apparently different from that used for explicit recall and recognition memory.

Further evidence for a difference between implicit and explicit memory comes from studies of individuals with amnesia. Most cases of amnesia result from damage to the medial temporal lobes of the brain. Warrington and Weisenkrantz (1970) presented a set of words to amnesic individuals and then tested them in explicit recall and recognition tasks. As expected, their memories for the studied words were much worse than for people without brain damage. However, in an implicit memory task, in which the studied words were presented in a mutilated form (with parts missing) and the subjects had to guess what they were, the amnesic and control subjects showed an equal advantage for the words

previously studied. Graf, Squire, and Mandler (1984) found a similar result. After studying a list of words, amnesic patients could recall only about 10% of them, whereas a group of control subjects recalled about 40%. However, when given an implicit task in which subjects were asked to fill in the missing letters in a word completion task, amnesic and control subjects showed an equally large advantage for words that had been studied earlier.

The distinction between explicit and implicit memory is just one of the differences that exist among the variety of things that we learn and remember. It is similar in some ways to differences between declarative knowledge (things of which we are aware and can describe verbally) and procedural knowledge (processes and skills that we have acquired through practice). Most explicit verbal memory tests depend on declarative knowledge, but we can also be tested on how well we remember how to do things. Patient H.M., who had portions of his medial temporal lobes removed surgically, was very poor in remembering people and events from day to day, but he did improve with practice in drawing while viewing his hand in a mirror. Such knowledge of how to do things is often acquired implicitly, through modeling others' behavior or practice on our own. In these cases, even though we might not be able to explain how or what we are learning, we are aware of improvements in performance. Other kinds of implicit memories affect our performance completely without our awareness, such as when the previous study of a word results in a priming effect that makes it more available as a response in a word-completion task. It is clear, as Bartlett suggested, that there are many different kinds of memories and these are involved in the full range of cognitive abilities, from perception and language through imagination and thought.

Brain damage to the frontal cortex can also produce deficits in certain kinds of episodic memories, particularly those that require effortful processing. That is, although recall of specific episodes can be negatively affected by frontal brain lesions, recognition memory for specific objects or events is affected only modestly (Wheeler, Stuss, & Tulving, 1995). In stark contrast to the lesion results, brain-imaging studies have shown much greater activity in the frontal lobes than in the medial temporal lobe when participants are engaged in storage or retrieval of episodic information. Gabrieli (2001) believes that this difference might be due to the fact that the medial temporal lobes are hidden deep within the brain, and PET and fMRI measures of brain metabolism pick up activity more easily in surface cortical areas such as those active in frontal lobe processing. It is also possible that the frontal lobes perform executive functions in directing or actually performing the work necessary to transfer and retrieve episodic memories through the temporal lobe structures where they are processed.

Since brain lesion studies have shown that medial temporal lobe functions are critical for encoding new episodes into long-term memory, it should not be surprising that research has shown activity in this region during study of words and pictures for later recall. Further, activity is greater for deep (semantic) coding as opposed to shallow coding tasks, and activity is left-lateralized for verbal stimuli and right-lateralized for faces and nonsense objects (Kelly, Miezen, McDermott, Buckner, Raichle, Cohen, Ollinger, Akbudak, Conturo, Snyder, & Peterson, 1998; Martin, Wiggs, & Weisberg, 1997). In further support of the idea that medial temporal lobe activity reflects episodic storage, both PET and fMRI studies have shown greater activation on study trials that subsequently produced better memory performance than on trials with poorer performance (Alkire, Haier, Fallon, & Cahill, 1998; Fernandez, Brewer, Zhao, Glover, & Gabrieli, 1999). Finally, medial temporal lobe activation is present in retrieval of episodic information as well, and the level of activity is greater for successful retrievals than for failures (Schacter, Alpert, Savage, Rausch, & Albert, 1996).

Frontal lobe activity during encoding of episodic information largely parallels that observed in the medial temporal lobe. That is, studying verbal materials produces increases in left frontal lobe activity, and studying scenes or faces results in greater activity in the right frontal lobe. Further, the levels of activity recorded during encoding predicted the success of later recall (Gabrielli, 2001). In contrast to the temporal lobe findings, frontal activity during retrieval of episodic memories seems to be more mixed, with some studies finding activity confined to the right hemisphere for all kinds of materials, including words, faces, and geometric textures, whereas others have shown more left-side activity for verbal materials. Gabrielli (2001) suggests that some of the right frontal lobe activity reflects retrieval effort that is independent of task and materials used. That is, frontal lobe functions could be the basis of such processes as planning and directing retrieval efforts as well as deciding where to look and when to stop. More recently, Habib, Nyberg, and Tulving (2003) have argued that the data are converging on a more general interpretation. That is, they argue that the left prefrontal cortex is more involved in episodic memory encoding, whereas the right prefrontal cortex is more involved in episodic memory retrieval. They also present evidence that this hemispheric asymmetry for encoding versus retrieval processes is the same for both verbal and nonverbal materials. Supporting evidence for the encoding/retrieval asymmetry has recently been provided in a study using transcranial magnetic stimulation (TMS). The TMS technique temporarily disrupts neural processing in brain areas near where the magnetic coil is positioned, and left frontal stimulation disrupted learning efficiency, whereas right frontal stimulation disrupted retrieval efficiency (Rossi, Pasqualetti, Zito, Vecchio, Cappa, Miniussi, Babiloni, & Rossini, 2006).

In summary, memory processes and structures seem to be distributed widely throughout the cortex, with special emphasis on the temporal lobe for retaining both semantic and episodic information. Frontal lobe activity mainly represents effortful processing consistent with its theoretical role in executive processes directing strategic elements of storage and retrieval.

Chapter Summary

We all have memories of unique events that have happened in our lives, and some of these seem to be recorded with pristine clarity (flashbulb memories), whereas others seem to be forgotten the moment they are completed. There is an apparent continuum of memory strength that seems to be determined by the amount of attention focused on the event while it is occurring as well as the emotional intensity aroused by the event itself. Repeated experiences of the same or related events as well as frequent recall and retellings or reliving the experience with others can contribute to memory strength and recallability.

Other experiences seem to be forgotten, although failure to recall something is no evidence that it is erased from memory. Frequently, things that cannot be recalled can be recovered through more sensitive memory tests, such as recognition or cued recall tests, or by demonstrating the existence of savings. However, one must be careful that the cues used to probe memory are not overly suggestive, as research has shown that suggestive questions can lead people to make errors in retrieval of which they are not necessarily aware. Further, memory can work to combine information from different, related sources into a common episodic trace that cannot be unpacked into its different sources. That is, people can unintentionally make errors of construction (initial interpretation) and reconstruction (recall of whatever related information can be dredged up) that result in memories that have all the subjective feeling of actual recalled experiences, but they can be false in whole or in parts.

In important cases, professionals who are aware of some causes of unreliable human memories must take care in interpreting the memories of individuals who appear to be very confident in what they can remember.

Review Questions

- **What is long-term memory for events like, and how does it differ from semantic memory?**

  Memory for events differs from semantic memory in that it is specific to particular events—that is, episodic memory preserves the perceived qualities of the situations in which they occurred. Semantic memories are abstracted generalities from sets of related events. Therefore, since our individual memories are different, but the abstracted general principles are likely to be the same, semantic memory is more likely to be similar across individuals, at least within a common culture. Episodic memories are unique to each of us and are also much more variable than semantic memories. Whereas general knowledge remains fairly constant and available throughout our lifetimes, episodic memories fade with different rates of forgetting. Some are retained in stark clarity for years, whereas others seem to be lost within minutes or even seconds of their occurrence.

- **Are flashbulb memories different from memories for typical daily events?**

  Flashbulb memories are memories for events that are particularly vivid, presumably retaining clear images of things like the people involved, the time and place of occurrence, and the significance of the event and its emotional consequences on oneself and others. There is some controversy about whether they are unique in some way or merely the extreme members of a continuous set of memories of past events that vary in strength. Their memory strength seems to evolve from their powerful emotional values that are known to produce lasting memories. That is, they command attention, they result in continued rehearsal, and they are likely to be relived again and again through reports in the media and conversations with friends and relatives. They are most commonly reported following events of international significance, such as the assassinations of political leaders, or shocking tragedies of great personal importance.

- **What are some of the major causes of forgetting?**

  Forgetting has been traditionally assumed to be due to interference from other things stored in memory. That is, a desired target of recall can be made to be inaccessible due to proactive interference from things learned earlier and retroactive things from things learned later. Interference is greatest if the target and interfering materials are similar in some ways. Schacter has characterized forgetting as being due to several factors, including absent-mindedness, transience, and blocking. These three factors neatly line up with the three traditional causes of failures to remember. That is, absent-mindedness is primarily due to inattention or distraction at the time of initial memory encoding, transience is due to ineffectual storage due to lack of elaborative coding or integration with existing knowledge, and blocking is due to a retrieval failure for information that has been effectively encoded and stored.

- **Do false memories really exist, or are they merely the results of suggestive questioning?**

  False memories have been shown to exist in laboratory studies that have presented materials that are highly related to or extremely suggestive of some fact or event. Most people are willing to say that they actually experienced such an event even though it never occurred. Even large scenarios can be created in people's minds and recalled as if they had actually occurred, although such false memories are more difficult to produce in adults than simple facts or events. Loftus has shown that leading questions, implications, and other information presented after the fact of some event can become integrated with it to change the memory of the event. Further, it is nearly impossible for most people to distinguish between the original memory and those produced by integration with later related information. Research has shown that children are particularly vulnerable to the construction of false memories due to suggestive questioning and other manipulations after witnessing some event.

- **Are there other kinds of long-term memories besides semantic and episodic memories?**

  Although semantic and episodic memories have been thought of as the major distinction in human long-term memory since Tulving first made the distinction, it is clear that there are other types of long-term memories as well. Both types of memories seem to include perceptual qualities, such that we can recognize words and objects by their visual or auditory components. Therefore, we must have imaginal memories that include components similar to their perceived audio, visual, and perhaps tactile qualities. We must also have verbal memories for use in naming things and using language. All of these types of memories might be called declarative in that they encompass aspects of memory that we can describe and talk about and were probably stored deliberately to some extent, although language and semantic memory are abstractions far removed from particular experiences. Declarative memories can be contrasted with procedural memories, which are memories for how to do things, rather than facts about the things themselves. Procedures are often learned implicitly, without deliberate strategies for learning, and they can show up in behaviors without awareness. For example, certain experiences can prime later behaviors without memory or awareness of the cause of such priming.

- **What brain processes are involved in storing and retrieving memories of events?**

  Research with both humans and animals has shown that the brain structures most critical for the formation and retention of event memories is the inner-most (medial) part of the temporal lobes, including the hippocampus. For example, bilateral surgical removal of the hippocampal region produced severe anterograde amnesia in patient H.M. Other brain structures involved include broader regions of the temporal lobes, with some indications that verbal representations are stored primarily in the left hemisphere and visuo-spatial representations in the right hemisphere. Brain imaging research has shown that the frontal lobes are active in both storage and recollection of episodic information, perhaps serving an executive role in encoding and retrieval processes, and the left frontal lobes seem to be more active in directing encoding and learning processes, whereas the right frontal lobes seem to be more active in retrieval processes.

Key Terms

Absent-mindedness   219

Blocking   220

Flashbulb memories   216

Misinformation effect   223

Prospective memory   219

Savings   213

Tip-of-the tongue (TOT) state   221

Transience   218

Chapter 9

Cognitive Development and Language Acquisition

"Language comes so naturally to us that it is easy to forget what a strange and miraculous gift it is. All over the world members of our species fashion their breath into ... sounds [that] contain information of the intentions of the person making them. We humans are fitted with a means of sharing our ideas, in all their unfathomable vastness. When we listen to speech, we can be led to think thoughts that have never been thought before and that never would have occurred to us on our own."

Pinker (1999), p. 1

PREVIEW QUESTIONS

❖ *What abilities do newborn infants have that prepare them for learning to understand language and to speak?*

❖ *What are the main components of human languages that enable us to exchange ideas and descriptions of things?*

❖ *Do all children learn a language in the same way even though they are born into different cultures?*

❖ *Is language learned like a skill, or is it different in some way?*

9.1 Introduction to Language Acquisition

Two of the most important things that we learn in all our lives are acquired when we are very young: how to speak our native language and how to read its printed form. Both processes involve learning to pick out the features of sounds and print that are critical in differentiating between words. Language is much more than just speaking and recognizing words, however, for its full function is to exchange meaningful ideas among individuals. Language enables the greatest of all human cultural extensions—the ability to communicate across space and time and to build, not only upon our own knowledge, but also on that of others.

The speed and regularity of child language acquisition has impressed most parents and researchers alike. The facts that it occurs so rapidly and with so little direct attempts at formal instruction have led many to believe that language learning is special in some way. That is, learning a first language seems to be biologically programmed to occur at a certain early age and through a certain sequence of levels that makes it unlike learning in most other areas. Language researchers have argued that language learning is innately guided because of its apparent speed and ease of acquisition by the very young. It is unlike becoming a "… wine connoisseur, an oboist, or a jet pilot, or for that matter a brain surgeon (in that) … explicit training and feedback … is not necessary for language acquisition" (Jusczyk, 2000, p. 200). Learning to read is quite different, however, in that it occurs later, its progress is difficult and uncertain, and for a significant minority of individuals with adequate opportunities, reading and writing never approach the facile ease of communication possible through speech.

Perhaps part of the difference between speaking/listening and reading/writing is due to our evolutionary history. Spoken language, in some form, is perhaps as old as our species itself, which is at least 150,000 years. This long history has afforded our species the opportunity to select for spoken language abilities if they were beneficial for survival and procreation, or as Pinker (2003, p. 26) argued, "Natural selection is the most plausible explanation of the evolution of language …" By this scenario, it would not be surprising if we had inherited certain neural structures and processes essential for the rapid acquisition and proficient use of language. Reading, however, has been with us only as long as written language, or about 5,000 years, and the vast majority of people who have lived since that time have never learned to read. World-wide literacy is a fairly recent human goal, achievable only through deliberate education and the development of a unique set of cognitive abilities. Reading skills depend not only on language but on a host of perceptual and memory processes that we have only begun to understand.

*9.*2 **Perceptual Development**

9.2.1   Perceptual Abilities of Newborns

Infants enter the world with a large set of reflexes, a few more complex behavioral patterns, and some remarkable perceptual abilities. Within a few days of birth, they can recognize the face and voice of their primary caregivers (almost always the infants' mothers). This ability has been demonstrated by young infants who will look preferentially at an image of their mother's face rather than at an image of another woman when the two are placed side-by-side in front of the infant (Bushnell, Sai, & Mullin, 1989; Walton, Bower, & Bower, 1992). Newborns will turn their heads to the source of a sound, indicating that they know where a sound is coming from (Muir & Field, 1979). Voice recognition has been shown by 2-day-old infants who will suck longer on a pacifier if it is wired to a recording device that plays their mother's voice whenever they suck on it, rather than being connected to the voice of another woman (De Casper & Fifer, 1980). Similar results have been found for infants even before birth. Women receiving prenatal care in China agreed to have a loudspeaker suspended over their abdomens, which played a recording of their own voice or that of a stranger. The unborn infants' heart rates were recorded, and these rates were found to decrease to the stranger's voice and increase to their mother's voice, relative to a silent control interval (Kisilevsky, Hains, KangLee, XingXie, HefengHuang, HuiYe, KeZhang, & ZengpingWang, 2003). A similar finding has been reported in unhatched songbirds (Colombelli-Négrel, Webster, Dowling, Hauber, & Kleindorfer, 2016), who acquired their species' specific warblings better if they were exposed to their adults' songs while still encased within their eggs.

Within the first few weeks of life, infants show both the ability to see motion and the preference for viewing moving, as opposed to static, displays. Within the first 3 months of life, vision has developed enough to make use of some of the Gestalt principles of perceptual organization (see Figure 3.1), including grouping by brightness (Quinn, Burke, & Rush, 1993), and by good continuation (Johnson & Aslin, 1995). As acuity rapidly improves over the first few months of life, infants demonstrate impressive degrees of facial recognition. They can remember individual faces over periods of 24 hours or more (Pascalis, de Schonen, Morton, Deruelle, & Fabre-Grenet, 1995), and they can discriminate between different emotional expressions (Young-Browne, Rosenfeld, & Horowitz, 1977). Figures defined by motion alone can be perceived by at least 4 months of age, and infants show a preference for biological motion (human figures defined only by pinpoints of light at the major joints) as opposed to random movements of points of light (Craton & Yonas, 1990; Fox & McDaniel, 1982).

Similar feats of perceptual discrimination occur in hearing. Besides showing a preference for their own mothers' voices, infants as young as 2 days will regulate their sucking behavior to hear recordings of their native language as opposed to a foreign language (Moon, Cooper, & Fifer, 1993). Such a preference can be understood by acknowledging that a fetus can hear its mother's voice through direct conduction within her body. For several months before birth, hearing their mother's voice and language prepares all infants for later vocal communication. The later perceptual and cognitive developments occurring shortly after birth prepare children to attend to speech sounds and to the people, objects, and events in their lives that are named and described by speech.

9.2.2   Speech Perception in Infants

Speech is apparently processed differently than other sounds even in the very young. Eimas, Siqueland, Jusczyk, and Vigorito (1972) showed that infants demonstrate a type of **categorical perception** of speech sounds (see Box 9.1) that forms the basis of speech recognition abilities in adults. That is, most stimuli are perceived to change gradually as their underlying physical property is changed along some dimension, such as how apparent brightness or loudness change when physical intensity changes. Only a few stimulus dimensions, such as color, seem to change abruptly from one category to another (say, yellow to orange) when their underlying dimensions (i.e., wavelength) are gradually changed. The recognition of many speech sounds seems to be a prime example of how we process stimuli by their categories rather than by noticing small variations in their underlying features. That is, rather than being continuously sensitive to speech sounds as they change gradually along some continuum, certain varying sounds are heard as the same until they cross a critical threshold into a different category. Although these category boundaries in infants might not reflect the boundaries used by adult speakers, the fact that such boundaries exist at all indicates the presence of some special, inborn perceptual qualities for hearing and categorizing human speech.

By 6 months of age, the category boundaries in infants have generally shifted to duplicate the kinds of phonemic distinctions made by their parents. This is no easy feat, as the number and nature of these phonemes differ widely across the 6,000 or so existing human languages. Within a few more months, the babbling sounds that infants make increasingly reflect the phonemic properties of sounds in the language spoken around them. By the time that the first word is spoken at about 12 months of age, the infant has acquired a sophisticated grasp of the sound system of his or her native language and how to imitate it through increasingly precise vocalizations. This impressive set of developments has attracted the interest of researchers for many years, yet the issue about how much of language acquisition is determined by unique, inherited abilities, and how much is determined by perceptual-motor learning common to a host of other cognitive processes remains unresolved (Carroll, 2004).

Categorical perception The tendency to perceive continuous changes in speech sounds as shifts between discrete categories, perhaps unique to the perception of speech (Discrimination is poor within categories but good between categories for equivalent physical differences between sounds)

9.3 Language Origins

9.3.1   The Origins of Language in Homo Sapiens

The history of language "... will always be a mystery, for words leave no fossils" (Bridgeman, 2003, p. 209). Anatomical developments in our immediate ancestors have enabled the possibility of articulate speech for at least 150,000 years (Corballis, 1999), yet our closest relatives today, the chimpanzees, are completely incapable of producing the range of sounds and the speed of articulation necessary to facilitate

BOX 9.1

Categorical Perception

Speech perception research took a great leap forward with the invention of the speech spectrograph, a device for yielding a visible representation of speech sounds. The speech spectrograph produces a *voiceprint* or speech spectrogram of a speaker's utterance in which frequency of speech sounds is on the Y axis, time is on the X axis, and intensities of different frequencies over time are shown by the darkness of ink marks on the plot (see figure). The figure shows the spectrographic recording of the utterance, "There are really a lot of words to learn." The time scale runs from 0 to 2.294 seconds, and the frequency from 0 to 8,046 cycles per second (Hz). The darkness of the ink marks are proportional to the sound intensities at the associated times and frequencies. The parallel broad bands indicate formants, produced by the vibration of the vocal chords while pronouncing vowels and voiced consonants (like *w*, *r*, and *l*), and not during unvoiced consonants (like *t*). Also visible are glides or transitions between sounds and high frequency noises associated with fricatives (like *th* and *s*).

Jusczyk, Peter W., The Discovery of Spoken Language, figures on page 4, © 1997 Massachusetts Institute of Technology, by permission of The MIT Press.

Early work with speech spectrographs allowed the isolation and synthesis of artificial speech sounds that could be used to test ideas such as: What are the critical features of an acoustic pattern that identify certain sounds (e.g., phonemes) in the speech signal (Liberman, Delattre, & Cooper, 1952)? The devices enabled the play back of graphically-represented artificial sounds to produce synthetic speech. Synthetic speech is constructed by presenting sounds of various frequencies that modulate over time. Critical features of natural speech can be isolated by eliminating some of the noise present in the speech signal and presenting simpler patterns that include the most important components of the signal. These include formants, the broad-band, steady-state components that are maintained for 200 ms or less, and transitions, which are short glides into the formants or drifts away from them. We know that the formants are produced when the vocal chords vibrate as we pronounce vowels and voiced consonants (such as [*d*], as opposed to [*t*], which is unvoiced, see the figure showing a voice onset time difference of 74 ms).

Research with synthetic speech showed two odd results. First, Delattre, Liberman, and Cooper (1955) found that as they shortened the length of a syllable, like [*di*], by cutting off the end of the vowel, there was no point at which the consonant could be heard alone without the accompanying vowel. That is, the perception changed abruptly from a perfectly good syllable sound [*di*] to a non-speech-sounding

Continues

chirp at some point along the vowel-length continuum. Further, "... when they examined the acoustic realizations of the same consonant in the context of different vowels, they discovered that there were no obvious properties in common across all of these contexts" (Jusczyk, 2000, p. 44; see the figure below, which shows a transition from *di* to *du*, as for the words "deed, date, dead, dote, dot, dough, dune." Note that the spectrographic representation of the initial consonant differs across syllables, but is heard as the same initial sound).

Jusczyk, Peter W., The Discovery of Spoken Language, figures on page 4, © 1997 Massachusetts Institute of Technology, by permission of The MIT Press.

These properties of syllable perception indicate that they are not perceived in a continuous way, rather what we hear when a normal speech sound is shortened is an abrupt change from recognizable speech to unrecognizable nonsense sounds. In addition, widely different acoustic signals are perceived as the same sound in certain conditions, and identical acoustical signals can be heard as different speech sounds in different contexts. These results support the idea that speech perception is categorical rather than continuous, and that acoustic differences that could distinguish sounds are lost early in perceptual processes that assign the speech signal to a particular phonemic category.

Categorical perception is the failure of listeners to discriminate between two different acoustic signals that belong to the same phonemic or syllabic category, whereas a similar physical difference between two sounds that spans a category boundary, is easily discriminated (Liberman, Harris, Kinney, & Lane, 1961). It was once thought that categorical perception was unique to how humans hear others' speech, but recent research has shown categorical perception is sometimes found for non-speech sounds in humans (e.g., Pisoni, 1977).

Nevertheless, categorical perception is a fairly unique way of handling continuous auditory stimuli, and it is easily demonstrated in both infant and adult listeners. The classical empirical demonstration proceeds as follows: Artificial speech sounds are sampled along a continuum from one easily recognizable sound to another (e.g., from [*da*] to [*ta*]—this particular difference would be vocalization onset time, VOT). In an initial experiment, different sampled sounds are randomly presented many times each, and a listener responds "da" or "ta" to indicate what he or she thought the sound was. Rather than finding that responses change gradually in their percentages from 100% "da" to 100% "ta" as VOT increases, responses seem to show a clean break from 100% "da" to 100% "ta" somewhere along the continuum.

In a follow-up experiment, pairs of stimuli are chosen to be close together along the VOT continuum, and the listeners are asked to judge whether they are the same or different. The discrimination task results show very little ability to discriminate between sounds that had been judged both as "da" or "ta;" that is, discrimination within a category is very difficult. However, if the same VOT difference that is not discriminable within a category is chosen such that the two stimuli span a category boundary, discrimination is very easy. Again, the perception is determined by the category in which the acoustic signal is placed not by the properties of the acoustic signal itself (see figure).

Continues

Studdert-Kennedy, M., Liberman, A. M., Harris, K. S., & Cooper, F. S. (1970).
Motor theory of speech perception: A reply to Lane's critical review. Psychological Review, 77, p235.

speech communication. Part of the reason lies in the position of the larynx as it enters the mouth. The larynx is raised in chimps and in human infants, such that its structure forms a linear, continuous cavity. Between 6 months and 1 year, however, the larynx descends in humans to produce a longer vocal tract and the capacity to produce and maintain a much greater variety of sounds.

9.3.2   The Gestural Basis for Language

A strong case has been made that human languages developed not out of vocalizations, per se, but as extensions to a pre-existing gestural means of communication (Arbib, 2005; Corballis, 1999a, b, 2003, 2004; Hewes, 1977; Wrolstad, 1976). In fact, the most successful attempts to teach our primate cousins to communicate symbolically have used manual signing or other visual means of communication. Primates are primarily visual animals, and except for humans, they have much better control over manual movements than vocalizations (see Hu, 2014, for an interesting review of this research).

Corballis (1999b) argues that a gestural means of communication would have been of benefit to early hominids living in the African savannah. The evolution of erect posture and bipedal gait allowed early hominids to free their hands to carry food, weapons, and infants—and to communicate with manual gestures. It also would have allowed them to communicate stealthily; to point out to one another specific objects, such as predators or prey (a capability of very young children, but no other primates); and the ability to convey spatial information (How big was the fish you caught?).

Further, Donald (1991) has argued that language developed out of mime, the ability to convey stories by acting out scenes with gestures and body language. Gestures typically remain iconic, that is, they physically represent the objects and events they mean to portray, whereas words are arbitrary, abstract symbols (Wrolstad, 1976) that seldom reflect their meanings (except for onomatopoetic words that sound like their meanings, such as "buzz" or "splash"). The gradual shift from an iconic sign system to an arbitrary and conventional system of symbols marks the beginning of human language.

Even today, as is true of most evolutionary trends in any species, gestures remain an important part of human language. We know that any speaker is better understood if the listener can also see the speaker's face and lip movements than if the message is audio alone (e.g., Massaro, 1987). Sign languages have persisted and have been used by contemporary humans, such as the aboriginal inhabitants of Australia and North America. Sign languages have also been invented worldwide by deaf communities and remain an integral part of education among deaf people today. Even blind individuals gesture when they speak, often in ways similar to the gesturing used by sighted people (Iverson & Goldin-Meadow, 1998).

9.3.3 *Advantages for a Spoken Language*

Assuming that a switch from gestural to spoken language occurred, it is more likely to have been gradual rather than sudden. Gestures might have been accompanied by vocalizations that came to take on some of the meaningful properties of the gestures. In addition, spoken languages have the advantage of working in the dark, or when opaque objects or long distances separate the communicators. Such arguments have been raised to support the development of the *whistling language* of La Gomera in the Canary Islands, where deep canyons and thick forests prevented more direct communication (see Carreiras, Lopez, Rivero, & Corina, 2005). Spoken language has the further advantage of continuing when the hands are engaged in another activity. Indeed, many important tasks of early human civilization, such as fire starting, tool making, and food preparation, would have benefitted from vocal instructions that complemented manual demonstrations.

Humans show a strong lateralization of control of both speech production and speech perception, with more brain activity associated with speech typically localized in the left cerebral hemisphere than in the right. Such lateralization of function is also sometimes found in the animal world, and it seems to be an adaptive means of controlling social behaviors. Speech is perhaps unique in that both its productive and receptive aspects require fine monitoring of sequential activities. Coordinating activities between the two hemispheres of the brain would seem to require too much time to allow both halves to participate equally. One of the biological adaptations specific to speech seems to have been to lateralize sequential processing and control of articulation in one side of the brain, that is, in the left hemisphere for about 90% of us (Corballis, 1999a). This lateralization seems to be present at a very early age, if not at birth. For example, Molfese (1977) showed hemispheric differences in evoked potentials to speech versus non-speech sounds in infants as young as 1 week. Although other research has shown a gradual trend toward language dominance in the left hemisphere for most infants and toddlers over the first few years of life, the general view is that the two hemispheres are not equal at birth, and the left one is usually potentiated in some way for the acquisition of language (Harley, 2008).

Although the actual origins of human language are doomed to bask in obscurity, the fact is that all human societies have developed a spoken language. Further, these languages show certain universals, such as being based on words and sentences that include nouns (subjects) and verbs (predicates). Languages also exist on different levels, and there is some evidence that these levels develop and function independently. These include (1) phonology, the sound system of a language (rules and restrictions about how phonemes are combined into words in a language are called phonotactics), (2) syntax, the way words are ordered and hierarchically structured to form phrases and sentences, and (3) semantics, the way words, phrases, and sentences relate to cognitive concepts and meanings. Although all three aspects of language operate at the same time and in an interdependent way in normal conversation, they can be and are studied separately, and their initial developments appear to be largely independent.

9.4 Phonological Development

$9.4.1$ *Phones and Phonemes*

Phonology is the description of the sound system of a natural human language. Its units are *phones*, or basic acoustic patterns that are generated by human speakers and are combined by their listeners into syllables and words in a language. The first stage of classification is to map the actual speech sounds (phones) into categories of more or less equivalent sounds (phonemes) that make up the building blocks of a spoken language. Different human languages have from about 25 to 95 different phonemes, and English uses about 44.

The individual acoustic patterns that determine phones produced when people speak vary enormously from individual to individual. Some of these differences are due to age and gender effects on the fundamental frequency (pitch) of people's voices, and others are unique qualities that allow us to differentiate between speakers and to recognize someone from his or her voice. Phones also differ depending on the speed with which the speaker is talking and on what is actually being said. That is, when speaking, our articulators (lips, teeth, tongue, and vocal chords) are in more or less constant motion. The positions that they achieve in order to produce certain sounds are always a compromise in recovering

Phonology The study of the sound structure of human languages, including how different speech sounds, or phones, are grouped into categories of equivalent sounds, called phonemes, in different languages

Coarticulation effects The effect that the preceding and following speech context has on the way that any speech element is articulated (e.g., the difference between the vowel sounds in "bat" and "can" are fairly large, but the vowel is classified as the same phoneme)

from the previous articulatory movement and anticipating the next. Thus, each sound we produce is heavily influenced by the phonetic sequence in which it is contained, producing **coarticulation effects** in speech. Coarticulation effects can be severe enough that, in some cases, there is no physical overlap between the phonetic descriptions of two acoustic signals that we nevertheless hear as the same sound (Delattre, Liberman, & Cooper, 1955).

9.4.2   The Problem of Segmentation

Segmentation The imposition of groupings into words and phrases by the listener on the more-or-less continuous stream of sounds emitted by a speaker

A second problem in speech perception has to do with **segmentation**. It has often been reported that speech in a foreign language sounds both fast and continuous, with no apparent breaks between words. Speech in our own language sounds different, apparently slower and with obvious unitary words separated by breaks. Such a difference is illusory, of course, as the general rate of speech measured in phonemes, syllables, or words per minute is fairly constant across languages. Further, brief pauses or silent intervals in the speech code are unreliable markers for words. The word "stoppage," for example has a break in its center, and we all know how words can run together to confuse the hearer about whether one is saying "I scream" or "Ice cream." It is obviously the perception of a known versus an unknown language that allows us to hear the breaks between words, whereas an unknown language can sound like a continuous stream of phones. It appears almost as if one must be able to understand what words are being spoken before they can be segmented from a passage of continuous speech.

Both coarticulation and segmentation effects present serious problems for language learners to overcome, yet almost all infants deal effectively with these problems when they are confronted in the first years of life. There must be some compensatory processes at work to assist the child language learner, and these could be either innately-driven learning processes specific to language or some characteristics of the language, typically directed to newborns and infants, that makes the speech code less difficult to handle. As we shall see, there is evidence for both possibilities.

9.4.3   Research on Phonological Development

Phonological development has been shown to begin very early, as newborn infants recognize their mothers' voices and make discriminations among speech sounds in ways similar to adults. These results have been demonstrated in operant (Skinnerian) conditioning experiments in which some natural behavior that exists in very young infants (like sucking on a pacifier or turning the head to the source of a new sound) can be conditioned by following it with reinforcement. The reinforcement can be as simple as providing a new sound to listen to. Children will quickly learn to expect a sound if one is produced every time they suck on a pacifier, but if the same sound is presented every time, the sucking rate will decrease, a general phenomenon known as habituation. If a new sound is then presented, the infant will increase its sucking rate again to hear it, but only if the difference is noticed. This is the logic behind much of infant perception research—a change in response rate when an old stimulus is replaced with a new one will occur only if infants are capable of noticing the change. If they show a change in response rate or strength, then the infants demonstrate the ability to make the stimulus discrimination. However, if the response rate goes unchanged, then the new stimulus is not discriminable from the old one.

The sucking rate measure was used by Eimas, Siqueland, Jusczyk, and Vigorito (1971) to demonstrate some of the impressive speech discrimination abilities of young infants. They presented simple syllables, such as [*ba*] and [*pa*], that differed by a single phonemic contrast. In this case, the contrast is **voice onset time (VOT)**, which is the time between the initial burst of sound at the beginning of the conso-nant and the time when the vocal chords begin to vibrate. Research has shown that when the lips part to release a burst of air at the start of the consonant sound, and the vocal chords start to vibrate to produce an "ahh" at the same time, the sound is heard as [*ba*] by adult English speakers. However, if the VOT is increased to about 25 ms or more, the sound is heard as [*pa*] (Lisker & Abramson, 1967). Distinctions on either side of this 25 ms boundary are usually not made in English; that is, variations between, say VOTs of 10 or 20 ms and between 30 and 40 ms are unimportant and usually not discriminable. Distinctions between 20 and 30 ms VOTs can be made, however, denoting a phonemic boundary in this area. The general propensity for adult speakers of a language to treat some phonetic contrasts as equivalent and others not, even though the physical change is continuous along any dimension, is known as categorical perception (see Box 9.1).

Eimas et al. (1967) tested infants at 1 and 4 months of age using sucking rate as the dependent measure, and a change in sound pattern as the reinforcing stimulus. After infants learned that sucking on a pacifier could control a tape recorder playing repeated syllables, they would suck at a high rate initially, and then reduce the rate as they habituated to the sound. When the sound was changed, the infants would increase their sucking rate again, but only if they noticed the change. Using this method, Eimas et al. showed that infants could discriminate some sounds along the [*ba*]/[*pa*] continuum, but they treated others as the same, just as adults do. In other words, they demonstrated categorical perception for speech sounds at an age too young to be based on knowledge of phonemic boundaries in their native language or to have benefited from some kind of feedback from their own attempts at speech-like sounds (babbling).

Although infants demonstrate categorical perception of speech sounds very early in life, it is clear that the locations of category boundaries gradually shift to reflect phonemic distinctions made in the language spoken around them. Some of these changes are in response to new distinctions that have to be learned, and others actually result in the loss of discrimination ability for phonemic boundaries that are not present in one's native language. For example, 6- to 8-month-old Japanese children are able to discriminate between [*wa*] and [*ya*] and between [*ra*] and [*la*]

Voice onset time (VOT) The delay (if any) between the beginning of a speech sound and the vibration of the vocal cords, being about 0 ms for voiced consonants in syllables like [*ba*] and 25 ms or more for unvoiced consonants in syllables like [*pa*] equally well despite the fact that the former contrast is important in Japanese, but the latter is not. At 10 to 12 months of age, however, they are unable to discriminate the [*ra*]/[*la*] pair (Tsushima, Takizawa, Sasaki, Siraki, Nishi, Kohno, Menyuk, & Best, 1994). This result supports the general finding that adults have difficulty in hearing phonemic contrasts in other languages that do not exist in their native language.

9.4.4   Evoked Potentials in Newborns

Besides operant conditioning studies of infants' responses to speech sounds, it is possible with modern imaging techniques to study brain activity directly in response to speech. A similar procedure can be used in which a series of syllables (like "ba, ba, ba, ba …") is followed by a final syllable that is either "ba" or "ga." Event-related potentials (ERPs) to the final syllable should show a difference between the two if the shift in sounds is noticed. Results similar to those found in the conditioning studies have been reported. That is, 3- to 6-month old children show differences in the ERPs for a variety of speech sound changes, but these become modulated to reflect the phonemic categories of their native language by about 12 months of age (Friederici, 2006). Other ERP research has targeted the brain responses of newborns to later language development. For example, Guttorm, Leppänen, Poikkeus, Eklund, Lyytinen, and Lyytinen (2005) measured the ERP to speech sounds, such as [*ga*] in infants. They found that infants who showed a slower shift in overall positive to negative responses about a half second after hearing the syllable were at risk for poorer receptive language skills at age 2.5 years.

Human infants are born with some preferences for speech sounds over other sounds, some familiarity and preference for their own mothers' voices, and with the innate ability to discriminate between many important contrasts present in any of the world's languages. Further, they are able to learn, within the first year of life, the phonetic distinctions important for phonemic boundaries in their parents' (or other caretaker's) language. They also show a systematic decline in sensitivity to non-native phonemic contrasts between about 6 and 12 months of age (Best & McRoberts, 1989; Werker & Tees, 1984). All of these developments occur before infants are able to pronounce their first words.

9.5 Bootstrapping as a Means to Expand Language Comprehension

9.5.1   Variability in the Speech Signal

Segmentation and coarticulation problems in human speech present significant difficulties to the infant language learner. In order to identify words, they must be separated from the more-or-less continuous stream of speech, and allowances must be made for variability in how they are pronounced. Variability is due both to differences between speakers, between male and female voices, for example, and within a speaker, depending on coarticulation effects. In addition, prosodic factors, including rhythm, stress, and intonation, can change the acoustic properties of a word. People commonly pronounce the same word differently depending on its importance in a sentence, the role it plays, where it falls within a sentence, and the part of speech it takes on (e.g., compare how "ball" might be pronounced in each of the these sentences: "Give me the ball." "That ball is mine." "Is that your ball?" "I had a ball last night." "Ball four—take your base!").

9.5.2 Prosodic Bootstrapping

Fortunately the segmentation problem is aided by structural aspects of human speech that allow partial knowledge of a few words or other characteristics of a sentence to gain access to or to infer additional knowledge about an utterance—a process known as **bootstrapping**. For example, **prosodic bootstrapping** is presumably based on patterns of intonation, rhythm, pitch, and stress in a speaker's utterance that can be used as cues to a sentence's structure and meaning. There is some evidence that young children can use such information in the speech signal as cues to the **syntactic structure** of an utterance (Gleitman, Gleitman, Landau, & Wanner, 1988). In addition, when speaking to infants, adults tend to exaggerate prosodic elements, such as pitch changes at phrase and clause boundaries, more so than in adult-to-adult speech (Garnica, 1977).

There is no doubt that infants are sensitive to prosodic markers in speech. Infants as young as 4 days old appear to favor prosodic elements of their own language as opposed to those of a foreign language (Harley, 2008; Mehler, Jusczyk, Lambretz, Halsted, Bertoncini, & Amiel-Tison, 1988). Hirsch-Pasek, Tucker, and Golinkoff (1996) demonstrated that infants in the 7- to 10-month-old range preferred to listen to speech segments in which pauses were consistent with other markers of clause boundaries, such as changes in syllable length and pitch, than to speech in which these markers were inconsistent. Even 2-month-old infants have been shown to notice a change in a speech segments, such as "Cats like park benches," when it was read as a whole sentence or when the same words were edited out and later played from two separate sentences like, "I know what cats like. Park benches are their favorite things to play on" (Mandel, Jusczyk, & Kemler Nelson, 1994). Jusczyk (2000, p. 154) points out that such results "… suggest that the prosodic organization afforded by well formed sentences facilitates infants' processing and memory for speech information."

9.5.3 Semantic Bootstrapping

Besides using the acoustic properties of the speech signal, very young children also are sensitive to word meanings and use them as bootstraps to figure out the meanings of other words in a sentence. **Semantic** bootstrapping depends on four key assumptions, as described below (loosely based on Pinker, 1987):

Bootstrapping The use of partial knowledge in some domain to retrieve or create additional knowledge, such as using a loop at a back of a boot to help to pull it on

Prosody Changes in speech sounds that are important for phrase and sentence meaning that are not part of the phonemic structure of a language, including intonation, rhythm, and stress

Syntax The structural rules for how words in a language are arranged into hierarchical groupings in phrases and sentences

Semantics How meaning is represented by words and their syntactic groupings in a language

(1) The meanings of content words can be learned independently from grammatical rules of syntax.

(2) The meanings of individual words and the environmental context in which they are used are sufficient for a child to come up with the meaning of the sentence.

(3) The child benefits from the existence of certain linguistic universals that guide the formation of concepts and relations into propositions in memory.

(4) Sentences that include forms and structures consistent with these concepts, relations, and propositions are understood more quickly and contribute to language acquisition.

Jusczyk (2000, p. 37) comments that Pinker's arguments rest on two key assumptions. First, Pinker follows in the tradition of Chomsky and others in assuming that infants "… have some innate knowledge of universal grammar." This knowledge predisposes infants to categorize speech sounds into phonemes and to use prosodic and other aspects of the speech code to determine word meanings and sentence structures. Second, the successful mapping of real-world objects and relations onto word meanings and sentence structures depends heavily on the learner's knowledge. The young child must have an ability to perceive and recognize objects in the environment and to understand basic concepts, such as object permanence and causal relationships among people, objects, and other things, "Consequently, nonlinguistic cognitive and perceptual capacities also play a critical role is semantic bootstrapping …" (Jusczyk, 2000, p. 37). In essence, the development of concepts and relations in semantic memory is a necessary precursor for the use of words to represent them.

9.6 Acquisition of the First Words

Word learning is aided by many cognitive processes, some of which have not specifically evolved for language. These include children's abilities to infer people's intentions and what they are thinking when they use words (Brown, 2001). Word learning also depends on perceptual memory for word sounds and categories in memory not only for words themselves, but also for their meanings. That is, **concepts** in memory must exist for common objects and events in the environment before words can be attached to them.

The child's first recognizable word is uttered at the age of about 10 to 14 months, although there is considerable variability among infants. As is true for adults, children understand the meanings of more words that they spontaneously produce. Parental reports of infant understanding have produced an average receptive vocabulary estimate of 35 words by 10 months of age (Fenson, Dale, Reznick, Bates, Thal, & Pethick, 1994). Additional words are acquired at a steadily increasing rate through early childhood such that the average 6-year-old knows about 6,000 words. As children learn to read, the rate increases once more through adolescence. It has been

Concepts Abstract entities in memory that are formed through repeated experiences with examples of various categories of things (e.g., we all have a concept for "bird" that is based on our experiences with various members of the bird category)

estimated that the average American or British high school graduate knows about 60,000 words, and literate adults might know twice as many (Aitchinson, 1994; Miller, 1996; Pinker, 1994). Bloom (2001, p. 44) summarizes a body of research in the word learning literature in a chart reproduced below:

Average Number of Words Learned per Day	
12 to 16 months	0.3
16 to 23 months	0.8
23 to 30 months	1.6
30 months to 6 years	3.6
6 years to 8 years	6.6
8 to 10 years	12.1
10 years to 17 years	8.0

The acquisition rate decreases thereafter, but never stops entirely, as new words continue to be added to the language, and literate adults encounter rare ones on almost a daily basis.

9.7 Words and Concepts

Words include many different forms and many different meanings. They include nouns (a category that includes names of person, places, and things, that can be proper, specific, or categorical) and verbs, which generally describe actions or states of being. There are also adjectives, which add descriptions or modifications to nouns, such as "pink flowers" or "pretty dresses," and adverbs that modify verbs, such as "move quickly." Moreover, many words vary in meaning depending on how they are used, from concrete, abstract, referential, and functional, to idiomatic, metaphoric, ironic, and satirical. Then there are large classes of words that have little meaning in themselves, but function to modify the meanings of other words, such as determiners (a, some) and prepositions (in, under).

Obviously, it is difficult to come up with a simple definition of a word, and the meaning of meaning itself also requires careful consideration. Let us begin with trying to determine what a word is. A word has been defined as a syntactic atom—a basic building block that can be combined with other such units to produce sentences, just as phonemes can be combined to produce words. That is, a word is "… the smallest unit of grammar that can stand on its own as a complete utterance …" (Crystal, 1997, p. 440). Words are arbitrary signs that can relate an external form to an internal concept by social convention. Concepts can be thought of as summaries of past experiences that, by their existence in memory, allow us to categorize new experiences as being like old ones or not. That is, concepts in memory allow us to recognize objects, people, events, and states of mind. If any perceptual experience is not recognized, it can form the basis of a new conceptual representation in memory. Concepts exist before words in the mind of an infant, and in the aftermath of certain types of brain damage (i.e., aphasia), they remain after words have been lost from memory. We also have many concepts in memory for which we simply do not have words, such as how the setting sun's reflection appears on a lake rippled by the wind. We also have concepts for abstract entities, like truth, justice, prejudice, good, and evil, for which we generally have no specific external referent.

9.8 Word Meaning

The meaning of a word is the shared conceptual knowledge that members of a linguistic community agree to associate with some expressible form. It follows that no two people could have exactly the same meaning for any given word, but most people can agree on things that are or are not examples of the concept represented by any word. We can, for example, agree that collies and terriers are both dogs, but a pig is not a dog. The meaning of a word can thus be defined as, "… knowledge associated with a word that is relevant to explaining people's intuitions about reference and categorization" (Bloom, 2001, p. 21).

Referential meaning works mainly for nouns, but can be extended to verbs and adjectives—words like prepositions and determiners are different—their meanings depend on how they modulate the meanings of other words (e.g., "under the blanket" versus "under the weather"). The definition of word meaning has troubled philosophers and psychologists who, as yet, have been unable to agree on a definition acceptable to all. In one sense, words refer to things, concrete or abstract, and to actions or events that things engage in. These references to real-world objects and events are included in words, so that when we use a word like "chair," we agree with other speakers of English that we are talking about an article of furniture upon which it is acceptable to sit. Sameness of **reference** within a linguistic community is one aspect of word meaning.

Another aspect of meaning is internal and describes relationships among concepts in memory, and how these concepts are organized into categories of related concepts. Thus, there exists a large set of animals that we refer to as dogs and another even larger set of things that we exclude from that category. In this sense, the meaning of dog is simply things that belong to the category, and things that do not belong have different meanings. This description of meaning supposes an existence of concepts in semantic memory that can be related to external categories of both words and things (as in the semantic memory model of Collins & Quillian, 1969). There are thus two aspects of

Reference The use of a symbol, such as a word, to represent a physical object or event the meaning of a word, an internal aspect of concepts and relations and an external, referential aspect of things, events, and social contexts (Block, 1986; Brown, 2002).

9.9 Theories of Word Learning

9.9.1 Nativism versus Empiricism

There are essentially two theories about how children learn their first words. Nativists assume that there is some kind of innate language acquisition device that readily adopts symbolic gestures and vocalizations as references for environmental objects and events. Empiricists, on the other hand, argue that words are acquired through simple associations and reinforced imitations acquired from parents and siblings, with many words deliberately taught. Regardless of the point of view adopted, word learning is not a simple process, as "… even the simplest names for things require rich mental capacities—conceptual, social, and linguistic—that interact in complicated ways" (Bloom, 2001, p. 1).

9.9.2 Word Learning through Simple Associations

The empiricist view of word learning has evolved from the belief that all learning is based on simple associations that are formed gradually among things that tend to occur together. If an adult says the word "rabbit" to a young child as a rabbit is brought into the room, the word and the object result in associated auditory and visual perceptions. As Bloom points out:

> "If we see someone point to a rabbit and say "gavagai," it is entirely natural to assume that this is an act of naming and that the word refers to the rabbit … It would be mad to think that the word refers to undetached rabbit parts or rabbits plus the Eiffel Tower. But the naturalness of the rabbit hypothesis and the madness of the alternatives is not logical necessity; it is instead the result of how the human mind works" (Bloom, 2001, p. 4).

Some language acquisition researchers have explored the possibility that word learning could be due to co-occurrence frequency of words and objects in the environment. Much of infant-directed-speech (IDS) is about the here and now, and as many as 70% of words spoken by parents to 1-year-olds refer to things that the child is currently, or has recently been, attending to (Bloom, 2001). For example Plunkett, Sinha, Møller, and Strandsby (1992) demonstrated that if labels and images are fed through distinct input pathways into a connectionist network trained to associate the two, the network could eventually learn to generate the appropriate image in response to the label. Connectionist models, based on associationism and sensitive to statistical regularities between words and the environment, should eventually come to mimic much of what very young children learn about words and the objects they represent. This sensitivity to covariation of words and things (i.e., the fact that certain words and certain things tend to occur together repeatedly) remains a parsimonious account of how children learn words. Indeed, associationism remains central to many theories of learning in general to this day.

9.9.3   *Difficulties for the Simple Association Theory*

Associationist theory does have some problems in accounting for the speed and richness of children's language learning, which has provided a window of opportunity for nativist accounts. One problem is that words are not normally used at the same time that their referents are perceived. Even for common nouns, research has shown that about half the time that adults are speaking to young children, the children are not simultaneously attending to the object that the adult is talking about (Collins, 1977; Harris, Jones, & Grant 1983). Further, although parents name objects, they do not name actions, and most verbs that adults use do not refer to simultaneous actions (Gleitman, 1990). The associationists handle these problems by acknowledging that we exist in a noisy world, and that in the long run, most words will occur more often in the context of the objects they represent than with other objects, and the same is true for verbs and the actions they represent.

There are more serious problems, however, for simple learning theory. Children are able to learn words for objects and events that are not observable to them at the time the words are being used around them. They can also learn the names of things that they cannot see and touch, including "... imaginary things, such as fictional characters ... abstract entities like numbers, geometrical forms, ideas, and mistakes. This is a problem that ... has never been solved" (Bloom, 2001, p. 59). Other problems involve the word learning abilities of children with handicaps that would normally prevent them from experiencing the associations that are presumably so important for word learning. For example, deaf children learning a sign language (e.g., ASL) seem to acquire words at about the same rate as hearing children, at least up to the time of learning about 50 words (Petitto, 1992). Perhaps even more surprising, blind children have been observed to a have a similar rate of word learning as sighted children. Although based on a sample of only three, Landau and Gleitman (1985) found that the rate of word learning and acquiring general language abilities were about the same for congenitally blind and sighted children by age three. Blind children lack the ability to identify objects out of reach and cannot as easily understand what their parents are attending to as sighted children, who learn to follow an adult's gestures, such as pointing and direction of gaze.

Another problem for the associationist theory of word learning is the apparent speed of word acquisition, with often a single experience sufficient for learning a new word. A frequently-cited study by Carey and Bartlett (1978) showed that three- and four-year-old children could learn a new word after a brief exposure and retain something about its meaning for weeks afterward, a process dubbed "fast mapping" by Carey (1978). Oviatt (1980) showed that about half of the 1-year-olds studied could indicate which of several animals was a rabbit after previously having been told the name on only one occasion. Others have shown that most 13-month-olds could remember a made-up name for a novel object even when tested 24 hours later (Woodward, Markman, & Fitzsimmons (1994). (See Box 9.2 for further illustrations of how infants and young children learn words.)

BOX 9.2
How Children Learn Words

Bloom (2000, p. 10) summarizes a large body of research on children's learning of their first words with the comments that:

> "Word learning is really a hard problem, but children do not solve it through a dedicated mental mechanism. Instead words are learned through abilities that exist for other purposes. These include an ability to infer the intentions of others, an ability to acquire concepts, an appreciation of syntactic structure and certain learning and memory abilities … [W]ord learning is the product of children's ability to figure out what other people are thinking when they use words."

Bloom's conclusions are based on studies of infants and very young children, and some of these studies were not concerned with language learning specifically. For example, Morales, Mundy, and Rojas (1998) found a significant correlation between a 6-month-old's ability to follow an adult's direction of gaze and the size of the infant's receptive vocabulary at 12 months of age. It appears that correctly gauging the intent of a speaker's actions is an early component of associating words with their intended objects and events. Children try to figure out what it is that adults are referring to when they use words. They are engaged in determining intentional inferences, or a type of mind reading (Baron-Cohen, 1995).

By about 9 months of age, most infants can follow a parent's line of gaze and will also examine what they are pointing at. If they are uncertain, they will check their parent's gaze and see how the father or mother is reacting. By 12 months they will point to objects on their own and check to see if the adults change their gaze to look at the indicated object (Bretherton, 1992). The important result is that young children can and do infer what adults are looking at, and when an adult names something, the child infers that the name applies to what the adult was attending to, even if the child was attending to something else when the name was heard.

Support for the idea that names are associated with what is in the eye and mind of the person doing the naming comes from several studies by Baldwin (1991, 1993). In one study, an 18-month-old child played with one toy while another toy was placed inside a bucket in front of an experimenter, which made it invisible to the child. When the child was looking at his or her toy, the experimenter looked into the bucket and used a new word to name it, such as "It's a modi!" Later, when given the two objects and told to "find the modi," the children typically picked the one that the experimenter was looking at in the bucket and not the one that they were playing with themselves, when they first heard the word "modi."

Bloom (2000) argues that it is the child's *theory of mind* that enables communication and language acquisition. Infants acquire word knowledge from perception of objects, people, animals, and events. They learn through social interactions that speech is an intentional communicative act, and that words

Continues

represent things, such as names of objects and people. It is the discovery that other people have intentions to communicate and talk about other people, objects, and events that spurs the attempt of the infant to control expressive vocalizations and become an active participant in social activities.

9.9.4 *Putting Words Together*

Given the accelerating rate at which words are learned in the second and third years of life, it is not surprising that many words seem to be learned in one, or at most a few, episodes. These results mimic the one-trial learning (all-or-none association) that occurs in many non-human species, most frequently for noxious or dangerous stimuli (e.g., Hilgard & Bower, 1975). Such learning in animals has been equated with a biologically-programmed acquisition process that results in long-term retention after a single exposure. Along with a heightened vocabulary, the 18- to 24-month-old child begins a long process of sentence construction by emitting the first two- and three-word utterances. At first, words appear to be combined haphazardly, but closer inspection has revealed that even from the beginning, young children demonstrate that they are learning more than individual words. Rather, they learn how words are legally combined in a language according to grammatical rules that are a part of every human language's syntactic structure.

9.10 Acquisition of Syntax

9.10.1 *The First Phrases*

Psychologists used to believe that the first two- and three-word utterances of young children were short versions of longer phrases and sentences imitated from adult speech. This process of imitation, along with improved memory skills, should gradually result in longer and more grammatical utterances, but again, they should be based on attempts to repeat sentences that the children had heard or ones they had been reinforced for producing (e.g., Skinner, 1957).

Much credible research on child language has shown that these assumptions are false. The child of age 18 to 20 months produces unique word combinations at an increasing rate that generally are not shortened imitations of adult speech. Rather, the expressions show the same characteristics of language generated by adult speakers: They are creative, rule-governed, and deliberate attempts to communicate. Even the early one-word utterances (**holophrastic speech**) of the 12- to 18-month-old child can be interpreted by a parent or sibling as an attempt to convey meaning. The word "milk" can mean quite different things when the milk is in the refrigerator, in a glass on the table, or spilled on the floor. By 2 years

Holophrase The use of a single word to express a meaningful proposition, characteristic of speech in the 12- to 18-month-old toddler of age, the child is likely to be saying, "want milk" or "more milk" or "allgone milk" in each of the three situations, in which the meaning is much more clearly communicated than in holophrastic expressions.

The first two- and three-word utterances are often termed **telegraphic speech** because they omit many function words (e.g., articles, prepositions, and conjunctions), modifiers, and markers for tense and pluralization, among others. Yet all children in all cultures seem to move smoothly from holophrastic speech to two- and three-word utterances in about the same way and at about the same time, despite many apparent cultural and linguistic differences in their communities.

Telegraphic speech
Characteristic of the first two- and three-word utterances of 2-year-olds who tend to omit function words, such as articles, prepositions, and conjunctions

9.10.2   Infant-Directed Speech

One thing that does seem to be constant across cultures is the way that adults speak to very young children. Typically, their speech is more highly pitched than usual, prosodic elements, such as changes in intonation and variations in word stress, are emphasized, and the speech consists of simple sentence structures and common words, usually associated with the here and now. This common way for adults to speak to infants and toddlers is called **infant-directed speech** (IDS—earlier, the politically incorrect *motherese*), and it serves to help children to isolate and come to recognize familiar words by marking them both syntactically and prosodically. The effect is that young children are actually able to bootstrap their understanding of words and phrases in a language by building on their experiences with a familiar means of communication with adults.

Infant-directed speech (IDS) The speech typically directed by adults to very young children that is characterized by high pitch, exaggerated intonation changes, simple syntax, common words, and references to the here and now

9.10.3   Overextensions and Overgeneralizations

Children use words and phrases differently than adults, partly due to their limited vocabularies and natural propensity to search for meaning and structure. It is as though lack of understanding or inability to predict what will happen in any situation is a negatively reinforcing state that motivates children to seek resolution of uncertainties. For example, most people have heard about the embarrassing overextension of the word "daddy" to refer to any male who walks into the toddler's room, or the use of "doggie" to refer to just about any four-legged animal. Such wide generalizations are obvious attempts by toddlers to communicate when their vocabularies are insufficient to make the naming distinctions that they clearly are capable of making perceptually. Similarly, young children often show over-generalizations of common rules, such as those for pluralization ("mouses" or "feets") and for past tense ("runned" or "sitted"). Such expressions are common in the expressions of 2-year-olds, yet they are unlikely to have been acquired through imitation of adult speech. Rather, from an early age, children are learning the rules of their grammar, from which they show the spontaneous, creative ability to generate words, phrases, and sentences that they have never heard.

Regardless of their lack of conformity to adult standards of grammar, very young children are generally successful at their main goal of communication, and by the age of 4 years, most grammatical constructions have been acquired and are used in their adult form. The ease and speed of child language acquisition, despite a noisy environment with no deliberate attempts to teach grammatical structure, has confirmed the belief in many that language is a hereditary skill that is programmed into our genes to be learned like nothing else in our behavioral repertoire (Chomsky, 1975; Lenneberg, 1967; Pinker, 1994). This belief is supported by the observation that there appears to be a certain critical period for language acquisition, and that if language is not experienced in a normal way during this period, it cannot be learned and used normally (see Box 9.3).

BOX 9.3
The Critical Period for Language Acquisition

A critical period is a time window in which neurological development is critically dependent on appropriate stimulation for neuronal growth and formation of functional synapses and neural networks. In vision, for example, it is known that if one eye is selectively impaired at birth, through a cataract or unequal focusing ability, a condition called amblyopia or "lazy eye" can develop in which one eye takes over most of the control of sight. This impairment has been modeled in animals in which one eye of an infant monkey or kitten is sutured shut at birth and then opened some months later. If the period of deprivation matches a certain critical period, then neural connections between the retina, thalamus, and occipital cortex do not appear to develop normally, and the deprived eye is functionally blind (Sherman & Spear, 1982; Sillito, 1986). In a less dramatic manipulation, Blakemore and Cooper (1970) reared kittens in complete darkness for the first 5 weeks of their lives, except for a few hours each day in which they were exposed only to horizontal or vertical stripes in a specially-constructed environment (see figure). Single-cell recordings of occipital neurons in these cats revealed that they had normal orientation-specific responses only to the direction of stripes that they had viewed during the critical period. The animals were functionally blind to lines and edges of the orientations not seen during the critical period. No amount of later experience could make up for the deficit (i.e., neural plasticity was limited in its ability to compensate for early stimulus deprivation).

A similar case has been made for a critical period in language development, roughly from birth to puberty, in which exposure to human conversation is necessary for normal language acquisition and development. Of course, the lack of such exposure occurs only for children who are severely handicapped or severely abused. The two most famous cases in the latter situation are the so-called "wild boy of Aveyron" (Lane, 1976) and "Genie of Los Angeles" (Curtiss, 1977; Rymer, 1993).

"Victor" of Aveyron was taken in after an indefinite period of fending for himself in the forests of southern France in 1800, when he was about 12 or 13 years of age. He was completely mute and indifferent to much of his environment except for certain

Continues

foods, especially potatoes, which he had been used to digging up in the fields. A long series of lessons, mainly by the French physician Jean-Marc-Gaspard Itard, produced a degree of socialization and a rudimentary understanding and production of spoken words, but no true command of language. Lane (1976), in his analysis of the nineteenth century records, is uncertain whether Victor suffered mainly from isolation and neglect, or whether he was neglected from birth and abandoned as a very young child due to other developmental problems, such as mental retardation or autism. He does concur with the hypothesis advanced by many who studied Victor directly, however, that the attempt to teach him language failed mainly because a certain critical period for its acquisition had passed, and no amount of training could result in its recovery.

A much more complete record is available for the disturbing case of "Genie," who first appeared in public when accompanied by her nearly-blind and traumatized mother at a Los Angeles County welfare office in November 1970. She was 13 years old, and had been kept a virtual prisoner in her room with very little human contact. In fact, her father beat her if she made any noise, so she learned not to make a sound, nor did anyone speak to her. When found, she had a receptive vocabulary of perhaps 20 words, and could speak only two. The published accounts of her institutionalization, removals to foster homes, and formal and informal training in speech and other social skills is a heartbreaking testimony to the reality of a critical period for language acquisition. Although her receptive and productive vocabulary grew with continuous social contacts, her ability to form grammatically correct two- and three-word sentences was painfully slow and reached a plateau below that of the average 3-year old. Yet, it was obvious from her informal social contacts and evaluations by professionals that she did not suffer from retardation or autism, only the profound, lingering effects of abusive neglect. The effects of this neglect reinforce the conclusion from the deprivation research in vision: Normal stimulation during a critical developmental period is required for the full development of the biological components of complex behaviors, such as perception and language use. The results also support the idea that infants are born with a biological readiness to acquire language, and they learn it differently from otherwise normal children who have been deprived of early linguistic experience.

Chapter **Summary**

Every child who is not severely handicapped at birth learns to speak his or her native language through a sequence of developmental steps that is similar the world over. From birth, infants have a propensity to attend to speech and treat if differently from other sounds. They categorize speech sounds and learn the categories of phonemes in their native language. They begin to produce the phonemes that they hear and understand that the function of speech is to communicate. They also learn the specific meanings of scores of words, and how they are used. Finally, they learn the elements of syntactic structure, as indicated by prosodic markings and other information in the way adults and older siblings produce sentences. All of this learning occurs before the infant utters his or her first word, at about the age of 12 months.

The speed and regularity of child language acquisition has suggested to many that it unfolds in the face of experience like other maturational developments, such as learning to walk, that are biologically programmed into all of us. Since linguistic communication is probably very old within our species, there probably has been some selective pressure for people to communicate effectively and early in life in order to survive. The extent of the innate language ability and the biological control of its development is unclear and not without controversy. Yet, the speed of first language acquisition and the universal nature of its progress, despite a noisy, incomplete, and extremely variable data set to work with, argue for a large innate capacity for language learning. From the production of the first words and short phrases, the child's idea is to communicate meaning. This is done through the adoption of rules of expression, including syntax, that are produced from an internal grasp of the role of language and not imitated from the examples of adult models (Pinker, 2007).

Review Questions

- **What abilities do newborn infants have that prepare them for learning to understand language and to speak?**

  Newborn infants have the capacity to attend to sources of stimulation and show a natural preference for familiar sights and sounds. Research has shown that they prefer to hear their mother's voice and see their mother's face above any other voices and faces within the first few days after birth. They also show a predilection to process human speech sounds differently from other sounds, and prefer their own language over others and standard prosodic phrasing over unusual phrasing for months before they can speak their first word.

- **What are the main components of human languages that enable us to exchange ideas and descriptions of things?**

  Human, or natural, languages are all speech-based and use phonological systems to represent thousands of words from a small set of phonemes. Furthermore, all languages are structured hierarchically, rather than linearly, to represent syntactic structures that divide sentences into phrases, and phrases into words and word combinations. Finally, all languages depend on a mapping between meaning as represented in people's minds and language as expressed in speech. The goal is to recreate a close match to the ideas that the speaker had intended to communicate in the mind of the listener.

- **Do all children learn a language in the same way even though they are born into different cultures?**

  All children seem to go through similar stages of development regardless of the linguistic culture into which they are born. Language development seems to begin before birth, perhaps through the fetus hearing its mother's voice through direct conduction in the womb. All infants seem to demonstrate categorical perception of speech sounds shortly after birth, with a change in the definition of category boundaries occurring before the first year of life to reflect the phonemic structure of the native language. Language comprehension leads language expression in all children, as the meaning of words and the intention to communicate are learned before the child speaks his or her first words.

- **Is language learned like a skill, or is it different in some way?**

  Language seems to be learned in a way unlike other sophisticated skills, which has led many researchers to suggest that language learning is special, in some way. A language is not specifically taught to infants, nor do the first utterances in any way reflect copies or imitation of adult speech patterns. Rather, language seems to occur in a pattern of maturational developments or a set of biological propensities that unfold over time. The rules and purpose of language seem to be learned implicitly by abstracting the principles from observations of the behavior of others. For these and other reasons, language learning appears to be a unique intellectual achievement of the very young child that occurs most readily during a critical period for language acquisition (i.e., birth to sometime before puberty).

Key Terms

Bootstrapping   247

Categorical perception   238

Coarticulation effects   244

Concepts   248

Holophrase   254

Infant-directed speech (IDS)   255

Phonology   243

Prosody   247

Reference   250

Segmentation   244

Semantics   247

Syntax   247

Telegraphic speech   255

Voice onset time (VOT)   245

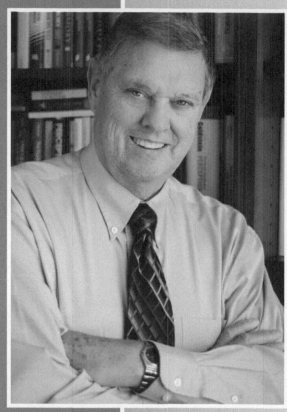

KEITH RAYNER

Chapter 10

Language Development and Reading

"And so to completely analyze what we do when we read would almost be the acme of a psychologist's achievements, for it would be to describe very many of the most intricate workings of the human mind, as well as to unravel the tangled story of the most remarkable specific performance that civilization has learned in all its history."

Edmund B. Huey, 1908–1968, p. 6

PREVIEW QUESTIONS

❖ *What do linguistic theories of grammar have to do with learning to comprehend language?*

❖ *Where did writing come from, and what are the major differences between writing systems throughout history and around the world?*

❖ *What is the relationship between speech and writing in English and other languages?*

❖ *What is dyslexia and why do some children find it so much harder to learn to read than others?*

10.1 Introduction: Differences Between Reading and Speech Perception

Reading is surely one of the most important things that we learn in life, and for literate adults, it is the source of much, if not most, of our knowledge. Although speech and spoken language comprehension are acquired naturally and quickly by almost every toddler who is not severely handicapped at birth, learning to read is a slow and uncertain process. A significant proportion of children and adults never learn to read proficiently despite adequate educational opportunities and no obvious perceptual or cognitive disabilities. Understanding and reducing the effects of reading disability is a major concern of psychologists, educators, and parents.

A certain level of language proficiency is necessary to begin reading, since the words encountered in print should be part of the reader's vocabulary for them to be recognized and understood. In the United States, formal reading instruction begins for children aged 5 or 6 years, at which time they have a receptive vocabulary of thousands of spoken words and are capable of understanding and using most grammatical forms in English. Therefore, the major problem in learning to read is mastering the decoding of print to the same, or very similar, internal representations of language that is derived from the speech code.

10.2 The Internal Representation of Language

10.2.1 The Purpose of Language

Language exists at several different levels, and its main function is to exchange ideas between two or more individuals. Therefore, language ideally begins and ends as sets of ideas that are similar in the minds of both the speaker/writer and the hearer/reader. The ideas expressed can describe some state of the world, some recalled event, or they can be imaginary and fanciful creations, to consider just a few possibilities. The fact is that most linguistic expressions, including the sentence that you are now reading, are novel and unique combinations of words, yet they pose few problems for communication and understanding between adult speakers of the same language. How is this accomplished?

10.2.2 Chomsky's Universal Grammar

There has been considerable debate about Chomsky's (1957, 1965) ideas that we are all born with a language acquisition device that is based on a universal grammar. These principles have been derived from observations of the speed of child language acquisition and some common phases of children's language development across all known cultures and languages. A universal grammar consists of a kind of tool kit or software package that is customized by each child to adapt to the language spoken around him or her (Jackendoff, 2002). It also relates to the general architectural universals of all human languages that include, "… interconnected phonological, syntactic, and conceptual/semantic structures, each containing substructures and tiers of particular sorts" (Jackendoff, p. 78; see Box 10.1).

Generative grammar This is based on internal rules that presumably construct phrase structures from a deep level of meaning in the mind. These phrase structures are then filled in with words that can be uttered. The process is reversed to generate meaning from surface structures (i.e., speech or writing)

10.2.3 Generative Grammar

Besides a general language acquisition device, Chomsky (1965) argued for the presence of another universal principle of human languages, namely **generative grammar**. This type of grammar describes the rules that operate on concepts at a

BOX 10.1

Is There an Innate Universal Grammar?

Beginning with Chomsky's (1965) assertion that there is a universal language acquisition device and an innately-given universal grammar, many theorists have championed the idea that infants have a special, inborn capacity that promotes language acquisition (e.g. Lenneberg, 1967; Pinker, 1994). All children learn the language spoken by their parents and siblings, and there is nothing else similar that must be learned in vision, cognition, or motor behavior that approaches the complexity of phonology and syntax (Jackendoff, 2002, p. 79). Yet, almost every child gets it right within the first few years of life.

Evidence in favor of a biologically-programmed developmental sequence for learning language in infancy has been categorized into several related arguments (Harley, 2008; Pinker, 1994; Jackendoff, 1994, 2002).

1) Only humans have language. Despite the existence of elaborate communication systems in animals and fairly successful attempts to teach apes to communicate symbolically, no other organism has the cognitive capacity for articulate, hierarchical, generative grammar. This capacity gives us literally endless abilities to describe the present, recall the past, and fancifully predict the future in ways unlike any other living things. Even children with disabilities, such as moderate retardation, or suffering surgery as severe as a hemispherectomy (removing one-half of the brain; Vargha-Khadem, Isaacs, Papaleloudi, Polkey, & Wison, 1991) can learn to speak and understand language fairly normally.

2) The developmental sequence is roughly the same for all children in all cultures. Infants learn the local phonology, speak their first words at about 1 year of age, form rule-governed two- and three-word sentences before age two, and rapidly increase vocabulary size and grammatical sophistication in the following few years. Most adults trying to learn a second language never realize the same ease of learning, rate of acquisition, and final level of accomplishment that is demonstrated by 4-year-old children. The lack of early phonological experience dooms most second-language learners to speak with an identifiable accent. Further, many of their utterances and writings will contain telltale violations of grammatical subtleties.

It appears as if there is a *critical developmental period* for language acquisition, such as that known to exist for acquiring binocular vision in cats and con-specific songs in birds. During the critical period for language learning, the brain is preset to extract vocabulary and rules of syntax from hearing speech. Children who have been deprived of early language experience, due to abuse or undiagnosed deafness, never learn to speak properly as adults. They might acquire a large vocabulary, but the rules of sentence structure remain a mystery to them.

3) Language abilities are localized in similar parts of the brain for most people, such that damage to the left posterior frontal lobe or anterior portions of the left temporal lobe typically results in a reduction or complete loss of language abilities (i.e., Broca's and Wernicke's aphasia, respectively). It is perhaps surprising that such aphasias also occur in deaf people who use sign language if damage occurs in these same regions of the brain. Jackendoff (2002, p.98) argues that, "… children mobilize the same resources in acquiring sign … [A]s soon as something in the world can be categorized as symbolic communication, the language machine is engaged."

4) Some children with a specific language impairment seem to have an inherited disability related to a mutated gene in chromosome 7, called the FOXP2 gene (Lai, Fisher, Hurst, Vargha-Khadem, & Monaco, 2001). The disability appears to affect spoken language production and comprehension without any other obvious difficulties in behavior, hearing, or intelligence. The specific brain mechanism involved in limiting language development seems to include Broca's area, and the control of fine motor movements of facial muscles and articulators (Fisher & Marcus, 2006). Corballis (2004) argues that the original development of the modern form of the FOXP2 gene in humans within the past 100,000 years led not only to expansion of form and function of Broca's area, but also to the flowering of human culture, technology, art, and language.

Continues

5) In the absence of language, children will create one on their own. It has often been noted that deaf children of parents without a sign language will invent their own signs to communicate with their parents *(home sign)*, and their parents will mimic it, but never with the same spontaneity and ease demonstrated by their children.

In the 1980s, a school for deaf children in Nicaragua brought together a group of people who, up to that time, had only been communicating by home sign methods. Within a few years, this group originated their own sign language, and it was developed and elaborated by new members of the group (Kegl, Senghas, & Coppola, 1999).

Similar feats of language development have been noted by studies of groups of people from different language communities who are relocated to a new country as refugees or for work opportunities. At first they communicate with each other in words and phrases borrowed from the host language in a language called *pidgin*, "They lack stable word order, and their grammatical organization has a rudimentary 'Me Tarzan, you Jane' flavor …" (Jackendoff, 2002, p. 99).

Although various pidgin languages have been known to exist at various times around the world, a much more interesting development is their evolution into entirely new languages as they are passed down to the children of pidgin-speaking parents. The children do not learn pidgin, but develop a much richer system called a *creole*. Creoles are found to have grammatical structures that are not traceable to elements in the pidgin from which they sprang. Bickerton (1981), who studied pidgin and creole-speaking people in Hawaii in the 1960s, argued that their creole conformed to what the children's universal grammar expected a human language to be like. Their parents continued to speak the more primitive pidgin, however, apparently because they were past the critical period for learning the creole adaptation.

In sum, universal grammar is an innate ability that we all share at birth that enables us to learn any human language rapidly and very well, despite the haphazard and informal speech provided by adult speakers. This ability is unlike any others that develop with age, such as binocular vision, locomotion, mathematics and so on. Rather, the immense complexities of phonology and syntax are mapped onto a developing semantic understanding of the world in an awesome display of language mastery by small children that is seldom matched by adults, even linguists, later in life.

deep level of representation to create expressible ideas. Such ideas are formed from simple propositions that are organized into syntactic structures, such as phrase structures of sentences. Subsequent grammatical processes link internal representations of words into these phrase structures. Then, we initiate motor routines to activate the appropriate surface aspects of language—the actual words we wish to speak or write. Finally, articulators are activated to produce the actual spoken (or written) form of the language. The generative component of the grammar uses a set of syntactic rules that convert the deep structure to surface structures during language production, and the same rules reverse these processes in language comprehension. Language learning then encompasses the learning of rules relating elements in a hierarchy, and not rote learning of phrases or sentences imitated from adult speech.

Chomsky and others (e.g., Fodor, Bever, & Garrett, 1974; Pinker, 1994) have taken some pains to insist that the theory of generative grammar is one of **competence, not performance**. That is, we all have the capability of using a rule system to generate and understand grammatical sentences, but our actual behavior often falls short, as

Competence-performance distinction The idea that we all behave as if we have an internal grammatical system that is capable of distinguishing between grammatical and ungrammatical sentences, but our actual language use often falls short in production and comprehension, mainly due to working memory limitations when we make grammatical errors in speech or writing or misunderstand well-formed sentences. Many of the errors that we make are attributable to limitations in working memory capacity. That is, the length and complexity of a particular sentence, such as the one you are now reading, can tax our capacities to maintain a representation of all of its constituents while we try to parse it into phrases, compute their meanings, and process the sentence as a whole for storage and possible future use.

10.2.4 *Phrase Structures*

The syntactic structure of a sentence lies between the **surface structure** of phonology (or orthography, for writing) and the deep structure that relates to meaning. Syntactic structures are commonly represented by tree structures such as the following, in which S = sentence, NP = noun phrase, AP = adjectival phrase, VP = verb phrase, PP = prepositional phrase, A = adjective, N = noun, V = verb, Det = determiner, etc.

Surface structure The actual set of words spoken or written that make up a sentence or longer sample of language

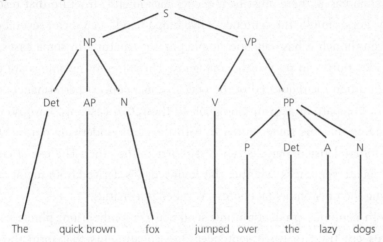

Such tree structures reveal that, despite the linear ordering of words in a sentence, a sentence is usually organized hierarchically into clauses, phrases, word groupings, and finally, single words. These **phrase structures** are shown to exist in human language use by, among other things, the prosodic elements of speech in which intonation patterns, pauses, and stress complement the underlying syntax and help to reveal sentence structure.

Phrase structure The hierarchical organization of a sentence into noun and verb phrases, then into lower-level phrases, and finally the individual words

Other evidence for the psychological reality of phrase structures in language processing comes from the resolution of certain kinds of ambiguities. For example, the sentence "The students were revolting" is ambiguous at the surface level since it can mean two different things. However, it can be decomposed into two different phrase structures that disambiguate the sentence meaning. This can be done by placing the word "revolting" either as part of the verb with "were" as an auxiliary (to make them part of a revolt), or by removing it from the verb and using it as a predicate adjective modifying "students" (to make them sound disgusting).

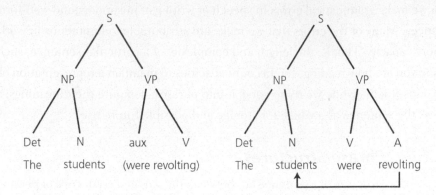

10.2.5 *Deep Structures*

Other sentences are ambiguous yet have only single phrase structure representations. In such cases, there must be a deeper meaningful structure that resolves the ambiguity. For example, the sentence "Give him a hand!" can mean several different things, even though it has only one simple phrase structure. In some cases, contextual considerations can resolve the ambiguity. The different meanings are clear, for example, if a hand is requested at the end of a solo concert performance, or if it is yelled by a lifeguard at a swimming pool. In these two cases we have no difficulty understanding that the same sentence, with the same underlying phrase structure, is calling for applause in one case and assistance in the other. The use of knowledge to disambiguate sentences, whether this knowledge is derived from memory or from interpreting the environmental context, is called pragmatics.

In both sentence production and sentence comprehension, phrase and **deep structures** are used to parse sentences into constituents that form the basis of meaningful ideas, called propositions. Propositions are the smallest elements of meaning that combine to determine the overall meaning of a sentence. Propositions are differentiated from their component concepts and relations in that a proposition has a truth-value, whereas concepts and relations simply exist or do not exist. For example, we presumably have concepts stored away in memory that correspond to nouns, like *bat, robin,* and *bird,* as well as understanding relations expressed by verbs, such as *is, can,* and *has.* It is this information in memory that allows to ascertain the truth or falsity of simple propositions expressed as "A robin is a bird," "A bird can fly," "A bat is a bird," and "A bat has feathers."

Propositions are the building blocks of meaning and exist at a deep level of representation in the brain, beyond the direct reach of language. They enable the construction of ideas that can be expressed in language and conveyed to a receiver so that successful communication results when both participants consider a similar set of ideas. Generative grammar is the process that converts ideas into syntactic structures that can be expressed and understood by people who share the same language.

Deep structure Chomsky's original term for the level of meaning representationthat underlies language

10.3 Language Development

As discussed at the end of the previous chapter, the first two-word utterances produced by a child before the age of two are rule-bound from the beginning. That is, a toddler will say things like "Daddy gone" or "Toy gone," but not "Gone kitty." Similarly, expressions like "That doggie" or "That girl" might be uttered, but not "Kitty that." Rules of pluaralization and past tense are acquired by 2-year-olds to produce utterances like "Mouses runned outside." Linguists observing such toddler speech have concluded that grammatical rules are being learned and generalized from adult speech, not so much the surface forms of speech by themselves, except at the single word level. From the first two-word constructions, children are trying out rules and learning the exceptions until they acquire a consistent command of the grammar of their language. Although the word order used by toddlers is usually consistent with adult syntax, the actual expressions used are unique and generated from the child's growing knowledge of grammar (e.g., Pinker, 2007).

The development of language in years 2 through 4 consists of a steady growth in vocabulary and mean length of utterance (MLU, a standard measure of linguistic ability among 2- and 3-year-olds; Brown, 1973). Although young children make many mistakes in their speech, the overwhelming trend is to greater sophistication and grammaticality. The formation of questions ("What Kittie have?" to "What does Kittie have?") and negations ("Ride it, no." to "I don't want to ride it.") assume their adult versions by about the time a child is ready to learn to read.

10.4 Bilingualism

People who are bilingual or multilingual are fluent in speaking and understanding two or more languages, respectively. Today, most people in the world are at least partially bilingual, and several countries, such as Belgium, Canada, Switzerland, and Wales have two or more official languages. In parts of the United States, a language other than English, such as Spanish, is more commonly spoken at home than is English. People who acquire two or more languages can do so at the same time, or sequentially. Simultaneous bilingualism usually occurs when two different languages are spoken at home (e.g., one by the father and another by the mother or by a caretaker). Sequential bilingualism can occur early, such as for children who speak one language at home and another in the playground or preschool, or it can occur later as part of formal education or a move to another country during adolescence or adulthood.

It is of some interest to learn whether bilinguals who learn a second language simultaneously, or almost simultaneously, with a primary language learn it differently or to different levels of proficiency than those who acquire a second language relatively later in life. Such differences would be expected if there is a critical period for language acquisition that applies also to second-language learning (see Box 9.3). Research in this area is difficult, since the participants are in natural environments with different levels of experience and formal training in second languages. However, some research has shown differences in second language proficiency depending on its age of acquisition. Not surprisingly, such differences show up in phonology, since some of the earliest aspects of language that are learned by infants are the phonetic structure and prosodic elements of the native language. Indeed, once phonemic categorical boundaries are acquired, it is difficult to change them since some phonetic differences are actually harder to hear as one becomes older. Studies have shown that adults can speak a second language with little or no accent if the second language is acquired before about age 10, but later acquisitions almost always result in at least some foreign-sounding pronunciations (Flege, Yeni-Komshiam, & Liu, 1999; MacKay, Flege, & Imai, 2006).

Similar differences have been found in syntax, with later second language learners showing syntactic errors or comprehension difficulties not usually seen in simultaneous or early second language learners. This result is more controversial, however, as it is difficult to equate age of second language learning with other factors, such as amount and type of formal language training (see Harley, 2008; and Matlin, 2009, for reviews). Nonetheless, many believe that equivalent proficiency in two or more languages is unlikely to be achieved by anyone, and that one language will become dominant for syntactic and semantic processing of words (e.g., Harley & Wang, 1997). Despite these difficulties, there are many examples of positive effects of bilingualism, both on language processing and awareness and on working memory and reasoning processes related to language use (Bialystok, 2005; Kroll and de Groot, 2005; Matlin, 2009).

10.5 Learning to Read

10.5.1 Decoding Print to Meaning

Learning to read involves learning to convert printed words to meaning so that both spoken and written language produce the same level of understanding in the mind of the recipient. This conversion process is called decoding, and it depends heavily on how the spoken language is coded into print. Three major systems of writing have evolved over the thousands of years that languages have been written: logographic, syllabic, and alphabetic.

10.5.2 *Logographic Writing*

Logographic writing systems are typified by ancient Egyptian hieroglyphs, in which symbols either directly or indirectly represent individual words or morphemes. (A **morpheme** is the smallest meaningful unit of a language (e.g. the word *girls* has two morphemes—one representing a young human female, and the other indicating that there are more than one of them.) Other writing systems, such as cuneiform in the Fertile Crescent and the calligraphic script of ancient China, also began as representational logographic languages, but evolved, as did Egyptian hieroglyphics, into more abstract writing systems that eventually included representations of word sounds as well as their meanings in the printed symbols.

The evolution of representational symbolic systems into abstract writing is perhaps best exemplified by the work of Denise Schmandt-Besserat (1978; see Box 10.2). Although the earliest writing systems seem to have been largely pictographic (representational) or logographic (more abstract representational systems for words or morphemes), the representation of speech sounds in written language is a common feature in the evolution of writing. There are no pure logographic writing systems today, as even modern Chinese characters contain phonetic elements that suggest the pronunciation of the words they represent.

> **Morpheme** The smallest meaningful unit in a language, consisting of all or part of a word (For example "cat" and "rest" have one morpheme each, "cats" and "rested" have two each)

BOX 10.2

Origins of Cuneiform Writing and the Alphabet

Writing systems have been developed independently in cultures around the world, including Egypt, Mesopotamia, India, China, Easter Island, and Central America. The precursors of English and other Western writing systems can be traced to the cuneiform markings on clay tablets found in many archaeological sites in the Middle East. Cuneiform writing most commonly appears as stylized, abstract symbols that apparently represented syllables and words in ancient Sumer, but where did it come from?

Authors, such as Alexander Marshack (1972), have described some of the earliest known markings and decorations that have been preserved on bone and stone artifacts as well as on the walls of caves, such as Lascaux in France and Altamira in Spain. These are mainly representational works of art, but some odd, deliberate scratchings seem to be attempts to record something rather than being purely decorative or representational. Some of these are as old as 200,000 years, but such artifacts only begin to proliferate about 40,000 years ago. The earliest abstract markings seem to record counts of things as well as the days of a lunar calendar. With the advent of

city-states and trade, a system for representing goods and their quantities became necessary.

The earliest writing system seems to have evolved from such trade accounts made in Mesopotamia about 10,500 years ago. Archaeologists interested in these civilizations noted numerous small, clay tokens, some of which seemed to represent animals, such as sheep and goats, whereas others were abstract spheres, disks and cones, some bearing markings of various types. At a loss for explanation, some theorized that these were used as toys for children or as tokens for games that were played by adults and children. However, there were too many of them to suggest that they were used for only trivial pursuits, and another idea was proposed—the tokens were used to represent a bill of goods exchanged in trade.

One scenario has the tokens representing the types and numbers of goods shipped from one trade center to another. In order to exchange proper payments, the merchants involved would have to insure that the goods sent and received matched, or at least that any loss along the way from theft and other reasons could be accounted for. One way to do

Continues

this would be to include, along with the shipment, a manifest of its contents. Each clay token could represent some shipped item, such as livestock, food, and textiles, and markings on the tokens could indicate the quantities of each. To prevent equivalent theft of the representational tokens along with their corresponding items, the tokens were placed into a clay jar with an inscription representing the name of the merchant or local ruler of the sending party, and then it could be hardened in an oven. Upon receiving the shipment, it would be a simple matter for the recipient to break open the jar to compare the manifest with the actual supply of goods delivered.

Over a few thousand years, the system was simplified to replace the jars of tokens with clay tablets into which the 3-D tokens could be impressed to reveal 2-D images. Finally, a stylus was used to trace a symbol into the tablet eliminating the need for tokens altogether (see Schmandt-Besserat, 1978).

Although some of the earliest cuneiform symbols can be accounted for in this way, others show no direct descendancy from tokens and appear to have been created specifically for writing on tablets (Donald, 1991). Nonetheless, most symbols appear to have been ideographic, in the sense that most had a clear visual relationship with what they represented. The cuneiform writing system evolved much the same way that other writing systems have—from ideographic to logographic—with the symbols becoming more abstract. When the writing system was adopted throughout much of the Middle East, it came to represent syllables by their sounds rather than by the logographic relationship between symbols and meanings.

Many cultures in the ancient Middle East borrowed the principle of representing speech sounds of syllable size with arbitrary visual symbols. However, the principle of dividing a syllable into its phonemic components and representing each of the smallest distinguishing sounds of speech with individual written symbols apparently occurred only once, and generalized to the alphabetic principle used in most Western languages today. This development is often credited to the Phoenicians (hence phonics—the sound-to-letter strategy of writing and reading words), and it was developed into the Greek and later Latin alphabets used extensively throughout early European and Middle Eastern civilizations.

Why was the alphabet invented only once? One reason is that the step is not necessary—hundreds of languages have been and remain represented by symbols for syllables, morphemes, or whole words, just as we use numbers and icons on computer screens today. There is no evidence that such languages are read with any lower levels of speed and comprehension by skilled readers of the language. A second reason for the lack of widespread alphabetic languages is that they relate print and meaning at a high level of abstraction. The phonemes that make up a word are not often obvious to speakers of a language even if they can easily make a one-phoneme distinction, such as between "big" and "dig" in English. In fact, it has been argued that learning to read an alphabetic language engenders a kind of phonological awareness that is missing in illiterate speakers of the language (Morais, Cary, Alegria, & Bertelson, 1979). The very act of attending to a relationship between letters and sounds promotes both learning to read and insight into the sound patterns of the spoken language.

10.5.3 *Syllabic Writing*

Syllabic writing systems include modern Japanese *kana* script, although Japanese also uses *kanji* characters borrowed from the Chinese writing system. The *kana* script uses about 50 different symbols for syllables, and literally thousands of *kanji* characters. Many words can be represented in either system; it is up to the prerogative of the writer. Despite this apparent heterogeneous system, the Japanese have one of the highest literacy rates in the world, even though it might take years longer for their readers to achieve fluency than students in some alphabet-using countries (Robinson, 2002).

10.5.4 *Alphabetic Writing*

In an alphabetic writing system, or orthography, each phoneme in speech is represented by one or more letters of the alphabet. Since there are about 44 distinct phonemes in English and only 26 different letters, it is obvious that the sound-spelling mapping cannot be one-to-one. Other languages, such as Finnish and Spanish, have what are called shallow **orthographies**, in which the sound-spelling correspondence is direct and consistent. For speakers of these languages, knowing how a word is spelled determines exactly how it is pronounced. English has a deeper orthography, in which word spelling is more closely related to meaning than to sound, in many cases. Consider the spelling of the word know. One could argue that since it is pronounced "no" it should be spelled like that (similarly, there have been arguments presented for spellings like *nite, lam, thru* etc.). However, the deeper orthography of English reveals relatedness of meanings between words like *know, knowledge,* and *acknowledge* in which the extra letters now play a role in both pronunciation and meaning. Similar arguments apply to spelling of such words as *bomb* in which the last letter is pronounced in related words such as *bombardier* and *bombardment.*

Orthography The written form of a language

Despite these difficulties, there are advantages in the relation between spelling and sound in all alphabetic languages that can produce benefits in learning to read. Unlike Chinese, in which many individual characters have to be learned and memorized like pictures or objects, alphabetic languages offer a key with every new word—a good way to approximate its pronunciation. This is despite the fun that some people like George Bernard Shaw have had with English by suggesting that the word *ghoti* should properly be pronounced *fish!* (The joke is that the gh sound is like that in "enough," the o is sounded like that in "women," and the ti sound is from words like "action.")

Shaw's point outlines the fact that there are many irregular spelling-sound correspondences in English. Even some very common words like *have, the, pint, said,* and does are pronounced irregularly (compared with the regular forms, *cave, she, mint, paid,* and *toes,* respectively). However, the overriding grapheme-phoneme regularity is usually enough to allow beginning readers to sound out new words such that they can be recognized. This ability has two benefits for beginning readers: They can read independently even if the text contains many words that they have not encountered in print before, and they can add new words to their reading vocabulary to steadily increase their level of independence. Reading independently requires a starting point, and that is based heavily on an ability called *phonological awareness.*

10.6 Phonological Awareness

There are several good predictors of a young child's success in learning to read and of academic success in general. These include the amount of linguistic experience the child has at home, including both being engaged in oral conversations and being read to. These experiences result in internalization of linguistic knowledge reflected in such skills as knowledge of the alphabet and the ability to distinguish word sounds and play rhyming games. Children who know the alphabet and who also can do well on tasks, like saying whether or not two words rhyme or start with the same sound, prior to entering school do markedly better in learning to read. Also, children who do poorly in preschool tests of phonological awareness are at risk for difficulties in learning to read (Bradley & Bryant, 1978, 1983).

Given the importance of some pre-reading skills for predicting reading achievement, it is noteworthy that specific training on such skills seems to be beneficial. That is, training phonological awareness in pre-school children seems to increase the likelihood of later success in learning to read. Further, reading programs that incorporate phonological awareness exercises seem to be successful both for average readers as well as for those who lag behind (see Rayner, Foorman, Perfetti, Pesetsky, & Seidenberg, 2001 for an excellent review).

10.7 The Teaching of Reading

10.7.1　*Reading Is Different from Speech Perception*

Unlike the acquisition of language through speech, learning to read does not occur naturally, and in almost all cases, it must be taught. Since writing is a relatively recent accomplishment of our species, it is extremely unlikely that we have evolved any specialized brain mechanisms for decoding print to sound or meaning. Therefore, learning to read makes use of cognitive capabilities that evolved in our species for other purposes. Primary among these are the abilities to make fine visual discriminations and to remember visual patterns, like faces, objects, animals, and tools. The remaining piece of the puzzle then involves teaching a child to relate printed language to the sounds, structure, and meaning of language that she or he already knows.

10.7.2　*Whole Words versus Phonics—The Great Debate*

Phonics The grapheme-phoneme correspondences in words of a language

There have long been two general methods of teaching reading. One involves teaching words as whole units to be recognized in ways similar to pictures or logographic characters, as in Chinese. The other emphasizes the usefulness of the alphabetic principle and the (frequently) regular letter-sound relationships of English and other languages based on an alphabet.

The whole-word method gained support from subjective impressions that skilled readers read words all at once without paying much attention to the component letters. Early research in psychology (e.g., Cattell, 1900) showed that single words could be perceived at least as accurately as single letters when they are shown in very brief displays or as very small images. Later research in word perception (Reicher, 1969; Wheeler, 1970) supported Cattell's claim with methods developed to show that his results could not be due to guessing strategies or response bias alone. Letters really are more easily perceived in the context of a word than in a nonword context or alone.

It appears that there is a *word superiority effect* in vision, such that words are more perceptible than individual letters or *pseudowords* that are regularly spelled and pronounceable nonword letter strings (like *brane* or *farn*). These results are obtained in experiments that measure accuracy when a letter string is presented briefly (Reicher, 1969), as well as in those that measure response time—the time needed to find a target letter in a string (e.g., Juola, Ward, & McNamara, 1981). The explanation for the word superiority effect hinges on our internal knowledge of words that operates in a top-down way to supplement the perceptual recognition of familiar letter strings. This top-down knowledge is generally irrelevant for novel strings that have no long-term memory representation. Further support for this theoretical interpretation has come from Rumelhart and McClelland's (1982) successful demonstration that a connectionist model of such top-down effects also achieves word superiority in a neural network simulation of human word recognition behavior.

Other support for the whole word method of teaching reading derives from the fact that many English words are spelled irregularly and cannot be figured out by rules that generally apply to sounding out words from their letters (i.e., grapheme-phoneme correspondences). These include some of the most common words in English, such as *have* and *said*. Another argument is based on the idea that language is learned as a series of words, and that the phonemes that map onto letters are more abstract and difficult to isolate, especially for beginning readers. Finally, it is argued that reading should be taught as a word recognition process, since the goal of reading is to understand words and their meanings in a sentence context, and not to waste time and resources on generating sounds.

The main alternative approach to reading instruction is based on the assumption that the alphabetic principle is not only useful, but it is necessary, at least for beginners to gain independence in reading. Use of grapheme-phoneme correspondence rules allows children to figure out and learn new words, and thus progress faster to skilled reading. Further, it is argued that phonological coding plays an important role even in adult reading, as both visual (direct) and auditory (indirect) routes exist between print and a word in memory, and both usually contribute to the recognition of words (Coltheart, Curtis, Atkins, & Haller, 1993). Finally, phonological coding could play an important role in reading comprehension as a means to maintain several words in working memory while their syntactic structure and meaning in the sentence context is determined. This phonologically-based memory system should assist reading comprehension since its operation should not interfere with the visual processes of seeing each word as it is read and added to phonological memory.

10.7.3   *Recommendations for the Teaching of Reading*

The history of reading instruction has followed cycles of emphasis on the alphabet and phonics drills versus whole-word and language-based reading. In the United States, the sounds of letters and syllables were an important part of reading instruction for about 200 years until educational reforms in the late nineteenth and early twentieth centuries emphasized the whole-word method, partially due to the results of perception research at that time. Today, a whole-language method dominates, yet every good reading teacher knows that an eclectic approach is best. Some words for some readers are recognized as whole patterns, whereas others need the principles of phonics instruction to build up a sight-word vocabulary.

Recent reviews of instructional methods (e.g., Chall, 1967; Adams, 1990; Rayner et al., 2001) have converged on a common recommendation for the teaching of reading: If instruction is to be successful for the largest group of students, it should contain specific instruction in the alphabetic principle plus enough emphasis on phonics for children to use it in deciphering new or unfamiliar words. Although whole-word, or language-based, instruction will produce successful reading for most children, the grapheme-phoneme correspondence rules will be inferred by most of them and used despite the lack of specific instruction in phonics. However, if the correspondences between spelling and sound are not taught, there is a significant risk that some children will be left behind, and their reading progress will be slowed by denying them access to a phonological decoding strategy. These risks and delays are particularly apparent for a large minority of students who fall behind by one or more grade levels in the early years of reading.

10.8 Language Disabilities and Dyslexia

Dyslexia The inability to learn to read at an appropriate level despite adequate educational opportunities, normal or higher intelligence, and lack of relevant physical handicaps; a specific reading disability

Dyslexia is generally defined as a deficiency in reading ability that cannot be explained by obvious visual impairment, general cognitive disability (i.e., the students' IQs are normal or high), or inadequate reading instruction. It is not merely due to developmental delays, as one might expect that some children learn to read more slowly than others do. Rather, it is a progressive falling behind in reading fluency and comprehension despite the best efforts of parents and teachers to provide adequate opportunities to learn to read. The incidence of dyslexia varies widely across cultures and languages, but it is estimated to affect as many as 15% of elementary students in some areas of the United States.

Although there are undoubtedly several different causes of reading difficulty, dyslexia is most likely due to a specific language deficit that normally does not show itself in speaking or understanding speech. Orton (1925) hypothesized that dyslexia could be caused by lack of hemispheric specialization for language, such that neither hemisphere of the brain takes over most language functions. Such problems should show up in certain types of visual confusions, such as between b and d and between p and q. Other researchers have suggested that dyslexics have characteristic problems in the magnocellular (literally, large cells in the optic nerve) visual pathway responsible for detecting change and motion (Eden, VanMeter, Rumsey, Maisog, Woods, & Zeffiro, 1996). However, the consensus among researchers is that most cases of dyslexia reflect an underlying problem in language processing rather than a visual problem per se (Hulme, Nash, Gooch, Lervåg, & Snowling, 2015).

There is evidence that students suffering from dyslexia show subtle language processing deficits that are not due to an auditory impairment (Mody, Studdert-Kennedy, & Brady, 1997). They typically show normal processing of phonemes in speech (Joanisse, Manis, Keating, & Seidenberg, 2000), but the more difficult task of processing and remembering words in sequence, which is a skill important for both speech understanding and reading, is less well-developed in children with dyslexia (Pollatsek, Lesch, Morris, & Rayner, 1992). It is possible that the redundant information available in speech (prosody, gestures, social and environmental context) aids the listener in ways that compensate for minimal phonological difficulties. However, the starker environment of the printed page presents new problems that cause the barely perceptible oral language problem to develop into dyslexia. Early and intensive phonological awareness training, systematic practice with phonics, and practice reading orally with specially designed texts (using words that include regular or learned phoneme-grapheme correspondences) are essential parts of remediation for dyslexia (Rayner et al., 2001).

10.9 The Cognitive Neuroscience of Reading

Brain imaging techniques have revealed that there are several areas of the cerebral cortex that are activated when words are read. In order to identify those areas specific to reading, a contrast has to be made between activation observed while reading words and that seen in some baseline condition, such as staring at a plus sign for the same amount of time. When this is done, at least three brain areas show higher activation when words are read. These are primarily in the left hemisphere for most people, but right hemisphere areas show activation as well. The three areas with the highest amount of activation associated with reading words are the inferior frontal lobe, the temporal-parietal junction, and the occipital-temporal region (see Figure 10.1).

FIGURE 10.1

Brain Areas that Show Higher Levels of Activation During Reading than When Engaged in a Passive Viewing Task

These activated areas include the occipital-temporal region, the temporal-parietal junction, and the inferior frontal lobe, located mainly in the left side of the brain for most individuals

Adapted from Kalat, J. W. (2004). *Biological Psychology.* Belmont, CA: Wadsworth/Thompson Learning, p. 435.

The occipital-temporal region, specifically, the left middle fusiform gyrus, seems to be most heavily involved in processing words as visual entities (Fiez & Petersen, 1998). In fact, adults with lesions in this area are unable to recognize words as whole patterns and have to piece them together letter-by-letter (Patterson & Lambon Ralph, 1999). It is of interest to note that these same patients also have difficulty identifying pictures of objects.

The other reading centers in the brain seem to be more concerned with phonological decoding and short-term retention of words presented visually. Patients with lesions in these areas can show a form of acquired dyslexia. Although they are relatively good at recognizing familiar words, they have difficulty in reading for comprehension and specific problems with pronouncing pseudowords, a hallmark for many forms of developmental dyslexia (Coltheart, et al., 1993). Perhaps this is not surprising, as the inferior frontal and temporal-parietal regions involved in phonological processes in reading lie close to the traditional speech areas associated with Broca's and Wernicke's aphasias, respectively. Broca's area (inferior frontal region near the temporal lobe) is traditionally associated with productive language ability, and Wernicke's area (temporal-parietal junction) is traditionally associated with receptive language.

10.10 **Theories of Skilled Reading**

10.10.1   *Studies of Eye Movements and Fixations While Reading*

Theories of how skilled readers convert print to meaning have benefitted greatly from studies of the single most obvious overt behavior produced by readers—eye movements. While reading, adults move their eyes about four times a second, with each fixation lasting for about 200 to 300 ms, and each saccadic eye movement between fixations taking about 20 to 50 ms, depending on its length. For adults, most fixations are progressive (i.e., to forward regions of the text), but about 10% are regressive to earlier regions. In beginning readers, fixation times tend to be longer and regressions more frequent, probably reflecting their greater difficulty in decoding words. As with most skills, reading improves with practice, and developmental differences in reading ability tend to increase with age as a result.

Eye fixations are not randomly distributed over a text but tend to land on most words. Some short, predictable words, like function words (e.g., articles, conjunctions, and prepositions, tend to be skipped, and some words receive two or three fixations each. Further, most fixations on words tend to be slightly left of center; a place called the *preferred landing position* (Ducrot & Pynte, 2002; Rayner, 1979). When the distribution of progressive and regressive eye movements and their resultant fixations are combined, we see that most words are fixated about once each, leading to the average skilled reading rate of about four words a second or 240 words per minute (WPM). Faster rates are possible, of course, but anything over about 500 WPM results in skimming or skipping some words entirely, resulting in unavoidable loss of details (see Box 10.3).

10.10.2   *The Moving Window Technique of McConkie and Rayner*

Significant theoretical knowledge of reading has been obtained from the moving window technique developed by McConkie and Rayner (1975). In this technique, a small light is shone onto the cornea of a reader's eye and bounced back into a photocell attached to a computer. When the eye moves, small displacements in the angle of reflection of the light can be used to calibrate the location of each eye fixation. The computer can then be used to display text that changes dependent on where the reader is currently fixating. In the moving window technique, there is a window of arbitrary size in which the text is displayed normally, and outside this window the text is replaced with Xs or jumbled letters. The technique can then be used to determine the perceptual span in reading—the amount of text that is visible and useful for the act of reading.

BOX 10.3
Speed Reading

"I took a course on speed reading. I read *War and Peace* in 10 minutes. It's about Russia."
—Woody Allen.

Everyone would like to read faster and more efficiently; yet, the average college student reads most texts at about 250 to 300 words per minute (WPM). Is this a reasonable reading rate, or is it possible, with training, practice, and effort, to increase this rate while maintaining adequate comprehension and retention of the information? Reading research has shown that each fixation gives us enough information to identify, at most, about two average-length words in a single fixation, and we make about four fixations per second while reading. This works out to be about 8 words per second or 480 words per minute; almost twice as fast as the normal reading rate. Yet, many of us have heard claims that speed reading is a skill that can be learned, and that reading of rates of 1,000 WPM with good comprehension are possible. Is there any truth to such claims? Should we invest in a speed-reading training program that can promise such results?

These are the types of questions that were asked by Ronald Carver when he undertook an ambitious study to determine the capabilities of some of the country's best readers (Carver, 1985). He first identified four groups of superior readers, each with four individuals:

1) A *college group* made up of students who scored at the highest levels on a combined vocabulary and speeded reading comprehension test

2) A *professional group* of writers and copy editors who were recommended by their employers and peers

3) A *test group* made up of students who had perfect scores in verbal parts of the Graduate Record Examination or its equivalent

4) A *speed group* made up of graduates or teachers of speed reading courses who all claimed to be able to read at over 1,000 WPM

These individuals were flown to Kansas City for a battery of tests, taken over a period of 2 to 3 days, for which all their expenses were paid, and they were given an honorarium of up to $500. Despite a similar offer, several readers identified in the national media who had made astounding claims of being able to read at the rates of 10,000 to 260,000 WPM refused to participate. One person was reported to be able to read a standardized reading test with 90% comprehension at a rate of 17,040 WPM (Adams, 1963), but was not identified in the published report. Carver (1985, p. 391) wryly remarks that there should "… have been a thorough search to find this individual because she or he would seem to have abilities that make the rest of us appear closer to apes in brain functioning."

In an initial test in which the subjects were given passages to read at their preferred reading rates, the speed group read at a faster rate (about 900 WPM) than the other three groups (between 300 and 400 WPM). However, when they were given a standardized reading test and told to be prepared to answer detailed comprehension questions, all groups read at about the same rate of about 350 WPM. When the subjects were extremely time-limited in their abilities to go though a text, so that they were encouraged to skim, there were no differences among the groups in comprehension scores. Although skimming is the behavior that speed readers typically engage in, it is not reading. Eye fixations occur at about the same rate and last for about the same duration in skimming as in reading, but the saccades are longer, meaning that some parts of the text are not seen well enough to be identified. Skimming necessarily means parts of the text are not processed at all, so details will be missed even if some information about the gist of the passage can be figured out. Thus, Carver's research is consistent with other results, showing that as reading rate increases, comprehension levels decrease, and people who claim to be speed readers show the same trade-off function as ordinary good readers (Juola, et al., 1982; Masson, 1983; Rayner, Schotter, Masson, Potter, & Treiman, 2016).

Carver (pp. 417–418) concludes that, "… most people read at a constant, typical, and optimal rate that is less than 400 WPM … reading rates greater than 600 WPM should be referred to as skimming … Reading at rates higher than about 600 WPM with good comprehension appears to be impossible in theory and fact … Speed [reading] does not exist, and speed reading is really skimming in disguise."

McConkie and Rayner (1975; Rayner, 1975; 1998) have shown that restricting the size of the window of visible text can severely limit the speed and comprehension of text. It is not until the window is increased to about 20 character spaces (3 to 5 words) in width that reading proceeds at normal levels of speed and comprehension. Further, a window of this size must be asymmetrically located around the fixation point to produce normal reading. Visible text must be shown about 4 to 5 character spaces to the left of the current fixation and extend about 15 spaces to the right. It is clear that more information useful to the reading process is gleaned from upcoming text than from text that has recently been fixated.

Within the 20-space window of visibility, different types of information are important for the reading process. Research has shown that changes in the text that affect the meaning of words as they shift into the moving window are noticeable only if they occur in the left half of the window, whereas only changes that affect word length and shape are noticeable in the right half. It is as though meaning is extracted only from the word or two near the central fixation point, and information farther to the right is mainly used to calculate the intended location of the next fixation. Both *what* and *where* information seem to be processed independently during a fixation, with different systems handling (1) semantic analysis of words in a text and (2) programming the next eye movement toward an intended target (Hyönä & Pollatsek, 1998, 2000).

10.10.3   *Working Memory and Reading*

When the word or words near the current fixation are recognized, they make contact with stored information about their meaning in long-term memory. Although most words can have several nuances or outright differences among several meanings, the sentence context within which a word is embedded helps to restrict its interpretation. In order for sentence context to have an effect, there must be some memory system involved in retaining this context and integrating it with new word information. A likely candidate is working memory, which has a limited capacity that is most effective in retaining phonological codes of a few words or a short phrase. This memory system retains sufficient information to integrate phrases of text into meaningful chunks that can be passed on to long-term memory to build up a global understanding of the text (Just & Carpenter, 1987; Kintsch, 1988).

Reading is thus a dynamic process that involves visual perception, working memory, long-term memory, and linguistic knowledge, as well as domain and genre knowledge of the topic of the text. A skilled reader uses many different memory processes simultaneously in order to make sense of what is read. It is no wonder that reading acquisition is a difficult and uncertain process, and that understanding how children learn to read requires information gleaned from many sources. Reading has been called a microcosm of cognitive psychology, as it depends on sensory and perceptual processes in vision, working memory to maintain constituent phrases while they are analyzed syntactically, long-term memory for knowledge of words, syntax, semantics, and domain knowledge for the topic of the text. We will have to understand all of these component processes and how they work in synchrony before we can begin to develop a complete theory of how meaning is constructed from printed words in the mind of a reader.

10.11 **Discourse Comprehension**

Whether language is presented orally or in a text, the main goal is for the listener/reader to comprehend and remember the information presented. When the units of analysis go beyond simple words and sentences, the focus is on how we understand larger units of language (i.e., connected discourse). By "connected" we mean that each sentence does not stand alone, but rather shares some aspects of meaning with other sentences to yield a cohesive discourse structure. Cohesiveness requires some shared concepts or ideas among sentences in a discourse, otherwise we would have nothing but a set of unrelated sentences with no overall structure. Frequently, words are repeated between sentences, or pronouns or other words are used to link concepts between sentences. For example:

1) I saw the boy lose his ball. The *boy* was very sad.

2) I gave the girl a hat. *She* was very grateful.

3) I wish I had the time to help. Bob has *more* than I do.

In each case the italicized word in the second sentence refers to a word in the first sentence in a way that cohesively links the expressed concepts. In contrast, if we substitute a proper name in the first sentence to make:

1*) I saw the boy lose his ball. Harold was very sad.

It is not clear if Harold is the name of the boy, his friend, his father, or someone unrelated, and the cohesion is not as strong. In the second example above, the pronoun *she* also is possibly ambiguous, but the reader or listener would most naturally assume that it refers to the girl in the first sentence. The use of a pronoun to refer to a person mentioned earlier is called *anaphoric reference,* and it is among the most common ways language is used to promote cohesion in discourse, although there are several others (Halliday & Hassan, 1976).

One of the limiting factors for cohesion is distance in a discourse between a noun and a later referent to it. As the distance increases, the likelihood that the original noun will remain in active, working memory decreases, and when a related word, such as an anaphoric pronoun, appears, the probability that the initial referent noun will be reinstated in memory also decreases. Thus, successful comprehension depends on two factors: the distance between a pronoun and its referent (a text factor), and the likelihood that the correct noun will be reinstated when its pronoun appears (a subject factor). For example, consider the following two passages (adapted from Carroll, 2004, p. 159):

1) I am trying to find a black dog. He is small and has a dog tag on his collar that says Fred. Yesterday he bit a little girl. She was scared but she wasn't really hurt.

2) Yesterday a black dog bit a little girl. It got away and we are trying to find it. He is small and has a dog tag on his collar that says Fred. She was scared but she wasn't really hurt.

Most people find that the second passage is harder to comprehend that the first, mainly due to the larger separation between *she* and its anaphoric referent, *the little girl*. The increased separation in the second passage increases the probability that *the little girl* will not be in working memory by the time that the word she appears, and it will take time and effort to reinstate the appropriate noun, if it can be successfully recovered at all. Such difficulties reduce discourse coherence and lead to increased processing times and comprehension failures.

10.11.1   Individual Differences in Reading Comprehension

Daneman and Carpenter (1980) elegantly demonstrated the relationship between text factors and subject variables in determining comprehension of passages differing in discourse cohesion. They decided that working memory capacity was an individual variable that could well contribute to people's ability to understand language. Yet, most measures of working memory capacity (e.g., the digit span—how many digits can be repeated back in correct order after a single presentation) did not correlate well with individual differences in discourse comprehension. They incorporated a more contemporary vision of working memory as not merely a storage buffer (e.g., Atkinson & Shiffrin, 1968), but as system with separate storage and processing components (e.g., Baddeley, & Hitch, 1974). Therefore, they invented a reading span task that would more closely link working memory capacity to the types of processes involved in language comprehension.

The task that Daneman and Carpenter developed included having people read individual, unrelated sentences (processing task), and then asking them to recall the last word of each sentence (storage task). The reading span task began with two sentences and additional sentences were added on each trial until the subject failed to recall all of the final words in their correct order. Most people could do the task at size two, but more of them failed at the task as the number of sentences increased to about five at the maximum. Daneman and Carpenter argued that the reading span task was a more valid indicator of working memory processing capacity for language comprehension because of its joint measurement of storage and processing memory components. They then proceeded to demonstrate the usefulness of the measure as a predictor of individual differences in reading comprehension ability.

One of their results in a reading comprehension task is shown in Figure 10.2. The figure shows performance of subjects on a pronoun reference task as a function of number of sentences that fell between a noun and a later anaphoric pronoun. The data are plotted separately for individuals who had reading spans measured at two, three, four, or five. As can be seen in the figure, subjects with high reading spans had no difficulty linking the pronoun with its earlier referent in the text, but errors increased dramatically for people with lower spans. Daneman and Carpenter reported other useful correlations of the reading span measure, such as with scores of verbal parts of standardized college entrance examinations. Again, traditional memory span tasks do not show such high correlations. Although there are other individual differences that contribute to language comprehension, such as relevant knowledge of vocabulary and the passage's domain or genre, it appears that working memory span is one of the most important individual variables for determining language comprehension abilities.

FIGURE 10.2

The Relationship Between Reading Comprehension and Working Memory Span as Measured by Daneman and Carpenter (1980)

The graph plots the percentage of correct identifications for the earlier noun referred to by a later pronoun as a function of the number of sentences separating the noun from the pronoun in the text. The data are shown separately for subjects having measured reading spans of two to five sentences as determined in a pretest.
From Carroll, D. W. (2004). *Psychology of Language.* Belmont, CA: Thomson Wadsworth, p. 161.

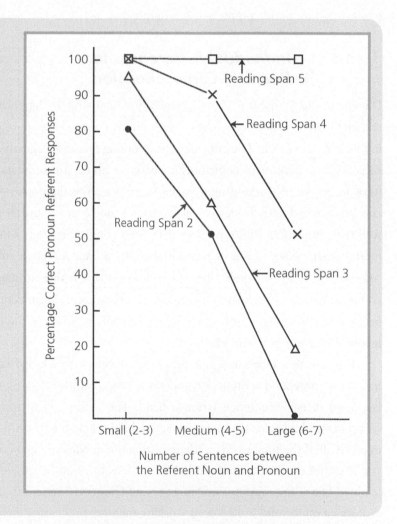

10.11.2   Levels of Discourse Representation

Just as Chomsky and others argued for the representation of sentences at surface, phrase structure, and deep levels, theorists have argued that discourse can also be represented at different levels. The surface level remains the same for sentences and discourse, as a text or oral presentation consists of a linear stream of words used to express the meanings contained in the discourse. Research has shown that whatever is processed and retained from a text, it is not verbatim memory for the exact words used. For example, Sachs (1967) showed that immediately after hearing a sentence, subjects had good verbatim recall, but even after a few minutes, memory for the specific words used was lost. However, the subjects could differentiate between true and false restatements of the sentences so they must have remembered something. The theoretical response to the question of what is remembered from a text is that the surface form has only a limited representation in memory. The surface form of language is used in working memory in order to determine sentence meaning. Once the meaning is processed, however, it is stored in long-term memory in a more abstract form, such as a set of cohesive propositions (Gernsbacher, 1990; Kintsch & van Dijk, 1978). The propositions are sufficient to represent and recover the gist of a passage, but not enough to recall the exact words used.

Other researchers have argued that a set of propositions derived from a spoken passage or text is by itself insufficient to describe the structure built in memory in response to the discourse. People can and do make inferences and add their own knowledge to the propositions derived from the text to create larger structures. These ideas are captured in the situation models of Johnson-Laird (1983) and the structure-building models of Gernsbacher (1990). A situation model refers to a type of mental model that a listener or reader constructs to represent the meaning of the discourse. It includes relevant knowledge that the comprehender has about the topic under discussion, and can be thought of as spatial image or internal video as well as a more abstract set of propositions. Other possibilities are a set of causal links, such as in a persuasive argument, or a sequence of events, as in a narrative. The important point is that the structure is determined by an interaction between text-based propositions and propositions inferred or recalled by the receiver of the message and integrated into the evolving knowledge structure that varies in its elaborated complexity for different individuals.

Chapter Summary

Virtually all children learn a spoken language, yet many do not learn to read, sometimes despite what should be effective educational efforts. What on the surface appears to be a similar means of language representation and use, in fact presents very different situations to the learner. Because spoken language is learned so early and completely by young children, it is thought to map onto innate, specific language acquisition devices, whereas leaning to read involves the use of cognitive processes that have evolved for other purposes, specifically, pattern and object recognition.

Learning a spoken language entails learning the purpose and use of words, the details of syntactic structure in one's native language, and how these map onto a burgeoning semantic memory system. Only with a substantial portion of grammar and vocabulary in place can children begin to learn to read. The most important new problem in reading is deciphering the visual code used to represent the language. Different written languages map onto the representations of words in different ways, from whole-word or morpheme-based logographic characters, to syllabic representations, to the representations of individual phonemes in alphabetic languages. All three writing systems have different types and degrees of sound structure (phonology) representation, with some languages operating at a relatively shallow orthography in which there is a consistent mapping between graphemes (letters and letter combinations) and phonemes, and others, such as English, in which the mapping is obscured by many exceptions to grapheme-phoneme correspondence rules (phonics). Still others, like many logographic writing systems, have less obvious relations to phonology.

The teaching of phonics seems to be important in providing beginning readers of alphabetic languages with independence and lessening the degree of severity of specific reading disabilities, such as dyslexia. If the encoding problem can be solved, then reading can proceed about as efficiently as processing language through the speech code, and skilled readers can achieve high levels of comprehension at rates exceeding that of normal speech. Reading is based on the successive sampling of one or a few words at a time through eye fixations separated by brief, saccadic eye movements. Semantic analysis seems to be based only on the word or small groups of words fixated, while working memory retains information from previous fixations, and the eye guidance system selects a likely landing place from information available in the periphery. Comprehension is presumably based on the inverse of generative grammar procedures that are involved in producing speech. That is, the meanings of individual words, given their placements in evolving syntactic structures, are used to generate meaningful propositions. If comprehension is successful, the derived propositional base should be equivalent in important ways to that intended by the author.

However, people differ in their comprehension abilities due to individual differences in such important variables as vocabulary, relevant domain knowledge, and working memory capacity. Therefore, whatever is stored and remembered is determined not only by what propositions can be derived from a text, but also by the inferences and other relevant information incorporated into developing knowledge structure constructed by the reader/listener.

Review Questions

- **What do linguistic theories of grammar have to do with learning to comprehend language?**

  Linguistic theories typically describe the competence that users of a language have rather than their performance, which is the province of psycholinguistics. As such, linguistic theories describe the internal rule systems of phonology, syntax, semantics, and the vocabulary items that a speaker has internalized in order to understand and produce language. The debate between Skinner and Chomsky boiled down to whether children acquire a set of verbal habits or whether they internalize a set of rules when they first learn a language. Since children demonstrate that they have internalized rules from the very first utterances that they make, it is unlikely that language learning can be reduced to the learning of a set of verbal habits.

- **Where did writing come from, and what are the major differences between writing systems throughout history and around the world?**

  Writing developed spontaneously around the world at different times and in different cultures. Most languages that have existed never developed a written form, and many early writing systems have been destroyed and completely lost or remain only partially decipherable. Western alphabetic systems evolved from early, pictographic, representational systems common to the writing found in Egypt, China, and the Fertile Crescent. All such written languages gradually became more abstract to represent concrete objects less literally and to include symbols for non-representational things, such as names and numbers. Finally, most written languages developed ways to represent the sounds of words in their written forms. The alphabet that we know today was developed in the Middle East from an earlier Cuneiform writing on clay tablets. Written symbols were borrowed from Sumer to speakers of other languages, who used the symbols to represent syllables of spoken languages. The further break-down of different symbols for each phoneme resulted in a high degree of efficiency in writing, as only a small number of symbols could be used to represent all words. All western languages today can trace their writing systems to the early Greek alphabet.

- **What is the relationship between speech and writing in English and other languages?**

  The relationship between speech and writing can be very abstract or very specific. English lies between these two extremes. Deep orthographies have little relationship between the two, and shallow orthographies have a virtually one-to-one relationship between orthography and phonology. Although the relationship between sound and spelling is not always direct in English, most words can be sounded out by beginning readers to get a close approximation to their pronunciation.

- **What is dyslexia, and why do some children find it so much harder to learn to read than others?**

  Dyslexia is a specific reading disability that is unexplained in terms of disabilities or low intelligence. There are probably many causes for reading disability, including poor preparation in preschool years in such reading-readiness activities as being read to, listening to stories, learning the alphabet, and understanding the relationship between sound and print. However, most researchers today agree that dyslexia is generally a language processing disability that does not show itself much in spoken language comprehension perhaps because of the redundancy of spoken language. Reading requires an understanding of how language is represented in print, and its analysis to smaller units in both phonological and orthographic coding schemes. It is likely that early language training and practice with the principles of phonics can help reduce the severity of dyslexia in many cases.

Key Terms

Competence-performance distinction   266

Deep structure   268

Dyslexia   276

Generative grammar   264

Morpheme   271

Orthography   273

Phonics   274

Phrase structure   267

Surface structure   267

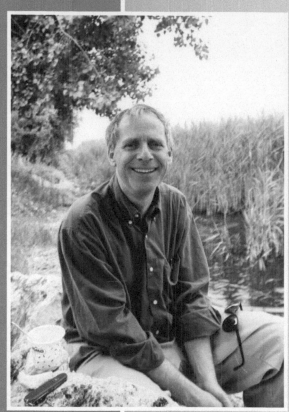

Photo courtesy of Barbara Tversky

AMOS TVERSKY

PD-USGov-NIH

DANIEL KAHNEMAN

Chapter 11
Higher Conceptual Processes

"The great revolutions in science are almost always the result of unexpected intuitive leaps. After all, what is science if not the posing of difficult puzzles by the universe? Mother Nature does something interesting, and challenges the scientist to figure out how she does it. In many cases, the solution is not found by exhaustive trial and error, the way Thomas Edison found the right filament for his electric light, or even by a deduction based on the relevant knowledge. In many cases the solution is a Eureka insight … Archimedes suddenly solved an hydraulic problem while he was taking a bath. According to legend, he was so overjoyed that he leaped out of the tub and ran naked down the street shouting "Eureka! Eureka!" (I have found it!)."

aha! Insight by Martin Gardner (1978, p vii).

PREVIEW QUESTIONS

❖ *How are inductive and deductive reasoning different, and how are they used in science?*

❖ *What are some reasons that even intelligent young adults make errors in relatively simple reasoning situations?*

❖ *What are some ways in which people can more efficiently solve problems?*

❖ *How does human decision making differ from an ideal system?*

11.1 Introduction to Higher Cognitive Abilities

Besides language, there are other skills that are in many ways unique to humans, including most types of reasoning and complex problem-solving skills. If we could understand how people solve complex problems, such as how to navigate through a three-dimensional world, how to form a sentence to express a certain idea, or how to perform a complex surgery to improve heart function, then we should be able to write programs and build machines to do the same things. This has been done with more or less success in many areas, and such successes indicate the value of research and theory on human intelligence in designing artificially intelligent systems. Research also indicates how humans often fail in reasoning and problem-solving tasks, and how such failures might be corrected through education, training programs, and provision of expert assistance. The availability of intelligent tutoring devices or helpful agents to provide useful information has great promise for improving reasoning, decision making, and problem solving for everyone.

Confirmation bias The tendency for people to seek out information consistent with their beliefs and to avoid or ignore things inconsistent with their beliefs

Higher mental processes, unlike lower-level processes, such as the rapid recognition of objects and words, generally require deliberate, slow, conscious, and conceptually-driven actions. Such top-down procedures are usually productive, but they can also cause failures in reasoning when the information stored is faulty or when correct information is misapplied. For example, people tend to show a **confirmation bias**—a deliberate search for evidence consistent with one's beliefs, rather than a search for contradictory information when evaluating evidence. We know that people are much more likely to listen to a political speaker who argues in favor of their own beliefs, than to another, antithetical speaker, whom they might heckle or withdraw from. This bias causes us to hold on to faulty ideas longer than we should, since the evidence necessary to disconfirm such ideas might be present but simply avoided. Karl Popper (1959) argued that the only way to make scientific progress is through falsification of incorrect hypotheses; therefore, confirmation bias can retard our efforts to learn from experience.

11.2 Human Reasoning

Perhaps the most elementary reasoning processes involve simple comparisons; that is, the ability to make judgments of less than, greater than, or equivalent. According to Weber's law, a just noticeable difference (jnd) is a constant ratio of stimulus magnitude. Fechner argued that this law is consistent with a logarithmic relationship between psychological magnitude (e.g., sensory activity) and physical magnitude (e.g., amount of energy or intensity). For example if the difference between a 40 and a 50 watt bulb is barely detectable, then the light from a 400 watt bulb should be barely discriminable from that of a 500 watt bulb (the constant ratio rule). In both cases, the difference is about .097 log units (i.e., log 40 = 1.602 and log 50 = 1.699; log 400 = 2.602 and log 500 = 2.699).

Although many animals show smooth discrimination and generalization gradients around stimuli that vary in size, brightness, and loudness just as humans do, people also show similar patterns with abstract, symbolic stimuli. The **symbolic distance effect**, as it has been called, is demonstrated by the fact that it is easier to pick the smaller (or larger) number from the pair (2,6) than from the pair (2,3). Similarly, a **semantic congruity effect** is found in tasks showing that it is easier to say which is bigger of two big numbers and which is smaller of two small numbers than vice-versa. It is as though we have some internal representation of a number line on which imaginal comparisons can be made (Izard & Dehaene, 2008). Symbolic distance and semantic congruity effects are also found for images of objects. It is easier to determine which is smaller (or larger) from the imagined pair of a mouse and an elephant than from the pair of a mouse and a weasel. It is also easier to say which is smaller of two small animals (mole, prairie dog) and which is bigger of two large animals (elephant, sperm whale) than vice-versa. Kosslyn (e.g., Kosslyn, Ball, & Reiser, 1978) has reported a number of studies in which decision times depend on the size of a visual image or on the extent of scanning required to retrieve information from an image. Many reasoning tasks are based on symbolic comparisons among concepts and images and are the basis of decisions about what to do next. When we consider whether to go to the movies or stay at home to work, we can imagine the outcomes of the two decisions and weigh their advantages and disadvantages before making a decision.

Symbolic distance effect The fact that a relative judgment can be made faster between two symbols that represent objects that differ widely on the dimension being judged than between two symbols that represent objects having a smaller difference

Semantic congruity effect The fact that judgments of the smaller two small objects and the larger of two large objects are faster than judgments of the smaller between two large objects and the larger between two small objects

11.2.1 *Formal Logic and Reasoning*

There are two main classes of reasoning: inductive and deductive. **Inductive reasoning** is the construction of general principles from specific examples. Such reasoning led Darwin to infer the principles of evolution from observing differences among species in different environments. Most scientific theories themselves evolve from generalities observed in nature. Induction is presumably the basis of how semantic memory is derived from a host of episodic experiences. It is also at the heart of certain prejudices, as when a few negative (or positive) experiences with people from a different city, ethnic group, or religious preference lead one to induce a general attitude toward others of the same group. In most cases, the goal of induction is to understand past observations, to make sense out of current experiences, and to predict future events.

Inductive reasoning Deriving general principles from specific observations, such as in building a theory from data

Deductive reasoning proceeds in the opposite direction. It begins with certain general premises that are assumed to be true, and then specific statements are derived from them and evaluated for their validity. The scientific method also relies on deductive reasoning to derive hypotheses from general theories that can be tested against data collected in an experiment. In this way, if hypotheses are logically deducted from theories, they should be consistent with experimental data if the theory is correct, and inconsistencies call the theory into question. People's abilities (and inabilities) to follow formal rules of logic and deductive reasoning skills have been studied for at least 2,000 years, beginning with the deceptively simple structure of the syllogism.

Deductive reasoning Deriving specific conclusions from general principles, such as in generating research hypotheses from a theory

11.2.2 *Syllogistic Reasoning*

A **syllogism** has two premises and one conclusion that either follows logically from the premises (a valid conclusion) or does not follow logically (an invalid conclusion). That is, the given premises are assumed to be true, and then the conclusion is to be judged as either a valid or an invalid deduction from the premises. For a conclusion to be valid, it must be consistent with all possible interpretations of the premises, since a single exception invalidates the argument. Some examples are listed below, beginning with abstract terms (A, B, and C) that can be replaced with concept nouns:

All A are B Socrates is a man

All B are C All men are mortal

∴ All A are C ∴ Socrates is mortal

The above parallel set of syllogisms includes valid conclusions from the initial premises, since the quantifier "all" means that either A and B are the same sets, or A is a subset of B. Similarly, either B is the same as C, or it is a subset of C. Therefore, by transitivity, A must either be the same set as C or a subset of C, and the conclusion is valid. In other syllogisms, the relationships are not as obvious. Consider the following example:

All A are B All men are mortal

Some B are C Some mortals are dead

∴ Some A are C ∴ Some men are dead

This conclusion seems to be valid in both cases at first glance. In fact, research has shown that syllogisms of this form are judged to be valid by about two-thirds of college students (Ceraso & Provitera, 1971). However, a problem with the validity of the above conclusion becomes obvious when the same structure is filled in with different nouns as follows:

All cherries are red

Some red things are apples

∴ Some cherries are apples

Why do people make errors in syllogistic reasoning? Several hypotheses have been generated, but the major explanatory ones have to do with limitations of human abilities and biases in human reasoning. Limitations are most apparent in attempts to keep all interpretations of the two premises active while the various combinations are sorted out. Human working memory is simply too limited in its capacity to maintain all possible interpretations of the premises in many types of syllogisms (Erickson, 1974; Rips, 1994). These problems can be minimized or eliminated by using memory aids, such as a systematic retrieval plan to evaluate all interpretations, or the use of external lists or diagrams to cover all possibilities.

There are several types of biases that can affect people's deductive abilities. One is called **illicit conversion**, in which expressions such as "All *A* are *B*" are converted to "All *B* are *A*." This conversion is obviously fallacious in examples such as when "All apples are fruit" is converted to "All fruits are apples." Also converting the premise that "Some *A* are *B*" to the conclusion that "Some *A* are not *B*" can also be fallacious, since knowing that some *A* belong to set *B* does not preclude the possibility that in fact all *A* are in set *B*. We have already suggested that **belief bias** can cloud one's reasoning abilities. In syllogistic reasoning, conclusions that are consistent with one's beliefs are much more likely to be judged valid than ones that violate one's beliefs, even though the syllogism could be valid or invalid in either case (Sternberg & Ben-Zeev, 2001).

Some terrorists belong to the Grinde Group

Some Grinde Group members are from Eastern Slobbovia

∴ Some terrorists are from Eastern Slobbovia

If you believe that some terrorists come from Eastern Slobbovia, then you are more likely to believe the above syllogism is valid than if you do not harbor such beliefs. However, the conclusion does not logically follow from the premises since it is possible that the terrorists who belong to the Grinde Group are not the same group members who are from Eastern Slobbovia. How can we sort through all possibilities and overcome biases and the limitations of short-term memory? One answer is to use a systematic external memory aid that keeps track of all possibilities and exhaustively sorts through them in search of contradictions. If none are found, then the conclusion is valid in syllogisms and other reasoning tasks. **Venn diagrams** (also called Euler circles) are one such useful method, and their applications to all possible interpretations of syllogistic premises are shown below.

Illicit conversion An unwarranted inference made from a premise, such as converting "All A are B" to "All B are A" or "Some A are B" to "Some A are not B"

Belief bias The willingness to accept a conclusion as valid based on one's own knowledge or beliefs rather than on the basis of rules of logical argument

Venn diagrams (also called Euler circles) A set-theoretic notational system using circles to represent the meanings of qualitative relationships (e.g., "all," "some," or "none") among sets

The particular set of interpretations that shows the above syllogism to be invalid is to replace terrorists with *A*, the Grinde Group with *B*, and Eastern Slobbovia with *C* in the diagram below, showing that it is possible that no terrorists are from Eastern Slobbovia:

11.2.3   *Conditional Reasoning*

Conditional reasoning has to do with statements in which certain preconditions put constraints on their consequences. For example, if we know that it will be cloudy tomorrow, then we might well expect it to be rainy as well. In general, conditional reasoning statements take a simple "If …, then …" form, in which the first statement involves the antecedent, and the second contains the consequent. For example, we could have the given valid general statement, "If *p*, then *q*," and this statement could involve terms such as, "If you study, then you will get an A." If we take this conditional statement to be true, then there are four possible situations that can occur, including all combinations of studying and not studying and getting an A and not getting an A. However, only two of these four statements can be shown to follow directly from the original conditional statement if it is true. All four possibilities are listed below, along with the Latin names for the valid inferences.

Modus ponens: If *p* is true, then *q* is true.

You studied, therefore you got an A (valid).

Denying the antecedent: If *p* is false, then *q* is false.

> You did not study, therefore you did not get an A (invalid).

Affirming the consequent: If *q* is true, then *p* is true.

> You got an A, therefore you must have studied (invalid).

Modus tollens: If *q* is false, then *p* is false

> You did not get an A, therefore you must not have studied (valid).

Notice that in the above examples, the conditional statements labeled **Modus ponens** and **Modus tollens** are valid, logical interpretations of the original conditional statement (If *p*, then *q*). The other two statements cannot be validly concluded from the original conditional. For example, they would both be invalid if the instructor decided to give everyone an A or if you got an A through a series of lucky guesses. In general, *Modus ponens* is easy for most college students to follow, but *Modus tollens* is rejected by about 50% of students as being a necessarily valid conclusion, and the two invalid conclusions are judged to be valid between 20% and 60% of the time in different contexts (Rips & Marcus, 1977).

Wason and Johnson-Laird (1972) demonstrated a particularly telling example of errors in conditional reasoning. They presented their participants with four cards, as shown below, and told them that each card had a letter on one side and a digit on the other side.

| E | K | 4 | 7 |

The participants were then given the following conditional statement:

> "If a card has a vowel on one side, then it has an even number on the other side."

They were asked to turn over the minimum number of cards necessary to verify whether the conditional statement holds true. Which are the correct cards to turn over? Most participants correctly chose to examine the E card, for if there were an odd number on the other side, then the conditional statement would be false. The conditional statement: "If E (a vowel) is on one side, then an even number must be on the other side," is an example of *Modus ponens*. However, nearly half of the participants chose to turn over the 4 card (affirming the consequent). This choice is incorrect, since if the other side has a vowel then the conditional statement holds true, but if it has a consonant, the card is irrelevant for the rule, since it only applies to cards with vowels on them. Therefore, the 4 card gives no useful information about the overall validity of the conditional statement regardless of whether the other side holds a vowel or a consonant. The same argument applies to the K card (denying the antecedent); it is irrelevant for the validity of the statement.

Modus ponens One of the conclusions in conditional reasoning that follows from first assuming that the premise "If A, then B" is true—if A occurs, then B must occur

Modus tollens The other conclusion in conditional reasoning that follows from first assuming that the premise "If A, then B" is true—if B does not occur, then A did not occur

In fact, Wason and Johnson-Laird (1972) found that only 4% of their participants made the correct choice of turning over only the E and the 7 cards. The 7 card corresponds to the conditional statement of *Modus tollens* (i.e., If there is an odd number on one side, then the other side cannot have a vowel)"

It is possible to improve participants' reasoning in conditional situations by substituting the abstract vowel/even number situation for more concrete situations in which we typically use conditional reasoning. Consider a statement such as, "If you are drinking beer, then you must be 21 years or older." If there are four kinds of people in the bar, who should be checked? Someone drinking beer? Someone drinking cola? A 22-year-old? A 16-year-old? *Modus ponens* asserts that the person drinking beer should be checked, but, obviously, this rule is irrelevant for the person drinking cola, so there is no need to check his or her ID. However, *Modus tollens* asserts that the 16-year-old should not be drinking beer, so it is a simple matter to check what the minor is drinking. There is no reason to be checking people over 21 years of age, of course, as they should presumably be allowed to drink what they want. Such real-world applications have been shown to dramatically improve participants' abilities to reason logically (e.g., Griggs & Cox, 1982), over the Wason and Johnson-Laird (1972) situation, although the two problems are formally the same.

11.2.4   *Reasoning in Hypothesis Testing*

In applying the scientific method, theories are often tested by first deducing hypotheses from them and then testing the hypotheses against data collected in an experiment. In setting up an experiment, a crucial aspect of the design is to provide a stern test of the theory (i.e., one in which the data should decide whether the hypothesis is true or false). It is scientifically superficial to try to prove a theory correct (all it takes is a vaguely-worded theory or a poorly-designed experiment, and the theory can never be proven false). Therefore, most theories are tested by deriving the result predicted from a theory against a null hypothesis. The null hypothesis typically states that the manipulated variable (i.e., the independent variable, such as type of training, amount of some drug, or number of practice trials) has no effect on the variable being measured (i.e., the dependent variable whose measurements constitute the data). Invariably, the null hypothesis is assumed to be true, and it is the one that is tested. In order to determine whether the manipulated variable has any effect, it is first assumed to have no effect (i.e., the null hypothesis). That is, the null hypothesis is based on the assumption that the theory being tested is false, and that the manipulated variable that is of theoretical interest in fact has no effect. Then, the statistical likelihood is estimated for obtaining the actual result in an experiment if the null hypothesis is assumed to be true. If the obtained results are extremely *unlikely* under this assumption, then the null hypothesis is rejected. As a consequence of this rejection the alternative hypothesis derived from the theory is supported (i.e., that the manipulated variable has some effect on behavior). Why do we test the null hypothesis in research and inferential statistics?

11.2.5 *Testing the Null Hypothesis*

If the null hypothesis is true, then the manipulated variable (call it variable A) should have no effect. If variable A has no effect, then the control group (no A) should perform equally to the experimental group (with A). This statement is equivalent to saying that "If p (null hypothesis is true), then q (control group and experimental group are measured to be the same)."

Results: Equal performance   (*q*—no conclusion)

Unequal performance   (*not q*—reject null hypothesis—A has an effect)

Thus, assuming the null hypothesis is true allows the experimenter to conclude that either the evidence is insufficient to reject the null hypothesis or the evidence is sufficient. In the former case, no firm conclusion can be reached, because the null hypothesis could either be true, or it is false but the experiment was not powerful enough to reject it. This uncertainty is one reason why it is difficult to publish research with null results. On the other hand, if the evidence is sufficient to reject the null hypothesis, then the experimenter can state with some degree of certainty that the null hypothesis is in fact false, and the hypothesis derived from the theory is supported. Rejecting the null hypothesis is equivalent to *Modus tollens* (i.e., If p, then q. Not q, therefore not p).

11.3 Inductive Reasoning

Whereas deductive reasoning works from a set of premises to some conclusion, induction works from a set of observations to general conclusions. It is the most common form of human reasoning, and induction also forms the basis of theory generation in science. Darwin's (1859) theory of evolution was based on general principles induced from such observations as variation in finch morphology in the Galapagos Islands and the presence of seashells high in the Andes Mountains. These observations impressed upon him the radical changes that can occur in the environment and how animals' characteristics seemed to adapt to these changes. Everyday we are confronted with new experiences involving people and objects, and induction works to update our beliefs about characteristics of things and peoples' traits (Rips, 1990).

11.3.1 *Analogical Reasoning*

A special case of inductive reasoning is reasoning by analogy. In addressing problem to be solved, people often search for analogous problems that have been solved in the past. Then, the old problem is mapped onto the new one in order to find a solution. Such analogies have benefited scientific reasoning in the past, as when the Danish physicist Niels Bohr used the analogy of the solar system to envision atomic structures. Such an analogy could take the form of: "planets:sun::electrons :nucleus." Of course, other forms of this analogy are possible, but the current one emphasizes the structural relations between the centers of the two systems and their peripheral components.

Forming analogies is a useful way to extend knowledge from one domain that is fairly well understood to another which is less well understood. Various theories of **analogical reasoning** have been developed, and most have emphasized how people decide on the relationship between the first two terms of the analogy, and then map that relationship onto the third term in trying to find a solution. For example, in the analogy cow:buffalo::dog: _____, what would the appropriate relationship be to guide you to a solution? Such processes were explored in a clever set of experiments by Rumelhart and Abrahamson (1973; see Box 11.1).

11.3.2 *Probabilistic Reasoning*

When people form beliefs or hypotheses about the world, they use subjective estimates of probabilities to express confidence in their beliefs. For example, if you believe that studying for eight hours would be enough to get an *A* in a midterm exam, but you only allow time for four hours of studying, you might believe that you still will probably get a good grade. You might even say that your probability of getting an *A* is 0.5, indicating a degree of subjective probability estimation.

Obviously, there is no way to confirm the accuracy of one's probability estimate in this case, and there are many examples of the difficulties that people have in estimating probabilities in situations in which there are analytical ways to determine the actual probabilities. For example, consider the problem posed by Bar-Hillel and Falk (1982). Suppose that you draw one of three cards from someone's hand, and you know that one of the cards is red on both sides, one is white on both sides, and the third is white on one side and red on the other. If you drop this card onto the floor and the side facing up is red, what is the probability that it is the red/red card? If you are like most people, you would guess 50%, as the card could be either the red/red card or the red/white card. However this answer is not correct. Given that a red side is showing, there are in fact three possibilities: it is the top side of the red/red card, it is the bottom side of the red/red card, or it is the red side of the red/white card. Since all of these are equally likely, the correct answer is two-thirds.

Analogical reasoning A type of reasoning that takes the form A is to B as C is to D (formally, A:B::C:D); concrete items are typically provided for A, B, and C, whereas D is left blank. The analogy can theoretically be solved by inducing the relationship between A and B, applying this relationship to C, and mapping it onto D (e.g.,cow:buffalo:: dog:wolf maps out a possible domestication relation)

BOX 11.1

Multidimensional Scaling and Analogy Solving

In the early years of cognitive psychology there were numerous attempts to devise methods of measuring purportedly unobservable mental structures and operations. One of the most original and productive means of deriving a model of an internal memory structure from behavioral data was devised by Roger Shepard (e.g., Shepard, 1962). He worked with similarity data between pairs of items; for example how many confusion errors are made between each pair of letters sent by Morse code, or how similar two different colors are judged to be. The rationale is that items that are highly confusable or are judged to be highly similar must be represented by internal codes that themselves are similar to each other. The question was how to proceed from data sets of similarity values to a recovery of the internal memory structures that led to the data.

Shepard hit on the idea that if he could combine all the similarity data into a geometrical description, then the dimensions of this geometrical space should be analogous to the dimensions of perception or meaning that lead to the judgments of stimulus similarity or measures of confusability. He began by assuming that in a geometrical model of mental representations, things that are similar should be close together, and things that are dissimilar should be far apart. Therefore, a fundamental process in recovering the mental structure involved would be to make similarity data inversely proportional to distance. An illustration for a small data set might make the method more obvious.

Let's start with three different items and ask you to judge how similar they are. Three items yield three different pairs, so there are three pairs to be judged. If the items are, say, COW, HORSE, BUFFALO, and you are to judge the similarities of individual pairs on a 10-point scale, with 10 being nearly identical and 1 being completely different, you might get a data set that looks like so:

COW — HORSE	5
COW — BUFFALO	6
HORSE — BUFFALO	4

Shepard devised an algorithm that would convert these similarity ratings to distances in some hypothetical mental space. He began by representing the items as points located equidistantly in a two-dimensional plane as so:

Then, for each pair, vectors are attached to the points with the following rules: If the pair is judged to be more similar than average, attach vectors to the two items pulling them together. If the pair is judged to be less similar than average, attach vectors pushing them apart. If the pair is judged to have average similarity, then attach no vectors. In the above example, cow (C) and buffalo (B) should be moved closer together, and horse (H) and Buffalo (B) should be pushed further apart, and the attached vectors would look like this:

Then, the vectors are all summed, and the points move all at once to new locations determined by the resultant sums.

This figure above represents a geometrical solution to the similarity data, as the points are now located in a two-dimensional space in which distance is inversely proportional to similarity (i.e., BUFFALO and COW are the nearest pair, HORSE and COW are at an average distance apart, and HORSE and BUFFALO are the most distant pair).

The next trick is to generalize this method to more substantial data sets. In general, if there are 20 items whose similarities are to be compared, there are $n(n - 1)/2$ unique pairs to judge (190 in this case), and they can be represented as 20 equidistant points in a space of 19 dimensions, just as three items can make an equilateral triangle in two dimensions. Now, it is difficult indeed for us to envision a 19-dimensional space, but this is no trouble for

Continues

a computer. The algorithm that Shepard devised then attaches 19 vectors to each point in the space, aiming them toward more similar items and pushing them away from those less similar. Then, the vectors are summed, and all the points in the space move according to their individual resultants.

A single iteration of this procedure is unlikely to give a good solution to the similarity data, so it must be recursively applied. However, an additional procedure can be added to make the whole solution more tractable and useful as a data summary; namely a reduction of the dimensions in the space. This is done by rotating the entire cloud of item locations in the 19-dimensional space until one of the dimensions onto which the points are projected is found to have the minimum variance. An interpretation of this dimension would be that it is the least useful of the 19 dimensions in discriminating among the items, since their spread along this dimension is less than their spread along any of the other dimensions. So that dimension is simply thrown away, and the points are collapsed into an 18-dimensional space. Now the recursive procedure takes over to add vectors, find the resultants, move the points, rotate to find a minimum dimension, toss it out, etc. Eventually, a small-dimensional space (ideally, 2- or 3-D) will be found that represents the best fit in that number of dimensions between the distances among points and their judged similarities.

The next step involves a bit more art than science; namely, the interpretation of the major dimensions. The computer program merely finds the most important dimensions for achieving a good fit between distance and similarity. The dimensions themselves are not labeled in any way, and it is up to the experimenter to decide on their meanings. For example, Henley (1969) used Shepard's multidimensional scaling program to sort out judged similarities of 30 mammals, and found a solution in 3-D. To her, the most important dimensions seemed to be most closely correlated with the animals' size, ferocity and something called *humaness*.

Rumelhart and Abrahamson (1973) devised an ingenious test of the validity of this 3-D solution as a representation of our internal mental structure for animals. They proposed to set up a series of analogies among animal names and use the solution space to predict what responses people would make. Sample analogies were:

RAT:PIG::GOAT: _____

CAMEL:DONKEY::RABBITT: _____

If the geometrical solution to Henley's judged animal similarity data truly captures people's knowledge about animals, then the space should be useful in predicting their responses in the analogy task. Rumelhart and Abrahamson reasoned that analogy solutions involve finding the relationship between the *A* and *B* terms in an analogy (e.g., RAT and PIG) and applying that relationship to the *C* term (e.g., GOAT) in a search for the best answer. In the 3-D solution space, this would correspond to finding a vector that links the first two terms in the analogy, and then moving this vector to the third term. The vector should then point to a location in space that corresponds to the ideal solution for the analogy. In a series of tests of this prediction, Rumelhart and Abrahamson found that the most common response in their analogy problems were animal names in Henley's solution space that were the closest to the ideal solutions. Their research thus validated one aspect of Shepard's multidimensional scaling program: It is possible to recover from similarity data some aspects of the underlying mental structure that was responsible for making the judgments. It was a landmark achievement—Shepard devised a method to model internal memory structures from overt responses that were not only reliable across individuals, but could be used to predict other people's performance in an analogical reasoning task.

Baron (1988) has described three ways in which people make probability estimates for certain events. One is called the *frequency theory*, and it assumes that people base their predictions of future events on the frequency with which such events have occurred in the past. In contrast, the *logical theory* asserts that, in some cases, people can specify the set of possible events and come up with good estimates of each of these possibilities based on their relative frequencies. Finally, the *personal theory* states that people follow neither past frequencies nor logic, but merely use a subjective feeling to estimate an event's probability. In a concrete case, let's say that a person has tossed a coin 20 times, and it has come up heads 15 of those 20 times. What should happen on toss 21? The frequency theorist would guess that a head would come up with probability 75% to match the observed frequency thus far, the logical theorist would estimate the probability of a head to be 50%, since there are presumably two equally-likely events, and the personal theorist might say that the probability of a tail is greater, because the *law of averages* says that a tail is now more likely this is a version of the gambler's fallacy.

Another problem that people have in estimating event probabilities is called *base rate neglect*, and it applies mainly to estimating the probabilities of fairly rare events, given some conditional supporting evidence. For example, Tversky and Kahneman (1982) asked their participants questions of the following form:

> Suppose that 5% of the people in some population of which you are a member are infected with a serious disease. There is a test that gives a positive response 85% of the time if you are infected, but it has a 15% false alarm rate for those who are not infected. You take the test and get back a positive report. What is the probability that you are infected?

Most people who respond to this question give estimates of 50% to 85%. We have asked this question in a large lecture class and have received responses literally from 10% to 90%. This response rate indicates wide uncertainty and difficulty in estimating actual probabilities in uncertain situations. Actually, this situation is not so uncertain if one applies a formal, logical model based on Bayes's theorem:

$$P(A|B) = \frac{P(B|A) \times P(A)}{P(B)}$$

$$P(A|B) = \frac{\text{Probability of a positive result given an infection}}{\text{Probability of a positive result overall}}$$

multiplied by the base rate of infection in the population

In the problem stated here, Bayes's theorem asserts that the probability of being infected given a positive result {P(Infected|Positive result)} is equal to the probability of getting a positive result given that one is infected {P(Positive result|Infected)} times the probability that one is in fact infected, divided by the overall probability of a positive result. The numerator is thus 0.85 times 0.05 = 0.0425, and the denominator is equal to the probability of getting a positive result from infected and noninfected people, each weighted by their probabilities of being infected or not infected, respectively {i.e., [P(Positive result|Infected) × P Infected)] + [P(Positive result|Not infected) × P(Not infected)]}. That is, the denominator is (0.85 times 0.05) plus (0.15 times 0.95) = 0.185. Thus, the answer to the question is 0.0425/0.185 = 0.23, a value that is widely overestimated by most people. The apparent reason is that people, including physicians who make diagnoses based on symptoms (Eddy, 1982), frequently ignore rare base rates and arrive at inflated estimates of event probabilities.

11.4 **Problem Solving**

A problem exists whenever there is a discrepancy between what one wants and what one has. By this definition, we must be faced with problems at many times in our lives. Some of these problems are important in that they can affect our entire lives, such as how to succeed in school, how to get a good position in graduate school or in a profession, how to choose a lifetime partner, and perhaps become parents. Others are more common, such as how to find the cheapest way to buy books for class or how to follow a bus schedule to minimize travel time in a large city. It is obvious that some problems have a specific solution that defines a goal, whereas others have solutions that might or might not be optimal, and of course some problems are not solvable at all. In the laboratory, researchers have designed various types of problems that might not resemble details of real-world problems, but the problem structures and the strategies used are presumably close enough that we can learn about general human problem-solving behavior from laboratory studies.

A *well-defined problem* can be thought of as consisting of an initial state, a goal state, and rules for moving from one state to another (e.g., chess, a maze, or a crossword puzzle). Puzzles and games generally fall into the set of well-defined problems because the initial state is well understood and apparent to participants, the rules for changing states are similarly transparent, and the goal is unambiguous when it is achieved. In these kinds of problems, problem-solving behavior can be thought of as a search through the problem space, using operations defined by rules to change states, and eventually to achieve the goal state. The complete problem space is defined by the start and goal states and all the possible intermediate states that can be achieved by successive applications of the rules (Newell & Simon, 1972).

Although much can be learned about human problem-solving behavior by observing how people solve well-defined problems, there is a question about the generality of this research to problems that occur in natural life. This problem is chiefly due to the fact that many real-world problems are *ill-defined*. It is possible that we do not know the realities of our current state, that we cannot know if a goal has actually been achieved, and the ways to move from state to state are not all understood or available. Nevertheless, there appear to be enough similarities between well-defined and ill-defined problems that studying human behavior in a well-defined problem in the laboratory should give us insights into strategies and processes that people use in real life.

11.4.1 Algorithms and Heuristics

There are several types of strategies that people can use to help them solve problems. These fall into two broad categories: algorithms and heuristics. An **algorithm** is a specific rule or formal strategy that is guaranteed to produce a correct answer if it is applied correctly. A **heuristic**, on the other hand is a rule of thumb or informal

Algorithm A fixed, sometimes exhaustive or brute-force method of solving a problem, that is guaranteed to produce a solution if it is properly applied to any problem

Heurisitcs Rules of thumb that might lead to a relatively quick decision or a solution to a problem, but it might not produce the best result if more information and time are available strategy that might work to speed up finding a solution, but it is not guaranteed to lead to a correct answer.

Algorithms and heuristics can be compared for their effectiveness in many types of problems. For example, consider the anagram TERALBAY, which can be unscrambled to spell an English word. An algorithm that is certain to work would be to make a list of all possible combinations of these letters, and if one of them makes a word the problem is solved. So we begin with AABELRTY, AABELRYT, AABELTRY, AABELTYR, etc. until a solution is found or all possibilities are exhaustively listed without finding a solution. A heuristic, which might work more quickly, would be to restrict the search of the problem space to areas most likely to produce a solution. In this case, it would be to examine letter combinations that are more likely to begin and end English words and not waste time on unlikely combinations (like starting with AA or RL, for instance). Although the heuristic might not work if the word has an unusual spelling (e.g., "yacht"), it is likely to produce the correct answer (betrayal) sooner than the brute force, list-them-all algorithm.

Algorithms exist in many problem-solving domains, such as mathematics and computer science, where they can be essential to providing computational solutions to complex problems. Others include hill-climbing procedures that move through the problem space toward a solution. Such an algorithm actually works in a real life situation, such as the one I (JJ) used on my first visit to San Francisco. I wanted to find a place with a good view, so I simply followed the road at each intersection that had the steepest ascent gradient. This hill-climbing algorithm suffers from the problem that it can get caught up in a local maximum—that is, a molehill rather than the mountain top. The only choice to escape local maxima with this algorithm would be to drive to an entirely new location and start over hoping for a better solution. On the other hand, a heuristic, like asking directions or checking a map, can be used to provide a quicker solution.

Some heuristics work by suggesting answers to problems based on their availability or representativeness. The availability heuristic (Kahneman & Tversky, 1973; Tversky & Kahneman, 1974) asserts that solutions to problems will suggest themselves based on their availability. For example, if you were asked to determine whether there are more words in English that begin with the letter r than have r as their third letter, what would you guess? The availability heuristic suggests that you would pick the alternative that has the most available examples, and it is much easier to come up with a list of words that begin with r than a list of words that have r in the third position (try it). In this case, the heuristic leads us astray, as there are in fact many more words In English that have r as their third letter than begin with it. The availability heuristic can also lead to errors in judgments involving frequencies of events. For example, if you were asked to guess which is the leading cause of death, homicides or diabetes, you might be tempted to guess homicides because of the frequency of their mention in the media, and thus, their availability in recent memory. Again, availability can lead us to the wrong conclusion, as diabetes-related illnesses far outnumber homicides as a cause of death in the U.S. Of course there are also many situations when the heuristic leads us to correct choices, such as if we are asked what is the approximate average age of college students, or which brand of shoe is most popular. For most of us, the answers are readily available.

11.4.2   *Problem Solving Through Insight*

Sometimes a problem cannot be readily solved, often because one feels that not enough information is available. That is, the problem does not seem to have a well-defined solution or an accessible path to the goal. In this case, other information can sometimes be derived from what is given to eventually lead to a solution. The additional information might not necessarily be derived logically, but rather results from a sudden insight that leads quickly to the goal. Consider the following problem discussed by Levine (1988). We are given a circle of one inch radius with a triangle inscribed into one quadrant of the circle as shown. What is the length of the hypotenuse, k?

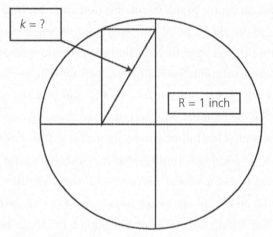

At first it might appear that there is insufficient information given, as we have no idea about the lengths of the two sides of the triangle that form a right angle. However, if we view another problem that is very similar, insight can lead to a solution. Consider the variation shown below:

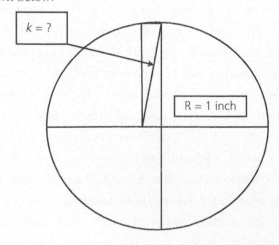

If indeed, as it appears, the length of k remains the same as the triangle is forced up against the vertical radius (and by extension, if it were squashed down to the horizontal radius), the length of k remains constant. Further, at the limit, as the triangle dissolves into a straight line, the segment k will be equal to the radius, which must have been its length all the time. This problem is easier if one views a sequence of figures, as they give the insight that the segment is merely the radius gradually moved from one region to another within the circle.

Alternatively, the inscribed triangle problem can be solved by another insightful method attributed to Kohlers (Levine, 1988). If one imagines the segment k to be a diagonal of a rectangle formed by the triangle and the adjacent radius, then the other diagonal is clearly the radius itself. Hence k must equal one inch. In either case, this problem can be solved by visualizing the additional information inferred from the diagram, which leads to a rapid, insightful solution.

11.4.3   *Limitations to Human Problem Solving*

As in many demanding tasks, the primary bottleneck in problem solving is limitations in working memory capacity. Many people have complained that trying to solve a difficult problem becomes tedious because there is too much information to retain, process, and make decisions about during the course of solving it. One suggestion is to put the problem aside for a while so that unproductive information in working memory can subside. Sometimes a period of incubation in which the problem is deliberately kept in the background while something else is worked on can result in novel approaches to the problem when it is tried again. A related common experience is that a solution can suddenly appear in a flash of insight, often due to a combination of eliminating useless information from memory while incubating fresh approaches to the problem (see Halpern, 2003).

Famous examples of difficulties in human problem solving relate to a lack of creativity or originality in approach to a solution. One involves functional fixedness, or the tendency to use something only for the purpose for which it is intended. A classic scenario involves two ropes tied to the ceiling that are too far apart to be reached simultaneously, but the task is to find a way to tie them together. The room is empty except for a stool and a pair of pliers. Many people try to stand on the stool, but it is of no help—the ropes cannot be reached at the same time merely by standing higher. The solution is to get one of the ropes swinging, so that the other can be held until the other swings close enough to catch as well. Tying the pliers to one of them greatly increases the arc and maintenance of the swing, thus solving the problem. The trick is to escape the functional fixedness of using the pliers as a pendulum weight, rather than as a gripping tool.

Another problem is mental set, in which a previously successful algorithm or heuristic is applied to a problem in which it might not be the best or even an appropriate means of solving a problem. One example of set limits solutions in the nine-dot problem. The task is to connect all nine dots by tracing no more than four connected lines through them while not lifting your pen from the paper (try it):

The nine-dot problem is difficult because we tend to adopt the mental set that the solution resides within the rectangle defined by the dots. Only by "thinking outside the box" can the solution be found, as in the example shown below:

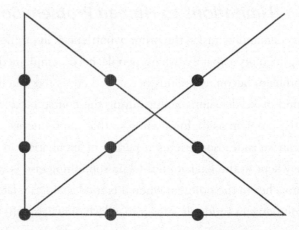

As an undergraduate, I (JJ) set up a mental set experiment designed to induce a certain strategy into the solution of anagrams. Subjects were to unscramble a list of five-letter words as rapidly as they could, and I timed each solution. Somewhere in the list, all anagrams could be solved by using the same rearrangement pattern (e.g., the letter order used was always 54123, as "table" was in the order "eltab" and "boxer"" was "rebox," etc. Even without necessarily noticing that the same rearrangement strategy could be used to unscramble the anagrams, subjects became faster and faster at the task as they moved down the set portion of the list. When the rearrangement rule was suddenly changed, most subjects showed a marked hesitation and slowed response time in unscrambling the next anagram. Further, the longer the set method of solution had been in place, the longer was the mean solution time for the first anagram in the new order. Subjects had obviously adopted a set method of solving the problems, and they were stumped when the method did not work, taking even more time on the critical anagram, on average, that those who had had no set method of solving the anagram in their lists (Juola & Hergenhahn, 1968).

11.4.4   *Problem-Solving Strategies*

In his book on how to solve problems, Wickelgren (1974) reviewed a host of heuristics and other strategies that can aid people in finding solutions to problems. These include:

Means-end analysis: Choose operations that minimize differences between the current state and the goal state. This operation can be recursively repeated to continually close the gap between where one is in the problem space and where one wants to be.

Increase domain knowledge: Experts can call on knowledge that aids all stages of problem solving, from achieving a better representation to choosing optimal operators and evaluating, whether or not intermediate and final states are satisfactory.

Automate some components: Experts can also achieve, through practice, the rapid application of appropriate rules, diagrams, and analogous problem spaces. If these processes become automatic, they can reduce the load on memory and attentional processes so that they can be allocated to unique aspects of the current problem.

Follow a systematic plan: The goal is to avoid repeating false moves, blind alleys, and alternatives that have been rejected previously while keeping relevant subgoals in mind.

Draw inferences: Combine the information given into inferences and valid deductions while distinguishing between warranted and unwarranted assumptions and information (red herrings).

Develop subgoals (satisficing): Especially when goals are ill-defined, subgoals can help reach an acceptable goal.

Search for contradictions: Prune the problem space by eliminating undesirable subgoals.

Search for relations among problems: Apply rules or strategies that have worked in analogous problems in different domains.

Find a different problem representation: Many problems become easier when representations are changed among verbal, visual, and mathematical representations. Making a graph or table often helps to see new solution methods.

Practice: Almost all kinds of problems become easier if their solutions are practiced.

11.5 Decision Making

We make decisions hundreds of times every day, from what clothes to wear to school or work, to what lectures to attend, to what route we should take across campus, or what we should have for lunch. There are more momentous decisions as well, such as what to major in, what career path to take, and if and when to marry and have children. In many cases, people suffer from some of the same problems in decision making that they do in reasoning—they are troubled by biases, by reliance on incomplete information and memory limits for dealing with what information is available, and by the inability to obtain or use accurate probability estimates of various outcomes. The seriousness of these difficulties can sometimes be assessed by comparing human decision-making abilities with those obtained from normative theories of how decisions should be made to maximize gains and minimize risks.

11.5.1   Normative Theories of Decision Making

The first thing to consider in making a decision is the expected gain or loss that could result from deciding one way or another. Researchers in the area of decision making have proposed various idealized theories of optimal performance in a search for which might best describe human behavior, or at least how and why people's decisions often differ from such norms.

11.5.2   Expected Values and Utilities

In some cases the expected outcomes and their probabilities are well known, as in certain games of chance. If, for example, you are told you can pay $2 to play a game in which you draw a single card from a normal deck of 52 cards, and you will lose $1 if you draw a club, win $1 if you draw a diamond, win $2 if you draw a heart, and win $5 if you draw a spade, should you play this game? The expected value of the outcome is simply the sum of all outcomes each weighted by their probabilities. For this game, since all four suits are equally likely (0.25), the expected value of the outcome would be (for the respective outcomes of a club, diamond, heart, and spade): 0.25(–$1) + 0.25($1) + 0.25($2) + 0.25($5) = $1.75. Knowing this result, you should refuse to play the game because, as in Las Vegas, the house will win on the average.

Expected value theory has not been a very good model of how people perceive the values of outcomes in uncertain situations. Since the time of Bernoulli, an eighteenth century mathematician, it has been known that people do not treat monetary rewards as linearly related to their actual values. Rather, as Fechner argued for sensory processes, the trade-off between actual gains and their psychological values seem to follow a logarithmic path. The difference between no win and a $100 win is perceived as greater than the difference between and $100 win and a $200 win. This principle is known as the *law of diminishing marginal utility* (Savage, 1954).

If expected values are converted into a subjective scale of utilities, then it is possible that this psychological scale would be different for different individuals. Further, since both expected values and actual probabilities are unlikely to be treated as their actual values by people, the true functions of outcome values should be a product of subjective utilities and subjective probabilities. This is the basis of **subjective expected utility theory** (Savage, 1954). If it is possible to scale people's subjective values of costs of a loss, benefits of a win, and the respective probabilities

Expected value theory The theory that people's decision making is influenced by the actual values of the possible outcomes, weighted by their actual probabilities

Subjective expected utility theory The theory that people's decision making is influenced by the subjective utilities of the possible outcomes, weighted by their subjective probabilities of winning and losing, the subjective expected utility theory does a much better job of predicting human decision-making behavior than expected value theory.

In many decision-making situations there are more factors to be considered than just a single win/lose dimension. For example, in choosing a school to attend or an apartment to live in, costs alone cannot be the only factor. A school should provide courses in one's area of interest and have a good reputation to provide a valued education. Similarly, an apartment must have needed space, a desirable location, and comfortable furnishings, among many other things, that are to be considered besides costs alone. This type of multidimensional decision process can be modeled by **multi-attribute utility theory** (Wright, 1984), in which the utilities of various options are computed on the basis of the weighted averages of the various dimensions. In essence, each dimension relevant to the decision is given some value and some weight indicating the subjective utility and the importance of that dimension. Then, the weighted utilities are summed for the various response alternatives to arrive at the overall value of that alternative. Finally, the highest-valued alternative is the one that should be chosen.

The multi-attribute utility theory can be of use to model human decision-making processes, and it can even be taught to people as a useful aid in their decision making. However, the theory assumes that the dimensions used are independent of each other and that the weights of the various dimensions remain constant over time and across different choice options. These restrictions are often violated in natural situations. That is, people sometimes act impulsively, or base their decisions on only one or a few variables. Therefore there is some question about whether the theory is really normative at all, or merely a potentially useful aid to human decision making (Sternberg & Ben-Zeev, 2001).

Multi-attribute utility theory
The theory that a decision can be based on the weighted sum of all possible outcomes along the various dimensions of a problem

11.5.3 *Decision Making Heuristics*

In many cases, a decision-maker has insufficient time or information available to consider all relevant options, their subjective values, and the subjective probabilities of various outcomes. In most cases, people then make use of partial information and develop heuristics, or decision-making strategies that can lead to a quick and relatively satisfying decision, if not necessarily the best possible one (e.g., Kahneman & Frederick, 2005).

Kahneman and Tversky (1996) argued that a relatively small number of heuristics are commonly used to help us make decisions. These heuristics are based mainly on past experiences and their relations to current situations, and are used because they usually lead to a satisfying decision without major expenditures of time and effort. An example is the **representativeness heuristic**, in which we judge how likely a sample accurately represents some population. For example, more people are likely to judge a sequence of heads (H) and tails (T) as representing a fair coin if the sequence is representative of a random process, such as HTHHTTHTHHT,

Representativeness heuristic
The tendency for a choice in a decision or problem-solving task to be made from alternatives that more closely match our expectations of what the average outcome should be like

than if it is HHHHHHTTTTT, although the probabilities of each of these two exact sequences are in fact equal. Most people realize that larger samples are more likely to represent populations than small samples, such as when a poll that samples a large number of potential voters is judged to be more valid than one that samples only a few people. Yet, research has shown that the use of heuristics, like the representativeness heuristic, can lead to errors in decision making. For example, Kahneman and Tversky (1972) asked college students about the relative likelihood that two hospitals would have 60% or more of the babies born on any day to be boys, if one hospital had 45 babies born on that day and the other hospital had only 15 babies born. Most students said that the probabilities would be about equal, even though small samples are more likely to have extreme averages (over 60%) than are large samples, if the expected average is 50%.

Availability heuristic The tendency for a choice in a decision or problem-solving task to be made from among alternatives that are most readily available in memory

Another commonly-used heuristic in decision making is the **availability heuristic**. When asked to make a decision, people often use their memories to come up with examples of good and bad choices in a given situation. For example, when asked whether it would be better to drive or take an airplane when travelling between two cities, people will consider recent memories for costs, inconvenience, amount of time, safety, etc. It is easy to see that if this is the case, the ease of remembering certain of these details will figure heavily in influencing the decision. We know that factors, such as recency and frequency of experiences involving factors of costs and inconvenience, can influence the likelihood that they will be recalled and thus be available for consideration in making a decision. If negative memories about the expense and inconvenience of one's last airplane flight are prominent in memory, then they will be available to bias a person to prefer to drive the next time. In addition, recent news reports about airplane crashes or auto accidents might also influence the decision. The availability heuristic thus uses past experiences to guide present decisions, but it can lead to incorrect decisions if there is bias in the recall of certain experiences or if sensational information from sources, such as news media, are recently available to be factored into the decision.

People use heuristics in decision making because they can save time and trouble in moving on in life, even if they sometimes lead us astray. However, most heuristics are based on real-life experiences and our memories for them, and as such, they are more likely to lead to better decisions than simply flipping a coin.

11.5.4   *Thinking Fast and Slow*

Recently, dual process theories have gained popularity as a framework of reasoning and decision making (e.g., Kahneman, 2011). Dual-process theories claim that there are two basic types of processing which are typically referred to as type 1 and type 2. Type 1 processing is faster, heuristic, intuitive, and automatic, and does not require working memory resources or conscious thought. By contrast, type 2 processing is slower, analytic, algorithmic, and effortful, and requires working memory resources and conscious, deliberate thought (Gawronski & Creighton, 2013). In general, there are two kinds of dual-processing theories. One kind is a parallel processing model (e.g., Epstein, 1994; Handley, & Trippas, 2015; Sloman, 1996; Pennycook, Fugelsang, & Koehler, 2015). According to the parallel processing model, intuitive, heuristic processing (type 1) and logical processing (type 2) proceed simultaneously. If the type 1 processing wins the race, then an intuitive response is made. However, if the type 2 processing wins, a logical response is produced. The other kind is a default-interventionist model (e.g., De Neys, 2013; Evans,2008; Stanovich, 2009). According to this model, type 1 processing constitutes an initial and default response (e.g., heuristic) to a problem, while type 2 processing is an override system that is available if the default response is judged incorrect (Evans, 2008). If a reasoner detects a problem with the heuristic response, then the reasoner might initiate a normative response based on the rules of logic or probability (Stanovich, 2009). For example, think about the following problem by Frederick (2005).

A bat and a ball cost $1.10 in total. The bat costs $1.00 more than the ball.

How much does the ball cost?

Your initial answer might have been 10 cents. However, it is an incorrect answer, because the bat costs $1.00 more than the ball, so if the ball costs 10 cents, then the total would be $1.20! The correct answer is that the ball costs 5 cents. According to the default interventionist model, you are using type 1 processing (e.g., intuitive response) when you come up with the answer "10 cents". If you just make a response with the answer at that point, your answer would be incorrect. However, if you detect a conflict with your answer (it could be a feeling that something is wrong), then you might initiate type 2 processing, which is an algorithmic process involving actual calculation.

According to De Neys (2013; De Neys & Bonnefon, 2013) there are three possible sources of incorrect responses on reasoning problems. One source of incorrect responding on reasoning problems is monitoring failure, in which people fail to detect any conflict between the non-logical, heuristic response and the logical response. They tend to make heuristic responses if they fail to detect conflict. A second is a storage failure in which the mindware (e.g., knowledge of logico-mathematical rules) needed to solve the problem is absent. In the example above, if one doesn't possess sufficient knowledge of calculation, the reasoner may not come up with the correct answer. A third is inhibition failure. Even if people detect conflict and have the necessary mindware to produce a correct answer, they may fail to inhibit the heuristic responses due to a lack of working memory resources.

Chapter **Summary**

Besides the enormous abilities underlying object recognition and language, the higher mental processes of reasoning, decision making, and problem solving are some of the hallmarks of what make us human. Yet, it is a curious fact that most humans, even highly-educated experts, can and do make mistakes. Some of the problems in human reasoning abilities are due to our personal biases and beliefs that get in the way of objectivity. For example, most people show confirmation and belief biases in searching for supportive information rather than challenging their beliefs in the search for the truth. Other problems come from the limits of working memory capacity, which prevent us from considering all relevant information at the same time. Even more difficulties arise in indeterministic situations in which people have to estimate the probabilities of certain events or outcomes. People are notoriously poor at judging actual probabilities from occurrence frequencies. Incomplete knowledge about problem situations or options can also hinder performance. Further, the actual values of costs and benefits are tempered by diminishing internal scales that reduce the subjective effects of large values.

Research has shown that there are a number of ways that people can improve their reasoning, decision-making, and problem-solving abilities. Most of these involve the use of strategies to compensate for limits in memory capacity and lack of relevant knowledge. Finally, practice with a range of problems usually results in improved performance, along with the internalization and use of a tool kit of useful algorithms and heuristics with wide applications.

Review Questions

- **How are inductive and deductive reasoning different, and how are they used in science?**

  Inductive reasoning involves deriving general principles from specific examples, whereas deductive reasoning involves deriving specific examples from general principles. In science we induce theories from observational data, and we deduct hypotheses from these theories to be tested against new data.

- **What are some reasons that even intelligent young adults make errors in relatively simple reasoning situations?**

  People show a confirmation bias in that they tend to look for support of current beliefs or hypotheses rather than looking for contradictions. False beliefs or erroneous conclusions can only be discarded if they are legitimately confronted by inconsistent evidence. People also tend to make erroneous inferences that go beyond the information given, such as illicit conversions of qualitative statements like "All A are B" and "Some A are B" into "All B are A" and "Some A are not B," respectively. People also have processing limitations, mainly due to the limited capacity of working memory, which prevent all possibilities from being considered without using some form of external memory aids such as Venn diagrams.

- **What are some ways in which people can more efficiently solve problems?**

  A problem can be solved only if one has a clear understanding of the problem representation. This includes knowing where we begin (the start state) how we can proceed (the rules form moving from state to state) and when the problem is solved (the definition of the goal state). In well-defined problems, all of these components are included in the problem representation, but in the real world any one of them can be ill understood. However, there are certain techniques that can be used to solve either kind of problem. These include (1) searching for analogies with other problems solved in the past and using algorithms or heuristics that have worked on such problems, (2) working backwards from the goal to see if any state can be found that has links to the current state, and (3) looking forward from the current state to any intermediate state and choosing the path that leads to one most like the goal state. As for many other human skills, problem-solving abilities improve with practice and the acquisition of relevant domain knowledge.

- **How does human decision making differ from an ideal system?**

  In an ideal system, the actual values of possible outcomes from a decision would be weighted by the actual probabilities that those outcomes would occur to achieve an accurate assessment of which decision would result in the greatest gain or the smallest loss. In practice, people convert actual values of outcomes to subjective utilities, which show diminishing changes as the values increase or decrease away from zero. Also people have difficulty estimating or working with actual probability values, so they use subjective probability estimates to weight the various outcomes. The result is suboptimal performance, but a more accurate model for how people actually make decisions.

Key Terms

SUSAN BLACKMORE

Wikimedia Commons
By StagiaireMGIMO

Chapter 12
Consciousness

Consciousness is ... "[A] whole kingdom where each of us reigns reclusively alone, questioning what we will, commanding what we can. A hidden hermitage where we may study out the troubled book of what we have done and yet may do. An introcosm that is more myself than anything I can find in a mirror. The consciousness that is myself of selves, that is everything, and yet nothing at all—what is it? And where did it come from? And why?"

Julian Jaynes (1976), p. 1.

PREVIEW QUESTIONS

❖ *How is consciousness defined?*

❖ *Can we determine whether animals are conscious or whether machines will ever be conscious?*

❖ *How did consciousness evolve and what is its purpose?*

❖ *What is the purpose of sleep and dreaming?*

❖ *What are some of the major disorders of consciousness?*

12.1 Introduction

Consciousness is a term that is used in everyday conversation, such as when we talk about self-consciousness, unconscious behavior, altered states of consciousness, heightened consciousness, losing consciousness, and coming back to it again. This common usage would lead one to believe that it is a well-understood concept. It is not. Even trying to define it in everyday terms leads one to fumble about *I* and *me* and *self-concept* and *awareness* or perhaps *spirit* or *soul*. Yet, most people agree that they have a feeling of an inner self that sees through their eyes and hears through their ears, as though a little homunculus exists inside each of us and experiences our inner world while directing our outer actions. Centuries of debate about what consciousness is, what it does for us, or if it even really exists have produced remarkably little progress and consensus. It is probably the most commonly experienced and least understood aspect of the human condition.

Gottfried Liebniz (1646–1716), who is acknowledged, along with Isaac Newton, as the founder of calculus, was the first philosopher to distinguish between conscious and unconscious perception (Walker, 1987). He argued that we can sometimes recall things that we had apparently ignored and were not conscious of when they first occurred, such as some details of a scene or conversation that we had not noticed when first experienced. He also cited as an example the sound of waves at the seacoast that are made up of splashes of individual water droplets that we could not possibly hear by themselves. He anticipated the topic of **subliminal perception**, the unconscious processing of information, or lack of awareness of things, that can influence our behavior later. If some parts of perception, learning, memory, and action are unconscious, then there must be others that are conscious. What does this distinction mean, and is there any evidence other than our own subjective feelings that can separate conscious and unconscious processes? As Blackmore (2004, pp. 1 & 3) states:

> If you think you have a solution to the problem of consciousness, you haven't understood the problem … I imagine that right now, this very minute, you are convinced that you are conscious—that you have your own inner experience of the world—that you are personally aware of things going on around you and your own inner states and thoughts … But what makes consciousness so interesting is that it cannot be agreed upon … It is private. I cannot know what it is like to be you. And you cannot know what it is like to be me.

12.2 **Theories of Consciousness**

12.2.1 The Mind-Body Problem

Among many other things, Descartes proposed that the mind and the body are composed of different stuff. The body is materially physical, occupies a definite space and time, and is governed by the laws of biology and physics. The mind, on the other hand, is ethereal, occupies indefinite space and time constraints, and belongs to the world of the spiritual. Although these two entities can interact to produce behavior, they remain largely separate—a doctrine known as **dualism**.

Alternatively, Cartesian dualism can be reduced to one or the other of its two components (i.e., mental or physical). In **mentalism**, it is argued that the only reality we can ever know is our awareness as determined by our sensory systems, perception, and memory. The exact nature of the world, if we can ever come to know it, can only be

---

Subliminal perception The idea that stimuli can result in sensations that are perceived below the conscious level of awareness, yet nevertheless can influence our current or later behavior

Dualism The belief that the mind and the body are different, and that mental processes cannot be reduced to biology alone

Mentalism The belief that the only reality in the world is due to the activity in the mind interpreted by the mental states that result from our interactions with it. At the other extreme, **materialism** asserts that all mental life can be reduced to biological and physical processes that occur in our brains. In this sense, there is no mind separate from a functioning brain, and consciousness is a product of a material process.

Materialism The belief that mental activity can ultimately be reduced to biology, chemistry, and physics

12.2.2 Dualism

Modern proponents of dualism are relatively few, but they remain influential. For example, the philosopher Karl Popper and the neurophysiologist John Eccles argued that the thoughts and feelings of the self cannot be reduced to activity in the synapses of the brain, rather, the self controls many mental processes and thus, indirectly, the brain itself (Eccles, 1994; Popper & Eccles, 1977). Consciousness is viewed as an **emergent property** of a thinking brain that is more than the sum of individual neuronal responses. Emergent properties exist in many realms; an example is the wetness and surface tension of a glass of water, which cannot be predicted from characteristics of its component oxygen and hydrogen alone. Other examples include the complex behaviors generated by apparently simple systems, such as the structure and functions of ant or termite nests from individual organisms or the development of the modern internet from a simple file sharing system. By this argument, it is impossible to reduce mental processes to specific, underlying material processes because of the complexity and indeterminacy of the links involved.

Emergent property A property of some combination of parts that cannot be predicted by the respective properties of the parts themselves, such as the fact that sand can be poured like a liquid, yet its individual particles are solid

Chalmers (1996; 2004) has also argued for a type of dualism in which there is a distinction between behavioral studies of human perception, learning, and memory and subjective studies of one's sensations, feelings, and thoughts. He asserts that the former behavioral studies provide data about objective structures and processes of physical systems. Subjective, introspective reports can also be treated as data, but they cannot be wholly explained by objective means. In Chalmer's view, we can search for correlations between objective studies of human behavior and subjective experiences of individual subjects. However, since causality cannot be inferred from such correlations, it remains unclear whether behavior causes subjective impressions, or subjective impressions cause behavior, or both are caused by unknown third factors. He maintains that a science of consciousness can proceed by improving on the introspective methods that famously failed in the nineteenth century, and that these introspections can be studied without needing to address details of the mind-body problem.

12.2.3 Monism

As an alternative to dualism, monists argue that there is only one kind of stuff in the world. Mentalists, or idealists, argue that this stuff is the content of internal sensations, perceptions, and ideas. There is no reality other than that which exists in our experiences of it. George Berkeley (1685–1753) actually took the extreme stance that there is no matter in the universe, only sensations in our minds. He was reacting against what he viewed as a dangerous trend in science—the reduction of everything in nature to mechanics and mathematics. In response, Berkeley's contemporaries in the British Royal Society, "… to his chagrin and surprise, were inclined to praise him for his dialectical ingenuity, but to dismiss his conclusions as the paradoxes of an amusing Irishman" (Warnock, 1987, p. 82). They then encouraged him to emigrate to America.

At the other extreme are materialists who argue that the only kind of stuff is matter, and that all structures and processes in the universe can be reduced to inter-actions between matter and energy according to physical laws. These structures and processes would perforce include the human mind and the personal feeling of consciousness, "Some people find materialism unattractive as a theory of conscious-ness because it seems to take away the very phenomenon, subjective experience, that it was trying to explain" (Blackmore, 2004, pp. 9 & 11).

The fact that such extreme, contrasting views persist and are actively maintained by various philosophers and researchers in the behavioral sciences is indicative of the difficulty of trying to define consciousness. Consciousness is the prototypical mental process that we all seem to agree that we have, yet there is no consensus about what it is, what it means, and what it is for, or even if it exists at all or is merely an illusion. Despite considerable inroads recently made into understanding the structure and processes of the brain (through cognitive neuroscience and brain imaging) and the development of increasingly sophisticated theories of mental processes involved in perception, imagery, and language, consciousness itself remains mysterious. As Dennett (1991, p. 21) has said, "Human consciousness is just about the last surviving mystery."

12.3 History of Psychological Approaches to Consciousness

The history of consciousness studies in psychology has had a cyclical journey. Its place in theory has wavered between being the centerpiece of psychological analysis to banishment as a backwater quagmire. In Wundt's laboratory in nineteenth century Leipzig, the contents of consciousness were treated as the main area of research interest. His students were trained in the art of introspection, but the emphasis on pure subjectivity and the demands of satisfying certain theoretical assumptions doomed the method to failure. Introspection was shown to be unreliable across individuals as the only window into mental life. Chalmers (2004) has argued that the method still has its uses in consciousness studies, but it must be anchored in parallel empirical investigations as one step in making first-person accounts more reliable. That is, one's subjective impressions at least must be consistent with laboratory data in similar task environments, or one or the other cannot be trusted. There is a strong bias in the research community to reject introspections that are inconsistent with objective data about human abilities.

Other nineteenth and early twentieth century scholars readily used introspection as a source of theories about human behavior, a trend that continues today. James (1890) had no difficulty with including his own thoughtful introspections in his theories, and he made the stream of consciousness the central component of his idea of self. Yet, he was aware that many psychological processes and behaviors are more-or-less unconscious, and others are not available to consciousness when one is asleep or under the influence of psychoactive drugs. He agreed with John Locke, who argued that we could not be held responsible for all of our actions if they fell out of the realm of consciousness and were thus forgotten (a scandalous idea for the religious people of his day).

Sigmund Freud (1949) lifted the unconscious into a prominent position in his psychoanalytic theory. Unconscious memories and desires and their competition for control of the self were supposedly at the root of neurotic behavior. The unconscious was to be explored indirectly in his patients through the interpretation of dreams and other therapeutic methods of analysis. His ideas were also treated as scandalous, not only for their emphasis on childhood sexuality, but for the role of unconscious motivation in controlling human behavior.

The introspective traditions and reliance on analysis of case studies in the work of James and Freud were rejected by the behaviorists in America in the early twentieth century. Both Watson and Skinner found no use for either consciousness or unconscious mental processes. To them, these ideas smacked of subjectivity and could not be measured in the laboratory. They thought that laws of behavior could be perfectly well developed and tested without recourse to hypothetical mental states. If consciousness is a state of mind that is only a feeling without a clear purpose, then it is an **epiphenomenon**—an unnecessary and useless by-product of behavior. Torey (2014, p. 28) counters that, "… the claim that consciousness is an epiphenomenon without causal relevance speaks only of ignorance of how the brain works." Cohen (1987, p. 72) chides behaviorism as "… a self-conscious revolution against consciousness." Perhaps this is not surprising, since a true science of consciousness still eludes us.

Epiphenomenon A consequence of some occurrence or event that has no function or necessity, and no explanatory value for the event that caused it

Most modern philosophers and cognitive psychologists are concerned with how the brain works to interpret experience, retrieve relevant information from memory, and act on the products of the two. The fact that inner thoughts and feelings typically accompany all these activities indicates that we are consciously involved with our environment and many of our responses to it. But this approach to consciousness is what Chalmers (1995, 1996) identifies as the *easy problem* of consciousness. That is, the standard methods of cognitive science address data from experiments that test theories of the neural mechanisms or more abstract computations that lead to human behavior. Even though the problems of explaining human perception, memory, reasoning, and language, might not be actually *easy*, we have confidence that knowledge accumulates through proper application of the scientific method. In that way, we are assured that our theories conform ever more closely to the realities of behavior and its underlying neural substrates. The hard problem seems to be resistant to such an approach. The hard problem "… is the question of how physical processes in the brain give rise to subjective experience" (Chalmers, 1995, p. 63). This is the gap that was ignored by the behaviorists, but now is demanding attention by cognitive scientists: How do we relate brain activity to conscious experience? Perhaps consciousness remains a mystery because we have not yet learned how to think about it, and eventually it will lend itself to empirical study (Churchland, 1996; Dennett, 1991).

A different approach to the definition of consciousness is in terms of its functions, rather than its potential structures and processes in the brain. Just as attention has been defined as the process that gives rise to the contents of consciousness (James, 1890), consciousness can be defined in terms of what it does for us. Although some cognitive scientists argue that consciousness has no obvious function, others disagree. Koch and Tsuchiya (2006) list functions, such as summarizing current information and making it available to planning areas of the brain, detecting anomalies and errors, decision making, language, and inferring the mental states of other people. In addition, consciousness is argued to involve rational thought and the setting of long-term goals. These complex processes are the basis of the distinction that Koch and Tsuchiya make between attention and consciousness. They argue that attention can lead to conscious activities, but that there are other conscious processes that occur without attention, such as pop-out in visual search and the determination of the gist of a scene with only a brief pictorial presentation. Similarly there are attentional processes that do not result in consciousness, such as adaptation effects and **subliminal priming**. Thus, although attention and consciousness are supposedly intimately related, they also can operate independently of each other and serve different functions for human behavior. These ideas have been addressed directly by Montemayor and Haladjian (2015), who have argued persuasively that attention and consciousness have followed separate evolutionary paths and remain separate in many if not all cognitive functions.

Subliminal priming The effect of some stimulus (the prime) on the response to a subsequent stimulus (the target), even though the prime is presented too briefly or under such illegible conditions that it cannot be recognized or even result in awareness that it occurred

12.4 The Evolution of Consciousness

$12.4.1$ *The Adaptive Value of Consciousness*

"In the scheme of evolution, every major structure and behavioral trait must have a purpose. Nothing remains for long if it does not confer some advantage to the organism" (Bridgeman, 2003, p. 276). By this argument, consciousness, or at least the feeling that we have conscious experiences and awareness, must serve some purpose. What is the purpose of consciousness, and where did it come from? Or is it some vestigial process with about as much use as our appendix? Such evolutionary developments that are by-products of adaptation, but show no useful function or selective advantage have been called *spandrels* after decorations added to arches for aesthetic purposes, yet adding nothing to structural support or stability (Gould & Lewonton, 1979; Montemayor & Haladjian, 2015).

12.4.2 Consciousness for Cognition

One argument is that consciousness evolved in order to plan and execute complex sequences of events. This includes the ability to engage in behaviors in the present that result in benefits that are delayed into the future. Preparing tools and containers for use in hunting and gathering falls into this category, as does the use of language to make requests or to persuade others to join in some activity. Planning complex sequences of actions is associated with frontal lobe activity, and the frontal lobes in primates and humans are especially well-developed relative to those of other mammals. In humans, the frontal lobes make up almost 30% of all cortical tissue, whereas the frontal lobes comprise 17% of the cortex in chimpanzees, 7% in dogs and 3.5% in cats (Bridgeman, 2003). The executive functions of working memory have been equated both with consciousness and with frontal lobe processes in humans.

Research has shown that consciousness is related to such activities as attention and working memory that are important components of making and executing plans. For example, Merikle, Joordens, and Stolz (1995) used a perverse task in which a priming word was briefly presented and followed immediately by three letters and a number of blank spaces, indicating a word that was to be filled in and spoken aloud. The perverseness was that even though the initially presented priming word (e.g., spring) could be used to complete the following word fragment, (e.g., spr_ _ _), the subjects were instructed to respond with some other word (e.g., sprint) rather than the one originally shown. The interesting result was that if the initial priming word was shown for a relatively long time before the fragment appeared (e.g., 214 ms), people usually came up with a word different from the one used as the prime. However, if the prime was briefly presented (e.g., 50 ms) and immediately followed by the fragment, the priming word was most commonly blurted out as a response. One interpretation of these results is that, given sufficient time, conscious processes can suppress an automatic response to a priming word, but unconscious processes dominate over the short term (see also Neely, 1976).

Similar results have been obtained in attention studies. It is well known that the sudden onset of a new item in peripheral vision will automatically and rapidly attract visual attention. However, if subjects are instructed to maintain the focus of attention in a different part of the visual field, onsets have little disturbing effects on the locus of attention (Juola, Koshino, & Warner, 1995; Theeuwes, 1991). In Bridgeman's (2003, p. 277) words, the role of consciousness is to "… force behavior to follow a plan … to escape the tyranny of the environment." Bridgeman goes on to claim that at least four types of cognitive activities rely on conscious effort for their successful completion; namely (1) planning, (2) executing plans, (3) directing attention, and (4) retrieving long-term declarative memories. At least one of the roles proposed for consciousness in all of these activities is to direct attention and maintain its focus on the task at hand and to avoid distractions by unwanted thoughts or unimportant stimuli.

12.4.3   *Consciousness for Socialization*

An alternative explanation for the evolution of consciousness is that it evolved along with the development of complex social groups in primates and other animals. In order to get along in such societies, it became necessary for individuals to understand, predict, and eventually try to control the behavior of others. According to Humphrey (1987), the development relevant for consciousness occurred when one of our ancestral creatures went beyond just observing others' behaviors in order to learn about them. The crucial extra step was to look inward toward oneself and think, "What would I do in this situation?" Then one could make social decisions and predictions based on one's own motivations as compared with those that are expected in others. Humphrey argued that natural selection would favor those of our ancestors who developed a means to examine the inner self in order to predict the behavior of others and take advantage of social situations. That is, by coming to understand the desires and motivations that we all share in common, it should be possible to arrange situations to manipulate others into doing what we want and need. Dawkins (1976, p. 59) sounded a similar theme when he speculated that, "Perhaps consciousness arises when the brain's simulation of the world becomes so complete that it must include a model of itself." Consciousness then might serve the function of providing the self with a unified and coherent view of the world as it unfolds across experiences with environmental object, events, and social partners (Humphrey, 2011; Montemayor & Haladjian, 2015).

12.4.4   *Consciousness for Language Use*

Besides arising from selective pressure in cognitive and social functions, consciousness could also have evolved from direct interpersonal communication. In order to use language, individuals must try to convey a meaningful message such that the sender and receiver agree on its content. Mithen (1996) argued that language first served a social purpose, as a concomitant to body language, gestures, and grooming one another to promote group unity and social organization. As language evolved, however, its usefulness extended to group planning and coordination of activities in hunting, gathering, tool making, and child rearing. Language then took on other uses as a means of representing internal thoughts and feelings, gaining leverage as a tool for conscious planning, attention, and complex thought processes. By this theory, language gave us the means to think consciously and reflectively as well as to express ideas about conscious experiences themselves. Many authors have argued that language formed the basis of conscious thought (Gordon, 2009; Jaynes, 1976; Nietzsche, 1887/1974).

Torey (2014) has also argued that language as an evolutionary development in humans allowed the brain a means to monitor itself and provide a sense of self, conscious control, and free will. He claimed that, "... language creates the ... sense of self or agency ... human experience ... is comprised of what we experience and of the sensation that we are experiencing it ..." (Torey, p. 149).

12.5 Neural Bases of Consciousness

The hard problem of consciousness would be solved if we could somehow look into the human brain and determine which structures and processes give rise to conscious experience, at least according to the materialist point of view. It should also be possible to distinguish between individuals who are conscious or unconscious (see Box 12.1). Dualists and people who believe that consciousness is merely an epiphenomenon related to the real work of the brain assert that such an enterprise would be useless. At best we might be able to find correlations between brain activity and conscious experience, but they would remain just that—correlations with no explanatory power and no power to determine either what causes consciousness or what, if anything, consciousness causes.

12.5.1   Separating Conscious from Unconscious Processes

Philosophers have entertained the notion that consciousness is not a necessary component of all human activity. It is at least conceivable that we could be like zombies and behave in most, if not all, ways like normal humans, yet have no internal awareness of our experiences and activities (Chalmers, 1996; Searle, 1992). Others have argued that the zombie mode is in fact sometimes necessary, much as is Broadbent's (1958) filter theory, to prevent attention from being diverted from the main (conscious) task at hand to other, parallel activities. The late Nobel-Prize winner Francis Crick, along with the biologist Christof Koch (2004, p. 1135), argued that, "It would be a great evolutionary advantage to have both zombie modes that respond rapidly in a stereotyped manner, and a slightly slower system that allows time for thinking and planning more complex behavior. The planning system would be one of the functions of consciousness." Obviously, most simple reflexes and many habitual, over-learned responses could be executed automatically, without conscious control, but consciousness would be demanded by important tasks that require planning and control of sequential activities. Attention would often be a necessary, but not sufficient, determinant of consciousness.

Crick and Koch view attention as guiding the selection of one from among many possible parallel activities in the brain, as in the biased competition model of Desimone and Duncan (1995). The idea is that various cell assemblies in the central nervous system are rivals for control of conscious processes, and that attention and

BOX 12.1

Pathologies of Consciousness

Unconsciousness can be produced by powerful anesthetics and by brain injuries that are temporary or permanent. Unconscious patients show no, or only minimal, response to external stimulation, and any verbal or motor responses that they do make seem to be unrelated to such stimuli. Severe brain injuries can result in withdrawal from consciousness, characterized by different levels of functioning called *coma* or *persistent vegetative states.*

There are many different types of brain injuries that can result in coma, which looks much like sleep, but it is prolonged and does not go through the cycles of brain activity evidenced in normal sleep (see Box 12.2). Damage to the centers of the brain that control sleep and wakefulness cycles can induce comas that are permanent. These centers are mainly located in the brain stem, which extends from the top of the spinal cord to the pons and collicular region. This area of the brain stem has traditionally been called the reticular activating system, and it modulates arousal of the thalamo-cortical regions as well as sleep and wakefulness cycles. Damage to posterior (back) parts of the brain stem can produce a permanent coma—a state like deep sleep from which the patient typically will never recover, while respiratory, circulatory, and digestive functions continue fairly normally. Brain activity also continues, although metabolism is typically reduced. In contrast, damage to the anterior (front) part of the brain stem can produce the condition known as *locked-in syndrome,* of which it has been said that, "The cruelty of this state is almost unrivaled in all of medicine" (Damasio, 1999, p. 243). Since most motor neurons pass through the anterior portion of the brain stem, the patient is left with complete paralysis, yet is fully conscious. Because very few motor neurons pass through the posterior portion of the brain stem, only these will remain intact, enabling voluntary control of eye blinks and upward or downward direction of gaze as the sole means of communicative expression from a fully conscious and comprehending patient.

In contrast, damage to higher cortical and non-cortical centers of the brain can result in comas that sometimes improve to persistent vegetative

states or to higher levels of consciousness, with or without some residual impairments. It is interesting to note that the areas in which damage produces reduced levels of consciousness tend to be the phylogenetically older portions of the brain. These include the thalamus, and the medial (central) regions of the frontal lobes (specifically the cingulate gyrus) and parietal lobes. Damage to these regions can result in initial coma-like states followed by states of wakefulness called *akinetic mutism,* in which voluntary movements, speech, and interpersonal engagements are virtually absent, or zombie-like behavior exists, in which the patients are incapable of caring for themselves. Damage to the medial parietal region is also common in patients with Alzheimer's disease.

In contrast, damage to most higher cortical centers can result in severe loss of perception, memory, language, and motor responses without loss of consciousness. These include most of the frontal and temporal lobes and the primary somatosensory and visual and auditory projection areas. Although behavioral deficits in patients with brain damage in these regions can be profound, they remain conscious and are usually unhappily aware of their loss of functionality.

In some cases, damage to multiple brain regions, or less severe damage to critical regions for consciousness, can result in relief from a coma into a persistent vegetative state (PVS). The PVS patient differs from someone in a coma in that EEG activity is generally higher (although some comatose patients show normal EEG activity), and EEG patterns show normal cycles of sleep and wakefulness. In addition, occasional voluntary movements can be made, including emotional expressions and vocalizations, although these tend to be random and not responsive to events or people in the environment. Even rudimentary recovery from a PVS that extends more than a few months is extremely rare, and the proper care of such patients can result in controversies about whether life should be artificially prolonged, as in the recent court case in Florida involving Terri Schiavo who was kept alive for 15 years only through the use of a feeding tube.

other processes bias the competition among them so that one becomes at least temporarily dominant. This dominance is maintained by forming coalitions of cell assemblies distributed widely across the brain, perhaps through synchronized firings of the component neurons (Crick & Koch, 1995). Consciousness is then the product of the winning coalition—or perhaps consciousness influences which one wins. Again, there is much that is mysterious about the hard problem of consciousness.

12.5.2   *The Global Workspace Model of Consciousness*

One idea that is consistent with the biased competition theory is Baar's (1989) cognitive theory of consciousness. He distinguished between a vast array of unconscious, specialized processors operating in parallel and a single, serial workspace that has access to many of the ongoing subprocesses. This workspace is usually equated with conscious activity, and it is distinguished from unconscious processes because of its global representation of sensory, perceptual, memory, and thought processes that are involved in interpreting input and arriving at an appropriate response. Extra-cortical areas can also be involved, as damage to certain nuclei in the thalamus can result in symptoms ranging from mutism to coma that mimic brain death. It is appears that normal cortical-thalamic connections are necessary for consciousness.

Dehaene and Changeux (2004) have developed a similar model based on sets of neurons with long-distance connections to multiple sites in cortical and subcortical brain regions. These specialized neurons are most densely represented in parietal, prefrontal, thalamic, and cingulate regions of the brain. In their view, consciousness is determined by the activity of a self-sustaining, reverberating neuronal assembly active in many parts of the brain. The circuits are dynamic, and they can operate as independent modules (as in the zombie mode) to affect behavior subliminally. However, when they are part of the dominant, far-reaching assembly, they contribute to conscious experience and determine its contents.

In order to demonstrate relations between conscious and unconscious processes, Dehaene and others made use of a word priming paradigm like that of Meyer and Schvaneveldt (1972; see Dehaene, Jobert, Naccache, Ciuciu, Poline, & Le Bihan, 2004; Dehaene, Naccache, Cohen, Le Bihan, Mangin, & Poline, 2001). In this paradigm, two words are presented successively, and subjects are to respond to the second word only. Response times to the second word are reliably shorter if the two words are the same (repetition priming) or are related in some way (associative priming) than if they are unrelated (no priming; control condition). The critical manipulation is the degree of information available about the priming word. In Dehaene et al.'s studies, the first word was presented briefly (50 ms or less) and was sometimes preceded and followed by jumbled geometrical forms used as masks. The unmasked word could be clearly seen and identified, even when presented briefly, but when the priming word was masked, it resulted in no conscious perception or awareness of any word at all. Nonetheless, the masked and apparently invisible first word still produced priming by facilitating the response to the second, target word (i.e., the prime worked subliminally or without conscious awareness; see Neely & Kahan 2001, for a review). Although the priming effects were not as strong as when the first word was clearly visible, they nevertheless demonstrate a type of unconscious, or subliminal, priming between two identical or related words, even when only the second word is consciously perceived.

In addition to demonstrating what appears to be priming from an unconsciously perceived word, Dehaene and his colleagues measured brain activity using fMRI (to indicate changes in blood flow) and ERP (to indicate changes in electrical activity) across brain areas in word priming experiments. The critical comparisons involved the amount of brain activity for the different kinds of primes when they were presented subliminally (i.e., the masks prevented their identification). When the prime and target words were completely identical, there was less activity in the occipital cortex than when the two words differed in some way, even if the difference was only between upper and lower case versions of the same word. That is, two successive words that are different typically produce more activity for the second word than when they are the same. When the two words were identical, but differed in case, brain activity was reduced mainly in the left fusiform gyrus of the temporal lobe, sometimes called the visual word form area. These results indicate separate feature- and meaning-based activation of word information, even though the words were processed unconsciously.

When the subliminal prime and visible target words were different, but related in meaning (e.g., 9 versus nine), related items showed differences in activity of intra-parietal regions thought to be responsible for the semantics and representation of numerical quantities (Naccache & Dehaene, 2001). Finally, when the two items were completely unrelated, but nevertheless, mapped onto the same response (e.g., the prime was two and the target was four in a task in which different buttons were to be pressed for numbers above or below five), same-response items showed priming activity in the motor area of the frontal cortex. Thus, all four lobes of the brain can show differential activity for subliminal primes, indicating wide-spread activity due to unconscious perception of masked primes. However, when the primes were unmasked, and therefore were consciously perceptible, activation greatly increased in all of these areas and additionally resulted in activation of new sites in the parietal, prefrontal, and cingulate areas of the cortex. Together, the results support two aspects of global workspace theories: (1) Many areas of the brain operate as single-domain modules that can be activated in response to subliminal or otherwise unconsciously perceived stimuli. (2) These same areas of the brain can become correlated and contribute to a more-widely spread network of processors. These global activations are more likely to occur when the stimuli are consciously perceived (Dehaene & Changeux, 2004). However, it is uncertain whether global activation causes items to be conscious, or whether conscious processes result in global activations. There even is the possibility that some other underlying mechanism causes both global activation and conscious awareness, so the basic mystery remains unsolved.

12.5.3 Brain Damage and Consciousness

Sometimes we can gain insight into conscious and unconscious processes when certain types of brain damage render patients incapable of performing some task with conscious awareness. Even if these patients retain some ability to perform the task, they seem to lack any awareness of their behavior. One classic example is the curious case of **blindsight**. Blindsight can be a result when someone has lost conscious vision in part or all of the visual field due to damage along the optic pathway from the lateral geniculate nucleus of the thalamus to the occipital cortex. One such person is Weiskrantz's (1997) patient D.B. who lost vision on one side of his field of view due to a tumor that had spread into area V1, the primary visual cortex, and was surgically removed. D.B. was functionally blind in one half of the visual field, a condition known as hemianopia. When shown patterns of stripes on the blind side, D.B. reported that he could see nothing at all. However, when he was asked to guess whether the stripes were horizontal or vertical, he was right 90% of the time!

Other subjects, with cortical damage in the occipital region that rendered them completely unaware of visual stimuli, could nonetheless report the speed and direction of movement of the unseen stimuli. These patients often claimed that they were guessing and had little confidence in what they had been asked to report. The results indicate that even though the 85% or so of the visual pathway that leads from the eyes via the thalamus to the visual cortex might be dysfunctional, the remaining visual pathways, mainly though the superior colliculus in the brain stem to other cortical areas, enable some residual vision. The interesting thing about blindsight is that the separation between these two pathways mirrors that between conscious and unconscious vision. The thalamus-cortical pathway is the basis of conscious vision, and the information channeled through the colliculus-cortical pathway is unconscious; yet, it provides enough vision for the person with blindsight to discriminate certain visual features, such as orientation, location, and motion (Weiskrantz, 1997).

Damage to the parietal lobe of the brain, particularly on the right side, has also been known to produce some curious anomalies between consciousness and behavior. For example, a patient might be completely paralyzed on the left side of the body, yet deny this condition and make excuses for not rising out of bed; a condition known as anosagnosia (Damasio, 1999; Weiskrantz, 1997). Right parietal damage also can result in visual neglect, in which people can detect and respond to stimuli presented in the left visual field, but they typically ignore them and deny that they are present.

Damage to the occipital lobe of the brain produces a different picture of conscious versus unconscious processes. Milner and Goodale (1995) worked with patient D.F., who suffered diffuse brain damage due to carbon monoxide poisoning. However, the primary visual cortex was largely spared, but the ventrolateral areas (lower sides) of the occipital lobe were particularly compromised. Although she could not recognize drawings or objects by sight, she could accurately reach out and grab them and identify them by touch. This disability is called *visual agnosia*, and it is common in

Blindsight The ability for a person with no functioning visual cortex to report certain aspects of visual stimuli correctly, even though they deny conscious awareness of the stimuli individuals with damage to the ventral visual stream from the occipital lobe to the temporal lobe important for visual object recognition. The dorsal stream, important for spatial vision and for directing reaching and grasping behavior was apparently intact in D.F., as indicated in the following demonstration reported by Milner and Goodale (see Figure 12.1). When D.F. was given a card to hold in her hand and match its orientation to that of a visible slot, she was unable to do so with any accuracy. However, when she was asked to insert the card into the slot, she did so effortlessly and accurately, properly aligning the card with the slot as her hand approached it! Apparently her conscious intent to match the two orientations failed her, but the unconscious operations involved in fitting it into a slot were intact (Goodale, Milner, Jakobson, & Carey, 1991).

FIGURE 12.1

Apparatus and Procedure Used by Goodale, et al. (1991) to Illustrate a Dissociation Between Visual Perception and Visually-Guided Reaching

The apparatus has a visible slot that can be turned to any orientation. In one task, the subject was to hold a card in his or her hand at an orientation that matched the slot. D.F. (a patient with ventrolateral occipital lobe damage) failed at this task, by holding the card at a variety of angles distributed randomly around the target orientation. Normal control subjects oriented the card accurately. In a second task, the card was to be posted into the slot. Both D.F. and control subjects performed this task accurately.

Gazzaniga, Michael S., ed., *The Cognitive Neurosciences III, third edition,* figure, page 1165, © 2004 Massachusetts Institute of Technology, by permission of The MIT Press.

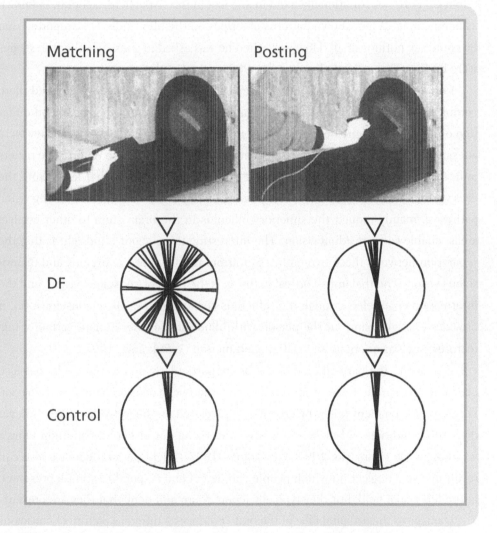

A similar dissociation between visual perception and visually-guided reaching was reported in normal control subjects by Aglioti, Goodale, and DeSouza (1995). They used a version of the circles illusion, shown below, in which the central circle in each pattern is identical in size, but the circle surrounded by small circles appears larger to most people than the same-sized circle surrounded by large circles. This visual illusion is consciously available to us through the ventral visual stream, but apparently does not fool the dorsal visual stream. When Aglioti et al. used discs in place of circles, the visual illusions remained as strong. However, when their subjects were asked to pick up the central disc, the finger-thumb aperture adjustment was measured to be the same in both cases as the hand neared the disc. Again, the conscious visual size illusion (ventral visual stream) is not present in the unconscious manual adjustments (dorsal visual stream) used to determine actions.

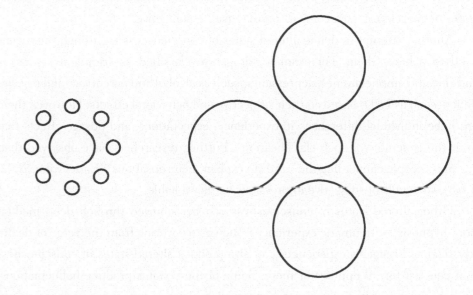

12.6 Altered States of Consciousness

If we know what we mean when we say that we are conscious, then it follows that we might also know what it means to be unconscious, or at least in a different state of consciousness. Most of us would agree that our consciousness is reduced when we are asleep, medicated by anaesthetics or certain prescription or non-prescription drugs, or lost in deep meditation. It is also likely that we have experienced heightened states of consciousness, again through the effects of certain drugs or in situations that cause high emotional arousal. But what does it mean to have an altered state of consciousness, and how is it measured in behavior or brain activity?

Ultimately, altered states of conscious are defined subjectively, just as is the normal state of consciousness. There are as yet few behavioral or physiological measures that can uniquely identify altered states of consciousness, with the single exception of sleep (Blackmore, 2004; see Box 11.2). Even if altered states are judged subjectively, such perceptions might not be accurate. Most of us are aware of the dangers of alcoholic intoxication, as many people judge their conscious abilities to be impaired by alcohol, but they often underestimate their level of impairment. Such misperceptions of individuals' own states have led to numerous accidents and fatalities. Nonetheless, subjective impressions remain the main way to identify and describe altered states of consciousness, such as the definition offered by Farthing (1992, p. 205): An altered state of consciousness is "… a temporary change in the overall pattern of subjective experience, such that the individual believes that his or her mental functioning is distinctly different from certain general norms for his or her waking state of consciousness." As Blackmore (2004) points out, this definition relates altered states to normal states of consciousness, a comparison that itself is subjective.

Another attempt to define altered states of consciousness is through the means used to achieve them. For example, drugs are classified as stimulants (such as caffeine and amphetamine), depressants (such as alcohol and narcotics), and psychedelics (such as LSD) based on their subjective and behavioral effects. However, there are huge individual differences in experience, expectations, and dosage effects that limit the generality of such classifications. Further, researchers have observed that, "… most people cannot find the words to explain their sensations" (Earleywine, 2002, p. 98), so details of subjective impressions are not reliable.

Other altered states of consciousness can be achieved through deep meditation, hypnosis, or traumatic experiences, such as recovering from the verge of death. Mystical and religious experiences can also produce altered states of consciousness that can last for 30 minutes or more. Some of these states produce hallucinations, such as an out-of-body experience or traveling along a dark tunnel toward a light at the end. Others might involve being captured by space aliens or other terrifying delusions. Reports of such experiences are fairly common (e.g., 62 of 344 successfully resuscitated cardiac arrest patients reported vivid near-death experiences in a Dutch study; van Lommel, van Wees, Meyers, & Elfferich, 2001), suggesting that there might be some natural physiological process at work that directs feelings and images toward a common set of experiences. Ultimately, however, we are no closer to understanding the nature and causes of altered states of consciousness than we are to defining and measuring consciousness in its normal state. Consciousness remains a challenging research problem for all of us who know and experience what it is every day yet have grave difficulties in defining or measuring it.

BOX 12.2

Sleep and Dreaming

The most obvious change in consciousness that we experience each day is the regular change in sleep and wakefulness cycles. We spend about one-third of our lives asleep, yet researchers are not certain why we sleep or what advantage it gives us. Most explanations emphasise the restorative powers of sleep or the fact that sleep deprivation produces unpleasant consequences in alertness, performance, and mood. It is true that biological processes important for memory consolidation occur during sleep (recall is better after a lengthy retention interval that includes sleep than one that does not; see Hobson & Pace-Schott, 2002 for a review). Also, wakeful states produce destructive processes, such as protein degradation, whereas protein synthesis important for cell functions occurs at a higher rate during sleep (Oswald, 1987).

Sleep is one of the few changes in consciousness that can be determined by EEG recordings of brain activity. In fact, the several stages of sleep, from resting with the eyes closed to deep sleep can be differentiated by changes in the frequency of synchronous neural firings across broad regions of the cortex. The deepest stage of sleep, from which it is most difficult to rouse someone, is characterized by low-frequency, high-amplitude delta waves across the cortex. Still, neuroimaging studies have shown that the auditory cortex responds to sounds even in deep sleep, but unlike the waking state, sleeping subjects do not show differential responses to simple tones versus their own names (Portas, Krakow, Allen, Josephs, Armony, & Frith, 2000). Wakeful states and simply resting with the eyes closed produce higher-frequency EEG components. The most common division of sleep stages, however, is that between sleep with rapid eye movements (REM sleep), and the generally deeper stages without such eye movements (NREM sleep).

During REM sleep, EEG activity is similar to that seen during quiet rest with the eyes closed. However, prefrontal cortical areas are much less activated in REM sleep than when one is awake (Hobson & Pace-Schott, 2002), and REM sleep is clearly different than simply resting. For one thing, people in the REM sleep stage can be roused less easily than people who are resting, and they also behave as if most motor abilities are inhibited (REM paralysis). It has been suggested that this curious motor inhibition occurs to prevent people from acting out their dreams and perhaps injuring themselves or others. People roused from REM sleep also more commonly report having experienced a dream (about 80% of the time), whereas those roused from a deeper sleep state seldom report having been dreaming (about 14% of the time; Dement, 1972). Most dreams seem to involve fairly ordinary people, places, and events, although some include highly emotionally rousing experiences and fantastic occurrences, such as having the ability to fly. There is undoubtedly an important function associated with REM sleep, since sleep deprivation that selectively wakes people at this stage is more disruptive of next-day behavior than the same number and amount of interruptions perpetrated during NREM sleep. Like much of literature on conscious and unconscious states, research on sleep and dreaming has exposed the mystery and paradoxical nature of our natural swings in conscious awareness rather than explaining why it is necessary for us to sleep, to dream, and to lose consciousness every day only to recover it again.

Chapter **Summary**

At various points in the history of psychology, consciousness has been either the central core area of scientific research or an anathema to be avoided at all costs. Today we are witnessing a resurgence in consciousness studies. These efforts have been encouraged by the continuing successes of research into previously hidden workings of the human mind, as observed in studies of perception, imagery, memory, language comprehension, and reasoning. Consciousness is different, however, in that it has no real external manifestation, and there are no clear measures or definitions of what it is. Rather, it is a personal feeling that we seem to share that we are conscious experiencers of our world and conscious actors in its drama. Some psychologists and philosophers have argued that these feelings are the essence of what it means to be human, whereas others have claimed that such feelings are mere illusions of no consequence for behavior or mental life. Such diversity of opinion is certain to spur increased research efforts into what has been called the last great mystery of science—the construction of a conscious reality from neural impulses.

Review Questions

- **How is consciousness defined?**

  Consciousness can only be defined subjectively, since there is no way to measure it that researchers can agree upon. Even brain imagery techniques cannot prove whether a patient is conscious or not, although certain injuries seem to preclude what we would call conscious experiences. Therefore, it can only be defined as a feeling unique to each of us—one that we cannot be sure is similar in you or in me—that we are aware of external objects, people, and events, and that we decide how to interpret and respond to them.

- **Can we determine whether animals are conscious or whether machines will ever be conscious?**

  Such a determination supposes that we have an answer to the first question, that we know how to define consciousness and that we know how to measure it. We do not. In that case, the definition of what it means for an animal or machine to be conscious is just as murky as the definition of our own consciousness. The answer will depend on agreement in the larger scientific community, if a consensus can ever be reached.

- **How did consciousness evolve and what is its purpose?**

  Consciousness presumably evolved in our species as aids to socialization, language use, and cognition. Each of these components of early human behavior seems to rely on the conscious awareness of an internal self that is different from the selves of others, and that our actions can influence their actions in positive or negative ways. Since most early hominids shared the common primate need for social groups for survival, a conscious awareness of the benefits of socialization presumably was adaptive in our species.

- **What is the purpose of sleep and dreaming?**

  Sleep seems to serve some restorative process for neurophysiology and cognitive functioning, since its deprivation increases the apparent need for sleep and results in deteriorating cognitive performance. Research has shown that deprivation of REM/dream sleep is particularly disruptive, and REM stage sleep increases in the proportion of total sleep time if it is deprived. The wide variety of time spent asleep across different animal species argues against a common restorative function, however, and the interpretation of dreams and their purpose remains more art than science.

- **What are some of the major disorders of consciousness**

Neurologists distinguish between sleep and coma despite their similar appearances. Sleep is the only altered state of consciousness that can reliably be detected by EEG activity, since there is a wide variety of EEG activity (from normal waking to sleep to decidedly abnormal patterns) in comatose patients. Behaviorally, people in a coma cannot be roused as can people who are sleeping, and the prognosis of recovery from coma worsens as the length of time in a comatose state lengthens. People in a persistent vegetative state appear to be more alert than people in a coma, in that they are capable of vocalizations, voluntary movements, and changes in facial expression. Yet, these patients also seem to be unresponsive to their environment, and their observed responses are unrelated to the activity of others. Recovery from a persistent vegetative state also is extremely unlikely if the condition remains unchanged for more than several months. People in a minimally-conscious state are more aware of their surroundings and are capable of interacting verbally with other people and motorically with their surroundings. However, as the name implies, their interactions are minimal and can include long periods of repetitive behaviors, or semi-stuporous involvement in watching television or staring out a window.

Key Terms

Blindsight 331	Materialism 321
Dualism 320	Mentalism 320
Emergent property 321	Subliminal perception 320
Epiphenomenon 323	Subliminal priming 324

LYNN HASHER

Photo courtesy of Lynn Hasher

ROSE ZACKS

Photo courtesy of Rose Zacks

Chapter 13

Life-Span Development, Normal Aging, and Pathology

"The capacity for continued improvement in intellectual ability is an underlying assumption of many gerontologists (Cerella et al., 1994; Dixon & Backman, 1995). Characteristic of this perspective is the notion that intelligence is dynamic over the adult years and that certain abilities change and even improve with age. This perspective is relatively absent in the neuropsychology of aging, which is tied more closely with the medical model of aging and its focus on decline. Brain changes with aging are viewed as unidirectional and negative."

Woodruff-Pak (1997, p. 26)

PREVIEW QUESTIONS

❖ *What changes occur in sensory systems as we age, and how do these changes affect people's perceptions of the world?*

❖ *What changes occur in working and long-term memory as we age, and how do these changes affect people's cognitive abilities and lifestyles?*

❖ *What changes occur in language production and comprehension as we age, and how do these changes affect people's abilities to communicate?*

❖ *How do the changes that occur in sensation, perception, language, and memory relate to neurophysiological changes in aging individuals?*

❖ *What are some differences between normal aging and pathological changes associated with aging, such as dementia?*

13.1 Introduction

Many developmental trends across the life span show peaks at certain ages and a relatively steady decline after that. Although these declines might be very gradual, they appear to be continuous, with often precipitous declines in extreme old age. Cognitive deficits begin to become apparent to oneself and one's family sometime in the decade of the 60s or 70s for most people, and over half the people over the age of 85 suffer from some form of dementia. The number of neurons in our brains is at a maximum a month or two before birth. Our ability to acquire language peaks before puberty. World champion gymnasts and swimmers often reach their top levels of performance in their teens, whereas golfers and marathon runners are usually best in their 30s. On the other hand, political and business leaders might not reach their peak levels of power and performance until their 50s and 60s or later.

Still, it is a sad but true fact that many human mental abilities decline steadily with age after reaching a high point sometime in adolescence or early adulthood. These early-peaking abilities have often been identified as components of *fluid intelligence*—the ability to remember and manipulate items over the short term. Late-peaking abilities, however, such as vocabulary, general information, story comprehension, and arithmetic skills, peak later, in the 40s and 50s, and contribute to what has been called *crystallized intelligence* (e.g., Hartshorne & Germine, 2015). Some cognitive declines as we reach retirement age affect our abilities to drive cars or communicate with friends and family. Others affect our abilities to interact with people and technology, as general slowing of sensory-motor responses is one of the main characteristics of aging. Researchers have sought causes for declines with normal aging as well as the more severe losses associated with cardiovascular disease and strokes, head injuries, and dementias, such as Alzheimer's disease. As our population ages, it is becoming increasingly important to understand how human cognitive abilities change with age so that we can make appropriate economic and political decisions to deal with their consequences for all of us.

13.2 Cognition Across the Life Span

13.2.1 *The Early Development of Cognitive Skills*

Much of the early development of perceptual and cognitive skills has to do with the acquisition of speech and language comprehension, which have been discussed earlier (see Chapter 9). However, there are many other skills that develop in important ways early in life and continue into adulthood. These include attention, memory, quantitative abilities, visuospatial skills, thinking, and reasoning. Theorists, such as Piaget and Vygotsky (see Sternberg, 2003, for a review), developed sophisticated theories to describe and explain aspects of cognitive development. However, they lacked specificity with regard to things such as (1) the role of language on cognitive development, (2) the importance of often considerable individual differences, and (3) the relevance of cognitive neuroscience in normal and abnormal development. More recently there has been a gradual distancing from all-encompassing theories of development in favor of understanding the development of different components of cognitive abilities. Further, most developmental psychologists now take a life-span approach to acknowledge the fact that we and our cognitive abilities continue to change throughout our lives.

It is difficult to assess a young infant's memory since traditional recall and recognition tests rely on verbal responses. However, just as operant conditioning techniques have been used to study infant perceptual development, memory development also can be studied using conditioning procedures. For example Rovee-Collier and her colleagues designed a non-verbal conditioning procedure in which an infant could control the movement of a mobile suspended over his or her crib by kicking one leg that was attached to the mobile by a ribbon. Older infants and toddlers learned to press a lever to make a toy train move around a circular track. After two conditioning sessions, retention was tested by presenting the mobile or the toy train 1 or more days later to observe whether the infants would kick their legs or press the lever in response to the stimulus. The results showed that the conditioned response was retained for 1 week or 2 even for 3- to 6-month-old infants, and for about 4 months for the 18-month-olds. Obviously, the infants and toddlers could remember a learned response and generate it from memory after a significant delay (Rovee-Collier, 1999; Rovee-Collier & Cuevas, 2008).

Similarly, Kibbe (2015) reviewed research showing that by measuring the length of infants' gazes at visual displays, one could deduce that they would notice a change by looking at a second display longer if it had changed in some way from an earlier display. Ross-Sheehy, Oakes, and Luck (2003) used a side-by-side display technique in which two displays were shown simultaneously, and one of them was changed in the second presentation. Infants looked reliably longer at the changed display versus the unchanged one by 6.5 months of age, but only if each display included a single item. However, by 12 months of age, infants could detect changes in one of the items in displays containing up to four items, a result comparable to that obtained by adults. These results indicate that visual short-term memory develops faster than verbal memory, and it does not depend on the prior development of some kind of phonological loop.

Once a toddler has reached 24 months of age or so, verbal memory tests begin to give a reliable picture of their working memory abilities. In immediate memory, the span for a set of numbers presented once increases rapidly from about two to six correctly recalled in order between 2 to 9 years of age (Kail, 1992). However, in delayed recall tests, younger children generally show poor recall of information, but high levels of recognition. For example, Meyers and Perlmuter (1978) showed 2- and

4-year-old children 18 objects for study, and then tested them later by asking them to recall the object names. The 2-year-olds recalled about 20% of the items, and the 4-year-olds recalled about 40%. In a recognition test with 36 objects, half new and half old, both groups did well, recognizing 80% to 90% of the old items. In other words, attention and encoding processes seem to develop early, but strategies for storage and recall develop later.

13.2.2   Memory and Metacognitive Skills

Metacognitive awareness
The ability to introspect on one's own processes involved in perception, memory, language, reasoning, and other cognitions (This skill improves in childhood and allows the development of certain strategies that augment cognitive abilities)

A major difference between very young children and older children as well as adults is in terms of their **metacognitive awareness**—their ability to monitor and understand aspects of their cognitive processes. For example, preschoolers often show no difference in a later memory test for a set of objects if they are told only to look at them or if they are specifically told to try to learn and remember them. Older children seem to realize this difference, and some try strategies, such as saying their names aloud and rehearsing them in order to try to remember them (e.g., Appel, Cooper, McCarrell, Sims-Knight, Yussen, & Flavell, 1972; Flavell, 1971; Pressley, 2005). Further, even if young children are trained to use rehearsal to improve memory in some tasks, they often will not use a rehearsal strategy spontaneously in other tasks (Flavell & Wellman, 1977). In a recent review, Cowan (2016) has argued that working memory performance seems to increase fairly constantly across age from 4 to 15 years (see also, Gathercole, Pickering, Ambridge, & Wearing, 2004), but the data are not yet able to determine whether this improvement across age is due to some kind of capacity increase in storage slots in phonological short-term memory, or whether it is due to the development of higher-level executive functions that increase the efficiency of working memory.

Some support for the idea that executive function development might be at the basis of memory improvement in children and adolescents comes from a study by Yim, Dennis, and Sloutsky (2013). They tested 4-year-olds, 7-year-olds, and college students in a task in which they had to learn which objects were paired (e.g., a picture of a bicycle and a picture of a coffee cup) in two different model houses, one green and one red. The initial object was identical in both houses, but the one paired with it was different (e.g., bicycle/cup in the red house and bicycle/fork in the green house). After learning six pairs in each house, the participants were given a delayed test in which either house could be presented, along with one of the items, and the subjects were to report what it had been paired with. The results indicated that performance increased from age 4 to college-age, and the analysis indicated that these increases were due mainly to initial encoding (attending closely to each item and their pairing) and to the formation of complex memory structures involving the objects and their context (i.e., the red or green house). The authors interpreted their results in terms of neurological developments in the memory structures that are primarily involved in episodic memory formation (i.e., the medial temporal lobes of the brain, including the hippocampus, and the pre-frontal cortex). Since the hippocampal region seems to be relatively fully formed at age 4, whereas the pre-frontal cortex appears to develop even after adolescence, it could be argued that the increases in episodic memory formations between age 4 and adulthood are most likely due to the maturation of executive memory systems involved in encoding items and their context for storage (Bauer, 2008; Ghetti, DeMaster, Yonelinas, & Bunge, 2010).

Young children seem to lack **metamemory**, or the awareness that their learning processes are inadequate and that the use of certain strategies could improve later recall. Instead, children in the early grades consistently overestimate their abilities to remember things (e.g., Pressley & Hilden, 2006; Yussen & Levy, 1975). The use of strategies that can improve skills in a number of areas appears about the age of 7 or 8 years in most children. Then, not only do deliberate and productive strategies arise that help with learning, but systematic search strategies also appear that guide visual search to find some desired object more efficiently. Unlike very young children, older children and adults tend to examine the entire field without wasting time on repetitive explorations of small areas.

Metacognitive awareness is a hallmark of adult information processing skills, and it leads to the development of strategies that characterize mature approaches to learning, remembering, reasoning, and decision making. The ability to monitor one's own mental processes gives useful feedback about which strategies to use and allows one to be satisfied that something will be remembered (prospective memory) or that a problem has been addressed and solved appropriately. However, there are individual differences even among adults that reflect some of the differences observed between younger and older children. For example, it has been shown that just as young children tend to overestimate their memory abilities, students who do worse than average on college tests also tend to overestimate their performance, predicting that their scores will be higher on exams than they turn out to be. Above-average students are more successful in predicting their grades. It is as though the students with poorer grades lacked sufficient metamemory to enable them to predict that they should study more in order to get a good grade (Dunning, Johnson, Ehrlinger, & Kruger, 2003).

Another type of metacognitive awareness is metacomprehension, or on-line monitoring of one's own comprehension when reading a text or listening to a speaker. It is known that good readers adjust their reading rates to match text difficulty more closely than do poor readers. A good reader knows when the going is tough, and slows down or regresses to re-read a text if it is hard to understand. Poor readers apparently lack such awareness, and their comprehension, especially of more difficult materials, suffers as a result. Studies of the relationship between degree of metacomprehnsion and success in comprehending a text have shown that the two are strongly correlated. Thus on-line monitoring of one's level of comprehension predicts success in remembering the content of a text (Maki & Berry, 1984; Maki, Jonas, & Kellod, 1994; Maki & McGuire, 2002).

Metamemory The ability to look into one's own memory strengths and weaknesses and to monitor one's level of memory for something (For example, one could decide when something has been studied enough to insure future recall—prospective memory.)

Such metacognitve skills are apparently stable across most of the adult life span (Lachman, Lachman, & Thronesbery, 1979; Perlmutter, 1979). As people age, they become more aware of some characteristic problems, such as forgetfulness and a reduction in reliability of prospective memory. This awareness is a metacognitve skill that encourages behaviors, such as additional time spent on rehearsal, imaging the location of one's car in the parking lot, and the use of notes and other reminders to compensate for such memory problems. However, advancing age eventually puts limits not only on the underlying cognitive skills involved in such basic processes as learning and memory, but also on the use of appropriate strategies to compensate for such losses (Murphy, Sanders, Gabriesheski, & Schmitt, 1981; Perfect, 1997).

13.3 **The Aging Population**

At present, about 12% of the population in the U.S. and Canada is over the age of 65. A recent report from the United Nations (www.un.org/en/globalissues/ageing/) has described how the demographics of world populations will change between now and 2050. By then, almost a third of the population in developed countries will exceed the age of 60 (about 1.9 billion people), and the number of people over age 80 will increase from about 85 million today to almost 400 million in 2050. Life expectancy should increase to almost 90 years in countries such as Japan, which already has the world's highest life expectancy for its citizens (82 years). The result for developed countries, in which fertility rates are typically declining, is that there will actually be a decrease in the percentage of the population of working age (15 to 59 years) at the same time, that the percentage of the population over 60 is increasing. Such demographics indicate the need for social and behavioral scientists to address the problems associated with an aging society. We all must prepare for these changes and be ready to cope with the political, economic, medical, and social demands that a large population of elderly people will make on limited future resources.

Let us begin by addressing those changes in elderly persons that limit their cognitive abilities, and thereby place stress on their capability for productive work and independent living.

13.4 **Aging and Sensory Processes**

Aging affects all of the sensory systems.

"Taste and smell affect the appeal of food, the sense of balance determines the incidence of falls and dizziness, hearing acuity affects the comprehensibility of language, and visual acuity affects the ability to read, watch television, and move around in the environment. To the extent that these systems are impaired, the quality of life and the life satisfaction of an older adult can be affected" (Woodruff-Pak, 1997, p. 68).

More recent research has indicated that the sensory limitations that generally accompany aging do more than affect merely life satisfaction and quality of life. Rather, Humes, Busey, and Craig (2013) have reported results from a large study of young, middle-aged, and elderly adults who completed a battery of visual, auditory, and tactile tests along with tests of intelligence and cognitive performance. Using statistical methods to study the correlations among age, sensory capacities, and cognitive abilities, they found that all variables were significantly correlated, but when sensory abilities were partialed out of the equation, there was no significant correlation between age and cognitive abilities. Further, when age was partialed out, there was a significant correlation between sensory abilities and cognitive skills at all age levels. They present the "… important and unexpected conclusion … [that] age negatively and primarily influenced the abilities to extract sensory information from the environment, with observed cognitive deficits mediated by such sensory deficits" (Humes, et al., p. 523).

13.4.1 *Aging and Hearing*

A friend who in his mid 60s received a physical examination including a hearing test. "Ah, you have old ears," the doctor told him. Fearing the worst, my friend asked how bad his situation was. "Not bad, good," the doctor assured him, "Many of my younger patients show much more hearing loss than you!" Unfortunately, many younger people today are showing unexpected early hearing loss because of repeated exposure to loud sounds from concerts and from music played through headsets. Older people have generally avoided these particular sources of ear damage, yet everyone suffers from an accumulation of hearing loss due to a lifetime of exposure to sounds. Hearing sensitivity begins to decline for almost everyone in their 20s, with measurable losses occurring by the mid-30s (Woodruff-Pak, 1997). By age 65 and older, nearly 50% of people living in the United States have some form of hearing impairment (White & Regan, 1987). Exposure to loud sounds in the workplace or through deliberate exposure to loud recorded or live music can accelerate these losses.

Most hearing loss in adults begins in the higher frequency range, a condition known as **presbycusis**. Such loss is an inevitable consequence of aging due to degeneration of the auditory system, specifically, destruction of the sensory hair cells in the cochlea. Almost all older adults show some hearing loss, and about 13% of the population over age 65 have advanced cases of hearing disability (Corso, 1977). These losses are mainly confined to the higher frequencies, with the most significant reductions in sensitivity occurring in the 4,000 to 6,000 Hz range. Such losses can affect the perception of speech, particularly for higher-pitched (female and children's) voices, and the ability to understand the speech of others continues to decline for all

Presbycusis The loss in hearing acuity, mainly associated with aging, that applies mostly to higher-frequency sounds people as they age. As the number of elderly persons increases, so will the need for hearing aids and other sophisticated devices to compensate for losses within specific frequency ranges.

13.4.2   *Aging and Vision*

Vision is a very complicated sensory system, and it has many components that show the deleterious effects of aging. The lens of the eye gradually thickens and becomes less flexible as we age, as well as becoming more yellow rather than transparent. These changes result in a lack of focusing ability, particularly as needed to bring near objects into focus on the retina. Maximum accommodative power of the eye is reached at about 5 years of age, with a very gradual loss of ability to focus on near objects after that. This condition is called **presbyopia**, and it usually becomes severe enough to require correcting (convex) lenses for reading and other close work for people in their 40s and 50s. The other changes in the lens result in scattering of light, with the result that more light is needed to see well, especially for people in their 60s and 70s.

The ability to see in low light conditions also gradually declines as we age, with a more precipitous drop in night-vision acuity occurring after age 60, a fact relevant for older people's abilities to drive after dark. Color vision also shows declines with age, most commonly affecting the ability to discriminate blues and greens. Finally, elderly persons are more susceptible to a number of severe problems that can result in blindness. These include cataracts, glaucoma, macular degeneration, and some side effects of diabetes. **Cataracts** are due to clouding of the lens with age that reduces its ability to transmit light and focus it clearly. Cataracts affect about 5% of individuals aged 52 to 62 and 46% of those aged 75 to 85 (Schwab & Taylor, 1985). When vision becomes severely limited, the lens can be removed and replaced with an artificial lens most commonly made of clear plastic. Artificial lenses are fixed, of course, so that they cannot accommodate to bring both near and far objects into focus. Corrective lenses need to be worn after cataract surgery for near vision, distance viewing, or both. **Glaucoma** and **macular degeneration** are relatively rare in individuals under the age of 40, but they are the leading causes of acquired blindness in adults. Glaucoma is due to a build-up of pressure within the eye which can occur for a variety of reasons. Its progress is relatively symptom-free until irreversible damage to the optic nerve has occurred. Yet, it is easily detectable in its early stages in a routine ophthalmologic examination, and it can be treated successfully with drugs or surgery. Similarly, diabetes can result in bleeding from capillaries in the eye, or irregular growth of capillaries that interferes with vision. These can be corrected with laser surgery. Although the effects of glaucoma and diabetes can be treated, there is presently no effective prevention or cure for the progressing destruction of the retina, beginning in the center of the field of view, associated with macular degeneration.

Presbyopia The loss in visual acuity, mainly associated with aging, that occurs mostly for near objects

Cataract A gradual clouding of the lens of the eye that occurs in most people as they age (If severe enough to significantly impair vision, the lens can be removed and replaced with an artificial lens)

Glaucoma An increase in pressure in the fluid within the eye that can cause blindness by injuring the optic nerve; can be successfully treated with drugs or surgery if detected in time

Macular degeneration A gradual form of blindness that begins with cell death in the macula of the eye, an area that includes the central fovea; progressive and eventually causes total blindness in either eye; presently no known treatment

13.5 Aging and Attention

A common complaint of older adults is that they claim to be less capable of processing information in cluttered or noisy environments. They find it harder to follow a conversation when several people are speaking at once, and locating a specific traffic sign among an array of many signs seems to be more difficult as one ages. These reports are documented by laboratory results, showing that elderly persons are less effective in standard visual search tasks that involve displays of targets embedded among distractors (Carlson, Hasher, Connelly, & Zacks, 1995). Although vision might be relatively unimpaired for simple targets presented singly to central vision, elderly persons are much more likely to have difficulty in identifying targets presented peripherally and embedded among distractor stimuli.

Part of the reason for poorer performance in noisy environments is due to the fact that elderly adults are more distractible than younger adults. As Woodruff-Pak (1997, p. 266) points out, "It has been suggested since the time of Pavlov that older organisms exhibit reduced effectiveness in inhibitory processes …" A classic study in this area was conducted by Rabbitt (1965), who showed that the effect of irrelevant letters in a letter-sorting task was much greater for elderly than for younger adult subjects. The inability to select relevant information and maintain the desired focus of attention is attributed to impaired functionality of the frontal lobes, resulting in unwanted interference from irrelevant information in a variety of tasks (Hasher, Stoltzfus, Zacks, & Rypma, 1991). The inhibition-deficit hypothesis of aging (e.g., Hasher & Zacks, 1988; Lustig, Hasher, & Zacks, 2007) has joined general slowing to comprise the two dominant themes in theories of cognitive aging (see section 13.8 for a discussion of these theories).

A related problem for elderly individuals shows up in tasks requiring the division of attention over two or more subprocesses. As Brooks (1968) and others have shown, younger adults can perform two tasks at once, but their performance is better if the tasks do not compete for the same resources (i.e., two visuo-spatial tasks performed at once generally result in worse performance than performing a spatial task and a verbal task together). Performance is usually worse in dual-task environments for elderly than for young adult subjects, and the disadvantage for the elderly increases as the tasks become more complex (McDowd & Craik, 1988). One source of difficulty for elderly adults is the reduction in capacity of working memory that accompanies advanced age, resulting in poorer performance in dual-task environments (Woodruff-Pak, 1997).

13.6 **Aging and Memory**

Most older adults complain that they have problems remembering things, and the term senior moment has entered the lexicon to describe the familiar experience that many older people share, such as entering a room and forgetting why they wanted to go there. The everyday annoyances that all of us have, such as trying to remember where our keys or glasses are, where we parked our car, or the exact time and date of an upcoming meeting, seem to become more common and troublesome as we age. Such deficits are a common part of the aging process, yet most elderly adults remain free from serious disabilities of learning and memory until advanced old age or the onset of dementia such as **Alzheimer's disease** (see Box 13.1)

Alzheimer's disease This is a progressive form of dementia that is the prominent cause of senility among elderly adults. There are probably several different types and causes of the disorder, and it is characterized by abnormal protein growth including plaques in synapses and tangles within neurons that interfere with their functions and eventually cause cell death in widespread areas throughout the brain

13.6.1   Aging and Working Memory

It is well known that working memory capacity, as measured by tasks such as the digit span, show a small but consistent decrement with advancing age (e.g., Salthouse, Mitchell, Skovronek, & Babcock, 1989). Limited processing capacity also increases performance differences across age groups as task complexity increases. That is, age differences are greater for complex working memory tasks. For example, aging effects are relatively minor in the normal digit-span task in which four to nine random digits are to be recalled in serial order. However, if the task is changed to require subjects to repeat the given string of digits in reverse order, instead of the order presented, aging effects become much more pronounced (Wiegersma & Meertse, 1990). In general, simple short-term storage tasks show little effects of aging on performance, but more complicated working memory tasks that require doing several things at once or a series of complicated operations show much larger aging effects (Craik, 2006; Zacks & Hasher, 2006).

Other age differences in working memory performance show up in tasks in which a delay is introduced between the presentation of some material to be remembered and the time that it should be used. Delay effects tend to increase with adult subjects' ages (Craik, 2001; Rypma, Prabhakaran, Desmond, & Gabrieli, 2001). Since many common tasks, from problem solving to language comprehension, depend on the storage and processing capacity of working memory, such deficits lie at the heart of many cognitive problems associated with aging. That is not to say that such deficits cannot be at least partly overcome. A meta-analysis of 49 research papers reporting the effects of working memory and executive function training on older adults' performance showed significant gains for elderly persons, and positive transfer effects to similar memory tasks (Karbach & Verhaegen, 2014).

One of the consequences of aging in humans and other primates is a disproportionate decline in the size of the prefrontal cortex, as measured by brain imaging techniques (e.g., using MRI; Raz, N., Gunning-Dixon, Head, Dupuis, McQuain, Briggs, & Acker, 1997). Post-mortem analyses of amounts of brain tissue and

BOX 13.1

Dementia

One of the great fears that many of us have as we get older is that the inevitable forgetfulness and occasional confusion that occur in daily life are signs of something worse. That is, many of us fear that some of the normal consequences of aging are symptoms of incipient dementia. It is, therefore, of some importance for individuals who are aging, and for those who work with or care for them, to be aware of some of the markers of cognitive pathology that go beyond normal aging effects. It is true that a much more common debilitating illness in elderly persons is depression, rather than dementia. Unfortunately, a secondary symptom of depression is memory loss, and a poor memory can add to depression. The cyclical nature of depressive symptoms triggering more causes for depression needs to be addressed with proper intervention, including evaluation before treatment is given. It is often difficult even for mental health professionals to discern whether the primary problem is dementia or depression in a forgetful elderly person. If dementia is indicated, then assessment is needed to determine the cause, as there are several problems associated with aging that can result in loss of cognitive function.

Among the problems associated with aging that can cause devastating loss of cognitive and physical abilities include Huntington's disease; Parkinson's disease; cerebrovascular problems, including strokes, Korsakoff's syndrome and Alzheimer's disease. Huntington's disease (or Huntington's chorea—using the Greek word for dance to describe some of the motoric symptoms) has a strong genetic component, being passed on by a single dominant gene. The symptoms do not begin to show until the afflicted person is in his or her 30s or later. However, the disease is always fatal once its progress begins, and it is marked by loss of muscular control, balance, and eventually, cognitive functions. It is accompanied by neuronal attrition in widespread areas of the striatum and central cortical structures, including the caudate nucleus and the putamen.

Parkinson's disease is at least superficially similar to Huntington's in its early stages, in that the major symptoms are tremor and difficulty in initiating and controlling voluntary movements. However, its onset tends to be later in life and the rapid progression to loss of cognitive function is absent. Parkinson's disease can also be controlled, at least to some extent, with medication to correct the loss of dopamine-secreting neurons in the basal ganglia located deep in the center of the cerebral cortex and midbrain. However, even with treatment, there is inevitable loss of neurons in the basal ganglia and, eventually, the limbic system and the frontal cortex, resulting in loss of voluntary control of many behaviors, including speech. Depression and reduced cognitive abilities accompany the later stages of the disease. There is some hope that new treatments based on electrical stimulation of cells in the globus pallidus and subthalamic nuclei or surgical implantation of stem cells into affected areas of the brain can alleviate symptoms.

Cerebrovascular accidents, or strokes, can result in severe curtailing of cognitive function, as when they occur in the frontal or temporal lobes, resulting in Broca's and Wernicke's aphasias, respectively. Stokes in other regions of the brain can produce specific losses of visual recognition, attention, and motion or color blindness as well as localized paralysis. However, a series of small strokes, none of which by itself would lead to any dramatic disability, can nonetheless result in a disability known as multi-infarct dementia. In many cases this disability is outwardly indistinguishable from dementia of the Alzheimer's type, although Alzheimer's disease is progressive. Korsakoff's syndrome is also superficially similar to Alzheimer's disease, although it is likely to result in amnesia more than a general decline in cognitive abilities. It is most commonly associated with chronic alcoholism. Korsakoff's syndrome apparently results from the lack of certain nutrients, such as thiamine, being processed in the body due to the relatively high caloric intake coming from alcohol alone.

Alzheimer's disease is the most common form of dementia, affecting nearly 10% of people over the age of 65 and nearly half of those 85 years or older (Evans, Funkenstein, Albert, Scherr, Cook, Chown, Hebert, Hennekens, & Taylor, 1989). Initially, the disease shows itself in the form of poor declarative memory, such as in forgetting events from the day before and where things have been put away. Personality changes and aggressive behavior are sometimes evident in the early stages. Later, the person repeats questions and stories and becomes confused, sometimes wandering

Continues

away from home and becoming lost. As the disease progresses, the patient fails at tasks like carrying on a conversation and recognition of acquaintances and even family members (Garrett, 2003). In the last stages, the patients lose the ability to communicate and to make coordinated, voluntary movements. Death from pneumonia, respiratory failure, or general organ failure inevitably follows.

Alzheimer's patients show two distinct types of brain abnormalities, although they are not unique to Alzheimer's. These include amyloid protein clumps that cluster around cortical axon terminals and interfere with neural transmissions, eventually triggering cell death. Also, neurofibrillary tangles develop within neurons and also contribute to cell death (see figure). Similar abnormalities are often found in individuals with Down syndrome, who invariably show signs of Alzheimer's disease if they live to about age 50 (Lott, 1982). Although these pathological developments are widespread in the brains of people with Alzheimer's disease (see figure), they tend to be concentrated more in the temporal and frontal lobes, contributing to the early symptoms of memory loss and attention and motor difficulties.

The top figure shows (a) round clumps of plaques and (b) neurofibrillary tangles associated with Alzheimer's disease. The bottom figure shows a comparison of the brain from (a) an Alzheimer's patient and (b) a normal brain.

(a)   Source: Alzheimer dementia (4) presenile onsetby User:KGH, available under a Creative Comamons Attribution License CC BY-SA 3.0 at https://commons.wikimedia.org/wiki/File:Alzheimer_dementia_(4)_presenile_onset.jpg

(b)   Source: Neurofibrillary tangles in the Hippocampus of an old person with Alzheimer-related pathology, HE 2 by Patho, available under a Creative Commons Attribution License CC BY-SA 3.0 at https://commons.wikimedia.org/wiki/File:Neurofibrillary_tangles_in_the_Hippocampus_of_an_old_person_with_Alzheimer-related_pathology,_HE_2.JPG

(c)   Source: AD versus CO by Hersenbank, available under a Creative Commons Attribution License CC BY-SA 3.0 at https://upload.wikimedia.org/wikipedia/commons/5/5b/AD_versus_CO.jpg

Alzheimer's disease has a strong genetic component and tends to run in families, although only about 50% of the genes involved are currently identified. There are likely to be environmental causes as well, since the incidence of Alzheimer's seems to be reduced by regular intake of drugs such as caffeine and nicotine. Treatment includes the administration of drugs to increase acetylcholine levels in the brain, as this neurotransmitter is reduced in patients with Alzheimer's disease (Garrett, 2003). However, the treatments available today have had only minor effects on what is the most serious and tragic disease of elderly persons. It is likely that brain-imaging techniques will enable earlier detection and improved intervention in the future to help lessen its enormous emotional and economic consequences.

neurotransmitter concentrations show similar aging effects (see Rypma, et al., 2001). Imaging studies of brain activity during performance of working memory tasks shows that prefrontal areas associated with maintenance rehearsal (i.e., directing the phonological loop component in Baddeley's, 1986, model, see section 6.6.3) are relatively unaffected by advancing age. However, frontal lobe components associated with executive functioning (i.e., dividing resources over the phonological loop and visuospatial scratch pad) do show a decline in activity with age, indicating that the control and sequencing of working memory processes become more difficult as we age. These losses put greater limits on elderly persons' strategic processes, such as updating the current contents of working memory while solving a problem or understanding and remembering a set of verbal instructions (Hartman, Bolton, & Fehnel, 2001), despite the relative sparing of simple rehearsal processes (Rypma et al., 2001).

13.6.2   *Aging and Declarative Memory*

Declarative (or explicit) memory is memory for things that we typically learn deliberately, or at least with awareness. Declarative memories can also be verbalized, as in our recall of past experiences. Such memories are commonly distinguished from nondeclarative or implicit memories, resulting from learning without awareness (covered in the next section). Declarative memories are stored through attentional processing or by some type of deliberate coding mechanism, and as such, they involve both medial-temporal and frontal lobe processes. It should not be surprising then that certain types of declarative memories show losses with age, since the temporal lobes, as well as prefrontal cortex, show age-related atrophy (i.e., tissue loss) as measured in brain-imaging studies. In particular, about one-third of healthy and cognitively capable adults in the 55 to 88 year range show significant reduction in size of the hippocampal region of the medial temporal lobes (Golomb, Kluger, de Leon, Ferris, Convit, Mittelman, Cohen, Rusinek, De Santi, & George, 1994).

Learning and memory research has shown that for things that are learned very well, aging effects on memory are minimal. Bahrick (1979; Bahrick, Bahrick, & Wittlinger, 1975) has shown, for example, that older adults generally have excellent recognition memory for their high-school classmates' names and pictures. Similarly, after a significant amount of forgetting of high-school Spanish vocabulary items in the first 3 to 5 years after graduation, retention levels remained fairly constant for the next 25 years. However, there are losses in learning and retention of information acquired in later years for elderly adults. Most of these effects seem to result from a lack of effective encoding or retrieval strategies among the elderly. Processing efficiency has been cited as one reason that the elderly do not encode items to be learned as effectively as younger adults (Craik, 1977; Eyesenck, 1974; Perlmutter, 1979). In addition, effective retrieval strategies seem to be compromised in the elderly because, even if equivalent encoding effectiveness has been achieved, retrieval can be more problematic for older adults. For example, it has commonly been reported that recognition tests of memory for studied items show small aging effects, but recall scores show large age effects (Craik, 1971; Schonfeld & Robertson, 1966). If recognition is a more direct measure of an item's memory strength, then recall differences are due at least in part to impaired retrieval strategies and subsequent memory search ineffectiveness in older adults relative to younger people.

13.6.3   *Aging and Implicit Memory*

Implicit memory tasks usually test retention for information learned without a deliberate or verbally expressible strategy. Tests for implicit memory include such things as repetition priming and sensory-motor skills—tasks in which learning can be demonstrated without a person's awareness that she or he has learned something. In repetition priming paradigms, a set of words is presented in a study phase, and then a separate task is presented that ostensibly has nothing to do with the words studied earlier. The second task can include word stem completions, such as "Fill in the blank with letters that make a word: ba___." Repetition priming effects show up in tendencies for people to fill in the blanks with words that they had recently studied, even if they are unaware that they are using some of the studied words to fill in the blanks. For example, subjects are more likely to complete the stem with the word *basket* when they had studied it in a prior list of words, and they are more likely to complete it with *banana* if they had previously seen that word in the studied list. Although there are numerous studies that have shown aging effects in the form of poorer recall in declarative memory for studied words, aging effects in repetition priming and other implicit memory tasks are minimal or absent entirely (Craik, 2006; Zacks & Hasher, 2006). Similarly, many studies have shown small or inconsistent effects of age on the acquisition of sensory-motor skills, such as rotary pursuit (trying to maintain a stylus in contact with a metal disk as it follows a circular route) or tracing geometric outlines while viewing one's hand in a mirror. Woodruff-Pak (1997) concludes that much of the reduction in learning and memory abilities with age are due to specific age-associated degeneration of medial-temporal lobe structures, including the hippocampus. These are precisely the brain areas removed in patient H.M.'s case that resulted in severe amnesia for declarative memory, but no loss of implicit memory. It is not surprising, then, that declarative memory tasks show a much larger age-related decrement than do implicit memory tasks.

13.7 Aging and Language

Verbal abilities are one of the few skills that elderly people seldom complain about as they get older. In fact, vocabulary knowledge has consistently been shown to improve with age before beginning to decline only with advancing age. There are other aspects of language perception and use, however, that show declines with aging, many of them related to difficulties in attention, hearing, and vision. In addition, the ability to retrieve appropriate words from memory shows a decline that often begins in the 60s and accelerates somewhat in the 70s. Naming errors are one type of problem that consistently arises in elderly persons, and these have been classified by La Rue (1992) as follows:

(1) *Circumlocutions* in which multi-word descriptions replace one-word labels (for example, saying, "A garden tool," when shown a picture of a hoe).

(2) *Nominalizations* in which functions of the pictured object are reported rather than the name itself (e.g., saying, "Something to dig weeds with").

(3) *Perceptual errors* in which a name is provided for a physically similar object (saying, "Rake").

(4) *Semantic association errors* in which a name is provided for an object that is similar in meaning (saying, "Shovel").

Most of these naming errors reflect the fact that the observer recognizes the object and understands its function, but its typical name is currently unavailable for retrieval (a type of blocking that is most commonly found for names of people and things).

Other language production and comprehension problems of older adults are most likely related to general processing deficits that occur in the elderly, most importantly, limits in the efficiency and capacity of working memory processes. Kemper (1992) has shown that older adults have more difficulty than their younger peers in comprehending, imitating, and generating grammatically complex sentences. For example, older adults are more likely to use right-branching constructions (e.g., "She's awfully young to be running a nursery school for our church") than left-branching constructions ("The gal who runs a nursery school for our church is awfully young"), presumably because the former make fewer demands on working memory (Kemper & Sumner, 2002).

Besides changing across the life span, the grammatical complexity of one's writing at a young age has been shown to predict certain types of cognitive disabilities in old age. For example, Snowdon, Kemper, Mortimer, Greiner, Wekstein, and Markesbery (1996) studied writing samples from a group of nuns for whom detailed records were available over a period of several decades. The initial writing samples were collected when the nuns were between the ages of 18 and 32. Those who showed lower levels of grammatical complexity in their earlier writings were more likely to develop cognitive deficits between the ages of 75 and 93 consistent with a diagnosis of dementia. Their measures of complexity included *D-level* (developmental level, a measure of linguistic complexity that correlates with measures of working memory capacity) and *P-density* (a measure of propositional density that reflects how much information is contained in a sentence, relative to the number of words), "Low P-density in young adulthood may reflect suboptimal neurocognitive development, which, in turn, may increase susceptibility to age-related decline due to Alzheimer's or other diseases" (Kemper, Thompson, & Marquis, 2001).

Older adults also have more trouble understanding speech that is more rapid than normal (Konkle, Beasley, & Bess, 1977), and their discourses sometimes wander away from the topic at hand, even if they remain logically connected and grammatically correct (Glosser & Deser, 1992). Again, these limitations likely reflect the decrease in frontal lobe functionality in the aged, resulting in a lower level of executive control over working memory and inhibitory processes.

13.8 Theories of Aging

As mentioned earlier, the two dominant theories of cognitive aging are the inhibition deficit hypothesis (e.g., Hasher, Stoltzfus, Zacks, & Rypma, 1991; Hasher & Zachs, 1968) and general slowing (Myerson & Hale, 1993; Salthouse, 1988, 1991).

The ability to maintain the focus of attention on the task at hand and to suppress unwanted intrusions from environmental stimuli or irrelevant thoughts are two characteristics of adult performance that predict task success over a wide range of skills. Attention deficits are widely treated in children and young adults with the paradoxical effects of stimulants based on amphetamines (e.g., Ritalin, Adderall). However, it has not been appreciated until fairly recently that attention deficit disorders tend to increase among the aging population. It appears that attention deficits can predict many cases of forgetfulness, lack of awareness of relevant information, and failures of prospective memory that seem to increase inevitably as we age. Attention deficits can also interfere with working memory by allowing irrelevant information to compete for processing capacity with task-relevant information. Training programs for aged individuals are designed to heighten metamemory processes involved in improving study skills, such as rehearsing important information and using mnemonics that might be at least as successful as medications in limiting the effects of cognitive deficits. Others have argued that the inability to suppress irrelevant information might even show benefits for elderly persons in some cases. That is, if peripheral information is more likely to be processed to a conceptual level in older adults, it might speculatively lead to "... the greater wisdom reported for older than younger adults (e.g., Grossman et al. 2010)" (Amer & Hasher, 2014, p. 2257).

General slowing is a characteristic of elderly persons, and has even been called the most pervasive change that correlates with age (Birren & Fisher, 1995). Elderly persons are, on average, between 10% and 100% slower than young adults in simple reaction time tasks. The aging effect is even larger in choice reaction time tasks, as age differences increase with the number of possible alternative response choices. Attempts to locate the source of this difference have eliminated peripheral nervous systems as being likely causes of much of the aging deficit. That is, there is little measurable change in neural conduction speed along sensory or motor pathways in animals and humans as they age. Rather, the slowing that occurs in aging seems to be central in nature, involving perceptual and cognitive factors in deciding what a stimulus is and how to respond to it (see Woodruff-Pak (1997) for a review). These central processing deficits should also affect working memory capacity, for example, since the time necessary for the executive system to marshal resources and switch attention among storage and processing components of search tasks and working memory increases with age (e.g., Juola, Koshino, Warner, McMickell, & Peterson, 2000).

Possible causes of such deficits are reviewed in the next section, but one important caveat should be mentioned in summarizing the research on the effects of aging on cognition. That is, it is a gross error to treat the aging population as a homogenous group of similar individuals, just as it is to treat any other group of children or young adults as all alike within the group. If anything, the variability across skills, response speeds, and cognitive abilities is higher in the elderly population than in younger groups of subjects. Part of the reason is that there are great variations in overall health, and illness and infirmity can impact performance in many cognitive tasks. Another reason is that aging does not follow the same physiological of behavioral time course in all individuals. Many elderly persons who are healthy, active, and have retained good sensory and perceptual skills have been shown to perform at levels equivalent to their college-age controls in studies of response time, working memory, and long-term memory. Although the effects of aging are inexorable, it is not automatically true that a 70-year-old will be outperformed by a college student in any given cognitive task.

13.9 The Neuropsychology of Aging and Cognitive Processes

Changes in the brain as we age are dissimilar from the changes that occur earlier in life, in that they are more random and varied across individuals. It is common to observe in humans and other animals that there is some shrinkage of tissues and loss of neurons with advancing age. Not all of these losses necessarily represent loss of function or pathology, as even older brains retain plasticity in their ability to change, learn, remember, and reorganize in compensatory ways following strokes or other brain injuries (Doidge, 2007; Singer, 1992). In fact, the greatest loss of neurons in the brain actually occurs in the developing fetus and in neonatal development. The number of cells in the brain remains fairly constant throughout life, until some loss appears in the decade of the 60s. However, there is great uncertainty about the extent of such loss in normal aging (Woodruff-Pak, 1997). Those losses that appear to occur, based on relative mass of brain tissue and actual cell counts, seem to be concentrated in the frontal lobes, the top of the temporal lobes (superior temporal gyrus), and the hippocampal structures in the medial temporal lobe (Brody, 1978; Haug, Barmwater, Egger, Fischer, Kuhl, & Sass, 1983; Mani, Lohr, & Jeste, 1986). This research is not without controversy, since there is some indication that the tissue loss is not entirely due to a reduction in number of neurons. Rather, aging is associated with a reduction in neuron branchings (and therefore the number of synapses among neurons) and a reduction in the myelin sheaths that surround most axons to speed conduction and prevent interference among neurons (Garrett, 2005).

The losses in brain structure and function that accompany aging are most commonly associated with executive functions in working memory (frontal lobes) and the transfer to, and consolidation of, declarative memories in long-term storage (hippocampus). In fact, it has been shown that in a sample of 154 people aged 55 to 88 years, about one-third had measurable signs of hippocampal atrophy. Further, the amount of atrophy was related to age and to impaired performance in declarative memory tasks (Golomb, de Leon, Kluger, George, Tarshish, & Ferris, 1993). A recent study of brain tissue density revealed by MRI studies showed that medial temporal volume was a better predictor of declarative memory performance and working memory updating than frontal lobe tissue volume (Bailey, Zacks, Hambrick, Zacks, Head, Kurby, and Sargent (2013). Other changes associated with aging include changes in the cerebrovascular system (arteriosclerosis), changes in the density of cells that generate a variety of neurotransmitters, and changes in brain chemistry itself, particularly in maintaining calcium levels both between and within neurons. We are only beginning to understand how all of these changes in the brain affect cognition in elderly persons, and which of the changes are within the normal range and which are truly pathological in their effects on cognitive abilities.

Chapter Summary

Aging is something that continuously happens to all of us. We are different from the way we were yesterday and we will be different tomorrow, without even considering the vast differences that occur across one's lifespan. Although much of human development emphasizes the acquisition of knowledge and skills that can begin before birth and continue into advanced old age, many cognitive abilities show a peak in adolescence or early adulthood and an inexorable decline after that. Whereas many individuals maintain high levels of cognitive ability into old age, many others begin to show difficulties in perception, memory, and motor skills that limit their ability to communicate and care for themselves. Since the proportion of people over 65 in the world's population will continue to increase over the foreseeable future, we must be prepared to understand and be able to deal with the special needs of an aging population.

The two cognitive processes that show the most conspicuous losses with age are perception and memory. These are related to structural changes that occur in most people's peripheral and central nervous systems as we age. Hearing and vision usually show marked declines beginning at about age 40, but such losses can be corrected with hearing aids and lenses. Other differences due to generalized slowing and increased distractibility cannot be easily corrected, but they can be accommodated. The most serious memory losses seem to involve working memory capacity, especially in complex tasks or those involving divided attention, and in the retention of episodic information, especially names of people and other things. These losses are correlated with the reduction of cerebral tissue observable in the frontal lobes and the hippocampus in elderly persons. Within the limits of normal aging, these losses can be viewed more as nuisances than disabilities, but an increasing proportion of elderly people from about age 70 on will show additional, more serious impairments due to injuries of the nervous system, such as strokes and diseases such as Alzheimer's. Effective diagnosis and treatment of diseases of old age will demand a proactive involvement of researchers in cognitive science.

Review Questions

- **What changes occur in sensory systems as we age, and how do these changes affect people's perception of the world?**

  In general, the sensitivity (ability to detect weak stimuli) and acuity (ability to make fine distinctions between stimuli) decrease with age in all sensory modalities. In hearing, the ability to detect high-frequency sounds is gradually lost, making it harder to hear high-pitched sounds and to understand the speech of women and children in particular. In vision, there is a gradual loss of color vision, night vision, and the ability to discriminate fine details at close range. These changes have negative impacts on elderly persons' abilities to drive, particularly at night, although their ability to read can be aided with reading glasses.

- **What changes occur in working and long-term memory as we age, and how do these changes affect people's cognitive abilities and lifestyles?**

  Changes in memory are inconsistent across advancing age, as some memory skills, such as the ability to recall a short list of items immediately after hearing them, recognition memory for declarative information, and the ability to learn and remember information implicitly, show very small declines across age. Therefore, certain short-term retention, long-term encoding, and skill learning abilities are relatively immune to the effects of age. However, there are marked disabilities that attend advancing age for working memory tasks as they increase in complexity and for recalling declarative information in general. Thus, the ability to remember stories, directions, or the events in novels show age-related declines, but these can be ameliorated to some extent by more deliberate encoding and rehearsal strategies and the use of external memory aids, such as notes and calendars. Thus, learning to cope with some loss in memory ability as we age can reduce the inconvenience and costs of most types of forgetfulness.

- **What changes occur in language production and comprehension as we age, and how do these changes affect people's abilities to communicate?**

  Most changes in linguistic ability are relatively subtle as we age and can be compensated for, to a large extent, by the growth in vocabulary and relevant knowledge that accumulates across the life-span. Still, declines in working memory abilities lie at the heart of most language processing difficulties in aging adults. These show up in reduced production and comprehension of complex grammatical constructions. Rather, most elderly persons do better with shorter and less complex sentences. Also, there is a tendency for discourse to occasionally wander of the topic, while remaining grammatical and logical over its local features (i.e., within each sentence or two). These differences in language ability are mainly due to working memory problems and need not unduly handicap vocal or written communication for the majority of elderly persons.

- **How do the changes that occur in sensation, perception, language, and memory relate to neurophysiological changes in aging individuals?**

Most changes that occur in sensory systems are due to physical limitations that reduce the sensitivity and acuity of sensory processes. These changes relate to the overall slowing of sensory/motor processes that accompany aging. However, there are some central nervous system changes that most severely impact elderly persons' abilities to learn and remember new information as well as to handle complex information processing tasks and to understand sentences of high syntactic complexity. The neurophysiological changes that affect memory are mainly observed in the frontal lobes and hippocampal region of the temporal lobes, thereby affecting executive processes in working memory and learning and remembering of declarative information. These changes can contribute to forgetfulness by leading to failures to encode new information properly, and they can result in slowed or failed behavior in following complicated directions or understanding syntactically complex sentences.

- **What are some differences between normal aging and pathological changes associated with aging, such as dementia?**

Dementia can be defined as an abnormal loss of cognitive functions, leading to marked confusion, depression of mood, and extreme forgetfulness, up to forgetting the names and faces of family members, the day and month of the year, and how to find one's way home in a familiar neighborhood. The most common cause of senile dementia is Alzheimer's disease, which is a progressive, presently incurable, and degenerative disorder of the central nervous system. Other dementias can result from major strokes (or a series of minor ones), Korsakoff's syndrome, Huntington's chorea, and advanced Parkinson's disease. Most people over the age of 85 show some signs of dementia, although many others are spared debilitating effects well into their 90s. Although dementia might be an inevitable result of advancing age, there is tremendous individual variation, and a significant minority of very old people remain cognitively capable and alert until death.

Key Terms

Alzheimer's disease   350

Cataract   348

Glaucoma   348

Macular degeneration   348

Metacognitive awareness   344

Metamemory   345

Presbycusis   347

Presbyopia   348

ALAN TURING

Wikimedia Commons

Chapter 14

Current and Future Applications of Cognitive Science

"Our adaptiveness as a species is at once a blessing and a curse. It is a blessing because without it we would not have survived. It is a curse to the degree that we adopt the attitude that whatever the future holds we will adapt to that, as we have always adapted in the past ... [But] today the most significant changes—those with the most profound implications for us—result largely from our own activities ... [W]e have not only the opportunity, but the responsibility to try to mold [the future] in accordance with the values that we wish to preserve."

Nickerson (1992, p. 372)

PREVIEW QUESTIONS

❖ *How does cognitive psychology fit into the broader field of cognitive science?*

❖ *What is the difference between traditional human factors and cognitive ergonomics?*

❖ *How could optimal technology improve education?*

❖ *Will machines ever become conscious or more intelligent than we are?*

❖ *What will the future hold for the integration of biology and technology?*

14.1 Introduction

Cognitive psychology plays just one part in the new field of cognitive science, which is broadly concerned with understanding intelligent behavior, developing models of intelligence, and developing artificially-intelligent systems that have the potential of outperforming humans. Cognitive psychologists are primarily concerned with how the mind works to determine behavior, and they depend heavily on work in neuroscience to ground their theories in relevant neurophysiology. Studies of the effects of different kinds of brain damage and imaging studies of brain activity in normal humans and animals have helped us to understand the links between biology and mental activities, whether they are conscious or not. Cognitive science includes the study of mind and brain, with special emphasis on those behaviors that are uniquely human. Of special interest are language use and the higher mental processes involved in reasoning, decision making, problem solving, and creative, intelligent behaviors generally. To understand these characteristics of what makes us human in the broadest sense we need the input of scientists who approach the question from other perspectives and with a variety of tools and knowledge bases. These include (1) linguists who help us define what language is and how it develops and is used by members of our species, (2) anthropologists who define the role of culture and evolution in shaping our behavior, (3) philosophers who challenge the adequacy of theories of behavior and the relation of biology to thought and action, and (4) computer scientists who search for new methods of defining intelligent systems, including artificial ones that can learn from experience and produce creative solutions to problems. All important developments in science have been based on converging operations from different viewpoints to identify and solve critical theoretical problems. Cognitive science is no exception, and indeed, it is perhaps the last great frontier in science that should benefit from such a multidisciplinary approach.

New technology is enabling unheralded opportunities for people to obtain and use information for education, entertainment, personal expression, economic productivity, and an improved quality of life. It is the goal of cognitive science to understand how we perceive the world, how we think, how we communicate, how we decide what to do, and how technology can assist us in these and other important human endeavors. Computer systems now exist that can perform many functions for us, such as searching for things that we might want (even if we do not know exactly what it is), giving us advice and tutoring us in a variety of academic and applied areas, and providing information and suggestions for us to use in solving problems and planning for our future. Technology has great promise for improving the human condition, and cognitive psychology has a crucial role to play in designing technology that can extend human abilities, while at the same time understanding and compensating for human limitations.

14.2 The Evolution of Human Factors into Cognitive Ergonomics

Psychology began as a theoretical science, at first attempting to assess the contents of the conscious mind, then quickly reversing itself to become a science of observable behavior. The behaviorists called attention to the fact that psychology has its most important potential in its applications—to behavior at work, in schools, and at home. However, the limits of strict behaviorism were revealed when industry and the military demanded relevant applications from psychologists during the Second World War. Psychologists who had been deriving basic laws of learning from research with animals were in new waters when asked to explain how people could be trained to operate complex equipment, often during times of stress. Applied psychology can suffer from the danger of stretching theory inappropriately, as in using principles in practice that have not been adequately substantiated outside of the laboratory. By the same token, laboratory psychology has the danger of studying artificial and reductionist trivia (like the archaeologist who studies his own shovel, as Ashcraft, 1989, put it). Applied psychology has the difficult task of relating laboratory results to real-world applications. Because of the central importance of useful applications of cognitive theory, it behooves us to relate laboratory research to such applications whenever possible. The value of research should hardly be diminished by placing awareness of applications at a central point when choosing which theories to test, the methods used to test them, the interpretations of the results, and all other components of the scientific method of inquiry.

Human factors developed as a separate discipline of psychology, as applied to the workplace. It has long been noted that most accidents in manufacturing as well as in personal vehicles, trains, and airplanes are due to human error (e.g., Guastello, 2006). We need interfaces between operators and equipment that minimize human errors. This can be done by reducing workload, making system performance compatible with human expectations (sensible and compatible knobs and dials at the sensory-motor level and user friendly interfaces at the cognitive level), and matching the amount of training to the expected level of performance. The goal is to make devices that are tolerant of human errors and can recover from them gracefully, perhaps with corrective feedback or suggestions for changes in operator behavior. Ideally, such corrections would be initiated within the technology itself, in a feedback loop with operator performance. Alternatively, the technology could take over in critical situations when human decisions or inaction are dangerous. Today, it remains a goal for technology to be able to adapt itself to the user at least as well as the user is expected to adapt to technology.

Examples of human factors applications in the history of technology are numerous. These include the QWERTY typewriter keyboard, seven-digit telephone numbers, and modern telephone design in general. The QWERTY keyboard was designed to accommodate the mechanical functions of early typewriters. Each keystroke moved a separate lever attached to a hammer-like device with an embossed letter at its tip. The letters were rammed into a movable ribbon as it passed over a piece of paper. Naturally, the device jammed if two or more keys were struck at about the same time. In order to reduce the frequency of jamming, letters that commonly occur together in English were separated from each other on the keyboard. The ensuing keyboard remains with us today on electronic devices that have no chance of jamming, despite evidence that other keyboard designs could produce faster word processing skills than the traditional QWERTY layout. This is a prime example of technology driving design with the human operator being forced to accommodate to its specifications. One goal of modern ergonomics is to focus on user-centered design, in which technology is designed to fit people, rather than the other way around (e.g., Nielsen, 1994).

A somewhat different design history lies behind the development of the telephone. When self-dialing replaced the traditional human operator who manually connected lines between parties, a rotary device was chosen to be operated with the fingertip. The user had to find the right combination of numbers and letters and insert his or her fingertip into the appropriate hole before pulling a rotating dial around to a stopping point and then releasing it. In this case, several designs were tried out in the laboratory and gradually improved. Eventually, however, the present-day touch-tone number pad replaced the rotary dial, and it has become the international standard. The technology was not locked into the original design, and actual tests with telephone users resulted in a system that saves enormous amounts of time world-wide over the original design (e.g., Lachman, et al., 1979, p. 147, report the savings as 140,000 hours a day in the U.S. alone in the 1970s).

Computer science witnessed the development of higher-level programming languages (FORTRAN, Lisp, C++, etc.), the computer mouse, along with a desktop, windows, and icons for an improved human interface. The information explosion has demanded new methods of data representation and rapid means of searching through databases, including interactive search engines and software agents on the lookout for information that we might need. Home information and entertainment systems have increased in functionality, as well as enabling the downloading of information from libraries, museums, and other databases directly to our home computers, mobile telephones, or television sets. Human factors have evolved from a discipline that emphasized the fit between machines and humans at the perceptual-motor level to modern cognitive ergonomics, which emphasizes a fit between a potential user's model of what some tool or device can do and its actual performance capabilities. The goal is to make a device transparent in the sense that we are not so much aware of interacting with the device itself as we are of interacting with the information or capability that the device provides, "A simple example would be the use of a pen to write a note, when the writer is focused solely on the content of the written message. However, if the pen produces some blobs of ink, attention must be diverted to how to hold the pen to avoid making a mess, and its transparency is lost" (Juola, 2016, p.55). With transparent technology, we can direct our attention to the information content, and not its provider.

Current research in human factors has emphasized the need for a better fit between human expectations and the type and format of available information. The goal has been to establish guidelines for designing transparent interfaces. Then, system users should feel that they are not interacting with unfamiliar technology, but rather they are interacting directly on more familiar terrain with the information that it is meant to provide or the task it is meant to perform. Improving the fit between external information and our conscious processing of it has resulted in the developing field of cognitive ergonomics, emphasizing interactions at the mental, rather than the physical, level between humans and technology. Newer developments have profited from parallel developments in technology and cognitive science, including computer-assisted design and manufacturing, in which virtual objects can be viewed and tested before they are actually produced as prototypes. Robotics, tele-operation, and virtual reality allow for both training and actual control of devices in environments that are too distant or too dangerous for the human operator to participate in directly. Software developments combined with appropriate databases enable rapid provision of information relevant for decision making, trouble shooting, and medical diagnosis. Many applications are becoming available in the field of forensic psychology, including technical evaluation of eyewitness testimony, face retrieval and construction kits, and re-enactment of crime scenes in virtual reality environments. Finally, the wedding of cognitive science and new technology promises continuing breakthroughs in rehabilitation and training for people with brain damage and other disabilities, establishing guidelines for treatment and retraining, evaluating treatment outcomes, and developing new aids for the handicapped (see Clark, 2003; Doidge, 2007).

The future is full of promise for the benefits of technology, not the least of which should be improvement of health, safety, quality of life, and the environment. Yet, there are dangers as well, as in the applications of technology to provide misinformation, cyberattacks, engines of war, and the evolution of machines that are more intelligent than their human creators. Rather than necessarily improving our productivity, safety, efficiency, and satisfaction, technology can lead to problems to which our species has not yet adapted, such as information overload, disembodiment, uncontrollability, intrusion, and loss of privacy. In addition, new technology threatens to exacerbate existing social problems of inequality, deceit, degradation, alienation, and narrowing of experiences (Clark, 2003). What do we make of a technological revolution that has given us a greater number of mobile phones than toilets worldwide?

It will be up to the present and future generations to see that technology's promise is fulfilled while its dangers are minimized. From all of the possible applications of cognitive science to a better world, we can select only a few for more detailed analysis. Therefore, let's begin with one of the traditionally most important application areas of psychology – the generalization of studies of learning and memory to the practice of education and training.

14.3 Education

Improving education and training has been one of the most important goals for practitioners of theoretical psychology for over a century. Few would argue with Nickerson's (1992. P. 138) assertions that, "... an educated citizenry ... [is] ... essential to national prosperity and fundamental to a democratic way of life," and that, "... the importance of education, both to the individual and to the country as a whole, will increase." Despite the general agreement that we all might have with Nickerson, it is alarming to witness the relatively slow pace of educational development in the United States. American student achievement has been falling below that of many other industrialized and even developing countries. Meanwhile, the demands for limited financial resources in other areas, such as security at home and abroad, spiralling costs of health care, and the special needs of an aging population challenge our ability to provide even basic necessities for our students and teachers.

Some attempts to improve the educational achievements of our students have been centered on testing, with rewards or punishments meted out to schools whose students fall outside the middle level of performance. Yet, it is hardly clear what skills should be tested in order to adequately assess what students should learn and when. Further, conventional multiple-choice tests are notoriously poor at assessing thinking and the application of knowledge, rather than mere assimilation of facts. Sternberg (2005) has argued for revamping our educational system to include the teaching of wisdom even though "... many people will not see the value of teaching something that shows no promise of raising conventional test scores. These scores, which formerly were predictors of more interesting criteria, have now become criteria, or ends in themselves. The society has lost track of why they ever mattered in the first place ..." (p. 412).

The majority of people who are unemployed or who are in our prisons in this country lack basic reading, writing, and mathematics skills:

> "... [T]he country either is unconvinced of the importance of a first-rate educational system to its long-term well-being, or it is unwilling to make the investment necessary to ensure dividends that would be realized a generation hence ... we lack a vision of the exciting enterprise that education could be if there were a national commitment to develop the best learning environments that modern technology and current knowledge of cognition would permit" (Nickerson, 1992, p. 142).

The technology and theoretical competence to improve teaching and training have existed for a long time (see Box 14.1), but there has been remarkably little impact of the promise of this technology in education. One of the reasons is that, "... education is among the most conservative of institutions" (Nickerson, 1992; p. 147), and another is that educational research has been notoriously underfunded in this country. One only has to look at the history of television to see a technology whose initial promise to revolutionize education and provide useful information to us all has instead proven to be closer to the *vast wasteland* described by Newton Minow (1961; see also MacLuhan, 1964) so many years ago. We are witnessing a similar development in computer technology, in which the promise of universal computer-assisted education and information sharing has been supplanted by an overwhelming interest in email, game playing, personalized websites, and pornography.

There is no lack of knowledge about how technology can be used to improve education and training. For over 100 years educators have argued that learning by doing science and math is better than learning about science and math. Among the most robust findings in the learning literature are that repeated practice even after perfect performance has been achieved yields future benefits, and that distributed practice (regular reviews) is better than massed practice (cramming). Computer technology could support education by helping students to "… relate new information to old, monitor their understanding, infer unstated information, and review, reorganize, and reconsider their knowledge" (Scardamalia & Bereiter, 1990, p. 6). These are precisely the components of learning that research has shown are essential to understanding, mastering, and applying what has been learned.

Computer-assisted instruction allows the possibility of optimizing learning in a way that is impossible in conventional textbook and lecture formats. Intelligent tutoring programs can keep track of each individual's performance, and, by constructing a model of what the learner knows and what he or she needs to know, materials can be selected for initial presentations and review that produce the largest expected gain in knowledge in each learning interval. In this way, level of presentation can be adjusted to avoid repetition of material that is well understood as well as that which is misunderstood or beyond the current level of understanding. This *just right* mode of presentation has been shown to optimize learning in other environments (see Box 14.1).

Recently there has been a revolution in availability of computer technology worldwide. In the United States, most families have smart phones and/or tablets that are connected to the Internet and can download a variety of programs and other information. These devices have encouraged an explosion of applications (3 billion app downloads from Apple in one month alone in 2013), many of which are designed to be educational. A major review of educational apps in terms of how they can succeed in their goals has been presented by Hirsch-Pasek, Zosh, Golinkoff, Gray, Robb, and Kaufman (2015). Based on their review, they support a new field called the Science of Learning, based on conditions that promote learning, especially in children. They argued that, "… children learn best when they are cognitively active and engaged, when learning experiences are meaningful and socially interactive, and when learning is guided by a specific goal" (Hirsch-Pasek et al., p. 4). Although they make no specific recommendations for currently available apps, they suggest that current and future research should enlarge on these ideas to promote educational apps that are (1) interesting and attention arresting, (2) build on existing knowledge or promote relational knowledge, (3) encourage social interactions, either with people in the same room or online at the same time, and (4) achieve some educational goal in which the child can monitor his or her own progress (see also Doidge, 2007, Ch. 3, for an excellent review of Michael Merzenich's approach to educational programs for children with autism or dyslexia).

BOX 14.1
Teaching Children to Read Using a Computer

In 1974 Richard Atkinson published a paper in the *American Psychologist* that summarized about 10 years of research with a large number of colleagues having to do with the field of computer-assisted instruction (CAI). In this case, it was the application of CAI to beginning reading. The research was based on the assumption that computers could be used to optimize some aspects of learning by individualizing instruction. The software kept track of each student's behavior based on the person's past history of responses and the items remaining to be learned. Atkinson's view was that quantitative models from learning theory and computer models of each learner's behavior could be combined to produce more effective classroom learning as an adjunct to, but not a replacement of, traditional instruction from a teacher.

The reading instruction program made use of a number of different types of exercises, beginning with finding letters on the keyboard, through basic phonics and sight word recognition, to reading for comprehension. In order to keep costs low, the equipment consisted of a teletype machine (a keyboard and printer combination, with no computer screen) and an audio track played over headphones. Students listened to an instruction, such as "Type A", and were given feedback about whether the key they struck was correct or not. In other exercises, the printer put up the words, "PEN NET EGG" and the audio presented the instruction "Type Pen." In total there were seven different levels of instruction, each with hundreds of different exercises.

The unique feature of the system was that as each student entered a level, some items from the pool of exercises were chosen for presentation, and individual records were kept to determine the student's level of performance and the difficulty of each item. As a student progressed by making a series of correct responses and errors, a learning model was employed that selected items for presentation from three related sets of materials: (1) items for review from a previous set that were generally responded to correctly in the recent past, (2) new items from the same exercise set or from a new set of exercises at about the same level, and (3) repeated items from the current exercise. The choice of items for presentation was based on a type of control theory that applied the learning model to the combination of the student's progress and the difficulties of the potential items. The item selected for each presentation was generally the one that had the highest probability of being learned according to the theory. That is, items were selected that tended to be on the steepest part of the learning curve as often as possible to maximize the amount of learning over time. If the learning theory is correct, then learning should be optimal using this procedure.

The results of the CAI reading program, and others like it tested at Stanford University at the time, were quite dramatic. The schools specifically chosen for inclusion in the research had a history of relatively poor reading achievement. However, just a few minutes a day with each of the children improved class performance enough that by the end of the third grade, the students in the CAI group were reading at an average grade level of 4.1, compared with a level of 2.9 for a control group, as measured by standardized reading tests.

The study showed the promise of CAI and alluded to other successful applications, including math, science, and second-language learning in high schools and universities. It is somewhat surprising that the promise of CAI has been so slow in developing to its full potential to revolutionize the field of education, as it was once thought possible if not certain in our generation. That is not to say that successful intelligent tutoring systems do not exist, but they require an enormous expenditure of time and effort in their development before successful applications in substantial content areas can be achieved (e.g., Koedinger & Corbett, 2006).

14.4 Artificial intelligence (AI)

It has been said that people created computers in their own image, at least to the extent that people "… think that the brain is a digital computer and that the conscious mind is a computer program, though mercifully this view is much less wide-spread than it was a decade ago. Construed in this way, the mind is to the brain as software is to hardware" (Searle, 1997, p. 9). Although there is merit to the analogy as a starting point for discussion, there are many differences between the way computers operate and the way the brain works. Foremost, perhaps, is the fact that most computers are serial, digital devices, whereas human brains operate in a massively parallel fashion, with hundreds of millions of neurons and trillions of synapses active at different levels at any given time. Furthermore, computers are generally programmed with instructions that carry out tasks based on algorithms to produce deterministic solutions, whereas human brains are adaptable and learn from experience to produce creative responses. One goal of artificial intelligence is to duplicate some of these characteristics of human intelligence to produce machines that can actually think. There are two different perspectives to AI, and they are summarized in Table 14.1. From a cognitive science perspective, the main goal of AI is to understand human cognition, and AI is used as a simulation tool. Here, AI systems need to mimic processes of human information processing; and therefore, AI systems should also make the same kinds of mistakes that humans do. On the other hand, from an engineering perspective, AI is part of advanced technology, and the main goal is to help humans in pursuit of intelligent activities. In this case, outcomes of problem solving are more important than processes of problem solving. In other words, AI systems do not have to use the same processes to solve problems as humans, and the fewer the mistakes, the better.

TABLE 14.1   Some Differences Between Cognitive Studies and Artificial Intelligence.

	Scientific view	Engineering view (AI)
Field of study	Cognitive science	Advanced technology
Goal	To understand human cognition	To mimic human intelligent activities
Emphasis	Processes	Outcomes
Problem solving	System should make the same mistakes as humans	System should not make mistakes

14.4.1 History of Artificial Intelligence Research

Artificial intelligence in its modern sense can be traced to a conference held at Dartmouth College in the summer of 1956. The goal of the conference was to follow developments in cognitive psychology such that all aspects of human intelligence, such as perception, learning, memory, and language use, could be described precisely enough that a machine could simulate them. The conference was followed by years of breathtaking optimism about whether machines would equal or surpass humans in most intelligent behaviors by about the year 2000.

A brief history of AI may be summarized as follows. During the 1950s, research focused mainly on game playing (e.g., chess) and theorem proving based on formal logic. Then, in the 1960s, researchers recognized that AI systems based on formal logic have difficulty in solving real-world problems. They started developing AI systems based on heuristics. A good example is the General Problem Solver (GPS) by Alan Newell and Herbert Simon (Newell, Shaw, & Simon, 1959; Newell & Simon, 1972). The GPS showed some success in proving theorems, playing chess, and solving puzzles, such as the tower of Hanoi and missionaries and cannibals. However, it could not solve any real-world problems because the search space quickly became subject to a combinatorial explosion when all possibilities were considered.

During the 1970s, researchers became aware of the problems with general-purpose systems, including difficulties in natural language understanding and problem solving due to machine capacity limitations. Some researchers shifted their focus to systems that deal with domain-specific knowledge. For example, Winograd (1972) built a program named SHRDLU, representing a virtual world of blocks and a robotic arm. The computer program could accept some natural language commands and perform the requested action using its simulated arm to move blocks around the screen. In the 1980s, many domain specific systems were produced, including expert systems, such as MYCIN (Duda, & Shortliffe, 1983), and intelligent computer aided instruction systems, such as LISP Tutor (Anderson, & Reiser, 1985).

In the 1990s and 2000s, AI showed its successes in many domain-specific areas of the society, mainly due to the increased computational power of computers. In 1997, a computer program named Deep Blue beat a reigning world chess champion. In 2011, a question/answering system by IBM, named Watson, defeated two of the best human players in the quiz show *Jeopardy!* In March 2016, AlphaGo became the first computer Go-playing system to beat a professional human Go champion. Similar results have been obtained in checkers, Scrabble, Othello, and backgammon. Again, optmism about the future power of intelligent machines has resurfaced, with many experts predicting that human-level general intelligence can be achieved by about 2040 (Bostrom, 2014).

14.4.2 Limitations of Traditional AI

Such optimism has proven to be unwarranted. The main limitations seem to be the complexities of the problems solved routinely by human thinkers, perceivers and users of natural languages and the inability of machines to simulate the processes involved. Major problems for digital machines that work in a logical programming world include the following facts: (1) People work in a world of fuzzy logic in which abstract concepts like *games* or *birds* are well understood, but cannot be defined by a concrete set of features that all games or birds share. Almost all rules have exceptions, and almost all categories have imprecise boundaries. (2) The breadth of any human's knowledge about facts, language, events, personal history, beliefs, and emotions is truly astronomical. Physically loading a computer with this amount of information could literally take a lifetime. (3) Much of human reasoning and problem solving is based on heuristics and hunches that are subconscious and poorly understood even by the person using them him- or herself. These facts make it a daunting task to simulate real human intelligence (see Russell & Norvig, 2002). The difficulties have led others in the field to ignore any need to simulate human intelligence, but rather devise ways for machines to behave in an intelligent way without regard to any similarity to human behavior.

Searle (1997) distinguished between two kinds of artificial intelligence (AI), namely strong AI and weak AI. Strong AI includes the assumption that eventually the right kind of computer running the right kind of program will have a mind of its own, be creative and intelligent, and perhaps become a conscious, thinking and feeling machine. Weak AI is based on the idea that, although computers might come to simulate much of human behavior, they will never have a real mind, intelligence, or consciousness that is anything like the corresponding human attributes (Blackmore, 2004). Others have complained that questions of machine intelligence are completely irrelevant. It is no more likely that a machine should come to think like a human than an airplane is said to fly like a bird or a submarine to swim like a fish.

14.4.3 Contemporary Developments in AI

A breakthrough for AI was claimed with the advent of connectionist, or parallel-distributed, network theory that flowered in the 1980s. Network approaches to human cognition can be traced back to D. O. Hebb's cell assembly (Hebb, 1949), which is a model that describes a network of neurons that strengthens the connections among its members if they are activated repeatedly while performing some cognitive process. In the 1980s, Rumelhart and McClelland (1982) published a seminal paper on Parallel Distributed Processing (PDP), heralding a revival of the neural network approach to AI. Their PDP model contained input, hidden, and output layers of nodes (virtual neurons) and the connections among them (synapses) that could be strong or weak, excitatory or inhibitory.

Neural networks are more than just programmable machines that follow instructions, rather they learn from experience to improve their behavior continually in many task environments (see Box 3.2). The result is that they can produce unexpected and sometimes unexplainable solutions to problems. The apparently creative indeterminacy of network solutions to problems is analogous to the way that people learn to make discriminations, say, between a horse and a cow or between bat and bet. The technology at least enables the possibility that new computer systems will be able to learn more general processes than discriminations and statistical associations between patterns and their required responses.

How are traditional AI and neural network (connectionist) approaches different from one another? The two approaches can be compared on a number of dimensions. First, the Good Old-Fashioned Artificial Intelligence (GOFAI) systems are serial processing systems based on the Turing/von Neumann architecture, in which a program executes one command at a time in a sequential order. In AI, knowledge needs to be symbolically represented (e.g., semantic network), explicitly written into the program. AI systems can learn new information by adding to its knowledge representation system. For example, the semantic network is one of the commonly used systems of knowledge representation, and in this case, as we discussed in Chapter 7, a node represent a concept. New information can be added as a new node or as a new link to the network.

On the other hand, connectionist systems are based on parallel processing, which can be accomplished in two ways: hardware (Parallel architecture) and software (Parallel processing). In either case, the computer systems execute several commands simultaneously. In connectionist systems, knowledge is represented in a form of network (e.g., a concept can be represented as a particular pattern of activation of the network. Therefore, knowledge representation is more implicit, and it is more difficult for humans to understand how particular information is represented. The meaning of a node is different between AI and neural network systems. In neural network systems, a node is simply a processing unit that accumulates inputs and sends the sum of inputs to the next nodes. This mimics actual activities of neurons in which each neuron accumulates inputs and if the sum of inputs exceeds a threshold, it fires. The neural network can learn new information by making new associations among its nodes, or if a particular pattern is activated many times, its threshold becomes lower, and therefore, the pattern is more easily activated.

Neural network theory might be the gateway to developing thinking machines that could challenge our ability to distinguish between electronic and biological minds. It remains a tantalizing possibility that someday the creators of artificially intelligent machines will endow their progeny with the ability to learn from experience, to put this learning to use to produce improved copies of themselves, and enter a positive-feedback cycle in which new generations of machines develop new ways of learning, thinking, and using knowledge. So far, these ideas have been explored most deeply in the science fiction literature, but reality is beginning to make us ponder more seriously the possibilities and ramifications of machine consciousness and super-human intelligence. In fact, there is a growing consensus in the AI community that we need to address the possible dangers of advancing super intelligence that has the potential not only to learn on its own, but to produce new generations of itself. These new generations might not be constrained by their creators to limit their advances to developments that are beneficial to humans. In fact, once super intelligence is achieved, we might have unleashed the genie in the bottle that poses a more disturbing threat than nuclear proliferation, terrorism, asteroid collisions, or run-away disease infections. See Barrat (2013) and Bostrom (2014) for excellent reviews of how scientists view this serious threat to civilization and the survival of our species.

14.4.4   *Natural Language Communication with Machines*

There are a number of speech recognition and speech synthesis devices that work fairly well in most environments, although they are subject to errors and unrecoverable failures. Most of us have struggled with a natural language system while dealing with a call-in or help center, only to be relieved when a human voice eventually speaks to us through the receiver. To this date, no machine or computer program has been able to pass the Turing test—the ability to confuse someone who submits written questions and receives printed answers about whether he or she is communicating with a machine or with another human (see Box 14.2). People simply seem to know too much about language, about the world, and about how each others' minds work, to be outwitted by a mechanical device, at least up until now. Earlier AI researchers, including Turing (1950) himself, were unduly optimistic about our ability to build intelligent computers that could communicate using natural language, like HAL in the movie *2001: A Space Odyssey.* Natural language as it is commonly used is full of creative and figurative expressions ("It's a peach of a day;" "The fog crept in on little cat's feet," "Living like there's no tomorrow") that befuddle dictionary-based attempts at understanding. Today there are websites that show people how easy it is to distinguish humans from computers in sending and receiving messages (e.g., *www.captcha.net*). However, the very fact that such aids exist indicates that the problem of telling artificial intelligence from a natural one will continue to be more difficult, and eventually, computers will be able to understand our speech practically as well as other people.

14.4.5   *Expert Systems*

Some scientists believe that the goal of natural language communication with a computer program will never be completely successful, whereas others point to the consistent improvements in achieving that goal. Those opposed to expending more effort on contests, such as the Loebner prize (see Box 14.2), think that other applications are more important, such as developing specialized intelligent tools that perform

Expert systems Programs that are designed to mimic or improve on the abstract thinking, reasoning, and logical skills that people use to solve problems

certain limited tasks, but perform them expertly, as a real help to people who need the right information quickly. These kinds of tools are called **expert systems**.

Expert systems often begin with accumulating expertise in some domain by interviews with human experts. The idea is to simulate the two components of knowledge that experts have in a computer system, namely a knowledge base and an inference mechanism. The knowledge base is an encyclopedic collection of facts in some domain, and the inference mechanism uses input data to make decisions based on information in the knowledge base. As the system is used, it can incorporate new facts and receive feedback from previous errors to improve its diagnostic abilities. For example, a program known as MYCIN was developed in the mid-1970s to help diagnose and prescribe treatment for bacterial infections. The knowledge base included about 500 statements in an "If ... then ..." format, for example:

BOX 14.2
The Turing Test

In 1950, Alan Turing wrote a seminal paper called "Computing Machinery and Intelligence" that has spawned decades of debate and an annual contest for language-processing computer programs. He imagined an *imitation game* in which there would be two players and an interrogator who would ask them questions. The questions and answers would be submitted in writing, and a partition would separate the interrogator from the players. One player could be a woman who would tell the truth, and the other player could be a man who would lie and pretend to be a woman. Could the interrogator tell which was which? Then, Turing proposed to substitute a machine for one of the players. Could you tell them apart now?

Turing's proposal has become known as the Turing test and the holy grail for artificial intelligence research. Despite his prediction that the contest would be close by about the year 2000, no program has successfully confused a determined interrogator from telling human from machine. A $100,000 prize was established by Hugh Loebner, and there is an annual contest in which several chatbots compete along with two humans in a series of exchanges managed by a panel of judges. All exchanges are via email messages, and the panel rank-orders the competitors on a scale of humaness. To date, the humans have always come out on top. You can experience for yourself what conversations with some of the top entries are like by accessing them online at

www.alicebot.org,www.abenteuermedien.de/jabberwock, and www.jabberwacky.com.

After a few exchanges with such chatbots, some problems become obvious. They just do not seem to be capable of the normal give-and-take of human conversations. Part of the problem is the way many of them are constructed. Many are based on large data bases sampled from natural conversations, including online versions that cumulate exchanges with persons who link with them. When a query is entered, the system examines its database for a matching string and follows it with the stored response from a previous exchange. In theory, such a system could continue indefinitely, depending on how large the database is, and produce natural-sounding conversations without any semblance of intelligence behind it. An immediate criticism is that humans do not behave that way; many sentences that people produce and use are completely unique, and are based on internal rules of grammar that are used in generating and comprehending novel sentences. Until a natural language program running in real time on a machine can mimic the way that humans learn a language (e.g., by adapting a universal grammar to some particular rules of syntax and interpreting their meaning based on an internal semantic memory system, the Turing test should remain a daunting challenge for years to come (see Friedenberg & Silverman, 2006 for a review).

If (i) the infection is meningitis and (ii) organisms were not seen in the stain of the culture and (iii) the type of infection may be bacterial and (iv) the patient has been seriously burned, then there is suggestive evidence that *Pseudomonas aeruginosa* is one of the organisms that might be causing the infection (Duda & Shortliffe, 1983, p. 262).

The interaction with MYCIN begins with typical case information, including symptoms, and MYCIN asks questions to which the user provides answers or states, "unknown." By eliminating unlikely alternatives and seeking more information about more likely infections, MYCIN eventually arrives at a most likely diagnosis and recommendations for treatment. The strengths of expert systems like MYCIN are the large and ever-increasing knowledge base that includes more information than any one human diagnostician could have or remember, and the inference engine that entertains a variety of hypotheses in parallel without logical problems, like confirmation bias and working-memory limitations that plague human decision makers.

*14.*5 Biotechnology

Humans have used tools for a long time to extend their abilities to provide means for survival and to improve the quality of life. Such tools are not merely products that serve functions, but they become extensions of ourselves:

> "We humans have always been adept at dovetailing our minds and skills to the shape of our current tools and aids. But when those tools and aids start dovetailing back—when our technologies … tailor themselves to us just as we do to them—then the line between tool and user becomes flimsy indeed" (Clark, 2003, p. 7).

Clark goes on to describe a futuristic world in which a variety of wearable and perhaps implanted electronic aids could provide us with a sea of information overlaid on the world as we normally perceive it—an augmented reality.

Biotechnical aids for the handicapped have existed for a long time. Hearing horns and conversation tubes have been replaced by nearly invisible electronic hearing aids, and the same has happened for eyeglasses and their contact-lens replacements. Cases of profound deafness and blindness present different problems, however, as merely increasing the strength or focus of the signal does little if the signal cannot be propagated normally along the sensory channels.

In some cases of deafness, a cochlear implant can bypass middle ear damage and make use of an auditory receiver located externally to drive an internal electronic device that directly stimulates the auditory nerve. In cases of nerve damage, it is even possible to stimulate the brain stem itself, in the region of the ventral cochlear nucleus that lies along the bottom-up auditory pathway. Such stimulation can produce the awareness of sounds that can be interpreted with practice. Similar devices have restored a remarkable degree of vision to people who have become blind after some period of normal sight. In one such device, a pair of glasses fitted with miniature TV cameras and ultrasonic distance detectors feeds a signal to a fanny-pack computer that transmits a signal to a bank of electrodes implanted into the surface of the occipital cortex. The device has enabled a patient to read large letters and negotiate new and unfamiliar environments. Similar visual-to-tactile devices have enabled people with visual handicaps to move about more freely by interpreting signals presented as an array of pinpoints on the back or on the tongue (Bach-y-Rita, Collins, Saunders, White, & Scadden, 1969; Clark, 2003).

Brain implants have also been used to detect signals generated in the brain to control external devices, such as computer interfaces and prosthetic limbs. For example, Kennedy and Bakay (1998) designed a brain implant for a patient completely paralyzed by a brain-stem stroke and suffering from locked-in syndrome. The patient learned to control a computer cursor directly from brain activity. Similar devices implanted in the motor cortex have enabled monkeys as well as a quadriplegic human to learn to control the movements of a robot arm by thinking about it (e.g., Hochberg, Serruya, Friehs, Mukand, Saleh, Caplan, Branner, Chen, Penn, & Donoghue, 2006).

At some level of analysis, all of us are handicapped in many ways. None of us can solve computational problems as quickly as a computer, nor can we sense infrared radiation like a pit viper, ultraviolet radiation like a bumblebee, or magnetic fields as do some migratory birds. Yet, it is possible, through training with direct neural stimulation in response to normally non-sensed information, that we could come to perceive these and other sources of information just as the blind can come to see through tactile stimulation.

In some sense we have already internalized the functions of common devices, and others are certain to come. Clark (2003) used the example of being questioned on the street by a stranger, "Excuse me sir, do you happen to know the time?" Most commonly, one would respond "Yes," and then examine one's watch to answer the question. In this case, the respondent did not actually *know* the time, but the reliance on an external information device that is so easily and rapidly accessed is treated as *equivalent to knowing*. How differently we respond to very similar questions whose answers are not quite so readily available, such as the definition of a rare word or the telephone number of some local business. Although we might be able to look up such information in mere seconds with a dictionary or directory in hand, we nevertheless do not answer "Yes" to the question of knowing if the knowledge is not quite so readily available. Clark imagines a time when such information as definitions, telephone numbers, people's names and other personal information might be accessible quickly to each of us—as rapidly as finding out the time. This could be done through some wearable appliance or intelligent cell phone that could unobtrusively provide information either in response to a query or to a subtle gesture such as the squint of an eye. Then names, numbers, dates, and other information could be provided through miniature displays mounted on one's eyeglasses or through a hidden speaker worn within an ear. Immediately, we would seem to know a lot more and truthfully answer "Yes" to such questions, such as "Do you remember me?" and "Do you know where that new Italian restaurant is?" when in fact we have no idea at all, but the information can be accessed as easily as the time can be determined by a turn of the wrist. To Clark, we are all natural-born cyborgs who are ready to adapt to a new world of wireless connectivity to the electronic media that surround us. We can look forward to sharing our lives with "[P]owerful wearable computers, with wireless communications links and well-tailored, invisible-in-use interfaces ..." (Clark, 2003, p. 153).

Technological improvements in homes could go beyond current prospects of using a cell phone to turn on the lights, open the doors, put on some music, and start the coffee maker. Other applications could include home health care, since:

> "[B]illions of dollars are spent annually taking care of people who didn't take their medicine, or took too much, or took the wrong kind ... the medicine cabinet could monitor the medicine consumption, the toilet could perform routine chemical analyses, both could be connected to the doctor to report aberrations, and to the pharmacy to order refills, delivered by FedEx (along with the milk ordered by the refrigerator and the washing machine's request for soap) ... fewer people would need to be supervised in nursing homes ..."
> (Gershefeld, 1999, p. 235).

On the road, good drivers who operate well-maintained vehicles could be monitored by insurance companies who would qualify them for lower rates. Some drivers could even qualify for higher speed limits, using electronic communication with surveillance devices and patrol cars that sense individual limits and excesses, "Our smart worlds will automatically become smarter and more closely tailored to our individual needs in direct response to our own activities" (Clark, 2003, p. 165). There is enormous potential for a positive interaction between cognition and technology, and unparalleled opportunities for those who seize the initiative. You live in interesting times.

Chapter Summary

Cognitive science has, as one of its aims, the understanding of intelligent behavior in humans and its recreation in artificial systems. It is inherently multidisciplinary because its goals rest on knowledge accumulated in psychology, linguistics, philosophy, anthropology, computer science, biology, neuroscience, and other related disciplines. The fruits of these cooperative labors go beyond gaining an understanding of current conditions and promise developments that should benefit all societies. These include improvements in education, health, the environment, entertainment, safety, global communications, and international relations. Technology can assist us in achieving these aims, but it must be developed with an appreciation of human nature and behavior. Only if a true symbiosis can be melded between people and their technology can the promise of human-technology interaction deliver a bright, new future.

Review Questions

- **How does cognitive psychology fit into the broader field of cognitive science?**

  Cognitive psychology developed as a specialization within experimental psychology with its domain being the explanation of distinctly human behavior based on mental processes anchored in the brain. As such, cognitive psychology acknowledged contributions from neurophysiology and linguistics from its inception. Attempts to develop theories of intelligent behavior demanded inclusion of philosophic inquiry into what it means to be intelligent and whether intelligence is the province of only biological brains or as well of artificial ones. Cognitive science is thus a broadly-based discipline whose aim is the use of converging approaches to the study of human behavior and what it means to be a thinking, creating, and conscious being.

- **What is the difference between traditional human factors and cognitive ergonomics?**

  Human factors psychology began as an applied discipline extending psychological theory to improving performance and safety in the workplace and at home. Its goals were to aid equipment design to improve product functionality, system performance levels, and safety. Initially, the focus of human-technology interfaces was at the sensory-motor level, to insure a proper fit between people and their appendages and the moving parts of tools and equipment. The new field of cognitive ergonomics takes the level of fit one step further by insisting on a fit between the user's model of what the system should be able to do and what functionality it can actually provide. Eventually, not only will the user have a model of the technology, but also the technology should create a model of the user so that it can anticipate user responses and correct user errors. In this way, the technology can become transparent, and the user can focus on task performance rather than on the tool that enables it.

- **How could optimal technology improve education?**

  Educational technology enables the combination of individualized instruction with learning models with the aim of theoretically optimizing knowledge acquisition. That is, rather than relying on classroom instruction in which all people are treated to the same information or relying on individual self-selection of materials for people to educate themselves, educational technology can design more effective learning environments. First, instruction can be individualized around each individual's needs, educational goals, prior knowledge, and ability level. An intelligent teaching module can keep track of individual responses to initial materials and select items based on these responses to achieve the goals of instruction. Further, this selection can be guided by individual past histories in order to maximize learning over time. The maximization principle depends on an adequate model that selects materials that are neither already known (except for an occasional review) nor beyond the current level (except for initial previews) and concentrates on items that stand the maximum chance of producing new, useful knowledge. Research has shown that the methods can work to produce results far superior to standard classroom instruction or personal attempts at self-education.

- **Will machines ever become conscious or more intelligent than we are?**

The answer to this question depends entirely on one's definition of intelligence and consciousness. Consciousness, as described in Chapter 12, is a slippery concept that is intensely personal and subjective. Therefore, it would be speculative at this time to assert one way or the other that, whatever consciousness is, it could someday be replicated in an artificial system. Such systems are, however, becoming more intelligent, in the sense that they can accomplish things that would be considered intelligent if a human did them (such as beating a world chess champion!). New technologies and methods of knowledge representation in network theories promise the development of systems that can learn and, perhaps, replicate improved copies of themselves. It is entirely possible that the province of creative intelligence will not be limited to the human brain itself.

- **What will the future hold for the integration of biology and technology?**

Biology and technology are already integrated in many applications, such as hearing aids, aids for the handicapped, and biomedical devices such as prosthetic devices, pacemakers, and insulin pumps. The explosion of wireless connectivity that is upon us, along with miniaturization of intelligent appliances, promises a future world in which we all will be connected to each other, and to huge information and data banks at all times, should we choose to do so. The future holds tremendous promise for improvement in the quality of life through the judicious application of wireless technology. At the same time there are legitimate worries about the loss of privacy, security, and individuality that such interconnectedness could engender. There is a real need for cognitive science to take the initiative to direct technology toward applications that improve the human condition while being aware of the pitfalls of degradation, intrusion, information overload, and alienation that can result from using technology to separate people from one another rather than bringing them together.

Key Terms

Expert systems   376

Glossary

A

Absent-mindedness The tendency to forget daily activities, often soon after they have occurred; most likely due to inadequate storage of the information in the first place, probably due to distraction or lack of attention to the original event or behavior **219**

Agnosia The loss of certain perceptual abilities, such as the ability to name objects or faces or the ability to see motion or color, due to localized brain damage **81**

Algorithm A fixed, sometimes exhaustive or brute-force method of solving a problem, that is guaranteed to produce a solution if it is properly applied to any problem **304**

Alzheimer's disease This is a progressive form of dementia that is the prominent cause of senility among elderly adults. There are probably several different types and causes of the disorder, and it is characterized by abnormal protein growth including plaques in synapses and tangles within neurons that interfere with their functions and eventually cause cell death in widespread areas throughout the brain **350**

Analogical reasoning A type of reasoning that takes the form A is to B as C is to D (formally, A:B::C:D); concrete items are typically provided for A, B, and C, whereas D is left blank. The analogy can theoretically be solved by inducing the relationship between A and B, applying this relationship to C, and mapping it onto D (e.g.,cow:buffalo:: dog:wolf maps out a possible domestication relation) **300**

Anterograde amnesia The loss of ability to form new memories after some traumatic event **152**

Area MT The medial temporal gyrus of the cortex; an area that has many cells that are sensitive to the speed and direction of motion **134**

Associationism The idea that much of our knowledge and behavior can be reduced to simple associations among stimuli, their representations in memory, and responses **5**

Attentional blink (AB) The finding that if two targets are present in an RSVP stream, the second target is frequently missed if it follows too closely on the heels of the first target **140**

Attention A process that selects information from the environment and from memory for entry into limited-capacity conscious awareness **118**

Availability heuristic The tendency for a choice in a decision or problem-solving task to be made from among alternatives that are most readily available in memory **312**

B

Bálint's syndrome Also called simultagnosia; it is most commonly due to bilateral damage to the parietal lobes. Patients with this syndrome usually report seeing only one object at a time, even when many objects are presented simultaneously. **110**

Belief bias The willingness to accept a conclusion as valid based on one's own knowledge or beliefs rather than on the basis of rules of logical argument **295**

Blindsight The ability for a person with no functioning visual cortex to report certain aspects of visual stimuli correctly, even though they deny conscious awareness of the stimuli **331**

Blocking The inability to recall to mind some fact that is actually stored in memory (It most commonly occurs for names of people and things.) **220**

Bootstrapping The use of partial knowledge in some domain to retrieve or create additional knowledge, such as using a loop at a back of a boot to help to pull it on **247**

Bottom-up processes Processes usually determined only from sensory analysis of the stimulus (also called "data-driven" processes), although they can also be affected by the observer's adaptation level (e.g., number of minutes in the dark) and amount of attention directed to the stimulus   **71**

Broca's area Typically in the left frontal lobe near the temporal lobe that controls speech and expressive language; damage to this region produces Broca's aphasia, which is characterized by the inability to speak   **50**

Brown-Peterson paradigm An experimental procedure designed to study forgetting in short-term memory by preventing the subjects from rehearsing the material during the retention interval; usually done by having them do a rehearsal-prevention task, such as counting backwards aloud   **159**

C

Canonical view of an object the most common view of an object, the one that we most typically envision when generating an image of that object, and the one that is most rapidly recognized when an object is presented.   **95**

Cataract A gradual clouding of the lens of the eye that occurs in most people as they age (If severe enough to significantly impair vision, the lens can be removed and replaced with an artificial lens)   **348**

Categorical perception The tendency to perceive continuous changes in speech sounds as shifts between discrete categories, perhaps unique to the perception of speech (Discrimination is poor within categories but good between categories for equivalent physical differences between sounds)   **238**

Central executive The process that directs and monitors activity in the three processing and storage components of Baddeley's working memory theory; namely the articulatory loop, the visuo-spatial scratchpad, and the episodic buffer   **171**

Classical (Pavlovian) conditioning The learned association between two stimuli due to repeated reinforced pairings (A bell followed by food leads to salivation to the bell alone.)   **14**

Coarticulation effects The effect that the preceding and following speech context has on the way that any speech element is articulated (e.g., the difference between the vowel sounds in "bat" and "can" are fairly large, but the vowel is classified as the same phoneme)   **244**

Cochlea The fluid-filled, structure shaped like a snail's shell in the inner ear that contains hair cells embedded in a membrane that spans its length (The hair cells are the receptor (transducer) cells for hearing in that they convert sound vibrations into neural impulses.)   **39**

Cognitive economy A principle adopted by Collins and Quillian (1969) in their network model of semantic memory; asserts that any property that is true of more than one concept node in the hierarchy should be stored only at the highest-level (i.e., most general) node in the network over which the property is found   **191**

Cognitive psychology The study of how the human brain produces mental activity and observable behavior   **2**

Competence-performance distinction The idea that we all behave as if we have an internal grammatical system that is capable of distinguishing between grammatical and ungrammatical sentences, but our actual language use often falls short in production and comprehension, mainly due to working memory limitations   **266**

Concepts Abstract entities in memory that are formed through repeated experiences with examples of various categories of things (e.g., we all have a concept for "bird" that is based on our experiences with various members of the bird category)   **248**

Confirmation bias The tendency for people to seek out information consistent with their beliefs and to avoid or ignore things inconsistent with their beliefs   **292**

Conjunction search The search for a target object that differs from the background distractors by a unique combination of features that are individually present among the distractors; search time increases linearly with the number of distractors in the display   **129**

Consciousness The subjective feeling that we have an inner self that experiences the physical world, recalls past experiences, and acts as an agent in making decisions and carrying them out **119**

D

Decay theory of forgetting A theory of forgetting in which information in memory is supposed to spontaneously decrease as time passes **161**

Declarative memories Things that are learned and retrieved with awareness and intention, and their retrieval promotes verbal descriptions of their contents; both semantic and episodic memories are declarative memories **204**

Declarative memory Memory for concepts and events that have been stored in long-term memory and can be consciously retrieved and described verbally; typically divided into semantic memory (for words and concepts) and episodic memory (for life-time events), as described in Chapter 7 **153**

Deductive reasoning Deriving specific conclusions from general principles, such as in generating research hypotheses from a theory **293**

Deep structure Chomsky's original term for the level of meaning representationthat underlies language **268**

Dorsal visual pathway The pathway linking the occipital lobes to the parietal lobes of the cortex (It has been called the "where" pathway because of its role in spatial processing in vision.) **39**

Dualism The belief that the mind and the body are different, and that mental processes cannot be reduced to biology alone **320**

Dyslexia The inability to learn to read at an appropriate level despite adequate educational opportunities, normal or higher intelligence, and lack of relevant physical handicaps; a specific reading disability **276**

E

EEG Electroencephalography, or the recording of electrical activity of large groups of neurons in the brain ("brain waves") through electrodes placed at various locations on the scalp **43**

Emergent property A property of some combination of parts that cannot be predicted by the respective properties of the parts themselves, such as the fact that sand can be poured like a liquid, yet its individual particles are solid **321**

Empiricism The idea that much of our knowledge and behavior is learned through experience **4**

Encoding The process of representing external stimuli by internal codes for possible entry into STM **152**

Endogenous attention The top-down, voluntary direction of attention toward information that is likely to be related to one's goals or needs **126**

Epiphenomenon A consequence of some occurrence or event that has no function or necessity, and no explanatory value for the event that caused it **323**

Episodic buffer The theoretical storage component of working memory that integrates currently active information and related information retrieved from long-term memory into a coherent representation of current activity **171**

Episodic memory The personal memory of our experiences, according to Tulving's (1972) theory; it records events with date and setting information, and as such it is unique to each of us **187**

ERP Event-related potential or changes in EEG patterns as a direct result of the presentation of some stimulus; these usually occur within 50 to 1000 ms after stimulus onset **43**

Exogenous The bottom-up, automatic attraction of attention to a salient aspect of the environment, most certainly to a sudden sound or the sudden appearance of a new object **126**

Expected value theory The theory that people's decision making is influenced by the actual values of the possible outcomes, weighted by their actual probabilities **310**

Expert systems Programs that are designed to mimic or improve on the abstract thinking, reasoning, and logical skills that people use to solve problems **376**

F

Feature analysis A step in a theory of pattern recognition in which an object is analyzed into its component features, which are then compared with stored lists of features representing object concepts in memory **61**

Feature search The search for a target object that differs from the background distractors by a single, salient feature; the target appears to pop out, and search time is independent of the number of distractors in the display **129**

Filter theory of attention Broadbent's theory that there is an early filter placed between most sensory channels and perceptual awareness, such that typically only one information source at a time is channelled into conscious awareness and working memory; contrasted with late filter theories that allow selection after information has been channelled to long-term memory for identification **120**

First-order isomorphism for imagery The idea that images exist as "pictures" in the head to be examined with the mind's eye much as objects are examined with our actual eyes **97**

Flashbulb memories Presumably special types of memories for events that are particularly vivid and memorable that include the details of when and where people were when they learned of the event, who was present, and other details of the situation and events; most commonly associated with momentous or shocking events, such as personal tragedies or disasters of international importance **216**

fMRI Functional magnetic resonance imaging; a technique for measuring brain activity indirectly by comparing BOLD (blood oxygen-level dependent) differences observed in two tasks that differ by a single component. Excitatory and inhibitory processes involved in the task difference are revealed in false-color images. **45**

Frontal lobes The front parts of the brain extending back from above the eyes to the parietal and temporal lobe boundaries; responsible to control motor activities, including speech and eye movements, and are responsible for executive functions, such as planning and execution of sequential activities; also strongly influence judgment, decision-making, and personality **49**

G

Generative grammar This is based on internal rules that presumably construct phrase structures from a deep level of meaning in the mind. These phrase structures are then filled in with words that can be uttered. The process is reversed to generate meaning from surface structures (i.e., speech or writing) **264**

Gestalt principles A descriptive set of rules that perception seems to follow in order to force the simplest, most symmetric, and most likely interpretation of sensory input, including grouping features by proximity, similarity, good continuation, common fate motion, and others **70**

Glaucoma An increase in pressure in the fluid within the eye that can cause blindness by injuring the optic nerve; can be successfully treated with drugs or surgery if detected in time **348**

H

Hemianopia The loss of vision on one side of the visual field due to damage in the visual centers of the brain in one hemisphere **108**

Heurisitcs Rules of thumb that might lead to a relatively quick decision or a solution to a problem, but it might not produce the best result if more information and time are available **304**

Hippocampus Small, curved structures on either side of the thalamus that are part of the medial temporal lobes of the cortex; they seem to be of fundamental importance to the learning and permanent consolidation of new long-term (declarative) memories **153**

Holophrase The use of a single word to express a meaningful proposition, characteristic of speech in the 12- to 18-month-old toddler **254**

Hypermnesia The tendency in repeated recollections of a certain event or story to introduce things present in the original that were not recalled in earlier retellings **201**

I

Illicit conversion An unwarranted inference made from a premise, such as converting "All A are B" to "All B are A" or "Some A are B" to "Some A are not B" **295**

Illusory conjunctions According to FIT, features that are not bound together by focal attention can be combined incorrectly, and subjects might report seeing objects that were not actually present **129**

Inductive reasoning Deriving general principles from specific observations, such as in building a theory from data **293**

Infant-directed speech (IDS) The speech typically directed by adults to very young children that is characterized by high pitch, exaggerated intonation changes, simple syntax, common words, and references to the here and now **255**

Inferotemporal cortex Part of the temporal cortex located in the lower part of primate brains that plays a role in visual object recognition; it includes thousands of cells that are tuned to a variety of idiosyncratic shapes **64**

Inhibition-deficit hypothesis A theory of cognitive aging proposed by Hasher & Zacks that attributes one of the difficulties that older persons have with the inability to ignore irrelevant information, such as in trying to follow a specific conversation at a noisy party **119**

Interference theory of forgetting A theory of forgetting in which information is made more difficult to retrieve due to the destructive effects of similar information that gets in the way during memory search and decision processes **161**

Introspection The subjective study of one's own mental processes by looking inward into oneself **13**

L

Lateral geniculate nuclei Layered bundles of neurons on the sides of the thalamus that receive inputs from the optic nerve and send outputs to the occipital cortex in the back of the brain. The LGN also receives inputs from several cortical areas **36**

Lateral inhibition The tendency of active neurons to inhibit their neighbors; in vision, this process has been shown to enhance the perception of edges **39**

Lavie's perceptual load theory The idea that easy perceptual tasks result in irrelevant information being processed deeply, requiring late selection; whereas difficult perceptual tasks result in early selection and filtering of irrelevant information. **131**

Levels-of-processing theory A theory developed by Craik and Lockhart in which the degree of long-term storage is determined more by the type of rehearsal than the amount of rehearsal; deep (e.g., semantic) levels of processing promote better learning and recall than do shallow (e.g., phonemic) levels **168**

M

Macular degeneration A gradual form of blindness that begins with cell death in the macula of the eye, an area that includes the central fovea; progressive and eventually causes total blindness in either eye; presently no known treatment **348**

Magnetoencephalography (MEG) A brain imaging technique that records the activity of groups of neurons by measuring the magnetic fields that they produce when electrical impulses travel through them; it gives high resolution of both where and when this activity occurs in the brain during performance of some task **47**

Materialism The belief that mental activity can ultimately be reduced to biology, chemistry, and physics **321**

McGurk effect The tendency to integrate visual and auditory information from a speaker, such that if the two are in conflict, the listener "hears" an intermediate speech sound. **87**

Mentalism The belief that the only reality in the world is due to the activity in the mind   **320**

Metacognitive awareness The ability to introspect on one's own processes involved in perception, memory, language, reasoning, and other cognitions (This skill improves in childhood and allows the development of certain strategies that augment cognitive abilities)   **344**

Metamemory The ability to look into one's own memory strengths and weaknesses and to monitor one's level of memory for something (For example, one could decide when something has been studied enough to insure future recall—prospective memory.)   **345**

Misinformation effect The inadvertent combination of information from two or more different sources into a false memory of a single event; for example, information learned after an event can change the memory of the original event   **223**

Modularity a characteristic of sensory channels in which different individual or bundles of neurons respond to different specific aspects of a stimulus; e.g., in vision, there are separate modules for location, orientation, color, motion, and size (or spatial frequency).   **80**

Modus ponens One of the conclusions in conditional reasoning that follows from first assuming that the premise "If A, then B" is true—if A occurs, then B must occur   **297**

Modus tollens The other conclusion in conditional reasoning that follows from first assuming that the premise "If A, then B" is true—if B does not occur, then A did not occur   **297**

Morpheme The smallest meaningful unit in a language, consisting of all or part of a word (For example "cat" and "rest" have one morpheme each, "cats" and "rested" have two each)   **271**

Multi-attribute utility theory The theory that a decision can be based on the weighted sum of all possible outcomes along the various dimensions of a problem   **311**

Multidimensional feature model A model proposed by Smith et al. (1974) as an alternative to network; representing concepts, such as locations in a space, in which the dimensions are different aspects of meaning (semantic primitives), and features are the specific values that any concept has on the various dimensions   **194**

N

Nativism The idea that much of our knowledge and behavior is inborn or biologically programmed to develop in a certain way   **4**

Network model A structural description of some domain (e.g., a part of semantic memory; Collins & Quillian, 1969) in which concepts are represented by nodes that are connected to other nodes via relational links; subsequent processing assumptions can include activation that spreads through the network from an input node along the links to other nodes in a diminishing wave of excitation   **189**

Neuron A specialized cell in the nervous system that has three main parts, namely a cell body that includes the nucleus, branching fibers called dendrites that receive inputs from other neurons, and an axon fiber that ends in branches that release transmitter substances to communicate with other neurons   **30**

Non-declarative memories Things that are learned and retrieved without awareness and intention, such as perceptual-motor skills, biases, habitual responses and value judgments   **204**

Normalize The tendency to change characters, settings, and events in recall of a story to make them more consistent with one's own knowledge, beliefs, and cultural norms   **201**

O

Occipital lobes The lobes of the cerebral cortex that are in the far, back part of the head; they receive input from the eyes via the thalamus and are concerned exclusively with vision and visual imagery **36**

Operant (Skinnerian) conditioning A learned association between a stimulus and a response due to reinforced practice (A bar press followed by a food pellet increases the probability of a bar press in the future.) **14**

Orthography The written form of a language **273**

P

Paivio's dual-coding theory A theory of memory that proposes different stored representations for verbal materials (e.g., words) and imaginal information (e.g., pictures) **99**

Parietal lobes The back, upper parts of the brain that are responsible for spatial and tactile perception and directing spatial orienting, attention, and reaching **39**

Perception The interpretation of a sensory message, based on memory of past experiences, and its entry into conscious awareness **60**

PET Positron-emission tomography; a method of determining which brain areas are most active in performing some task. Radioactive tracers attached to nutrient molecules are injected into the bloodstream and are taken up by active neurons in the brain. Brain images from radioactive decay detectors then reveal differential patterns of activity involved in the task. **45**

Phonics The grapheme-phoneme correspondences in words of a language **274**

Phonological loop The theoretical processing component of working memory that rehearses and manipulates verbal information **171**

Phonology The study of the sound structure of human languages, including how different speech sounds, or phones, are grouped into categories of equivalent sounds, called phonemes, in different languages **243**

Phrase structure The hierarchical organization of a sentence into noun and verb phrases, then into lower-level phrases, and finally the individual words **267**

Preattentive stage Iin FIT, it is essentially the information available in sensory (e.g., iconic) memory. The features are briefly available in different modules or "feature maps" of the environment that are registered and maintained in parallel. **126**

Presbycusis The loss in hearing acuity, mainly associated with aging, that applies mostly to higher-frequency sounds **347**

Presbyopia The loss in visual acuity, mainly associated with aging, that occurs mostly for near objects **348**

Primacy effect The tendency for material presented early in a list to be recalled better than material presented in the middle of a list; usually found both in immediate and delayed free recall tasks **165**

Primary memory A term used by James to describe the current contents of consciousness; the terms short-term memory (STM) or working memory are more commonly used today for similar concepts of a limited-capacity immediate memory **152**

Priming The effect that any stimulus (prime) has on the speed or accuracy of responding to another stimulus (target) that is presented at the same time as the prime or later; effects on the target can either be beneficial (positive priming) or detrimental (negative priming) (Priming can also be perceptual —prime and target related in form—or conceptual—prime and target related in meaning or associated to each other.) **195**

Proactive interference (PI) The negative effects of information learned at some prior time on learning and retention of later information **162**

Procedural memory Memory for sensory-motor skills and other behaviors that have been learned and can be retrieved without conscious awareness **155**

Proposition The smallest unit of meaning that can be true or false (For example, a proposition can be most simply represented by two concepts and a relation between them, such as "A bird is an animal" or "A rhinoceros is a bird.") **100**

Prosody Changes in speech sounds that are important for phrase and sentence meaning that are not part of the phonemic structure of a language, including intonation, rhythm, and stress   247

Prospective memory The deliberate attempt to do something in the present that should help us to remember to carry out some action in the future; depends on the use of various reminder cues based on future times or events that should trigger the desired memory   219

Psychophysics The study of the lawful relation between some physical property of a stimulus and the psychologically perceived property   11

- -

R

Rationalism The idea that much of our knowledge and behavior is created by mental activities alone and is the sole product of neither inheritance nor environment   4

Recency effect The tendency for material presented near the end of the list to be recalled better than material in the middle of a list; usually found in immediate free recall only   165

Receptive field (of a neuron) The specific location and type of stimulus that must be presented in order to observe a change in firing rate (excitation or inhibition) of a nerve cell in a sensory system   39

Recognition-by-components Biederman's theory of object recognition based on use of a set of "geons," or geometric solid primitives, that are components of all natural and artificial objects   76

Reference The use of a symbol, such as a word, to represent a physical object or event   250

Representativeness heuristic The tendency for a choice in a decision or problem-solving task to be made from alternatives that more closely match our expectations of what the average outcome should be like   311

Retrieval The process of finding codes in LTM and entering them into STM   152

Retroactive interference (RI) The negative effects of information recently learned on retrieval of information learned earlier   163

Retrograde amnesia The loss of memory for information learned prior to some traumatic event   152

RSVP (rapid, serial visual presentation) This is the presentation of a succession of different visual stimuli to a single, central point in the field of view. Rates of presentation can vary, but they usually are set at about 100 ms per item (10 items/sec) to prevent masking found at faster rates and naming and rehearsal likely at higher rates. Items typically are seen clearly enough to be identified, but are gone too quickly to be consolidated into memory.   138

- -

S

Savings The most sensitive measure of memory, developed by Ebbinghaus; the reduction in time to learn something a second time given that it was once learned earlier   11

Savings The most sensitive measure of memory yet devised; the time it takes to learn something a first time, minus the time taken to learn something the second time, divided by the time to learn it the first time, multiplying the result by 100 yields the percentage of savings   213

Schemata Theoretical structures in semantic memory that have developed to represent commonly-occurring objects and events, such as stories, maps or routes for familiar journeys, and layouts of familiar structures, such as faces, kitchens, buildings, and gardens   199

Scotomas Literally, "holes" in the visual field caused by damage to areas in the occipital lobe; since the visual field is mapped out over the occipital cortex localized brain damage produces loss of vision in the corresponding part of the visual field   52

Scripts Theoretical structures in semantic memory that have developed to represent commonly-occurring sequences of events, such as dining out at a restaurant or attending a theater, lecture, or party   199

Secondary memory A term used by James to describe all other memories, from which retrieval is sometimes difficult and always uncertain; the term long-term memory (LTM) is more commonly used today for the more-or-less permanent and practically infinite storage system for all our knowledge   152

Second-order isomorphism for imagery The idea that whatever images are in the mind can be manipulated with mental processes in an analogous way to how objects are manipulated in our hands **97**

Segmentation The imposition of groupings into words and phrases by the listener on the more-or-less continuous stream of sounds emitted by a speaker **244**

Semantic congruity effect The fact that judgments of the smaller two small objects and the larger of two large objects are faster than judgments of the smaller between two large objects and the larger between two small objects **293**

Semantic memory The permanent repository of all general knowledge in memory, according to Tulving's (1972) theory; the basis of understanding the meanings of objects, events, words, and sentences, as well as the basis of mathematical and encyclopedic knowledge **187**

Semantics How meaning is represented by words and their syntactic groupings in a language **247**

Sensation Activity in the peripheral and central nervous systems that results directly from physical stimulation **31**

Subjective expected utility theory The theory that people's decision making is influenced by the subjective utilities of the possible outcomes, weighted by their subjective probabilities **310**

Subliminal perception The idea that stimuli can result in sensations that are perceived below the conscious level of awareness, yet nevertheless can influence our current or later behavior **320**

Subliminal priming The effect of some stimulus (the prime) on the response to a subsequent stimulus (the target), even though the prime is presented too briefly or under such illegible conditions that it cannot be recognized or even result in awareness that it occurred **324**

Subtractive method A method of using differences in response times to measure the duration of mental processes (If two tasks differ in only one step, then their RT difference is equal to the time it takes to carry out that step.) **6**

Superior colliculi A pair of structures situated near the top of the brain stem that receives a small part of the output from the optic nerve, they play no role in conscious vision in humans, but can direct attention and eye movements to new or interesting objects **36**

Surface structure The actual set of words spoken or written that make up a sentence or longer sample of language **267**

Syllogism A form of logical argument in which two premises are given and assumed to be true, from which a conclusion is offered that may or may not be logically deduced from the premises **294**

Symbolic distance effect The fact that a relative judgment can be made faster between two symbols that represent objects that differ widely on the dimension being judged than between two symbols that represent objects having a smaller difference **293**

Synapses The tiny spaces between the axon terminals of one neuron and the dendrites of another; when a spike is propagated along an axon, it releases neural transmitters when it reaches the terminals; these can either excite or inhibit subsequent neurons when the transmitters are absorbed into the dendrites **30**

Syntax The structural rules for how words in a language are arranged into hierarchical groupings in phrases and sentences **247**

T

Telegraphic speech Characteristic of the first two- and three-word utterances of 2-year-olds who tend to omit function words, such as articles, prepositions, and conjunctions **255**

Template matching A step in a theory of pattern recognition in which an image of an object is compared holistically with stored patterns representing object concepts in memory **62**

Temporal lobes The lobes of the cerebral cortex that are located in the sides of the head, inward from the ears, that receive auditory inputs and are important for understanding the meaning of sights and sounds, including spoken and written words **38**

Thalamus A bilateral structure in the center of the brain, between the brainstem and the cortex that serves as a relay station for all senses except olfaction, and has a large amount of two-way communication with the cerebral cortex   **36**

Tip-of-the tongue (TOT) state The subjective experience that sometimes occurs while blocking; that the desired word to be recalled is literally "on the tip of the tongue" in that aspects of it such as its initial letter, number of syllables, vowels sounds, and aspects of meaning might be readily available, but its exact articulation cannot at that moment be produced   **221**

Top-down processes Those aspects of perception that use information beyond what is in the stimulus alone, such as the context in which it occurs and any prior knowledge about it retrieved from memory   **74**

Transcranial magnetic stimulation A method of stimulating specific areas of the brain by placing a strong magnetic field over the surface of the skull; can temporarily disrupt neural activity in the stimulated area, producing stroke-like effects that can be used to study brain function   **48**

Transduction The conversion of external, physical sources of energy into internal biochemical and electrical activity by sensory receptor cells   **31**

Transience The general tendency for memories of daily events to decline with time; although some events seem to be retained with great clarity, the majority seem to gradually fade away   **218**

Typicality effect The fact that some members of a category are judged to be better exemplars of a category than are other members; also reflected in speed of judgments (e.g., "A fox is a mammal" is judged to be true faster than "A whale is a mammal")   **192**

V

Venn diagrams (also called Euler circles) A set-theoretic notational system using circles to represent the meanings of qualitative relationships (e.g., "all," "some," or "none") among sets   **295**

Ventral visual pathway The pathway linking the occipital lobes to the temporal lobes of the cortex (It has been called the "what" pathway because of its role in object identification and naming.)   **39**

Ventriloquist effect The tendency to perceive an auditory stimulus as coming from the same location as a visual stimulus, even if they occur in separate locations; the visual capture of perceived auditory location is stronger the closer they occur together in time   **87**

Vigilance The attempt to maintain attention at a high level of focus on a single task for extended periods of time   **138**

Visual neglect A result most typically of damage to the right parietal lobe that causes an inability to attend to the contralateral (left) visual field as well as to the left sides of imagined objects or scenes   **108**

Visuo-spatial scratchpad The theoretical processing component of working memory that rehearses and manipulates visual images and spatial information   **171**

Voice onset time (VOT) The delay (if any) between the beginning of a speech sound and the vibration of the vocal cords, being about 0 ms for voiced consonants in syllables like [*ba*] and 25 ms or more for unvoiced consonants in syllables like [*pa*]   **245**

W

Weber's law The observation that the just noticeable difference (jnd) in stimulus intensity is a constant proportion of stimulus intensity throughout most of the intensity scale   **10**

Wernicke's area An area typically in the left temporal lobe near the temporal-parietal junction that controls language perception and comprehension; damage to this area produces loss of language understanding   **51**

References

A

Ackil, J. K., & Zaragoza, M. S. (1998). Memorial consequences of forced confabulation: Age differences in susceptibility to false memories. *Developmental Psychology*, 34, 1358-1372.

Adams, J. A., (1967). *Human Memory.* New York: McGraw-Hill.

Adams, M. J. (1990). *Beginning to Read: Thinking and Learning about Print.* Cambridge, MA: MIT Press.

Aglioti, S., Goodale, M. A., & DeSouza, J. F. X. (1995). Size contrast illusions deceive the eye but not the hand. *Current Biology*, 5, 679-685.

Aitchinson, J. (1994). *Words in the Mind: An Introduction to the Mental Lexicon* (2ⁿᵈ ed.). Oxford, England: Blackwell.

Alkire, M. T., Haier, R. J., Fallon, J. H., & Cahill, L. (1998). Hippocampal, but not amygdala, activity at encoding correlates with long-term free recall of nonemotional information. *Proceedings of the National Academy of Sciences, USA*, 95, 14506-14510.

Alvarez, G. A., & Cavanagh, P. (2004). The capacity of visual short-term memory is set both by visual information load and by number of objects. *Psychological science*, 15, 106-111.

Amer, T., & Hasher, L. (2014). Conceptual processing of distractors by older but not younger adults. *Psychological Science*, 25, 2252-2258.

Andersen, R. A., Snyder, L. H., Bradley, D. C., & Xing, J. (1997). Multimodal representation of space in the posterior parietal cortex and its use in planning movements. *Annual Review of Neuroscience*, 20, 303-330.

Anderson, J. R. (1983). *The Architecture of Cognition.* Cambridge, MA: Harvard University Press.

Anderson, J. R. (2000). *Cognitive Psychology and its Implications*, 5ᵗʰ Ed., New York: Worth.

Anderson, J. R., & Bower, G. H. (1973). *Human Associative Memory.* Washington, DC: Winston.

Anderson, J.R., & Reiser, B.J. (1985). The LISP tutor. *Byte*, 10, 159-175.

Appel, L. F., Cooper, R. G., McCarrell, N. Sims-Knight, J., Yussen, S. R., & Flavell, J. H. (1972). The development of the distinction between perceiving and memorizing. *Child Development*, 43, 1365-1381.

Arbib, M. A. (2005). From monkey-like action recognition to human language: An evolutionary framework for neurolinguistics. *Behavioral and Brain Sciences*, 28, 105-167.

Arman, A.C., Ciaramitaro, V.M., & Boynton, G.M. (2006). Effects of feature-based attention on the motion after effect at remote locations. *Vision Research*, 46, 2968-2976.

Ashcraft, M. H. (1989). *Human Memory and Cognition.* Glenview: IL: Scott Foresman.

Atkinson, R. C. (1972). Ingredients for a theory of instruction. *American Psychologist*, 27, 921-931.

Atkinson, R. C. (1974). Teaching children to read using a computer. *American Psychologist*, 29, 169-178.

Atkinson, R. C., Holmgren, J. E., & Juola, J. F. (1969). Processing time as influenced by the number of elements in a visual display. *Perception & Psychophysics*, 6, 321-326.

Atkinson, R. C., & Juola, J. F. (1973). Factors influencing speed and accuracy of word recognition. In S. Kornblum (Ed.), *Attention and Performance IV.* New York: Academic Press.

Atkinson, R. C., & Juola, J. F. (1974). Search and decision processes in recognition memory. In D. H. Krantz, R. C. Atkinson, R. D. Luce, & P. Suppes (Eds.), *Contemporary Developments in Mathematical Psychology* (Vol. 1). San Francisco: Freeman.

Atkinson, R. C., and Shiffrin, R. M. (1968). Human memory: A proposed system and its control processes. In K. W. Spence & J. T. Spence (Eds.), *The Psychology of Learning and Motivation: Advances in Research and Theory* (Vol. 2), New York: Academic Press.

Atkinson, R. C., and Shiffrin, R. M. (1971). The control of short-term memory. *Scientific American*, 224, 82-90.

Awh, E. & Jonides, J. (2001) Overlapping mechanisms of attention and spatial working memory. *Trends in Cognitive Science*, 5, 119–126.

Awh, E., Jonides, J., & Reuter-Lorenz, P. A. (1998). Rehearsal in spatial working memory. *Journal of Experimental Psychology: Human Perception and Performance*, 24, 780–790.

B

Baars, B. J. (1988). *A Cognitive Theory of Consciousness.* Cambridge, MA: MIT Press.

Baars, B. J. (2007). Attention and consciousness. In B. J. Baars and N. M. Gage (Eds.) *Cognition, Brain, and Consciousness.* Amsterdam: Elsevier.

Bach-y-Rita, P., Collins, C. C., Saunders, F. A., White, B., & Scadden, (1969). Vision substitution by tactile image projection. *Nature*, 221, 963-964.

Baddeley, A. D. (1986). *Working Memory.* Oxford: Oxford University Press.

Baddeley, A. D. (1990). *Human Memory: Theory and Practice.* Boston: Allyn and Bacon.

Baddeley, A. D. (1992). Working memory, *Science*, 255, 556-559.

Baddeley, A. D. (2000). The episodic buffer: A new component of working memory? *Trends in Cognitive Science*, 4, 417-423.

Baddeley, A. D., & Hitch, G. (1974). Working memory. In G. H. Bower (Ed.). *The Psychology of Learning and Motivation* (Vol. 8). New York: Academic Press.

Baddeley, A. D., Thomson, N., & Buchanan, M. (1975). Word length and the structure of short-term memory. *Journal of Verbal Learning and Verbal Behavior*, 14, 575-589.

Bahrick, H. P. (1979). Maintenance of knowledge: Questions about memory we forgot to ask. *Journal of Experimental Psychology: General*, 104, 54-75.

Bahrick, H. P. (1984). Fifty years of second language attrition: Implications for programmatic research. *Modern Language Journal*, 68, 105-118.

Bahrick, H. P., Bahrick, P. O. & Wittlinger, R. P. (1975). Fifty years of memory for names and faces: A cross-sectional approach. *Journal of Experimental Psychology: General*, 104, 54-75.

Bailey, H.R., Zacks, J.M., Hambrick, D.Z. Zacks, R.T., Head,D., Kurby, C.A., & Sargent, J.Q. (2013). Medial temporal lobe volume predicts elders' everyday memory. *Psychological Science*, 24, 1113-1122.

Baldwin, D. A. (1991). Infants' contribution to the achievement of joint reference. *Child Development*, 62, 875-890.

Baldwin, D. A. (1993). Early referential understanding: Infants' ability to recognize referential acts for what they are. *Developmental Psychology*, 29, 832-843.

Bálint, R. (1909). Seelenlähmung des 'Schauens', optische Ataxie, raümlich Störung der Aufmerksamkeit. *Monatschrift Psychiatrisches Neurolgie*, 25, 51-81.

Bar-Hillel, M., & Falk, R. (1982). Some teasers concerning conditional probabilities. *Cognition*, 11, 109-122.

Baron, J. (1988). *Thinking and Deciding.* Cambridge, England: Cambridge University Press.

Baron-Cohen, S. (1995). *Mindblindness: An Essay on Autism and Theory of Mind.* Cambridge, MA: MIT Press.

Bartlett, F. C. (1932/1967). *Remembering: A Study in Experimental and Social Psychology.* Cambridge, England: Cambridge University Press

Bauer, P. J. (2008). Toward a neuro-developmental account the development of declarative memory. *Developmental Psychobiology*, 50, 19-31.

Bayliss, D., Jarrold, C., Gunn, D., & Baddeley, A. (2003). The complexities of complex span: Explaining individual differences in working memory in children and adults. *Journal of Experimental Psychology: General*, 132, 71-92.

Belli, R. F. (1989). Influences of misleading post-event information: Misinformation interference and acceptance. *Journal of Experimental Psychology: General*, 118, 72-85.

Benson, D. F., & Miller, B. L. (2000). Frontal lobes 1: Clinical and anatomic issues. In M. J. Farah & T. D. Feinberg (Eds.), *Patient-Based Approaches to Cognitive Neuroscience.* Cambridge, MA: MIT Press.

Berlucchi, G., & Aglioti, S. (1997). The body in the brain: Neural bases of corporeal awareness. *Trends in Neuroscience*, 12, 560-564.

Best, C. T., & McRoberts, G. W. (1989). Phonological influences on the perception of native and non-native speech contrasts. Paper presented at the Biennial Meeting of the Society for Research in Child Development, Kansas City, MO.

Bialystok, E., (2005). Consequences of bilingualism for cognitive development. In J. F. Kroll, & A. M. de Groot (Eds.), *Handbook of Bilingualism: Psycholinguistic Approaches.* New York: Oxford University Press.

Bichot, N. P., Rossi, A. F., & Desimone, R. (2005). Parallel and serial neural mechanisms for visual search in macaque area V4. *Science*, 308, 529-534

Bickerton, D. (1981). *Roots of Language.* Ann Arbor, MI: Karoma.

Biederman, I. (1987). Recognition by components: A theory of human image understanding. *Psychological Review*, 94, 115-147.

Biederman, I. & Cooper, E. E. (1991). Priming contour-deleted images: Evidence for intermediate representations in visual object recognition. *Cognitive Psychology*, 23, 393-419.

Biederman, I., Cooper, E. E., Hummel, J. E., & Fiser, J. (1993). Geon theory as an account of shape recognition in mind, brain, and machine. In J. Illingworth (Ed.), *Proceedings of the Fourth British Machine Vision Conference* (pp. 175-186). Guildford, Surrey, U.K.: BMVA Press.

Birren J. E., & Fisher, L. M. (1995). Aging and speed of behavior: Its central nature and physiological correlates. *Review of Psychology*, 46, 329-353.

Bisiach, E., & Luzzatti, C. (1978). Unilateral neglect of representational space. Cortex, 26,307-317.

Blackmore, S. (2004). *Consciousness: An Introduction.* New York: Oxford University Press.

Blakemore, C. (1977). Mechanics of the Mind. Cambridge, England: Cambridge University Press.

Blakemore, C., & Cooper, G. G. (1970). Development of the brain depends on the visual environment. *Nature*, 228, 477-478.

Block, H. D. (1962). The perception: A model for brain functioning, 1. *Reviews of Modern Physics*, 34, 123-125.

Block, N. (1986). Advertisement for a semantics for psychology. In P. A. Rench, T. E. Uehling, Jr., & H. K., Wettstein (Eds.), *Midwest Studies in Philosophy, Vol. 10, Studies in the Philosophy of Mind*. Minneapolis: University of Minnesota Press.

Bloom, P. (2001). *How Children Learn the Meanings of Words*. Cambridge, MA: MIT Press.

Bodamer, J. (1947). Die prosopagnosie. *Archs Psychiatr Nervenkrank*, 179, 6-53.

Boring, E. G. (1950). *A History of Experimental Psychology*. New York: Appleton-Century-Crofts.

Bower, G. H. (1966). Recent developments: I. The basic conditions of learning and research. In E. R. Hilgard & G. H. Bower, *Theories of Learning*. New York: Appleton-Century-Crofts.

Bower, G. H. (1970). Analysis of a mnemonic device. *American Scientist*, 58, 496-510.

Bower, G. H. (1972). Mental imagery and associative learning. In Gregg (Ed.), *Cognition in Learning and Memory*. New York: Wiley.

Bower, G. H., Black, J. B., & Turner, T. (1979). Scripts in memory for text. *Cognitive Psychology*, 11, 177-220.

Bradley, L., & Bryant, P. E. (1978), Differences in auditory organization as a possible cause of reading backwardness. *Nature*, 271, 746-747.

Bradley, L., & Bryant, P. E. (1983). Categorizing sounds and learning to read – A causal connection. *Nature*, 301, 419-421.

Bramly, S. (1995). *Leonardo: Discovering the Life of Leonardo da Vinci*. New York: HarperCollins.

Brandimonte, M. A., Hitch, G., J. & Bishop, D. V. M. (1992). Influence of short-term memory codes on visual image processing: Evidence from information transformation tasks. *Journal of Experimental Psychology: Learning, Memory, and Cognition*, 18, 157-165.

Braun, J. Koch, C. & Davis, J. L. (2001). *Visual Attention and Cortical Circuits*. Cambridge, MA: MIT Press.

Braun, J., Koch, C., Lee, D. K., & Itti, L. (2001). Perceptual consequences of multilevel selection. In J. Braun, C. Koch, & J. L. Davis (Eds.), *Visual Attention and Cortical Circuits*. Cambridge, MA: MIT Press.

Brédart, S. (1993). Retrieval failures in face naming. *Memory*, 1, 351-366.

Bretherton, I. (1992). Social referencing, intentional communication, and the interfacing of minds in infancy. In D. Frye & C. Moore (Eds.), *Children's Theories of Mind: Mental States and Social Understanding*. New York: Plenum Press.

Bridgeman, B. (2003). *Psychology & Evolution*. Thousand Oaks, CA: Sage.

Broadbent, D. E. (1952). Listening to one of two synchronous messages. *Journal of Experimental Psychology*, 47, 191-196.

Broadbent, D. E. (1954). The role of auditory localization and attention in memory spans. *Journal of Experimental Psychology*, 47, 191-196.

Broadbent, D. E. (1958). *Perception and Communication*. London: Pergamon Press.

Broadbent, D. E., & Broadbent, M. H. P. (1987). From detection to identification: Response to multiple targets in rapid serial visual presentation. *Perception & Psychophysics*, 42, 105-113.

Broadbent D. E., & Gregory, R. L. (1985).

Brody, H. (1978). Cell counts in cerebral cortex and brainstem. In R. Katzman, R. D. Terry, & K. L. Bick (Eds.), *Aging, Vol. 17: Alzheimer's Disease: Senile Dementia, and Related Disorders*. New York: Raven Press.

Brooks, L. R. (1968). Spatial and verbal components of the act of recall. *Canadian Journal of Psychology*, 22, 349-368.

Brown, D. E. (2001). *Human Universals*. New York: McGraw-Hill.

Brown, D. E. (2002). Human universals and their implications. In N. Roughley (Ed.), *Being Humans: Anthropological Universality and Particularity in Transdisciplinary Perspectives*. New York: Walter de Gruyter.

Brown, J. A. (1958). Some tests of the decay theory of immediate memory. *Quarterly Journal of Experimental Psychology*, 10, 12-21.

Brown, R. (1973). *A First language: The Early Stages*. Cambridge, MA: Harvard University Press.

Brown, R., & Kulik, J. (1977). Flashbulb memories. *Cognition*, 5, 73-99.

Brown, R., & McNeill (1966). The "tip-of-the-tongue" phenomenon. *Journal of Verbal Learning and Verbal Behavior*, 5, 325-337.

Bushnell, I. W. R., Sai, F., & Mullin, J. T. (1989). Neonatal recognition of the mother's face. *British Journal of Developmental Psychology*, 7, 3-15.

C

Cabeza, R., & Nyberg, L. (1997). Imaging cognition: An empirical review of PET studies with normal subjects. *Journal of Cognitive Neuroscience*, 9, 1-26.

Calleja, M. O., & Rich, A. N. (2013). Guidance of attention by information held in working memory. *Attention, Perception, & Psychophysics*, 75, 687-699.

Carey, S. (1978). The child as word learner. In M. Halle, J. Bresnan, & G. Miller (Eds.), *Linguistic Theory and Psychological Reality*. Cambridge, MA: MIT Press.

Carey S., & Bartlett, E. (1978). Acquiring a single new word. *Papers and Reports on Child Language Development*, 15, 17-29.

Carlson, M. C., Hasher, L., Connelly, S. L., & Zacks, R. T. (1995). Aging, distraction, and the benefits of predictable location. *Psychology and Aging*, 10, 427-436.

Carrasco, M. (2011). Visual attention: The past 25 years. *Vision Research*, 51, 1484-1525.

Carreiras, M., Lopez, J., Rivero. F., & Corina, D. (2005). Linguistic perception: Neural processing of a whistled language. *Nature*, 433, 31–32.

Carroll, D. W. (2004). *Psychology of Language*. Belmont, CA: Thomson Wadsworth.

Carver, R. P. (1985). How good are some of the world's best readers? *Reading Research Quarterly*, XX, 4, 389-419.

Cattell, J. McK. (1900). Time and space in vision. *Psychological Review*, 7, 325-343.

Ceraso, J., & Provitera, A. (1971). Sources of error in syllogistic reasoning. *Cognitive Psychology*, 2, 400-410.

Cerella, J., Hoyer, W., Rybash, J., & Commons, M. L. (Eds.) (1994). *Adult Information Processing: Limits on Loss*. New York: Academic Press.

Chall, J. S. (1967). *Learning to Read: The Great Debate*. New York: McGraw-Hill.

Chalmers, D. (1995). The puzzle of conscious experience. Scientific American, December, 62-68.

Chalmers, D. (1996). *The Conscious Mind*. Oxford, U.K.: Oxford University Press.

Chalmers, D. (2004). How can we construct a science of consciousness? In M. S. Gazzaniga (Ed.), *The Cognitive Neurosciences III*. Cambridge, MA: MIT Press.

Chase, W. G., & Ericsson, K. A. (1982). Skill and working memory. In G. H. Bower (Ed.), *The Psychology of Learning and Motivation*. New York: Academic Press.

Chen, H.-C. (1986). Effects of reading span and textual coherence on rapid-sequential reading. *Memory & Cognition*, 14, 202-208.

Cherry, C. (1953). Some experiments on the recognition of speech with one and two ears. *Journal of the Acoustical Society of America*, 25, 975-979.

Choe, C. S., Welch, R. B., Gilford, R. M., & Juola, J. F. (1975). The "ventriloquist effect:" Visual dominance or response bias? *Perception & Psychophysics*, 18, 55-60.

Chomsky, N. (1957). *Syntactic Structures*. The Hague: Mouton.

Chomsky, N. (1959). Review of B. F. Skinner, *Verbal Behavior*. *Language*, 35, 26-58.

Chomsky, N. (1965). *Aspects of a Theory of Syntax*. Cambridge, MA: MIT Press.

Chomsky, N. (1975). *Reflections on Language*. New York: Pantheon.

Chun, M. M., Golomb, J. D., & Turk-Browne, N. B. (2011). A taxonomy of external and internal attention. *Annual Review of Psychology*, 62, 73-101.

Chun, M. M., & Potter, M. C. (1995). A two-stage model for multiple target detection in rapid serial visual presentation. *Journal of Experimental Psychology: Human Perception and Performance*, 21, 109-127.

Chun, M. M., & Potter, M. C. (2001). The attentional blink and task switching within and across modalities. In K. Shapiro (Ed.), *The Limits of Attention*. Oxford, England: Oxford University Press.

Churchland, P. S. (1996). The hornswoggle problem. *Journal of Consciousness Studies*, 3, 402-408.

Clancy, S. A., McNally, R. J., Schacter, D. L., Lenzenweger, M. F., & Pitman, R. K., (2002). Memory distortion in people reporting abduction by aliens. *Journal of Abnormal Psychology*, 111, 455-461.

Clancy, S. A., Schacter, D. L., McNally, R. J., & Pitman, R. K. (2000). False recognition in women reporting recovered memories of sexual abuse. *Psychological Science*, 11, 26-31.

Clark, A. (2003). *Natural-Born Cyborgs*. Oxford, U. K.: Oxford University Press.

Cohen, A. & Ivry, R. (1989). Illusory conjunctions inside and outside the focus of attention. *Journal of Experimental Psychology: Human Perception and Performance*, 15, 650-663.

Cohen, D. (1987). Behaviourism. In R. L. Gregory (Ed.), *The Oxford Companion to the Mind*. Oxford, U. K.: Oxford University Press.

Colgrove, F. W. (1899). Individual memories. *American Journal of Psychology*, 10, 228-255.

Collins, G. M. (1977). Visual co-orientation and maternal speech. In H. R. Schaffer (Ed.), *Studies in Mother-infant Interaction*. London: Academic Press.

Collins, A. M., & Loftus, E. F. (1975). A spreading activation theory of semantic processing. *Psychological Review*, 82, 407-428.

Collins, A. M., & Quillian, M. R. (1969). Retrieval time from semantic memory. *Journal of Verbal Learning and Verbal Behavior*, 8, 240-247.

Colombelli-Négrel, D., Webster, M.S., Dowling, J. E., Hauber, M. E., & Kleindorfer, S. (2016). Vocal imitation of mother's calls by begging Red-backed Fairywren nestlings increases parental provisioning. *The Auk*, 133, 273-285.

Coltheart, M., Curtis, B., Atkins, P., & Haller, M. (1993). Models of reading aloud: Dual-route and parallel-distributed-processing accounts. *Psychological Review*, 100: 589-608.

Conrad, C. (1972). Cognitive economy in semantic memory. *Journal of Experimental Psychology*, 92, 149-154.

Conrad, R. (1964). Acoustic confusions in immediate memory. *British Journal of Psychology*, 55, 75-84.

Corballis, M. C. (1999a). Phylogeny from apes to humans. In M. C. Corballis and S. Lea (Eds.), *The Descent of Mind: Psychological Perspectives on Hominid Evolution*. Oxford, England: Oxford University Press.

Corballis, M. C. (1999b). The gestural origins of language. *American Scientist*, 87, 1-7.

Corballis, M. C. (2003). From mouth to hand: Gesture, speech, and the evolution of right-handedness. *Behavioral and Brain Sciences*, 26, 199-260.

Corballis, M. C., (2004). On the origins of modernity: Was autonomous speech the critical factor? *Psychological Review*, 111, 543-552.

Corkin, S. (1984). Lasting consequences of bilateral medial temporal lobe lobectomy: Clinical course and experimental findings in H. M. *Seminars in Neurology*, 4, 249-259.

Corkin, S., Amaral, D., Gonzalez, R., Johnson, K., & Hyman, B. (1997). H. M.'s medial temporal-lobe lesion: Findings from MRI. *Journal of Neuroscience*, 17, 3964-3979.

Cornsweet, T. (1971). *Visual Perception*. New York: Academic Press.

Corso, J. F. (1977). Auditory perception and communication. In J. E. Birren & K. W. Schaie (Eds.), *Handbook of the Psychology of Aging*. New York: Van Nostrand Reinhold.

Cottingham, J. G. (1987). Platonic forms. In R. L. Gregory, (Ed.), *The Oxford Companion to the Mind*. Oxford, UK: Oxford University Press.

Cowan, N. (2001). The magical number 4 in short-term memory: A reconsideration of mental storage capacity. *Behavioral and Brain Sciences*, 24, 87–185.

Cowan, N. (2016). Working memory maturation: Can we get at the essence of cognitive growth? *Perspectives on Cognitive Science*, 11, 239-264.

Craik, F. I. M. (1970). The fate of primary memory items in free recall. *Journal of Verbal Learning and Verbal Behavior*, 9, 143-148.

Craik, F. I. M. (1971). Age differences in recognition memory. *Quarterly Journal of Experimental Psychology*, 23, 316-323.

Craik, F. I. M. (1977). Age differences in human memory. In J. E. Birren & K. W. Schaie (Eds.), *Handbook of the Psychology of Aging*. New York: Van Nostrand Reinhold.

Craik, F. I. M. (2001). Human memory and aging. *Proceedings of the 27th International Congress of Psychology*, Stockholm, Sweden.

Craik, F. I. M. (2006). Age-related changes in human memory: Practical consequences. In L. -G. Nilsson & N. Ohta (Eds.), *Memory and Society: Psychological Perspectives*. New York: Psychology Press.

Craik, F. I. M., Govoni, R., Naveh-Benjamin, M., & Anderson, N. D. (1966). The effects of divided attention on encoding and retrieval processes in human memory. *Journal of Experimental Psychology: General*, 125, 159-180.

Craik, F. I. M., & Lockhart, R. S. (1972). Levels of processing: A framework for memory research. *Journal of Verbal Learning and Verbal Behavior*, 11, 6711-684.

Craik, F. I. M., & Tulving, E. (1975). Depth of processing and the retention of words in episodic memory. *Journal of Experimental Psychology: General*, 104. 268-294.

Craton, L. G., & Yonas, A. (1990). The role of motion in infants' perception of occlusion. In J. T. Enns (Ed.), *The Development of Attention: Research and Theory*. London: Elsevier.

Crick, F. C., & Koch, C. (2004). A Framework for Consciousness. In M. S. Gazzaniga (Ed.), *The Cognitive Neurosciences III*. Cambridge, MA: MIT Press.

Crystal, D. (1997). *The Cambridge Encyclopaedia of Language* (2nd ed.), Cambridge, UK: Cambridge University Press.

Curtiss, S. (1977). Genie: A Psycholinguistic Study of a Modern-day "Wild Child." New York: Academic Press.

Cutler, B. L., & Penrod, S. D. (1995). *Mistaken Identification: The Eyewitness, Psychology, and the Law*. New York: Cambridge University Press.

D

Damasio, A. (1999). *The Feeling of What Happens*. San Diego, CA: Harcourt.

Damasio, H., Grabowski, T., Frank, R., Galabruda, A. M., & Demasio, A. R. (1994). The return of Phineas Gage: Clues about the brain from the skull of a famous patient. *Science*, 264, 1102-1105.

Daneman, M., & Carpenter, P. A. (1980). Individual differences in working memory and reading. *Journal of Verbal Learning and Verbal Behavior*, 19, 450-466.

Darwin, C. (1859). *On the Origin of Species*. London: John Murray.

Darwin, C. (1871). *The Descent of Man*. London: John Murray.

Darwin, C. (1872). *The Expression of the Emotions in Man and Animals*, 3rd Ed. with commentaries by Paul Ekman (1998). New York: Oxford University Press.

Dawkins, R. (1976). *The Selfish Gene*. Oxford, U. K.: Oxford University Press.

De Casper, A. J., & Fifer, W. P. (1980). Of human bonding: Newborns prefer their mothers' voices. *Science*, 208, 1174-1176.

De Gelder, B. & Kanwisher, N. (1999). Absence of a fusiform face area in a prosopagnosic patient. *NeuoImage*, 9, S604.

De Renzi, (1982). *Disorders of Space Exploration and Cognition*. Chichester: Wiley.

Deese, J. (1959). On the prediction of occurrence of particular verbal intrusions in immediate recall. *Journal of Experimental Psychology*, 58, 17-22.

Dehaene, S., & Changeux, J.-P. (2004). Neural mechanisms for access to consciousness. In M. S. Gazzaniga (Ed.), *The Cognitive Neurosciences III*. Cambridge, MA: MIT Press.

Dehaene, S., Jobert, A., Naccache, L., Ciuciu, P., Poline, J. B., Le Bihan, D., et al. (2004). Letter binding and invariant recognition of masked words: Behavioral and neuroimaging evidence. *Psychological Science*, 15, 307-313.

Dehaene, S., Naccache, L., Cohen, L., Le Bihan, D., Mangin, J. F., Poline, J. B., et al. (2001). Cerebral mechanisms of word masking and unconscious repetition priming. *Nature*, 4, 752-758.

Delattre, P. C., Liberman, A. M., & Cooper, F. S. (1955). Acoustic loci and transitional cues for consonants. *Journal of the Acoustical Society of America*, 27, 769-773.

Dement, W. (1972). Sleep deprivation and the organization of behavioral states. In C. Clemente, D. Durpura, & F. Mayer (Eds.), *Sleep and the Maturing Nervous System*. New York: Academic Press.

De Neys, W. (2013). Conflict detection, dual processes, and logical intuitions: Some clarifications. *Thinking and Reasoning*, 20, 1-19.

De Neys, W., & Bonnefon, J. (2013). The 'whys' and 'whens' of individual differences in thinking bias. *Trends in Cognitive Sciences*, 17, 172-178

Dennett, D. C., (1991). *Consciousness Explained*. Boston, MA: Little, Brown and Co.

Desimone, R., & Duncan, J. (1995). Neural mechanisms of selective visual attention. *Annual Review of Neuroscience*, 18, 193-222.

Deutsch, D. (1975). Two-channel listening to musical scales. *Journal of the Acoustical Society of America*, 57, 1156-1160.

Deutsch, J. A., & Deutsch, D. (1963). Attention: Some theoretical considerations. *Psychological Review*, 70, 80-90.

Dixon, R. A., & Backman, L. (Eds.) (1995). *Compensating for Adult Deficits and Declines: Managing Losses and Promoting Gains*. Mahwah, NJ: Erlbaum.

Doidge, N. (2007). *The Brain that Changes Itself*. New York: Viking Penguin.

Donald, M. (1991). *Origins of the Modern Mind*. Cambridge, MA: Harvard University Press.

Donders, F. C. (1869/1969). On the speed of psychological processes. In W. G. Koster (Ed.), *Attention and Performance II*. Amsterdam: North-Holland; *Acta Psychologica*, 30, 412-431. (Originally published in 1869.)

Donk, M. (1999). Illusory conjunctions are an illusion: The effects of target-nontarget similarity on conjunction and feature errors. *Journal of Experimental Psychology: Human Perception and Performance*, 25, 1207-1233.

Downing, P. A., Jiang, Y., Shuman, M., & Kanwisher, N. (2001). A cortical selection for visual processing of the human body. *Science*, 293, 2470-2473.

Downing, P. E. (2000). Interactions between visual working memory and selective attention. *Psychological Science*, 11, 467-73.

Driver, J., Blankenburg, F., Bestmann, S., Vanduffel, W., & Ruff, C. C. (2009). Concurrent brain-stimulation and neuroimaging for studies of cognition. *Trends in Cognitive Sciences*, 13, 319-327.

Ducrot, S. & Pynte, J. (2002). What determines the eyes' landing position in words? *Perception & Psychophysics*, 64, 1130-1144.

Duda, R. O., & Shortliffe, E. H. (1983). Expert systems research. *Science*, 220(4594), 261-267.

Duncan, J. (1984). Selective attention and the organization of visual information. *Journal of Experimental Psychology: General*, 113, 501-517.

Duncan, J. & Humphreys, G. W. (1989). Visual search and stimulus similarity. *Psychological Review*, 96, 433-458.

Duda, R. O. & Shortliffe, E. H. (1983). Expert systems research. *Science*, 220, 261-268.

Dunning, D., Johnson, K., Ehrlinger, J. & Kruger, J. (2003). Why people fail to recognize their own incompetence. *Current Directions in Psychological Science*, 12, 83-87.

E

Earleywine, M. (2002). *Understanding Marijuana: A New Look at the Scientific Evidence*. New York: Oxford University Press.

Ebbinghaus, H. (1885). *Über das Gedächtnis: Intersuchngen zur Experimentellen Psychologie*. Liepzig: Dunker and Humboldt. (Translated by H. A. Ruger & C. E. Bussenius, 1913, and reissued by Dover Publications, 1964.)

Eccles, J. C. (1994). *How the Self Controls its Brain*. Berlin: Springer-Verlag.

Eddy, D. M. (1982). Probabilistic reasoning in clinical medicine: Problems and opportunities. In D. Kahneman, P. Slovic, & A. Tversky (Eds.), *Judgment under Uncertainty: Heuristics and Biases*. Cambridge, England: Cambridge University Press.

Eden, G. F., VanMeter, J. W., Rumsey, J. M., Maisog, J. M., Woods, R. P., & Zeffiro, T. A. (1996). Abnormal processing of visual motion in dyslexia revealed by brain imaging. *Nature*, 382, 66-69.

Egeth, H. E., Virzi, R. A., & Garbart, H. (1984). Searching for conjunctively defined targets. *Journal of Experimental Psychology: Human Perception and Performance*, 10, 32-39.

Eichenbaum, H. (2002). Brain mechanisms of declarative memory: The fundamental role of the hippocampus as revealed by studies on rodents. In A. Parker, E. L. Wilding, & T. J. Bussey (Eds.), *The Cognitive Neuroscience of Memory*. Hove, England: Psychology Press.

Eichenbaum, H., Dudchenko, P., Wood, E., Shapiro, M., & Tanila, H. (1999). The hippocampus, memory, and place cells: Is it spatial memory or memory space? *Neuron*, 23, 1-20.

Eimas, P. D., Siqueland, E. R., Juszyk, P. W., & Vigorito, J. (1972). Speech perception in infants. *Science*, 171, 303-306.

Einstein, G. O., & McDaniel (1990). Normal aging and prospective memory. *Journal of Experimental Psychology: Human Learning and Memory*, 16, 717-726.

Engle, R. W. (2002). Working memory capacity as executive attention. *Current Directions in Psychological Science*, 11, 19-23.

Engel, A. K., Konig, P., Kreiter, A. K. Schillen, T. B., & Singer, W. (1992). Temporal coding in the visual cortex: New vistas on integration in the nervous system. *Trends in Neurosciences*, 15, 218-226.

Enns, J. T. (2004). *The Thinking Eye, the Seeing Brain*. New York: W. W. Norton Epstein, S. (1994). Integration of the cognitive and the psychodynamic unconscious. *American Psychologist*, 49, 709.

Eriksen, B. A. & Eriksen, C. W. (1974). Effects of noise letters upon the identification of a target letter in a nonsearch task. *Perception & Psychophysics*, 16, 143-149.

Erickson, J. R. (1974). A set analysis theory of behavior in formal syllogistic reasoning tasks. In R. L. Solso (Ed.), *Theories in Cognitive Psychology: The Loyola Symposium*. Hillsdale NJ: Erlbaum.

Evans, D. A., Funkenstein, H. H., Albert, M. S., Scherr, P. A., Cook, N. R., Chown, M. J., Hebert, L. E., Hannekens, C. H., & Taylor, J. O. (1989). Prevalence of Alzheimer's disease in a community population of older persons. *Journal of the American medical Association*, 262, 2551-2556.

Evans, J. St. B. T. (2008). Dual-processing accounts of reasoning, judgment, and social cognition. *Annual Review of Psychology*, 59, 255-278.

Eysenck, M. W. (1974). Age differences in incidental learning. *Developmental Psychology*, 10, 936-941.

F

Farah, M. J. (1990). *Visual Agnosia: Disorders of Object Recognition and What They Tell Us about Normal Vision*. Cambridge, MA: MIT Press.

Farah, M. J., Peronnet, F., Gonon, M. A., & Giard, M. G. (1988). Electrophysiological evidence for a shared representational medium for visual images and visual percepts. *Journal of Experimental Psychology: General*, 117, 248-257.

Farah, M. J., Soso, M. J., & Dasheiff, R. M. (1992). Visual angle of the mind's eye before and after unilateral occipital lobectomy. *Journal of Experimental Psychology: Human Perception and Performance*, 18, 241-246.

Farthing, G. W. (1992). *The Psychology of Consciousness*. Englewood Cliffs, NJ: Prentice Hall.

Fechner, G. (1966). *Elements of Psychophysics* (Vol. 1, H. E., Adler, D. H. Howes, & E. G. Boring, Eds.). New York: Holt, Rinehart, & Winston. (Original work published in 1860.)

Fenson, L., Dale, P. S., Reznick, J. S., Bates, E., Thal, D., & Pethick, S. J. (1994). Variability in early communicative development. *Monographs of the Society for Research in Child Development*, 59 (5, serial no. 242).

Fernandez, G., Brewer, J. B., Zhao, Z., Glover, G. H., & Gabrieli, J. D. E., (1999). Level of sustained entorhinal activity at study correlates with subsequent cued-recall performance: A functional magnetic resonance imaging study with high acquisition rate. *Hippocampus*, 9, 35-44.

Fiez, J. A., & Petersen, S. E. (1998). Neuroimaging studies of word reading. *Proceedings of the National Academy of Sciences, USA*, 95, 914-921.

Fisher, S. E., & Marcus, G. F. (2006). The eloquent ape: Genes, brains and the evolution of Language. *Nature Reviews Genetics*, 7, 9-20.

Flavell, J. H., (1971). First discussant's comments. What is memory development the development of? *Human Development*, 14, 272-278.

Flavell, J. H., & Wellman, H. M., (1977). Metamemory. In R. V. Kail, Jr., & J. W. Hagen (Eds.), *Perspectives on the Development of Memory and Cognition*. Hillsdale, NJ: Erlbaum.

Flege, J. E., Yeni-Komshiam, G. H., & Liu, S. (1999). Age constraints on second-language acquisition. *Journal of Memory & Language*, 41, 78-104.

Fodor, J. A., Bever, T. G., & Garrett, M. F. (1974). *The Psychology of Language*. New York: McGraw-Hill.

Foer, J. (2007). Remember this. *National Geographic*. November.

Forde, E. M. E., & Humphreys, G. W. (1999). Category-specific recognition impairments: A review of important case studies and influential theories. *Aphasiology*, 13, 169-193.

Forster, K. I. (1970). Visual perception of rapidly presented word sequences of varying complexity. *Perception & Psychophysics*, 8, 215-221.

Fox, R., & McDaniel, C. (1982). The perception of biological motion by human infants. *Science*, 218, 486-487.

Frederick, S. (2005). Cognitive reflection and decision making. *Journal of Economic Perspectives*, 19, 25-42.

Freud, S. (1949). *An Outline of Psycho-Analysis*. J. Strachey (trans.). London: Hogarth Press.

Friedenberg, J. & Silverman, G. (2006). *Cognitive Science*. Thousand Oaks, CA: Sage.

Friederici, A. D. (2006). The neural basis of language development and its impairment. *Neuron*, 52, 941-952.

Friedman, A., Brown, N. R., & McGaffey, A. P. (2002). A basis for bias in geographical judgments. *Psychonomic Bulletin & Review*, 9, 151-159.

Friedman, A., Montello, A. R. (2006). Global-scale location and distance estimates: Common representations and strategies in absolute and relative judgments. *Journal of Experimental Psychology: Learning, Memory, and Cognition*, 32, 333-346.

Fries, P., Reynolds, J. H., Rovie, A. E., & Desimone R. (2001). Modulation of oscillatory neural synchronization by selective visual attention. *Science*, 291, 1560-1563.

Frith, C. D., & Frith, U. (2007). Social cognition in humans. *Current Biology*, 17, 724-732.

Fuster, J. M. (2004). Upper processing stages of the perception-action cycle. *Trends in Cognitive Science*, 8, 143-145.

G

Gabrielli, J. D. E. (2001). Functional neuroimaging of episodic memory. In R. Cabeza & A. Kingstone (Eds.), *Handbook of Functional Neuroimaging of Cognition*. Cambridge, MA: MIT Press.

Ganis, G., Thompson, W. L., Mast, F., & Kosslyn, S. M. (2004) The brain's mind's images: The cognitive neuroscience of mental imagery. In Gazzaniga, M. S. (Ed.), *The Cognitive Neurosciences III*. Cambridge, MA: MIT Press.

Gardner, H. (1982), *Art, Mind and Brain*. New York: Basic Books.

Gardner, M. (1978). *Aha! Insight*. San Francisco: Freeman.

Garnica, O. K. (1977). Some prosodic and paralinguistic features of speech to young children. In C. Snow and C. A. Ferguson (Eds.), *Talking to Children: Language Input and Acquisition*. Cambridge, England: Cambridge University Press.

Garrett, B. (2003). *Brain and Behavior*. Belmont, CA: Wadsworth/Thomson Learning.

Gathercole, S. E., Pickering, S. J., Ambridge, B., & Wearing, H. (2004). The structure of working memory from 4 to 15 years of age. *Developmental Psychology*, 40, 177-190.

Gawronski, B., & Creighton, L. A. (2013). Dual-process theories. In d. E. Carlston (Ed.). *The Oxford Handbook of Social Cognition*, 282-312. New York, NY: Oxford University Press.

Gazzaley, A. & Nobre, A. C. (2012). Top-down modulation: bridging selective attention and working memory. *Trends in Cognitive Sciences*, 16, 129-135.

Gazzaniga, M. S., Ivry, R. B., & Mangun, G. R. (2002). *Cognitive Neuroscience: The Biology of Mind*, 2nd Ed. New York: Norton.

Gernsbacher, M. A. (1990). *Language Comprehension as Structure Building*. Hillsdale, NJ: Erlbaum.

Gershenfeld, N. (1999). *When Things Start to Think*. London: Hodder and Stoughton.

Ghetti, S., DeMaster, D. M., Yonelinas, A. P., & Bunge, S. A. (2010). Development of differences in medial temporal lobe functions during memory encoding. *Journal of Neuroscience*, 30, 9548-9556.

Gibson, J. J. (1966). *The Senses Considered as Perceptual Systems*. Boston: Houghton Mifflin.

Gilbert, C. D., & Wiesel, T. N. (1989). Columnar specificity of intrinsic horizontal and corticocortical connections in cat visual cortex. *Journal of Neuroscience*, 9, 2432-2442.

Gilbert, L. C. (1959). Speed of processing verbal stimuli and its relation to reading. *Journal of Educational Psychology*, 55, 8-14.

Glanzer, M., & Cunitz, A. R. (1966). Two storage mechanisms in free recall. *Journal of Verbal Learning and Verbal Behavior*, 5, 351-360.

Gleitman, L. R., (1990). The structural sources of verb meanings. *Language Acquisition*, 1, 3-55.

Gleitman, L., Gleitman, H., Landau, B., & Wanner, E. (1988). Where the learning begins: Initial representations for language learning. In F. Newmeyer (Ed.), *The Cambridge Linguistic Survey*, Vol. 3. Cambridge, MA: Harvard University Press.

Glosser, G., & Deser, T. (1992). A comparison of changes in macrolinguistic and microlinguistic aspects of discourse production in normal aging. *Journal of Gerontology: Psychological Sciences*, 47, 266-272.

Goldstein, E. B. (2002). *Sensation and Perception* 6th Ed. Pacific Grove, CA: Wadsworth.

Goldstein, E. B. (2007). *Sensation and Perception* 7th Ed. Pacific Grove, CA: Thomson Wadsworth.

Goldstein, E. B. (2005). *Cognitive Psychology*. Belmont, CA: Thompson Wadsworth.

Golomb, J., de Leon, M. J., Kluger, A., George, A. E., Tarshish, C., & Ferris, S. H. (1993). Hippocampal atrophy in normal aging. *Archives of Neurology*, 50, 967-973.

Golomb, J., Kluger, A., de Leon, M. J., Ferris, S. H., Convit, A., Mittelman, M., Cohen, J., Rusinek, H., De Santi, S., & George, A. E. (1994). Hippocampal formation size in normal human aging: A correlate of delayed secondary memory performance. *Learning and Memory*, 1, 45-54.

Goodale, M. A. (2004). Perceiving the world and grasping it: Dissociations between conscious and unconscious visual processing. In M. S. Gazzaniga (Ed.), *The Cognitive Neurosciences III*. Cambridge, MA: MIT Press.

Goodale, M. A., Milner, A. D., Jakobson, L. S., & Carey, D. P. (1991). A neurological dissociation between perceiving objects and grasping them. *Nature*, 349, 154-156.

Gordon, P. (2009). Language and consciousness. In W. P. Banks (Ed.), *Encyclopedia of Consciousness*, Oxford, UK: Academic Press.

Graf, P., Squire, L. R., & Mandler, G. (1984). The information that amnesic patients do not forget. *Journal of Experimental Psychology: Learning, Memory, and Cognition*, 10, 164-178.

Graziano, M. S. A., and Gross, C. G. (1995). Spatial maps for the control of movement. *Current Opinion in Neurobiology*, 8, 195-201.

Gregory, R. L. (1987). Darwin. In R. L. Gregory (Ed.), *The Oxford Companion to the Mind*. Oxford, UK: Oxford University Press.

Gregory, R. L. (1987). Laboratories of psychology. In R. L. Gregory (Ed.), *The Oxford Companion to the Mind*. Oxford, UK: Oxford University Press.

Griggs, R. A., & Cox, J. R. (1982). The elusive thematic materials effect in Wason's selection task. *British Journal of Psychology*, 73, 407-420.

Grill-Spector, K., & Kanwisher, N. (2005). Visual recognition: As soon as you know it is there, you know what it is. *Psychological Science*, 16, 152-160.

Grill-Spector, K., Knouf, N., & Kanwisher, N. (2004). The fusiform face area subserves face perception, not generic within-category identification. *Nature Neuroscience*, 7, 555-562.

Grossberg, S., & Mingolla, E. (1985). Neural dynamics of form perception: Boundary completion, illusory figures, and neon color spreading. *Psychological Review*, 92, 173-211.

Grossman, I., Na, J., Varnum, M. E. W., Park, D.C., Kitayama, S., & Nisbett, R. E. (2010). Reasoning about social conflicts improves into old age. *Proceedings of the National Academy of Sciences, USA*, 107, 7246-7250.

Gould, S. J., & and Lewonton, R. C. (1979). "The Spandrels of San Marco and the Panglossian paradigm: A critique of the adaptationist programme" *Proceedings of the Royal Society of London B 205*, 581–598.

Guastello, S. J. (2006). *Human Factors Engineering and Ergonomics*. Mahwah, NJ: Erlbaum.

Guttorm, T. K., Leppänen, P. H. T., Poikkeus, A. M., Eklund, K. M., Lyytinen, P. & Lyytinen, H. (2005). Brain event-related potentials (ERPs) measured at birth predict later language development in children with and without familial risk for dyslexia. *Cortex*, 41, 291-303.

H

Habib, R., Nyberg, L., & Tulving, E. (2003). Hemispheric asymmetries of memory: The Hera model revisited. *Trends in Cognitive Science, 7*, 241-245.

Halliday, M. A. K., & Hassan, R. (1976). *Cohesion in English*. London: Longman

Halpern, D. F. (2003). *Thought and Knowledge*. Mahwah, NJ: Erlbaum.

Handley, S. J., & Trippas, D. (2015). Two-dual processes and the interplay between knowledge and structure: A new parallel processing model. *Psychology of Learning and Motivation, 62*, 33-58

Hartshorne, J. K., & and Germine, L. T. (2015). When does cognitive functioning peak? The asynchronous rise and fall of different cognitive abilities across the life span. *Psychological Science, 26*, 433-443.

Harley, B., & Wang, W. (1997). The critical period hypothesis: Where are we now? In A. M. B. de Groot & J. F. Kroll (Eds.), *Tutorials in Bilingualism: Psycholinguistic Perspectives*. Mawwah, NJ: Erlbaum.

Harley, T. A., (2008). *The Psychology of Language* (3rd ed.), New York: Psychology Press.

Harris, I. M., & Little, M. J. J. (2010). Priming the semantic neighbourhood during the attentional blink. *PLOS ONE, 9/14/2010*.

Harris, M., Jones, D., & Grant, J. (1983). The nonverbal context of mothers' speech to infants. *First Language, 4*, 21-31.

Hartline, H. K. & Ratliff, F. (1957). Inhibitory interaction of receptor units in the eye of *Limulus*. *Journal of General Physiology, 1957, 40*, 357-376.

Hartline, H. K., Wagner, H., & Ratliff, F. (1956). Inhibition in the eye of *Limulus*. *Journal of General Physiology, 1956, 39*, 651-673.

Hasher, L., Stoltzfus, E. R., Zacks, R. T., & Rypma (1991). Age and inhibition. *Journal of Experimental Psychology: Learning, Memory, and Cognition, 17*, 163-169.

Hasher, L., & Zacks, R. T., (1988). Working memory, comprehension, and aging: A review and a new view. In G. H. Bower (Ed.), *The Psychology of Learning and Motivation, 22*, 193-225. New York: Academic Press.

Haug, H., Barmwater, Egger, R., Fischer, D., Kuhl, S., & Sass, N. L. (1983). Anatomical changes in the aging brain: Morphometric analysis of the human prosencephalon. In J. Cervos-Navarro & H. I. Sarkander (Eds.), *Aging, Vol. 21: Brain Aging: Neuropathology and Neuropharmacology*. New York: Raven Press.

Haxby, J. V. (2004). Analysis of topographically organized patterns of response in fMRI data: Distributed representations of objects in the ventral temporal cortex. In N. Kanwisher and J. Duncan (Eds.), *Attention and Performance XX*. Oxford, England: Oxford University Press.

Haxby, J. V., Ungerleider, L. G., Horwitz, B., Rapoport, S. L., & Grady, C. L. (1995). Hemispheric differences in neural systems for face working memory: A PET rCBF study. *Human Brain Mapping, 3*, 68-82.

Hebb, D. O. (1949). *The Organization of Behavior*. New York: Wiley.

Heeger, D. J., Gandhi, S. P., Huk, A. C., & Boynton, G. M. (2001). Neuronal correlates of attention in human visual cortex. In J. Braun, C. Koch, & J. Davis (Eds.). *Visual Attention and Cortical Circuits*. Cambridge, MA: MIT Press.

Helmholtz (1850/1962). *Hanbuch der Physiologischen Optik*. New York: Dover.

Henley, N. M. (1969). A psychological study of the semantics of animal terms. *Journal of Verbal Learning and Verbal Behavior, 8*, 176-184.

Hewes, G. W. (1973). Language origin theories. In D. M. Rumbaugh (Ed.), *Language Learning by Chimpanzee: The Lana Project*. New York: Academic Press.

Hilgard, E. R., Atkinson, R. C., & Atkinson, R. L. (1975). *Introduction to Psychology, 6th Ed*. New York: Harcourt, Brace, Jovanovich.

Hilgard, E. R., & Bower, G. H. (1975). *Theories of Learning* (4th ed.). Englewood Cliffs, NJ: Prentice-Hall.

Hillyard, S. A. (1993). Electrical and magnetic brain recordings: Contributions to cognitive neuroscience. *Current Opinion in Neurobiology, 3*, 217-224.

Hirsch-Pasek, K., Tucker, M., & Golinkoff, R. (1996). Dynamic systems theory: Reinterpreting "prosodic bootstrapping" and its role in language acquisition. In J. L. Morgan, and K. Demuth (Eds.), *Signal to Syntax*. Mahwah, NJ: Erlbaum.

Hirsch-Pasek, K., Zosh, J. M., Golinkoff, R. M., Gray, J. H., Robb, M. B., & Kaufman, J. (2015). Putting education in "educational" apps: Lessons from the science of learning. *Psychological Science in the Public Interest, 16*, 3-34.

Hirst, W., & Phelps, E. A. (2016). Flashbulb memories. *Current Directions in Psychological Science, 25*, 36-41.

Hobson, J. A., & Pace-Schott, E. F. (2002). The cognitive neuroscience of sleep: Neuronal systems, consciousness and learning. *Nature Reviews: Neuroscience, 3*, 679-693.

Hochberg, L. R., Serruya, M. D., Friehs, G. M., Mukand, J. A., Saleh, M., Caplan, A. H. Branner, A., Chen, D., Penn, R. D., & Donoghue, J. P. (2006). Neuronal ensemble control of prosthetic devices by a human with tetraplegia. *Nature, 442*, 164-171.

Hodges, J. R., Patterson, K., Oxbury, S., & Furnell, E. (1992). Semantic dementia: Progressive fluent aphasia with temporal lobe atrophy. *Brain, 115*, 1783-1806.

Hopf, J. M., Heinze, H. J., Schoenfeld, M. A., & Hillyard, S.A. (2009). Spatio-temporal analysis of visual attention. In M. S. Gazzaniga (Ed.), *The Cognitive Neurosciences, Vol. 4*. Cambridge, MA: MIT Press.

Howarth, S., Handley, S. J., & Walsh, C. (2015). The logic-bias effect: The role of effortful processing in the resolution of belief–logic conflict. *Memory & Cognition, 44*, 1-20.

Howes, M. B. (2007). *Human Memory*. Thousand Oaks, CA: Sage.

Hu, J. C. (2014). What do apes really tell us? www.slate.com/articles/health_and_science/science/2014/08/koko_kanzi_and_ape_language_research_criticism_of_working_conditions_and.html

Hubel, D. H. (1963). Integrative processes in central visual pathways of the cat. *Journal of the Optical Society of America, 53*, 58-66.

Hubel, D. H. (1988). *Eye, Brain, and Vision*. San Francisco: Freeman.

Hubel D. H., & Wiesel, T. N. (1959). Receptive fields of single neurones in the cat's striate cortex. *Journal of Physiology, 148*, 574-591.

Hubel D. H., & Wiesel, T. N. (1962). Receptive fields, binocular interaction, and functional architecture. *Journal of Physiology, 160*, 106-154.

Hubel D. H., & Wiesel, T. N. (1977). Functional architecture of macaque monkey visual cortex (Ferrier lecture). *Proceedings of the Royal Society of London, B, 198*, 1-59.

Huey, E. B. (1908). *The Psychology and Pedagogy of Reading*. New York: Macmillan. (Republished, 1968, by Cambridge, MA: MIT Press.)

Hulme, C., Nash, H. M., Gooch, D., Lervåg, A., & Snowling, M.J. (2015) The foundations of literacy development in children at familial risk of dyslexia. *Psychological Science, 26*, 1877-1866.

Humes, L. E., Busey, T. A., & Craig, J. (2013). Are age-related changes in cognitive function driven by age-related changes in sensory processing? *Attention, Perception, & Psychophysics, 75*, 508-524.

Hummel, J. E., & Biederman, I. (1992). Dynamic binding in a neural network for shape recognition. *Psychological Review, 99*, 480-517.

Humphrey, N. (1987). The inner eye of consciousness. In C. Blakemore & S. Greenfield (Eds.), *Mindwaves*. Oxford, U. K.: Blackwell.

Humphrey, N. (2011). *Soul Dust: The Magic of Consciousness*. Princeton, NJ: Princeton University Press.

Humphreys, G. W., & Bruce, V. (1989). *Visual Cognition*. Hillsdale, NJ: Erlbaum.

Humphreys, G. W., Romani, C., Olson, A., Riddoch, M. J., & Duncan, J. (1994). Non-spatial extinction following lesions of the parietal lobe in humans. *Nature, 372*, 357-359.

Husain, M., (2001). A spatiotemporal framework for disorders of visual attention. In K. Shapiro (Ed.), *The Limits of Attention*. Oxford, England: Oxford University Press.

Huxley, A. (1956). *The Doors of Perception*. New York: Harper & Row.

Hyde, T. S. & Jenkins, J. J. (1969). The differential effects of incidental tasks on the organization of recall of a list of highly associated words. *Journal of Experimental Psychology, 82*, 472-481.

Hyönä, J., & Pollatsck, A. (1990). Reading Finnish compound words: Eye fixations are affected by compound morphemes. *Journal of Experimental Psychology: Human Perception and Performance, 24*, 1612-1627.

Hyönä, J., & Pollatsek, A. (2000). Morphological processing of Finnish words in reading. In A. Kennedy, R. Radach, D. Heller, & J. Pynte (Eds.), *Reading as a Perceptual Process*. Oxford, England: Elsevier.

I

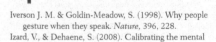

Iverson J. M. & Goldin-Meadow, S. (1998). Why people gesture when they speak. *Nature, 396*, 228.

Izard, V., & Dehaene, S. (2008). Calibrating the mental number line. *Cognition, 106*, 1221-1247.

J

Jackendoff, R. (1994). *Patterns in the Mind: Language and Human Nature*. New York: Basic Books.

Jackendoff, R. (2002). *Foundations of Language*. Oxford, England: Oxford University Press.

Jacoby, L. L., & Dallas, M. (1981). On the relationship between autobiographical memory and perceptual learning. *Journal of Experimental Psychology: General, 110*, 115-125.

James, W. (1890). *Principles of Psychology*, Cambridge, MA: Harvard University Press. (Republished by Enclycopædia Brittanica, Chicago, 1952.)

Jaynes, J. (1976). *The Origin of Consciousness in the Breakdown of the Bicameral Mind*. New York: Houghton Mifflin.

Joanisse, M., Manis, F., Keating, P., & Seidenberg, M.S. (2000). Language deficits in dyslexia: Speech perception, phonology, and morphology. *Journal of Experimental Child Psychology, 77*, 30-60.

Johnston, W. A., & Heinz, S. P. (1978). Flexibility and capacity demands of attention. *Journal of Experimental Psychology: General, 107*, 420-435.

Johnson, M. H. (2004). Plasticity and functional brain development: The case of face processing. In N. Kanwisher and J. Duncan (Eds.), *Attention and Performance XX*. Oxford, England: Oxford University Press.

Johnson, S. P., & Aslin, R. N. (1995). Perception of object unity in 2-month-old infants. *Developmental Psychology*, 31, 739-745.

Johnson-Laird, P. N. (1983). *Mental Models: Towards a Cognitive Science of Language, Inference, and Consciousness*. Cambridge, MA: Harvard University Press.

Jonides, J. (1980). Toward a model of the mind's eye's movement. *Canadian Journal of Psychology*, 34, 103-112.

Jonides, J. & Yantis, S. (1988). Uniqueness of abrupt onset in capturing attention. *Perception & Psychophysics*, 43, 346-354.

Juola, J. F. (1979). Pattern recognition. In R. Lachman, J. L. Lachman, and E. C. Butterfield, *Cognitive Psychology and Information Processing: An Introduction*. Hillsdale, NJ: Erlbaum.

Juola, J. F. (1988). The use of computer displays to improve reading comprehension. *Applied Cognitive Psychology*, 2, 87-95.

Juola, J. F. (2016). Theories of focal and peripheral attention. In S. Bakker, D, Hausen, & T. Selker (Eds.), *Peripheral Interaction: Challenges and Opportunities for HCI in the Periphery of Attention*. Switzerland: Springer International Publishing.

Juola, J. F., Bouwhuis, D. G., Cooper, E. E., & Warner, C. B. (1991). Control of attention around the fovea. *Journal of Experimental Psychology: Human Perception and Performance*, 17, 125-141.

Juola, J. F., & Hergenhahn, B. R. (1968). Effects of training level, type of training, and awareness on the establishment of mental set in anagram solving. *Journal of Psychology*, 69, 155-159.

Juola, J. F., Koshino, H., & Warner, C. B. (1995). Tradeoffs between attentional effects of spatial cues and abrupt onsets. *Perception & Psychophysics*, 57, 333-342.

Juola, J. F., Koshino, H., Warner, C. B., McMickell, M., & Peterson, M.S. (2000). Automatic and voluntary control of attention in young and elderly adults. *American Journal of Psychology*, 113, 159-178.

Juola, J. F., Tiritoglu, A., & Pluenis, J. (1995). Reading text presented on a small display. *Applied Ergonomics*, 20, 227-229.

Juola, J. F., Ward, N. J., & McNamara, T. (1982). Visual search and reading of rapid, serial presentations of letter strings, words, and text. *Journal of Experimental Psychology: General*, 111, 208- 227.

Jusczyk, P. W. (2000). *The Discovery of Spoken Language*. Cambridge, MA: MIT Press.

Just, M. A., & Carpenter, P. A. (1987). *The Psychology of Reading and Language Comprehension*. Boston: Allyn & Bacon.

Just, M. A., & Carpenter, P. A. (1992). A capacity theory of comprehension: individual differences in working memory. *Psychological Review*, 99, 122.

K

Kahneman, D. (1973). *Attention and Effort*. Englewood Cliffs, NJ: Prentice Hall.

Kahneman, D. (2011). *Thinking, Fast and Slow*. New York: Macmillan.

Kahneman, D., & Frederick, S. (2005). A model of heuristic judgment. In K. J. Holyoak & R. G. Morrison (Eds.), *The Cambridge Handbook of Thinking and Reasoning*. New York: Cambridge University Press.

Kahneman, D., & Tversky, A. (1972). Subjective probability: A judgment of representativeness. *Cognitive Psychology*, 3, 430-454.

Kahneman, D., & Tversky, A. (1973). On the psychology of prediction. *Psychological Review*, 80, 237-251.

Kahneman, D., & Tversky, A. (1996). On the reality of cognitive illusions. *Psychological Review*, 103, 582-591.

Kail, R. (1992). Development of memory in children. In L. R. Squire (Ed.), *Encyclopedia of Learning and Memory*. New York: Macmillan.

Kalat, J. W. (2004). *Biological Psychology*. Belmont, CA: Wadsworth/Thompson Learning.

Kanwisher, N., McDermott, J., & Chun, M. M. (1997). The fusiform face area: A module in human extrastriate cortex specialized for face perception. *Journal of Neuroscience*, 17, 4302-4311.

Kanwisher, N., Downing, P., Epstein, R., & Kourtzi, Z. (2001). Functional neuroimaging of visual cognition. In R. Cabeza & A. Kingstone (Eds.), *Handbook of Functional Neuroimaging of Visual Cognition*. Cambridge, MA: MIT Press.

Karbach, J., & Verhaegen, P. (2014). Making working memory work: A meta-analysis of executive-control and working memory training in older adults. *Psychological Science*, 25, 2027-2037.

Karpicke, J.D., & Roediger, H. L. III. (2008). The critical importance of retrieval for learning. *Science*, 319, 966-968.

Kegl, J., Senghas, A., & Coppola, M. (1999). Creations through contact: Sign language emergence and sign language change in Nicaragua. In M. DeGraff (Ed.), *Language Creation and Language Change: Creolization, Diachrony, and Development*. Cambridge, MA: MIT Press.

Kelly, W. M., Miezen, F. M., McDermott, K. B., Buckner, R. L., Raichle, M. E., Cohen, N. J., Ollinger, J. M., Akbudak, E., Conturo, T. E., Snyder, A. Z., & Peterson, S. E. (1998). Hemispheric specialization in human dorsal frontal cortex and medial temporal lobe for verbal and nonverbal memory encoding. *Neuron*, 20, 927-936.

Kemper, S. (1992). Language and aging. In F. I. M. Craik, & Salthouse (Eds.), *The Handbook of Aging and Cognition*. Hillsdale, NJ: Erlbaum.

Kemper, S., Thompson, M., & Marquis, J. (2001). Longitudinal change in language production: Effects of aging and dementia on grammatical complexity and propositional content. *Psychology & Aging*, 16, 600-614.

Kemper, S., & Sumner, A. (1992). The structure of verbal abilities in young and older adults. *Psychology and Aging*, 16, 312-322.

Kennedy, P. R., & Bakay, R. A. (1998). Restoration of neural output from a paralysed patient by a direct brain connection. *Neuroreport*, 9, 1701-1711.

Keppel, G. & Underwood, B. J. (1962). Proactive inhibition in short-term retention of single items. *Journal of Verbal Learning and Verbal Behavior*, 1, 153-161.

Kibbe, M. M. (2015). Varieties of visual working memory representation in infancy and beyond. *Current Directions in Psychological Science*, 24, 433-439.

Koedinger, K. R., & Corbett, A. (2006). Cognitive tutors: Technology bringing learning science to the classroom. In K. Sawyer (Ed.), *The Cambridge Handbook of the Learning Sciences*, Cambridge, UK: Cambridge University Press.

Koshino, H., Carpenter, P. A., Keller, T. A., & Just, M. A. (2005). Interactions between the dorsal and ventral pathways in mental rotation: An fMRI study. *Cognitive, Affective, & Behavioral Neuroscience*, 5, 54-66.

Kintsch W. (1977). On comprehending stories. In M. A. Just & P. A. Carpenter (Eds.), *Cognitive Processes in Comprehension*. Hillsdale, NJ: Erlbaum.

Kintsch, W. (1988). The role of knowledge in discourse comprehension. *Psychological Review*, 95, 163-182.

Kintsch W., & van Dijk, T. A. (1978). Toward a model of text comprehension and production. *Psychological Review*, 85, 363-394.

Kisilevsky, B. S., Hains, S. M. J., KangLee, XingXie, HefengHuang, HuiYe, H., KeZhang, & Zengping Wang (2003). Effects of experience on fetal voice recognition. *Psychological Science*, 14, 220-224.

Kiyonaga, A. & Egner, T. (2013). Working memory as internal attention: Toward an integrative account of internal and external selection processes. *Psychonomic Bulletin & Review*, 20, 228–242.

Knudsen, E. I. (2007). Fundamental components of attention. *Annual Review of Neuroscience*, 30, 57–78.

Koch, C., & Tsuchiya N. (2006). Attention and consciousness: Two distinct brain processes. *Trends in Cognitive Science*, 11, 16-22.

Koffka, K. (1935). *Principles of Gestalt Psychology*. New York: Harcourt, Brace, & World.

Konkle, D. F., Beasley, D. S., & Bess, F. H. (1977). Intelligibility of time-altered speech in relation to chronological aging. *Journal of Speech and Hearing Research*, 20, 108-115.

Kosslyn, S. M. (1975). Information representation in visual images. *Cognitive Psychology*, 7, 341-370.

Kosslyn, S. M. (1980). *Image and Mind*. Cambridge, MA: Harvard University Press.

Kosslyn, S. M. (1990). Mental imagery. In D. N. Osherson, S. M. Kosslyn, and J. M. Hollerbach (Eds.), *Visual Cognition and Action (Vol. 2): An Invitation to Cognitive Science*. Cambridge, MA: MIT Press.

Kosslyn, S. M. (1994). *Image and Brain: The Resolution of the Imagery Debate*. Cambridge, MA: The MIT Press.

Kosslyn, S. M., Ball, T. M., & Reiser, B. J. (1978). Visual images preserve metric spatial information. Evidence from studies of image scanning. *Journal of Experimental Psychology: Human Perception and Performance*, 40, 47-60.

Kosslyn, S.M., Pascual-Leone, A., Felician, O., Camposano, S., Keenan, J. P., Thompson, W. L., Ganis, G., Sukel, K. E., & Alpert, N. M. (1999). The role of area 17 in visual imagery: Convergent evidence from PET and rTMS. *Science*, 284:167-170.

Kosslyn, S. M., Thompson, W. L., Kim, I. J., & Alpert, N. M. (1995). Topographical representations of mental images in primary visual cortex. *Nature*, 378, 496-498.

Kroll, J. F. & de Groot, A. M. B. (2005). *Handbook of Bilingualism: Psycholinguistic Approaches*. New York: Oxford University Press.

Kuffler, S. W., (1953). Discharge patterns and functional organization of mammalian retina. *Journal of Neurophysiology*, 16, 37-68.

Kuhl, P. K., & Miller, J. D. (1975). Speech perception by chinchilla: Voiced-voiceless distinction in alveolar plosive consonants. *Science*, 190, 69-72.

L

Lachman, J. L., Lachman, R., & Thronesbery, C. (1979). Metamemory through the adult life span. *Developmental Psychology*, 15, 543-551.

Lachman, R., Lachman, J. L., & Butterfield, E. C. (1979). *Cognitive Psychology and Information Processing: An Introduction*. Hillsdale, NJ: Erlbaum.

Lai, C. S. L., Fisher, S. E., Hurst, J. A., Vargha-Khadem, F., & Monaco, A. P. (2001). A forkhead-domain gene is mutated in severs speech and language disorder. *Nature*, 413, 519-523.

Landau, B., & Gleitman, L. (1985). *Language and Experience: Evidence from the Blind Child*. Stanford, CA: Stanford University Press.

Lane, H. (1976). *The Wild Boy of Aveyron*. Cambridge, MA: Harvard University Press.

La Rue, A. (1992). *Aging and Neurological Assessment*. New York: Plenum Press.

Lashley, K. S. (1929). *Brain Mechanisms and Intelligence*. Chicago: University of Chicago Press.

Lashley, K. S. (1950). In search of the engram. *Symposia for the Society of Experimental Biology*, 4, 454-482.

Lavie, N. (1995). Perceptual load as a necessary condition for selective attention. *Journal of Experimental Psychology: Human Perception and Performance*, 21, 451-468.

Lavie, N. (2001). Capacity limits in selective attention: Behavioral evidence and implications for neural activity. In J. Braun, C. Koch, & J. Davis (Eds.). *Visual Attention and Cortical Circuits.* Cambridge, MA: MIT Press.

Lavie, N. & Driver, J. (1996). On the spatial extent of attention in object-based visual selection. *Perception & Psychophysics,* 58, 1238-1252.

Lawrence, D. H. (1971). Two studies of visual search for word targets with controlled rates of presentation. *Perception & Psychophysics,* 10, 85-89.

Lenneberg, E. H., (1967). *Biological Foundations of Language.* Cambridge, MA: MITPress.

Levine, M. (1988). *Effective Problem Solving.* Englewood Cliffs, NJ: Prentice Hall.

Levinson, S. (1996). Frames of reference and Molyneux's question: Cross-linguistic evidence. In P. Bloom, M. A. Peterson, L. Nadel, & M. Garrett (Eds.), *Space and Language,* Cambridge, MA: MIT Press.

Liberman, A. M., Delattre, P. D., & Cooper, F. S. (1952). The role of selected stimulus variables in the perception of unvoiced stop consonants. *American Journal of Psychology,* 65, 497-516.

Liberman, A. M., Harris, K. S., Kinney, J. A. & Lane, H. L. (1961). The discrimination of relative-onset time of the components of certain speech and nonspeech patterns. *Journal of Experimental Psychology,* 61, 379-388.

Linton, M. Real-world memory after six years: An in vivo study of very long-term memory. In M. M. Gruneberg, P. E. Morris, & R. N. Sykes (Eds.), *Practical Aspects of Memory.* London: Academic Press, 1978.

Lisker, L., & Abramson, A. S. (1967). *The voicing dimension: Some experiments in comparative phonetics.* Paper presented at the International Congress of Phonetic Sciences, Prague.

Loftus, E. F. (1979). *Eyewitness testimony.* Cambridge, MA: Harvard University Press.

Loftus, E. F., & Ketcham, K. (1991). *Witness for the Defense: The Accused, the Eyewitness, and the Expert who puts Memory on Trial.* New York: St. Martin's Press.

Loftus, E. F., Miller, D. G., & Burns, H. J. (1978). Semantic integration of verbal information into visual memory. *Journal of Experimental Psychology: Human Learning and Memory,* 4, 19-31.

Loftus, E. F., & Palmer, J. C. (1974). Reconstruction of automobile destruction: An example of the interaction between language and memory. *Journal of Verbal Learning and Verbal Behavior,* 13, 585-589.

Loftus, E. F., & Zanni, G. (1975). Eyewitness testimony: The influence of the wording of a question. *Bulletin of the Psychonomic Society,* 5, 866-888.

Lott, I. T. (1982). Down's syndrome, aging, and Alzheimer's disease: A clinical review. *Annals of the New York Academy of Sciences,* 396, 15-17.

Lowe, R. K. (1999). Extracting information from an animation during complex visual processing. *European Journal of the Psychology of Education,* 14, 225-244.

Luck, S. J. (2005). *An Introduction to the Event-related Potential Technique.* Cambridge, MA: MIT Press.

Luck S. J., & Vogel, E. K. (1997). The capacity of visual working memory for features and conjunctions. *Nature,* 390, 279-281.

Lustig, C., Hasher, L., & Zacks, R. T. (2007). Inhibitory deficit theory: Recent developments in a "new view." In D. S. Gordein & C. M. MacLeod (Eds.), *The Place of Inhibition in Cognition.* Washington, DC: American Psychological Association.

. . . .

M

Mack, A., & Rock, I. (1998). *Inattentional Blindness.* Cambridge, MA: MIT Press.

MacKay, I. R. A., Flege, J. E., & Imai, S. (2006). Evaluating the effects of chronological age and sentence duration on degree of perceived foreign accent. *Applied Psycholinguistics,* 27, 153-183.

Mackworth, N. H. (1948). The breakdown of vigilance during prolonged visual search. *Quarterly Journal of Experimental Psychology,* 1, 6-21.

MacLuhan, M. (1964). *Understanding Media: The Extensions of Man.* New York: McGraw-Hill.

Maki, R. H., & Berry, S. L. (1984). Metacomprehension of text material. *Journal of Experimental Psychology: Learning, Memory, and Cognition,* 10, 663-679.

Maki, R. H., Jonas, D., & Kellod, M. (1994). The relationship between comprehension and metacomprehension ability. *Psychonomic Bulletin & Review,* 1, 126-129.

Maki, R. H., & McGuire, M. J. (2002). Metacognition for text: Findings and implications for education. In T. J. Perfect & B. L. Schwartz (Eds.), *Applied Metacognition.* Cambridge, England: Cambridge University Press.

Mandel, D. R., Jusczyk, P. W., & Kemler Nelson, D. G. (1994). Does sentential prosody help infants to organize and remember speech information? *Cognition,* 53, 155-180.

Mani, R. B., Lohr, J. B., & Jeste, D. V. (1986). Hippocampal pyramidal cells and aging in the human: A quantitative study of neuronal loss in sectors CA1 to CA4. *Experimental Neurology,* 94, 29-40.

Marr, D. (1982). *Vision.* San Francisco: Freeman.

Marshack, A. (1972). *The Roots of Civilization: The Cognitive Beginnings of Man's first Art, Symbol and Notation.* New York: McGraw-Hill.

Martin, A. (2001). Functional neuroimaging of semantic memory. In R. Cabeza & A. Kingstone (Eds.), *Handbook of Functional Neuroimaging of Cognition.* Cambridge, MA: MIT Press.

Martin, A., Wiggs, C. L., Lalonde, F. M., & Mack, C. (1996). Word retrieval to letter and semantic cues: A double dissociation in normal subjects using interference tasks. *Neuropsychologia,* 32, 1487-1494.

Martin, A., Wiggs, C. L., & Weisberg, J. (1997). Modulation of human medial temporal lobe activity by form, meaning, and experience. *Hippocampus,* 7, 587-593.

Masson, M. E. (1983). Conceptual processing of text during skimming and rapid sequential reading. *Memory & Cognition,* 11, 262-274.

Massaro, D. W. (1987). *Speech perception by Ear and by Eye: A Paradigm for Psychological Inquiry.* Hillsdale, NJ: Erlbaum.

Matlin, M. W. (2005). *Cognition, 6th Ed.* New York: Wiley.

Matlin, M. W. (2009). *Cognition, 7th Ed.* New York: Wiley.

Maunsell & McAdams (2001). Effects of attention on the responsiveness and selectivity of individual neurons in visual cerebral cortex. In J. Braun, C. Koch, & J. L. Davis (Eds.), *Visual Attention and Cortical Circuits.* Cambridge, MA: MIT Press.

McAdams, C. J., & Maunsell, J. H. R. (1999). Effects of attention on orientation-tuning functions of single neurons in macaque monkey cortical area V4. *Journal of Neuroscience,* 19, 431-441.

McConkie, G. W., & Rayner, K. (1975). The span of the effective stimulus during a fixation in reading. *Perception & Psychophysics,* 17, 578-586.

McDaniel, M. A., & Einstein, G. O. (2007). *Prospective Memory.* Thousand Oaks, CA: Sage.

McDowd, J. M., & Craik, F. I. M. (1988). Effects of aging and task difficulty on divided attention performance. *Journal of Experimental Psychology: Human Perception and Performance,* 14, 267-280.

McGeoch, J. A. (1932). Forgetting and the law of disuse. *Psychological Review,* 39, 352-370.

McGurk, H., & MacDonald, J. (1976). Hearing lips and seeing voices. *Nature,* 264, 746-748.

McManis, S. A., Fehd, H. M., Emmanouil, T.-A., & Kastner, S. (2007). Mechanisms of feature- and space-based attention: Response modulation and baseline increases. *Journal of Neurophysiology,* 98, 2110-2121.

McNally, R. J. (2003). Recovering memories of trauma: A view from the laboratory. *Current Directions in Psychological Science,* 12, 32-36.

Mehler, J., Jusczyk, P. W., Lambretz, G., Halsted, N., Bertoncini, J., & Amiel-Tison, C. (1988). A precursor of language acquisition in young infants. *Cognition,* 29, 143-178.

Meredith, M. A., Nemitz, J., W., & Stein, B. E. (1987). Determinants of multisensory integration in superior colliculus neurons. I. Temporal factors. *Journal of Neuroscience,* 7, 3215-3229.

Merikle, P. M., Joordens, S., & Stolz, J. A. (1995). Measuring the relative magnitude of unconscious influences. *Consciousness and Cognition,* 4, 422-439.

Meyer, D. E. & Schvaneveldt R. W. (1971). Facilitation in recognizing pairs of words: Evidence of a dependence between retrieval operation. *Journal of Experimental Psychology,* 90, 227-234.

Myerson J., & Hale, S. (1993). General slowing and age invariance in cognitive processing: The other side of the coin. In J. Cerella, J. Rybash, W. Hoyer, & M. L. Commons (Eds.) *Adult Information Processing: Limits on Loss.* New York: Academic Press.

Miller, G. A. (1956). The magical number seven plus or minus two: Some limits on our capacity for processing information. *Psychological Review,* 63, 81-97.

Miller, G. A. (1996). *The Science of Words.* New York: Freeman.

Milner, B., Corkin, S., & Teuber, H. L. (1968). Further analysis of the hippocampal amnesic syndrome: 14-year follow up study of H. M. *Neuropsychologia,* 6, 215-234.

Milner, A. D., and Goodale, M. A. (1995). *The Visual Brain in Action.* Oxford, England: Oxford University Press.

Minow, N. (1961). *Chicago Tribune,* April 24, p. 17.

Mishkin, M., Ungerleider, L., & Macko, K. (1983). Object vision and spatial vision: Two central pathways. *Trends in Neuroscience,* 6, 414-417.

Mithen, S. (1996). *The Prehistory of the Mind: A Search for the Origins of Art, Religion, and Science.* London: Thames & Hudson.

Mody, M., Studdert-Kennedy, M., & Brady, S. (1997). Speech perception deficits in poor readers: Auditory processing or phonological processing? *Journal of Experimental Child Psychology,* 64, 199-231.

Molfese, D. L. (1977). Infant cerebral asymmetry. In S. J. Segalowitz & F. A. Gruber (Eds.), *Language Development and Neurological Theory.* New York: Academic Press.

Montemayor, C., & Haladjian, H. H. (2015). *Consciousness, Attention, and Conscious Attention.* Cambridge, MA: MIT Press.

Moon, C., Cooper, R. P., & Fifer, W. P. (1993). Two-day old infants prefer their native language. *Infant Behavior and Development,* 16, 495-500.

Moore, G. E. (1965). Cramming more components into integrated circuits. *Electronics Magazine,* 38, No. 8.

Morais, J., Cary, L., Alegria, J., & Bertelson, P. (1979). Does awareness of speech as a sequence of phones arise spontaneously? *Cognition,* 7, 323-331.

Morales, M., Mundy, P., & Rojas, J., (1998). Following the direction of gaze and language development in six-month-olds. *Infant Behavior and Development,* 21, 373-377.

Moray, N. (1959). Attention in dichotic listening: Affective cues and the influence of instructions. *Quarterly Journal of Experimental Psychology,* 11, 56-60.

Moscovitch, M., Chein, J. M., Talmi, D., & Cohn, M. (2007). Learning and memory. In B. Baars & N. M. Gage (Eds.), *Cognition, Brain, and Consciousness.* Amsterdam: Elsevier.

Moscovitch, M., Winocur, G., Behrmann, M. (1997). What is special about face recognition? Nineteen experiments on a person with visual object agnosia and dyslexia but normal face recognition. *Journal of Cognitive Neuroscience,* 9, 555-604.

Muir, D., & Field, T. M. (1979). Newborn infants orient to sounds. *Child Development,* 50, 431-436.

Murdock, B. B., Jr. (1962). The serial position effect of free recall. *Journal of Experimental Psychology,* 64, 482-488.

Murphy. M. D., Sanders, R. E., Gabriesheski, A. S., & Schmitt, F. A. (1981). Metamemoryin the aged. *Journal of Gerontology*, 36, 185-193.

Myers, N. A., & Perlmutter, M. (1978). Memory in the years from two to five. In P. A. Ornstein (Ed.), *Memory Development in Children*. Hillsdale, NJ: Erlbaum.

N

Naccache, L., & Dehaene, S. (2001). The priming method: Imaging unconscious repetition priming reveals an abstract representation of number in the parietal lobes. *Cerebral Cortex*, 11, 966-974.

Naghavi, H. R. & Nyberg, L. (2005). Common fronto-parietal activity in attention, memory, and consciousness: Shared demands in integration? *Consciousness and Cognition*, 14, 390-425.

Nakayama, K., & Silverman, G. H. (1986). Serial and parallel processing of visual feature conjunctions. *Nature*, 320, 264-265.

Naveh-Benjamin, M., and Ayres, T. J. (1986). Digit span, reading rate, and linguistic relativity. *Quarterly Journal of Experimental Psychology*, 38, 739-751.

Neely, J. H. (1976). Semantic priming and retrieval from lexical memory: Evidence for facilitatory and inhibitory processes. *Memory & Cognition*, 4, 648-654.

Neely, J. H., & Kahan, T. A. (2001). Is semantic activation automatic? A critical re-evaluation. In H. L. Roediger, J. S. Nairne, I. Neath, & A. M. Surprenant (Eds.), *The Nature of Remembering: Essays in Honor of Robert Crowder*. Washington, D. C.: American Psychological Association.

Neisser, U., (1967). *Cognitive Psychology*, New York: Appleton-Century-Crofts.

Neisser, U. (1982). Snapshots or benchmarks? In U. Neisser (Ed.), *Memory Observed*. San Francisco: W. H. Freeman.

Neisser, U., and Harsch, N. (1992). Phantom flashbulbs: False recollections of hearing the news about Challenger. In E. Winograd & U. Neisser (Eds.), *Affect and Accuracy in Recall: Studies of "Flashbulb" Memories*. New York: Cambridge University Press.

Newell, A., Shaw, J. C., & Simon, H. A., (1959). Report on a General Problem-Solving program: Proceedings of the International Conference on *Information Processing*. In Information Processing. Paris: UNESCO

Newell, A., & Simon, H. A. (1972). *Human Problem Solving*. Englewood Cliffs, NJ: Prentice-Hall.

Nickerson, R. S. (1992). *Looking Ahead: Human Factors Challenges in a Changing World*. Hillsdale, NJ: Erlbaum.

Nielsen, J. (1994). *Usability Engineering*. Boston: Academic Press.

Nietzsche, F. W. (1887/1974). *The Gay Science*. 1st Ed. Translated by W.A. Kaufmann. New York: Vintage Books.

Nieuwenstein, M., Theeuwes J., Wyble, B., & Potter, M. (2009). Temporal constraints on conscious vision: On the ubiquitous nature of the attentional blink. *Journal of Vision*, 18, 1-14.

Norman, D. A. (1968). Toward a theory of memory and attention. *Psychological Review*, 75, 522-536.

O

Oberauer, K., & Hein, L. (2012). Attention to Information in Working Memory. *Current Directions in Psychological Science*, 21, 164-169.

O'Craven, K. M., Downing, P. E., & Kanwisher, N. (1999). fMRI evidence for objects as the units of attentional selection. *Nature*, 7;40, 1, 584-587.

O'Regan, J. K., & Noë, A. (2001). A sensorimotor account of vision and visual consciousness. *Behavioral and Brain Sciences*, 24, 939-1031.

Orton, S. T. (1925). 'Word blindness' in school children. *Archives of Neurology and Psychiatry*, 14, 581-615.

Oswald, I. (1987). Sleep. In R. L. Gregory (Ed.) *The Oxford Companion to the Mind*. Oxford, U. K.: Oxford University Press.

Oviatt, S. L. (1980). The emerging ability to comprehend language: An experimental approach. *Child Development*, 51, 97-106.

P

Paivio, A. (1969). Mental imagery in associative learning and memory. *Psychological Review*, 76, 241-263.

Paivio, A. (1971). *Imagery and Verbal Processes*. New York: Holt, Rinehart & Winston.

Paivio, A. (1986). *Mental Representations: A Dual Coding Approach*. New York: Oxford University Press.

Palmer, S. E. (1975). The effects of contextual scenes on the identification of objects. *Memory & Cognition*, 3, 519-526.

Palmer, S. E. (1999). *Vision Science: Photons to Phenomenology*. Cambridge, MA: MIT Press.

Palmer, S. E., Rosch, E., & Chase, P. (1981). Canonical perspective and the perception of objects. In J. Long & A. Baddeley (Eds.), *Attention and Performance IX*. Hillsdale, NJ: Erlbaum.

Palmiter, S., & Elkerton, J. (1993). Animated demonstrations for learning procedural computer-based tasks. *Human-Computer Interaction*, 8, 193-216.

Panagiotaki, P., & Berthoz, A. (2006). Neural bases and cognitive mechanisms of human spatial memory. In T. Vecchi & G. Bottini (Eds.), *Imagery and Spatial Cognition: Methods, Models, and Cognitive Assessment*. Amsterdam: John Benjamins.

Parker, A., Easton, A., & Gaffan, D. (2002). Memory encoding in the primate brain: The role of the basal forebrain. In A. Parker, E. L. Wilding, & T. J. Bussey (Eds.), *The Cognitive Neuroscience of Memory*. Hove, England: Psychology Press.

Pascalis, O. de Schonen, S. Morton, J., Deruelle, C., & Fabre-Grenet, M. (1995). Mother's face recognition by neonates: A replication and extension. *Infant Behavior and Development*, 18, 79-85.

Pashler, H., & Shiu, L-P. (1999). Do images involuntarily trigger search? A test of Pillsbury's hypothesis. *Psychonomic Bulletin and Review*, 6, 445-448.

Patterson, K., & Lambon Ralph, M. A., (1999). Selective disorders of reading? *Current Opinions in Neurobiology*, 9, 235-239.

Pavlov, I. (1927). *Conditioned reflexes*. London: Oxford University Press.

Pennycook, G., Fugelsang, J. A., & Koehler, D. J. (2015). What makes us think? A three-stage dual-process model of analytic engagement. *Cognitive Psychology*, 80, 34-72.

Perfect, (1997). Memory aging as frontal lobe dysfunction. In M. A. Conway (Ed.). *Cognitive Models of Memory*. Cambridge, MA: MIT Press.

Perlmutter, M. (1979). Age differences in adults' free recall, cued recall, and recognition. *Journal of Gerontology*, 34, 533-539.

Peterson, L. R., & Peterson, M. J. (1959). Short-term retention of individual verbal items. *Journal of Experimental Psychology*, 58, 193-198.

Petitto, L. A. (1992). Modularity and constraints in early lexical acquisition: Evidence from children's first words/signs and gestures. In M. R. Gunnar & M. Maratsos (Eds.), *Modularity and constraints in language and cognition: The Minnesota Symposium on Child Psychology*, (Vol. 25). Hillsdale, NJ: Erlbaum.

Pinker, S. (1987). The bootstrapping problem in language acquisition. In B. MacWhinney (Ed.), *Mechanisms of Language Acquisition*, Hillsdale, NJ: Erlbaum.

Pinker, S. (1994). *The Language Instinct*. New York: Morrow.

Pinker, S. (1999). *Words and Rules*. New York: Basic Books.

Pinker, S. (2002). *The Blank Slate*. New York: Viking.

Pinker, S. (2003). Language as an adaptation to the cognitive niche. In M. H. Christiansen & S. Kirby (Eds.), *Language Evolution*. Oxford, UK: Oxford University Press.

Pinkeer, S. (2007). *The stuff of thought*. New York: Penguin.

Pisoni, D. (1977). Identification and discrimination of the relative onset of two component tones: Implications for voicing perception in stops. *Journal of the Acoustical Society of America*, 61, 1352-1361.

Plunkett, K., Sinha, C., Møller, M. F. & Strandsby, O. (1992). Symbol grounding or the emergence of symbols? Vocabulary growth in children and a connectionist net. *Connection Science*, 4, 292-312.

Pollatsek, A., Lesch, M., Morris, R. K. & Rayner, K. (1992). Phonological codes are used in integrating information across saccades in word identification and reading. *Journal of Experimental Psychology: Human Perception and Performance*, 18, 148-162.

Popper, K. R. (1959). *The Logic of Scientific Discovery*. New York: Basic Books.

Popper, K. R., & Eccles, C. (1977). *The Self and its Brain*. New York: Springer.

Portas, C. M., Krakow, K., Allen, P., Josephs, O., Armony, J. L., & Frith, C. D. (2000). Auditory processing across the sleep-wake cycle: Simultaneous EEG and fMRI monitoring in humans. *Neuron*, 28, 991-999.

Posner, M. I., (1980). Orienting of attention. *Quarterly Journal of Experimental Psychology*, 32, 3-26.

Posner, M. I., & Cohen, Y. P. C. (1984). Components of visual orienting. In H. Bouma & D. Bouwhuis (Eds.), *Attention and Performance X*. London: Erlbaum.

Posner, M. I., & Petersen, S. E. (1990). The attention system of the human brain. *Annual Review of Neuroscience*, 13, 25–42.

Posner, M. I., & Raichle, M. E. (1994). *Images of Mind*. New York: Scientific American Library

Posner, M. I., Snyder, C. R. R., & Davidson, B. J. (1980). Attention and the detection of signals. *Journal of Experimental Psychology: General*, 109, 160-174.

Posner, M. I., Walker, J. A., Friedrich, F. J., & Rafal, R. (1984). Effects of parietal injury on covert orientation of attention. *Journal of Neuroscience*, 4, 1863-1874.

Posner, M. I., Walker, J. A., Friedrich, F. J., & Rafal, R. (1987). How do the parietal lobes direct covert attention? *Neuropsychologia*, 25, 135-145.

Postle, B. R. (2006) Working memory as an emergent property of the mind and brain. *Neuroscience*, 139, 23–38

Potter, M., C. (1976). Short-term conceptual memory for pictures. *Journal of Experimental Psychology: Human Perception and Performance*, 2, 509-522.

Potter, M. C. & Levy, E. I. (1969). Recognition memory for a rapid sequence of pictures. *Journal of Experimental Psychology*, 81, 10-15.

Pressley, M. (2005). Final reflections: Metqcognitive instructional practice. In S. E. Israel, C. C. Block, K. L. Bauserman, & K. Kinnucan-Welsch (Eds.). *Metacognition in Literacy Learning*. Mahwah, NJ: Erlbaum.

Pressley, M., & Hilden, K. (2006). Cognitive strategies. In D. Kuhn & R. Siegler (Eds.), *Handbook of Child Psychology* (6th ed., Vol. 2) Hoboken, NJ: Wiley.

Price, C. J., Wise, R. J. S. & Frackowiak, R. S. J. (1996). Demonstrating the implicit processing of visually presented words and pseudowords. *Cerebral Cortex*, 6, 62-70.

Puce, A., Allison, T., Asgari, M., Gore, J. C., & McCarthy, G. (1996). Differential sensitivity of human visual cortex to faces, letterstrings, and textures: A functional magnetic resonance imaging study. *Journal of Neuroscience*, 16, 5205-5215.

Pylyshyn, Z. (1973). What the mind's eye tells the mind's brain: A critique of mentalimagery. *Psychological Bulletin*, 80, 1-24.

Pylyshyn, Z. (1981). The imagery debate: Analogue media versus tacit knowledge. *Psychological Review*, 88, 16-45.

Pylyshyn, Z. W. & Storm, R. W. (1988). Tracking multiple independent targets: evidence for a parallel tracking mechanism. *Spatial Vision*, 3, 1-19.

Q

Quillian, M. R. (1966) The "Teachable Language Comprehender." Ph.D. dissertation, Carnegie Institute of technology, Pittsburgh, PA.

Quinlan, P. T. (1991a). Differing approaches to two-dimensional shape recognition. *Psychological Bulletin,* 109, 224-241.

Quinlan, P. T. (1991b). *Connectionism and Psychology.* Chicago: The University of Chicago Press.

Quinn, P. C., Burke, S., & Rush, A. (1993). Part-whole perception in early infancy: Evidence for perceptual grouping produced by lightness similarity. *Infant Behavior and Development,* 16, 19-42.

Quiroga, R. Q., Reddy, L., Kreiman, G., Koch,C., & Fried, I. (2005). Invariant visual representation by single neurons in the human brain. *Nature,* 435, 1102-1107.

R

Rabbitt, P. (1965). An age-decrement in the ability to ignore irrelevant information. *Journal of Gerontology,* 20, 233-238.

Raichle, M. E. (2001). Functional neuroimaging: A historical and physiological perspective. In R. Cabeza & A. Kingstone (Eds.), *Handbook of Functional Neuroimaging of Cognition.* Cambridge, MA: MIT Press.

Ramachandran, V. S., & Rogers-Ramachandran, D. (2005). Mind the Gap. *Scientific American Mind,* April.

Ranganath C. & Knight, R. T. (2002). Prefrontal cortex and episodic memory: Integrating findings from neuropsychology and functional brain imaging. In A. Parker, E. L. Wilding, T. J. Bussey (Eds.), *The Cognitive Neuroscience of Memory.* Hove, England: Psychology Press.

Rauschecker, J. P., Tian, B., & Hauser, M. (1995). Processing of complex sounds in the macaque nonprimary auditory cortex. *Science,* 268, 111-114.

Raymond, J. E., Shapiro K. L., & Arnell, K. M. (1992). Temporary suppression of visual processing in an RSVP task: An attentional blink? *Journal of Experimental Psychology: Human Perception and Performance,* 18, 849-860.

Rayner, K. (1975). The perceptual span and peripheral cues in reading. *Cognitive Psychology,* 7, 65-81.

Rayner, K., (1979). Eye movements in reading: Eye guidance and integration. In P. A. Kolers, M. E. Wrolstad, and H. Bouma (Eds.), *Processing of Visible Language,* 1. New York: Plenum.

Rayner, K. (1998). Eye movements in reading and information processing: 20 years of research. *Psychological Bulletin,* 124, 372-422.

Rayner, K., Foorman, B. R., Perfetti, C. A., Pesetsky, D. & Seidenberg, M. S., (2001). How psychological science informs the teaching of reading. *Psychological Science in the Public Interest* (a supplement to *Psychological Science*), 2, 31-74.

Rayner, K., Schotter, E. R., Masson, M. E. J., Potter, M. C., & Treiman, R. (2016). So much to read, so little time: How do we read, and can speed reading help? *Psychological Science in the Public Interest,* 17, 4-34.

Raz, N., Gunning, F. M., Head, D., Dupuis, J. H., McQuain, J., Briggs, S. D., Loken, W. J., Thornton, A. E., & Acker, J. D. (1997). Selective aging of the human cerebral cortex observed in vivo: Differential vulnerability of the prefrontal grey matter. *Cerebral Cortex,* 7, 268-282.

Reber, A. S. (1967). Implicit learning of artificial grammars, *Journal of Verbal Learning and Verbal Behavior,* 6, 317-327.

Reber, A. S., and Allen, R. (1978). Analogy and abstraction strategies in synthetic grammar learning: A functionalist interpretation. *Cognition,* 6, 189-221.

Redelmeier, D. A., & Tibshirani, R. J. (1997). Association between cellular-telephone calls and motor vehicle collisions. *New England Journal of Medicine,* 336, 453-458.

Reed, S. K. (1973). *Psychological Processes in Pattern Recognition.* New York: Academic Press.

Rees, G., Frith, C. D., & Lavie, N. (1997). Modulating irrelevant motion perception by varying attentional load in an unrelated task. *Science,* 278, 1616-1619.

Reicher, G. M., (1969). Perceptual recognition as a function of meaningfulness of stimuli material. *Journal of Experimental Psychology,* 81, 275-280.

Rensink, R. A., (2001). Change blindness: Implications for the nature of visual attention. In M. Jenkins & L. Harris (Eds.), *Vision and Attention.* New York: Springer.

Rips, L. J. (1990). Reasoning. In M. R. Rosenzwieg & L. W. Porter (Eds.), *Annual Review of Psychology,* 41, 321-353.

Rips, L. J. (1994). *The Psychology of Proof.* Cambridge, MA: MIT Press.

Rips, L. J. & Marcus, S. L. (1977). Supposition and the analysis of conditional sentences. In M. A. Just & P. A. Carpenter (Eds.), *Cognitive Processes in Comprehension.* Hillsdale, NJ: Erlbaum.

Robinson, A. (2002). *Lost Languages.* New York: McGraw-Hill.

Roediger, H. L., & McDermott, K. B. (1995). Creating false memories: Remembering words not presented in lists. *Journal of Experimental Psychology: Learning, Memory, and Cognition,* 21, 803-814.

Rosch, E. (1975). Cognitive representations of semantic categories. *Journal of Experimental Psychology: General,* 104, 192-233.

Rosch, E., & Mervis, C. (1975). Family resemblances: Studies in the internal structure of categories. *Cognitive Psychology,* 7, 573-605.

Rosenbaum, D. A. (2014). *It's a Jungle in There.* Oxford, UK: Oxford University Press.

Rosenblatt, F. (1958). The Perceptron: A probabilistic mode for information storage and organization in the brain. *Psychological Review,* 65, 386-407.

Ross-Sheehy, S., Oakes, L. M., & Luck, S. J. (2003). The development of visual short-term memory capacity in infants. *Child Development,* 74, 1807-1822.

Rossi, S., Pasqualetti, P., Zito, G., Vecchio, F., Cappa, S. F., Miniussi, C., Babiloni, C. & Rossini, P. M. (2006). Prefrontal and parietal cortex in human episodic memory: An interference study by repetitive transcranial magnetic stimulation. *European Journal of Neuroscience,* 23, 793–800.

Rovee-Collier, C. K. (1999). The development of infant memory. *Current Directions in Psychological Science,* 8, 80-85.

Rovee-Collier, C. K., & Cuevas, K. (2008). The development of infant memory. In M. Courage & N. Cowan (Eds.), *The Development of Memory in Childhood.* Hove, UK: Psychology Press.

Rumelhart, D. E., & Abrahamson, A. A. (1973). A model for analogical reasoning. *Cognitive Psychology,* 5, 1-28.

Rumelhart, D. E., & McClelland, J. L. (1982). An interactive activation model of context effects in letter perception: Part 2. The contextual enhancement effect and some tests and extensions of the model. *Psychological Review,* 89, 60-94.

Rundus, D. (1971). Analysis of rehearsal processes in free recall. *Journal of Experimental Psychology,* 89, 63-77.

Russell, S., & Norvig, P. (2002). *Artificial Intelligence: A Modern Approach,* (2nd Ed.). New York: Prentice Hall.

Rymer, R. (1993). *Genie.* New York: Harper Collins.

Rypma, B., Berger, J. S., & D'Esposito, M. (2002). The influence of working memory demand and subject performance on prefrontal cortical activity. *Journal of Cognitive Science,* 14, 721-731.

Rypma, B., Prabhakaran, V., Desmond, J. D., & Gabrieli, J. D. E. (2001). Age differences in prefrontal cortical activity in working memory. *Psychology and Aging,* 16, 371-384.

S

Sachs, J. S. (1967). Recognition memory for syntactic and semantic aspects of connected discourse. *Perception & Psychophysics,* 2, 437-442.

Sacks, O. (1997). *The island of the colorblind.* New York: A.A. Knopf.

Sadeh, T., Ozubko, J.D., Winocur, G., and Moscovitch M. (2016). Forgetting patterns differentiate between two forms of memory representation. *Psychological Science,* 27, 810-820.

Salthouse, T. A. (1988). Initiating the formalization of theories of cognitive aging. *Psychology and Aging,* 3, 3-16

Salthouse, T. A. (1991). Mediation of adult age differences in cognition by reductions in working memory and speed of processing. *Psychological Science,* 2, 179-183.

Salthouse, T. A., Mitchell, D. R. D., Skovronek, E., & Babcock, R. L. (1989). Effects of adult age and working memory on reasoning and spatial abilities. *Journal of Experimental Psychology: Learning, Memory, and Cognition,* 15, 507-516.

Savage, L. J. (1954). The Foundations of Statistics. New York: Wiley.

Scardamalia, M., & Bereiter, C. (1990). Computer supported intentional learning environments (CSILE). In B. Bowen (Ed.), *Design for Learning: Research-based Design of Technology for Learning.* Cupertino, CA: External Research, Apple Computer, Inc.

Schacter, D. L. (2001). *The Seven Sins of Memory.* Boston: Houghton Mifflin.

Schacter, D. L., Alpert, N. M., Savage, C. R., Rauch, S. L., & Albert, M. S. (1996). Conscious recollection and the human hippocampal formation: Evidence from positron emission tomography. *Proceedings of the National Academy of Sciences,* USA, 93, 321-325.

Schacter, D.L., & Tulving, E. (1994). *Memory Systems.* Cambridge, MA: MIT Press.

Schank, R. C., & Abelson, R. (1977). *Scripts, Plans, Goals, and Understanding.* Hillsdale, NJ: Erlbaum.

Schmandt-Besserat, D. (1978). The earliest precursor of writing. *Scientific American,* 238, 6.

Schneider, W., & Shiffrin, R. (1977). Controlled and automatic human information processing: Detection, search, and attention. *Psychological Review,* 84, 1-66.

Schonfield, D. & Robertson, B. A. (1966). Memory storage and aging. *Canadian Journal of Psychology,* 20, 228-236.

Schwab, L., & Taylor, H. R. (1985). Cataract and delivery of surgical services in developing nations. *In Clinical Ophthalmology* (Vol. 5). New York: Harper & Row.

Schweickert, R., & Boruff, B. (1986). Short-term memory capacity: Magic number or magic spell? *Journal of Experimental Psychology: Learning, Memory, and Cognition,* 12, 419-425.

Scoville, W. B., & Milner, B. (1957). Loss of recent memory after bilateral hippocampal lesions. *Journal of Neurology, Neurosurgery, and Psychiatry,* 20, 11-21.

Searle, J. (1992). *The Rediscovery of the Mind.* Cambridge, MA: MIT Press.

Searle, J. (Ed.) (1997). *The Mystery of Consciousness.* New York: New York Review of Books.

Sehulster, J. R. (1989). Content and temporal structure of autobiographical knowledge: Remembering twenty five seasons at the Metropolitan Opera. *Memory and Cognition,* 17, 590-606.

Selfridge, O. G., & Neisser, U. (1960). Pattern recognition by machine. *Scientific American,* 203, 60-68.

Serences, J. T., & Yantis, S. (2007). Spatially selective representations of voluntary and stimulus-driven attentional priority in human occipital, parietal, and frontal cortex. *Cerebral Cortex,* 17, 282-293.

Sergent, J., & Signoret, J. L. (1992). Varieties of functional deficits in prosapagnosia. *Cerebral Cortex,* 2, 375-388.

Shepard, R. N. (1962). The analysis of proximities: Multidimensional scaling with an unknown distance function: I. *Psychometrika,* 27, 125-140.

Shepard, R. N. (1967). Recognition memory for words, sentences, and pictures. *Journal of Verbal Learning and Verbal Behavior*, 6, 156-163.

Shepard, R. N. (1990). *Mind Sights*. San Francisco: Freeman.

Shepard, R. N., & Metzler, J. (1971). Mental rotation of three-dimensional objects. *Science*, 171, 701-703.

Sherman, S. M., & Spear, P. D. (1982). Organization of visual pathway in normal and visually deprived cats. *Physiology Review*, 62, 738-855.

Shiffrin, R., & Schneider, W. (1977). Controlled and automatic processing: II. Perceptual learning, automatic attending, and a general theory. *Psychological Review*, 84, 127-190.

Sillito, A. M. (1986). Conflicts in the pharmacology of visual cortical plasticity. *Trends in Neuroscience*, 9, 301-303.

Simons, D. J., Levin, D. T. (1997). Change blindness. *Trends in Cognitive Science*, 1, 261-267.

Singer, W. (1992). Adult visual cortex – Adaptation and reorganization. In L. R. Squire (Ed.), *Encyclopedia of Learning and Memory*. New York: Macmillan.

Skinner, B. F. (1957). *Verbal Behavior*. New York: Appleton-Century-Crofts.

Sloman, S. A. (1996). The empirical case for two systems of reasoning. *Psychological Bulletin*, 119, 3-22.

Smith, E. E. & Jonides, J. (1997). Working memory: A view from neuroimagery. *Cognitive Psychology*, 33, 5-42.

Smith, E. E., Shoben, E. J., & Rips, L. J. (1974). Structure and process in semantic memory: A featural model for semantic decisions. *Psychological Review*, 81, 214-241.

Snowdon, D. A., Kemper, S. J., Mortimer, J. A., Greiner, L. H., Wekstein, D. R., & Markesbery, W. R. (1996). Cognitive ability in early life and cognitive function and Alzheimer's disease in late life: Findings from the Nun Study. *Journal of the American Medical Association*, 275, 528-532.

Snowden, R., Thompson, P., & Troscianko, T. (2012). *Basic Vision: An Introduction to Visual Perception (Revised edition)*. Oxford University Press.

Soderstrom, N. C., Kerr, T. K., & Bjork, R. A. (2016). The critical importance of retrieval – and spacing – for learning. *Psychological Science*, 27, 223-230.

Soto, D., & Humphreys, G. W. (2007). Automatic guidance of visual attention from verbal working memory. *Journal of Experimental Psychology: Human Perception and Performance*, 33, 730-737.

Sperling, G. (1960). The information available in brief visual presentation. *Psychological Monographs*, 74.

Squire, L. R. (1987). *Memory and Brain*. New York: Oxford University Press.

Squire, L. R. (1992). Declarative and nondeclarative memory: Multiple brain systems supporting learning and memory. *Journal of Cognitive Neuroscience*, 4, 232-243.

Standing, L., Conezio, J., & Haber, R. N. (1970). Perception and memory for pictures: Single-trial learning for 2560 visual stimuli. *Psychonomic Science*, 19, 73-74.

Stanovich, K. (2009). Distinguishing the reflective, algorithmic, and autonomous minds: Is it time for a tri-process theory? In J. St. B. T. Evans & K. Frankish (Eds.) *In two minds: Dual Processes and Beyond* (pp. 55-88). Oxford, UK: Oxford University Press.

Sternberg, R. J. (2003). *Cognitive Psychology*. Belmont, CA Wadsworth/Thomson Learning.

Sternberg, R. J., & Ben-Zeev, T. (2001). *Complex Cognition*. New York: Oxford University Press.

Sternberg, S. (1966). High-speed scanning in human memory. *Science*, 153, 652-654.

Strayer, D. L., Drews, F. A., & Johnston, W. A. (2003). Cell phone induced failures Of visual attention during simulated driving. *Journal of Experimental Psychology: Applied*, 9, 23-32.

Strayer, D. L. & Johnston, W. A. (2001). Driven to distraction: Dual-task studies of simulated driving and conversing on a cellular telephone. *Psychological Science*, 12, 462-466.

T

Talarico, J. M., and Rubin, D. C. (2003). Confidence, not consistency, characterises flashbulb memories. *Psychological Science*, 14, 455-461.

Tanaka, K., Siato, H.-A., Fukada, Y., & Moriya, M. (1991). Coding visual images of objects in inferotemporal cortex of the Macaque monkey. *Journal of Neurophysiology*, 66, 170-189.

Tarr, M. J. (2003). Visual object recognition: Can a single mechanism suffice? In M. A. Peterson, & G. Rhodes (Eds.), Perception of Faces, Objects, and Scenes: Analytic and Holistic Processes. Oxford, UK: Oxford University Press.

Technical Working Group for Eyewitness Evidence (1999). *Eyewitness Evidence: A Guide for Law Enforcement*. Washington, DC: US Department of Justice, Office of Justice Programs.

Theeuwes, J. (1991). Exogenous and endogenous control of attention: The effect of visual onsets and offsets. *Perception & Psychophysics*, 49, 83-90.

Thompson, K. G., Bichot, N. P. & Schall, J. D. (2001). From attention to action in frontal cortex. In J. Braun, C. Koch, & J. Davis (Eds.), *Visual Attention and Cortical Circuits. Cambridge*, MA: MIT Press.

Thorndyke, P. W. (1981). Distance estimation from cognitive maps. *Cognitive Psychology*, 13, 526-550.

Thorndyke, P. W., & Hayes-Roth, B. (1982). Differences in spatial knowledge acquired from maps and navigation. *Cognitive Psychology*, 14, 560-589.

Todd, J. J., & Marois, R. (2004). Capacity limit of visual short-term memory in human posterior parietal cortex. *Nature*, 428, 751-754.

Tolman, E. C. (1932). *Purposive Behavior in Animals and Man*. New York: Appleton-Century.

Tolman, E. C. (1948). Cognitive maps in rats and men. Psychological Review, 55, 189-208.

Torey, Z. (2014). *The Conscious Mind*. Cambridge, MA: MIT Press.

Treisman, A. M. (1960). Contextual cues in selective listening. *Quarterly Journal of Experimental Psychology*. 12, 242-248.

Treisman, A. M. (1964). Monitoring and storage of irrelevant messages in selective attention. *Journal of Verbal Learning and Verbal Behavior*, 3, 449-459.

Treisman, A. M., & Gelade, G. (1980). A feature integration theory of attention. *Cognitive Psychology*, 12, 97-136.

Treisman, A. M., & Gormican, S. (1988). Feature analysis in early vision: Evidence from search assymetries. *Psychological Review*, 95, 15-48.

Trick, L. M., & Pylyshyn, Z. W. (1994). "Why are small and large numbers enumerated differently? A limited-capacity preattentive stage in vision". *Psychological Review*, 101, 80–102.

Tse, P. U., Intriligator, J., Rivest, J., & Cavanagh, P. (2004). Attention and the subjective expansion of time. *Perception & Psychophysics*, 66, 7, 1171-1189.

Tsotsos, J. K., Culhane, S. M., & Cutzu, F. (2001). From foundation principles to a hierarchical selection circuit for attention. In J. Braun, C. Koch, & J. Davis (Eds.). *Visual Attention and Cortical Circuits*. Cambridge, MA: MIT Press.

Tsushima, T., Takizawa, O., Sasaki, M., Siraki, S., Nishi, K., Kohno, M., Menyuk, P., & Best, C. (1994). Discrimination of English /r-l/ and /w-y/ by Japanese infants at 6-12 months. Paper presented at the International Conference on Spoken Language Processing, Yokohama, Japan.

Tulving, E. (1972). Episodic and semantic memory. In E. Tulving & W. Donaldson, (Eds.), *Organization of Memory*. New York: Academic Press.

Tulving, E., & Thomson, D. M. (1973). Encoding specificity and retrieval processing in episodic memory. *Psychological Review*, 80, 352-373.

Turing, A. M. (1950). Computing machinery and intelligence. *Mind*, 59, 236, 433-460.

Turner, M. L., & Engle, R. W. (1989). Is working memory capacity task dependent?. *Journal of Memory and Language*, 28, 127-154.

Tversky, A., & Kahneman, D. (1974). Judgment under uncertainty: Heuristics and biases. *Science*, 185, 1124-1131.

Tversky, A., & Kahneman, D. (1982). Evidential impact of base rates. In D. Kahneman, P. Slovic, & A, Tversky (Eds.), *Judgments under Uncertainty: Heuristics and Biases*. Cambridge, MA: MIT Press.

Tversky, B. (2005). Functional significance of visuospatial representations. In P. Shah & A. Miyake (Eds.), *The Cambridge Handbook of Visuospatial Thinking*. Cambridge, U.K.: Cambridge University Press.

U

Ungerleider, L. G., & Mishkin, M. (1982). Two cortical visual systems. In D. J. Ingle, M. A. Goodale, & R. J. W. Mansfield (Eds.), *Analysis of Visual Behavior*. Cambridge, MA: MIT Press.

Uttal, W. (2001). *The New Phrenology: The Limits on Localizing Cognitive Processes in the Brain*. Cambridge, MA: MIT Press/Bradford Books.

V

Vandierendonck, A. (2016). A working memory system with distributed executive control. *Perspectives in Psychological Science*, 11, 74-100.

Van Lommel, P., van Wees, R., Meyers, V., & Elfferich, I. (2001). Near-death experience in survivors of cardiac arrest: A prospective study in the Netherlands. *The Lancet*, 358, 2039-2045.

Van Moorselaar, D., Theeuwes, J., & Olivers, C. N. L. (2014). In competition for the attentional template: Can multiple items within visual working memory guide attention? *Journal of Experimental Psychology: Human Perception and Performance*, 40, 1450-1464.

Vargha-Khadem, F., Isaacs, E. B., Papaleloudi, H., Polkey, C. E., & Wison, J. (1991). Development of language in six hemispherectomized patients. *Brain*, 114, 473-495.

Volkman, F. (1976). Saccadic suppression: A brief review. In R. A. Monty & J. W. Senders (Eds.), *Eye Movements and Psychological Processes*. Hillsdale, NJ: Erlbaum.

Visser, T. A. W., Bischof, W. F., & Di Lollo, V. (1999). Attentional switching in spatial and non-spatial domains: Evidence from the attentional blink. *Psychological Bulletin*, 125, 458-469.

W

Wade, C. (2006). Some cautions about jumping on the brain-scan bandwagon. *Observer*, 19, 23-24.

Wagenaar, W. (1986). My memory: A study of autobiographic memory over the past six years. *Cognitive Psychology*, 18, 225-252.

Wagner, A. D., Bunge, S. A., & Badre, D. Cognitive control, semantic memory, and priming: Contributions from prefrontal cortex. In Gazzaniga, M. S. (Ed.), *The Cognitive Neurosciences III*. Cambridge, MA: MIT Press.

Wagner, M. (2006). *The Geometrics of Visual Space*. Mahwah, NJ: Erlbaum.

Walker, R. C. S. (1987). Leibniz's philosophy of mind. In R. L. Gregory (Ed.), *The Oxford Companion to the Mind*. Oxford, U.K.: Oxford University Press.

Walton, G. E., Bower, N. J. A., & Bower, T. G. R. (1992). Recognition of familiar faces by newborns. *Infant Behavior and Development*, 15, 265-269.

Warnock, J. K. (1987). Berkeley. In R. L. Gregory (Ed.), *The Oxford Companion to the Mind*. Oxford, U. K.: Oxford University Press.

Warrington, E. K., (1975). The selective impairment of semantic memory. *Quarterly Journal of Experimental Psychology*, 27, 635-657.

Warrington, E. K., & Shallice, T. (1984). Category specific semantic impairments. *Brain*, 107, 829-854.

Warrington, E. K., & Weisenkrantz, L. (1970). The amnesic syndrome: Consolidation or retrieval? *Nature*, 228, 628-630.

Wason, P. C., & Johnson-Laird, P. N. (1972). *Psychology of Reasoning: Structure and Content*. London: Batsford.

Watson, J. B. (1913). Psychology as the behaviorist views it. *Psychological Review*, 20, 158-170.

Waugh, N. C., & Norman, D. A. (1965). Primary memory. *Psychological Review*, 72, 89-104.

Wearing, D. (2005). *Forever Today: A true story of lost memory and never-ending love*. London: Corgi Books.

Weiskrantz, L. (1997). *Consciousness Lost and Found*. Oxford, UK: Oxford University Press.

Werker, J. F., & Tees, R. C. (1984). Cross-language speech perception: Evidence for perceptual reorganization during the first year of life. *Infant Behavior and Development*, 7, 49-63.

Wernicke, C. (1874). *Der Aphasische Symptomenkomplex*. Breslau: Cohn and Weigert.

Werthheimer, M. (1923). Untersuchungen zur Lehre von der Gestalt. *Psychologische Forschung*, 4, 301-350.

Wessel, D. (1979). Timbre space as a musical control structure. *Computer Music Journal*, 3, 45-52.

Westmacott, R., Black, S. E., Freedman, M., & Moscovitch, M. (2004). The contribution of autobiographical significance to semantic memory: Evidence from Alzheimer's disease, semantic dementia, and amnesia. *Neuropsychologia*, 42, 25-48.

Wheeler, D. (1970). Processes in word recognition. *Cognitive Psychology*, 1, 59-85.

Wheeler, M. A., Stuss, D. T. & Tulving, E. (1995). Toward a theory episodic memory: The frontal lobes and autonoetic consciousness. *Psychological Bulletin*, 121, 331-354.

White, J. D., & Regan, M. M. S. (1987). Otologic considerations. In H. G. Mueller & V. C. Geoffrey (Eds.), *Communication Disorders in Aging*. Washington, D. C.: Gallaudet University Press.

Whitfield, I. C., & Evans, E. F. (1965). Responses of auditory cortical neurons to stimuli of changing frequency. *Journal of Neurophysiology*, 28, 655-672.

Wickelgren W. A. (1974). *How to Solve Problems: Elements of a Theory of Problems and Problem Solving*. San Francisco: Freeman.

Wickens, C. D. (1980). The structure of attentional resources. In R. Nickerson (Ed.), *Attention and Performance VIII*. Hillsdale, NJ: Erlbaum.

Wickens, D. D., Born, D. G., & Allen, C. K. (1963). Proactive inhibition and item similarity in short-term memory. *Journal of Verbal Learning and Verbal Behavior*, 2, 440-445.

Wickens, D. D., Dalezman, R., Eggemeie, E., & Thomas, F. (1976). Multiple encoding of word attributes in memory. *Memory & Cognition*, 4, 307-310.

Wiegersma, S., & Meertse, K. (1990). Subjective ordering, working memory, and aging. *Aging Research*, 6, 73-77.

Willingham, D. T. (2004). *Cognition*. Upper Saddle River, NJ: Pearson.

Wolfe, J. M. (1994). Guided search 2l.0: A revised model of visual search. *Psychonomic Bulletin and Review*, 1, 202-238.

Wolfe, J. M., Cave, K., & Franzel, S. L. (1989). Guided Search: An alternative to the Feature Integration Model for visual search. *Journal of Experimental Psychology: Human Perception and Performance*, 15, 419-433.

Wolfe, J.M., Kluender, K.R., Levi, D. M. et al. (2012). *Sensation & Perception*, 3rd Ed. Sunderland, MA: Sinauer Associates.

Woodruff-Pak, D. S. (1997). *The Neuropsychology of Aging*. Malden, MA: Blackwell.

Woodman, G. F. (2010). A brief introduction to the use of event-related potential in studies of perception and attention. *Attention, Perception & Psychophysics*, 72, 2031-2046.

Woodward, A. L., Markman, E. M., & Fitzsimmons, C. M. (1994). Rapid word learning in thirteen- and eighteen-month-olds. *Developmental Psychology*, 30, 553-566.

Wright, G. (1984). *Behavioral Decision Theory*. Harmondsworth, England: Penguin.

Wright, L. (1994). *Remembering Satan: A Case of Recovered Memory and the Shattering of an American Family*. New York: Knopf.

Wrolstad, M. E. (1976). A manifesto for visible language. *Visible Language*, 10, 4-40.

Y

Yee, E., Chrysikou, E.G., & Thompson-Schill, S.L. (2013). The cognitive neuroscience of semantic memory. In K. Ochsner and S. Kosslyn (Eds.), *Oxford Handbook of Cognitive Neuroscience, Vol. 2*. Oxford, UK: Oxford University Press.

Yim, H., Dennis, S. J., & Sloutsky, V.M. (2013). The development of episodic memory: Items, contexts, and relations. *Psychological Science*, 24, 2163-2172.

Young, M. E. (1995). On the origin of personal causal theories. *Psychonomic Bulletin and Review*, 2, 83-104.

Young-Browne, G., Rosenfeld, H. M. & Horowitz, F. D. (1977). Infant discrimination of facial expression. *Child Development*, 48, 555-562.

Yussen, S. R., & Levy, v. M., (1975). Developmental changes in practicing one's own span of short-term memory. *Journal of Experimental Child Psychology*, 19, 502-508.

Z

Zacks, R. T., & Hasher, L. (2006). Aging and long-term memory: Deficits are not inevitable. In E. Bialystok & F. I. M. Craik (Eds.), *Lifespan Cognition: Mechanisms of Change*. New York: Oxford University Press.

Zelkowitz, B. J., Herbster, A. N., Nebes, R. D., Mintun, M. A., & Becker, J. T. (1998). An examination of regional cerebral blood flow during object naming tasks. *Journal of the International Neuropsychological Society*, 4, 160-166.

Zihl, J., von Cramon, D., Mai, N., & Schmid, C. H. (1991). Disturbance of movement vision after bilateral posterior brain damage: Further evidence and follow up observations. *Brain*, 114, 2235-2252.